Intelligent Music Information Systems:
Tools and Methodologies

Jialie Shen
Singapore Management University, Singapore

John Shepherd
University of New South Wales, Australia

Bin Cui
Peking University, China

Ling Liu
Georgia Institute of Technology, USA

Information Science REFERENCE
(Formerly known as Idea Group Reference)

INFORMATION SCIENCE REFERENCE

Hershey · New York

Acquisitions Editor:	Kristin Klinger
Development Editor:	Kristin Roth
Assistant Development Editor:	Meg Stocking
Editorial Assistant:	Deborah Yahnke
Senior Managing Editor:	Jennifer Neidig
Managing Editor:	Sara Reed
Copy Editor:	Erin Meyer
Typesetter:	Michael Brehm
Cover Design:	Lisa Tosheff
Printed at:	Yurchak Printing Inc.

Published in the United States of America by
Information Science Reference (an imprint of IGI Global)
701 E. Chocolate Avenue, Suite 200
Hershey PA 17033
Tel: 717-533-8845
Fax: 717-533-8661
E-mail: cust@igi-pub.com
Web site: http://www.igi-global.com/reference

and in the United Kingdom by
Information Science Reference (an imprint of IGI Global)
3 Henrietta Street
Covent Garden
London WC2E 8LU
Tel: 44 20 7240 0856
Fax: 44 20 7379 0609
Web site: http://www.eurospanonline.com

Library of Congress Cataloging-in-Publication Data

Intelligent music information systems : tools and methodologies / Jialie Shen ... [et al.], editors.

     p. cm.

  Summary: "This book provides comprehensive description and analysis into the use of music information retrieval from the data management perspective, and thus provides libraries in academic, commercial, and other settings with a complete reference for multimedia system applications"--Provided by publisher.

  Includes bibliographical references and index.

  ISBN-13: 978-1-59904-663-1 (hardcover)

  ISBN-13: 978-1-59904-665-5 (ebook)

  1. Information storage and retrieval systems--Music. I. Shen, Jialie.

  ML74.I55 2008

  025.06'78--dc22

                               2007023436

British Cataloguing in Publication Data
A Cataloguing in Publication record for this book is available from the British Library.

All work contributed to this book set is new, previously-unpublished material. The views expressed in this book are those of the authors, but not necessarily of the publisher.

Table of Contents

Section III
P2P and Distributed System

Section IV
Music Analysis

Table of Contents

Section I
Indexing and Retrieving Music Database

Chapter I

Indexing is the core component of most information retrieval systems because it allows for a compact representation of the content of a collection of documents aimed at efficient and scalable access and retrieval. Indexing techniques can be extended also to music, providing that significant descriptors are computed from music documents. These descriptors can be defined as the "lexical units" of music, and depend on the dimensions that are taken into account – melody, harmony, rhythm, timbre – and are related to the way listeners perceive music. This chapter describes some relevant aspects of indexing of symbolic music documents, giving a review of its basic concepts and going in more detail about some key aspects, such as the consistency at which candidate index terms are perceived by listeners, the effectiveness of alternative approaches to compute indexes, and how individual indexing schemes can be combined together by applying data fusion approaches.

Chapter II

Marsyas is an open source audio processing framework with specific emphasis on building Music Information Retrieval systems. It has been under development since 1998 and has been used for a variety of projects in both academia and industry. In this chapter, the software architecture of Marsyas will be described. The goal is to highlight design challenges and solutions that are relevant to any MIR software.

Chapter III

This chapter discusses key issues of building and using a system designed to search and query a music collection through the input of the actual or perceived melody of a song. It presents a detailed survey and discussion of studies, algorithms, and systems created to approach this problem, including new contributions by the author. Emphasis is placed on examining the abilities and likely errors of those with little or no formal musical training to remember and reproduce melodic phrases, as these must be taken into account for any music information retrieval system intended for use by the general public. The chapter includes an extensive discussion on human humming as an intuitive input method for the musically untrained person and an examination of several music information retrieval systems designed for this type of input query.

Section II
Music Identification and Recognition

This chapter describes logic and computer algebra based Expert System that automates identification and recognition of the cult music styles of the XVII century - beginning of the XX century. It uses a table that contains a list of characteristics (identifiers) of the music styles of the epoch, developed after interacting with a panel of experts. The user, during or after analysing a score, introduces the identifiers and the expert system returns the score's style. These tentative identifications and recognitions could be interactively compared with those of experts. Therefore it may be a useful tool for teaching and learning history of music. The objectives are to organize the musical knowledge in any way admissible by the inference engine, to adapt and implement the inference engine (based on a powerful tool for effective polynomial computations named Gröbner bases) and to implement a GUI.

We describe a novel approach to the task of identifying performers from their playing styles. We investigate how professional Jazz saxophonists express and communicate their view of the musical and emotional content of musical pieces and how to use this information in order to automatically identify performers. We study deviations of parameters such as pitch, timing, amplitude, and timbre both at an internote level and at an intranote level. Our approach to performer identification consists of establishing a performer dependent mapping of internote features to a repertoire of inflections characterized by intranote features. We present and discuss some results of our approach and comment on future trends in this exciting research area.

State-of-the-art MIR issues are presented and discussed both from the symbolic and audio points of view. As for the symbolic aspects, different approaches are presented in order to provide an overview of the different available solutions for particular MIR tasks. This section ends with an overview of MX, the

IEEE standard XML language specifically designed to support interchange between musical notation, performance, analysis, and retrieval applications. As for the audio level, first we focus on blind tasks like beat and tempo tracking, pitch tracking and automatic recognition of musical instruments. Then we present algorithms that work both on compressed and uncompressed data. We analyze the relationships between MIR and feature extraction presenting examples of possible applications. Finally we focus on automatic music synchronization and we introduce a new audio player that supports the MX logic layer and allows it to play both score and audio coherently.

Section III
P2P and Distributed System

Chapter VII

Today, large audio collections are stored at computers, and machine learning can support organization. This demands a more abstract representation than is the time series of audio values. We have developed a unifying framework which decomposes the complex extraction methods into their building blocks. This allows us to move beyond the manual composition of feature extraction methods. Several of the well-known features as well as some new ones have been composed automatically by a genetic learning algorithm. While this has delivered good classifications it needs long training times. Hence, we additionally follow a metalearning approach. We have developed a method of feature transfer which exploits the similarity of learning tasks to retrieve similar feature extractions. This method achieves almost optimal accuracies while it is very efficient. Nemoz, an intelligent media management system, incorporates adaptive feature extraction and feature transfer which allows for personalized services in peer-to-peer settings.

Chapter VIII

This chapter presents a model enabling content providers to successfully sell digital music. We show that content providers must overcome three main hurdles to successfully sell digital music. The first is to establish an efficient and economically viable distribution channel. Second, they need to develop a secure and interoperable framework for protecting copyrighted digital music from piracy by integrating Digital Rights Management Systems into the distribution channel. The third hurdle is to set-up a robust payment mechanism that meets the content providers' needs for revenue capturing and the consumers' needs for hassle-free and legal content acquisition and usage. This chapter finally presents a DRM supported peer-to-peer network which could address and overcome the three hurdles. We conclude that a DRM supported P2P network gives content providers as well as consumers the secure, legal and most cost-efficient and user friendly digital distribution channel they have been searching for.

In this chapter we present the most significant trends in recent research in the field of content-based music information retrieval in peer-to-peer networks. Despite the diminished attention the area has received in general terms, the relatively close area of metadata MIR in P2P is by far new. As metadata prove to be inefficient for the purposes of MIR as well as the peculiarities of music in comparison to text and image data, developing dedicated solutions for CBMIR in P2P networks becomes a necessity while the challenges faced therein, unique. Depending on the type of P2P network, a number of prominent research works are presented and compared in this chapter.

This chapter introduces the DART (Distributed Audio Retrieval using Triana) project as a framework for facilitating the distributed processing and analysis of audio and Music Information Retrieval. The chapter begins by discussing the background and history of Grid and P2P technologies, the Triana framework, the current tools already developed for audio-rate signal processing, and also gives a description of how Triana is employing a decentralized P2P framework to support MIR applications. A music recommendation system is proposed to demonstrate the DART framework, and the chapter also documents the DART team's progress towards the creation of a working system. The authors hope that introducing the DART system to the MIR community will not only inform them of a research tool that will benefit the entire field of MIR, but also establish DART as an important tool for the rest of the audio and research communities.

Section IV
Music Analysis

This chapter offers an overview of computational research in motivic pattern extraction. The central questions underlying the topic, concerning the formalization of the motivic structures, the matching strategies and the filtering of the results, have been addressed in various ways. A detailed analysis of these problems leads to the proposal of a new methodology, which will be developed throughout the study. One main conclusion of this review is that the problems cannot be tackled using purely mathematic or geometric heuristics or classical engineering tools, but require also a detailed understanding of the multiple constraints derived by the underlying cognitive context.

Chapter XII

This chapter deals with pen interaction and its use for musical notation composition and editing. The authors first present existing pen-based musical notation editors and argue that they are dedicated to classical musical notations and are often constraining for the user. They then focus on their generic method that is in particular based on a formalism that models how to interpret the strokes drawn in online structured documents. To analyze an element, it models a coupling of a global vision (its position relatively to the other elements of the document) with a local vision (its shape and that of its components). The authors also present the hand-drawn stroke analyzer associated to this formalism. Finally they demonstrate how the presented method can be used to design pen-based systems not only for classical musical score notations, but also for plainchant scores, drum tablatures and stringed-instrument tablatures.

This chapter covers some of the challenges in storytelling with music. We describe the MusicStory system which creates music videos from personal media (audio and image) collections. Using a song's lyrics, MusicStory finds and presents word/image associations. It takes the emotional experience of listening to music, amplifies it and heightens its visceral appeal by externalizing concrete and visual imagery intrinsic in the music. The retrieved images vary in their association – some semantically on point and some distant. The flow of imagery moves with the pace of the song: providing quick transitions through fast songs, and leisurely transitions through slower songs. In addition, MusicStory uses vocal segmentation to direct the video and alter how images are displayed. We discuss the creative and technical challenges in this work as well as how it was deployed in several fashions.

In this chapter, we will analyze the heterogeneous contents involved in a comprehensive description of music, organizing them according to a multilayer structure. Each layer we can identify corresponds to a different degree of abstraction in music information. In particular, our approach arranges music contents in six layers: General, Music Logic, Structural, Notational, Performance, and Audio. In order to reflect such organization, we will introduce a new XML-based format, called MX, which is currently undergoing the IEEE standardization process (IEEE SA PAR1599). In an MX file, music symbols, printed scores, audio tracks, computer-driven performances, catalog metadata, and graphic contents related to a single music piece can be linked and mutually synchronized within the same encoding. The aforementioned multilayer structure allows us to gather and organize heterogeneous contents, leaving them encoded in well-known and commonly used formats aimed at music description.

Preface

INTRODUCTION

As an important form of human expression and creativity, music data has permeated into every corner of our daily life. At the beginning of 21st century, empowered by advances in networking, data compression and physical storage, modern information systems deal with ever-increasing amounts of musical data. However, effective searching and retrieving continue to be one of the most challenging research problems. The development of new technology to facilitate music information retrieval and management has gained considerable momentum. However, relatively less attention has been paid in this field. In comparison with data from other application domains, music information enjoys many unique characteristics and the most important ones are:

1. **Rich semantics:** Music data contains a large amount of information relative to its high-level semantic meaning. On the other hand, most user queries are semantically-based (e.g., "find all music items with guitar and drums performed by Michael Jackson"). How to generate a concise comprehensive representation for such information is an important but challenging problem. Any useful solution must be efficient in term of computation cost and effective in calculating a content descriptor that represents the semantics of the data item.

2. **Large volume:** In music applications, the size of data is huge (each item is much larger than a tuple in a conventional (relational) data repository). Dealing with such data items requires large amounts of computer resources such as storage and data processing power. A typical example is that audio and video data may exceed gigabytes on personal computers. Storage and data management solutions provided by state-of-art relational database management systems (DBMSs) are generally not adequate in such cases. New techniques for managing such large data sets need to be developed to provide economic and effective access and management.

3. **High dimensionality:** Representations of low-level acoustic features are high-dimensional in nature. Typical examples are the feature vectors for properties such as pitch and timbre extracted from raw audio data. In extreme cases, it could require thousands of dimensions to represent a particular feature, and dozens of dimensions are typical. It is extremely difficult for the current techniques to deal efficiently with such kinds of data. As a consequence, dimensionality reduction becomes an important technique in dealing with music data. However, it is important that the reduction does not lose useful discriminative information for indexing and classification.

4. **Complex structure:** Music can be treated as a nonlinear composite of various kinds of characteristics from different sources. Applying traditional solutions developed for the extraction of knowledge and querying results from structured data (e.g., tabular data) is not feasible in this case. Further, it appears that knowledge discovery and retrieval in music data cannot be simply based on the concatenation of the partial information obtained from each part of the target object. Therefore, developing multimodal techniques to integrate different kinds of information seamlessly is essential for effective knowledge discovery and information retrieval.

All of these musical characteristics make information retrieval, knowledge discovery and content management on music data challenging. Indeed, modern information technologies lag far behind in their support for efficiently accessing and managing music data.

The main objective is to assemble together, in a single volume, contributions on the topic of modern music information retrieval and management, including tools, methodologies, theory and frameworks. The book will present and provide insights into both the state-of-the-art music information retrieval issues and techniques and future trends in the field. It will also serve as a useful guide for researchers, practitioners, developers and graduate students who are interested or involved in the design, state-of-the-art development, and deployment of in music retrieval, music data management, music knowledge discovery and other related applications.

TARGET AUDIENCE

The primary target audience for the book includes researchers, graduate students, developers and users who are interested in designing, using, and/or managing complex music information systems. Potential users can be music researchers, entertainers or professionals from the music industry or amateur music lovers. The book will provide reviews of the concerned modern technology and insights for music information retrieval. It can be used as a comprehensive reference for both professional and amateur users or a textbook for graduate and senior undergraduate students who are specializing or taking a course in multimedia information systems.

ORGANIZATION OF THE BOOK

The book contains 14 chapters organized under 4 sections. Each section addresses a topic or main research theme, which is relevant to music information systems. Detail arrangement is as follows:

Section I: Indexing and Retrieving Music Database

Chapter I: Content-Based Indexing of Symbolic Music Documents. The chapter gives a review on basic concept and describes some relevant aspects of indexing of symbolic music documents. The effectiveness of different approaches is discussed and authors show how individual indexing can be combined together by applying data fusion methods.

Chapter II: MARSYAS-0.2: A Case Study in Implementing Music Information Retrieval Systems. The author presents that Marsyas, is an open source audio processing framework with specific emphasis on building Music Information Retrieval systems. It has been been under development since 1998, and has been used for a variety of projects in both academia and industry. In this chapter, the software architecture of Marsyas will be described.

Chapter III: Melodic Query Input for Music Information Retrieval Systems. The chapter gives a comprehensive discussion on key issues of building and using a system designed to search and query a music collection through the input of the actual or perceived melody of a song. Author also presents a detailed survey and discussion of studies, algorithms, and systems created to approach this problem, including new contributions by the author. Emphasis is placed on examining the abilities and likely errors of those with little or no formal musical training to remember and reproduce melodic phrases, as these must be taken into account for any music information retrieval system intended for use by the general public.

Section II: Music Identification and Recognition

Chapter IV: An Expert System Devoted to Automated Music Identification and Recognition. This chapter describes an expert system based on logic and algebra that automates identification and recognition of the cult music styles of the XVII century - beginning of the XX century. It uses a table that contains a list of characteristics (identifiers) of the music styles of the epoch, developed after interacting with a panel of experts. The user, while or after analyzing a score, introduces the identifiers and the expert system returns the score's style.

Chapter V: Identifying Saxophonists from their Playing Styles. The chapter focuses on the task of identifying performers from their playing style using high-level semantic descriptors extracted from audio recordings. The identification of performers by using the expressive content in their performances raises particularly interesting questions but has nevertheless received relatively little attention in the past.

Chapter VI: Tools for Music Information Retrieval and Playing. The chapter focuses on the advanced tool and analysis technique for music information retrieval and playing. The authors introduce and analyze the symbolic level of music: some of the main models and techniques developed up to now. The chapter also gives detail survey on musical feature extraction for music content representation.

Section III: P2P and Distributed System

Chapter VII: Collaborative use of Features in a Distributed System for the Organization of Music Collections. The chapter introduces a method of feature transfer which exploits the similarity of learning tasks to retrieve similar feature extractions. This method achieves almost optimal accuracies while it is very efficient. Nemoz, an intelligent media management system, incorporates adaptive feature extraction and feature transfer which allows for personalized services in peer-to-peer settings

Chapter VIII: A P2P based Secure Digital Music Distribution Channel: The Next Generation. This chapter presents a model enabling content providers to successfully sell digital music. Authors show that content providers must overcome three main hurdles to successfully sell digital music. The first is to establish an efficient and economically viable distribution channel. Second, they need to develop a secure and interoperable framework for protecting copyrighted digital music from piracy by integrating Digital Rights Management Systems into the distribution channel. The third hurdle is to set-up a robust payment mechanism that meets the content providers' needs for revenue capturing and the consumers' needs for hassle-free and legal content acquisition and usage.

Chapter IX: Music Information Retrieval in P2P Networks. In this chapter, authors present the most significant trends in recent research in the field of content-based music information retrieval in peer-to-peer networks. Despite the diminished attention the area has received in general terms, the relatively close area of metadata MIR in P2P is by far new. As metadata prove to be inefficient for the purposes of MIR as well as the peculiarities of music in comparison to text and image data, developing dedicated solutions for CBMIR in P2P networks becomes a necessity while the challenges faced therein, unique. Depending on the type of P2P network, a number of prominent research works are presented and compared in this chapter.

Chapter X: DART: A Framework for Distributed Audio Analysis and Music Information Retrieval. The chapter present DART framework designed for distributed audio analysis and music information retrieval. The associate project is being researched jointly between Cardiff University and the Laboratory for Creative arts and Technologies (LCAT) in Louisiana State University that capitalises on these developments to provide a decentralised overlay for the processing of audio information for application in Music Information Retrieval (MIR).

Section VI: Music Analysis

Chapter XI: Motivic Pattern Extraction in Symbolic Domain. In this chapter, author gives an overview of computational research in motivic pattern extraction. The central questions underlying the topic, concerning the formalization of the motivic structures, the matching strategies and the filtering of the results, have been addressed in various ways. A detailed analysis of these problems leads to the proposal of a new methodology, which will be developed throughout the study. One main conclusion of this review is that the problems cannot be tackled using purely mathematic or geometric heuristics or classical engineering tools, but require also a detailed understanding of the multiple constraints derived by the underlying cognitive context.

Chapter XII: Pen-Based Interaction for Intuitive Music Composition and Editing. This chapter present pen interaction and its use for musical notation composition and editing. The authors first review existing pen-based musical notation editors and argue that they are dedicated to classical musical notations and are often constraining for the user. Then a novel generic method is present and they also demonstrate how the presented method can be used to design pen-based systems not only for classical musical score notations, but also for plainchant scores, drum tablatures and stringed-instrument tablatures.

Chapter XIII: MUSICSTORY: An Autonomous, Personalized Music Video Creator. The chapter describes the MusicStory system which creates music videos from personal media (audio and image) collections. Basic idea for MusicStory is to search and present word/image associations based on a song's lyrics. It takes the emotional experience of listening to music, amplifies it and heightens its visceral appeal by externalizing concrete and visual imagery intrinsic in the music. The retrieved images vary in their association – some semantically on point and some distant. The flow of imagery moves with the pace of the song: providing quick transitions through fast songs, and leisurely transitions through slower songs.

Chapter XIV: Music Representation of Score, Sound, MIDI, Structure and Metadata All Integrated in a Single Multilayer Environment based on XML. The chapter presents an analysis of issues and concerns in music representation. The authors give very comprehensive literature review, analyze the requirement from real life applications and address the weakness of existing approaches. New content representation based on XML is design and present to support access of music. The authors also present application of this framework.

CONCLUDING REMARKS

Intelligent music information systems, which aim to provide effective searching and management on a large number of music data, offers an important platform to access and manage the vast amount of music contents for various kinds of application domains. In spite of large amount of output from the most recent research in the field of music retrieval, mining, management, current state-of-the-art technology is still in its infancy to fit real requirements from users in daily applications. Thus, it has always been a great challenge to develop useful tools, methodologies, theory and frameworks. In this book, we try to present some of the recent research progress undertaken during the past years. In case that the past is a guide to the future, these articles could serve as the seeds of new concepts and research ideas invigorating the field. In coming days, we hope to see the combination of different technologies and research areas to address the problem.

Acknowledgments

We would like to acknowledge the people for their kindness and support in making this book possible. Among them, peer reviewers who have volunteered their time, efforts and experience are listed below. In particular, we would like to express our great appreciation to them for their valuable contribution to the success of this book.

- Gao Cong (Miscroft Asia)
- Ioannis Karydis (Aristotle University of Thessaloniki)
- Bo Li (Beihang University)
- Orio Nicola (University of Padova)
- Namunu Chinthaka Maddage (Institute for Inforcomm Research, Singapore)
- Anirban Mondal (University of Tokyo)
- Lidan Shou (Zhejiang University)
- Wei-Ho Tsai (National Chiao-Tung University)
- George Tzanetkis (University of Victoria, Canada)
- Steffen Pauws (Philips Research)
- Linhao Xu (National University of Singapore)
- Qiankun Zhao (Pennsylvania State University)
- Yongwei Zhu (Institute for Inforcomm Research, Singapore)

We also would like to thank University of Glasgow, the University of New South Wales, Peking University and Georgia Institute of Technology (Gatech). Finally we wish to thank our families for their love and support.

Section I
Indexing and Retrieving Music Database

Chapter I
Content–Based Indexing of Symbolic Music Documents

Nicola Orio
University of Padova, Italy

ABSTRACT

Indexing is the core component of most information retrieval systems, because it allows for a compact representation of the content of a collection of documents, aimed at efficient and scalable access and retrieval. Indexing techniques can be extended also to music, providing that significant descriptors are computed from music documents. These descriptors can be defined as the "lexical units" of music, depend on the dimensions that are taken into account – melody, harmony, rhythm, timbre – and are related to the way listeners perceive music. This chapter describes some relevant aspects of indexing of symbolic music documents, giving a review of its basic concepts and going in more detail about some key aspects, such as the consistency at which candidate index terms are perceived by listeners, the effectiveness of alternative approaches to compute indexes, and how individual indexing schemes can be combined together by applying data fusion approaches.

INTODUCTION

The core problem of Information Retrieval (IR) is to effectively retrieve documents which convey content being relevant to the user's information needs. Effective and efficient techniques have been developed to index, search and retrieve documents from collections of hundreds of thousands, or millions of textual items. The most consolidated results have been obtained for collections of documents and user's queries in *textual* form and in English language. In order to provide a *content-based multimedia* access, the development of new techniques for indexing, searching and retrieving multimedia documents have been the focus of many researchers in IR. The research projects in digital libraries, and specifically those carried out in cultural heritage domain, have shown that the integrated management of diverse media—text, audio, image, video—is a necessary step (Moen, 1998). As stressed in Sparck Jones and Willett (1997), the problem with content-based access to multimedia data is twofold. On the one hand, each media requires specific techniques that cannot be directly employed for other media. On the other hand, these specific techniques should be integrated whenever different media are present in an individual item. The core information retrieval (IR) techniques based on statistics and probability theory may be more generally employed outside the textual case and within specific nontextual application domains, like music. This is because the underlying models, such as the vector-space and the probabilistic models, are likely to describe fundamental characteristics being shared by different media, languages and application domains (Sparck Jones & Willett, 1997).

The requirement for a music content-based IR has been stressed, since many years, within the research area of music information systems as well. The developments in the representation of music "suggest a need for an information retrieval philosophy directed toward non-text searching and eventual expansion to a system that encompasses the full range of information found in multimedia documents", as stressed by McLane (1996). As IR has dealt with the representation and the disclosure of content from its early days (van Rijsbergen, 1979), it is natural to consider that IR techniques should be investigated to evaluate their application to music retrieval. By concluding his survey, McLane stressed that "what has been left out of this discussion, and will no doubt be a topic for future study, is the potential for applying some of the standard principles of text information retrieval to music representations". Since 1996, many approaches have been applied to music access, browsing, retrieval, personalization, both proposing original techniques tailored to the music domain and adapting IR techniques (Downie, 2003). Many approaches to music retrieval are related to the field of digital libraries (Bainbridge, Nevill-Manning, Witten, Smith & Mc-Nab, 1999; Agosti, Bombi, Melucci & Mian, 2000). Because of their multimedia and multidisciplinary nature, digital libraries may profit from results in music indexing and retrieval. In particular, projects on the preservation and dissemination of cultural heritage can be the result of the combination of digital library and information indexing techniques (Ferrari & Haus, 1999). Yet most of the projects involving digital libraries, such as Harmonica (2006), are still based on bibliographic values rather than on indexing document contents, meaning that research on content-based approaches is required.

Indexing

One of the main components of an IR system is *indexing* (Baeza-Yates & Ribeiro-Neto, 1999). Indexing can be defined as "the process of analyzing the informational content of records of knowledge and expressing the informational content in the language of the indexing system. It involves: (1) selecting indexable concepts in a document; and (2) expressing these concepts in the language of the indexing system (as indexing items)" (Borko & Bernier, 1978). An *indexing system* is composed of a number of automatic procedures that allows for the organization of document contents, and for their access, retrieval and dissemination.

Indexes are used as guidance towards items in a collection of documents. In particular, the fact that indexes can be ordered, stored in complex data structures, and accessed with fast techniques such as hashing functions or tree searches, allows for efficient retrieval of documents in a collection. The effectiveness of indexes is part of everyday life, when looking up a dictionary or looking for the content of a book through its list of relevant names and concepts (which is precisely called "index"). Because it allows fast access to a synthetic description of documents content, indexing allows for the scalability of an IR system. Efficient data structures, such as *inverted files* (Baeza-Yates & Ribeiro-Neto, 1999) have been proposed to connect the indexes—which are used for retrieval—to the documents—which are of interested for the user.

Many approaches to music retrieval are based on online searches, where the user's query is compared with the documents in the collection using approximate string matching. For example, approximate string matching has been proposed in one of the earliest paper on music retrieval (Ghias, Logan, Chamberlin & Smith, 1995) while Dynamic Time Warping has been proposed in Hu and Dannenberg (2002). Statistical approaches have been proposed as well, in particular Markov chains (Birmingham, Dannenberg, Wakefield, Bartsch, Bykowski & Mazzoni, 2001) and hidden Markov models (Shifrin, Pardo, Meek & Birmingham, 2002). The advantage of these approaches is that the difference between the query and the documents can be modeled, considering explicitly all the possible mismatches. Thus very high performances in terms of retrieval effectiveness can be achieved. On the other hand, all these techniques require that the string representing the query is matched against all the documents in the collection, giving a complexity that is linear with the number of documents in the collection. Scalability to large collections of millions of documents becomes then an issue.

For this reason alternative approaches have been proposed that take advantage from indexing (Doraisamy & Rüger, 2004; Downie & Nelson, 2000; Melucci & Orio, 2004; Pienimäki, 2002). Moreover, other IR techniques can be applied to music retrieval. For instance, Hoashi, Matsumoto and Inoue (2003) applied relevance feedback to a melodic retrieval task, with the main goal of personalization of the results. The metaphor of navigation inside a collection of documents, which corresponds to document browsing, has also been proposed (Blackburn & DeRoure, 1998). On the other hand, indexing is also widely used to retrieve or recognize music in audio format, in particular for audio fingerprint and audio watermarking techniques (Cano, Batlle, Kalker & Haitsma, 2005).

This chapter describes some aspects of content-based indexing, as opposed to metadata indexing, giving a review of its basic concepts and going in more detail about some key aspects, such as

the consistency at which candidate index terms are perceived by listeners, the effectiveness of alternative approaches to compute indexes, and how individual indexing schemes can be combined together by applying data fusion approaches.

METADATA VS. CONTENT-BASED INDEXING

The first problem that arises when choosing an indexing scheme for a music collection regards the most effective representation of documents content, in particular whether documents have to be described by external metadata or directly by a synthetic representation of their content. Both approaches have positive and negative aspects. Metadata usually requires extensive manual work for retrieving external information on the documents and for representing in a compact way most of the subtleties of document content, but it increases the cost of indexing and does not guarantee consistency when different documents are indexed by different persons. Automatic computation of metadata based on external resources has been proposed in systems for collaborative filtering aimed, for example, at recommendation systems, but the results are in terms of similarity between documents and are biased by the presence of scattered data (Stenzel & Kamps, 2005). At the state of the art they do not seem suitable for a retrieval task. Content-based indexing is carried out starting from a set of features extracted automatically from the document itself, and it is the main focus of this chapter.

Metadata

For most media, such as images and video, the choice of textual metadata proved to be particularly effective. Textual metadata as a tool to describe and indexing music is a natural choice that has been made for centuries (Dunn & Mayer, 1999). In general metadata, especially in the form of semantic labels, are a very compact representation of the document content, because they can summarize a complete document with few keywords. Though not the main subject of this discussion, it is hence worth spending few words on music indexing through metadata and on its limitations for an efficient and effective retrieval task. A number of music digital libraries are accessible through the use of metadata. For instance, Cantate (2006) and Musica (2006) allow users to access to choral music using metadata and lyrics. Another project based on the use of metadata is Jukebox (Harvell & Clark, 1995).

As for many other media, music metadata addresses different characteristics of document content. In the particular case of music, it can be roughly divided in three categories:

- **Bibliographic values:** Suthor's name, performer's name (in the case of audio recordings), title, year of publication, editor, cataloguing number.
- **General information on document content:** Time and key signatures, musical form, structure, music genre, orchestration.
- **Additional available information:** Lyrics and, if applicable, related documents that create a context for the music work (e.g., a drama, a movie, a poem).

The search through bibliographic values can be very effective in terms of retrieval effectiveness, even if in this case a database approach to match exact values in predefined fields would be more suitable than an IR approach. On the other hand, the user is required to have a good knowledge of the music domain, being able to clearly describe the documents of interest. In the case of tonal Western music, the title of a music work is often nondescriptive, describing part of the general information on document content, and it is typical to have titles such as "Sonata in D flat, Op. 5" or "Fugue". The title can be based on

some music features also in other music genres: terms like "bossa", "waltz", and "blues" appear often in jazz compositions with that particular feature, and terms like "jig" and "reel" are often part of the title of the respective dances in Irish music tradition.

General information is often too generic to be a good discriminator between different music works. For example in tonal music there are only 21 major and 21 minor different tonalities, while thousands of compositions of tonal Western music can be labelled with the term "cantata" or "concerto", and the same applies with terms such as "up tempo" or "slow" for pop and rock genres. The genre information itself groups together hundreds of thousands of different works. Another problem that arises with metadata on general information is that the terminology is not consistent across genres and historical periods. For example, the term "sonata" has different meanings for Baroque and Romantic repertoires and the term "ballad" refers to different characteristics in jazz and in folk music. This kind of metadata can be useful to refine the description of a music information need, but it can hardly be used to completely define it. Moreover, a preliminary study on users information needs (Lee & Downie, 2004) showed that users are interested in retrieving songs by their specific content.

Additional information in the form of lyrics, when present, can be particularly useful to describe an information need, yet in this case the retrieval of music documents becomes an application of textual IR. Contextual information, such as the movie where a particular soundtrack has been used, or the poem that inspired a particular composition, can be very helpful as well to describe a user information need. In many cases the information need is motivated by the contextual information itself—that is, a user may be searching for the theme song of a TV series or for the music of a known ballet—yet this kind of contextual information applies only to a small percentage of music documents.

What is normally missing in music metadata is a textual description of the document content other than its musical structure, which is a peculiar situation of the music language that is due to the fact that music is not aimed at describing something with a known semantic—like text, images, speech, video or 3D models. This is probably the main limitation of the use of metadata for music indexing, and it is the motivation for the number of content-based approaches proposed in the last years, compared to textual metadata approaches. Moreover, it has to be considered that music representation is aimed at giving directions to performers and, at least for Western music, is biased by the characteristics of the music scores that allows a limited representation of high level characteristics (Middleton, 2002).

Music Dimensions

Music has a multidimensional nature. Rhythm, melody and harmony are all well-known dimensions that capture distinctive features of a music document. These dimensions are conveyed explicitly by music scores and recognized easily by listeners of audio recordings, and can be defined as the *canonical dimensions* of music, because they are used extensively by music theorists and musicologists as tools to describe, analyze, and study music works. Another perceptually relevant music dimension is timbre, which is related to the quality of sounds and is conveyed only by audio recordings. Yet timbre is a multidimensional feature by itself, and can be described using a set of continuous parameters, such as spectral power energy or Mel-Cepstrum Coefficients, and by perceptually based features such as spectral centroid, roughness, and attack time. As stated by Krumhansl (1989), timbre remains a difficult dimension to understand and represent, though studies have been carried out on the perception of timbre similarity (Berenzweig, Logan, Ellis & Whitman, 2004). The discussion on content-based music indexing will be limited to canonical dimensions, in particular the ones that may have a symbolic representation, which is more suitable for the creation of an index of a music collection. For any chosen dimension, the indexing scheme has to be based on a suitable definition of the particular lexical units of the dimension and their representation. A taxonomy of the characteristics of music and their potential interest for users is reported in Lesaffre, Leman, Tanghe, De Baets, De Meyer and Martens (2003).

The representation of the melody can build upon traditional score representation, which is based on the drawing of a sequence of notes, each one with a given pitch and a duration relative to the tempo of the piece. This symbolic representation is particularly suitable for indexing, providing that the melodic lexical units are highlighted. This is a more difficult task also for musicians and music scholars; the results of a perceptual study on manual segmentation are presented in a following section. The representation of rhythm can be considered as a variation of melodic representation, where pitch information can be discarded or substituted with the information of the particular percussive instrument that plays each rhythmic element. Also the indexing of the harmonic dimension can be based on common chord representation. In this case there are alternative representations, from figured bass to functional harmony and chord names. An overview of chord representations, aimed at their annotation, is presented in Harte, Sandler, Abdallah and Gómez (2005). The segmentation of chords in their lexical units can be based on notions of harmony, including modulations, cadences, and the use of particular chord progressions in different music genres.

The analysis of different dimensions and their representation as building blocks of music documents may be of interest also for musicologists, composers and performers. To this end, it is interesting to cite Humdrum (Huron, 1995), which apart from retrieval allows a number of manipulations for analyzing music scores.

BASIC CONCEPTS OF INDEXING

Early models and experiments on textual information retrieval date back to the 1970'S. Textual information retrieval, which for years has been simply addressed information retrieval (IR) *tout-court*, has a long history, where many different approaches have been experimented and tested. Being indexing one of the core elements of an IR system, many approaches have been proposed to optimize indexing from the computational cost, memory storage, and retrieval effectiveness points of view and, most of all, these approaches have been extensively tested and validated experimentally using standard test collections, in particular in the framework of the Text REtrieval Conference (TREC). For this reason, the main ideas underlying textual indexing will be reviewed, together with possible applications to music indexing.

Textual indexing is based on four main subsequent steps, which are respectively:

- Lexical analysis
- Stop-words removal
- Stemming
- Term weighting

It has to be noted that existing IR systems may not follow all these steps; in particular the effectiveness of stemming has been often debated, at least for languages with a simple morphology such as English.

Lexical Analysis

The first step of indexing consists in the analysis of the content of a document in order to find its candidate index terms. In the case of textual documents, index terms are the words that form the document, thus lexical analysis corresponds to document parsing for highlighting its individual words. Lexical analysis is straightforward with European languages, where blanks, commas, dots, are clear separators between two subsequent words. Attention has to be paid in some particular cases, for example an acronym where letters are separated by dots has to be considered as a single term and not a sequence of one-letter terms. The creation of a lexical analyzer for these languages can be done through regular expressions, and normally poses only implementation issues. For other languages, such as Chinese and Japanese, the written text does not have necessarily to be divided in terms by special characters, and the compounding of ideograms in different words has to be inferred from the context. Automatic lexical analysis for these languages is nontrivial, and it has been a research area since years.

Application to the Music Domain

As discussed in the previous section, the first issue on music indexing is the choice of the dimensions to be used as content descriptors. This choice influences also the approaches to the lexical analysis. For instance, if rhythm is used to index music documents, attack time of the different notes has to be automatically detected and filtered, which is an easy task for symbolic documents and can be carried out with good results also for documents in audio format. On the other hand, if harmony is used to compute indexes, lexical analysis has to rely on complex techniques for the automatic extraction of chords from a polyphonic music document, which is still an error prone task especially in the case of audio documents, even though encouraging results have been obtained (Gómez & Herrera, 2004). The automatic extraction of high level features from symbolic and audio music formats is a very interesting research area, studied by a very active research community, but it is beyond the aims of this discussion. For simplicity, it is assumed that a sequence of features is already available, describing some high-level characteristics of a music documents, related to one or more of its dimensions. It is also assumed that the feature extraction is affected by errors that should be taken into account during the design of the indexing scheme.

Figure 1. Possible outcomes of the lexical analysis of a simple melody; the bars in grey are alternative segmentations in melodic lexical units

Even after a sequence of features has been extracted automatically from a music document, lexical analysis of music documents remains a difficult task. The reason is that music language lacks of explicit separators between candidate index terms for all of its dimensions. Melodic phrases are not contoured by particular signs or sounds that express the presence of a boundary between two phrases. The same applies to harmonic progressions, or rhythmic patterns. In all these cases there is no additional symbol that expresses the ending of a lexical unit and the beginning of the next one. This is not surprising, because the same concept of lexical unit is borrowed from the textual domain, and it is not part of the traditional representation of music documents. Even if there is a wide consensus in considering music as a structured organization of different elements, and not just a pure sequence of sounds, there was no historical need to represent directly this aspect. Music is printed for musicians, who basically need the information to create a correct performance, and who could infer the presence of basic elements from the context. Different approaches have been proposed for lexical analysis, considering musical patterns (Hsu, Liu & Chen, 1998), main themes (Meek & Birmingham, 2003), or musical phrases (Melucci & Orio, 1999).

The consistency between musicians in performing the lexical analysis of some monophonic written scores has been investigated in a perceptual study, which is presented in the next section. The lexical analysis of music documents is still an open problem, both in terms of musicological analysis because alternative theories have been presented, and in terms of indexing and retrieval effectiveness. As an example, Figure 1 reports possible segmentations of the same musical excerpt.

Stop-Words Removal

Many words that are part of a textual document have only a grammatical function, and do not express any semantics. In most languages articles, conjunctions, prepositions and so on, can be deleted without substantially affecting the comprehension of the text. Moreover, if after indexing a document is described by a simple list of terms in a given order (i.e., alphabetical), the fact that the documents contained a particular conjunction does not give any additional information on the document content. These words can thus be removed, or *stopped* from which the term "stop-words", from the output of the lexical analysis without affecting the overall performance of an indexing system. Given that stop-words of this kind are very frequent in textual documents, their removal improves the system performances in terms of storage needed for the indexes and thus on the computational cost of the retrieval. For any particular language a list of stop-words, named *stop-list*, can be derived from a priori knowledge of the grammatical rules.

Stop-words removal can be applied also to words that, though carrying a semantic that could be used to describe the document content, are extremely frequent inside a collection of documents. For example, the lexical analysis of a set of documents on music processing will very likely show that all documents contain words such as "music", "computer", "note", "algorithm", and so on. Moreover, these words are probably evenly distributed across the collection, and their contribution to specify the content of a particular document in respect to the others is very low. Also in this case, a collection dependent stop-list can be created, and words belonging to the stop-list can be ignored in subsequent phases of document indexing. The stop-list can be computed automatically by analyzing a representative sample of the collection, adding to the stop-list all the words that consistently appear in all (or in a high percentage) of the analyzed documents. Clearly, this kind of analysis would highlight also the words that have a grammatical function and no semantic as described above, thus a two-step removal of stop-words can be avoided. Nevertheless, the designer of an IR system can choose to remove only the frequent and uninformative words, keeping the ones that are only frequent.

Application to the Music Domain

It is difficult to state whether or not a musical lexical unit has a meaning in order to create a priori a stop-list of musical lexical units that can be ignored during indexing. It is preferable to face the problem considering how much a particular unit is a good discriminator between different music documents. For instance, in the case of indexing of melodic intervals, a lexical unit of two notes that form a major second is likely to be present in almost all of the documents, and thus not being a good index in the case of a collection of "cantate" of tonal Western music, and probably for any collection of music documents. A single major chord is unlikely to be a good discriminator as well. Depending on the particular set of features used to index a music collection, the designer of the indexing and retrieval engine can make a number of choices about the possible stop-list of lexical units.

The choice of the particular stop-list to use, if any, could be driven by both musicological and computational motivations and by the characteristics of the music collection itself. A statistical analysis of the distribution of lexical units across documents may highlight which are the potential stop-words that can be used. It has to be noted that this approach is not usually exploited in the literature of music indexing and retrieval. The term "stop-list" is quite infrequent in music retrieval, and the common approach is to select carefully the parameters to avoid the computation of lexical units that are believed to be uninformative about the document content. What it is important for this discussion is to highlight the fact that not all the lexical units are equally informative about the document content and its differences with other documents in the collection (which is aim of term weighting described below) and that some lexical units may be totally uninformative as a sort of background noise.

Stemming

Many words, though different in the way they are spelled, can be considered as different variants that *stem* from a common morphological root. This is the case of the English words "music", "musical" (adjective and substantive), "musicology", "musician"; the number of variants may increase if singular and plural forms are taken into account, together with the gender information (which does not apply to English but applies to most European languages) and other possible variants which are peculiar of some languages. Moreover, in many languages verbs are conjugated, that is the root of the verb is varied depending on mode, person and time. Thus a textual document may contain different word variants, which are identified as different from lexical analysis but share a similar meaning. Intuitively, it can be considered that a textual document could be relevant for a given information need even if it does not contain the exact term chosen by the user for his query, but it contains other variants. For example, a document that contains many times the words "computing", "compute", and "computation" is likely to address the subject of "computers" even if this exact word is missing. On the other hand, many words, even though stemming from the same root, evolved to express different meanings.

The basic idea of stemming is to conflate into a single index all the words that have slightly different meaning but stem from a common morphological root. The positive effects are a generalization of the concepts that are carried by the stems and not by the single words, and a lower number of index terms. The higher generalization is expected to improve recall, at a probable cost of lowering precision. There are different approaches to automatic stemming, depending on the morphology of the languages, and on the used techniques. The research on stemming is still very active, in particular for languages different from English and that have a rich morphological structure, with derivations expressed by prefixes, infixes and suffixes.

Application to the Music Domain

The idea behind stemming is that two indexes may be different but can be perceived/considered similar. Analogously, two musical lexical units may be slightly different, yet listeners can perceive them as almost identical, or confuse one from the other when recalling from memory, or consider that they play a similar role in the musical structure. For instance, two identical rhythmic patterns played with a different tempo and small variations in the actual onset time, two musical phrases that differ only for one interval that from major turns minor, chords progressions where one chord is substituted by another with a similar function as it is routinely done in jazz music, are all situations where stemming may become useful. In practice, all the perceptually similar variants could be conflated into a common stem.

It can be noted that the analogous of stemming is regularly carried out in many approaches to music retrieval, and it is normally addressed as feature *quantization*. The main motivation of feature quantization in music processing is probably related to the fact that each feature extraction process is error prone: quantization partially overcomes this problem if erroneous measurements are reported to the same quantized value of the correct one. For example, because pitch detectors are known to produce octave errors, a solution that has been often proposed in the literature is to represent only the name of the notes, with eventual alterations, and not their actual octave (Birmingham et al., 2001). Automatic chord detection from polyphonic audio signals is still very error prone, thus quantization to a fixed number of chords—for example triads only—may help removing part of the measurement noise. Yet quantization can be useful when the automatic detection is reliable, but it is known in advance that the signal itself may have variations, like in the case of onset notes and note durations even for performances of the same score.

Quantization can be useful also as a stemming procedure. It is well known that many compositions are based on a limited number of music materials, which is presented and then varied and developed during the piece. In this case, the conflation of different thematic variations into a single index will improve the recall because the user may choose any of these variations to express the same information need. Quantization can be carried out on any music dimension, and at different levels. Table 1 shows possible approaches to the quantization of melodic intervals, some of them already proposed in the literature, from the more fine-grained to the more-coarse. Figure 2 gives a graphical representation on the amount of information that is lost through quantization, in particular when melodic or rhythmic information is quantized in a single level and thus discarded.

Table 1. Number of different indexes when quantization is applied to ascending and descending intervals within an octave (including unison)

Quantization Level	#symbols
Cents	2401
Semitones: *0, +1, +2, ...*	25
Music intervals: *unison, second, third, ...*	15
Perceptual intervals: *unison, small, medium, large*	9
Direction: *up, down, same*	3

As for stemming, quantization may improve recall because more documents may contain a quantized lexical unit. The increase in recall usually correspond to a lowering in precision, because a quantized lexical unit is usually more generic and it describes less precisely a user information need. From a computational point of view, quantization may also speed up retrieval, because the decrease of the number of different symbols used as building blocks of the index correspond to a decrease in the computational cost to perform the matching. This characteristic has been exploited in system for melodic retrieval (Ghias et al., 1995) where only three levels have been used. Authors reported that, in order to overcome the problem of generic information needs the user had to provide more complete information, in particular using long melodic excerpts to create his query.

A similar approach to quantization can be carried out on rhythmic information. In this case it has to be noted that the same score representation is a quantized version of possible performances, because it is not expected that onset times and duration are played using the exact values computed from the beats per minute (when that happens the performance sounds mechanic). In the case of scores that are transcriptions of pre-existing performances, the transcriber chooses which is the level of quantization as a compromise between the readability of the score and the precision of the reported times. Rhythmic quantization for index conflation can be carried out with an approach similar to melodic quantization, from milliseconds to very coarse levels (such as the levels *long* and *short*). A number of approaches to melodic indexing do not take into account note durations, but are based only on pitch information, and they can be considered as a limit case where there is only one level of quantization for note onsets and durations.

Figure 2. Graphical representation of the information loss when increasing levels of quantization of pitch and duration are applied (from top: original score, removal of rhythm, pitch quantization, removal of pitch)

Term Weighting

The last phase of an indexing process is related to a main consideration: inde terms do not describe the content of a document to the same extent. It has already been mentioned that stop-words, which are frequent inside the collection, are not good descriptors because they do not allow the differentiation between documents. On the other hand, it can be argued that a particular set of terms that are peculiar of a particular documents, in which they are extensively used, are very good descriptors of that document because they allow its exact identification. Clearly, the importance of a term in describing a document varies along a continuum that ranges from totally irrelevant to totally relevant.

For textual documents it has been proposed that the frequency at which a word appears in a document is directly proportional to its relevance, while the frequency at which it appears in the collection is inversely proportional to its relevance. These considerations gave birth to a very popular weighting scheme, called *term frequency—inverse document frequency*, in short *tf·idf*. There are a number of different variants of this scheme, which share the same principles:

- Term frequency is computed, for each term *t* and each document *d*, from a monotonic increasing function of the number of counts of *t* appearing in *d*.
- Inverse document frequency is computed, for the set of documents d_t that belong to collection *C* and contain at least one occurrence of term *t*, from a monotonic decreasing function of the size d_t normalized by the size of *C*.

A widely used implementation of the two monotonic functions for the computation of *tf·idf* is reported in the following formula:

$$tf \cdot idf_{t,d} = w_{t,d} = \frac{freq(t \in d)}{\max_l freq(l \in d)} \times \log \frac{|C|}{|d_t|}$$

A special case of term weighting can be found in *binary weighting*, which is normally used when Boolean searches are carried out. In binary weighting an index term has a weight of *false* if it does not appear in the document, *true* otherwise. Retrieval is carried out as the solution of a Boolean expression, where the values true or false correspond to the value of the proposition "the term *t* belongs to document *d*" and are combined with Boolean operators—that is, "and", "or", "not"—in order to create complex queries. Binary weighting is still very popular because it is easy to implement and allows for a great expressivity in describing the user information need through a query.

Application to the Music Domain

If a musical lexical unit, for any chosen dimension, appears frequently inside a given document, it is very likely that listeners will remember it. Moreover, a frequent lexical unit can be part of the music material that is proposed and developed by the composer, or can be also part of the composer's personal style. Finally, frequent lexical units have good chances to be part of a user query. Thus, the term frequency seems to be a reasonable choice also for music documents. On the other hand, a lexical unit that is very common inside a collection of documents can be related to style of a thematic collection—the chord progression of blues songs, the accent on the up beat in reggae music—or can correspond to a simple musical gesture—a repeated note, a major scale—or can be the most used solution for particular passages—the descending bass connecting two chords, a seventh chord introducing a modulation. Moreover, a user may not use frequent lexical units as parts of a query because it is clear that they will not address any particular document. Thus, inverse document frequency seems to be a reasonable choice as well.

Yet, some care has to be paid to a direct application of a *tf·idf* weighting scheme to music indexing because of the evident difference between textual and musical communication. One thing that is worth mentioning is that users access the two medias very differently. In particular, music documents are accessed many times by users, who may choose to not listen to the complete song, but only to a part of the song. Moreover, it is common practice of radio stations to broadcast only the parts of the songs with the sung melody, skipping the intro and the coda, and fading out during long guitar solos. The computation of the relative importance by which a lexical unit describes a document should deal also with these aspects. Moreover, listeners are likely to remember and use in their queries the part of the song where the title is sung, which becomes more relevant disregarding its frequency inside the documents and inside the collection. Yet, there have been very few studies that investigate the best weighting scheme for music indexing, and in many cases a direct implementation of the *tf·idf* (such as the one presented in this section) is used.

It is important to note that the possibility to give different weights to lexical units is an important difference between information retrieval and approaches based on recognition—such as approximate string matching techniques. The former allows users to rank the documents depending on the relevance of their lexical units as content descriptors, while the latter allows for document ranking depending on the degree at which an excerpt of each document matches the query. In other words, a good match with an almost irrelevant excerpt may give a higher rank than a more approximate match with a highly relevant excerpt. It could be advisable to extend weighting approaches also to methods other than indexing. To this end, a mixed approach of indexing with approximate matching has been proposed in Basaldella and Orio (2006), where each index term was represented by a statistical model and the final weight of each index term of the query was computed combining the *tf·idf* scheme with the probability by which it was generated by the model.

Retrieval Techniques

Once indexes have been built through the four steps described earlier, and both the collection of documents and the user query have been indexed, it is possible to perform retrieval. It is important to note that also the query has to be analyzed and indexed in order to retrieve relevant documents, because the similarity between the query and the documents is carried out using indexes only.

Different approaches can be applied to retrieval; the one that is more intuitive, and that has been extensively applied in the experiments reported in the following sections, is the Vector-Space Model (VSM). Accordingly to the VSM, both documents and queries are represented as K-variate vectors of descriptor weights $w_{t,d}$, provided that K is the total number of unique descriptors or indexes. Then, document d_i is represented as $d_i = (w_{i1},...,w_{iK})$, while query q is represented as $q = (q_1,...,q_K)$. The weight $w_{t,d}$ of index term t within document d are computed according to the *tf·idf* scheme already described. Query descriptor weights are usually binary values, then $q_t = 1$ if term t occurs within query q, 0 otherwise.

The retrieval status value (RSV) is the cosine of the angle between the query vector and the document vector. That is:

$$RSV(d,q) = \cos(\vec{d},\vec{q}) = \frac{\vec{d} \cdot \vec{q}}{|\vec{d}| \cdot |\vec{q}|}$$

where d and q are the document and the query respectively, with their vectorial representations, and $|x|$ is the norm of vector x. As the cosine function normalizes the RSV to the query and document lengths, long documents have the same chance of being retrieved than short ones.

In order to be comparable, both documents and queries need to be transformed. This process usually corresponds to the segmentation of music documents in their lexical units, and to a more complex query processing. The latter can

Figure 3. Parallel processing of documents and queries aimed at retrieval of potentially relevant documents

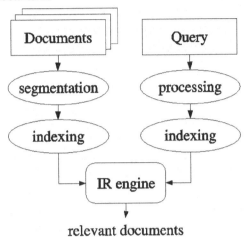

Retrieval can be then carried out by measuring the similarity (or the distance) between the two strings, ranking the retrieved documents according to their decreasing similarity (or decreasing distance) from the query. The complexity of these techniques is linear with the size of the document collection, because all the documents have to be matched against the query.

Indexing techniques does not require this exhaustive comparison, and in fact the main motivation behind indexing is its efficiency and scalability also for very large collections of documents. Let us consider each index term as a pointer to the list of the documents that contain it. It is assumed that the number of documents in each list is small if compared to the number of documents in the collection, apart from stop-words that are usually not used as index terms. This assumption is surely true for textual documents, but it applies also to music documents because melodies have different thematic material. Index terms can then be stored in efficient data structures, such as *hash tables* that can be accessed in constant time or *binary search trees* that can be accessed in logarithmic time.

The efficiency implied by indexing is somehow balanced by the retrieval effectiveness. The main issue is that, in order to be efficient, the access to the data structure requires an exact match between documents and query indexes. While this assumption is reasonable for textual documents, because the user is expected to spell correctly the words of the query, in the music domains there are many sources of mismatch that may affect retrieval effectiveness. A melodic query can either contain errors, due to imprecise recall of the melody, or be a different variant of a particular theme. These differences may affect the way index terms are computed from the query and the way they are represented. For this reason, some peculiar aspects of music document indexing are addressed in more detail.

involve the application of noise reduction and pitch tracking techniques (de Cheveigné & Baskind, 2003), in the case of audio queries, followed by an approach to segmentation that can be carried out with the same technique used for document segmentation or with different techniques tailored to the peculiarities of the queries. Figure 3 represents the parallel processing of documents and queries aimed at computing the RSV for ranking relevant documents.

Efficiency and Effectiveness

It can be argued that all these steps, although useful for indexing textual documents, are not necessary for a music retrieval task that can be solved directly within an *approximate string matching* framework, as mentioned in the introduction of this chapter. For instance, the main melodies of music documents can be represented by arrays of symbols, where the number of different symbols depends on the kind of quantization applied to melodic and rhythmic information. The user's query is normally an excerpt of a complete melody and thus can undergo the same representation.

AN EXPERIMENT ON THE PERCEPTION OF LEXICAL UNITS

It is normally assumed that the dimensions that form the music flow can be divided in their lexical units by listeners, depending on the characteristics of the music structure (Lerdhal & Jackendoff, 1983; Narmour, 1990). This means that it is assumed that listeners are able to single out one or more dimensions of interest and to segment them. Segmentation can be considered the process by which listeners recognize boundaries of lexical units, being able to recognize the presence of boundaries according to a number of perceptually and culturally based strategies. Given these assumptions, it is not clear the degree by which listeners agree in recognizing the exact positions of these boundaries. A similar situation applies to other application domains of media segmentation, like text, image, and video segmentation. For instance, experiments on manual text segmentation showed that subjects might have different concepts of the meaning of a textual segment, and thus recognize boundaries at different locations, or not agree at all about the presence of a given boundary.

A perceptual study has been carried out on a number of subjects to verify the degree of consistency of manual melodic segmentation. Melodic information has been used as the preferred dimension for the segmentation task, even if it has to be noted that melody carries information also about rhythm and harmony that can be inferred at least by experienced musicians and musicologists. This choice is motivated by the fact that most of the approaches to music retrieval are based on the melodic dimension, with few exceptions such as exploiting harmonic information (Lavrenko & Pickens, 2003).

Experimental Setting

An expert musicologist was asked to highlight 20 melodic excerpts that he considered representative of the styles of 4 well-known composers of tonal Western music, namely Bach, Mozart, Beethoven and Chopin. The criterion for the choice was to have a good sampling of different kinds of melodic structure, in which they were all present the different cues that listeners may use for segmenting the melodies.

Each melodic excerpt was transcribed on a separated sheet, without reporting composer and composition names. The excerpts had different tempos, different time and key signatures, which were all maintained in the transcriptions. Moreover, the transcribed melodies had different length, ranging from 7 to 26 bars and from 36 to 192 notes. The musicologist indicated the length of each excerpt, which depended on the melodic structure and on the length of the main theme. Finally, in each sheet there were four lines for comments, whether the subjects would like to describe the reasons of a particular choice. The complete list of the music works, from which excerpts were taken, is reported in Table 2. Another short melodic excerpt was used as a graphical example of the segmentation task.

A group of 17 subjects participated in the experiment. Subjects were asked to perform the segmentation task directly on the paper where the music scores were printed. They were provided with the melodic excerpts plus one page of instructions on their task. Instructions also included a short explanation about the motivation of the research work and its application to music retrieval. All subjects were professional or semi-professional musicians. The choice of including only musicians in the group is due to a main consideration. A musician is able to relate himself directly with the written score, without the need of someone else's performance. This avoids the possible bias in the recognition of melodic contours given by an intermediate interpretation. Moreover, musicians are more familiar with the concepts of phrases in music. Beside of the segmentation task, subjects were required to give some information about their background in music

Table 2. Complete list of the music works used for the segmentation test; for each score is reported the length in bars.

No.	Title	Bars
J. S. Bach		
1	Sinfonia Cantata no. 186, Adagio	7
2	Orchestral Suite no. 3, Aria	6
3	Orchestral Suite no. 2, Bourreé	13
4	Cantata BWV 147, Choral	26
5	Preludium n. 9, BWV 854	8
L. Van Beethoven		
6	Symphony n. 5, 4th movement	22
7	Symphony n. 7, 1st movement	21
8	Sonata n. 14, 3rd movement	12
9	Sonata n. 7, Minuetto	17
10	Sonata n. 8, Rondò	18
F. Chopin		
11	Ballade no. 1, op. 23	11
12	Impromptu op. 66, 2nd movement	16
13	Nouvelle Etude no. 3	21
14	Waltz no. 7	16
15	Waltz no. 9	17
W. A. Mozart		
16	Concerto no. 1, K313	10
17	"Don Giovanni", Aria	18
18	"Le Nozze di Figaro", Aria	10
19	Sonata no. 11, K331	18
20	Sonata no. 9, K310	22

concerning: played musical instrument, years of music practice, expertise on music analysis and knowledge of the proposed melodic excerpts.

The major direction given to the subjects was an operative definition of lexical units, which were expressed as "the *musical phrases*, or *musical gestures*, in which a melody can be divided during its performance, playing a similar role of words in the spoken language." The example annexed to the test showed some possible musical phrases, while stating that subjects may disagree with the particular choices. Instructions suggested to use two different graphic signs to be drawn at the end of a musical phrase, a simple and a double bar respectively indicating the presence of a normal or of a strong boundary between lexical units.

The test package was given to the subject, who had a complete freedom in the development of the test. There was no maximum time for giving back the compiled tests. Moreover, they were allowed to help themselves by playing the excerpts on their instrument, and to make corrections of previous choices. Even if it was roughly calculated that the development of the test would take about 20 minutes for each excerpt, subjects had the test at their homes for more than one month. This was because almost all of them claimed that the task of segmenting the excerpt was tiring and time-consuming.

Analysis of the Results

The first, quite surprising, result was that more than half of the subjects followed the given instructions only partially and provided indirectly useful feedback. As reported in the previous section, subjects were asked to put a marker, by drawing a single or double bar, between two subsequent notes of the score to highlight the presence of a boundary in the melodic surface. Hence, instructions had the implicit assumption that melodic lexical units do not overlap.

Some subjects, that is, 8 out of 17 subjects, disregarded this assumption and invented a new sign (different among subjects, but with the same meaning) that clearly indicated that some notes were both the last of a lexical unit and the first of the next one. This result implies that, at least for these subjects, the concept of melodic contour cannot be applied, unless we take into account the fact that contours may overlap of at least one note. Another result is that subjects very seldom highlighted the presence of a strong boundary by drawing a double marker. The number of double markers represents the 4.5% of the overall number of markers (including also the ones used for overlapping phrases), thus preventing for a quantitative analysis of strong separators between musical phrases. This result can be partially explained considering that, in most cases, musical excerpts were too short to allow the presence of strong separators. It is likely that the musicologist who suggested which music works should be used for the test, decided to truncate the excerpt in coincidence with the first strong separator.

A visual representation of the position and number of markers along the score helped in visualizing the subjects behavior. Arrays of weights have been assigned to each subject, one for each score; the elements of the arrays correspond to the spaces between two subsequent notes. The following weighting rules were applied for array $a_s[i]$ of subject s, where the index i indicates the position in the score, $m(i)$ is the kind of eventual marker, M_n a normal and M_o an overlapping marker, at position i in the score:

$$a_s[i] = \begin{cases} 1 & \text{if} \quad m(i) = M_n \\ 0.5 & \text{if} \quad m(i) = M_o \quad \text{or} \quad m(i+1) = M_o \\ 0 & \text{elsewhere} \end{cases}$$

For each score, the sum of all the weights assigned by each subject has been computed, allowing for the representation of each score as a histogram (or a curve) where notes numbers are on X-axis and weights sums are on the Y-axis. Peaks in the histograms correspond to positions where many of the subjects put a marker, while low values that is the *noise* between peaks, correspond to positions where subjects disagreed. Figure 4 reports two representative histograms of subjects' choices. Excerpt No. 3 (on the left) shows that subjects substantially agreed in putting markers in a single positions, which corresponded to the only three-quarters note in a continuous flow of one-octave notes, while their concordance is very low even though all of them perceived the presence of boundaries (weights are nonzero). An opposite behavior can be observed for excerpt No. 15, where there is a high concordance among subjects around particular notes, corresponding to long notes with a duration about four times the surrounding notes. An important characteristics, highlighted by Figure 4, is that often peaks are contoured by positions with high concordance: most of the subjects perceived the presence of a boundary in the melodic contour, but they often disagreed by judging a given note either as the last of a phrase, or as the first of the next one (or both in case of overlapping markers).

Figure 4. Frequency by which subjects highlighted a boundary between lexical units for Excerpt No. 3 (left) and Excerpt No. 15 (right)

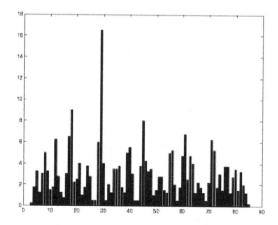
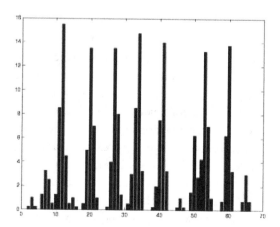

Quantitative analysis has been carried out computing a distance measure between subjects. To this end a symmetric matrix of distances **D** between couple of segmentations made by the subjects has been computed for each excerpts, according to the formula:

$$\mathbf{D}[s,t] = 1 - \frac{\mathbf{P}[s,t]}{\sqrt{\mathbf{P}[s,s]^2 + \mathbf{P}[t,t]^2}} \quad \text{with} \quad \mathbf{P}[s,t] = a_s^T \cdot a_t$$

Hence **D**[s,t] = 0 means that judgments of subjects *i* and *t* are perfectly equal and **D**[s,t] = 1 means that judgments of subjects *s* and *t* do not have any marker in common. Cluster analysis and multidimensional scaling have been carried out using the proposed distance function, highlighting that the group of subjects was uniform, without any cluster of subjects.

A feature of interest for application in the information retrieval domain is the typical length of lexical units. The average length varied considerably depending on the subject and on the excerpt. Yet, no one of the subjects indicated a lexical unit of unitary length. Furthermore, only two subjects indicated lexical units of two notes length, while for four subjects the minimum length of a lexical unit was three notes. The rest of the subjects indicated a minimum length between four and five notes. On the other hand, subjects did not show the same agreement regarding the maximum length of musical phrases. Apart from subject No. 11, who indicated a musical phrase of 38 notes in excerpt No. 4 (clearly indicating the reasons of this choice, which then cannot be considered an error), the maximum length of musical phrases is within the range of 8 and 18 notes.

Results of the Perceptual Study

The results of the perceptual study showed that subjects agree on perceiving a boundary between lexical units only when there are strong cues. In particular, the presence of long notes surrounded by short ones seems to give the strongest evidence

of a boundary between two lexical units. In other cases, like the example shown in Figure 4 for excerpt No. 3, different strategies can be applied by subjects in defining the presence of a boundary between lexical units. The fact that cluster analysis did not highlight any particular group of subjects suggests that subjects changed their strategies according to the excerpt to be segmented, but no trend can be highlighted.

These results show that melodic segmentation is a complex task, and that the concept of lexical unit is not well defined as it is for text where, at least for most Western languages, the organization of sentences in words, and the existence of clear separators between them, allows for an easy computation of indexing terms. It has to be considered that the perceptual study has been carried out only using melodic information, and results could be different for other dimensions. For instance, the segmentation of the harmony may take advantage, at least for musicians and musicologists, by the theory on chord progressions and cadences, while the segmentation of rhythm may be carried out considering that rhythmic patterns tend to repeat almost exactly, allowing for an easier identification and subsequent segmentation.

AN EXPERIMENTAL COMPARISON OF MELODIC SEGMENTATION TECHNIQUES

Given that music is a continuous flow of events without explicit separators, automatic indexing needs to rely on automatic segmentation techniques, that is techniques that detect automatically the lexical units of music documents. Different strategies of melodic segmentation can be applied, each one focusing on particular aspects of music information. A study has been carried out on the effectiveness, in terms of retrieval performances, of different approaches to segmentation. The study has been limited to melodic segmentation, because as already stressed melody is the most used dimension in music retrieval. Another interesting comparison of approaches to music retrieval has been presented in Hu and Dannenberg (2002), where the focus was on alternative representations for a dynamic programming approach, both from the retrieval effectiveness and from the computational cost points of view. In the presented study the computational costs of the tested approaches were comparable, and thus result are not reported.

The organization of a number of evaluation campaigns by the research community working on the different aspects of music access, retrieval, and feature extraction (IMIRSEL, 2006), which started in 2005 (preceded in 2004 by an evaluation effort on audio analysis), will increasingly allow for the comparison of different approaches to music indexing, using standard collections (Downie, Futrelle & Tcheng, 2004).

Approaches to Melodic Segmentation

The approaches to music segmentation can be roughly divided in two main groups: the ones that highlight the lexical units using only the document content, and the ones that exploit prior information about the music theory and perception. Four different approaches, two for each group, have been tested.

Fixed-Length Segmentation (FL)

The simplest segmentation approach consists of the extraction from a melody of subsequences of exactly N notes, called *N-grams* (Downie & Nelson, 2000). N-grams may overlap, because no assumption is made on the possible starting point of a theme, neither on the possible repetitions of relevant music passages. The strength of this approach is its simplicity, because it is based neither on assumption on theories on music composition or perception, nor on analysis of complete melodies. The exhaustive computation of FL units is

straightforward, and can be carried out in linear time. The idea underlying this approach is that the effect of musically irrelevant N-grams will be compensated by the presence of all the musically relevant ones. It is common practice to choose small values for N, typically from 3 to 7 notes, because short units give higher recall, which is considered more significant than the subsequent lowering in terms of precision. Fixed-length segmentation can be extended to polyphonic scores, with the aim to extract all relevant monophonic tokens from concurrent multiple voices (Doraisamy & Rüger, 2004).

Data-Driven Segmentation (DD)

Segmentation can be performed considering that typical passages of a given melody tend to be repeated many times (Pienimäki, 2002). The repetitions can simply be due to the presence of different choruses in the score or can be related to the use of the same melodic material along the composition. Each sequence that is repeated at least K times—normally twice—is usually defined a *pattern*, and is used for the description of a music document. This approach is called data-driven because patterns are computed only from the document data without exploiting knowledge on music perception or structure. This approach can be considered as an extension of the N-grams approach, because DD units can be of any length, with the limitation that they have to be repeated inside the melody—subpatterns that are included in longer patterns are discarded, if they have the same multiplicity. Patterns can be computed from different features, like pitch or rhythm, each feature giving a different set of DD units to describe document content. Patterns can be truncated by applying a given threshold, to reduce the size of the index and to achieve a higher robustness to local errors in the query (Neve & Orio, 2004). The extension to polyphonic scores can be carried out similarly to the FL approach.

Perception-Based Segmentation (PB)

Melodies can be segmented accordingly to theories on human perception. Listeners have the ability to segment the unstructured auditory stream into smaller units, which may correspond to melodic phrases, motifs or musical gestures. Even if listeners may disagree on the exact location of boundaries between subsequent units, as highlighted by the perceptual experiment described above, it is likely that perceptually-based units are good descriptors of a document content because they capture melodic information that appears to be relevant for users. The ability of segmenting the auditory stream may vary depending on the level of musical training of listeners and their knowledge of rules on music theory. Yet, a number of strategies can be generalized for all listeners, in particular the ones related to the detection of clear changes in the melodic flow such as large pitch intervals or note durations. This behavior can be partially explained by the principles of Gestalt psychology. Computational approaches have been proposed by music theorists for the automatic emulation of listener's behavior (Tenney & Polansky, 1980). PB units do not overlap and are based on information on note pitch and duration of monophonic melodies.

Musicological-Oriented Segmentation (MO)

Another approach to segmentation is based on knowledge on music theory, in particular for classical music. According with music theorists, music is based on the combination of musical structures (Lerdhal & Jackendoff, 1983; Narmour, 1990), even if its actual notation may lack of clear representations of such structures. Yet, they can be inferred by applying a number of rules, and part of the analysis of compositions consists in their identification. It is likely that the same approach can be extended to less structured music, like popular or ethnic music. It is assumed that a hierarchical relationship exists among music structures, from musical phrases at the lower level to movements at the higher level. MO units are computed by analyzing the musical score, applying rules for structure identification and segmenting the score in units that correspond to low-level structures. The computation of MO units should be carried out using the global information of the score, but it has been proposed an algorithm that uses only local information and gave results comparable to more complex ones (Cambouropoulos, 1997). Structures may overlap in principle, but the current implementations do not take into account this possibility.

Figure 5. Graphical representation of different automatic segmentation (from the top: PB, a statistical approach not tested, and MO)

The effect of alternative approaches to segmentation is shown in Figure 5, where the lexical units highlighted by different algorithms are graphically shown. The algorithms are the ones included in the MidiToolbox (Eerola & Toiviainen, 2004) and correspond, from the top, to PB, to a probabilistic approach not tested in the present study, and to MO.

Characteristics of the Index Terms

The comparison has been carried out according to the Cranfield model for information retrieval. A music test collection of popular music has been created with 2310 MIDI files as music documents. MIDI is a well-known standard for the representation of music documents that can be synthesized to create audible performances (Rothstein, 1991). MIDI is becoming obsolete both as a format for the representation of music to be listened to because of the widespread diffusion of compressed audio formats such as MP3, and as a format for representing notated music because of the creation of new formats for analyzing, structuring and printing music (Selfridge-Field, 1997). The availability of large collections of music files in MIDI is the main reason why this format is still widely used for music retrieval experiments.

From the collection of MIDI files, the channels containing the melody have been extracted automatically and the note durations have been normalized; the highest pitch has been chosen as part of the melody for polyphonic channels (Uitdenbogerd & Zobel, 1998). After preprocessing, the collection contained complete melodies with an average length of 315.6 notes. A set of 40 queries, with average length of 9.7 notes, has been created as recognizable examples of both choruses and refrains of 20 randomly selected songs. Only the theme from which the query was taken was considered as relevant, considering a query-by-examples paradigm where the example is an excerpt of a particular work that needs to be retrieved. This assumption simplifies the creation

Table 3. Main characteristics of the index terms obtained from the different segmentations techniques

	FL	DD	PB	MO
Average length	3.0	4.8	4.0	3.6
Average units/document	52.1	61.9	43.2	45.0
Number of units	70093	123654	70713	67893

of the relevance judgments that can be built automatically. Alternatively, relevance judgments can be created using a pool of excerpt that may find that more than a document is relevant to a particular query (Typke, den Hoed, de Nooijer, Wiering & Veltkamp, 2005). The initial queries did not contain errors and had a length that allowed for a clear recognition of the main theme. The robustness of errors has been tested by modifying notes pitch and duration, while the effect of query length has been tested by shortening the original queries.

Table 3 shows the main characteristics of lexical units, and thus of the index terms, extracted with the segmentation approaches, giving a preliminary idea on how each segmentation approach describes the document collection. The values reported in the table have been computed with the following experimental setup: FL has been computed with N-grams of three notes; DD has been computed applying a threshold of five notes; PB and MO have been computed using the algorithms presented in Eerola and Toiviainen (2004). For these four approaches, units were sequences of couples of values, pitch and duration, and the index is built with one entry for each different sequence.

The approaches gave comparable results in terms of average length of lexical units, which is about three to four notes, and also in the average number of different units per document. This behavior is different from the results given by the perceptual study on manual segmentation,

Table 4. Retrieval effectiveness of the different approaches

	FL	DD	PB	MO
Av.Prec.	0.98	0.96	0.80	0.83
= 1	97.5%	92.5%	72.5%	77.5%
≤ 3	97.5%	100%	87.5%	87.5%
≤ 5	97.5%	100%	87.5%	92.5%
≤ 10	100%	100%	90.0%	95.0%
not found	0.0%	0.0%	10.0%	2.5%

which for many subjects gave a minimum length of lexical units of about four to five notes. Another interesting feature is the average number of different lexical units for documents that range from 43.2 for PB to 61.9 for DD. Given that these values are computed for complete music documents, even if only on the melodic line, music indexing is based on a very compact description of document contents, at least compared with indexing of textual documents that, also in the case of short documents, have hundreds of different index terms. The last row reports the number of different lexical units that corresponds to the number of entries in the index file. As it can be seen, segmentation with overlapping units with different lengths (DD) has the drawback of an increase of the index size and in memory requirements.

Retrieval Effectiveness

All the retrieval experiments have been carried out using the same retrieval engine, which is based on the Vector Space Model and implements the *tf·idf* weighting scheme described previously. The results in terms of retrieval effectiveness are presented in Table 4, where the average precision (Av.Prec.), the percentage of queries that gave the relevant document within the first k positions (k with values in [1,3,5,10]), and the ones that did not retrieve the relevant document at all ("not found"), are reported. It has to be noted that retrieval effectiveness is usually reported through precision/recall plots, using the rank list of retrieved documents. The particular choice of parameters adopted in this experiment depends on the fact that there was only one relevant document for each query in the test collection.

FL and DD had comparable results, because they have close average precision and both approaches always retrieved the relevant document within the first ten positions (DD within the first three, but with a lower percentage of queries that retrieved the relevant document at top rank). Also PB and MO had comparable results in terms of average precision; with slightly better performances of MO, in particular because PB did

Figure 6. Retrieval effectiveness of the different approaches depending on the number of errors added to the query (left) and on the shortening of query length (right)

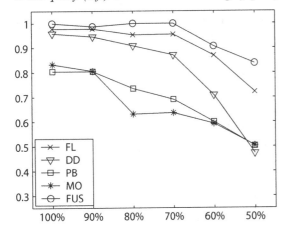
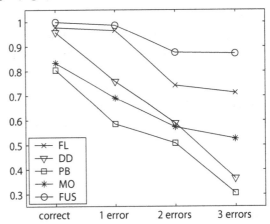

not retrieve at all the relevant document in 10% of the queries. This is a negative aspect of PB, due to the fact that its units do not overlap and, for short queries, it may happen that none of the note sequences match with the segmented units. A similar consideration applies also to MO, but this effect seems to be bounded by the fact that MO units are shorter.

The performances of the different approaches depending on the presence of errors in the query are shown on the left of Figure 6, which reports the average precision of the approaches. Apart from FL, the other segmentation techniques had a clear drop in the performances, also when a single error was introduced. In particular, PB and MO showed a similar negative trend, almost linear with the number of errors. It is interesting to note that DD, even if its performances are almost comparable to FL in the case of a correct query, had a faster degradation in performances. The average precision depending on query length is shown on the right of Figure 6. Similar considerations can be made on the trends of the different approaches. PB and MO had a similar behavior, and also in this case FL was the one with the best performances. It can be noted that, when the queries are moderately shortened, the average precision of FL and DD is almost constant. The drop in performances appears earlier, and more remarkably, for DD than for FL.

From the analyses, it appears that simple approaches to segmentation, which have redundant information through overlapping units, give better performances than approaches based on music perception or music theory. Moreover, fixed-length segmentation was more robust to errors in the queries and to short queries than data-driven segmentation. From these results, it seems that for music indexing an approach that does not filter out any information, improves recall without degrading precision. The good performances of FL can be also due to the fact that it has the shortest average length of index terms (actually, being N-grams, the average correspond to the length of all the index terms), and hence local perturbations due to errors in the query do not affect a high number of indexes.

The fact that a simple approach to melodic segmentation such as FL outperforms all other ones that are based on content specific characteristics is somehow counterintuitive. For this reason, a number of experiments have been carried out in order to highlight the best configuration of the parameters for each approach. The results reported in Table 4 and Figure 6 are the best ones achieved by each approach. It has to be noted that the overall performances are biased by the particular implementation of the different segmentation algorithms, and this is particularly true for PB and MO. The aim of the study was not to state which is the best approach, but to compare the experimental results of different implementations using a common testbed.

In addition to the results of the segmentation algorithms, Figure 6 reports also the average precision of a fifth approach, named FUS, which with this particular setting outperforms all the others in terms of robustness to errors and short queries. The approach is discussed in the next section.

PARALLEL INDEXES

Up to this point, the discussion has been carried out assuming that only one index is built on a document collection, eventually using a combination of features. In general, this is a reasonable approach, because the creation of an index file is computationally costly, and may require a remarkable amount of memory storage. On the other hand, different indexes may capture different characteristics of a document collection, which usefulness may depend on the user information need, on the way the query is created, and on the approach to evaluation of retrieved documents carried out by the user. The presence of a number of alternative indexing schemes can be exploited by running a number of parallel retrieval sessions on the different indexing schemes, obtaining a number of ranked list of potentially relevant documents, and combining the results in a single ranked list using some strategies. The approach is named *data fusion* or *collection fusion*, where the latter term more precisely addresses the problem of combining together the results from indexing schemes built on different—and potentially non-overlapping—collections of documents.

Collection fusion techniques are quite popular in Web metasearch engines, which are services for the automatic parallel querying of a number the normal Web search engines where overall results are presented in a single ranked list (Lee, 1997). The advantages of a metasearch engines are an higher coverage of the Web pages, which is the union of the coverage of single search engines, and improvements of the retrieval effectiveness in terms of recall—because more documents are retrieved—and in terms of precision—because multiple evidences of the relevance of some documents are available. The crucial point in the development of a collection (or data) fusion technique is on the way different ranked lists are fused together. A number of constraints have to be considered for typical collection fusion applications, namely the indexing schemes of the different search engines are not known; there is a different coverage of the overall set of documents; the individual RSVs, or the similarity score, may not be known by the metasearch engine; if known, the RSVs may be expressed in different scales and have different statistical distributions. For this reason, some techniques have been proposed using the only information that is surely available: the rank of each retrieved document for each search engine (Fox & Shaw, 1994).

Most of these constraints do not hold when the parallel indexes are built within the same retrieval system, because there is complete control on each weighting scheme, on the range and distribution of each RSVs which can be obtained using the same retrieval engine that is run on the different indexes. Even if this aspect is more related to the retrieval rather than indexing of music documents, it is worth mentioning an experiment on data fusion of alternative indexing schemes.

Fusion of Different Melodic Descriptors

Even when a single dimension is used to extract content descriptors, there are a number of choices that have to be made on the way lexical units are computed that affect the effectiveness of an indexing scheme. Let us consider the common situation in which the melodic information is used as content descriptor, using an example of a complete evaluation of music indexing schemes.

The first choice in music indexing is how lexical units are computed, as described in the previous section. In the running example, the DD approach is used—Data Driven, where lexical units are computed using a pattern analysis approach presented in the preceding section—because it gives high performances in terms of retrieval while allowing for different lengths of the index terms. The second step consists of choosing whether using absolute or relative features. The third step regards the levels of quantization that has to be applied to each feature, that may range from one single level—meaning that the feature is not used in practice—to as many levels as the possible values—meaning that no quantization is applied. Table 5 represents the different combinations of time and pitch information of melodic lexical units; the three cells marked with an acronym in bold are the ones that have been used in the experiment on data fusion, the two cells marked with "---" highlight combinations that do not make sense.

As shown in Table 5, three indexing schemes have been used: PIT that uses only relative pitch information, with $N=9$ levels of quantization of melodic intervals; IOI that uses only absolute duration information, with $N=11$ levels the quantization of exact durations; BTH that uses both relative pitch and absolute duration. Having used

Table 5. Possible combinations of duration and pitch information, according to the absolute or relative representation and on the levels of quantization

			Duration					
			Abs.			Rel.		
			1	N	∞	1	N	∞
P i t c h	A b s.	1	---				IOI	
		N						
		∞						
	R e l.	1				---		
		N	PIT				BTH	
		∞						

the DD approach, lexical units may be different from an index to the other, because IOI patterns may not correspond to PIT or BTH patterns, and vice versa.

It can be noted that any combination reported in the table, eventually varying quantization, can be used to index music documents from melodic information. An extensive evaluation of the retrieval effectiveness of any combination of choice—and their merging with data fusion techniques—has not been carried out yet. The individual indexing schemes can be fused in any combination. In the presented evaluation, two data fusion approaches have been tested: Fuse2 that merges the results from PIT and IOI, and Fuse3 that merges all three indexing schemes.

Experimental Evaluation

The effect of data fusion has been tested on a small test collection of popular music, which has been created using 107 Beatles' songs in MIDI format downloaded from the Web. As for any test collection, documents may contain errors. In a preprocessing step, the channels containing the melody have been extracted automatically and the note durations have been normalized; in case of polyphonic scores, the highest pitch has been chosen as part of the melody. After preprocessing, the collection contained 107 complete melodies with an average length of 244 notes, ranging from 89 of the shortest melody to 564 of the longest. Indexes were built on complete melodies, because repetitions are important for the DD approach to melodic segmentation. A set of 40 queries has been created by randomly selecting 20 themes in the dataset and using the first notes of the chorus and of the refrain. The initial note and the length of each query were chosen to have recognizable motifs that could be considered representative of real users' queries. The queries had an average length of 9.75 notes, ranging from 4 to 21 notes. Only the theme from which the query was taken was considered as relevant.

Results are shown in Table 6, where the average precision (Av.Prec.), the percentage queries that gave the relevant document within the first k positions (k with values in [1,3,5,10]), and the ones that did not retrieve the relevant document at all ("not found"), are reported. As it can be seen, IOI gave the poorest results, even if for 90% of the queries the relevant document was among the first three retrieved. The highest average precision using a single feature was obtained by BTH, with the drawback of an on-off behavior: either the relevant document is the first retrieved or it is not retrieved at all (2.5% of the queries). PIT gave good results, with all the queries that found the relevant document among the first three documents.

The first interesting result is that Fuse2 gave an improvement in respect to the separate features—IOI and PIT—with an average precision of 0.96, hence with values comparable to BTH and without the drawback of not retrieving the relevant document for 2.5% of the queries. It is worth noting that even if the retrieval effectiveness of IOI is very low compared to PIT, nevertheless the combination of the two in a fused ranked list gave an improvement of the recognition rate (the relevant document retrieved at top rank) of 3%. It could be expected that adding BTH in the data fusion would not give further improvements, since BTH is already a combination of the first two. The set of BTH patterns is a subset of the union of set of IOI and PIT patterns, while it can be shown that set BTH includes the intersection of sets IOI and PIT, because of the choice of not considering subpatterns that have the same multiplicity of longer ones. Given these considerations, it is clear that BTH does not introduce new patterns in respect to IOI and PIT. Yet, as can be seen from column labeled with Fuse3 in Table 6 the use of all the three features allowed for reducing the drawbacks of the three single rankings. This result can be explained considering that BTH had different *tf·idf* weights, which were somehow more

selective than simple IOI and PIT and which gave a very high value score to the relevant document in case of a good match.

In these experiments, and with this particular setup, the best results for Fuse2 and Fuse3 have been obtained assigning equal weights to the single RSVs, thus computing the final similarity as the average of individual similarities. This setup was the one that gave the best results. Yet data fusion can be used also to allow the user a refinement of the query, by manually assigning which are the dimensions and the features that are more relevant for the user's information need. For instance, if the peculiarity of a song is on the rhythm of the melody rather than on the pitch contour, the user may choose a particular data fusion strategy that underlines this characteristic. Data fusion allows also to increases in robustness to errors in the query and to short queries, as shown in Figure 6 for the experiments on the comparison of different segmentation techniques. In this case, the values reported for FUS are obtained by fusing the individual results of the four techniques.

The drawback of data fusion techniques is that they require to create parallel indexing schemes, to carry out parallel retrievals, and finally to fuse the results together. Nevertheless, results are encouraging, and are worth to be tested extensively. A possible complete scheme for indexing, retrieval and data fusion is plotted in Figure 7.

Table 6. Retrieval effectiveness using single indexing schemes and data fusion approaches

	IOI	PIT	BTH	Fuse2	Fuse3
Av.Prec.	0.74	0.93	0.98	0.96	0.98
= 1	57.5%	87.5%	97.5%	92.5%	95.0%
≤ 3	90.0%	100%	97.5%	100%	100%
≤ 5	95.0%	100%	97.5%	100%	100%
≤ 10	97.5%	100%	97.5%	100%	100%
not found	0	0	2.5	0	0

Figure 7. Main components of a complete music retrieval engine where multiple indexing schemes are combined with a data fusion technique

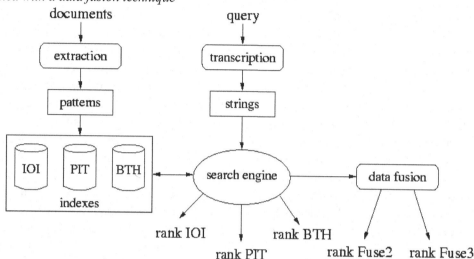

CONCLUSION

Indexing is based on the concept that documents become more accessible if a number of guidance tools are provided. This fact can be exploited to improve the retrieval effectiveness, reducing its computational cost because the content of a collection of documents is accessed through a set of pointers: instead of browsing all the documents to find which are relevant to the user's information need, the system may access only the ones that are potentially relevant, depending on the set of indexes that point to them. Indexing is the key to scalability.

The application of indexing to music retrieval is motivated by the need for a scalable system to access music documents, because music collections are increasingly growing, both in digital libraries systems at server side and in storage devices at user side. Given that the main ideas behind textual document indexing are quite general, a parallelism can be drawn between the phases of textual document indexing—namely, lexical analysis, stop-words removal, stemming and index weighting—and the phases that may be required for music document indexing.

Yet there are a number of factors that need to be taken into account when extending the indexing concept to the music domain. First of all, the fact that it is difficult to state which is the semantic of a music document, if a semantic exists. Thus the choice of which are the most representative index terms have to be carried out with a different approach. To this end, the concept of lexical units of the music language has been introduced, taking into account that music has a multidimensional nature, and that not all the dimensions may be of interest for the final user. Furthermore, it is not clear to which extent the users agree on the way they perceive lexical units.

To investigate this aspect, a perceptual study has been carried out on the way a number of musicians highlighted melodic lexical units of 20 excerpts of music scores. The analysis highlighted that, even if there are some common trends in user's behavior, the consistency among subjects depends on the availability of particular cues in the music documents. Even if subjects may not agree when they refer to lexical units, their use as index terms may be evaluated experimentally, using a test collection of documents, queries and relevance judgments. This is the goal of an experiment that has been reported, where four different approaches of melodic segmentation, aimed at highlighting lexical units, have been compared. Results showed that simple approaches outperform more complex ones that exploit a priori information either on music perception or on music theory. Simple approaches are based on the creation of a redundant index, where different elements (i.e., a given note) belong to more than one index term. From the experimental comparison it may be inferred that redundancy is an important aspect of music indexing. To this end, a final experiment has been proposed, where a data fusion approach has been exploited to mix together the results of alternative indexing schemes. Results showed that data fusion allows for an improvement of the retrieval effectiveness.

From this discussion it can be concluded that music indexing can inherit most of the advantages of textual indexing, which is still a promising approach to music access, provided that the peculiarities of the music language are taken into account. Even if research in music retrieval should not be limited to the extension of well-known techniques to the music domain, indexing can be considered as a core technique for building more complex systems. Furthermore, it has to be noted that the actual trends in the Music Information Retrieval (MIR) research community encompass a number of approaches that are beyond the pure retrieval task. The user of a MIR system may have different needs other than searching for a particular song that she has in mind. The user may need an *information filtering* system that allows the user to listen only to the music documents that the user (potentially) likes, or a *browsing* system for managing a personal music collection. Also in these cases, indexing can be used to increase the efficiency of new approaches to music access.

REFERENCES

Agosti, M., Bombi, F., Melucci, M. & Mian, G. A. (2000). Towards a digital library for the Venetian music of the eighteenth century. In J. Anderson, M. Deegan, S. Ross & S. Harold (Eds.), *DRH 98: Selected papers from digital resources for the humanities* (pp. 1-16). Office for Humanities Communication.

Baeza-Yates, R. & Ribeiro-Neto, B. (1999). *Modern information retrieval*. New York: ACM Press.

Bainbridge, D., Nevill-Manning, C. G., Witten, I. H., Smith, L. A. & Mc-Nab, R. J. (1999). Towards a digital library of popular music. *In Proceedings of the ACM Conference on Digital Libraries* (pp. 161-169).

Basaldella, D. & Orio, N. (2006). An application of weighted transducers to music information retrieval. *In Proceedings of Electronic Imaging* (pp. 607306/1-607306/10).

Berenzweig, A., Logan, B., Ellis, D. P. W. & Whitman, B. (2004). A large-scale evaluation of acoustic and subjective music-similarity measures. *Computer Music Journal, 28*(2), 63-76.

Birmingham, W. P., Dannenberg, R. B., Wakefield, G. H., Bartsch, M., Bykowski, D., Mazzoni, D., Meek, C., Mellody, M. & Rand, W. (2001). MUSART: Music retrieval via aural queries. *In Proceedings of the International Conference on Music Information Retrieval* (pp. 73-82).

Blackburn, S. & DeRoure, D. (1998). A tool for content-based navigation of music. *In Proceedings of the ACM Multimedia Conference* (pp. 361-368).

Borko, H. & Bernier, C. L. (1978). *Indexing concepts and methods*. New York: Academic Press.

Cambouropoulos, E. (1997). Musical rhythm: A formal model for determining local boundaries. In E. Leman (Ed.), *Music, gestalt and computing* (pp. 277-293). Berlin: Springer-Verlag.

Cano, P., Batlle, E., Kalker, T. & Haitsma, J. (2005). A review of audio fingerprinting. *Journal of VLSI Signal Processing, 41*, 271-284.

Cantate (2006). Computer access to notation and text in music libraries. Retrieved May 17, 2007, from *http://projects.fnb.nl/cantate/*

de Cheveigné, A. & Baskind, A. (2003). F0 extimation. *In Proceedings of Eurospeech* (pp. 833-836).

Doraisamy, S. & Rüger, S. (2004). A polyphonic music retrieval system using N-grams. *In Proceedings of the International Conference on Music Information Retrieval* (pp. 204-209).

Downie, S. & Nelson, M. (2000). Evaluation of a simple and effective music information retrieval method. *In Proceedings of the ACM International Conference on Research and Development in Information Retrieval* (pp. 73-80).

Downie, J. S. (2003). Music information retrieval. *Annual Review of Information Science and Technology, 37*, 295-340.

Downie, J. S., Futrelle, J. & Tcheng, D. (2004). The international music information retrieval systems evaluation laboratory: Governance, access and security. *In Proceedings of the International Conference on Music Information Retrieval* (pp. 9-14).

Dunn, J. & Mayer, C. (1999). VARIATIONS: A Digital Music Library System at Indiana University. *In Proceedings of ACM Conference on Digital Libraries* (pp. 12-19).

Eerola, T. & Toiviainen, P. (2004). MIR in Matlab: The Midi Toolbox. *In Proceedings of the International Conference on Music Information Retrieval* (pp. 22-27).

Ferrari, E. & Haus, G. (1999). The musical archive information system at Teatro alla Scala. *In Proceedings of the IEEE International Conference on Multimedia Computing and Systems* (Vol. 2, pp. 817-821).

Fox, E. A. & Shaw, J .A. (1994). Combination of multiple searches. *In The Second Text REtrieval Conference*, TREC-2 (pp. 243-249).

Ghias, A., Logan, J., Chamberlin, D. & Smith, B. C. (1995). Query by humming: Musical information retrieval in an audio database. *In Proceedings of the ACM Conference on Digital Libraries* (pp. 231-236).

Gómez, E. & Herrera, P. (2004). Estimating the tonality of polyphonic audio files: Cognitive versus machine learning modelling strategies. *In Proceedings of the International Conference on Music Information Retrieval* (pp. 92-95).

Harmonica (2006). Accompanying action on music information in libraries. Retrieved May 17, 2007, from *http://projects.fnb.nl/harmonica/*

Harte, C., Sandler, M., Abdallah, S. & Gómez, E. (2005). Symbolic representation of musical chords: A proposed syntax for text annotations. *In Proceedings of the International Conference on Music Information Retrieval* (pp. 66-71).

Harvell, J. & Clark, C. (1995). Analysis of the quantitative data of system performance. Deliverable 7c, LIB-JUKEBOX/4-1049: Music across borders. Retrieved May 17, 2007, from *http://www.statsbiblioteket.dk/Jukebox/edit-report-1.html*

Hoashi, K., Matsumoto, K. & Inoue, N. (2003). Personalization of user profiles for content-based music retrieval based on relevance feedback. *In Proceedings of the ACM International Conference on Multimedia* (pp. 110-119).

Hsu, J.-L., Liu, C. C. & Chen, A. L. P. (1998). Efficient repeating pattern finding in music databases. *In Proceeding of the International Conference on Information and Knowledge Management* (pp. 281-288).

Hu, N. & Dannenberg, R. B. (2002). A comparison of melodic database retrieval techniques using sung queries. *In Proceedings of the ACM/IEEE Joint Conference on Digital Libraries* (pp. 301-307).

Humdrum. The Humdram toolkit: Software for music research. Retrieved May 17, 2007, from *http://www.music-cog.ohio-state.edu/Humdrum/*

Huron D. (1995). *The Humdrum toolkit: Reference manual.*, Menlo Park, CA: Center for Computer Assisted Research in the Humanities.

IMIRSEL (2006). The international music information retrieval system evaluation laboratory project. Retrieved May 17, 2007, from *http://www. music-ir.org/evaluation/*

Krumhansl, C. L. (1989). Why is musical timbre so hard to understand? In S. Nielsen and O. Olsson (Eds.), *Structure and perception electroacoustic sound and music* (pp. 45-53). Amsterdam, NL: Elsevier.

Lavrenko, V. & Pickens, J. (2003). Polyphonic music modeling with random fields. *In Proceedings of the ACM International Conference on Multimedia* (pp. 120-129).

Lee, J. H. (1997). Analysis of multiple evidence combination. *In Proceedings of the ACM International Conference on Research and Development in Information Retrieval* (pp. 267-275).

Lee, J. H. & Downie, J. S. (2004). Survey of music information needs, uses, and seeking behaviours: Preliminary findings. *In Proceedings of the International Conference on Music Information Retrieval* (pp. 441-446).

Lerdhal, F. & Jackendoff, R. (1983). *A generative theory of tonal music.* Cambridge: The MIT Press.

Lesaffre, M., Leman, M., Tanghe, K., De Baets, B., De Meyer, H. & Martens, J.-P. (2003). User-dependent taxonomy of musical features as a conceptual framework for musical audio-mining technology. *In Proceedings of the Stockholm Music Acoustics Conference* (pp. 635-638).

McLane, A. (1996). Music as information. In M. E. Williams (Ed.), *Arist* (Vol. 31, pp. 225-262). American Society for Information Science.

Meek, C. & Birmingham, W. (2003). Automatic thematic extractor. *Journal of Intelligent Information Systems, 21*(1), 9-33.

Melucci, M. & Orio, N. (1999). Musical information retrieval using melodic surface. *In Proceedings of the ACM Conference on Digital Libraries* (pp. 152-160).

Melucci, M. & Orio, N. (2004). Combining melody processing and information retrieval techniques: Methodology, evaluation, and system implementation. *Journal of the American Society for Information Science and Technology, 55*(12), 1058-1066.

Middleton, R. (2002). *Studying popular music.* Philadelphia: Open University Press.

Moen, W. E. (1998). Accessing distributed cultural heritage information. *Communications of the ACM, 41*(4), 45-48.

Musica. The international database of choral repertoire. Retrieved May 17, 2007, from *http://www.musicanet.org/*

Narmour, E. (1990). *The analysis and cognition of basic melodic structures.* Chicago, MI: University of Chicago Press.

Neve, G. & Orio, N. (2004). Indexing and retrieval of music documents through pattern analysis and data fusion techniques. *In Proceedings of the International Conference on Music Information Retrieval* (pp. 216-223).

Pienimäki, A. (2002). Indexing music database using automatic extraction of frequent phrases. *In Proceedings of the International Conference on Music Information Retrieval* (pp. 25-30).

Rothstein, J. (1991). *MIDI: A comprehensive introduction*. Madison, WI: A-R Editions.

Selfridge-Field, E. (1997). *Beyond MIDI: The handbook of musical codes*. Cambridge: The MIT Press.

Shifrin, J., Pardo, B., Meek, C. & Birmingham, W. (2002). HMM-based musical query retrieval. *In Proceedings of the ACM/IEEE Joint Conference on Digital Libraries* (pp. 295–300).

Sparck Jones, K. & Willett, P. (1997). *Readings in information retrieval.*, San Francisco: Morgan Kaufmann.

Stenzel, R. & Kamps, T. (2005). Improving content-based similarity measures by training a collaborative model. *In Proceedings of the International Conference on Music Information Retrieval* (pp. 264-271).

Tenney, J. & Polansky, L. (1980). Temporal gestalt perception in music. *Journal of Music Theory*, *24*(2), 205-241.

TREC. Text REtrieval conference home page. Retrieved May 17, 2007, from *http://trec.nist.gov/*

Typke, R., den Hoed, M., de Nooijer, J., Wiering, F. & Veltkamp, R.C. (2005). A ground truth for half a million musical incipits. *Journal of Digital Information Management*, *3*(1), 34-39.

Uitdenbogerd, A. & Zobel, J. (1998). Manipulation of music for melody matching. *In Proceedings of the ACM Conference on Multimedia* (pp. 235-240).

van Rijsbergen, C. J., (1979). *Information retrieval* (2nd ed.). London: Butterworths.

Chapter II
MARSYAS-0.2:
A Case Study in Implementing Music Information Retrieval Systems

George Tzanetakis
University of Victoria, Canada

ABSTRACT

MARSYAS is an open source audio processing framework with specific emphasis on building music information retrieval systems. It has been under development since 1998 and has been used for a variety of projects in both academia and industry. In this chapter, the software architecture of Marsyas will be described. The goal is to highlight design challenges and solutions that are relevant to any MIR software.

INTRODUCTION

Advances in technology have always transformed music. Examples of technologies that transformed the way music was produced, distributed and consumed include musical instruments, music notation, recording and more recently digital music storage and distribution. Recently portable digital music players have become a familiar sight and online music sales have been steadily increas-ing. It is likely that in the near future anyone will be able to digitally access all of recorded music in human history. In order to efficiently interact with the rapidly growing collections of digitally available music it is necessary to develop tools that have some understanding of the actual musi-cal content. Music information retrieval (MIR) is an emerging research area that deals with all aspects of organizing and extracting information from music signals.

In the past few years, interest in music information retrieval (MIR) has been steadily increasing. MIR algorithms, especially when analyzing music signals in audio format, typically utilize state-of-the-art signal processing and machine learning algorithms. The large amounts of data that are processed together with the huge computational requirements of audio processing can stress current hardware to its limits. Therefore efficient processing is critical for building functional MIR systems that scale to large collections of music and eventually to all of recorded music. Moreover, MIR is an inherently interdisciplinary field with practitioners with varying degrees of computer and programming expertise (examples of fields involved include musicology, information science and cognitive psychology). Therefore it is desirable for MIR systems to support multiple hierarchical levels of usage and extensibility. These issues make the design and development of MIR systems and frameworks especially challenging.

MARSYAS (*M*usic *A*nalysis, *R*etrieval and *SY*nthesis for *A*udio *S*ignals) is an open source audio processing framework with specific emphasis on building MIR systems. It has been under development since 1998 and has been used for a variety of projects both in academia and industry. The guiding principle behind the design of *MARSYAS* has always been to provide a flexible, expressive and extensive framework without sacrificing computational efficiency. Addressing these conflicting requirements is the major challenge facing the software engineer of MIR systems.

The main objective of this chapter is to describe the software architecture of *MARSYAS* using examples from specific MIR applications. We highlight the design challenges and corresponding solutions that are probably relevant to any MIR software system. In many cases these solutions are informed by ideas originating from other fields of computer science and software engineering but have to be adapted to the particular needs and constraints of MIR research. After reviewing related work and background information, *MARSYAS* is described in the following subsections: History, Requirements, Architecture and Projects. The next section (Specific Topics) describes in more detail specific topics that we believe are especially important for audio processing and how we have tried to address them in the framework. The chapter concludes with a description of future trends in *MARSYAS* and audio processing software frameworks in general. One of the major dilemmas facing any MIR researcher is whether to use existing tools or develop their own. By describing the tradeoffs and challenges we have faced with the design of our system we hope to help researchers make more informed decisions. Finally an underlying theme of this chapter is the importance of open source software for research and how it is different from other areas of open source development.

BACKGROUND

Music Information Retrieval is a new area of content-based multimedia information retrieval. Although there was sporadic earlier work, a good reference starting point is the first international conference on MIR (ISMIR) which was held in 2000. These conferences (ISMIR) have been a forum for bringing together music researchers, audio engineers, computer scientists, musicologists, librarians and the music industry (Futrelle & Downie, 2002). MIR with audio signals typically requires signal processing and machine learning algorithms in order to achieve tasks such as classification, similarity-retrieval and segmentation.

MARSYAS 0.2, the software framework for audio analysis and synthesis described in this chapter, evolved from *MARSYAS 0.1* (Tzanetakis & Cook, 2000), a framework that focused mostly on audio analysis. One of the motivating factors for the rewrite of the code and architecture was the desire to add audio synthesis capabilities and was influenced by the design of the Synthesis Toolkit

(Cook & Scavone, 1999). Other influences include the powerful but more complex architecture of CLAM (Amatriain, 2005), the patching model and strong timing of Chuck (Wang & Cook, 2003), and ideas from Aura (Dannenberg & Brandt, 1996). The matrix model used in *Implicit Patching* was influenced by the design of SDIFF and the default-naming scheme for controls is inspired by the Open Sound Control (OSC) protocol (Wright & Freed, 1997). The code structure reflects many ideas from Design Patterns (Gamma, Helm, Johnson & Vlissides, 1995).

The idea of dataflow programming has been fundamental in the design of *MARSYAS*. Dataflow programming has a long history. The original (and still valid) motivation for research into dataflow was to take advantage of parallelism. Motivated by criticisms of the classical von Neumann hardware architecture such as (Ackerman, 1982) dataflow architectures for hardware was proposed as an alternative in the 1970's and 1980's. During the same period a number of textual dataflow languages such as Lucid (Wadge & Ashcroft, 1985) were proposed. Despite expectations that dataflow architectures and languages would take over from von Neumann concepts this did not happen. However during the 1990's there was a new direction of growth in the field of dataflow visual programming languages that were domain specific. In such visual languages programming is done by connecting processing objects with "wires" to create "patches". Successful examples include Labview (*http://www.ni.com/labview/*), SimuLink (*http://www.math-works/com/products/simulink/*) and in the field of Computer Music, Max/MSP (Zicarelli, 2002) and Pure Data (Puckette, 2002). A comprehensive overview of dataflow programming languages can be found in Johnston et al. (2004). Another recent trend has been to view dataflow computation as a software engineering methodology for building systems using existing programming languages (Manolescu, 1997). A comprehensive overview of audio processing frameworks from a Software

Engineering perspective can be found in (Amatriain, 2005). More recently frameworks specific to MIR have been introduced. They include ACE and JAudio (McEnnis et al, 2005) and D2K/M2K (Downie & Futrelle, 2005).

More detailed information about some of the topics discussed in this chapter can be found in conference publications. Implicit Patching was introduced in Bray and Tzanetakis (2005a) and Flexible Scheduling in Burroughs, Parkin and Tzanetakis (2006). Experiments with distributed audio feature extraction were described in Bray and Tzanetakis (2005b).

Description of MARSYAS

MARSYAS is a software framework for rapid prototyping, design and experimentation with audio analysis and synthesis with specific emphasis on processing music signals in audio format. In this section we examine the history and motivation behind the design and development of MARSYAS. Some of the requirements used to design the latest version that are applicable to any MIR system are also discussed. The section ends with an overview of the software architecture of the framework.

History

The design and development of *MARSYAS* was initiated by George Tzanetakis while he was studying at Princeton University as part of his graduate research under the supervision of Perry Cook. The motivating application was a reimplementation of a well-known music/speech discriminator work (Scheirer & Slaney, 1997). In general, implementing an existing algorithm provides a much deeper understanding of how it works and in many cases suggests directions for improvement or extensions. Even though the initial version was only used internally at Princeton it was designed to be a general framework with reusable components rather than a specific implementation. Gradually *MARSYAS* was used to conduct new research in audio analysis and retrieval. Since then every publication by George Tzanetakis and many by others have used *MARSYAS*. In 2000 it was clear that certain major design decisions needed to be revised. A major rewrite/redesign of the framework was initiated and the first public version was released (numbered 0.1). Soon after Sourceforge (http://sourceforge.net/index.php) was used to host *MARSYAS*. Version 0.1 is still widely used by a variety of academic groups and industry around the world. It is well known in Software Engineering that even though major rewrites can be time consuming they are inevitable for complex software and typically result in much better code structure and organization. A second major rewrite was initiated in 2002 while George Tzanetakis was a PostDoctoral Fellow at Carnegie Mellon University working with Roger Dannenberg. The motivation was the desire to port algorithms from the Synthesis Toolkit (STK) (Cook & Scavone, 1990) into *MARSYAS*. This effort, as well as many interesting discussions with Roger Dannenberg, informed the new design. The new version (numbered 0.2) uses a dataflow model of audio computation with general matrices (**Slices**) instead of 1-D arrays as data and an Open Source Control (OSC) (Wright & Freed, 1997) inspired hierarchical messaging system used to control the dataflow network. This is the version described in this chapter.

Even though not immediately obvious, supporting audio synthesis is important for a successful MIR software framework. The main reason is that the ability to hear the results of audio analysis algorithms can be very useful for debugging and understanding algorithms. For example the ability to listen to extracted chords or beat patterns can provide insights that are impossible to achieve just by looking at numbers or graphs.

Since the beginning, a major decision was to provide *MARSYAS* as free software under the GNU public license (GPL). Some of the common motivations and reasons behind free software in general are: (1) freedom to modify the software to suit the needs of individual users; (2) better quality by having many people working and looking at the source code; (3) support for multiple operating systems and porting by the ability to change the code appropriately; (4) easier adoption/lower cost compared to proprietary software. In addition to these motivations there are additional specific motivations behind free software when it is used in research. These include: (1) source code is a means of communication. This is especially important in research where publications can not possibly describe all the nuances and details of how an algorithm is implemented; (2) replication of experiments is essential for progress in research especially in new emerging areas such as MIR. For complex systems and algorithms it is almost impossible to know if a reimplementation is correct and therefore the ability to run the original code is crucial; (3) researchers have limited financial resources and therefore making the software free encourages adoption. One of the common objections to free software is why should someone invest all this time and effort into building something and then give it away for free. Most academics are comfortable with this idea as they do so with publications, reviewing and other activities. Even though many of these activities might not have direct financial reward they are part of the responsibilities of any academic. In addition, there are indirect benefits with developing research software such as peer recognition, opportunities for collaboration and international visibility. Finally, as will be describing in more detail in the section about projects, it is possible to use free software developed in academia in industrial settings and receive money for it.

A frequent dilemma facing graduate students and researchers is whether to build their own tools or use existing ones. This decision frequently involves a tradeoff between short and long term investment. For example using a combination of existing tools a particular task might be accomplished in 1 hour. By spending one week writing your own tool, the task might be accomplished

Figure 1. Audio feature extraction, segmentation and classification

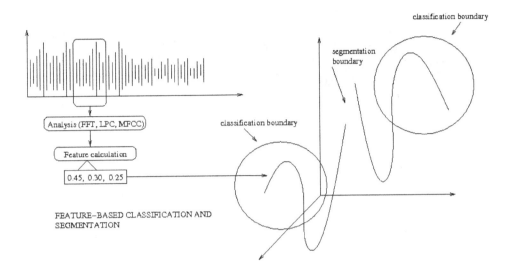

in 1 minute. Whether programming for a week is worth the trouble is a tough question. Even though it is impossible to provide a definite answer, we discuss how our experiences with *MARSYAS* can be informative. If the task at hand can take hours, as MIR algorithms frequently do, runtime performance becomes a critical issue that can affect research. For example, if an experiment that used to take 5 hours takes 10 minutes, it can be executed multiple times with different parameters to find the best choice. Programming is a very time consuming task so choosing to build your own tools works best if you have a large enough timeframe to do it. For example a PhD student has a better chance at completing a significant software framework than a Masters student pressed for time. A supportive advisor is also important and the best way to achieve this is to provide earlier proof that the time you spend developing software pays off in terms of research results. Finally, an important consideration is that the development of the software framework itself especially in emerging applications such as MIR is research in itself. *MARSYAS* has been used as

a test bed for many ideas in Software Engineering and Computer Science that arise based on the particular characteristics and constraints of audio processing.

MARSYAS can be obtained from *http://marsyas.sourceforge.net*. It is written in portable C++ (as much as possible) and it compiles in Linux, OS X, Cygwin and Windows Visual Studio 2003 and 2005. Subversion is used for version control and the latest unstable source code can be obtained from the Web page.

Requirements

The canonical application of MARSYAS is audio feature extraction (Tzanetakis & Cook, 2002) which forms the basis of many MIR algorithms such as classification, segmentation and similarity retrieval. Figure 1 shows a schematic diagram of audio feature extraction and how it can be used for segmentation and classification. The audio signal is broken into small slices and by performing some form of frequency analysis such as the Discrete Fourier Transform followed by

Figure 2. Frequency and time summarization in feature extraction

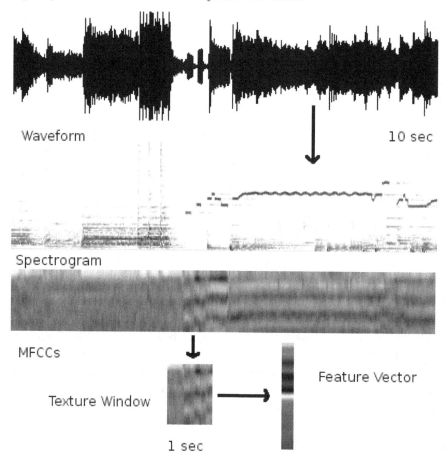

a summarization step a set numbers (the feature vector) is calculated. The feature vector attempts to summarize/capture the content information of that short slice in time. A piece of music can then be represented as a sequence of feature vectors. By detecting abrupt changes in the trajectory of the feature vectors segmentation can be performed and by detecting regions in feature space classification can be performed. Most audio features are extracted in three stages: (1) spectrum calculation, (2) frequency-domain summarization, (3) time-domain summarization. In spectrum calculation, a short-time slice (typically around 10 to 40 milliseconds) of waveform samples is transformed to a frequency domain representation. The most common such transformation is

the Short Time Fourier Transform (STFT). During each short-time slice the signal is assumed to be approximately stationary and is windowed to reduce the effect of discontinuities at the start and end of the frame. This frequency domain transformation preserves all the information in the signal and therefore the resulting spectrum has high dimensionality. For analysis purposes, it is necessary to find a more succinct description that has significantly lower dimensionality while still retaining the desired content information. Frequency domain summarization converts the high dimensional spectrum (typically 512 or 1024 coefficients) to a smaller set of number features (typically 10-30). A common approach is to use various descriptors of the spectrum shape such as the Spectral Centroid and Bandwidth. Another widely used frequency domain spectrum summarization is Mel-Frequency Cepstral Coefficients (MFCCs) which originated from speech and speaker recognition. The goal of time domain summarization is to characterize the musical signal at a longer time scale than the short-time analysis slices. Typically this summarization is performed across so called "texture" windows of approximately 2-3 seconds or it can be also performed over the entire piece of music. Figure 2 shows graphically frequency and time summarization. Later in this chapter we show how this process can be represented in *MARSYAS*.

MARSYAS 0.1 mainly supported audio analysis. One of the main motivations behind the redesign/rewrite of version 0.2 was the desire to also support audio synthesis. Even though not immediately obvious, audio synthesis can be very useful in MIR systems and applications. For example while researching an algorithm for drum transcription it is very useful to be able to hear a resynthesized sound contains only drum sounds. Listening to the result can reveal information that maybe hard to obtain from plots or just numeric results. Similarly synthesizing the result of pitch extraction can be very informative about the nature of pitch errors. Although it is possible to use a variety of different tools for these purposes, having them all integrated under one system can be very helpful.

The central challenge in the design of an audio processing framework is the need for very efficient runtime performance while retaining expressivity. Frequently audio researchers are faced with a hard dilemma. They can use interpreted programming environments such as MATLAB that provide a lot of necessary components but are not as efficient as compiled code or write code from scratch which requires a significant investment of time just to build the necessary infrastructure. *MARSYAS* attempts to balance these two extremes. As will be

described later in this chapter, a lot of flexibility and functionality is provided at run-time. For example, the user can easily create complicated networks of processing objects and control them without recompiling code. However the resulting system is still very efficient as it relies on compiled code. The only time that code recompilation is required is when new processing objects need to be written.

Two other important requirements for a successful audio framework are interoperability and portability. Most researchers utilize a large ecology of different tools to accomplish their task. To be useful, a framework must provide ways to communicate with other tools. For example *MARSYAS* provides a variety of tools for communicating with specific programs such as WEKA (for machine learning) and MATLAB (for numerical calculation) as well as general ways for communication with graphical user interfaces. Portability is also very important as operating systems and hardware change all the time. For example, initially *MARSYAS* was developed on SGI machines running IRIX which is not supported any more, but OS X which did not exist at the time is supported now.

These requirements make the development of audio processing frameworks challenging. However, there are some characteristics of audio that can help the designer. Audio processing has a strong notion of time. There is a constant flow of data through the system. In most cases there is little need for complicated dependencies between processing chunks of data. Therefore, for a specific application it is relatively easy to create efficient code with a fixed memory footprint. With a little bit more work it is possible to generalize the process so that most audio applications can be expressed easily without sacrificing run-time performance.

In the following sections we describe the general architecture of *MARSYAS* and how these requirements are addressed by specific design decisions and concepts. We believe that many of these concerns and their solutions are relevant not only to programmers and users of *MARSYAS* but developers of any MIR software system.

Architecture

Dataflow programming is based on the idea of expressing computation as a network of processing nodes/components connected by a number arcs/communication channels. Computer Music is possibly one of the most successful application areas for the dataflow-programming paradigm. The origins of this idea can possibly be traced to the physical rewiring (patching) employed for changing sound characteristics in early modular analog synthesizers.

Expressing audio processing systems as dataflow networks has several advantages. The programmer can provide a declarative specification of what needs to be computed without having to worry about the low-level implementation details of how it is computed. The resulting code can be very efficient and have a small memory footprint as data just "flows" through the network without having complicated dependencies. In addition, dataflow approaches are particularly suited for visual programming. One of the initial motivations for dataflow ideas was the exploitation of parallel hardware and therefore dataflow systems are particularly good for parallel and distributed computation.

The main goal of *MARSYAS* is to provide a general, extensible and flexible framework that enables experimentation with algorithms and provides the fast performance necessary for developing real-time audio analysis and synthesis tools. A variety of existing building blocks that form the basis of many published algorithms are provided as dataflow components that can be composed to form more complicated algorithms (black-box functionality). In addition, it is straightforward to extend the framework with new building blocks (white-box functionality).

In *MARSYAS* terminology the processing nodes of the dataflow network are called *MarSystems* and provide the basic components out of which more complicated networks are constructed. Essentially any audio processing algorithm can be expressed as a large composite *MarSystem*, which is assembled by appropriately connected basic *MarSystems*.

Some representative *MarSystems* provided are the following:

- Input/Output (Sources and Sinks)
    - SoundFile I/O for .wav, .au, .mp3 and .ogg files
    - Real-time audio I/O using RtAudio
    - Matlab, Weka, Octave I/O
- Feature Extraction
    - Short-Time Fourier Transform (STFT)
    - Discrete-Wavelet Transform (DWT)
    - Centroid, Rolloff, Flux, Contrast
    - Mel-frequency Cepstral Coefficients (MFCC)
    - Auditory Filterbanks
- Synthesis
    - Wavetable synthesis
    - FM synthesis
    - Phasevocoder
- Machine Learning
    - Gaussian Mixture Models (GMM)
    - K-Nearest Neighbor
    - Principal Component Analysis
    - K-Means Clustering
    - Support Vector Machine (SVM)

In addition to being able to process data, *MarSystems* need additional information that can change their functionality while they are running (processing data). For example a *SoundFileSource* needs the name of the sound file to be opened, and a *Gain* can be adjusted while data is flowing through. This is achieved by a separate message passing mechanism. Therefore, similarly to CLAM (Amatriain, 2005), *MARSYAS* makes a clear distinction between data-flow which is synchronous, and control flow which is asynchronous. Because *MarSystems* can be assembled hierarchically the control mechanism utilizes a path notation similar to OSC (Wright and Freed, 1997). For example *Series/playbacknet/Gain/g1/mrs_real/gain* is the control name for accessing the *gain* control of a *Gain MarSystem* named *g1* in a *Series* composite named *playbacknet*. A mechanism for linking top-level controls (with shorter names that act as aliases) to the longer full path control names is provided. For example a single gain control at the top-level can be linked to the gain controls of 20 oscillators in a synthesis instrument. That way, one-to-many mappings can be achieved in a similar way to the use of regular expressions in OSC (Wright & Freed, 1997).

Dataflow in Marsyas is synchronous which means that at every "tick" a specific slice of data is propagated across the entire dataflow network. This eliminates the need for queues between processing nodes and enables the use of shared buffers which improves performance. This is similar to the way Unix pipes are implemented but with audio specific semantics (see section on Implicit Patching).

One of the most useful characteristics of *MarSystems* is that they can be instantiated at run-time. Because they are hierarchically composable audio computation expressed as a dataflow, the network can be instantiated at run-time. For example, multiple instances of any complicated network can be created as easily as the basic primitive *MarSystems*. This is accomplished by using a combination of the *Prototype* and *Composite* design patterns (Gamma et al., 1995).

Projects

MARSYAS has been used for a variety of projects both in academia and industry. In this section we briefly describe some specific representative examples. The list is by no means exhaustive. An open source framework enables collaboration possibilities. Two research publications that resulted from such collaborations are Lippens et al (2004) and Li and Tzanetakis (2003). *Musicream* is a new music playback interface for streaming, sticking, sorting and recalling musical pieces that uses *MARSYAS* for calculating features and content-based audio similarity (Goto & Goto, 2005). The SndTools software also uses MARSYAS under the graphical user interface (Misra, Wang & Cook, 2005).

In industry MARSYAS has been used to design and prototype the audio fingerprinting software used by Moodlogic Inc. (http://moodlogic.com). After the fingerprinting was designed and evaluation experiments were conducted using MARSYAS a new proprietary source code just for the fingerprinting was written for the actual working product. This method of using research free software framework for prototyping and then providing a full proprietary rewrite is one possibility of how academic free software and industry can co-exist. Another possibility is the gender (male/female) voice detection scheme developed for *Teligence Communications Inc* (http://www.teligence.net/) using *MARSYAS*. In that case the developed software is part of the free software distribution. However it is based on machine learning and requires training data that is not publicly available and belongs to *Teligence Communications Inc.* As the company is mainly concerned in using the tool internally everything worked out ok for both parties. In both of these industrial collaborations it would have been possible for the company to just develop the software on their own. However, by collaborating and paying the companies benefit from fast turnaround and experienced knowledge and the free software, authors benefit from consulting payments. We hope that these strategies might provide some information about how industrial collaborations with academic free software projects can be established.

Specific Topics

In this section we discuss in more detail some specific topics that we believe are particularly interesting to the designer of audio processing frameworks.

Implicit Patching

The basic idea behind *Implicit Patching* (Bray & Tzanetakis, 2005) is to use object composition rather than explicitly specifying connections between input and output ports in order to construct the dataflow network. For example the following pseudo-code example (Figure 3) illustrates the difference between *Explicit* and *Implicit Patching* in a simple playback network.

The idea of *Implicit Patching* evolved from the integration if three different ideas that were developed independently in previous versions of *MARSYAS*. These three ideas and how they are integrated are described below. In addition, examples illustrating the expressive power of *Implicit Patching* are presented.

The first idea originated from the desire not to be constrained to fixed buffer sizes and to have proper semantics for spectral data. The majority of existing audio processing environments requires that all processing objects in a flow network/visual patch, process fixed buffers of audio samples (typical numbers are 64 and 128 samples). Having fixed buffers simplifies

Figure 3. Explicit and implicit patching

```
# EXPLICT PATCHING
create source, gain, dest

# connect the appropriate in/out ports
connect(source.out1, gain.in1);
connect(gain.out1, dest.in1);

#IMPLICIT PATCHING
create source, gain, dest

#create a composite that is the network
create series(source, gain, dest)
```

memory management and patching as all connections are treated the same way. However, some applications like audio feature extraction require a variety of different buffer sizes to flow through the network (for example feature vectors typically have much lower dimensionality than audio data). Even though it is possible to have dynamic buffer sizes in *Explicit Patching* it is complex to implement and frequently requires a lot of work from the programmer to appropriately set the connections. In addition, these fixed-sized buffers are reused for holding spectral data and it is up to the programmer to correctly connect the spectral data to objects that process such data. The result is that the exact details of the Short-Time Fourier Transform are encapsulated as a black box and the programmer has little control over the process. Our proposed solution to these two problems is to extend the semantics of the data that is processed. In *MARSYAS*, processing objects (*MarSystems*) operate on chunks of data called *Slices*. *Slices* are matrices of floating point numbers characterized by three parameters: number of samples (things that are "measured" at different instances in time), number of observations (things that are "measured" at the same time instance) and sampling rate. This approach is similar to the Sound Description Interchange Format (SDIF) (Schwarz & Wright, 1997).

Figure 4 shows a *MarSystem* for spectral processing that converts an incoming audio buffer of 512 samples of 1 observation at a sampling rate of 22050 Hz to 1 sample of 512 observations (the FFT bins) at a lower sampling rate of 22050/512 Hz. By propagating information about the sampling rate and number of observations through the dataflow network, the use of *Slices* provides more correct and flexible semantics for spectral processing and feature extraction. *MarSystems* are designed so that they can handle Slices with arbitrary dimensions with one important constraint: they need to be able to calculate their output Slice parameters from their input Slice parameters. For example it is possible to change the input number of samples

Figure 4. MarSystem and corresponding slices for spectral processing

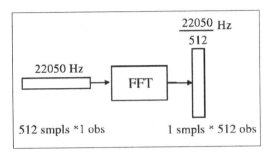

to the *MarSystem* shown in Figure 4 to 1024 and the *MarSystem* will automatically determine that the number of observations of the output *Slice* is also 1024.

The second major idea behind *Implicit Patching* is the use of the Composite design pattern (Gamma et al., 1995) as a mechanism for constructing dataflow networks. The extended semantics of Slices require careful manipulation of buffer sizes especially if run-time changes are desired. The most important composite is Series, which connects a list of *MarSystems* in series so that the output of the first one becomes the input to the second and so forth. (similarly to UNIX pipes). The pseudo-code in Figure 3 uses a Series composite. Initially composites were used as programming shortcuts. However, gradually we discovered that they offer many advantages and we decided to make them the main mechanism for constructing complicated *MarSystems* out of simpler ones. Their advantages include hierarchical encapsulation, automatic dynamic handling of all internal buffers and run-time instantiation. More specifically, any dataflow network, no matter how complicated, is represented as a single *MarSystem* that is hierarchically composed of simpler *MarSystems*. Multiple instance of any *MarSystem* can be instantiated at run-time and all internal patching and memory handling is encapsulated.

The third idea was the unification of *Sources* and *Sinks* as regular MarSystems that have both input and output. *Sources* are processing objects that have only output, and *Sinks* only have input. In order to be able to use them as any *MarSystem* we extend them in the following way: *Sources* mix their output with their input and *Sinks* propagate their input to their output while at the same time playing/writing their input as a side-effect. This way, for example, one can connect a *SoundFileSink* to an *AudioSink* in series and the data will be written both to a sound file and played using the audio device. Basically this way both *Sources* and *Sinks* can be used anywhere inside a network.

Implicit Patching is made feasible by the integration of these three ideas. In this approach, each *MarSystem* has only one input port and one output port and consumes/produces only one token. However because of the extended semantics of Slices one can essentially have multiple input/output ports (as observations) and consume/produce multiple tokens (as samples). This enables non-trivial *Composites* such as *Fanout* to be created. The expressive power of composition is increased and a large variety of complex dataflow networks can be expressed only using object composition and therefore no *Explicit Patching*. Another side benefit of *Implicit Patching* is that it enforces the creation of trees and therefore avoids problems with cycles in the dataflow graph.

Figure 5 shows how a *Series Composite* consisting of a *SoundFileSource src, Gain g* and *AudioSink dest* can be assembled in C++. At each iteration of the loop, the audio rate is incremented starting from 1 sample (similar to Chuck or STK) until the block size of 1000 samples is reached. All the intermediate shared buffers between the *MarSystems* are adjusted automatically and the sound plays without interruption. Even though this example might seem artificial the need for dynamically adjusting window sizes occurs frequently in audio analysis for example in pitch-synchronous overlap-add (PSOLA).

Figure 5. Dynamic adjusting of analysis window size

```
MarSystem* net = mng.create("Series", "net");
net->addMarSystem(src);
net->addMarSystem(g);
net->addMarSystem(dest);

for (int i=1; i<1000; i++)
{
    net->updctrl("natural/inSamples", i);
    net->tick();
}
```

Figure 6. Fanout composite

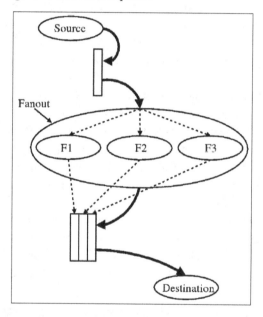

Figure 7. Fanout composite with implicit patching (left) and explicit patching (right)

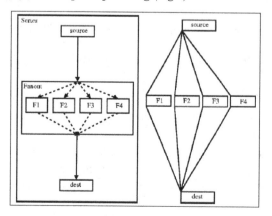

To illustrate this approach, consider the *Fanout Composite* which takes as input a slice and is build from a list of *MarSystems*. The input *Slice* is shared as input to all each internal *MarSystem* and their outputs are stacked as observations in the output *Slice* of the *Fanout*. For example a filterbank can be easily implemented as a *Fanout* where each filter is an internal component *MarSystem*. The filterbank will take as input a Slice of N samples by 1 observations and write to an output Slice of N samples by M observations, where M is the number of filters. Because the inner loops of MarSystems iterate over both samples and observations if we connect the filterbank with a *Normalize MarSystem* each row of samples corresponding to a particular observation (each channel of the filterbank) will be normalized accordingly. This can be very handy in large filterbanks as the part of the network after the filterbank does not need to know how many filter outputs are produced. This information is taken implicitly from the number of observations. Figure 6 shows graphically how *Slices* are used in *Fanout*. The dotted lines show the patching that is done implicitely by the *Fanout*. The black arrows show the main flow created implicitely by a *Series Composite*. In constrast, in environments with explicit patching such as Max/MSP each connection between the filters of the filterbank and the input would have to be created by the user. Figure 7 shows the difference between Implicit Patching (left) where the dotted lines are created automatically from the semantics of Composites, and Explicit Patching (right) where each connection must be created separately. Even though environments such as Max/MSP or PD provide sub-patching, the burden of internal patching is still on the user.

We conclude this section with a nontrivial example illustrating the expressive power of *Implicit Patching*. Figure 8 shows how a layer of nodes in an Artificial Neural Network (ANN) can be expressed using a *Fanout*. The input to the layer (the output of the previous layer) consists of 4 number x_1, x_2, x_3, x_4. These 4 numbers (obser-

Figure 8. Artificial neural network layer using the fanout composite

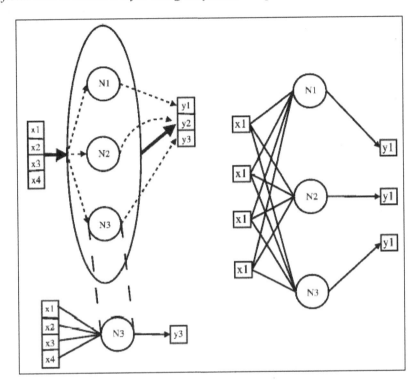

vations) based on the *Fanout* semantics become the input to each individual neuron (N_i) of the layer. Each neuron forms a weighted sum (with weights specific to each neuron) of the input, applies a sigmoid function to the sum and outputs a single output. The outputs using the *Fanout* semantics are stacked as observations y_1, y_2, y_3 (one for each neuron) ready for processing for the next layer. Figure 8 illustrates this process graphically (left side) and contrasts it with Explicit Patching (right side). In *MARSYAS,* creating an ANN using an *AnnNode MarSystem* is simply a *Series* of *Fanout* of *AnnNodes*. More specifically seriesNet(fanoutLayer1, fanoutLayer2, ..., fanoutLayerM) where fanoutLayer1(annNode11, annNode12, ...,annNode1N). All the connections are created implicitly.

Figure 9 shows a dataflow network for extracting audio features for real-time music/speech classification. *Series* connections are top to bottom and *Fanout* connections are shown by horizontal forking. For example the output of the *Spectrum* calculation is used as input to the *Centroid, Rolloff* and *Flux MarSystems*. The input to texture memory is 4 observations (the features) by 1 sample and the output is 4 observations by 40 samples consisting of the last 40 feature vectors (approximately corresponding to 1 second). Means and variances of the feature vectors over the texture window are calculated and the input to the classifier is an 8-dimensional feature vector (4 means and 4 vairances). The entire network can be created at run-time without requiring any code recompilation. The complete feature extraction front-end described in Tzanetakis and Cook (2002) has been implemented as a dataflow network in *MARSYAS* in a similar fashion.

Flexible Scheduling

Scheduling is central to any computer music system. A scheduling request consists of an event

Figure 9. *Music/speech classification as a dataflow network in MARSYAS*

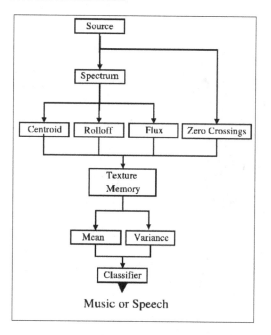

Music or Speech

Figure 10. *UML class diagram of the MARSYAS scheduler architecture*

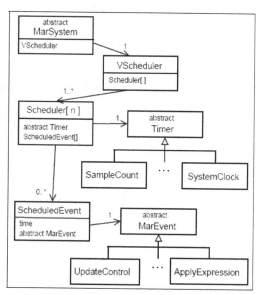

and a time. The scheduler keeps track of pending requests. Computer music schedulers use times which are typically references to a single clock that corresponds to real (physical) time. In addition to actual time, *MARSYAS* supports the notion of virtual time which is based directly on the data. This is especially important in nonrealtime applications. In addition it is often convenient to have a time reference or references that do not correspond to real time. For example consider scheduling events in beats that are defined in relation to tapping a MIDI keyboard to extract beat-synchronous audio features. In this section we show how multiple notions of time and events are supported through object orientation in *MARSYAS*.

Each *MarSystem* has its own *Virtual Scheduler* that manages an arbitrary number of *Event Schedulers*. Each *Event Scheduler* contains its own *Timer* that controls the rate at which time passes and events are dispatched. *Schedulers* themselves do not keep track of time, but leave

this task solely to the *Timer*. Structured this way events may be scheduled to any number of different *Timers*.

A *Timer* in *MARSYAS* is any object that can read from a time source and triggers some action on each tick. A *Timer* must also provide some way to specify units of time in its time base. The one restriction in a time source is that time must always advance. *Timers* are definable by the user, provided they support the *AbstractTimer* interface. The interface requires specification of the following: a method for determining the interval of time since the last reading, a method for comparing time intervals for that particular *Timer*, a trigger method which calls the Scheduler dispatch, and a method for converting time representations to the specific notion of time used by the *Timer*. This generalization of Timers allows for many different possibilities in controlling event scheduling. Linear and nonlinear advancing are both possible.

Figure 11. UML sequence diagram of event dispatch

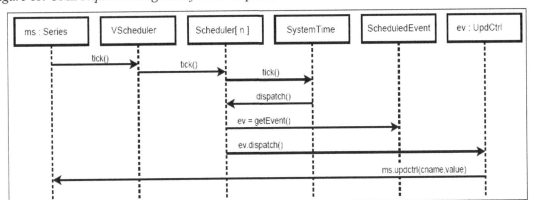

Events are user definable actions that are "frozen" until dispatched. They are distinct from the normal flow of audio data. There are no restrictions on the types of *Events* that can be defined. Perhaps the most common event is updating a *MarSystem* control (for example creating a new file with features every 1 minute). Another example is the "wire" event which updates the value of a control based on the value of another control (similar to a control wire in Max/MSP, PD). Events must supply a dispatch() method that the *Scheduler* can call at the appropriate time. *Events* may take place immediately or some time in the future. The time at which an *Event* happens may be specified by the user and depends on the Timer that the requested time is with respect to (for example the user might specify that an *Event* should happen after 4 beats using a tempo-based *Timer* or 3 seconds using a time-based *Timer*). The *Event* is then sent to the scheduler and removed when its time interval has passed. The *Scheduler* then calls the dispatch() method on the event.

Figure 10 shows a UML class diagram of the scheduling architecture. Notice how multiple, user-defined *Timers* and *Events* can be supported by abstraction and are decoupled from the *Scheduler*. The UML sequence diagram of Figure 11 shows the order of method calls between objects for performing a control update (a specific kind of *Event*).

MARSYAS Scripting Language

MSL is a scripting language for building and controlling *MarSystem* networks at runtime. It is more accessible and readable than writing raw C++ code. Essentially the interpreter translates MSL code into the corresponding C++ *Marsyas* code and then executes it. Lexical analysis (or scanning) is performed using the Flex scanner generator, and parsing performed using the Bison parser generator 2. The output of the parsing stage from Bison is an abstract syntax tree representation of the MSL script, which is then traversed to generate and execute the equivalent *Marsyas* C++ code. The "do" construct allows multiple events to be scheduled at particular times based on a Timer. Figure 12 shows a more complicated example with two-voice polyphony using a Fanout composite. Two sine oscillators are controlled by separate timers one based on SystemTimer and the other based on TempoTimer which is based on MIDI input.

Distributed Audio Processing

One of the most important challenges facing MIR of audio signals is scaling algorithms to large collections. Typically, analysis of audio signals utilizes sophisticated signal processing and ma-

Figure 12. MSL code example

```
Series net is [
Fanout mix is [ SineSource src1,
                SineSource src2 ],
Sum sum,
AudioSink dac
]

do [ (Math.rand() * 10000)+100 => net/mix/src/frequency
   ] every 2beats using TempoTimer

do [ (net/mix/src2/frequency + 400) % 10000
       => net/mix/src2/frequency
   ] every 0.5s using SystemTimer

run net run
```

chine learning techniques that require significant computational resources. Processing time is a major bottleneck. For example, the number of pieces utilized in the majority of existing work in audio MIR is at most a few thousand files. Computing audio features over thousands of files can sometimes take days of processing. The dataflow architecture of MARSYAS facilitates partitioning of audio computations over multiple computers. Using a declarative dataflow specification approach the programmer can distribute audio analysis algorithms with minimum effort. In contrast, distributing traditional sequential programs places a significant burden to the programmer who has to decide which parts of the code can be parallelized and deal with load distribution, scheduling, synchronization and communication.

There are two standard data communication protocols used on the Internet: transmission control protocol (TCP) and user datagram protocol (UDP). TCP provides reliability mechanisms to ensure that all packets are received exactly in the order they are sent; on the other hand, UDP provides no such mechanisms but is significantly faster due to less overhead. UDP is therefore the protocol of choice for real-time streaming applications where data is time critical.

MARSYAS supports both the UDP and TCP protocols. In order to send data to another machine,

a *NetworkSink MarSystem* is simply inserted somewhere in the "flow" of a *Composite MarSystem*. In order to receive data a *NetworkSource MarSystem* is inserted. Control flow and data flow are managed separately so that controls can be changed from the sender and propagate through the system. The idea is that the user can operate several "worker" machines and the view of the distributed system is abstracted as one large *Composite MarSystem*.

For the experiments described in this section a feature vector consisting the means and variances of smoothed Mel-Frequency Cepstral Coefficients (MFCC) as well as STFT-based features such as spectral centroid and rolloff was used. The data consists of 30-second audio clips and a single 35-dimensional feature vector is calculated for each clip. The actual audio waveform samples are transmitted over the network corresponding to a scenario where all the audio files reside on a single machine but multiple processing machines are available (for example the computers of a lab during nighttime). The experimentation was done on a 100Base-T Ethernet local area network of Apple G5 computers.

In the described experiments a dispatcher node (computer) sends separate audio clips from an audio collection to each worker node in the network. The job of a worker node is to simply calculate features for each clip it receives and then send the results to a collector process (possibly running on the same machine as the dispatcher) that gathers the results. The audio collection was partitioned into subcollections which were sent to each worker. All the audio clips are stored on the dispatcher. We found that the optimal number of worker nodes in this model was three, after which there was no time benefit of using extra machines. In fact, it was costly to add any more than five worker nodes due to the network capacity of the dispatcher collector. The use of multiple dispatchers in hierarchical fashion can improve results. More details can be found in Bray and Tzanetakis (2005b).

Table 1 shows results of using the collection dispatcher model, using up to 5 worker nodes and audio collections of up to 10,000 files. The format is *hours:minutes:seconds.*

The problem with the collection dispatcher approach is that some nodes may complete processing the features of their respective subcollection before others and have to sit idle. Thus the time it takes to process the entire collection is dependent on the slowest node in the system. In order to alleviate this problem and make sure of idle nodes, an adaptive approach is used where the dispatcher sends data as necessary to each worker. That way, each node in the system is working until the dispatcher has finished processing the files in the collection. Table 2 shows the increase in performance based on this approach.

Typically feature extraction tests run on audio collections of around 10,000 files. Based on our

Table 1. Parellelization results for collection dispatcher

	10	100	1000	10000
Local	00:05	00:58	09:39	1:36:49
1W	00:07	01:10	11:48	1:58:49
2W	00:03	00:38	06:01	1:10:46
3W	00:04	00:34	05:49	59:46
4W	00:03	00:34	05:52	1:04:56
5W	00:04	00:36	05:54	1:08:36

Table 2. Parellelization results for adaptive dispatcher

	10	100	1000	10000
Local	00:05	00:58	09:39	1:36:49
1W	00:07	01:10	11:48	1:58:49
2W	00:04	00:40	06:21	1:02
3W	00:03	00:33	05:33	57:10
4W	00:03	00:31	05:24	54:20
5W	00:03	00:31	05:25	54:15

results, we expect a linear trend as collection size increases. To test that hypothesis a large-scale test using the data-partitioning model (2 dispatchers with half the audio data each) with the adaptive dispatcher was conducted on 100,000 files. As expected, it took approximately 10 times the amount of time to complete the 100,000 clip test as it took to complete the 10,000 file test (5:00:44). Experimental results show that using 5 computers we can perform audio feature extraction for 100,000 30-second clips in 5 hours.

CONCLUSIONS AND FUTURE WORK

In this chapter we described MARSYAS a free software framework for audio applications with specific emphasis on MIR. We showed how *MARSYAS* addresses some of the requirements and challenges facing the designer of audio processing frameworks. It is our hope that the ideas and concepts presented in this chapter can be applied to other MIR software frameworks and tools. As a general conclusion dataflow architectures can help express easily complicated processing structures while retaining efficiency and being easy to parallelize. Finally the development of free software in an academic setting is not only possible, but has many benefits such as increase in visibility, collaboration opportunities, communication and even monetary rewards.

MARSYAS is an ongoing project and therefore there are always many directions of future work. In addition to obvious directions such as expanding the number of building blocks provided by the framework and improving reliability and performance, there a number of more large scale initiatives. A large effort is underway to build a visual patching environment and a library for creating widgets and audio processing graphical user interfaces (GUIs). Another initiative is to port *MARSYAS* to the Java programming language (the previous version 0.1 was partly ported). A more radical complete redesign and implementation are underway in the functional programming language OCAML. Audio programming in general provides a rich fertile area for ideas in Software Engineering as it combines many interesting areas such as digital signal processing, machine learning, efficient numerical processing and interactivity.

ACKNOWLEDGMENTS

There are many individuals that have helped in one way or another with the design and development of MARSYAS. These include in no particular order: Luis Gustavo Martins, Jennifer Murdoch, Start Bray, Neil Burroughs, Adam Tindale, Adam Parkin, Ajay Kapur, Manj Benniing, Douglas Turnbull, George Tourtellot, Taras Glek, Ari Lazier, Andreye Ermolinskyi, Carlos Castillo, Perry Cook, Malcolm Slaney, Mathieu Lagrango and Steven Ness.

REFERENCES

Ackerman, W. (1982). *Dataflow languages, IEEE Computer 15*(2), 15-25.

Amatriain, X. (2005). *An object-oriented metamodel for digital signal processing with a focus on audio and music.* Unpublished doctoral dissertation, Univesity of Pompeu Fabra, Spain.

Bray, S. & Tzanetakis, G. (2005a). Implicit patching for dataflow-based audio analysis and syntehsis. In *Proceedings of the International Computer Music Conference (ICMC).*

Bray, S. & Tzanetakis, G. (2005b). Distributed audio feature extraction for music. In *Proceedings of the International Conference on Music Information Retrieval (ISMIR).*

Burroughs, N., Parkin, A. & Tzanetakis, G. (2006). Flexible scheduling for dataFlow audio processing. In *Proceedings of the International Computer Music Conference (ICMC)*, New Orleans, USA.

Cook, P. & Scavone, G. (1999). The synthesis toolkit (STK) version 2.1. In *Proceedings of the International Computer Music Conference (ICMC)*, Beijing, China.

Dannengerg, R. & Brandt, E. (1996). A flexible real-time software synthesis system. In *Proceedings of the International Computer Music Conference (ICMC)* (pp. 270-273).

Downie, S. J. & Futrelle, J. (2005). Terascale music mining. In *Proceedings of the ACM/IEEE Super Computing Conference*, 2005.

Futrelle, J. & Downie, S. J. (2002). Interdisciplinary communities and research issues in music information retrieval. In *Proceedings of the International Conference on Music Information Retrieval (ISMIR)*, Paris.

Gamma, E., Helm, R., Johnson, R. & Vlissides, J. (1995). *Design patterns: Elements of reusable object-oriented software.* Addison Wesley.

Goto & Goto (2005). Musicream: New music playback interface for streaming, sticking, sorting and recalling musical pieces. In *Proceedings of the International Conference on Music Information Retrieval (ISMIR)*, London.

International Conferences on Music Information Retrieval, http://www.ismir.net

Johnston, W. Hanna, J.P., & Millar, R. (2004). Advances in dataflow programming languages. *ACM Computing Surveys, 36*(1), 1-34.

Lippens, S. et al. (2004). A comparison of human and automatic musical genre classification. In *Proceedings of the IEEE International Conference on Audio, Speech and Signal Processing,* Montreal, Canada.

Li, T. & Tzanetakis, G. (2003). Factors in automatic musical genre classification of audio signals. In *Proceedings of the IEEE Workshop on Applications of Signal Processing to Audio and Acoustics (WASPAA)* New Paltz, New York.

Manulescu, D. A. (1997). A dataflow pattern language. In *Proceedings of Pattern Languages of Programming,* Monticello, Illinois.

McEnnis, D., McKay, C., Fujinga, I., and Depalle, P. (2005). jAudio: A feature extraction library. In *Proceedings of the International Conference on Music Information Retrieval (ISMIR),* London.

Misra, A., Wang, G. & Cook, P. (2005). SndTools: Real-time audio DSP and 3D visualization. In *Proceedings of the International Computer Music Conference (ICMC),* Barcelona, Spain.

Puckette, M. (2002). Max at seventeen. *Computer Music Journal, 26*(4).

Schwarz, D. & Wright, M. (2000). Extensions and applications of the SDIF sound description interchange format. In *Proceedings of the International Computer Music Conf (ICMC).*

Scheirer, E. & Slaney, M. (1997). Construction and evaluation of a robust multi-feature music/speech discriminator. In *Proceedings of the IEEE Int. Conf. on Audio, Speech and Signal Processing (ICASSP).*

Tzanetakis, G. & Cook, P. (2000). MARSYAS: A framework for audio analysis. *Organized Sound, Cambridge University Press,* 4(3).

Tzanetakis, G. & Cook, P. (2002). Musical genre classification of audio signals. *IEEE Trans. on Speech and Audio Processing, 10*(5).

Wadge, W. and Ashcroft, E. (1985). Lucid, the dataflow programming language. *APIC Studies in Data Processing.* New York: Academic Press.

Wang, G. & Cook, P. (2003). Chuck: A concurrent, on-the-fly audio programming language. In *Proceedings of the International Computer Music Conference. (ICMC),* Singapore.

Wright, M. & Freed, A. (1997). Open sound control: A new protocol for communicating with sound synthesizers. In *Proceedings of the International Computer Music Conference (ICMC),* Thessaloniki, Greece.

Zicarelli, D. (2002). How I learned to love a program that does nothing. *Computer Music Journal, 26*(4), 44-51.

Chapter III
Melodic Query Input for Music Information Retrieval Systems

Richard L. Kline
Pace University, USA

ABSTRACT

This chapter discusses key issues of building and using a system designed to search and query a music collection through the input of the actual or perceived melody of a song. It presents a detailed survey and discussion of studies, algorithms and systems created to approach this problem, including new contributions by the author. Emphasis is placed on examining the abilities and likely errors of those with little or no formal musical training to remember and reproduce melodic phrases, as these must be taken into account for any music information retrieval system intended for use by the general public. The chapter includes an extensive discussion on human humming as an intuitive input method for the musically untrained person and an examination of several music information retrieval systems designed for this type of input query.

INTRODUCTION

An effective music information retrieval (MIR) system requires suitable mechanisms for specifying input queries. For queries of the nature of identifying a tune, theme or melody, providing query input in the form of a melody line or rhythm usually will be the most intuitive and powerful means of specifying such a search. Similarly, collections to be searched in this manner must have some available representation of the melody and

rhythm contained therein, such as that presented in written form or in formats such as MIDI (1993), rather than raw or processed digitized audio samples such as CD or MP3. In this chapter we will present many of the most important theories, algorithms, techniques and performed studies for capturing, representing and performing similarity or identification searches using melodic input query strings.

MIR systems requiring the highest search efficiencies generally must demand that the collection being searched and any given input queries are known to be error-free. There must be confidence in the quality of the songs comprising the search collection and error-free input can be reasonably expected only for systems built for and used by those with substantial musical training, researchers or publishers.

Systems designed for collections or input queries which are known or suspected to contain errors must be built with additional complexity, or a resulting loss of search efficiency, to take real or expected errors into account. These errors can come from many sources. For the collection being searched, errors may be introduced when digitizing manuscripts or when automated transcriptions are performed. For input queries, systems designed for those lacking in music training and those allowing for vocalized melody input, often called *query-by-humming* systems, are nearly certain to contain input errors. Some of these are due to the way nonmusicians perceive and recall music; others are due to performance errors; and still others due to imperfect transcription of acoustically-recorded vocal or instrumental input queries.

In this chapter we bring together the most relevant studies from the music literature in order to paint a clear picture of the allowances which must be made for input processing and searching of melodic queries. We then describe early and recent research efforts in creating error-tolerant melody-based MIR systems and highlight the best contributions of each. We conclude the chapter with a summary of the best practices presented and extrapolate likely avenues of further exploration in search of more efficient and successful MIR systems.

The discussion presented here refers specifically to music with an identifiable melody line, that is, a sequence of notes readily recognized as the dominant tune within a song that would be naturally reproduced by a listener able to play, sing or hum only a single note at a time. With vocal music, the melody is almost always associated with the notes sung by the primary vocalist. Even complex instrumental orchestral pieces typically have a theme or melody which is often played by a solo instrument and readily identified by casual listeners.

Regardless of whether a specific music collection being searched has been stored in a representational notation or digitized recordings with possible feature extraction, the ability to form musical queries based on a melody, via notation or by vocal or instrumental performance, will remain a powerful and needed option for many such MIR systems.

OBTAINING AND PROCESSING MUSIC

Many data formats have been created to store music and these fall into two basic categories. The average consumer is most familiar with music stored as a digital or analog audio recording, such as is found in cassettes, CDs, MP3 files, DRM-encrusted file formats and myriad other physical and digital formats. The recorded sounds can be stored in a single data stream or several; each channel can represent the output intended for a specific speaker upon playback (e.g., stereo or surround sound), or each channel can be devoted to a single instrument or vocalist, as is done for most professional audio recordings. This latter arrangement allows the greatest flexibility in processing the recording, affording the opportunity to select the relative emphasis given to various tracks through mixing before creating the published version.

The second method of storing music is a strictly logical or diagrammatic one. Rather than saving digitized waveforms of the actual acoustic sounds produced, information about the individual notes to be played or sung is recorded instead. The fundamental characteristics of a note include the time it should begin, its duration, its pitch value and the instrument or voice which is to intone the note.

Along with these, many secondary characteristics may also be stored, such as the volume at which the note should be performed, or performance variations such as trilling or vibrato which are dependent upon the specific instrument or voice involved. Finally, information about the song as a whole will be present, both musical (e.g., musical key(s), intended tempo or tempos or other performance notes) and metadata (e.g., title, composer or year published). Printed musical scores are the most familiar means of representing music in this manner, but many other formats exist to fulfill the same purpose. An excellent volume which describes most of the relevant data formats was edited by Selfridge-Field (1997).

One of the most popular of these high-level representation formats is known as MIDI. MIDI (Musical Instrument Digital Interface) (1993) was designed initially as a protocol for networking and control of electronic musical instruments, which at first consisted mainly of synthesizer keyboards but later included many other instruments and devices. Within the protocol is defined a series of messages which control timing and the playing of notes via events. MIDI can support the segmentation of music data into separate tracks, which typically are used to represent the individual instruments and voices needed for performance of the song being stored. These tracks are often given identifying labels to indicate the instrument or voice that represents the data within the track. The Standard MIDI Format (SMF) is the complementary data format developed to store MIDI information in individual files. In addition to the track and note data described, the storage format also accommodates additional information including song lyrics, time and key signatures, tempo(s), author and title. The MIDI standard has been universally adopted by manufacturers of synthesizer keyboards and other digital instruments. Rothstein's book (1995) describes the standard in detail and gives a discussion of its implementation in various products. Many thousands of MIDI song files have been pub-

lished in the public domain. Several research groups have assembled their own collections of MIDI files to create test databases for their MIR research systems, including those described by Jang, Chen and Kao (2001a), Kosugi, Nishihara, Sakata, Yamamuro, and Kushima (2000) and Uitdenbogerd and Zobel (1998).

Conversion of a logical description of music into an audible representation is quite straightforward: such a description needs only to be interpreted in a performance, whether it is done by live performers or a music synthesis system. On the other hand, automated transcription, or conversion of a digitized audio recording into a logical data representation, is a much more difficult problem. Klapuri is one of many researchers in this field, and he maintains an excellent literature review of this research area on his personal Web site (Klapuri, n.d.).

With the prospect of generalized automated music transcription likely many years away, an approach that should prove more successful in the short term is the introduction of new hybrid audio data formats which enable the association of logical descriptors along with representations of the digital waveforms in a common file. Examples of ongoing efforts in this area include MPEG-7 (Martinez, 2004). This type of format will afford the content creator the opportunity to include multiple representations of a piece of music in the same file, which could provide access to logical descriptors of the otherwise opaque digitized audio stream.

AUTOMATED TRANSCRIPTION OF THE HUMAN VOICE

While efforts continue in expanding the capabilities of music transcription in the coming years, systems now exist which can accurately transcribe music sources in which only one or very few instruments or voices are heard at one time.

In particular, systems which focus solely on single-note music transcription systems have progressed from early efforts such as those of Kuhn (1990), through those built into early MIR systems including Ghias, Logan, Chamberlin and Smith (1995), Kageyama, Mochizuki and Takashima (1993) Kageyama and Takashima (1994) and McNab, Smith, Witten, Henderson and Cunningham (1996), and finally to commercial products such as Wildcat Canyon Software's *Autoscore* and Emagic's *Logic* (now sold by Apple). Now that this technology has become sufficiently mature to be viable in the commercial marketplace, it is viable to build an MIR interface around it. Transcription systems such as these can produce accurate transcriptions of music much of the time, but consistently perfect transcriptions are by no means guaranteed. Many factors contribute to sources of error that inevitably creep into the resulting representations of acoustic input.

The individual notes produced by most instruments and the human voice are composed of sounds which resonate at a number of frequencies. The fundamental, or lowest, frequency is normally the strongest and the one we label as the pitch of a note. Besides the fundamental frequency, integral multiples of that frequency, known as harmonics or overtones, also appear but at lesser strengths than the fundamental. The relative strengths of the sounds centered at various harmonic frequencies are a characteristic of the instrument or voice making the sound. Occasionally, for a given note or some short subset of the duration of that note, one of the harmonic frequencies (normally the first harmonic) is identified incorrectly as the fundamental frequency. The note-tracking software interprets this as a jump in pitch of exactly one octave, as the first harmonic is twice the frequency of the true fundamental.

It is not uncommon for a person or an out-of-tune instrument to produce notes that are flat or sharp relative to the nearest key signature. A straightforward music transcription algorithm might use a strict cutoff halfway between two semitones, so that a note below the threshold is mapped to the nearest lower semitone and vice versa. A rendition whose notes occasionally cross this critical point would thus be recognized as if the user switched keys during the course of the input, perhaps many times back and forth.

There are a number of reasonable approaches to dealing with the tuning problem. If a representation scheme is designed to ignore small pitch differences, as may be reasonable with imprecise vocal input, it would be unaffected by the one-semitone differences we have discussed, and simply ignoring these anomalies is efficient and effective. Alternatively, an effective matching scheme may require to have the pitches of notes reported in more precise increments, as was suggested by Lindsay (1996) and eventually included in the MPEG-7 Melody Sequence DS representation (Gomez, Gouyon, Herrera & Amatriain, 2003). Another attempted remedy to this problem was the adaptive tuning method proposed by McNab et al. (1996) and implemented as part of their MELDEX system (McNab, Smith, Bainbridge & Witten, 1997): If the user's hummed note is sharp or flat relative to the Western tonal music scale, the algorithm adjusts its internal scale by an appropriate amount so that the note that follows will be assigned a pitch value relative to tuning of the prior note rather than by comparing to the absolute tonal scale. Unfortunately, they did not report if any formal testing had been performed to determine whether or not this method enables user input to be encoded more accurately, and Haus and Pollastri (2001) later found that this method actually decreased the accuracy of transcriptions compared to more naive algorithms. *Autoscore* incorporates as an option a simpler implementation of adaptive tuning which is performed only on the first note of an input phrase, so that all subsequent notes are assigned pitch values taking into account the degree to which the first note was out of tune. A more recent music transcription system produced by Haus and Pollastri (2001) utilizes some new techniques in identifying relative pitch errors in a user's hummed input over the entire length of the input phrase in order to adjust the tuning. They performed a limited study using five subjects, running a recording of the volunteers' hummed musical phrases through four different pitch transcription algorithms; their transcriber was shown to produce significantly more accurate results as compared to the other methods described earlier.

In addition to the issues of correctly identifying the fundamental frequency and of processing notes which are out of tune, a third class of errors has at its source the mechanisms used in note-tracking algorithms to determine note boundaries, particularly for successive notes having the same pitch. In sounding a long note, a user might change volume or shift position relative to the microphone over time, causing dropouts to occur which result in the single performed note being reported as several shorter notes. Conversely, a sequence of short notes intoned with little or no gaps between them might be reported with some of the notes grouped together incorrectly. The frequency and severity of these types of errors also depend on the environment in which the system is being used (e.g., the quality of the microphone used and the background noise it may pick up along with the intended vocal input), which may magnify the effects described here. Many systems such as *Autoscore* attempt to overcome the problems of note transition boundaries by requiring the user to intone each note with a consonant sound such as "da" rather than strict humming. Other researchers such as Hu and Dannenberg (2002) and Zhu and Shasha (2003) have created systems which do not rely on being able to correctly identify individual note boundaries, considering the time-series of successive pitch values directly and using different techniques to form representations appropriate for their respective search techniques.

Thus, the current state of automatic transcription of single-voice music is quite usable yet still susceptible to errors from a variety of sources. We can expect that the reliability and accuracy of automated transcription will continue to improve over time, but the issues of ambient noise, microphone positioning, and input quality will remain, and along with them, the errors they introduce into note sequences are likely to remain with us as well.

SURVEY OF RELEVANT STUDIES ON HUMAN HUMMING SKILLS

Aside from all of the sources of error possible from the process of recording and transcribing a person's vocal musical input, there remains the issue of the mistakes made by the person singing or humming with respect to the intended tune or musical phrase. In order to build an interface that can extract reliable information out of a typical user's singing or humming, we must first understand the processes by which humans perceive, recognize and remember musical information. A person's ability to reproduce music vocally rests squarely upon this foundation. We present here a number of studies in the areas of psychology and music cognition, most of which focused on the problems of music perception and recognition rather than reproduction. Through this exposition we will derive the motivations and sources of influence for our own experiments in music reproduction, which drew from the insights and techniques of several of these prior studies. From the collective results of these experiments, we will present data and conclusions which contribute to a more complete model of human humming ability.

Music Perception and Recognition

The way in which people remember both familiar and novel melodies clearly has a very strong influence on the way they will attempt to reproduce a tune that they have heard.

Along with several different contributors over the years, Dowling performed several studies to develop theories of how music is perceived, represented and remembered by the human mind. Dowling conducted experiments which have focused on exploring the roles *pitch contour* and *pitch interval* play as basic elements of the human memory model for music. Pitch contour refers to a measure of melody in which the relative pitch values of successive notes are compared using some metric. Several formal explorations of contour measures have been made by Friedman (1985), Marvin and Laprade (1987) and Polansky and Bassein (1992), among others. The most straightforward representation, often called ternary pitch contour, examines every pair of consecutive notes and compares the pitch values of a given pair; the transition from one note to the next is recorded as up, down or same, depending on the relative pitches. A pitch interval representation similarly examines every pair of consecutive notes but records the transition as the actual pitch distance from a given note to the one which follows it. This value is normally reported in semitones using the Western musical scale. Other pitch contour representations can be devised, dividing the general "up" and "down" designations into two or more possible value ranges and, in effect, giving the measure improved resolution over ternary pitch contour. In fact, a pitch interval representation can be seen as an extended case of applying additional resolution to a pitch contour scheme. Figure 1 gives an example of how a short musical phrase is represented using pitch intervals and ternary pitch contour.

Dowling's study with Fujitani (1971) identified pitch contour and pitch interval measures as relevant. Studies exploring the effect of using familiar vs. novel melodies (Dowling, 1978; Dowling & Fujitani, 1971), and a more recent study on novel melodies presented repeatedly over time (Dowling, Kwak & Andrews, 1995), revealed that most people move from a contour representation towards an interval representation as their familiarity with a song increases. Bartlett and Dowling (1980) pointed to earlier studies (Attneave & Olson, 1971; Cuddy & Cohen, 1976; Dowling, 1978) and concluded that "with unfamiliar melodies, subjects seemed to have little trouble reproducing or recognizing the melodic contour, but they had a great deal of trouble with the exact-pitch intervals among the notes" (p. 501). Another study (Dowling, 1986) showed that for recognizing transpositions of novel melodies, novices seemed to rely on interval representation, while moderately experienced subjects use a method involving contour and a representation of musical scale and professionals use more sophisticated strategies than those tested.

Edworthy (1985) explored the relative abilities of people with musical training to recognize pitch contour versus pitch intervals in unfamiliar musical phrases. In her study ten subjects listened to pairs of melodies which varied in length between 3 and 15 notes; the second of each pair was transposed to a different musical key, and in 75% of the trials, the melody was changed. For the interval tests, a single pitch interval in the phrase was altered by between one and four semitones;

Figure 1. An example of pitch contour and pitch interval representations for a musical phrase (Adapted from Minuet in G, J.S. Bach)

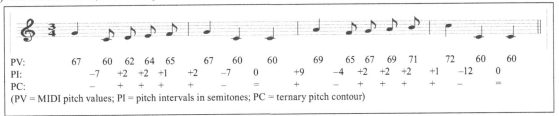

for the contour tests, intervals were allowed to vary slightly from the comparison phrase, but the pitch contour remained the same except for one note. She concluded from her results that musicians identify contour differences more easily for shorter phrases, while for longer phrases a changed interval was more easily recognized. She attributed this to the notion that longer musical passages afford listeners time to build up a "tonal framework" which facilitates memory for pitch intervals. It was not tested whether those with limited or no musical training establish a similar frame of reference when listening to music.

Trehub and colleagues (1987) conducted several studies with infants as young as six months to explore their understanding of music. They discovered that, even at this tender age, infants have the ability to distinguish between two similar musical phrases which differ in pitch contour. In some cases, they can also identify when the contour remains the same but a pitch interval has been changed, even if the altered melody was transposed to a different key from that of the reference melody.

Smith, Nelson, Grohskopf and Appleton (1994) performed a study which attempted to teach pitch interval recognition to two sets of nonmusical subjects using two different methods. One group was taught to compare the stimulus pitch intervals with intervals they already knew from the beginning notes of three familiar tunes: *Greensleeves*, which begins with a minor third interval, *Kumbahyah* (a major third), and *Bridal Chorus* ("Here comes the bride") (a fourth). The other group was taught using a more traditional method from music instruction. It was shown that the first group performed as well at their identification task as subjects with musical training, while the other group performed poorly as expected.

The work by Smith et al. (1994) also provides an excellent survey of musical perception studies as they relate to the nonmusical subject. The authors concluded this section by saying that

"novices often succeed in musical tasks when performance has the support of familiar musical tokens in long-term memory" (p. 46). For MIR systems designed to be useful to the musically untrained, this kind of informal music knowledge common to all could be incorporated in order to build a system that will be useful to this class of users.

In discussing some of the difficulties in obtaining accurate input phrases, McNab et al. (1996) referred to Sloboda's chapter on music performance in Deutsch's *The Psychology of Music* (1982): "Sloboda (1982) reports that people often distort and recombine melodic fragments in complex ways, changing melodic contours, intervals and tonalities; our own studies confirm this" (p. 14). The resulting challenge to a system designer is to create music recognition algorithms which are not overwhelmed computationally in their efforts to compensate for all of the possible permutations on a tune based on performance errors. It is clear that a successful system cannot rely upon recreating these myriad transformations from the user's input to the intended song in order to discover the correct match.

Music Reproduction

Several studies explored how well musicians and nonmusicians could manipulate a musical instrument, metronome, or synthesized tone generator in order to reproduce musical phrases or tempos.

Attneave and Olson (1971) performed experiments to test the ability of musical and of nonmusical subjects to reproduce note sequences played to them. This was accomplished by the use of tone generators under control of the subjects. In the first experiment subjects were asked to adjust the output of two tone generators to reproduce two-note sequences testing interval sizes from 1 to 12 semitones across 8 octaves. In the second experiment, a group of nonmusical subjects performed a series of trials in which they heard an anchor tone and manipulated two tone generators so that the three tones, played in sequence, reproduced the tones of the NBC chimes.

In the task of reproducing unfamiliar sequences, the subjects with musical training tested did well for most cases, while the others were very inconsistent in their responses. In sharp contrast, when reproducing a musical phrase known well to the subjects, the reported results were uniformly good across both groups. We must point out, though, that two of the six subjects in the second experiment were not allowed to proceed because they failed to give good results after attempting 20 practice trials for which the anchor tones were restricted to the key of C; this was significant because, unlike today, at that time NBC always played their identifying chime tones in the key of C.

This very early result shows that at least for short, familiar musical phrases, the majority of people can remember pitch sequences well enough to reproduce them fairly accurately. However, it does not necessarily follow that musically untrained people can manipulate their own voices with sufficient skill to reproduce with any accuracy the tunes they can remember well.

Halpern (1988) conducted two studies which explored the internal representation of musical tempo that subjects possessed for various familiar songs. The songs selected were chosen because they are normally rendered at various tempos. In the first study, subjects were given two tasks:

- To recall a familiar song presented to them only by name, and then to set a metronome to match the tempo at which they would expect the song to be played.
- To manipulate the playback tempo of a synthesized rendering of a song.

In the second study, subjects manipulated a metronome to discover the slowest and fastest tempos at which they could imagine a given song being played. In each study the result was clear that, both for individual subjects and as a group,

there were consistent preferences for specific tempos for different songs.

Drake, Dowling and Palmer (1991) studied the abilities of children and adult pianists to reproduce simple tunes. The subjects were given four sets of melodies, each of which consisted of a short theme followed by four variations of that theme. For each variation, at least one aspect of the tune—a metric (stress or loudness), melodic (pitch) or rhythmic (timing) accent—was modified to be out of sequence relative to the other elements. The subjects were then asked to reproduce the phrases: the adults played them on the piano, while the children were asked to sing them. The study revealed that the variations with altered metric accents were reproduced with fewer errors than those with changes to the melodic or rhythmic accents. It also showed that when reproduction mistakes were made, the errors were more likely to be in melody than in rhythm.

In a later study Drake (1993) tested children, adult musicians and adult nonmusicians for their ability to reproduce musical rhythms on a drum. The musical phrases used in the test were constructed with respect to two characteristics that, when used in combination, created four sets of rhythms. Two sets contained notes possessing only two possible duration values, while the others had three possible values; and two sets broke musical beats into only binary subdivisions while the other two used ternary subdivisions (i.e., triplets or a *3/4* time signature). The results showed that musicians could accurately reproduce all four rhythm types, while the other groups were accurate only for the simplest of the four sets: binary patterns with only two possible note durations. Interestingly, the performance of adult nonmusicians was statistically indistinguishable from that of seven-year-olds. It was also shown that all groups performed better with binary rather than ternary subdivisions, and similarly, with rhythms containing only two duration values rather than three.

VOCAL MUSIC REPRODUCTION

A more limited number of studies have been conducted which explored aspects of human humming or singing.

Halpern (1989) studied the ability of subjects to reproduce consistently the starting note of familiar songs, given only a song's title and its first line of lyrics. The songs chosen for the study were popular traditional or folk tunes which tend to be performed in varying keys, reducing the likelihood that subjects formed mental models of songs' performance keys solely through hearing them. Her results showed that subjects, both musical and nonmusical, made consistently similar choices for their starting pitches among different trials for the same song, and that the choices differed for different songs.

A complementary study was performed by Levitin (1994). His work tested subjects' ability to reproduce the starting notes of modern popular songs selected by the subjects. In contrast to Halpern's data set, the songs in this study were chosen because they are generally only heard in one key as recorded by the musical artist. In the experiment, subjects were shown a selection of 58 CDs and were asked to select two songs from among them. They were then to sing or hum a few notes from any point within the songs chosen. The result was that 40% of the subjects used the same pitch as the recorded song on at least one trial, and 12% matched the pitch for both trials. In addition, 81% were within 2 semitones of the pitch for at least 1 trial, and 44% were within 2 semitones for both trials. These results clearly are not due to chance and show that ordinary subjects have some memory skills for reproducing musical pitches.

Another study by Levitin and Cook (1996) explored subjects' ability to reproduce the tempo of familiar songs. The first experiment of this study utilized the data collected from Levitin's 1994 study, described above, which was performed using a set of popular songs with the characteristic

that they were invariably played on CD or radio stations at the same tempo. The subjects recalled and reproduced these tempos very well: 72% of the participants sang within 8% of the expected tempo for a given song. In a second experiment, volunteers hummed well-known folk tunes, which by their nature do not have a single performance tempo associated with them. The results showed that subjects' chosen tempos showed some consistency, but not to the same degree as was seen in the first experiment; tempo values typically varied between 10 – 20%. The authors note that this second result confirms observations made in the earlier study by Halpern (1988) on tempo. Further analysis of the results from their 1994 experiment showed that there was no correlation between subjects who scored well in estimating tempo and those who reproduced accurately the initial pitch of a song.

Lindsay's MS thesis work (1996) included a small study in which 6 subjects listened to a series of 32 five-note sequences, vocally reproducing each one after hearing it. These short phrases were carefully designed to test all 16 possible binary pitch contours as well as all pitch interval sizes between 1 and 7 steps. He measured how well the subjects were able to reproduce each phrase, and he proposed and tested several representations of the user input to see how well each matched the user input to the associated stimulus phrase. Based upon his experimental results, Lindsay proposed a straightforward representation of user input for which a musical phrase of n notes is represented directly by the $n – 1$ pitch interval values separating consecutive notes. (The intervals would be measured in cents, a more precise measure of pitch to describe notes which fall between two consecutive semitones in the Western tonal scale. The pitch space between any two adjacent semitones is divided into 100 cents.)

McNab et al. (1996) conducted a short study as part of their efforts to build an MIR system. Ten subjects sang or hummed ten familiar songs, which were measured to see how well the subjects were able to remain in key and whether their pitch contours remained correct over the course of their performances. Subjects were given time to practice each song before it was recorded, and they were asked to sing as much as they knew of the songs. They discovered that their subjects were able to sing at least one phrase of each song with two or fewer pitch contour errors, and that small pitch intervals were often exaggerated while large ones were often compressed. They described and analyzed how songs with large or unusual pitch intervals were much more likely to cause subjects to end their performance out of key. They also noted that singing experience played a larger factor than overall music training in the performance of the subjects. Unfortunately, most of these results were reported only anecdotally, with data reported only for how well subjects ended their singing in the same key in which they started.

The most recent study was performed by Unal, Narayanan, Shih, Chew and Kuo (2003) as part of their efforts to collect a corpus of hummed input queries from a variety of subjects. It is intended that their collection will be made available for further study, analysis and use in testing other MIR systems.

The collective insights of all of these studies paint a picture of our intended user, but not enough of the results apply to the vocal skills of the musically untrained. They provided the direction and many good ideas which we drew upon to develop and carry out our own study, which we describe in the next section. In addition to the intrinsic value of the knowledge gained through our experiments, we used this opportunity also to collect a significant body of sample queries with which to evaluate our later efforts at developing effective new MIR matching algorithms.

In summary, these are some of the important shortcomings of the available body of research which we attempted to address in the design and execution of our own study:

- The majority of the studies available from psychology and music cognition sources focus more on perception and recognition of music rather than its reproduction.
- Studies from these sources on music reproduction skills have typically been restricted to certain individual aspects such as selecting a starting pitch or tempo. Many of these have used instruments or other devices rather than subjects' voices.
- Some studies specifically targeting human humming ability have been performed anecdotally or used very small subject sets with a disproportionate number of highly skilled musicians represented.

OUR STUDY OF HUMAN HUMMING SKILLS

Our study consisted of four separate experiments in which subjects were asked to hum both familiar and unfamiliar melodies and rhythms. The experiments were conducted together under the same conditions and with the same group of subjects. For the first experiment, subjects hummed songs whose titles and lyrics were presented to them on paper. In the second, subjects first listened to recordings or MIDI renditions of songs, and then hummed them. The third experiment was a modified version of a study by Lindsay (1996) in which subjects heard 32 unfamiliar five-note phrases and hummed each one in turn. The fourth was a modified version of the Drake (1993) study on reproduction of rhythms. Space considerations allow us here to report on only the first and third experiments of the study, where most of our significant findings were discovered.

Subjects

A group of 15 subjects, all within the ages of 18-35, participated in the study. The subjects were unpaid volunteers who were undergraduate or graduate students at Rensselaer Polytechnic Institute in Troy, New York. At the beginning of each session, the subjects were asked about the amount of training and experience each had with musical instruments and with singing. Subjects were also asked informally about their familiarity with the tunes selected for the experiment.

Five of the subjects had more than five years experience with one or more musical instruments; the mean for this group was 14.8 years. In the reported results for each experiment, we referred to them collectively as the musician group, abbreviated as MUSI. Of the remaining ten subjects, six had between two and five years musical experience (mean 3.2 years); their results were grouped together as the inbetween (BTWN) group. The final four subjects had less than two years experience and were referred to as the nonmusician or NONM group. Five of the subjects were female, and they were evenly distributed among the groups with two musicians, two nonmusicians and one in the BTWN group. None of the subjects had formal voice training, though three of them had experience singing in volunteer community choirs. Of these, two were in the MUSI group and one was a nonmusician who had recently joined a choir.

Apparatus

All music played to the subjects during the course of the experimental trials was generated by a midrange sound card and played through inexpensive computer speakers (typically owned by home users) at a comfortable listening level in a quiet office. Almost all of the musical samples were synthesized MIDI renditions, though a few of the stimuli were presented as digitized audio (.wav) files made from original recordings.

The subjects' responses were recorded with an inexpensive computer microphone (again, equipment of the quality typically provided with computers used in the home) onto a medium-grade

cassette deck. The recorded input hummed by the subjects was digitized using Wildcat Canyon Software *Autoscore 2.0 Professional* music transcription software after the sessions.

All musical sequences played to the subjects during the course of the study were played out of tune relative to the key signature in which they were written. The degree to which the notes were out of tune was a randomly selected value in the range ± 100 cents. This technique was commonly used in the previously cited studies in order to eliminate any tonal basis among the trials. To facilitate accurate note segmentation by the transcription software, subjects were instructed to voice each note using the syllable *da* rather than by humming. This provides a consonant stopping sound between successive notes, which is another method *Autoscore* employs to improve transcription accuracy.

Experiment 1: Humming Familiar Tunes from Memory

The first two experiments explored how subjects hummed songs that were familiar to them. Several factors were taken into consideration when selecting the songs to be used for these two experiments. Many were selected from the Digital Tradition folksong collection (Greenhaus et al., n.d.). This collection was first used by McNab et al. (1997) as one of two components of their test database, and it has subsequently been used in other research as well, for example, Downie and Nelson (2000). Among our considerations in selecting the set of stimulus songs were these:

- Several of the songs chosen, such as Twinkle, Twinkle, Little Star (d02) and Yankee Doodle (d08), contain sequences in which consecutive notes continually increase or decrease in pitch by only one or two semitones.
- Care was taken to ensure that a wide variety of pitch interval sizes were represented in the selected tunes. For instance, Take Me

Out To The Ballgame (d01) and Somewhere Over The Rainbow (d06) both begin with the notes of the melody rising by an entire octave.

- Songs such as The Star-Spangled Banner (d09) were chosen because their melodies span a wide pitch range despite the fact they do not contain large pitch intervals. Attempting to hum such songs requires careful selection of the starting pitch in order to remain within a comfortable singing range when vocalizing subsequent notes.

- Also included were songs for which individual renditions frequently produce variations in notes or rhythm. For instance, the first two notes of The Star-Spangled Banner are commonly sung in one of two different rhythms: either both notes are given the same duration, or the first has twice the duration of the second. Another of the songs used here, Amazing Grace (d05), often has extra ornamental or grace notes added by individual performers.

The lack of constraints on how much the subjects were expected to hum, combined with the problem of occasional missing or extraneous notes as recorded by the transcription process, made it impossible to automatically measure in complete detail the subjects' performances with respect to the intended database song for features such as the ability to reproduce arbitrary pitch intervals. Formal analysis of these features was left for the more tightly controlled experimental trials utilized

in Experiment 3. Instead, general statistics are presented from these user trials, along the lines of the studies performed by Halpern (1989) and by Levitin (1994).

One important feature we analyzed was the relationship between the duration of a hummed note and the elapsed time from the beginning of that note to the start of the note that followed it. We refer to this as the *inter-note onset time* (INOT). Differences between these two values occur naturally in many songs when musical rests have been written into the tune (i.e., intentional gaps between successive notes). Testing this relationship was not part of the original design of the experiment, but informal analysis of the collected data revealed a significant difference between the two which we found important to quantify formally.

For one of the songs in this experiment, we manually produced our own transcriptions of each subject's humming by listening to the audio recordings. These were compared with those produced by the *Autoscore* software with the goal of quantifying the frequency and severity of errors introduced into the data by the music transcription process itself.

Method

Subjects were presented with the names of 12 popular tunes familiar to most Americans, along with a portion of the lyrics to the song (except for two of the songs which had no associated lyrics). They were asked to hum as much of the tune as they were comfortable in doing. A list of the set

Table 1. Songs used in Experiment 1

d01	Take Me Out To The Ballgame	d07	Bridal Chorus (Richard Wagner)
d02	Twinkle, Twinkle, Little Star	d08	Yankee Doodle
d03	Jingle Bells	d09	The Star-Spangled Banner
d04	Beethoveen's 5th Symphony, 1st Mvmt.	d10	Happy Birthday To You
d05	Amazing Grace	d11	Theme from *Gilligan's Island*
d06	Somewhere Over The Rainbow	d12	Main Theme, *Raiders of the Lost Ark*

of songs used for this experiment can be found in Table 1.

To prevent a subject's pitch selection for a given trial from being influenced by the previous trial, a sequence of 14 pseudo-random interfering notes was played in between each trial, as was done by Halpern (1989). The songs were presented to the subjects in one of two different orders, which were assigned randomly and equally to the subjects.

The *Autoscore* transcription software was run in its *Constrain* mode for this experiment. In this mode the program identifies the closest semitone to the user's hummed frequency for a given note, recording the note's pitch as that value. One consequence of using this mode is that occasionally a subject may hum two notes that sound very similar in pitch, but their frequencies differ enough that they straddle the cutoff between two semitones and end up being reported as two different pitches. We saw in our collected data several instances where this occurred.

Results

Nine of the subjects knew all 12 songs used in this experiment; 4 of them knew all but one, and 2 of

them knew all but two. Subjects did not attempt songs they did not know. In all but a few cases, subjects hummed exactly as much of each tune as was represented by the lyrics in front of them.

Table 2 illustrates the aggregate values of the starting pitches chosen by subjects for each of the performed songs. We report the data first averaged by song, then by subject. The reported average pitch values are given in the MIDI note scale (e.g., middle C is represented as 60 and consecutive semitones are separated in value by one). Since Halpern noted that women typically sing about an octave higher than men for the same song (1989), all of the pitch values for female subjects (denoted by italics in the table) were reported by their actual MIDI values but were reduced by 12 (semitones) when calculating averages to allow direct comparison to those of male subjects.

Both sections of the table show that the starting pitches chosen by MUSI subjects were consistently higher than those of the other two groups, whose values are roughly the same. When examining the values grouped by song, the MUSI group starting pitches were an average of 2.1 semitones higher than the BTWN group and 2.3 semitones higher

Table 2a. Average starting pitch selection and standard deviation, tabulated by stimulus song, from Experiment 1

Song	Subject Group							
	MUSI		BTWN		NONM		ALL	
	Pitch	S.D.	Pitch	S.D.	Pitch	S.D.	Pitch	S.D.
d01	45.75	2.87	43.60	1.52	44.25	0.50	44.46	1.94
d02	46.00	2.74	44.67	1.21	45.25	1.26	45.27	1.83
d03	44.75	2.22	44.00	2.97	43.75	0.96	44.14	2.21
d04	52.80	2.05	48.83	3.06	49.00	1.63	50.20	2.96
d05	43.50	1.29	44.20	1.79	42.50	1.73	43.46	1.66
d06	48.00	1.73	44.20	1.92	43.00	0.82	45.21	2.67
d07	45.80	3.27	44.83	2.56	43.75	2.63	44.87	2.75
d08	49.00	1.00	47.50	1.87	46.75	2.22	47.80	1.86
d09	50.60	1.52	47.67	1.51	49.00	3.16	49.00	2.30
d10	46.60	2.61	45.33	2.94	44.75	1.26	45.60	2.44
d11	49.50	5.45	45.83	2.14	46.50	1.91	47.07	3.47
d12	46.80	3.63	43.25	1.71	42.75	1.50	44.46	3.07

Note: Pitch values are given as MIDI note numbers; Female subjects are shown in italics.

than the NONM group. When considering all trials together, musicians chose starting pitches 2.1 semitones higher than BTWN subjects and 2.4 semitones higher than nonmusicians.

Perhaps more important than the actual starting pitches is the similarity of choices across subjects for a given song. In examining the starting pitches for a given song across all subjects, in most cases the standard deviation was quite small. When considering all subjects for a single song, the performances which resulted in the lowest standard deviation included both songs with small overall pitch ranges (i.e., d02, d08) and those with large ranges (i.e., d01, d05). In the same way, the songs with the largest deviation fell into both of these categories. Overall, four of the songs had a standard deviation below 2.0, while two songs had values over 3.0, and the remaining six were in between.

Table 2b. Average starting pitch selection and standard deviation, tabulated by subject, from Experiment 1

Subject	Avg.Pitch	Std.Dev.
1	48.83	3.71
2	46.33	2.71
3	47.30	3.27
12	50.60	1.96
14	*57.08*	*3.26*
MUSI	**47.54**	**3.53**
7	47.83	2.25
8	46.10	2.77
9	*56.92*	*2.43*
11	44.64	2.54
13	*55.91*	*1.22*
15	45.18	2.96
BTWN	**45.45**	**2.66**
4	44.33	2.77
5	*57.17*	*2.52*
6	45.83	2.98
10	*57.08*	*2.61*
NONM	45.10	2.69
ALL	46.04	3.15

Notes:Pitch values are given as MIDI note numbers;Female subjects are shown in italics.

When considering performance by subject group, the musicians showed the highest variability in pitch selection at 3.53, while the BTWN and NONM groups had standard deviations of 2.66 and 2.69, respectively. Only two subjects had variability below 2.0, one of who had the extremely low value of 1.22: this subject chose nearly the same starting pitch for every performance.

We meticulously compared the audio recordings of each subject's rendition of Take Me Out To The Ballgame (d01) with the automated transcriptions produced by *Autoscore* to determine the number of errors introduced through the pitch tracking process. On average, subjects hummed 26.5 notes of the melody. When compared to our manual transcriptions, the *Autoscore* transcriptions contained an average of 3.75 extraneous notes, while also failing to record 2.2 of the notes which were hummed. The transcription exactly matched the vocal rendition for only one subject. At least one extraneous note was introduced to the automatic transcription in 13 of 15 trials, and 10 of the 15 subjects' transcriptions were missing at least one hummed note clearly audible in the recording.

The difference between note durations and internote onset times was noticeable for all subjects and all groups. Overall, the average hummed note had a duration value 74% of the length of its corresponding INOT. Table 3 shows as percentages the ratio of note duration to INOT for all notes hummed by all subjects in the experiment. The values are shown categorized for each of the three subject groups, as well as in groups based on the INOT time value (reported in milliseconds). The different columns for each row give the percentage for all notes whose INOT values were in the ranges shown. The cutoff values were chosen based on the mean INOT value of 313ms for all notes in all trials. As expected, longer notes generally displayed a larger difference between the two values (both in absolute time and as a percentage) than exhibited by shorter notes.

Table 3. Note durations as a percentage of inter-note onset times (INOT) in Experiment 1

Subject Group	Percentages, ratio of (Duration / INOT), grouped by INOT value					
	0 < 150ms	150 < 300	300 < 600	600 < 1200	> 1200	ALL
MUSI	90.35	83.56	85.89	77.13	59.99	78.78
BTWN	92.09	79.40	80.26	60.86	55.04	72.13
NONM	91.61	78.28	79.09	63.79	37.20	70.59
ALL	91.43	80.46	81.75	67.75	53.60	74.08

Among the groups, musicians averaged 79% overall, while BTWN and NONM averaged 72% and 71%, respectively. The MUSI group score was pulled down by one subject who scored only 60%; otherwise, its average would have been over 82%. The largest difference among groups was seen with notes in the (600-1200ms) range.

Discussion

The data for this experiment show that both musicians and nonmusicians have some proficiency in choosing starting pitches so that they have a better likelihood of remaining in a comfortable singing range when vocalizing subsequent notes. The results confirm the general conclusions of Halpern (1989) and of Levitin (1994) that the choice of starting pitch for different subjects is dependent upon the song being sung and is not merely due to chance.

We had hypothesized that songs which required most of a subject's vocal range would show the smallest standard deviation, because the choice of starting pitch determines whether the melody will stay within the subject's vocal range or not. We were surprised to find no strong link between the two. We suggest that the differences in this case may be due to the natural differences in comfortable vocal range among subjects; further study would be required to prove this. In particular, a formal exploration of the vocal range of each subject would have given the ability to make more definitive statements about how well each subject chose starting pitches with respect to the subject's range.

When comparing the results of one subject group against another for a given song, we were also surprised that the group exhibiting the smallest standard deviation value changed from one song to the next with no consistent pattern we could discern. For instance, song d04 (Beethoven's Fifth) is nearly always heard in the same key, and we expected musicians in particular would tend toward reproducing the notes in the key in which it is usually played, but the MUSI group showed more variability in starting pitch choice than the NONM group. Alternatively, the starting pitches chosen for the folk song Yankee Doodle (d08) were most consistent with the MUSI group.

While the experiment showed that musicians in general have higher variability in their choices for starting pitch, we see from the inconsistent results of Table 2 that we cannot make any predictions about how musicians or nonmusicians will choose their pitches for any given song. Thus, providing information about starting pitch to any given song-matching algorithm is unlikely to improve search accuracy.

The large observed difference between note durations and INOTs from our subjects is very significant. While many songs do contain rests, most of the gaps between the time a note was voiced and the corresponding INOT were not intended to be rests, and the corresponding song transcriptions in the database lack rests at most of these points. This result clearly points to a requirement that any algorithms involving duration information must consider INOT as the more relevant measure of the user's intended duration values. It furthermore reduces confidence that searching algorithms could be made to account accurately for intended rests in hummed queries.

One might expect that some of the difference between durations and INOT values could be attributed to the manner of vocalization required by the note-tracking software. It is possible that the consonant sounds added by the subjects in singing *da* contributed to this difference in certain cases, but further analysis of the data collected makes this conclusion unlikely. Out of more than 4,000 notes recorded in this experiment, 42% have identical values for duration and INOT, meaning that *Autoscore* reported the time between the end of such a note and the start of the following note as zero. This measure was also fairly consistent across subjects; 9 of the 15 had between 37-47% of hummed notes exhibiting this equality.

Experiment 3: Humming Novel Melodic Phrases

Lindsay (1996) performed a small study with 6 subjects to see how well they could vocally reproduce a series of 32 five-note sequences. The sequences were carefully constructed so that, among all of them, each pitch interval between -7 and +7 semitones appeared approximately an equal number of times. He tested the subjects' accuracy by comparing their input phrases against all 32 test phrases; an edit distance was computed by summing the differences between the pitch interval values and the corresponding values of the target phrase, with the lowest-scoring phrase selected as the best match. For the five subjects with significant musical training, the correct phrase was identified on average 86% of the time. The sole nonmusician subject fared much worse, matching the intended stimulus in only 41% of the trials. Lindsay also tabulated how well the users' data matched when encoded using ternary pitch contours, finding that the musician group produced the correct contour in 96% of the trials, while the nonmusician was correct 72% of the time. These

results are compared with our own in Table 4 below. For the pitch interval representations, Lindsay also reported the percentage of trials for which the correct target phrase was ranked either first or second, since each possible five-note contour sequence appeared twice in the trials. We report this value under the column heading *1st/2nd*. In this and subsequent tables, we refer to the grouped results of Lindsay's musician subjects as LIN-M and the nonmusician as LIN-N.

Lindsay concluded from his subjects' excellent performance in the study that pitch intervals could be used as an accurate representation of hummed input, at least for those with significant musical training. Although his study was the most comprehensive of its kind we have found, it had a few limitations which caused us to question whether his proposed representation would lead to algorithms which would prove successful in identifying hummed queries from the average user:

- Only six subjects participated in the experiment; five of the six were musicians averaging 12 years of experience, and two of them had significant vocal training.
- From our own informal experience in hearing the singing and humming of random people, it appeared that attempts to intone larger pitch intervals were more likely to induce reproduction errors, but in the study the largest pitch interval tested was seven semitones.
- The representation scheme was tested by attempting to match individuals' input phrases against a music collection consisting only of the 32 test phrases used in the experiment.

With these ideas in mind, we expanded upon Lindsay's methodology for our experiment by testing a larger set of subjects and by including more variation in the pitch intervals used in the testing trials. We rewrote 50% of his test phrases to include the testing of larger pitch intervals. We also used a significantly larger group of subjects who possessed a much wider range of musical abilities.

Method

The stimulus data set was a series of 32 five-note sequences. The notes were all of equal duration, played at the rate of three notes per second. This is slightly slower than the four note-per-second rate used by Lindsay; the change was made after the faster tempo was tried in a few informal trials with nonmusicians before the study. We duplicated 17 of Lindsay's original sequences and the requirement that exactly 2 sequences represent each of the 16 possible five-note binary pitch contours. The remaining 15 sequences originally contained 1 or more instances of a six-semitone interval. This dissonant interval occurs rarely in Western popular and folk music because it is perceived as sounding unpleasant to many ears, and as a result, it is difficult for an untrained voice to reproduce it. Wherever this interval occurred, it was replaced equally by intervals of 9, 10 and 12 semitones. The resulting set of 32 sequences had approximately 9 intervals each of ± 1, 2, 3, 4, 5 and 7 semitones, and 3 each of ± 9, 10 and 12 semitones.

The sequences were presented in a pseudorandom order so that no trial was presented near another with similar contour or its opposite contour. Half of the subjects heard the sequences in one order, while the other half were presented them in exact reverse order, thus reducing the influence one trial has on the trial that followed it yet retaining the careful ordering based on contour distances. Subjects listened to each sequence in turn, and then vocalized the sequence just heard. They could begin humming whenever they were ready. Subjects were invited to request a short break after the first half of the trials if they wished it; seven of them did so.

In the first two experiments the music tracking software was run in its default *Constrain* mode of identifying the nearest semitone to the perceived frequency. For this experiment, in order to duplicate the reporting done by Lindsay, *Autoscore* was used in its *pitch bend* mode, in which it measures and reports the precise sound frequency many times per second. *Autoscore* typically reported about 20 distinct pitch-bend values per hummed note; these were averaged to come up with the pitch value we recorded.

Results

In several instances, the transcription process did not correctly output the exact five distinct notes hummed by the subjects. Most often, a single note was incorrectly identified as multiple notes at one or more pitch values. Each of these cases was edited by hand, comparing the transcription to the original recording to ensure the correct pitch values were retained. In a small number of instances, an individual trial had to be thrown out because of transcription difficulties or user errors such as humming only four notes. One of the subjects found this experiment too difficult to complete, so none of her results are included here.

Again here as before, we report results for subjects in three groups: musicians (MUSI), inexperienced musicians (BTWN) and nonmusicians (NONM). The MUSI group corresponds to the five musician subjects of Lindsay's study, while the BTWN group appears to correspond to the description of Lindsay's nonmusician subject.

Overall, the musician subjects in our study performed substantially worse than their counterparts in the Lindsay study, matching the intended sequence using pitch interval data 65% of the time, and giving the correct pitch contours in only 81% of the cases. The scores for BTWN and NONM were nearly identical to one another and were also very close to those of Lindsay's less experienced subject: combining these two groups, 48% of the trials matched correctly when

Table 4. Results of pitch interval and pitch contour performance in Experiment 3. Lower two rows are comparative results from Lindsay (1996)

Subject Group	Pitch Interval Matching		Contour Matching
	1st	1st/2nd	
MUSI	65.2%	77.2%	81.1%
BTWN	48.0%	64.0%	72.0%
NONM	47.1%	65.5%	69.7%
ALL	54.5%	69.7%	74.9%

LIN-M	86.3%	96.9%	95.6%
LIN-N	40.6%	68.8%	71.9%

Table 5. Results of pitch interval reproduction performance in Experiment 3, separated into trials common with Lindsay (1996) and modified trials

Subject Group	Common Trials		Modified Trials	
	1st	1st/2nd	1st	1st/2nd
MUSI	76.2%	84.5%	52.7%	68.9%
BTWN	64.7%	75.0%	28.1%	50.9%
NONM	56.7%	73.3%	37.3%	57.6%
ALL	67.0%	78.3%	40.5%	60.0%

Lindsay	Common Trials		6-semitone trials	
LIN-M	90.6%	94.1%	81.3%	94.7%
LIN-N	41.2%	64.7%	40.0%	73.3%

measuring by pitch intervals, and 71% matched the intended pitch contour. The values for each group are summarized in Table 4.

To better compare results between the two studies, it is helpful to break down the data into two groups: results based on the 17 unmodified note sequences which were common to both Lindsay's study and our own, and those based on the 15 modified phrases. When we consider these two components separately, we see clearly the effect of the larger intervals tested in our experiment, as shown in Table 5. In the unmodified trials, our MUSI group matched the correct phrase using pitch interval data 76% of the time, while Lindsay's musicians scored 91%; the difference between the groups is smaller than the 20% overall difference when including all 32 trials. The modified set of trials posed more of a difficulty to our subjects, as performance dropped dramatically to 53%; in comparison, Lindsay's musician group showed a significant but much less dramatic decrease to 81% for the trials involving six-semitone intervals. The BTWN and NONM groups showed the same behavior as the MUSI group. Interestingly, Lindsay's nonmusician was the only one to score equally well between the two subcategories.

Figure 2 illustrates the collective values of pitch intervals hummed by the MUSI group, the

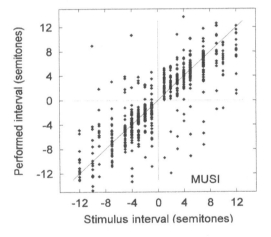

Figure 2. Performed intervals vs. stimulus intervals for MUSI subjects, all 32 trials, in Experiment 3

best performers of the three groups reported. This plot is helpful to illustrate instances where pitch contour errors occurred. Any points which appear in quadrants II or IV of the graph represent intervals which were in the opposite direction of the associated stimulus interval. It can be seen from the graph that contour errors occur against both large and small stimulus intervals, and they are distributed evenly between upward and downward intervals. Furthermore, when a contour mistake is made, the sizes of the incorrectly hummed intervals in these cases also vary

Figure 3. Average performed pitch intervals vs. stimulus intervals for each group (MUSI, BTWN, NONM) in Experiment 3

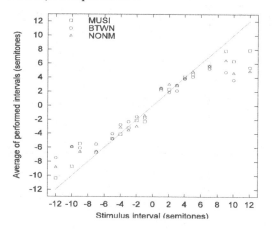

Table 6. Correlation of performed intervals with stimulus intervals for all subjects in Experiment 3

Subject	Correlation (r)	
	All Intervals	**Intervals ≤ ± 7**
1	0.91	0.88
2	0.69	0.58
3	0.87	0.91
12	0.79	0.79
14	0.92	0.80
MUSI	0.83	0.80
8	0.90	0.93
9	0.80	0.80
11	0.89	0.91
13	0.42	0.33
BTWN	0.75	0.74
4	0.87	0.82
6	0.84	0.84
7	0.81	0.75
10	0.55	0.69
NONM	0.75	0.77
ALL	0.78	0.77

widely. The plots for the BTWN and NONM groups look similar but demonstrate even more variation and contour errors. Figure 3 plots the average performed interval size for each of the three groups on the same graph.

Table 6 shows the correlation (r) values between stimulus interval and performed interval for each individual subject, each group and all subjects together. The correlation was computed first for the entire set of intervals and then a second time including only the smaller intervals of seven semitones or less. We expected to see better correlation values when considering only these smaller intervals, as they seemed likely to be easier to reproduce.

Discussion

Lindsay's LIN-M group of musician subjects performed significantly better than our MUSI group in their respective studies. We had hoped to attribute some of this difference to the two subjects in Lindsay's study who were trained vocally. However, further study of the results Lindsay reported for each of his five individual subjects demonstrated that the scores belonging to these two subjects did not score significantly higher than the other three. The differences may instead be due to the small sample sizes for each study.

The correlation scores of the BTWN and NONM groups are nearly identical to one another but below those of the MUSI group. While it might be expected that the correlation values would be higher when considering only intervals in the range ±7 semitones, the opposite is true for 8 of the 13 subjects, and in the MUSI group as a whole.

Another interesting observation is that the three subjects who scored most poorly came from all three of our subject groups, not (as one might guess) from only the NONM group. While the number of subjects in each group is not large enough for statistically significant generalizations, this result does confirm that musical training is no guarantee of good performance in reproducing pitch intervals.

Perhaps most importantly, this experiment has shown the similar degree to which both musicians and nonmusicians enlarge small pitch intervals and compress large ones, whether the intervals are moving upward or downward. It also showed that the accuracy of subjects' humming when measured even in a method as imprecise as ternary pitch contour was lower than reported in other studies. It must be remembered, though, that these results were obtained for unfamiliar melodic phrases, and informal inspection of the input queries for the first two experiments show better pitch contour performance than was seen in this experiment. In addition, some of the stimulus phrases used both in Lindsay's study and in our own contain dissonant intervals, which occur only rarely in popular vocal melodies and are more difficult to sing or hum.

STUDY CONCLUSIONS

Our experiments yielded several insights into characteristics which influenced our own development of algorithms for matching hummed input to a music database.

In almost every measured statistic, the relative performance of subjects with 2-5 years music experience as a group was indistinguishable from those with less than two years experience. On the other hand, in most cases those with more than five years of musical training performed significantly better than the other two groups. Of course, individual cases vary widely from the group norms; natural musical ability can make up for a lack of formal training.

We confirmed the results of Halpern (1989) and of Levitin (1994) that subjects make fairly consistent choices in selecting a starting pitch when humming a given song. We hypothesized that variation would be reduced when a song contained a large pitch range, but our data did not support it. An examination of the data for individual subjects showed that musicians chose a wider variety of starting pitches for different songs than the other two groups.

Musicians were more likely than the other groups to match the performance key of a song they had just heard when humming it, unless the song was beyond their comfortable vocal range. Nonmusicians were nearly equally adept as musicians when choosing a starting pitch for humming a song having a wide pitch range.

A significant difference was found between the duration a note was voiced and the inter-note onset time (INOT) corresponding to it. The difference increased as INOT increased. Musicians had a higher duration/INOT ratio than the other groups, but the improvement was seen mostly with notes longer than one-half second. INOT values are a more reliable representation of note timings for vocal input than note duration.

Pitch interval and pitch contour reproduction skills for musicians on unfamiliar musical phrases were lower than reported in an earlier study (Lindsay, 1996). Nonmusicians performed substantially worse than musicians in both studies. All subject groups tended to exaggerate the size of small pitch intervals and to compress large intervals, as reported informally by McNab et al. (1996). We further showed that subjects with musical training generally compress large intervals less than those without, and that for all subjects upward intervals are compressed more than downward intervals.

If the musically untrained cannot reliably reproduce even the simple pitch contour of a musical phrase, then representations using more complex contour schemes such as the five-category MPEG-7 Melody Contour description (i.e., a lot higher vs. a little higher) will not be effective for vocal input. Similarly, MIR systems expecting correct or nearly-correct contour information will not work successfully with input from this class of potential user.

MIR SYSTEM COMPARISONS AND TESTING

Our own efforts were directed toward developing effective schemes for representing hummed input queries to maximize search discrimination while minimizing the negative impact of query errors of all the types we have described. Hand in hand with an effective representation format goes the need for search algorithms able to match these search queries to a music database. We assembled our own test database of over 3,600 songs, consisting mostly of the Greenhaus Digital Tradition (n.d.) folksong database, which was also used in the MELDEX (McNab et al., 1996; 1997) system. As described above, the first two experiments of our study provided us with a set of 172 input test phrases from fifteen subjects of varying musical ability.

Contour-Based MIR

We created and tested many algorithms which made use of pitch contour information as a representation method for both input queries and database entries. Our goal was to produce a computationally efficient search mechanism that was still sufficiently robust to accommodate the types and quantity of errors we found in our experiments. The details of all of these efforts are beyond the scope of this chapter, but can be found in Kline (2002). We present here the most significant, general results of our work.

Among our accomplishments, we independently developed and tested the representation scheme known as *n-grams*, first developed by Ukkonen (1992), which were used at about the same time in MIR systems developed by Uitdenbogerd and Zobel (1998, 1999) and by Downie and Nelson (2000). We performed many tests using n-grams

of length three through six. With our input query set, we found matching accuracy to be completely unacceptable, even with a toy database of only 300 songs, for all but a few of the highest-quality input queries in our collection. The best of these poor results ranked the intended song only in the top 25% of the database on average for our MUSI subjects, and even lower for the other groups. As Downie and Nelson also reported, n-gram representation can be extremely sensitive to the presence of errors, and as we described earlier, our input collection contained an average of one false or incorrectly-recorded note for every five accurately transcribed notes. Shorter n-grams are less susceptible to errors, but they offer little discrimination power; for example, n-grams of size three represent clusters of just four consecutive notes, and there are only 27 (3 x 3 x 3) possible values for an n-gram of this length. Larger values mean that a single error propagates to progressively more consecutive individual n-grams in the encoded query string.

Since our study showed that one-semitone intervals were usually exaggerated by our subjects, we performed tests with our database songs encoded in two different ways: in one representation, only consecutive notes of the same MIDI pitch value were marked as "same" or "=" in pitch contour. In the other, we encoded intervals of one semitone as "same" as well, since we expected that most instances represented a subject who intended to hum the same pitch twice. This change did not show a significant improvement in the overall results for any of the algorithms we devised and tested.

In searching for ways to improve our results with this type of data representation and search, we chose to incorporate note duration information. We went on to create our own corresponding definition of *duration contour*, in which we marked consecutive pairs of notes as having increased in duration, decreased in duration or roughly equal duration. Analysis of the data collected in our experiments led us to define a contour transition as "same" when the two duration values were within 25% of one another. Based on the results of our first experiment, we additionally applied our duration contour scheme to INOT values rather than raw duration values as reported by our transcriber.

We found that these contour representations had even worse matching discrimination than the solely pitch-based ones. INOT-based contours using n-gram representation showed in the best case that the intended target song could be placed only in the top 33% of our 300-song database on average with our MUSI group input queries. Utilizing INOT values instead of note durations improved the overall results by approximately 10% using our search methods.

We further developed many other variants combining both pitch and INOT information in various ways to improve search accuracy, but none of these efforts proved fruitful in the end. Our conclusion was that contour-based representations are simply unlikely to work for MIR systems in the presence of input query errors caused by non-expert vocal input. We then turned to more computationally complex strategies, finding success with approximate matching algorithms based on the work of Smith and Waterman (1981) and also used by other MIR researchers.

Approximate Matching MIR

Kageyama et al. (1993, 1994) was one of the first groups to implement a voice transcription system and an integrated search mechanism with a 500-song test database in 1993. Hummed notes were translated into a scale-step (semitone) representation which was then subjected to an approximate pattern matching algorithm in order to locate a match between the transcribed input phrase and a song in the database. The accuracy of the system was reported to be fair, normally requiring 12 or more notes to find a match when testing against a database of 500 songs. Ghias et al. (1995) also created their own music transcription system and

used its output to build a musical database search mechanism in 1995, using an even smaller test database. Their system performed approximate matching searches using ternary pitch contour information. One of the ideas proposed by the authors to improve searching was to increase the resolution of the melodic contour data, so that a note transition is labeled not merely as increasing or decreasing, but some sense of magnitude is given as well (slightly increasing vs. significantly increasing). However, they did not perform any experiments to test the feasibility of such a representation or the limits of its resolution (i.e., how many distinct subdivisions of "increasing" can be used and where their boundaries lie). As we have shown, this kind of representation, which also forms the basis of the relatively new MPEG-7 Melody Contour description, will certainly not be effective for input queries with errors due to the combined effects of nonmusician humming skills and automated transcription errors.

The MELDEX system mentioned earlier became part of the New Zealand Digital Library project (Bainbridge, Nevill-Manning, Witten, Smith & McNab, 1999), which is currently available online (University of Waikato, n.d.). A Web-based interface allows for hummed input queries, and they use approximate matching algorithms incorporating pitch contour, pitch intervals, and/or rhythm information. Previous versions of the system allowed the user control over certain aspects of their search algorithm, but at the time of this writing, the current system has removed these options.

Hu and Dannenberg (2002) presented a series of approximate matching algorithms that took into account various input features of hummed input queries. They explored a promising technique in which no attempt is made to differentiate individual notes in the hummed input; instead, pitch values are reported in 100ms frames and then scaled to many different tempos and keys to run the matching algorithm many times. Preliminary testing was performed on a 598-song database with 37 query samples.

In our own work, we created and tested many existing and new music representations which we incorporated into various algorithms utilizing approximate matching techniques along the lines of the systems described here and below. As with our fast searching efforts described in the previous section, we made use of pitch data, duration data, and INOT data in our work. Here we describe only our most successful technique, which is named REPRED for relative-pitch, relative-duration. Further details of the most successful algorithms we developed can be found in Kline and Glinert (2003).

The key insight to REPRED came as a result of our development of a tempo estimator for our input query samples. Some of our algorithms made use of this estimator in order to transform note durations in terms of beats. The resulting REPSCAD (relative-pitch, scaled-duration) algorithm proved to be fairly effective, but analysis of our input data set through our tempo estimator revealed a pattern in INOT values. While we already knew anecdotally that subjects typically compress long notes when humming or singing, we found that the drop-off could be predicted fairly well with a logarithmic transformation.

The resulting REPRED algorithm represents note durations in this way: for a given note x, its duration component is given by taking the ratio of the INOT value for note x over the INOT value of the note following it, then taking the logarithm of the result, that is, $\log_2 (INOT_x / INOT_{x+1})$. The interval distance in semitones represents pitch values. REPRED then uses these two values within the approximate matching algorithm by means of a scaled linear combination.

We found that the REPRED algorithm successfully identified the target song within the top ten results of a 3,600-song database search in 67% of our trials. When removing from consideration the 3 subjects whose performances were consistently below par (one of which was from each of our three skill groups), success climbed to 78% of all trials.

A few other recent publications have suggested similar ideas to this. The matching algorithm described in the CubyHum MIR system by Pauws (2002) also incorporates a duration ratio as part of his work but does not involve log scaling and is used in a different manner. A more recent system by Unal, Narayanan and Chew (2004) similarly incorporates a duration ratio into their input representation. The MPEG-7 Melody Sequence description scheme, which was being developed independently from us as our work was being completed, uses exactly the same method as our REPRED implementation to encode and represent note duration information (Gomez et al., 2003, p. 3).

Other Systems and Techniques

As part of our testing of REPRED, we submitted to the MELDEX system a small subset of our input test queries as digitized audio (.wav) files, each containing at least twelve hummed notes, which were known to be in their database. For more than half of our tests, the system reported no matches whatsoever; others showed a list of results which did not contain the correct song; and in just one case did it correctly identify the song as the first title in the returned list of close matches. We cannot draw any definite conclusions from this informal test; it appears the most common problem was their transcriber missed some of the hummed notes in our queries, but enough remained that it seems the queries should have returned some results, even if incorrect.

Kosugi et al. (2000) and Kosugi, Sakurai and Morimoto (2004) produced an MIR system named SoundCompass. Their original version utilized a database of over 10,000 MIDI songs, while their latest version has over 20,000. Their initial system made use of Wildcat Canyon's *Autoscore* software to handle the pitch transcription task, though they have since made further improvements including replacing this with their own transcriber (Kosugi, personal correspondence, 2001). To our knowledge, this was the first published system designed to make significant use of duration information as an integral part of its matching algorithms by requiring users to select a metronome tempo before humming and creating beat-based representations of the input query note durations. Once the user input was recorded and encoded in this fashion, it was processed to create a series of feature vectors used for search and matching. Their newest SoundCompass version eliminates the need for the metronome. In 2002, Kosugi kindly shared with us 16 of his group's input query test samples and their system's matching results so we could compare the performance of REPRED. We found that REPRED correctly identified every sample as the highest-ranking match, even the seven which gave SoundCompass difficulty. However, the disparity in database size and composition prevents more definite conclusions from this small test. We have not compared the more recent version of the system, which utilized more feature extraction, incorporated INOT values rather than raw durations, and made other improvements such as multithreaded parallel searches.

We also were able to compare the performance of REPRED to the SuperMBox system from Jang et al. (2001a). They implemented their own pitch transcription component, which made use of some additional heuristics in an attempt to smooth out some of the pitch tracking errors we have described; they also eliminated the requirement of having a consonant stopping sound between successive notes, allowing continuous humming or even singing with words. (However, they did not report on the relative accuracy of their transcription process.) They assumed the tempo of the user's input is consistent, and they take advantage of this assumption by utilizing linear scaling on the resulting query representation to manipulate the effective tempo, creating several time-stretched copies searched in parallel through k-means clustering and a branch-and-bound tree

search on the resulting pitch vectors in order to identify and rank the closest matches to a hummed query. A follow-up system named MIRACLE (Jang, Lee & Kao, 2001b) enabled searches to run in parallel on several computers and a front-stage fast algorithm to prune the size of the database, the remainder of which is then searched by the more complex algorithm. We tested our input samples against the downloadable copy of SuperMBox available at Jang's personal Web site (Jang et al., n.d.). With databases of comparable size but largely different tunes, we found SuperMBox performed about as well as REPRED when it was constrained to match only against the start of songs; in its match-anywhere mode, it did not perform as well. Again, the small size of the test and the differences in database content preclude a formal performance comparison.

SUMMARY AND CONCLUSION

MIR systems which allow for melody-based search queries will be most useful to the average person if hummed or sung input is a means of specifying input queries. Given this allowance, there will always be errors due to the music transcription process itself, even with the anticipated continued improvement of such automated systems. Among the most significant sources of uncontrollable input error are these:

- The recording environment often cannot be controlled. MIR systems deployed in public spaces or which rely on wired or wireless telephone transmission invariably will be subject to ambient noise, generating false notes.
- Our own experience with test subjects showed the difficulty of properly adjusting the input level to minimize errors due to the natural volume of the subject as well as the subject's relative position with respect

to the microphone (which may also change over the course of a single input sample).

- The duration of a typical extraneous note in a transcription is long enough that it cannot be distinguished from genuine short notes as vocalized by the subject.

In addition to these likely sources of errors, additional errors from the human input source must also be anticipated.

Pitch and duration contour representations are not suitable for vocal input due to the relatively high number of input errors in a typical query. While this type of encoding affords fast and efficient search algorithms, query strings must have a lower error rate for this type of search to be effective.

Even in the absence of errors introduced by the transcription process, the reliability of pitch contour is dependent upon the user's familiarity with the phrase to be vocalized. For unfamiliar melodies, even a simple ternary pitch contour will likely contain several errors, regardless of the musical skills of the user. Contour representations with more than three gradations are unlikely to correctly capture the intended melody in the vocal rendition of a nonexpert user.

Rather than using actual note durations, systems can more accurately represent the rhythm of the user's input by encoding the times of the onsets of individual notes instead. Additionally, long notes are shortened, and the degree of compression depends on the musical ability of the user; representing onset times on a logarithmic scale rather than a linear scale reduces the negative effects of this phenomenon.

As we have seen, the most recent MIR systems which include query-by-humming components still utilize more complex approximate matching algorithms in order to perform their searches. Continued improvements in accuracy and in computational efficiency can be expected by finding new data representations, parallel searching and pruning techniques to reduce the area of the database which needs to be examined with the more complex search and matching algorithms. Our own work with REPRED shows the value of the independently-developed MPEG-7 Melody Sequence DS representation as a suitable means of encoding and representing hummed input queries.

There have been some efforts to assemble test suites of data as a common resource for MIR researchers, such as the vocal input query collection of Unal et al. (2003), the compendium of music collections maintained by Byrd (2006), and the audio description contest associated with the 2004 ISMIR symposium (Cano, Gomez, Gouyon, Herrera, Koppenberger, 2006; ISMIR, 2004). MIR systems and their relative performance advantages can be evaluated more objectively when they are compared using common criteria, databases or test input. The MIR community as a whole will benefit from continuing this trend to cooperate in the testing and evaluation of disparate systems and algorithms.

ACKNOWLEDGMENT

The author's work reported here was supported in part by research grants awarded by the National Science Foundation under contracts EIA-9214887, EIA-9214892, IIS-9213823, CCR-9527151 and EIA-9634485. The author gratefully acknowledges Naoko Kosugi of NTT Laboratories for providing a set of sample input queries from his group's research studies.

REFERENCES

Attneave, F. & Olson, R. K. (1971). Pitch as a medium: A new approach to psychophysical scaling. *American Journal of Psychology, 84,* 147-166.

Bainbridge, D., Nevill-Manning, C. G., Witten, I. H., Smith, L. A. & McNab, R. J. (1999). Towards a digital library of popular music. In *Proceedings of the Fourth ACM International Conference on Digital Libraries (DL'99)* (pp. 161-169). Berkeley, California.

Bartlett, J. C. & Dowling, W. J. (1980). Recognition of transposed melodies: A key-distance effect in developmental perspective. *Journal of Experimental Psychology: Human Perception and Performance*, 6(3), 501-515.

Byrd, D. (2006). Candidate music IR test collections: A list. Retrieved May 21, 2007, from *http://php.indiana.edu/~donbyrd/MusicTestCollections.HTML*

Cano, P., Gomez, E., Gouyon, F., Herrera, P., Koppenberger, M. et al. (2006). ISMIR 2004 audio description contest. Retrieved May 21, 2007, from *http://www.iua.upf.edu/mtg/publications/MTG-TR-2006-02.pdf*

Cuddy, L. L. & Cohen, A. J. (1976). Recognition of transposed melodic sequences. *Quarterly Journal of Experimental Psychology*, 28, 255-270.

Deutsch, D. (Ed.) (1982). *The psychology of music.* Academic Press.

Dowling, W. J. (1978). Scale and contour: Two components of a theory of memory for melodies. *Psychological Review*, 85(4), 341-354.

Dowling, W. J. (1986). Context effects on melody recognition: Scale-step versus interval representations. *Music Perception*, 3(3), 281-296.

Dowling, W. J. & Fujitani, D. S. (1971). Contour, interval, and pitch recognition in memory for melodies. *Journal of the Acoustical Society of America*, 49, 524-531.

Dowling, W. J., Kwak, S. & Andrews, M. W. (1995). The time course recognition of novel melodies. *Perception and Psychophysics*, 57(2), 136-149.

Downie, J. S. & Nelson, M. (2000). Evaluation of a simple and effective music information re-

trieval method. In *Proceedings of the 23rd ACM Conference on Research and Development in Information Retrieval (SIGIR '00)* (pp. 73-80) Athens, Greece.

Drake, C. (1993). Reproduction of musical rhythms by children, adult musicians, and adult nonmusicians. *Perception and Psychophysics*, 53(1), 25-33.

Drake, C., Dowling, W. J. & Palmer, C. (1991). Accent structures in the reproduction of simple tunes by children and adult pianists. *Music Perception*, 8(3), 315-334.

Edworthy, J. (1985). Interval and contour in melody processing. *Music Perception*, 2(3), 375-388.

Friedman, M. L. (1985). A methodology for the discussion of contour: Its application to Schoenberg's music. *Journal of Music Theory*, 29(2), 223-248.

Ghias, A., Logan, J., Chamberlin, D. & Smith, B. C. (1995). Query by humming: Musical information retrieval in an audio database. In *Proceedings of the 3rd ACM Conference on Multimedia (MM'95)* (pp. 231-236) San Francisco, California.

Gomez, E., Gouyon, F., Herrera, P. & Amatriain, X. (2003). Using and enhancing the current MPEG-7 standard for a music content processing tool. In *Proceedings of the Audio Engineering Society, 114th Convention*, Mar. 22-25, Amsterdam, NL. Retrieved May 21, 2007, from *http://www.iua.upf.es/mtg/publications/AES114-GomezEtAl.pdf*

Greenhaus, D. et al. (n.d.) Digital tradition folksong database. Retrieved May 21, 2007, from *http://www.mudcat.org*

Halpern, A. R. (1988). Perceived and imagined tempos of familiar songs. *Music Perception*, 6(2), 193-202.

Halpern, A. R. (1989). Memory for the absolute pitch of familiar songs. *Memory and Cognition*, 17(5), 572-581.

Haus, G. & Pollastri, E. (2001). An audio front end for query-by-humming systems. In *Proceedings of the Second International Symposium on Music Information Retrieval (ISMIR 2001)* (pp. 65-72) Bloomington, Indiana.

Hu, N. & Dannenberg, R. B. (2002). A comparison of melodic database retrieval techniques using sung queries. In *Proceedings of the 2nd ACM/ IEEE-CS Joint Conference on Digital Libraries* (pp. 301 – 307) Portland, Oregon.

ISMIR (2004). ISMIR 2004 audio description contest. Retrieved May 21, 2007, from *http://ismir2004.ismir.net/ISMIR_Contest.html*

Jang, J.-S. R., Chen, J.-C. & Kao, M.-Y. (2001a). MIRACLE: A music information retrieval system with clustered computing engines. In *Proceedings of the Second International Symposium on Music Information Retrieval (ISMIR 2001)* (pp. 11-12) Bloomington, Indiana.

Jang, J.-S. R., Lee, H.-R. & Kao, M.-Y (n.d.). SuperMBox computer software. Retrieved May 21, 2007, from *http://neural.cs.nthu.edu.tw/jang/demo*

Jang, J.-S. R., Lee, H.-R. & Kao, M.-Y. (2001b). Content-based music retrieval using linear scaling and branch-and-bound tree search. In *IEEE International Conference on Multimedia and Expo*, Tokyo, Japan.

Kageyama, T., Mochizuki, K. & Takashima, Y. (1993). Melody retrieval with humming. In *Proceedings of the 1993 International Computer Music Conference (ICMC'93)* (pp. 349-351) Tokyo, Japan.

Kageyama, T. & Takashima, Y. (1994). A melody retrieval method with hummed melody (language: Japanese). *Transactions of the Institute of Electronics, Information and Communication Engineers D-II, J77D-II(8)*, 1543-1551.

Klapuri, A. (n.d.) Automatic transcription of music: Literature review. Retrieved May 21, 2007, from *http://www.cs.tut.fi/~klap/iiro/literature.html*

Kline, R. L. (2002). Algorithms for error tolerant information retrieval from music databases using vocal input. Unpublished doctoral dissertation. Rensselaer Polytechnic Institute, Troy, NY.

Kline, R. L. & Glinert, E. P. (2003). Approximate matching algorithms for music information retrieval using vocal input. In *Proceedings of the 11ᵗʰ ACM Conference on Multimedia (MM'03)* (pp. 130-139) Berkeley, California.

Kosugi, N., Nishihara, Y., Sakata, T., Yamamuro, M. & Kushima, K. (2000). A practical query-by-humming system for a large music database. In *Proceedings of the 8th ACM Conference on Multimedia (MM'00)* (pp. 333-342) Marina del Rey, California.

Kosugi, N., Sakurai, Y. & Morimoto, M. (2004). SoundCompass: A practical query-by-humming system; Normalization of scalable and shiftable time-series data and effective subsequence generation. In *Proceedings of the 2004 ACM SIGMOD international Conference on Management of Data* (pp. 881-886) Paris, France.

Kuhn, W. B. (1990). A real-time pitch recognition algorithm for music applications. *Computer Music Journal, 14*(3), 60-71.

Levitin, D. J. (1994). Absolute memory for musical pitch: Evidence from the production of learned melodies. *Perception and Psychophysics, 56*(4), 414-423.

Levitin, D. J. & Cook, P. R. (1996). Memory for musical tempo: Additional evidence that auditory memory is absolute. *Perception and Psychophysics, 58*(6), 927-935.

Li, G. (1985). Robust regression. In D. C. Hoaglin, F. Mosteller & J. W. Tukey (Eds.), *Exploring data tables, trends, and shapes* (pp. 281-343). New York: John Wiley and Sons.

Lindsay, A. T. (1996). *Using contour as a mid-level representation of melody.* Unpublished master's thesis, Massachusetts Institute of Technology.

Manjunath, B. S., Salembier, P. & Sikora, T. (2002). *Introduction to MPEG-7.* New York: John Wiley and Sons.

Martinez, J. M. (Ed.) (2004). MPEG-7 overview (version 10). ISO/IEC JTC1/SC29/WG11, Palma de Mallorca. Retrieved May 21, 2007, from *http://www.chiariglione.org/MPEG/standards/mpeg-7/mpeg-7.htm*

Marvin, E. W. & Laprade, P. A. (1987). Relating musical contours: Extensions of a theory for contours. *Journal of Music Theory, 31*(2), 225-267.

McNab, R. J., Smith, L. A., Bainbridge, D. & Witten, I. H. (1997). The New Zealand digital library MELody inDEX. *D-Lib Magazine.* Retrieved May 21, 2007, from *http://www.dlib.org/dlib/may97/meldex/05witten.html*

McNab, R. J., Smith, L. A., Witten, I. H., Henderson, C. L. & Cunningham, S. J. (1996). Towards the digital music library: Tune retrieval from acoustic input. In *Proceedings of the First ACM Conference on Digital Libraries (DL'96)* (pp. 11-18) Bethesda, Maryland.

MIDI (1993). *MIDI 1.0 detailed specification, version 4.3.* Los Angeles, CA: International MIDI Association.

Mongeau, M. & Sankoff, D. (1990). Comparison of musical sequences. *Computers and the Humanities, 24*, 161-175.

Pauws, S. (2002). CubyHum: A fully operational query by humming system. In *Proceedings of the 3rd International Symposium on Music Information Retrieval (ISMIR'02)* (pp. 187-196). Paris, France.

Polansky, L. & Bassein, R. (1992). Possible and impossible melody: Some formal aspects of contour. *Journal of Music Theory, 36*(2), 259-284.

Rothstein, J. (1995). *MIDI: A comprehensive introduction* (2nd ed.). A-R Editions.

Selfridge-Field, E. (Ed.) (1997). *Beyond MIDI: The handbook of musical codes.*, Cambridge: MIT Press.

Smith, J. D., Nelson, D. G. K., Grohskopf, L. A. & Appleton, T. (1994). What child is this? What interval was that? Familiar tunes and music perception in novice listeners. *Cognition, 52*, 23-54.

Smith, T. F. & Waterman, M. S. (1981). Identification of common molecular subsequences. *Journal of Molecular Biology, 147*, 195-197.

Trehub, S. E. (1987). Infants' perception of musical patterns. *Perception and Psychophysics, 41*(6), 635-641.

Uitdenbogerd, A. & Zobel, J. (1998). Manipulation of music for melody matching. In *Proceedings of the 6th ACM Conference on Multimedia (MM'98)* (pp. 235-240). Bristol, UK.

Uitdenbogerd, A. & Zobel, J. (1999). Melodic matching techniques for large music databases. In *Proceedings of the 7th ACM Conference on Multimedia (MM'99)* (pp. 57-66) Orlando, Florida.

Ukkonen, E. (1992). Approximate string-matching with q-grams and maximal matches. *Theoretical Computer Science, 92*, 191-211.

Unal, E., Narayanan, S. S., Shih, H. H., Chew, E. & Kuo, C. C. (2003). Creating data resources for designing user-centric frontends for query by humming systems. In *Proceedings of the 5th ACM SIGMM International Workshop on Multimedia Information Retrieval (MIR'03)* (pp. 116-121) Berkeley, California.

Unal, E., Narayanan, S. S. & Chew, E. (2004). A statistical approach to retrieval under user-dependent uncertainty in query-by-humming systems. In *Proceedings of the 6th ACM SIGMM International Workshop on Multimedia Information Retrieval (MIR'04)* (pp. 113–118) New York, New York.

University of Waikato (n.d.). New Zealand digital library. Retrieved May 21, 2007, from *http://www.nzdl.org*

Zhu, Y. & Shasha, D. (2003). Warping indexes with envelope transforms for query by humming. In *Proceedings of the 2003 ACM SIGMOD international conference on Management of data (SIGMOD'03)* (pp. 181-192).

Section II
Music Identification and Recognition

Chapter IV
An Expert System Devoted to Automated Music Identification and Recognition

María Ángeles Fernández de Sevilla
Universidad de Acalá, Spain

Luis M. Laita
Universidad Politécnica de Madrid, Spain

Eugenio Roanes-Lozano
Universidad Complutense de Madrid, Spain

Leon González-Sotos
Universidad de Acalá, Spain

ABSTRACT

This chapter describes a logic and computer algebra-based expert system that automates identification and recognition of the cult music styles of the period XVII century—beginnings of the XX century. It uses a table that contains a list of characteristics (identifiers) of the music styles of the epoch, developed after interacting with a panel of experts. The user, while or after analysing a score, introduces the identifiers and the expert system returns the score's style. These tentative identifications and recognitions could be interactively compared with those of experts. Therefore it may be a useful tool for teaching and learning history of music. The objectives are to organize the musical knowledge in any way admissible by the inference engine, to adapt and implement the inference engine (based on a powerful tool for effective polynomial computations named Gröbner Bases) and to implement a GUI.

INTRODUCTION

This work describes a logic and computer algebra-based Knowledge Based Expert System, to be hereinafter denoted as "ES", for cult music styles identification of the period that lasts from the XVII century to the beginnings of the XX century. By introducing into the ES some music-related identifiers, that the user has selected while or after analyzing a score, the ES identifies both its style and, consequently, the epoch when it was composed.

Expert Systems have at least a "knowledge base", hereinafter denoted as "KB", which collects and represents formally expert knowledge, an "inference engine", hereinafter denoted as "IE", which extracts new knowledge from the KB, and a graphic user interface, hereinafter denoted as "GUI". An explanation of what KB, IE and GUI are in any ES shall be the topic of the section "Generalities about Rule-Based Expert Systems".

In order to build the KB of the ES, a list of characteristics, which are called in this chapter "identifiers", of the music styles of the epoch under consideration must be previously defined. The list used in this chapter is the list in Table 1. The user, during or after analyzing a score, introduces into the ES the identifiers that the user has selected from Table 1: the ES is supposed to output the identification and recognition of the score style.

A simple method builds, in three "levels" or steps, the formulae that constitute the KB, called "production rules" (the necessary definitions and concepts will presented in their adequate places in the chapter). For this purpose, tables that assign music related characteristics of an epoch to different consequents of the production rules are designed. This leads to the construction of a compact and coherent system of production rules.

The nonexpert users (an example of this type of user is a first year student of a conservatory or a cult music fan) of our ES are supposed to have some knowledge of the meaning of the "identifiers" included in Table 1. The interaction between users and experts improves, in successive steps—beginning with knowledge. This ES can be useful for cult music fans but, mainly, for both learning and teaching history of music and of composition (Fernández de Sevilla & Hilera, 2001; Fernández de Sevilla & Gutiérrez de Mesa, 2002; Fernández de Sevilla, 2001; Fernández de Sevilla, 2002; Fernández de Sevilla, 2003; Fernández de Sevilla & Fernández del Castillo, 2002; Fernández de Sevilla, 2005; Balaban & Ebcioglu, 1992).

It has to be emphasized at this point, that our purpose is to suggest and adapt a computational method illustrated with the corresponding implementation, rather than to present a selection of identifiers perfectly describing the characters of the different musical periods considered. If other experts judged that the identifiers should be chosen another way, only the input data to the system had to be altered, but not the rest of the system, that would be kept unchanged (obviously, the results given by the system could change). If a larger number of identifiers had to be considered, there would be no problem in dividing the system into subsystems, and to gather the partial results of those subsystems in a new one that would provide the final result.

Any ES (once constructed) must go through two processes: verification and validation. To verify the ES means to check that, syntactically, it does not contain inconsistencies. To validate the ES means that, after it has been verified, its outputs are in agreement with the "real" world, in our case, that the ES outputs reliable music styles identifications. Although the process of validation may improve our ES, the ES is very strong regarding verification because its IE is based on a sound computational method: Gröbner Bases.

The objectives of the chapter are the following:

- To organize the musical knowledge in any way admissible by the IE
- To adapt and implement the IE, based on a powerful tool for effective polynomial computations: Gröbner Bases
- To implement the GUI that will visually output the results of the system

The objectives outlined above will be developed in detail afterwards.

BACKGROUND

The general background of this chapter is a relatively new field of computer science named "symbolic computation". The authors have been working in this field for more than ten years. For instance, they have been the invited editors of a special volume of the Journal of the Royal Academy of Sciences of Spain (RACSAM) devoted to this topic, where many very good specialists from all around the world (Bruno Buchberger, Deepak Kapur, Jacques Calmet, John Campbell, Jochen Pfalzgraf, etc.) have collaborated (Laita, Roanes-Lozano & Alonso, 2004).

Inside symbolic computation, there is a subfield to which the topic of this chapter belongs: automated proving. We shall describe in section "Constructing the IE Using CoCoA" the particular theoretical background of our method. It is a theorem that links logical consequences with an algebraic result, and it is due to a team to which the authors belong. Prior related works are also detailed in that section.

MAIN THRUST OF THE CHAPTER

The main thrust of the chapter is to consider a system of music styles identification as an "expert system" based on symbolic computation. Moreover, such a computation uses Buchberger's Gröbner Bases and normal forms, theoretical

constructs that lead to powerful implementations for automated proving.

The method, original of the team to which the authors belong, has been applied to illnesses diagnoses, railway traffic control, automated theorem proving in geometry and so forth, as will be seen in the subsequent section. These applications have been considered quite original and different to others' approaches by the artificial intelligence and symbolic computation community. It seems that using this approach in music studies could be a new interesting approach to relate music topics with artificial intelligence.

A possible contrast with other methods is that ours is based on strong mathematical results, implemented in universally accepted algorithms: Gröbner Bases.

We give next some arguments to support the use of Gröbner Bases as our automated proving method.

In Clegg, Edmonds, and Impagliazzo (1996), a propositional Gröbner proving system is discussed. It is shown that this system polynomially simulates Horn clauses resolution and weakly exponentially simulates resolution. The authors say that this suggests that the Gröbner Bases algorithm might replace resolution as a basis for heuristics for NP-complete problems (Kapur & Narendran, 1984) already stated that using a Gröbner Bases approach subsumes resolution. Let us observe that there is an important difference between the average case and worst case complexities of Gröbner Bases computations.

In Clegg, Edmonds, and Impagliazzo (1996) there is also a comparison with other methods, which result only slightly superior. Thus, from the point of view of complexity, using a Gröbner Bases approach seems reasonable.

This was also the opinion of the referee of Laita, Roanes-Lozano, de Ledesma and Alonso (1999), an expert in automated theorem proving, who judged our approach as competitive, even though not the best for all types of problems. It is a fact that, among all known automated provers, some are good for some types of problems and not as god for other types of problems. Ours is not an exception. Our choice is mainly based on our previous experience in developing medium size expert systems and other related simulations.

There are two more advantages in our approach: first, it can deal with multivalued logics and, second, logical formulae can be written without any restrictions: they do not have to be Horn clauses (i.e., the symbol "or" can appear in both the antecedents and the consequents of the production rules).

A problem appears when the number of variables, in our case, those that refer to the musical characteristics of an epoch, is larger than 75-80. In these cases it is advisable to divide the system in two or more subsystems. In our chapter we have divided the whole system into three subsystems.

GENERALITIES ABOUT RULE-BASED EXPERT SYSTEMS

Expert systems have three components:

1. A knowledge base, "KB", composed by:
    *   A set "RB" (Rule Basis) of logic expressions, called "production rules". Production rules are, in this chapter, implications between a conjunction of literals (premises or antecedents), and a literal or a disjunction or a conjunction of literals (conclusions or consequents). The definition of "literal" comes next. A simple example of a production rule is:

        X1 and not-X2 and X3 implies A1

        that can be written in logical notation:

        $$X1 \land \neg X2 \land X3 \rightarrow A1$$

The logical connective "$\lor$" (or) is also allowed, both in the antecedents and in the consequents. The KB may also contain other items named integrity constraints, and any other additional information included by the experts, but these are not used here. Letters as X1, X2, X3 and A1 are called "propositional variables". Both the propositional variables and their negations are called "literals".

*   A set "F" of "potential facts". We call "potential facts" both the literals that are in the antecedents but not in the consequents of the production rules and their "contraries". For instance, if our RB consists of only the production rule written previously, the potential facts would be:

    X1, ¬X1, X2, ¬X2, X3, ¬X3

    In some cases the consequent of a rule may be part of the antecedent of another rule. These types of literals are called "derived facts".

2. An "inference engine" (IE). It is said that a rule can be "forward fired", if all the literals in the antecedent are, either potential facts (naturally, no pair of contrary potential facts are allowed in a same antecedent of any production rule) or "derived facts". Forward firing corresponds to the formal logic rule of "modus ponens". The "inference engine" performs such a forward firing. The IE is a procedure that extracts automatically consequences from the information contained in the KB. Ours, to be described in section "Construction of the IE using CoCoA", is based on a computer algebra theorem (Laita, Roanes-Lozano, de Ledesma, & Alonso, 1999; Roanes-Lozano, Laita, & Roanes-Macías, 1998), original to the team to which the authors belong. This theorem uses Hsiang

(1985) and Kapur-Narendran's (1984) ideas (Alonso, Briales & Riscos, 1990; Chazarain, Riscos, Alonso & Briales, 1991) and Gröbner Bases (GB) (Adams & Loustaunau, 1994; Buchberger, 1965; Buchberger, 1998; Cox, Little & O'Shea, 1992; Kreuzer & Robbiano, 2000) and is implemented in the computer algebra language CoCoA (Capani & Niesi, 1996; Perkinson, 2000). Although, in this chapter, the ES is based on classic Boolean logic, our method allows, as already said, to use p-valued (p being a prime number) modal logics.

3. A graphic user interface (GUI). It is a front-end that helps those users of the ES who do not necessarily master the mathematics and computer backgrounds on which the systems are based. By just pressing keys that correspond to potential facts (the identifiers, or their negations in this chapter), the user gets an output that is either the identification of a musical style in a time period or a statement asserting that the score under study does not belong to the period the user guessed.

OUR EXPERT SYSTEM

To decrease its computational complexity, we have divided our ES is into three subsystems: ES1, ES2 and ES3, which refer respectively to:

*   Baroque, Rococo and Classic (XVII-XVIII centuries)
*   Romanticism, Nationalism and Impressionism (XIX and beginnings of XX centuries)
*   Anti-Impressionism, Verism and Expressionism (chosen from many others styles of the XX century because they are among those having a best defined structure)

For the sake of space, only ES1 will be considered in this chapter, because both the construction and behavior of ES2 and ES3 are similar.

THE SUBSYSTEM ES1

Historical Introduction

ES1 is intended to identify musical styles of the period that lasts from 1600 to 1827.

In this time period three musical stiles arose and grew—Baroque, Rococo, and Classic (Groutald & Palisca, 2004; Marco, 2002; Zampronha, 2000). While Baroque and Classic are styles with well-defined characteristics, Rococo shares identifiers of both Baroque and Classic, sometimes in a not well-defined mixture, sometimes exaggerating the Baroque side.

The identifiers that have respectively been assigned in this chapter to Baroque, Rococo and Classic style (let us insist that this list of characters may be improved or changed) are the following ones.

Baroque's identifiers are ornamental, solemn, ceremonious, religious, harmonic complexity, counter point development (composed voices), polyphony, sound contrasts, continuous bass, use of wood wind instruments plus trumpet and chord (in this epoch metal wind instruments did not exist); it is also a sumptuous, over-elaborate, luxurious music, in which form and motif are more relevant than phrase.

Rococo is a transition epoch between Baroque and Classic, which developed, mainly, in France. It is a mixture of styles, and its identifiers are: sumptuous, refined, beautiful, devoted at its beginnings to selected audiences as the Royal Court, continuous bass, melodic complexity and ornamentation. The musical instruments are those of Baroque: wood wind instruments and trumpet, plus some use of chord. In this style, music compositions begun to have harmonic complexity. It is plenty of contrasts and importance is given to motif as well as to phrase.

Classicism identifiers are: equilibrium, clearness, regularity, simplicity, proportion, delicateness, beautifulness, brightness, reflects happiness and naturality, has bass Alberti, it uses metal wind instruments, importance is given to phrase and in many cases was devoted to the Royal Courts.

Construction of the Knowledge Base

As said above, all KB consist of a rule base RB and a fact base F. Although we said above that the elements of F are both the literals that are in the antecedents but not in any of the consequents of any of the production rules and their contraries, this does not mean that we must have the RB constructed before constructing F. Rather, as will be seen next, F is usually built first.

Description of the Set F of Potential Facts

The set F of potential facts consists of 23 + 23 elements (23 elements X1, X2, ..., X23, and 23 elements not-X1, not-X2, ..., not-X23). These elements, according to the opinion of the experts consulted, are the most relevant music identifiers which are present in the musical styles studied in this chapter.

As it will be seen, the RB of ES1, once constructed, remains unchanged, while *each* score under study by ES1 (the same would happen in ES2 and ES3) is characterized by just one subset A of F, each A consisting of 23 elements of F. Each one of the mentioned subsets A of F is a maximal consistent subset of the whole set F: "consistent" means that from each pair formed by a potential fact and its contrary at most one element of the pair is chosen (otherwise, a same style would be described by two contrary facts) and "maximal" means that such a selection must be done for all pairs.

The elements of F that the user judges that apply to the score under study are introduced as "Xi" (i = 1, 2, 3, ..., 23) and those the user judges the score does not have are introduced as "not-Xj" (j = 1, 2, 3, ..., 23).

We have divided the 23 pairs in F into five classes. For instance, X1 (which means religious), X2 (solemn) and X3 (sumptuous), together with X4 (finesse) and X5 (seemingly devoted to small selected audiences as Royal Courts) constitute, together with their negations, the class to be named *"musical-related characteristics of epoch"*; X14 (motif), X15 (phrase), X16 (bass Alberti),

Table 1. Classification of the potential facts

Musical-Related Characteristics of the Epoch
X1- Religious
X2- Solemn
X3- Sumptuous
X4- Finesse
X5- Seemingly devoted to a selected audience, like Royal Courts
Instrumentation
X6- Wood wind instruments plus trumpet
X7- Chord
X8- Remainder wind-chord
Characteristics of the Musical Style
X9- Proportion.
X10- Harmonic complexity
X11- Contrasts
X12- Clearness
X13- Equilibrium
Components of the Structure of the Music Work
X14- Motif
X15- Phrase.
X16- Alberti bass
X17- Continuous bass
X18- Melody
Compositional Analysis
X19- Regular structures
X20- Major tones
X21- Ornamentation
X22- Polyphonic development or counter point
X23- Melody accompaniment

X17 (continuous bass), X18 (melody), and their negations, constitute the class "*components of the structure of the music work*". The identifiers that in this chapter have been chosen to form these five classes are listed in Table 1 (the negation of the Xi (I = 1, ..., 23) are omitted for the sake of space). These classes shall be used both as frameworks for constructing the tables from which production rules will be written down and, later on, in the GUI.

Construction and Description of the RB of ES1

As already said, the RB remains unchanged whatever is the score being examined for its style characterization. The reason is that RB is a formal description of the characteristics of the musical period under consideration, but not of a particular score, while each score is described by one subset A of F. The RB of SE1 consists of 370 production rules (ES2 and ES3 consist of 706 and 923 respectively).

The process of construction of the RB of ES is explained in detail next and is summarized in the flowchart of Figure 1.

Table 2. A first level table

	X3	¬X3
X1∧X2	A1	A3
¬X1∧X2	A2	A3
X1∧¬X2	A1	A3
¬X1∧¬X2	A2	A3

First Level Production Rules

In a first stage we write what will be called "first level production rules" by building tables that relate potential facts with different Baroque, Rococo and Classic properties. For the sake of space and because all first level tables are built the same way, we only show in detail in this subsection, the first and the next to the last first level tables, together with their correspondent sets of production rules.

The first one of the first level tables, Table 2, relates the three characters, X1, X2 and X3, to the symbols: A1 which means "Baroque *tendency* I", A2 which means "Rococo *tendency* I", A3 which means "Classic *tendency* I" (Table 2). The assignations A1, A2 and A3 are decided by experts.

Figure 1. Flowchart of ES1

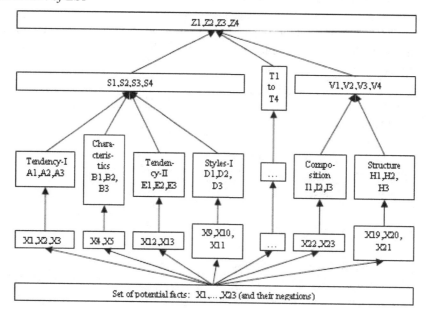

Table 2 gives rise to eight production rules. For instance, row X1∧X2 and column ¬X3, give rise to the production rule:

$$X1 \land X2 \land \neg X3 \to A3$$

("Rule 32" in ES1), which means:

"IF religious = yes AND solemn = yes AND sumptuous = no
THEN Classic tendency_I".

Another example is "Rule 5" of ES1:

$$X1 \land \neg X2 \land X3 \to A1$$

which means:

"IF religious = yes AND solemn = no AND sumptuous = yes
THEN Baroque tendency_I".

As a matter of fact, the eight rules obtained from Table 2 can be rearranged, using logic-based simplifications, into only three:

$$X1 \land X3 \to A1$$
$$\neg X1 \land X3 \to A2$$
$$\neg X3 \to A3$$

The remaining potential facts and their contraries are arranged in similar first level tables. It needs to be emphasized that these diagrams are not built arbitrarily, but always following the experts' opinions. Each first level table gives rise to a set of production rules.

- The combinations of X4, X5 and their contraries give rise to the literals B1, B2, and B3, which represent the Baroque, Rococo and Classic *characteristics*, respectively.
- The combinations of X6 to X8 and their contraries give rise to the literals C1, C2,

Table 3. Another first level table

	X21	¬X21
X19 ∧ X20	H3	H3
¬X19 ∧ X20	H2	H2
X19 ∧ ¬X20	H1	H3
¬X19 ∧ ¬X20	H2	H2

C3 and C4, which represent the Baroque, Rococo, Classic and "none of these *conditions*", respectively.

- The combinations of X9 to X11 and their contraries give rise to the literals D1, D2 and D3 which represent the Baroque *style*_I, Rococo *style*_I, and Classic *style*_I. D4 means "none of these styles_I".
- The combinations of X12, X13 and their contraries give rise to the literals E1, E2, and E3, which represent the Baroque *tendency* II, Rococo *tendency* II and Classic *tendency* II.
- The combinations of X14 to X16 and their contraries give rise to the literals F1, F2, F3 and F4, which represent the Baroque *style*_II, Rococo *style*_II, Classic *style*_II and "none of these styles_II".
- The combinations of X17, X18 and their contraries give rise to the literals G1, G2, and G3, which represent the Baroque, Rococo and Classic *qualities*, respectively.
- The combinations of X19 to X21 and their contraries give rise to the literals H1, H2 and H3 which represent the Baroque, Rococo, and Classic *structure*, respectively (see Table 3).

Table 3 gives rise to eight production rules, which are rearranged into the next five ones:

$$X19 \land X20 \to H3$$
$$\neg X19 \land X20 \to H2$$
$$X19 \land \neg X20 \land X21 \to H1$$
$$X19 \land \neg X20 \land \neg X21 \to H3$$
$$\neg X19 \land \neg X20 \to H2$$

For instance, the first and the fourth of these production rules respectively mean:

"IF regular structures = yes AND major tones = yes THEN Classic structure"

"IF regular structures = yes AND major tones = no AND sumptuousity = no THEN Classic structure"

- The combinations of X22, X23 and their contraries give rise to the literals I1, I2, I3 and I4, which represent the Baroque, Rococo, Classic and "none of these styles'" *composition*, respectively.

Second Level Production Rules

The literals A, D, E, F, G, H and I (each one having four elements, as A1, A2, A3, and A4 for A) are, on their side, arranged (by the experts!) into three tables, one for the A, B, D and E, one for the F, G and C, and one for H and I. Each of these three tables gives rise to a set of four literals each: {S1,...,S4}, {T1,...,T4} and {V1,...,V4}, respectively. These three sets of four literals are not particular characteristics of a musical style but rather, they are like valuations assigned to subsets of the sets of the characteristics A, D, … and H, in such a way that these valuations are approximations to the final identification of one of the three styles (or of no style at all).

First Second-Level Table

Let us denote by S1, S2, S3 and S4, the expressions "first approach to identification = Baroque", "first approach to identification = Rococo", "first approach to identification = Classic", "first approach to identification = none of these styles". The combinations of the A, B, D and E, give rise to Table 4.

For instance, two of the 162 second-level production rules corresponding to this table are:

$$A1 \wedge B1 \wedge E1 \wedge D1 \rightarrow S1$$
$$A3 \wedge B2 \wedge E3 \wedge \neg D1 \rightarrow S2$$

which, respectively, mean

"IF Baroque tendency_I = yes AND Baroque characteristics = yes

Table 4. First second-level table (note that first level rules lead neither to ¬D2 nor to ¬D4, so they do not appear as input in this table)

		E1	E1	E1	E1	E1	E1	E2	E2	E2	E2	E2	E2	E3	E3	E3	E3	E3	E3
		D1	¬D1	D2	D3	¬D3	D4	D1	¬D1	D2	**D3**	**¬D3**	D4	D1	**¬D1**	D2	D3	**¬D3**	D4
A1	**B1**	S1	S1	S1	S4	S1	S4	S1	S2	S2	S2	S2	S4	S4	S4	S4	S4	S4	S4
A1	**B2**	S1	S2	S1	S4	S2	S4	S1	S2	S2	S4	S2	S4	S4	S2	S2	S2	S2	S4
A1	**B3**	S1	S2	S2	S4	S2	S4	S2	S2	S2	S4	S4	S4	S4	S3	S2	S3	S3	S4
A2	**B1**	S1	S2	S2	S4	S2	S4	S2	S2	S2	S4	S2	S4	S2	S4	S4	S2	S4	S4
A2	**B2**	S1	S2	S2	S4	S2	S4	S2	S2	S2	S2	S2	S4	S2	S4	S2	S2	S2	S4
A2	**B3**	S2	S4	S3	S4	S4	S4	S4	S2	S2	S2	S2	S4	S2	S2	S2	S3	S2	S4
A3	**B1**	S2	S4	S4	S4	S4	S4	S4	S2	S2	S4	S2	S4	S4	S4	S4	S3	S4	S4
A3	**B2**	S2	S4	S4	S4	S4	S4	S4	S2	S2	S2	S2	S4	S4	S2	S2	S3	S4	S4
A3	**B3**	S4	S4	S4	S4	S4	S4	S2	S3	S2	S3	S4	S4	S4	S3	S3	S3	S4	S4

AND Baroque tendency_II = yes AND Baroque style_I = yes
THEN first approach to identification = Baroque"

and

"IF Classic tendency_I = yes AND Rococo characteristics = yes
AND Classic tendency_II = yes AND Baroque style_I = no
THEN first approach to identification = Rococo".

Note that the production rule

$$A3 \wedge B2 \wedge E3 \wedge \neg D1 \rightarrow S2$$

contains two Classic items (A3, B3), only one Rococo item (B2) and the specification that it does not contain any Baroque item (¬D1). At first sight, one might be inclined to assign S3 ("Classic") as the "second approach to identification", while the experts assigned S2 (Rococo) The reason was that, for assigning an approach as S3 or S2, experts were not just looking at S1, S2, S3, S4 as totally meaningless variables. Rather, they took into account that the meaning of these symbols result from the meaning of the symbols A,B,D,E which meanings, on their turn, depend on X1 to X23 (and their contraries). A careful consideration of all chaining

$$X \rightarrow \begin{matrix} A \\ B \\ D \\ E \end{matrix} \rightarrow S$$

has to be made because the literals X that characterize S can be so relevant that they sometimes substantially influence the results.

Table 5. Second second-level table

		C1	C2	C3	¬C3	C4	¬C4
G1	F1	T1	T1	T2	T1	T4	T1
G1	¬F1	T2	T2	T4	T2	T4	T2
G1	F2	T1	T2	T2	T2	T4	T2
G1	F3	T4	T2	T4	T4	T4	T4
G1	F4	T4	T4	T4	T4	T4	T1
G2	F1	T1	T2	T2	T2	T4	T2
G2	¬F1	T2	T2	T2	T2	T4	T2
G2	F2	T2	T2	T2	T2	T4	T2
G2	F3	T4	T2	T3	T2	T4	T2
G2	F4	T4	T4	T4	T4	T4	T2
G3	F1	T2	T2	T2	T4	T4	T2
G3	¬F1	T4	T2	T3	T4	T4	T3
G3	F2	T2	T2	T3	T2	T4	T2
G3	F3	T4	T2	T3	T4	T4	T3
G3	F4	T4	T4	T4	T4	T4	T3

Second Second-Level Table

Let us denote by T1, T2, T3 and T4, the expressions "second approach to identification = Baroque", "second approach to identification = Rococo", "second approach to identification = Classic", "second approach to identification = none of these styles". The combinations of the G, C and F, give rise to the Table 5.

For instance, the first and the last of the 90 second-level production rules corresponding to Table 5 are:

$$G1 \wedge F1 \wedge C1 \rightarrow T1$$
$$G3 \wedge F4 \wedge \neg C4 \rightarrow T3$$

which, respectively, mean

"IF Baroque qualities = yes AND Baroque style_II = yes
AND Baroque condition = yes
THEN second approach to identification = Baroque"

Table 6. Third second-level table

	I1	I2	I3	I4
H1	V1	V2	V4	V4
H2	V2	V2	V2	V4
H3	V4	V2	V3	V4

and

> "IF Classic qualities = yes AND none of the
> three styles_II = yes
> AND none of the conditions = no
> THEN second approach to identification =
> Classic".

Third Second-Level Table

Let us denote by V1, V2, V3 and V4, the expressions "third approach to identification = Baroque", "third approach to identification = Rococo", "third approach to identification = Classic", "third approach to identification = none of these". The combinations of the H and I, give rise to Table 6.

For instance, the first and the last of the 12 second-level production rules corresponding to Table 6 are.

$$H1 \wedge I1 \rightarrow V1$$
$$H3 \wedge I4 \rightarrow V4$$

which, respectively, mean

> "IF Baroque structure = yes AND Baroque
> composition = yes
> THEN third approach to identification =
> Baroque"

and

> "IF Classic structure = yes AND none of
> the three styles composition = yes THEN
> third approach to identification = none".

Table 7. Third-level table

		V1	V2	V3	V4
S1	T1	Z1	Z1	Z2	Z4
S2	T2	Z2	Z2	Z2	Z4
S2	T3	Z2	Z2	Z3	Z4
S2	T4	Z4	Z4	Z4	Z4
S3	T1	Z2	Z2	Z4	Z4
S3	T2	Z2	Z2	Z3	Z4
S3	T3	Z4	Z2	Z3	Z4
S3	T4	Z4	Z4	Z4	Z4
S4	T1	Z4	Z4	Z4	Z4
S4	T2	Z4	Z4	Z4	Z4
S4	T3	Z4	Z4	Z4	Z4
S4	T4	Z4	Z4	Z4	Z4

Third-Level Table

As said above, {S1,...,S4}, {T1,...,T4} and {V1,...,V4}, were three sets of literals that were called "first, second and third approaches" to the identification of a style. By combining them into Table 7, the user obtains the final identification, expressed by the letters Z1 (final identification = Baroque), Z2 (final identification = Rococo), Z3 (final identification = Classic), Z4 (final identification = none of these).

For instance, two examples, among 48 third-level production rules corresponding to Table 7 are.

$$S1 \wedge T1 \wedge V1 \rightarrow Z1$$
$$S3 \wedge T3 \wedge V1 \rightarrow Z4$$

which, respectively, mean

> "IF first approach to identification = Baroque
> AND second approach to identification = Baroque
> AND third approach to identification = Baroque
> THEN final identification = Baroque"

and

"IF first approach to identification = Classic

AND second approach to identification = Classic

AND third approach to identification = Baroque

THEN final identification = none".

CONSTRUCTION OF THE IE USING CoCoA

We shall refer in this section jointly to the theoretical background, the implementation and the user interface.

Background

Because different audiences are intended to read this chapter, its logical and mathematical background shall be described informally.

Figure 2. Theorem graphical illustration

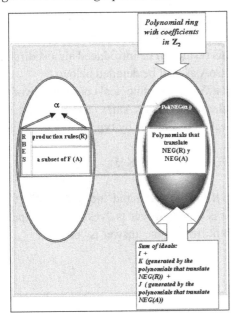

The logical and mathematical ideas to be presented in this section are based on our works on the application of GB to automated deduction in expert systems (Laita, Roanes-Lozano, de Ledesma, & Alonso, 1999; Roanes-Lozano, Laita, & Roanes-Macías, 1998) and the previous works on logic deduction (Alonso, Briales, & Riscos, 1990; Chazarain, Riscos, Alonso, & Briales, 1991; Hsiang, 1985; Kapur & Narendran, 1984). We have applied this technique to medical diagnoses (Laita, Roanes-Lozano, Maojo, de Ledesma, & Laita, 2000; Pérez Carretero, Laita, Roanes-Lozano, & Laita, 2002) and also GB-based techniques in other fields like railway interlockings (Roanes-Lozano, Roanes-Macías, & Laita, 2000) and to automated theorem proving in geometry (Roanes & Roanes, 2001). Recently, Pfalzgraf (2004) has designed a new methodology using logical fiberings.

Some Basic Algebraic and Logic Concepts

Definition: An "ideal" L of a commutative ring A is a subset of A that is also a ring and such the product of an element of L by an element of A is always in L.

Example: The multiples of 5 form an ideal in the ring of the integer numbers.

Remark: Given a set of polynomials {p, q, ..., s} of a polynomial ring A, their algebraic linear combinations, that is, the polynomials of the form:

$$u\,p + v\,q + ... + w\,s$$

where u, v, ..., w are polynomials of A, form an ideal of A (the so called "ideal generated by the set {p, q, ..., s}).

If L and M are ideals of a polynomial ring A, it is easy to prove that L+M, that is, the set of polynomials obtained by adding a polynomial of L and a polynomial of M, is also an ideal. Moreover, it is the minimum ideal containing $L \cup M$.

A process of reduction modulo an ideal L, denoted "normal form" (NF), can be applied to any polynomial, g, in A; g can then be expressed as a polynomial in L plus the normal form of g.

In the simple example of the multiples of 5 and the ring of integer numbers, the normal form of an integer would be the remainder of dividing it by 5.

Bruno Buchberger was able to build in 1965 a constructive method for calculating normal forms in polynomial rings using very particular "bases" (set of generators) of ideals (Gröbner Bases, named after his PhD advisor, Professor Gröbner) (Buchberger, 1965). If "L" denotes a polynomial ideal, the main result is:

$$g \in L \text{ if and only if } NF(g, L) = 0$$

and therefore the "ideal membership problem" was solved!

Definition: A logical formula α is a "tautological consequence" of a set S of formulae if and only if whenever all formulae in S are true, α is also true.

Application to Automated Extraction of Tautological Consequences

The basic two-valued logical formulae can be translated into polynomials the following way:

$\neg X1$ is translated into the polynomial $1+x1$

$X1 \vee X2$ is translated into the polynomial $x1+x2+x1*x2$

$X1 \wedge X2$ is translated into the polynomial $x1*x2$

$X1 \rightarrow X2$ is translated into the polynomial $1+x1+x1*x2$

They allow translation of any logical formula into a polynomial. The coefficients of these polynomials are just 0 and 1 (more formally, the coefficients of the polynomial ring A are in $Z/Z2$) and the maximum power of variables is 1, as greater powers are reduced to 1 (more formally, we are working in the quotient ring A/I, that is, simplifying modulo I, where I is the ideal generated by the polynomials of the form *variable²-variable*).

The inference engine is based on the following theorem, which is illustrated in Figure 2. The theorem is here referred to our ES, but is totally general.

Theorem: A formula (here a musical style assignation) "α", is a tautological consequence of the formulae in the union of the two sets {A1, A2, ..., Am} $\cup$ {B1, B2, ..., Bk} that represent, respectively, a maximal consistent subset A of the set F of potential facts (the subset that describes a melody) and the set of all production rules of ES1, if and only if the polynomial translation of the negation of "α" belongs to the ideal, sum of the three ideals, I+K+J generated, respectively, by the set of the polynomials {x1²-x1, x2²-x2, ..., i1²-i1, ..., z4²-z4}, by the set of the polynomial translations of the negations of A1, A2, ..., Am and by the set of the polynomial translations of the negations of B1, B2, ..., Bk.

This result can be introduced almost directly in CoCoA as will be detailed below.

That "α" is a tautological consequence of the formulae in {A1,A2,...,Am} $\cup$ {B1,B2,...,Bk}, can be checked in CoCoA by typing:

NF(NEG(alpha),I+K+J);

where NF is the command "normal form". If the output is 0, the answer is "yes"; if the output is different from 0, the answer is "no".

Application to Automated Verification

From the definition of ideal in a commutative ring with "1" above, if the polynomial "1" belongs to the ideal, the ideal is the whole ring.

If such is the case, then any formula "α", in particular a contradiction, would be a tautological consequence of the information contained in the ES.

But checking whether or not "1" belongs to the ideal (in this chapter's case the ideals are of the form I + K + J), is automatic, by just typing the command:

GBasis(NEG(alpha),I+K+J);

If the output is [1], the polynomial "1" belongs to the ideal and, thus, the ideal is the whole ring. Therefore any formulae (in particular contradictory formulae) are consequence of the ES, so that the ES would be found to be inconsistent (in an exact automated way). This is why it was said in the introduction to this chapter that this ES is sound regarding its verification.

CoCoA IMPLEMENTATION WORKING IN CONJUNCTION WITH THE GUI

We shall use Courier font for CoCoA code. We shall intermix the final parts of the program with screens of the user interface, in order to make our explanations more intuitive and better understood.

Definition of he ring A (all the two dots are CoCoA code):

```
A::=Z/(2)[x[1..23],a[1..3],c[1..4],
    d[1..4],e[1..3],f[1..4],g[1..3],
    h[1..3],i[1..3],s[1..4],t[1..4],
    v[1..4],s[1..4],t[1..4],z[1..4]];
USE A;
```

Definition of the basic ideal I ("..." are included for the sake of space, CoCoA requires writing all polynomials):

```
I:=Ideal(x[1]^2-x[1],x[2]^2-x[2],x[3]^2-x[3],...,
    x[23]^2-x[23],a[1]^2-a[1],...,a[3]^2-a[3],
    b[1]^2-b[1],...,b[3]^2-b[3],c[1]^2-c[1],...,
    c[4]^2-c[4],d[1]^2-d[1],...,d[4]^2-d[4],
    e[1]^2-e[1],...,e[3]^2-e[3],f[1]^2-f[1],...,
    f[4]^2-f[4],g[1]^2-g[1],...,g[3]^2-g[3],
    h[1]^2-h[1],...,h[3]^2-h[3],i[1]^2-i[1],...
    i[4]^2-i[4],s[1]^2-s[1],...,s[4]^2-s[4],
    t[1]^2-t[1],...,t[4]^2-t[4],v[1]^2-v[1],...,
    v[4]^2-v[4],...,z[1]^2-z[1],...,z[4]^2-z[4]);
```

Definition of the connectives corresponding to classic Boolean logic:

```
NEG(M):=NF(1+M,I);
OR1(M,N):=NF(M+N+M*N,I);
AND1(M,N):=NF(M*N,I);

IMP(M,N):=NF(1+M+M*N,I);
```

CoCoA Translation of the Production Rules

As already said, he total number of rules of ES1 is 370. CoCoA requires them to be written in "prefix form". For instance, the three production rules corresponding to Table 2:

$X1 \wedge X3 \rightarrow A1$
$\neg X1 \wedge X3 \rightarrow A2$
$\neg X3 \rightarrow A3$

are introduced as follows

```
R1:=NF(IMP(AND1(x[1],x[3]),a[1]),I);
R3:=NF(IMP(AND1(NEG(x[1]),x[3]),a[2]),I);
R10:=NF(IMP(NEG(x[3]),a[3]),I);
```

Similarly, the next two production rules corresponding to Table 3:

Figure 3. Selection corresponding to a Baroque composition

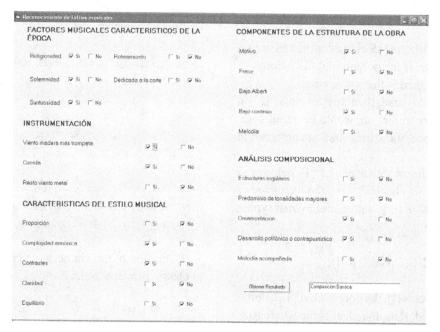

X19 ^ ¬X20 ^ ¬X21 → H3

¬X19 ^ ¬X20 ^ X21 → H2

are introduced as follows

```
R39:=NF(IMP(AND1(AND1(x[19],NEG(x[20])),NEG(x[21
])), h[3]),I);
```

```
R40:=NF(IMP(AND1(AND1(NEG(x[19],NEG(x[20])),x[21
]),h[2]),I);
```

Definition of potential facts: all the 23 pairs of potential facts and their negations should be declared. For the sake of space we only write down the first two and he last two pairs. "Fi" (i = 1,…,23) means "fact corresponding to literal Xi" and "FiN" (i = 1,..,23) means "fact corresponding to literal negation of XI".

```
F1:=x[1];          F1N:= NEG(x[1]);
F2:=x[2];          F2N:= NEG(x[2]);
...                ...
F23:=x[23];        F23N:= NEG(x[23]);
```

Ideal of production rules: the following ideal J corresponds to the RB. Recall that the theorem defines this ideal as the one generated by the polynomials that translate the negations of production rules (this is the reason of introducing "NEG" before the letters "R" denoting production rules). The same will be required later for the potential facts F1,…, F23,F1N,…, F23N:

```
J:=Ideal(NEG(R1),NEG(R2),NEG(R3),NEG(R4),NEG(R5)
,NEG(R6), NEG(R7),NEG(R8),NEG(R9),NEG(R10),
NEG(R11), NEG(R12),NEG(R13),NEG(R14),NEG(R1
5),NEG(R16), NEG(R17),NEG(R18),...,NEG(R292)
,NEG(R293),NEG(R294),...,NEG(R370));
```

Examples

We suppose that a History of Music teacher proposes to the students the next four scores for style identification. The argument in the four examples is similar. The identifiers of Table 1 appear in Spanish in the four screenshots of the GUI that follow, but the English translations are in most cases expressed by very similar words.

An expert teacher would probably use pieces of music which have well-defined identifiers. In a real session of practice with ES1, as advanced in the introduction, subjectivity or lack of a minimal knowledge of the meaning of the identifiers may cause the user(s) to introduce inaccurate identifiers.

First Example

We suppose that, during or after listening the first score, a student or a group of students using ES1, have distinguished, to the best of their knowledge, the following set of 23 identifiers—that is, a particular maximal consistent subset of the set of the 23 + 23 potential facts.

Actually, in the first example we have considered "Concert in La Minor" for violin by J.S. Bach.

- Regarding characterizing musical factors of the epoch, the user observed that the sound has certain religious flavor (potential fact denoted

as F1), it is solemn (potential fact denoted as F2) and sumptuous (potential fact denoted as F3). But it did sound neither exquisite (potential fact denoted as F4N, that is not-F4) nor devoted to a selected audience (potential fact denoted as F5N, that is not-F5).

- Instrumentation consisted fundamentally of wood wind instruments plus trumpet (potential fact denoted as F6).

- Regarding characteristics of the musical style, the user observed no proportion in the execution (potential fact denoted as F9N, that is, not-F9), while it did have harmonic complexity (potential fact denoted as F10) and significant contrasts (potential fact denoted as F11). Nevertheless, neither clearness (potential fact denoted as F12N, that is not-F12) nor equilibrium (potential fact denoted as F13N, that is not-F13).

- Regarding the structure, presence of motif is appreciated (potential fact denoted as F14), but no phrase (potential fact denoted as F15N, that is not-F15) neither Alberti bass

Figure 4. Selection corresponding to a Rococo composition

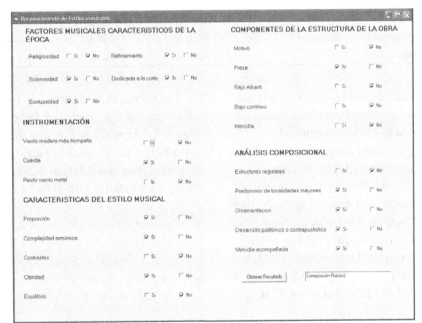

Table 8. Chosen identifiers for examples 2, 3 and 4

Musical-related Characteristics Of The Epoch	Example 2	Example 3	Example 4
X1- Religious	No (F1N)	No (F1N)	Yes (F1)
X2- Solemn	Yes (F2)	No (F2N)	Yes (F2)
X3- Sumptuous	Yes (F3)	No (F3N)	Yes (F3)
X4- Finesse	Yes (F4)	No (F4N)	Yes (F4)
X5- Seemingly devoted to a selected audience, like a Royal Court	Yes (F5)	Yes (F5)	Yes (F5)
Instrumentation			
X6- Wood wind instruments plus trumpet	No (F6N)	Yes (F6)	No (F6N)
X7- Chord	Yes (F7)	Yes (F7)	No (F7N)
X8- Remainder wind-chord	No (F8N)	Yes (F8)	No (F8N)
Characteristics Of The Musical Style			
X9- Proportion.	Yes (F9)	Yes (F9)	Yes (F9)
X10- Harmonic complexity	Yes (F10)	No (F10N)	Yes (F10)
X11- Contrasts	No (F11N)	Yes (F11)	No (F11N)
X12- Clearness	Yes (F12)	Yes (F12)	Yes (F12)
X13- Equilibrium	No (F13N)	Yes (F13)	Yes (F13)
Components Of The Structure Of The Music Work			
X14- Motif	No (F14N)	Yes (F14)	No (F14N)
X15- Phrase.	Yes (F15)	Yes (F15)	No (F15N)
X16- Alberti bass	No (F16N)	No (F16N)	No (F16N)
X17- Continuous bass	No (F17N)	No (F17N)	Yes (F17)
X18- Melody	No (F18N)	Yes (F18)	Yes (F18)
Compositional Analysis			
X19- Regular structures	No (F19N)	Yes (F19)	Yes (F19)
X20- Major tones	Yes (F20)	Yes (F20)	Yes (F20)
X21- Ornamentation	Yes (F21)	No(F21N)	Yes (F21)
X22- Polyphonic development or counter point	Yes (F22)	No(F22N)	No (F22N)
X23- Melody accompaniment	Yes (F23)	Yes (F23)	No (F23N)

(potential fact denoted as F16N, that is not-F16), although continuous bass (potential fact denoted as F16) is recognized.

- Regarding compositional analysis, neither regular structures (potential fact denoted as F19N, that is not-F19) nor over-stress of major tones (potential fact denoted as F20N, that is not-F20) appear. The music is ornamental (potential fact denoted as F21). Polyphony is part of it (potential fact denoted as F22) but there is not accompanying melody (potential fact denoted as F23N, that is not-F23).

The user(s) should choose in the GUI the 23 identifiers (that is, potential facts) as shown in Figure 3. The result of pressing these keys is the introduction of the following ideal K1 (generated by the polynomials that translate the negations of the 23 mentioned potential facts) into CoCoa.

```
K1:=Ideal(NEG(F1),NEG(F2),NEG(F3),NEG(F4N),NEG(
    F5N),NEG(F6),NEG(F7),NEG(F8N),NEG(F9N),NEG
    (F10),  NEG(F11),NEG(F12N),NEG(F13N),NEG(F
    14),NEG(F15N),NEG(F16N),NEG(F17),NEG(F18N)
    ,NEG(F19N),NEG(F20N),NEG(F21),NEG(F22),NE
    G(F23N));
```

Figure 5. Selection corresponding to a Classic composition

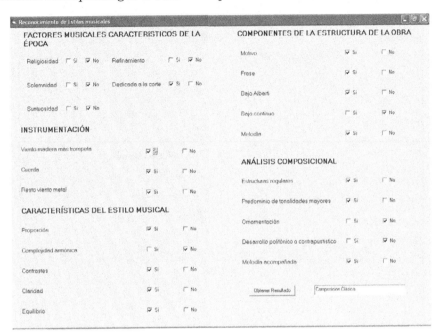

The answer to the question that for the ideal K1 corresponding to the keys pressed by the user, the score belongs to either Baroque style ($z[1]$), Rococo style ($z[2]$), Classic style ($z[3]$) or to none of them ($z[4]$), is provided when "0" is the output to (only one) of the four following commands.

```
NF(NEG(z[1]),I+J+K1);
NF(NEG(z[2]),I+J+K1);
NF(NEG(z[3]),I+J+K1);
NF(NEG(z[4]),I+J+K1);
```

In this case, the outputs are:

```
0
1 + z[2]
1 + z[3]
1 + z[4]
```

As "0" is the output to of the first command:

```
NF(NEG(z[1]),I+J+K1);
```

it means that the composition is Baroque.

Important Remark

For the sake of clarity and space, no text explaining what the user may feel and, consequently does, is explicitly written. Table 1, to which three columns of "yes" and "no" are added, summarizes in Table 8 the three lists of identifiers that the user may have chosen for the three scores considered in the second, third and fourth examples.

Second Example

The user presses 23 keys of the GUI as shown in Figure 4. The ideal K2 is then introduced to

Figure 6. This is not a score, at least of this period.

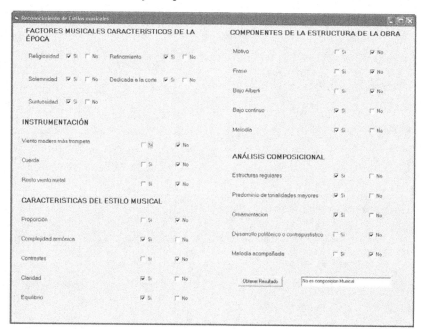

CoCoA and the corresponding normal forms are computed:

```
K2:=Ideal(NEG(F1N),EG(F2),NEG(F3),NEG(F4),NEG(F5)
    ,NEG(F6N),NEG(F7),NEG(F8N),NEG(F9),NEG(F10)
    ,NEG(F11N),NEG(F12),NEG(F13N),NEG(F14N),NEG
    (F15),NEG(F16N),NEG(F17N),NEG(F18N),NEG(F19
    N),NEG(F20),NEG(F21),NEG(F22),NEG(F23));


NF(NEG(z[1]),I+J+K2);
NF(NEG(z[2]),I+J+K2);
NF(NEG(z[3]),I+J+K2);
NF(NEG(z[4]),I+J+K2);
```

In this case, the outputs are:

```
1 + z[1]
0
1 + z[3]
1 + z[4]
```

As "0" is the output of:

```
NF(NEG(z[2]),I+J+K2);
```

it means that the composition is Rococo. Actually, the piece of music considered is the Hamburg Symphony No.1 Wq. 182 by C. P. E. Bach.

Third Example

The user presses 23 keys of the GUI as shown in Figure 5. The ideal K3 is then introduced to CoCoA and the corresponding normal forms are computed:

```
K3:=Ideal(NEG(F1N),EG(F2N),NEG(F3N),NEG(F4N),NEG
    (F5),NEG(F6),NEG(F7),NEG(F8),NEG(F9),NEG(F10
    N),NEG(F11),NEG(F12),NEG(F13),NEG(F14),NEG(F
    15),NEG(F16N),NEG(F17N),NEG(F18),NEG(F19),NE
    G(F20),NEG(F21N),NEG(F22N),NEG(F23));


NF(NEG(z[1]),I+J+K3);
NF(NEG(z[2]),I+J+K3);
NF(NEG(z[3]),I+J+K3);
NF(NEG(z[4]),I+J+K3);
```

In this case, the outputs are:

```
1 + z[1]
1 + z[2]
0
1 + z[4]
```

As "0" is the output of:

```
NF(NEG(z[3]),I+J+K3);
```

it means that the composition is Classic. Actually, the piece of music considered is the Concert for trump No. 4 by Mozart.

Fourth Example

The user presses 23 keys of the GUI as shown in Figure 6. The ideal K4 is then introduced to CoCoA and the corresponding normal forms are asked for:

```
K4:=Ideal(NEG(F1),NEG(F2),NEG(F3),NEG(F4),NEG(F5)
 ,NEG(F6N),NEG(F7N),NEG(F8N),NEG(F9),NEG(F10
 ),NEG(F11N),NEG(F12),NEG(F13),NEG(F14N),NEG
 (F15N), NEG(F16N),NEG(F17),NEG(F18),NEG(F19)
 ,NEG(F20),NEG(F21),NEG(F22N),NEG(F23N));
```

```
NF(NEG(z[1]),I+J+K4);
NF(NEG(z[2]),I+J+K4);
NF(NEG(z[3]),I+J+K4);
NF(NEG(z[4]),I+J+K4);
```

in this case, the outputs are:

```
1 + z[1]
1 + z[2]
1 + z[3]
0
```

As "0" is the output of:

```
NF(NEG(z[4]),I+J+K4);
```

it means that this is not a score of this period.

CONCLUSION

We have presented a prototype of an ES for musical styles identification, based on classical two-valued logic and computer algebra techniques. As a matter of interest, this study is representative of the wide range of topics that can be studied using Gröbner Bases.

Obviously the goal is not to substitute the specialist. There are two possible uses: first, helping in the process of detecting a style by nonspecialists, that must later consult specialists and, second, to allow specialists to compare their own opinions with those suggested by the system. We believe that the system is especially useful for learning and teaching history of music.

The KB of the system could be improved, detailed or updated without modifying either the inference engine or the method of knowledge management described in the chapter.

ACKNOWLEDGMENT

This work was partially supported by the research project MTM2004-03175 (Ministerio de Educación y Ciencia, Spain) and the grant of the research group *ACEIA* (Universidad Complutense de Madrid - Comunidad de Madrid).

We would like to thank the editors of the book and the anonymous referees of this chapter for their most valuable comments.

REFERENCES

Adams, W. W., & Loustaunau, P. (1994). *An introduction to Gröbner Bases*. Providende, RI: Graduate Studies in Mathematics, American Mathematical Society.

Alonso, J. A., Briales, E., & Riscos, A. (1990). Preuve Automatique dans le Calcul Propositionnel et des Logiques Trivalentes. In *Proceedings of the Congress on Computational Geometry and Topology and Computation* (pp.15-24). Seville, Spain: Universidad de Sevilla.

Balaban, M., Ebcioglu, K., & Laske, O. (1992). Understanding music with AI. *Perspectives on music cognition*. Boston: The MIT Press.

Buchberger, B. (1965). *An algorithm for finding a basis for the residue class ring of a zero-dimensional polynomial ideal*. Unpublished doctoral disseration. Insbruck, Austria: Math. Institute - University of Innsbruck.

Buchberger, B. (1988). Applications of Gröbner Bases in non-linear computational geometry. In J. R. Rice (Ed.), *Mathematical aspects of scientific software*. IMA Vol. 14 (pp. 60-88). New York: Springer-Verlag.

Capani, A., & Niesi, G. (1996). *CoCoA user's manual v. 3.0b*. Genova, Italy: Dept. of Mathematics, University of Genova.

Chazarain, J., Riscos, A., Alonso, J. A., & Briales, E. (1991). Multivalued logic and Gröbner Bases with applications to modal logic. *Journal of Symbolic Computation, 11*, 181-194.

Clegg, M., Edmonds, J., & Impagliazzo, R. (1996). Using the Groebner basis algorithm to find proofs of unsatisfiability. In *Proceedings of the twenty-eighth annual ACM Symposium on Theory of Computing*. Philadelphia.

Cox, D., Little, J., & O'Shea, D. (1992). *Ideals, varieties, and algorithms*. New York: Springer-Verlag.

Fernández de Sevilla, M. A. (2001). Desarrollo musical por medio de técnicas informáticas. Doce Notas, 28, 25-26.

Fernández de Sevilla, M. A. (2002). Informática musical al servicio de la formación de profesionales. *Música y Educación, 49*, 69-81.

Fernández de Sevilla, M. A. (2005). *Sistema Computacional para reconocimiento de Actitudes y Estilos en Música Culta*. Unpublished doctoral dissertation, Universidad de Alcalá, España.

Fernández de Sevilla, M. A., & Fernández del Castillo, J. R. (2002). Estudio Comparativo de editores musicales utilizando técnicas fuzzy. *Base Informática, 38*, 58-64.

Fernández de Sevilla, M. A., & Gutiérrez de Mesa, J. A. (2002). El software musical y su aplicación a la enseñanza de la música. *PCWorld, 7,* 194-202.

Fernández de Sevilla, M. A., & Hilera, J. R. (2001). Conservación y restauración del patrimonio musical. *Cuadernos de Documentación multimedia, 8,* 25-26.

Fernández de Sevilla, M. A., Jiménez, L., & Fernández del Castillo, J. R. (2003). Tool selection under uncertainty by fuzzy aggregation operators. In *Proceedings of AGOP 2003* (pp 67-72). Alcalá de Henares, España: Universidad de Alcalá.

Groutald, D. J., & Palisca, C. V. (2004). *Historia de la música occidental I, II*. Madrid: Alianza Editorial.

Hsiang, J. (1985). Refutational theorem proving using term-rewriting systems. *Artificial Intelligence, 25*, 255-300.

Kapur, D., & Narendran, P. (1984). *An equational approach to theorem proving in first-order predicate calculus* (Rep. No. 84CRD296). Schenectady, NY: General Electric Corporate Research and Development.

Kreuzer, M., & Robbiano, L. (2000). *Computational commutative algebra*. Berlin - Heidelgeberg, Germany: Springer-Verlag.

Laita, L. M., Roanes-Lozano, E., de Ledesma, L., & Alonso, J. A. (1999). A computer algebra approach to verification and deduction in many-valued knowledge systems. *Soft Computing, 3*(1), 7-19.

Laita, L. M., Roanes-Lozano, E., Maojo, V., de Ledesma, L., & Laita, L. (2000). An expert system for managing medical appropriateness criteria based on computer algebra techniques. *Computers and Mathematics with Applications, 51*(5), 473-481.

Laita, L. M., Roanes Lozano, E., & Alonso, J. A. (Guest Eds.). (2004). Symbolic computation in logic and artificial intelligence [Special Issue]. *RACSAM, Revista de la Real Academia de Ciencias de España, Serie "A" Matemáticas, 98*(1-2).

Marco, T. A. (2002). *Historia de la música occidental del siglo XX*. Madrid, España: Alpuerto.

Pfalzgraf, J. (2004). On logical fiberings and automated deduction in many-valued logics using Gröbner Bases. *RACSAM Revista de la Real Academia de Ciencias, Serie A "matemáticas", 98*(1-2), 213-228.

Pérez Carretero, C., Laita L. M., Roanes-Lozano, E., & Laita, L. (2002). A logic and computer algebra-based expert system for diagnosis of anorexia. *Mathematics and Computers in Simulation, 58*, 183-202.

Perkinson, D. (n.d.). *CoCoA 4.0 Online Help*. Genova, Italy: Dept. of Mathematics - University of Genova.

Roanes-Lozano, E., Laita, L. M., & Roanes-Macías, E. (1998). A polynomial model for multivalued logics with a touch of algebraic geometry and computer algebra. *Mathematics and Computers in Simulation, 45*(1), 83-99.

Roanes-Lozano, E., Roanes-Macías, E., & L.M. Laita. (2000). Railway interlocking systems and Gröbner Bases. *Mathematics and Computers in Simulation, 51*(5), 473-481.

Roanes-Macías, E., & Roanes-Lozano, E. (2001). Automatic determination of geometric loci. 3D-extension of Simson-Steiner theorem. In J. A. Campbell & E. Roanes Lozano (Eds.), *Artificial Intelligence and Symbolic Computation; International Conference AISC 2000*. Revised Papers. LNCS 1930 (pp.157-173). Berlin-Heidelberg, Germany: Springer-Verlag.

Zampronha, E. S. (2000). *Notação, Representação e Composição: Um Novo Paradigma da Escritura Musical*. Lisboa, Portugal: Annablume/FAPESP.

Chapter V
Identifying Saxophonists from Their Playing Styles

Rafael Ramirez
Pompeu Fabra University, Spain

ABSTRACT

We describe a novel approach to the task of identifying performers from their playing styles. We investigate how professional Jazz saxophonists express and communicate their view of the musical and emotional content of musical pieces and how to use this information in order to automatically identify performers. We study deviations of parameters such as pitch, timing, amplitude and timbre both at an internote level and at an intranote level. Our approach to performer identification consists of establishing a performer dependent mapping of internote features to a repertoire of inflections characterized by intranote features. We present and discuss some results of our approach and comment on future trends in this exciting research area.

INTRODUCTION

A key challenge in the area of music information, given the explosion of online music and the rapidly expanding digital music collections, is the development of efficient and reliable music search and retrieval systems. One of the main deficiencies of current music search and retrieval systems is the semantic gap between the simplicity of the content descriptors that can be currently extracted automatically and the semantic richness in music information. Conventional information retrieval has been mainly based on text, and the approaches to textual information retrieval have been transferred into music information retrieval. However, music contents and text contents are of a very different nature which very often makes textual information retrieval unsatisfactory in a musical context. It has been widely recognized that music retrieval techniques should incorporate high-level semantic music information.

In this chapter we focus on the task of identifying performers from their playing style using high-level semantic descriptors extracted from audio recordings. The identification of performers by using the expressive content in their performances raises particularly interesting questions but has nevertheless received relatively little attention in the past. Given the capabilities of current audio analysis systems, we believe expressive-content-based performer identification is a promising research topic in music information retrieval. After presenting the background to this area and briefly discussing the limitations of this approach to performer identification, we present an algorithm for identifying Jazz saxophonists using high-level semantic information obtained from real performances. This work is based on our previous work on expressive performance modeling (Ramirez & Hazan, 2005; Ramirez, Hazan, Maestre, & Serra, 2006). Finally, we discuss the results from the case study and draw some conclusions.

The data used in our investigations are audio recordings of real performances by Jazz saxophonists. The use of audio recordings, as opposed to MIDI recordings where data analysis is simplified, poses substantial difficulties for the extraction of music performance information. However, the obvious benefits of using real audio recordings widely compensate the extra effort required for the audio analysis. We use sound analysis techniques based on spectral models (Serra & Smith, 1990) for extracting high-level symbolic features from the recordings. The spectral model analysis techniques are based on decomposing the original signal into sinusoids plus a spectral residual. From the sinusoids of a monophonic signal it is possible to extract high-level semantic information such as note pitch, onset, duration, attack and energy among other information. In particular, for characterizing expressivity in saxophone we are interested in two types of features: *intranote* or *perceptual* features representing perceptual characteristics of the performance, and *internote* or *contextual* features representing information about the music context in which expressive events occur. We use the software SMSTools

(SMS) which is an ideal tool for preprocessing the signal and providing a high-level description of the audio recordings. Once the relevant high-level information is extracted we apply machine-learning techniques (Mitchell, 1997) to automatically discover regularities and expressive patterns for each performer. We use these regularities and patterns in order to identify a particular performer in a given audio recording. We discuss different machine learning techniques for detecting the performer's expressive patterns, as well as the perspectives of using sound analysis techniques on arbitrary polyphonic audio recordings.

The rest of the chapter is organized as follows: Section 2 sets the background for the research reported here. Section 3 describes how we process the audio recordings in order to extract both perceptual and contextual information. Section 4 presents our algorithm for identifying performers from their playing styles, as well as some results. Section 5 briefly discusses future trends in the context of this research, and finally, Section 6 presents some conclusions and indicates some areas of future research.

BACKGROUND

Music performance plays a central role in our musical culture today. Concert attendance and recording sales often reflect people's preferences for particular interpreters. The manipulation of sound properties such as pitch, timing, amplitude and timbre by different performers is clearly distinguishable by the listeners. Expressive music performance studies the manipulation of these sound properties in an attempt to understand *why*, *what*, *how* and *when* expression is introduced to a performance. There has been much speculation as to *why* performances contain expression. Hypothesis include that musical expression communicates emotions (Justin, 2001) and that it clarifies musical structure (Kendall, 1990), that is, the performer shapes the music according to her own intensions (Apel, 1972). In order to understand *what* is expressed in a performance it is necessary to understand *how* it is expressed.

Understanding and formalizing expressive music performance is an extremely challenging problem, which in the past has been studied from different perspectives (e.g., Bresin, 2002; Gabrielsson, 1999; Seashore, 1936). The main approaches to empirically studying expressive performance have been based on statistical analysis (e.g., Repp, 1992), mathematical modeling (e.g., Todd, 1992), and analysis-by-synthesis (e.g., Friberg, Bresin, Fryden, & Sunberg, 1998). In all these approaches, it is a person who is responsible for devising a theory or mathematical model which captures different aspects of musical expressive performance. The theory or model is later tested on real performance data in order to determine its accuracy. The majority of the research on expressive music performance has focused on the performance of musical material for which notation (i.e., a score) is available, thus providing unambiguous performance goals. Expressive performance studies have also been very much focused on (classical) piano performance in which pitch and timing measurements are simplified.

This chapter describes a machine learning approach to investigate how skilled musicians (saxophone Jazz players in particular) express and communicate their view of the musical and emotional content of musical pieces and how to use this information in order to automatically distinguish among interpreters. We study deviations of parameters such as pitch, timing, amplitude and timbre both at an internote level and at an intranote level. This is, we analyze the pitch, timing (onset and duration), amplitude (energy mean) and timbre of individual notes, as well as the timing and amplitude of individual intranote events. We consider both performances of musical material for which notation is available, and performances for which no notation is available, that is improvising and playing by ear. We focus on saxophone performance where timing, pitch

and timbre measurements present a greater challenge compared to the measurements in piano performances.

Previous research addressing expressive music performance using machine learning techniques has included a number of approaches. Lopez de Mantaras and Arcos (2002) report on SaxEx, a performance system capable of generating expressive solo saxophone performances in Jazz. Their system is based on case-based reasoning; a type of analogical reasoning where problems are solved by reusing the solutions of similar, previously solved problems. In order to generate expressive solo performances, the case-based reasoning system retrieves from a memory containing expressive interpretations, those notes that are *similar* to the input inexpressive notes. The case memory contains information about metrical strength, note duration, and so on, and uses this information to retrieve the appropriate notes. One limitation of their system is that it is incapable of explaining the predictions it makes and it is unable to handle melody alterations, for example ornamentations.

Ramirez et al. (2006) have explored and compared diverse machine learning methods for obtaining expressive music performance models for Jazz saxophone that are capable of both generating expressive performances and explaining the expressive transformations they produce. They propose an expressive performance system based on inductive logic programming which induces a set of first order logic rules that capture expressive transformation both at a note level (e.g., note duration, energy) and at an intranote level (e.g., note attack, sustain). Based on the theory generated by the set of rules, they implemented a melody synthesis component which generates expressive monophonic output (MIDI or audio) from inexpressive melody MIDI descriptions.

With the exception of the work by Lopez de Mantaras and Arcos (2002) and Ramirez et al. (2006), most of the research in expressive performance using machine learning techniques has focused on classical piano music where the tempo of the performed pieces is not constant. Thus, these works focus on global tempo and energy transformations while we are interested in notelevel tempo and energy transformations (i.e., note onset and duration).

Widmer (2001; 2002) reported on the task of discovering general rules of expressive classical piano performance from real performance data via inductive machine learning. The performance data used for the study are MIDI recordings of 13 piano sonatas by W.A. Mozart performed by a skilled pianist. In addition to these data, the music score was also coded. The resulting substantial data consists of information about the nominal note onsets, duration, metrical information and annotations. When trained on the data an inductive rule learning algorithm discovered a small set of quite simple classification rules (Widmer, 2001) that predict a large number of the note-level choices of the pianist.

Tobudic and Widmer (2003) describe a relational instance-based approach to the problem of learning to apply expressive tempo and dynamics variations to a piece of classical music, at different levels of the phrase hierarchy. The different phrases of a piece and the relations among them are represented in first-order logic. The description of the musical scores through predicates (e.g., *contains(ph1,ph2)*) provides the background knowledge. The training examples are encoded by another predicate whose arguments encode information about the way the phrase was played by the musician. Their learning algorithm recognizes similar phrases from the training set and applies their expressive patterns to a new piece.

Other inductive approaches to rule learning in music and musical analysis include (Dovey, 1995), (Van Baelen & De Raedt, 1996). In Dovey (1995), Dovey analyzes piano performances of Rachmaniloff pieces using inductive logic programming and extracts rules underlying them. In Van Baelen & De Raedt (1996), Van Baelen extended Dovey's work and attempted to discover

regularities that could be used to generate MIDI information derived from the musical analysis of the piece.

There are a number of approaches which address expressive performance without using machine-learning techniques. One of the first attempts to provide a computer system with musical expressiveness is that of Johnson (1992). Johnson developed a rule-based expert system to determine expressive tempo and articulation for Bach's fugues from *the well-tempered clavier*. The rules were obtained from two expert performers.

A long-term effort in expressive performance modeling is the work of the KTH group (Bresin, 2002; Friberg, 1998; Friberg, Bresin, & Fryden, 2000). Their *Director Musices* system incorporates rules for tempo, dynamic and articulation transformations. The rules are obtained from both theoretical musical knowledge, and experimentally from training using an analysis-by-synthesis approach. The rules are divided into *differentiation rules* which enhance the differences between scale tones, *grouping rules* which specify what tones belong together, and *ensemble rules* which synchronize the voices in an ensemble.

Canazza, De Poli, G., Roda, A., and Vidolin (1997) developed a system to analyze the relationship between the musician's expressive intentions and her performance. The analysis reveals two expressive dimensions, one related to energy (dynamics), and another one related to kinetics (rubato).

Dannenberg et al. (1998) investigated the trumpet articulation transformations using (manually generated) rules. They developed a trumpet synthesizer which combines a physical model with an expressive performance model. The performance model generates control information for the physical model using a set of rules manually extracted from the analysis of a collection of performance recordings.

Nevertheless, the use of expressive performance models for identifying musicians, either automatically induced or manually generated, has received little attention in the past. This is mainly due to two factors: (a) the high complexity of the feature extraction process that is required to characterize expressive performance, and (b) the question of how to use the information provided by an expressive performance model for the task of performance-based interpreter identification. To the best of our knowledge, the only group working on performance-based automatic interpreter identification is the group led by Gerhard Widmer. Saunders, Hardoon, Shawe-Taylor, and Widmer (2004) apply string kernels to the problem of recognizing famous pianists from their playing style. The characteristics of performers playing the same piece are obtained from changes in beat-level tempo and beat-level loudness. From such characteristics, general performance alphabets can be derived, and pianists' performances can then be represented as strings. They apply both kernel partial least squares and Support Vector Machines to this data.

Stamatatos and Widmer (2005) address the problem of identifying the most likely music performer, given a set of performances of the same piece by a number of skilled candidate pianists. They propose a set of very simple features for representing stylistic characteristics of a music performer that relate to a kind of "average" performance. A database of piano performances of 22 pianists playing two pieces by Frédéric Chopin is used. They propose an ensemble of simple classifiers derived by both subsampling the training set and subsampling the input features. Experiments show that the proposed features are able to quantify the differences between music performers.

MELODIC DESCRIPTION

In this section, we outline how we extract a description of a performed melody for monophonic recordings. We use this melodic representation to provide a contextual and perceptual description of the performances and apply machine learn-

ing techniques to these extracted features. This is, our interest is to obtain for each performed note a set of perceptual features (e.g., timbre) and a set of contextual features (e.g., neighboring notes pitch) from the audio recording. Thus, descriptors providing perceptual and contextual information about the performed notes are of particular interest.

Extraction of Contextual Features

Figure 1 represents the steps that are performed to obtain a melodic description from audio. First of all, we perform a spectral analysis of a portion of sound, called analysis frame, whose size is a parameter of the algorithm. This spectral analysis lies in multiplying the audio frame with an appropriate analysis window and performing a Discrete Fourier Transform (DFT) to obtain its spectrum. In this case, we use a frame width of 46 ms, an overlap factor of 50%, and a Keiser-Bessel 25dB window. Then, we compute a set of low-level descriptors for each spectrum: energy and an estimation of the fundamental frequency. From these low-level descriptors we perform a note segmentation procedure. Once the note

Figure 1. Block diagram of the melody descriptor

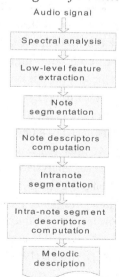

boundaries are known, the note descriptors are computed from the low-level values.

As mentioned before, the main low-level descriptors used to characterize note-level expressive performance are instantaneous energy and fundamental frequency.

Energy Computation

The energy descriptor is computed on the spectral domain, using the values of the amplitude spectrum at each analysis frame. In addition, energy is computed in different frequency bands as defined in (Klapuri, 1999), and these values are used by the algorithm for note segmentation.

Fundamental Frequency Estimation

For the estimation of the instantaneous fundamental frequency we use a harmonic matching model derived from the Two-Way Mismatch procedure (TWM) (Maher, 1994). For each fundamental frequency candidate, mismatches between the harmonics generated and the measured partials frequencies are averaged over a fixed subset of the available partials. A weighting scheme is used to make the procedure robust to the presence of noise or absence of certain partials in the spectral data. The solution presented in Maher (1994) employs two mismatch error calculations. The first one is based on the frequency difference between each partial in the measured sequence and its nearest neighbor in the predicted sequence. The second is based on the mismatch between each harmonic in the predicted sequence and its nearest partial neighbor in the measured sequence. This two-way mismatch helps to avoid octave errors by applying a penalty for partials that are present in the measured data but are not predicted, and also for partials whose presence is predicted but which do not actually appear in the measured sequence. The TWM mismatch procedure has also the benefit that the effect of any spurious components or partial missing from the measurement can be counteracted by the presence of uncorrupted partials in the same frame.

First, we perform a spectral analysis of all the windowed frames, as explained above. Secondly, the prominent spectral peaks of the spectrum are detected from the spectrum magnitude. These spectral peaks of the spectrum are defined as the local maxima of the spectrum which magnitude is greater than a threshold. The spectral peaks are compared to a harmonic series and a two-way mismatch (TWM) error is computed for each fundamental frequency candidates. The candidate with the minimum error is chosen to be the fundamental frequency estimate.

After a first test of this implementation, some improvements to the original algorithm where implemented to deal with some errors of the algorithm:

- **Peak Selection:** a peak selection routine has been added in order to eliminate spectral peaks corresponding to noise. The peak selection is done according to a masking threshold around each of the maximum magnitude peaks. The form of the masking threshold depends on the peak amplitude, and uses three different slopes depending on the frequency distance to the peak frequency.
- **Context Awareness:** we take into account previous values of the fundamental frequency estimation and instrument dependencies to obtain a more adapted result.
- **Noise Gate:** a noise gate based on some low-level signal descriptor is applied to detect silences, so that the estimation is only performed in nonsilent segments of the sound.

Note: segmentation is performed using a set of frame descriptors, which are energy computation in different frequency bands and fundamental frequency. Energy onsets are first detected following a band-wise algorithm that uses some psycho-acoustical knowledge (Klapuri, 1999). In a second step, fundamental frequency transitions are also detected. Finally, both results are merged to find the note boundaries (onset and offset information).

Note Descriptors

We compute note descriptors using the note boundaries and the low-level descriptors values. The low-level descriptors associated to a note segment are computed by averaging the frame values within this note segment. Pitch histograms have been used to compute the pitch note and the fundamental frequency that represents each note segment, as found in (McNab, Smith, & Witten, 1996). This is done to avoid taking into account mistaken frames in the fundamental frequency mean computation. First, frequency values are converted into cents, by the following formula:

$$c = 1200 \cdot \frac{\log(\frac{f}{fref})}{\log 2}$$

where f_{ref} = 8.176. Then, we define histograms with bins of 100 *cents* and hop size of 5 *cents* and we compute the maximum of the histogram to identify the note pitch. Finally, we compute the frequency mean for all the points that belong to the histogram. The MIDI pitch is computed by quantization of this fundamental frequency mean over the frames within the note limits.

Extraction of Perceptual (Intranote) Features

Once we segment the audio signal into notes, we perform a characterization of each of the notes in terms of its internal features.

Intranote segmentation. The proposed intranote segmentation method is based on the study of the energy envelope contour of the note. Once onsets and offsets are located, we study the instantaneous energy values of the analysis frames corresponding to each note. This study is carried out by analyzing the envelope curvature and characterizing its shape, in order to estimate the limits of the intranote segments.

When observing the note energy envelopes from the saxophone recordings, we identify that there are usually three segments (attack, sustain and release (Bernstein & Cooper, 1976)) needed to conform a description that fits the model schematically represented in Figure 2. We discarded the decay segment due to the general characteristics of the notes within the performances.

In order to extract these three characteristic segments, we study the smoothed derivatives in a similar way that presented in (Jenssen, 1999), where partial amplitude envelopes are modeled for isolated sounds. The main difference is that we analyze the notes in their musical context, rather than isolated. In addition, only three linear segments are considered. Moreover, instead of studying the contribution of all the partials, we obtain general intensity information from the total energy envelope characteristic. The procedure is carried out as follows.

Considering the energy envelope as a differentiable function over time, the points of maximum curvature can be considered as the local maximum variations of the first derivative of the signal energy (second derivative extremes), that is, the local maxima or minima of the second derivative.

Due to the characteristics of the audio signal, the energy envelope must be previously smoothed by low-pass filtering, since there are typically too many second derivative extremes. Several smoothing steps are carried out in order to find a good cut-off frequency of the smoothing filter. The smoothed envelope should not differ much to the original one to avoid loss of localization due to the filtering effect. Thus, for each smoothing step, the error e_m at smoothing step m between original and current envelope is computed. This is carried out by means of (1), where N is the length of the envelope in frames, *env* is the original envelope

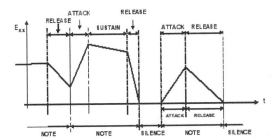

Figure 2. Schematic view of the proposed energy envelope-based intranote segmentation

and env_m is the smoothed envelope at step m.

$$e_m = \frac{1}{N} \sum_{k=1}^{N} \frac{|env(k) - env_m(k)|}{\overline{env}} \quad (1)$$

Starting from a low cut-off frequency f_{0init}, this frequency is increased each smoothing step until the error e_m gets lower than a certain threshold e_{th}, empirically selected. Then, we compute the three first derivatives of the last smoothed envelope. Frame positions and corresponding y-values of second derivative extremes are stored. Afterwards, these characteristic points are sorted by the second derivative modulus, and the n highest positions are selected to build up the set of characteristic points F. Of course, when the total number of third derivative zero-crossings is less than n, the set is F shortened.

Both note onset and offset are added as characteristic points to the set F. The slope defined by each pair of consecutive characteristic points on the envelope is computed (2), where i and j denote frame positions. A minimum slope duration (measured in frames) Δfr is defined relative to the note duration as the five per cent of the note length N for excluding the possible too high valued slopes near the note limits.

$$\forall i, j \in F \text{ such as } i \leq j + \Delta fr, s_{i,j} = \frac{env_m(j) - env_m(i)}{j - i} \quad (2)$$

Figure 3. Original and smoothed envelopes of a sax note for a value of eth=0.05 (top figure, solid and dashed thin lines, respectively); selected characteristic points are denoted with a square within extremes of the second derivative of the smoothed envelope

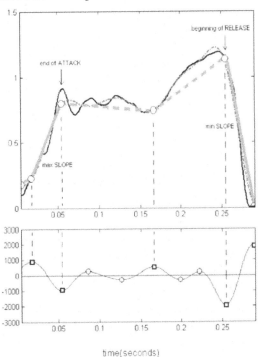

Finally, the two pairs of points defining, respectively, the most positive and most negative slope values from the remaining slopes after discarding are extracted. The end of the attack segment f_{AE} is defined as the frame position corresponding to second point of the maximum slope, while the start of the release segment position f_{RB} is defined as the first point of the minimum slope. This is stated in (3) and (4) and depicted in Figure 3.

$$s_M = s_{i_M, j_M} = \max(s_{i,j}), \ f_{AE} = j_M \quad (3)$$

$$s_m = s_{i_m, j_m} = \min(s_{i,j}), \ f_{RB} = i_m \quad (4)$$

The attack is defined as the segment between the note onset and the end of the most positive of the computed slopes, while the release segment

Figure 4. Energy envelope and its linear approximation of a real excerpt with intranote segment limits marked

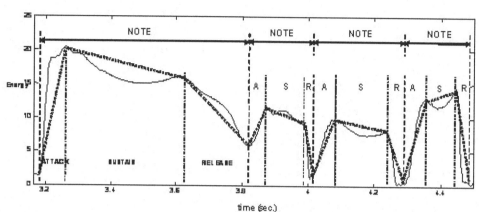

is defined as the segment between the start of the most negative of the computed slopes and the note offset. Sustain is restricted to the remaining segment. When the end of attack and the start of release limits of a note coincide, it is considered that the note does not present sustain segment.

Intranote segment characterization. Once we have found the intranote segment limits, we describe each one by its duration (absolute and relative to note duration), start and end times, initial and final energy values (absolute and relative to note maximum) and slope. For the stable part of each note (sustain segment), we extract an averaged spectral centroid and spectral tilt in order to have timbral descriptors related to the brightness of a particular execution. We compute the spectral centroid as the frequency bin corresponding to the barycenter of the spectrum, expressed as (5), where *fft* is the fast fourier transform of a frame, *N* is the size of the fast fourier tarnsform, and *k* is the bin index. For the spectral tilt, we perform a linear regression of the logarithmic spectral envelope between 2kHz and 6kHz, and get the slope expressed in dB/Hz.

$$SC = \frac{\sum_{k=1}^{N} k\left|fft(k)\right|}{\sum_{k=1}^{N}\left|fft(k)\right|} \qquad (5)$$

PERFORMANCE-DRIVEN INTERPRETER IDENTIFICATION

In this section, we describe our approach to the problem of recognizing saxophonists from their playing style. In particular, we introduce the different note descriptors we use to characterize the internal and contextual note properties (computed as described in the previous section), as well as the different algorithms we apply to identify interpreters from their playing style.

Note Descriptors

We characterize each performed note by the following two sets of features:

- Perceptual (intranote) features. The perceptual features represent perceptual properties of a note which are specified as intranote characteristics of the audio signal. The set of perceptual features we have included in the research reported here are the note's attack level, sustain duration, sustain slope, amount of legato with the previous note, amount of legato with the following note, mean energy, spectral centroid and spectral tilt. This is, each performed note is perceptually characterized by the tuple

(*AtackLev, SustDur, SustSlo, LegLeft, LegRight, EnergyM, SpecCen, SpecTilt*)

- Contextual (internote) features. The contextual features represent both properties of the note itself and aspects of the musical context in which the note appears. Information about the note includes note pitch and note duration, while information about its melodic context includes the relative pitch and duration of the neighboring notes (i.e. previous and following notes) as well as the Narmour structures to which the note belongs. The note's Narmour structures are computed by performing the musical analysis described in Section 4.2. Thus, each performed note is contextually characterized by the tuple

(*Pitch, Dur, PrevPitch, PrevDur, NextPitch, NextDur, Nar1, Nar2, Nar3*)

Musical Analysis

It is widely recognized that expressive performance is a multilevel phenomenon and that humans perform music considering a number of abstract musical structures. As a first step towards providing an abstract structure for the recordings under study, we decided to use Narmour's theory of perception and cognition of melodies (Narmour, 1990; 1991) to analyze the performances.

The Implication/Realization model proposed by Narmour is a theory of perception and cognition of melodies. The theory states that a melodic musical line continuously causes listeners to generate expectations of how the melody should continue. The nature of these expectations in an individual are motivated by two types of sources: innate and learned. According to Narmour, on the one hand we are all born with innate information which suggests to us how a particular melody should continue. On the other hand, learned factors are

due to exposure to music throughout our lives and familiarity with musical styles and particular melodies. According to Narmour, any two consecutively perceived notes constitute a melodic interval, and if this interval is not conceived as complete, it is an *implicative interval*, that is, an interval that implies a subsequent interval with certain characteristics. That is to say, some notes are more likely than others to follow the implicative interval. Two main principles recognized by Narmour concern *registral direction* and *intervallic difference*. The principle of registral direction states that small intervals imply an interval in the same registral direction (a small upward interval implies another upward interval and analogously for downward intervals), and large intervals imply a change in registral direction (a large upward interval implies a downward interval and analogously for downward intervals). The principle of intervallic difference states that a small (five semitones or less) interval implies a similarly-sized interval (plus or minus 2 semitones), and a large interval (seven semitones or more) implies a smaller interval. Based on these two principles, melodic patterns or groups can be identified that either satisfy or violate the implication as predicted by the principles. Such patterns are called structures and are labeled to denote characteristics in terms of registral direction and intervallic difference. Figure 5 shows prototypical Narmour structures. A note in a melody often belongs to more than one structure. Thus, a description of a melody as a sequence of Narmour structures consists of a list of overlapping structures. We parse each melody in the training data in order to automatically generate an implication/realization analysis of the pieces. Figure 6 shows the analysis for a melody fragment.

Algorithm

One of the first questions to be asked before attempting to build a system to automatically iden-

Figure 5. Prototypical Narmour structures

Figure 6. Narmour analysis of All of Me

tify a musician by his or her playing style is, how is this task performed by a music expert? In the case of Jazz saxophonists we believe that most of the cues for interpreter identification come from the timbre or "quality" of the notes performed by the saxophonist. That is to say, while timing information is certainly important and is useful to identify a particular musician most of the information relevant for identifying an interpreter is the timbre characteristics of the performed notes. In this respect, the saxophone is similar to the singing voice in which most of the information relevant for identifying a singer is simply his or her voice's timbre. Thus, the algorithm to identify interpreters from their playing style reported in this chapter aims to detect patterns of notes based on their timbre content. Roughly, the algorithm consists of generating a performance alphabet by clustering similar (in terms of timbre) individual notes, inducing for each interpreter a classifier which maps a note and its musical context to a symbol in the performance alphabet (i.e., a cluster), and given an audio fragment identify the interpreter as the one whose classifier predicts best the performed fragment. We are ultimately interested in obtaining a classifier *MC* mapping melody fragments to particular performers (i.e., the identified saxophonist). We initially segment all the recorded pieces into audio segments representing musical phrases. Given an audio fragment denoted by a list of notes $[N_1,...,N_m]$ and

a set of possible interpreters denoted by a list of performers $[P_1,...,P_n]$, classifier *MC* identifies the interpreter as follows:

$$MC([N_1,...,N_m], [P_1,...,P_n])$$
for each interpreter P_i
  $Score_i = 0$
  for each note N_k
    $PN_k = $ perceptual_features(N_k)
    $CN_k = $ contextual_features(N_k)
    $(X_1,...,X_q) = $ cluster_membership(PN_k)
    for each interpreter P_i
      Cluster$(i,k)=CL_i(CN_k)$
      $Score_i = Score_i + X_{Cluster(i,k)}$
  return P_M such that $Score_M = \max(Score_1,... ,Score_n)$

This is, for each note in the melody fragment the classifier *MC* computes the set of its perceptual features, the set of its contextual features and, based on the note's perceptual features, the cluster membership of the note for each of the clusters $(X_1,...,X_q$ are the cluster membership for clusters $1,...,q$, respectively). Once this is done, for each interpreter P_i its trained classifier $CL_i(PN)$ predicts a cluster representing the expected type of note the interpreter would have played in that musical context. This prediction is based on the note's contextual features. The score $Score_i$ for each interpreter i is updated by taking into account the cluster membership of the predicted cluster (i.e., the greater the cluster membership of the predicted cluster, the more the score of the interpreter is increased). Finally, the interpreter with the higher score is returned.

Clearly, the classifiers CL_i play a central role in the output of classifier MC. For each interpreter, CL_i is trained with data extracted from the interpreter's performance recordings. We have explored different classifier induction methods for obtaining each classifier CL_i. The methods we have considered are:

- **K-means Clustering:** Clustering techniques apply when there is no class to be predicted but rather when the instances are to be divided into natural groups. In k-means clustering (k is the number of clusters), k points are chosen at random as cluster centers, each instance is assigned to the nearest cluster center, for each cluster a new cluster center is computed by averaging over all instances in the cluster, and the whole process is repeated with the new cluster centers. Iteration continues until the same instances are assigned to each cluster in consecutive rounds. In this chapter, we apply fuzzy k-means clustering where Instances can belong to several clusters with different "degrees of membership".

- **Decision Trees:** A decision tree classifier recursively constructs a tree by selecting at each node the most relevant attribute. This process gradually splits up the training set into subsets until all instances at a node have the same classification. The selection of the most relevant attribute at each node is based on the information gain associated with each node of the tree (and corresponding set of instances). We have applied the decision tree building algorithm C4.5 (Quinlan, 1993).

- **Support Vector Machines (SVM):** SVM (Cristiani & Shawe-Taylor, 2000) take great advantage of using a nonlinear attribute mapping that allows them to be able to predict non-linear models (though they remain

linear in a higher dimension space). Thus, they provide a flexible prediction, but with a higher computational cost necessary to perform all the computations in the higher dimensional space. The classification accuracy of SVM largely depends on the choice of the kernel evaluation function and the parameters which control the amount to which deviations are tolerated (denoted by epsilon). In this chapter we have explored SVM with linear and polynomial kernels (2nd, 3rd and 4th order) and we have set epsilon to 0.05.

- **Artificial Neural Networks (ANN):** ANN learning methods provide a robust approach to approximating a target function. In this chapter we apply a gradient descent back propagation algorithm (Chauvin et al., 1995) to tune the neural network parameters to best fit the fMRI training set. The back propagation algorithm learns the weights for a multi layer network, given a network with a fixed set of units and interconnections. We set the momentum applied to the weights during updating to 0.2 and the learning rate (the amount the weights are updated) to 0.3. We use a fully-connected multilayer neural network with one hidden layer (one input neuron for each attribute and one output neuron for each class).

- **Lazy Methods:** Lazy Methods are based on the notion of lazy learning which subsumes a family of algorithms that store the complete set of given (classified) examples of an underlying example language and delay all further calculations until requests for classifying yet unseen instances are received. In this chapter we have explored the k-Nearest Neighbor (k-NN) algorithm (with $k \in \{1,2,3,4,7\}$) which is capable of handling noisy data well if the training set has an acceptable size. However, k-NN does not behave well in the presence of irrelevant attributes.

- **Ensemble Methods:** One obvious approach to making more reliable decisions is to combine the output of several different models. In this chapter we explore the use of methods for combining models (called ensemble methods) generated by machine learning. In particular, we have explored voting, stacking, bagging and boosting. In many cases they have proved to increase predictive performance over a single model. In voting a set of n different learning algorithms (in this chapter we applied decision trees, SVM, ANN, and 1-NN) are trained on the same training data, and prediction is performed by allowing all n classifiers to 'vote' on class prediction, final prediction is the class that gets the most votes. Stacking train n learning algorithms (here we applied decision trees, SVM, ANN, and 1-NN) in the same training data and train another learning algorithm, the "meta-learner", (we applied decision trees) to learn to predict the class from the predictions of the base learners. Bagging draws n bootstrap samples from the training data, trains a given learning algorithm (here we consider decision trees) on each of these n samples (producing n classifiers) and predicts by simple voting of all n classifiers. Boosting generates a series of classifiers using the same learning algorithm (here we applied decision trees) but differently weighted examples from the same training set, and predicts by weighted majority vote (weighted by accuracy) of all n classifiers.

The motivation for inducing the classifiers as described above is that we would like to devise a mechanism to capture which (perceptual) type of notes are played in a particular musical context by an interpreter. By clustering the notes of all the interpreters based on the notes' perceptual features, we intend to obtain a number of sets, each containing perceptually similar notes (e.g.,

notes with similar timbre). By building a classifier based on the contextual features of the notes of an interpreter, we intend to obtain a classifier which predicts what type of notes an interpreter performs in a particular musical context.

Evaluation

We evaluated the induced classifiers by performing the standard 10-fold cross validation in which 10% of the training set is held out in turn as test data while the remaining 90% is used as training data. When performing the 10-fold cross validation, we leave out the same number of examples per class (i.e., the same number of notes per performer). In the data sets, the number of examples is the same for each class (i.e., each interpreter) considered, thus by leaving out the same number of examples per class we maintain a balanced training set. In order to avoid optimistic estimates of the classifier performance, we explicitly remove from the training set all melody fragment repetitions of the hold out fragment. This is motivated by the fact that musicians are likely to perform a melody fragment and its repetition in a similar way. Thus, the applied 10-fold cross validation procedure, in addition to holding out a test example from the training set, also removes repetitions of the example.

A Case Study

We have applied our algorithm to a set of monophonic recordings obtained from professional saxophonists in a controlled studio environment. The musicians were instructed to interpret several Jazz standards by following the score of the piece.

Training Data

The training data used in this case study are monophonic recordings of four Jazz standards (*Body and Soul, Once I Loved, Like Someone in*

Love and *Up Jumped Spring*) performed by three different professional saxophonists. Each piece was performed at two different tempos. For each note in the training data, its perceptual features and contextual features were computed.

Results

There were a total of 792 notes available for each interpreter. We segmented each of the performed pieces in phases and obtain a total of 120 short phrases and 32 long phrases for each interpreter. The length of the obtained phrases and long phrases ranged from 5 to 12 notes and 40 to 62 notes, respectively. The expected classification accuracy of the default classifier (one which chooses randomly one of the three interpreters) is 33% (measured in correctly classified instances percentage). In the short phrase case, the average accuracy and the accuracy obtained for the most successful trained classifier was 97.03% and 98.42%, respectively. In the short long case, the average accuracy and the accuracy obtained for the most successful trained classifier was 96.77% and 98.07%, respectively. For comparative purposes, we have also experimented with 1-note phrases and have obtained poor results. The accuracy of the most successful classifier is 44.92%. This is an expected result since one note is clearly not sufficient for discriminating among interpreters. However, the results for short and long phrases are statistically significant which indicates that it is indeed feasible to train successful classifiers to identify interpreters from their playing style using the considered perceptual and contextual features. It must be noted that the performances in our training data were recorded in a controlled environment in which the gain level was constant for every interpreter. Some of the features (e.g., attack level) included in the perceptual description of the notes take advantage of this property and provide very useful information in the learning process.

Discussion

The difference between the results obtained in the case study and the accuracy of a baseline classifier, that is, a classifier guessing at random (33% in the case of the three-interpreter classification task) indicates that the perceptual and contextual features presented contain sufficient information to identify the studied set of interpreters, and that the machine learning methods explored are capable of learning performance patterns that distinguish these interpreters. It is worth noting that every learning algorithm investigated (decision trees, SVM, ANN, k-NN and the reported ensemble methods) produced significantly better than random classification accuracies. This supports our statement about the feasibility of training successful classifiers for the case study reported. However, note that this does not necessary imply that it is feasible to train classifiers for arbitrary performers.

We have selected three types of musical segment lengths: 1-note segments, short-phrase segments (4-12 notes), and long-phrase segment (30-62 notes). As expected, evaluation using 1-note segments results in poor classification accuracies, while short-phrase segments and long-phrase segment evaluation results in accuracies well above the accuracy of a baseline classifier. Interestingly, there is no substantial difference in the accuracies for short-phrase sand long-phrase segment evaluation which seems to indicate that in order to identify a particular performer it is sufficient to consider a short phrase segment of the piece, that is, the identification accuracy does not increase substantially by considering a longer segment.

FUTURE TRENDS

Given the capabilities of current audio analysis systems, we believe expressive-content-based performer identification is a promising research topic in music information retrieval. However, this area of study is still in its infancy and performance-based interpreter identification in a general setting is an extremely difficult task. The development of new signal processing techniques would certainly increase the generality of performance-based interpreter identification systems. One important reserch direction is the development of performance-based interpreter identification systems capable of dealing with polyphonic multi-intrument audio signals. We are currently investigating multi-instrument (sax, piano, double bass and drums) recordings by famous musicians. In this case, the input audio recordings have to be preprocessed in order to extract the melody (i.e., separate the saxophone) from the other instruments. Melody extraction is in general a complex task. In the context of this chapter, the melody extraction problem may be somehow simplified by taking into account some conditions often present in Jazz recordings. In many Jazz recordings, especially old recordings, the melody (in our case played by a saxophone) has higher loudness than the accompaniment and often the accompaniment consists of piano, bass and drums. Taking this in account, we have applied a monophonic fundamental frequency estimator to the audio recording in order to determine the predominant instantaneous pitch. This pitch usually corresponds to the pitch of the saxophone, because the sax is the predominant instrument (the one with higher loudness). We can consider that drums can be partially discarded by using a harmonic model, as it will be explained later, and the bass line can be removed considering only fundamental frequency candidates higher than a certain frequency. Discarding the piano components is a more difficult problem, but in the tested recordings the piano was usually playing chords with a lower loudness than the saxophone, so it normally does not mask the sax pitch. Once the fundamental frequency estimation was applied, we synthesized the harmonics that are multiples of the detected frequency in order

to obtain a monophonic audio containing only the saxophone melody. This process produces a lower quality saxophone sound compared with the original sound but still the resulting audio preserves important characteristics useful for distinguishing among different interpreters.

We employ a Sinusoidal plus Noise model which is able to decompose a sound into sinusoids plus a spectral residual signal (Serra, 1990). The analysis procedure detects partials by studying the time-varying spectral characteristics of a sound and represents them with time-varying sinusoids. These partials are then subtracted from the original sound and the remaining residual is represented as a time-varying filtered white noise component.

A short-time Fourier transform (STFT) is computed and the prominent spectral peaks are detected and incorporated into the existing partial trajectories by means of a peak continuation algorithm. A monophonic pitch detection step improves the analysis by using the fundamental frequency information in the peak continuation algorithm. Thus, the algorithm estimates the predominant fundamental frequency. The partials which are multiple of the fundamental frequency and have coherent trajectories are considered as sinusoids. The remaining components are considered as the residual part. Finally, the sinusoid components can be synthesized resulting on a monophonic signal. The STFT is performed using a Hamming window with 2048 samples, shifting it 256 samples before computing the next frame. By applying a harmonic analysis and taking into account continuous trajectories, we are able to remove most of the percussion components. The fundamental frequency detector is applied considering only the fundamental frequency candidates within the range 200Hz-1000Hz in order to discard the bass components. Once we have extracted the saxophone melody from the polyphonic recording, we can compute the note-level and the intranote-level descriptors in the same manner as described previously. Currently our saxophone separation method works only for a small subset of the polyphonic multi-intrument audio recordings. It remains a challenge the implementation of a more general method for obtaining the melody played by the saxophone from such recordings.

CONCLUSION

In this chapter we focused on the task of identifying performers from their playing style using note descriptors extracted from audio recordings. In particular, we concentrated in identifying Jazz saxophonists and explored and compared different machine learning techniques for this task. We characterized performances by representing each note in the performance by a set of perceptual features corresponding to the perceptual features of the note, and a set of contextual features representing the context in which the note appears. We presented successful classifiers for identifying saxophonists in recordings obtained in a controlled environment. The results obtained indicate that the perceptual and contextual features presented contain sufficient information to identify the studied set of interpreters, and that the machine learning methods explored are capable of learning performance patterns that distinguish these interpreters. We are currently extending our approach to performance-based interpreter identification in polyphonic multi-instrument audio recordings with encouraging preliminary results. We intend to pursue this research line. All in all, given the capabilities of current audio analysis systems obtained results, we believe expressive-content-based performer identification is a promising research topic in music information retrieval.

ACKNOWLEDGMENTS

This work was supported by the Spanish Ministry of Science and Education project ProSeMus (TIN2006-14932-C02-01). We would like to thank Esteban Maestre, Emilia Gomez, and Maarten Grachten for processing the data.

REFERENCES

Apel, W. (1972). *Harvard dictionary of music* (2nd ed.). Cambridge, MA: Belknap Press of Harvard University Press.

Bernstein, A. D., & Cooper E. D. (1976, July/August). The piecewise-linear technique of electronic music synthesis. *J. Audio Eng. Soc., 24*(6).

Bresin, R. (2002). Articulation rules for automatic music performance. In *Proceedings of the 2001 International Computer Music Conference*, San Francisco, California.

Canazza, S., De Poli, G., Roda, A., & Vidolin, A. (1997). Analysis and synthesis of expressive intention in a clarinet performance. In *Proceedings of the 1997 International Computer Music Conference* (pp. 113-120). San Francisco, California.

Cano, P. (1998). Fundamental frequency estimation in the SMS analysis. In *Proceedings of the Digital AudioEffects Workshop (DAFx)*, Barcelona, Spain.

Chauvin, Y. et al. (1995). *Backpropagation: Theory, architectures and applications.* Lawrence Erlbaum Assoc.

Colmenauer A. (1990). An introduction to PRO-LOG-III. *Communications of the ACM, 33*(7).

Cristianini N., & Shawe-Taylor J. (2000). *An introduction to support vector machines*. Cambridge University Press

Dannenberg, R. B., & Derenyi, I. (1998). Combining instrument and performance models for high-quality music synthesis. *Journal of New Music Research, 27*(3), 211-238.

Dannenberg, R. D., Pellerin, H., & Derenyi (1998). A study of trumpet envelopes. In *Proceedings of the International Computer Music Conference (ICMC)*, San Francisco, California.

Dovey, M. J. (1995). *Analysis of Rachmaninoff's piano performances using inductive logic programming*. European Conference on Machine Learning, Springer-Verlag.

Friberg, A., Bresin, R., Fryden, L., & Sunberg, J. (1998). Musical punctuation on the microlevel: Automatic identification and performance of small melodic units. *Journal of New Music Research, 27*(3), 217-292.

Friberg, A., Bresin, R., Fryden, L. (2000). Music from motion: Sound level envelopes of tones expressing human locomotion. *Journal of New Music Research, 29*(3), 199-210.

Gabrielsson, A. (1999). The performance of music. In D. Deutsch (Ed.), *The psychology of music* (2nd ed.) Academic Press.

Gomez, E., Gouyon, F., Herrera, P., & Amatriain, X. (2003). Using and enhancing the current MPEG-7 standard for a music content processing tool. In *Proceedings of the 114th Audio Engineering Society Convention*.

Herrera, P., & Bonada, J. (1998). Vibrato extraction and parameterization in the SMS framework. In *Proceedings of COST G6 Conference on Digital Audio Effects (DAFx)*. Barcelona, Spain.

Jenssen, K. (1999). Envelope model of isolated musical sounds. In *Proceedings of COST G-6 Workshop on Digital Audio Effects (DAFx)*, Trondheim.

Johnson, M. L. (1992). An expert system for the articulation of Bach fugue melodies. In D. L. Baggi (Ed.), *Readings in computer-generated music* (pp. 41-51). IEEE Computer Society.

Juslin, P. N. (2001). Communicating emotion in music performance: A review and theoretical framework. In P. N. Juslin, & J. A. Sloboda (Eds.), *Music and Emotion: Theory and Research*. Oxford University Press.

Kendall, R. A. & Carterette, E. C. (1990). The Communication of Musical Expression. *Musical Perception 8*.

Klapuri, A. (1999). Sound onset detection by applying psychoacoustic knowledge. In *Proceedings of the IEEE International Conference on Acoustics, Speech and Signal Processing, ICASSP*.

Lopez de Mantaras, R., & Arcos, J. L. (2002). AI and music, from composition to expressive performance. *AI Magazine, 23*, 3.

Maher, R. C., & Beauchamp, J. W. (1994). Fundamental frequency estimation of musical signals using a two-way mismatch procedure. *Journal of the Acoustic Society of America, 95*, 2254-2263.

McNab, R. J., Smith, L. l. A., & Witten I. H. (1996). Signal processing for melody transcription. (SIG Working Paper vol. 95-22).

Mitchell, T. M. (1997). Machine learning. Mc-Graw-Hill.

Narmour, E. (1990). *The analysis and cognition of basic melodic structures: The implication realization model.* University of Chicago Press.

Narmour, E. (1991). *The analysis and cognition of melodic complexity: The implication realization model.* University of Chicago Press.

Quinlan, J. R. (1993). *C4.5: Programs for machine learning.* San Francisco: Morgan Kaufmann.

Ramirez, R., & Hazan, A. (2005). In *Proceedings of the 18th Florida Artificial Intelligence Research Society Conference (FLAIRS 2005),* Clearwater Beach, Florida.

Ramirez, R., Hazan, A., Maestre, E., & Serra, X. (2006). A data mining approach to expressive music performance modeling. In *Multimedia data mining and knowledge discovery.* Springer.

Repp, B. H. (1992). Diversity and commonality in music performance: An analysis of timing microstructure in Schumann's "Traumerei". *Journal of the Acoustical Society of America, 104.*

Saunders C., Hardoon, D., Shawe-Taylor, J., & Widmer, G. (2004). Using string kernels to identify famous performers from their playing style. In *Proceedings of the 15th European Conference on Machine Learning (ECML'2004),* Pisa, Italy.

Seashore, C. E. (Ed.) (1936). *Objective analysis of music performance.* University of Iowa Press.

Serra, X., & Smith, S. (1990). Spectral modeling synthesis: A sound analysis/synthesis system based on a deterministic plus stochastic decomposition. *Computer Music Journal, 14*(4).

SMSTools. Retrieved May 26, 2007, from http://www.iua.upf.es/sms

Stamatatos, E., & Widmer, G. (2005). Automatic identification of music performers with learning ensembles. *Artificial Intelligence, 165*(1), 37-56.

Tobudic A., & Widmer, G. (2003). Relational IBL in music with a new structural similarity measure. In *Proceedings of the International Conference on Inductive Logic Programming.*

Todd, N. (1992). The dynamics of dynamics: A model of musical expression. *Journal of the Acoustical Society of America, 91.*

Van Baelen, E., & De Raedt, L. (1996). Analysis and prediction of piano performances using inductive logic programming. *International Conference in Inductive Logic Programming,* 55-71.

Widmer, G. (2002). Machine discoveries: A few simple, robust local expression principles. *Journal of New Music Research, 31*(1), 37-50.

Widmer, G. (2001). Discovering strong principles of expressive music performance with the PLCG rule learning strategy. In *Proceedings of the 12th European Conference on Machine Learning (ECML'01),* Freiburg, Germany.

Witten, I. H. (1999). Data mining, practical machine learning tools and techniques with JAVA implementation. Morgan Kaufmann Publishers.

Chapter VI
Tools for Music Information Retrieval and Playing

Antonello D'Aguanno
Universita degli Studi di Milano, Italy

Goffredo Haus
Universita degli Studi di Milano, Italy

Alberto Pinto
Universita degli Studi di Milano, Italy

Giancarlo Vercellesi
Universita degli Studi di Milano, Italy

ABSTRACT

State-of-the-art MIR issues are presented and discussed both from the symbolic and audio points of view. As for the symbolic aspects, different approaches are presented in order to provide an overview of the different available solutions for particular MIR tasks. This section ends with an overview of MX, the IEEE standard XML language specifically designed to support interchange between musical notation, performance, analysis, and retrieval applications. As for the audio level, first we focus on blind tasks like beat and tempo tracking, pitch tracking, and automatic recognition of musical instruments. Then we present algorithms that work both on compressed and uncompressed data. We analyze the relationships between MIR and feature extraction presenting examples of possible applications. Finally we focus on automatic music synchronization and we introduce a new audio player that supports the MX logic layer and allows users to play both score and audio coherently.

INTRODUCTION

This chapter deals with the state of the art of tools for music information retrieval (MIR) and playing.

First we focus on the symbolic level of music: some of the main models and techniques devel-oped up to now are introduced and analyzed. Three main approaches are discussed: functional, reductionistic, and structural. They all provide solutions for particular MIR situations and they are synergic to retrieval purposes.

We stress on the importance of identifying formal models in order to take into account the syntactic/semantic structures of musical data and the metric relationships between musical objects. In the context of structural similarity, we show that it is possible to extract some structural feature from the score that are invariant under a lot of standard and nonstandard musical transformations.

This section ends with an implementation of the model within the structural layer of MX, an IEEE standard XML language specifically designed to support interchange between musical notation, performance, analysis, and retrieval applications.

The second part deals with state of the art musical feature extraction. We make use of a bottom-up strategy. First we focus on three different blind tasks: beat and tempo tracking, pitch tracking, and automatic recognition of musical instruments; the attribute blind refers to the fact that these tasks deal with audio signals without paying attention to the symbolic information layer (score). Second we present the most useful algorithms which have proven to be most effective in solving these problems in general purpose situations, providing also an overview into specific task applications. These algorithms work both on compressed and uncompressed data; particular attention will be given to MPEG audio formats like AAC and MP3. We then introduce second level tasks, such as automatic genre extraction and score extraction, that make use of proprietary algorithms too, which will be described in the chapter. We analyze the relationships between MIR and feature extraction presenting examples of possible applications. Finally we focus on automatic music synchronization, a non-blind task on score and the corresponding audio performance, pointing out both solving algorithms and their applications in MIR, music playing, music education, and musicology. We introduce a new audio player that supports the MX logic layer and allows users to play both the symbolic score and the related audio file coherently, offering a new experience in music listening.

MUSICAL METRICS

Everyday experience tells us that the most outstanding music search engines deal with music-extraneous metadata like author's names, dates of publication, and so forth.

Music information retrieval (MIR) research has been producing numerous methods and tools, but the design of complete, usable working systems is still in its infancy (Hewlett & Selfridge-Field, 2005). The urgent need for such systems is strongly felt, in particular by cultural heritage institutions that possess large music holdings.

Up to date, different musical similarity metrics or similarity functions have been applied to music contents. As an example, this approach has been implemented in a software module which has been providing an effective environment for querying music scores in the Musical Archive Information System (MAIS) of the Italian theatre "Teatro Alla Scala" (Figure 1).

This module supports both standard and content-based queries in order to allow both metadata and semantic queries.

Musical Archive Information System is an integration of many research efforts developed at Laboratorio di Informatica Musicale (LIM). It is a system that allows to organize, manage, and utilize information of an heterogeneous set of music source material.

The main functionalities are database management and content data navigation. Database management allows the consultation of structured and unstructured multimedia information. Structured information is retrieved through traditional queries. Unstructured information is retrieved by nontraditional queries such as humming or playing of a melody (content queries). Content data navigation allows the nonsequential synchronized rendering of retrieved audio and score sources.

Three main modules compose the framework of this information system: a multimedia database, an archive of musical files, and a set of interfaces.

Figure 1. MAIS query environment: Functional metrics matching mode

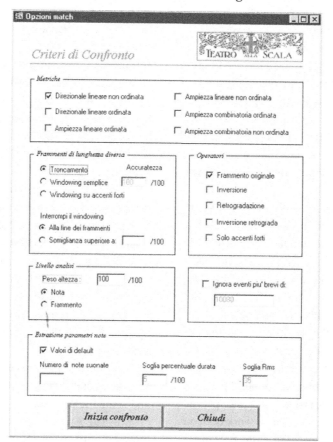

The multimedia database has been implemented with object relational technology.

Metadata, links to archive material and content indexes are stored as MAIS database objects.

Content indexes are musical features extracted from the source material in preprocessing phase. Furthermore, in this phase all the source material is analyzed for the automatic inclusion into the information system. The results are then included into a description XML file that works as an umbrella for the entire source files.

The approach adopted is typically functional, as we are going to describe in the next section.

In the query form (see Figure 1) is it possible to choose among different kind of functional metrics in order to allow different kind of content queries oriented to different musicological needs.

The Functional Approach

Functionalism is one of the most consolidated approaches in the treatment of music comparisons. In this context musical data (such as melodies, rhythms, spectra, etc.) are finite sequences of pitches, rhythms, and so forth, therefore distance concepts are inherited by metrics defined in functional spaces whose points are functions (Polansky, 1996).

Given two continuous real valued functions f(t) e g(t), defined on a subset of the real line

Figure 2. Comparison of melodic fragments using the functional model

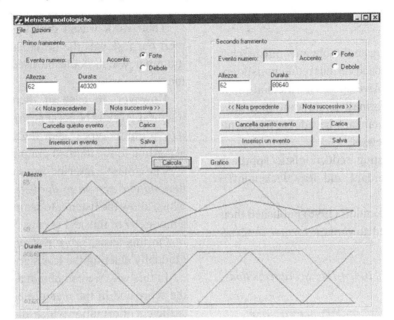

[m,n], it is possible to define different metrics; for example the maximal (sup) difference between the two functions or the "area" between the two functions viewed as curves:

$$d(f, g) = \sup\{|f(t) - g(t)|\}$$

and

$$d(f, g) = \int_n^m |f(t) - g(t)| dt$$

Generalizing the concept, it is possible to make an average of the higher order derivatives, like in the Sobolev metric:

$$d(f, g) = \sum_{i=0}^n \left[\sqrt{\int (f(t)^i - g(t)^i)^2} \right]$$

where *i* is the order of derivative.

This is a very interesting metric because it allows it to ignore differences between melodic sequences given by transpositions.

In fact, starting from *i=1* implicates the exclusion of the elements of *f* and *g*, so for example, transposition of melodic sequences have zero distance.

Reductionistic Approach

A typical mismatch of the functional approach leads to be too much "note sensitive" in the sense that themes with the same musical content may appear very different from a functional point of view.

As an example, in the following couple of themes, the second is a very simple variation of the first obtained by the introduction of a repeated "a" between couples of notes.

In order to mitigate the obvious mismatches typical of this approach various reductionistic approaches has been developed. This method aim to reduce musical information into some "primitive types" and then to compare the reduced fragments with functional metrics.

A very interesting reductionistic approach refers to Fred Lerdahl and Ray Jackendoff's studies.

Lerdahl and Jakendoff (1996) published their researches oriented towards a *formal descrip-*

Figure 5. J. S. Bach, B.A. 4,186: Score reductions

tion of the musical intuitions of a listener who is experienced in a musical idiom.

Their work wasn't directly related to MIR, their purpose was the development of a formal grammar which could be used to analyze any tonal composition.

However, in case of thematic fragments (themes), it would be possible to reduce the themes into "primitive types", showing formal similarities according to the defined grammar.

The aim is to describe, in a simplified manner, the *analytic system of the listener*, that is rules which allow the listener to segment and organize a hierarchy of musical events.

On this basis, *score reductions* are applied, gradually deleting the less significant events.

In this way we can obtain a simplification of the score and in the meantime we can preserve sufficient information which allows for maintaining recognizability.

The study of these mechanisms allows the construction of a grammar able to describe the fundamental rules followed by human mind in the recognition of the underlying structures of a musical piece.

In Figure 5 there is an example of score reductions provided by Lerdahl and Jackendoff (1996).

Figure 6. W.A. Mozart, KV 550: Correct analysis

Figure 7. W.A. Mozart, KV 550: Improbable correct analysis

In Figure 6 we provide an example of analysis based on the incipit of Mozart's Symphony in G Minor KV 550.

Grammar rules allow analysis such that sketched in Figures 7.a and 7.b.

Both analyses are grammatically correct but no musician would subscribe them.

The main difficulty with Lerdahl's and Jackendoff's work is that their view of music is overly simplified. Even with melodic themes numerous examples can be pointed out where different components of music form independent structures that overlap and cannot fit in only one hierarchy.

A musical theme does not submit to just one interpretation, and a piece of music with artistic value may call forth several independent and even contradictory sets of intuitions in an experienced listener.

The problem is that the preference rules cannot be used at all without a judgment by the analyst, and even the well-formed rules contain terms that are not formalized, for example "cadence" and "consonant".

The end result of this is that the theory cannot be expressed as a computer program that would analyze pieces by itself without any additional input by a human analyst.

The Structural Approach

Functional approaches are useful in a lot of different contexts but not, for example, for structural similarity queries, because they induce a lot of musically false-true due to the lack of an intrinsic structural coding.

In fact, how may be possible to find similarities among the melodic sequences of Figure 8?

In many contexts of musicological analysis, structural features are essential in order to find similarities among musical data. This raised the need for music information retrieval models oriented to structural information.

Here, the most important concept we are dealing with is transformations of themes.

Figure 8. Identically structured themes

A motif can be transformed in a great number of ways: the most important ones are rigid transformations, that is to say, one to one correspondences of the set of notes. However a theme could surely undergo transformations due, for example, to insertion of notes (passing tones, embellishments, etc.), as in the previous example.

Just to sketch the problem, look at the three themes in Figure 8. They sound actually similar even if, viewed as functions, they are quite different.

Nevertheless, from a structural point of view, they are undistinguishable as they are obtained by a simple permutation of notes.

So is evident that such similarities could not be looked at just like "mistakes".

Themes can undergo a lot of musical transformations: (rigid) standard ones are transpositions, inversions and retrogradations.

Now we sketch those transformations in the simple case, when the space of musical notes is the Z_{12} ring, in order to provide a brief tutorial to nonmusical experts.

Transposition (T) is the adding of a constant n to a given pitch class sequence: $T_n[x]=[x+n]$.

Given the theme in Figure 9, one of its transpositions can be seen in Figure 10.

Inversion (I) consists in a sign changement: $I[x]=[-x]$. The transposed inversion will be $T_nI[x]=[-x+n]$.

The (tonal) inversion of the theme shown in Figure 9 is shown in Figure 11.

Retrogradation (R) is the inversion of the temporal flow: given a pitch sequence $S=\{s_1,s_2...,,s_n\}$, its retrogradation R is the operator that maps S into $S^{-1}=\{s_n, s_{n-1}, \ldots, s_1\}$, $s_i \in Z_{12}$.

The retrogradation of the theme in example shown in Figure 9 is shown in Figure 12.

The class of nonstandard rigid musical transformations contains obviously all the *automorphism* of the pitch class set.

If we consider the 1-cycle permutation (A,E) the theme in example shown in Figure 9 becomes the theme shown in Figure 13.

The goal is to study a musical object "up to transformations" which preserve its inner structure, that is, the connections among notes (viewed as pitch, rhythm, or accent sequences).

A very useful trick in those situations is to find quantities related to the object that are *invariant* under particular transformation groups (Pinto, 2003).

In this context, we consider a structured set of themes (a database of indexes) and a theme (the query) which has to be compared with every set-element. The idea is to exploit the typical mathematical structure apt to formalize relations between objects, graphs, in order to build a representative graph for every theme and then work with graphs instead of themes.

In this way, is it possible to recognize a lot of relevant structural musical similarities and also to reduce the number of themes which should be compared.

So to summarize, the first step is the classification of themes by their representative graphs. The next step is mining graphs in a database isomorphic to the given one, and this can be done through graph invariants in order to reduce the computational cost of this operation; for a treatment of the isomorphism problem see for example Bollobas (1998) and Godsil and Royale (2001).

In Haus (2005) the graph-construction is throughout discussed for purely melodic sequences. A simple sketch of the graph construction is shown in Figure 14.

The notion of similarity function between graphs, which provide an estimation of the "distance" between two musical objects, is the following (for a throughout discussion see Buckley & Harary, 1990; Haus, 2005; Pinto, 2003).

Let M and M' be two music objects (for example melodic sequences) with representative graphs $G=G(M)$ and $H=H(M)$. Given $r \in N$ the r-order similarity function is

$$\sigma(M, M') = \sigma(G, H) = \max_\phi \sum_{i=1}^r \alpha_i \frac{|G| - |G \setminus H^i \setminus H^{i-1}|}{|G|}$$

Figure 9. Theme

Figure 10. Theme transposition

Figure 11. Tonal inversion of theme

Figure 12. Retrogradiation of theme

Figure 13. Theme after 1-cycle permutation

Figure 14. Graph representation of a melodic sequence

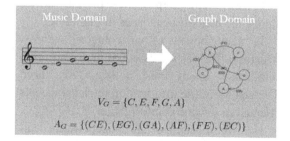

where $H^0 = \varnothing$, and the alpha coefficients are positive coefficients which depend upon the weights assigned to the different trail lengths in the power graphs H^i and phi varies among all the possible isometries of the vertex sets.

In the next section we introduce the MX environment that allows for handling of symbolic music and audio as well.

MX: AN XML MULTILAYER ENVIRONMENT FOR MUSIC

In MX music information is represented according to a multi-layered structure and to the concept of space-time construct. In fact, music information can be structured by a layer subdivision model, as shown in Figure 15.

Each layer is specific to a different degree of abstraction in music information: General, Structural, Music Logic, Notational, Performance, and Audio. Longari (2005) gives an exhaustive description of this format and the issue of the integration between MX and other formats is covered in Longari (2003).

The main advantage of MX is the richness of its descriptive features, which are based on other commonly accepted encodings aimed at more specific descriptions.

The multilayered music information structure is kept together by the concept of *spine*. Spine is a structure that relates time and spatial information (see Figure 16), where measurement units are expressed in relative format. Through such a mapping, it is possible to fix a point in a layer instance (e.g., Notational) and investigate the corresponding point in another one (e.g., Performance or Audio).

The *Structural* layer contains explicit descriptions of music objects together with their causal relationships, from both the compositional and musicological point of view, that is how music objects can be described as transformation of previously described music objects.

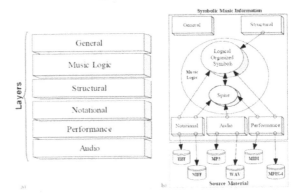

Figure 15. (a) Music information layers and (b) relations among them

An example of a particular structural object is Theme which represent exactly the concept of musical theme of the musical piece (or part of it) under consideration.

Theme objects may be whether the output of an automatic segmentation process (Haus, Longari, & Emanuele, 2004) or the result of a musicological analysis.

A content-based information retrieval method must take advantage of the presence of new metadata specifically oriented to retrieval in order to improve processes and algorithms.

Within IEEE WG on musical application of XML it is under development an XML language, named MX, specifically designed to support interchange between musical notation, performance, analysis, and retrieval applications.

The goal is the integration of audio and symbolic contents into the same framework through a search engine for music files that can handle standard XML music metadata (such as author, title, album, etc.) as well as new metadata provided by MX such as structural information, analysis, harmony, theme, melody, rhythm, and so forth, and structural audio features extracted from audio formats like PCM, MP3, and AAC.

MX Layers

XML organizes information in a hierarchic structure, so MX represents each layer as a secondary

Figure 16. Spine: Relationships between Notational, Performance and Audio layer

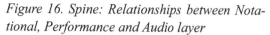

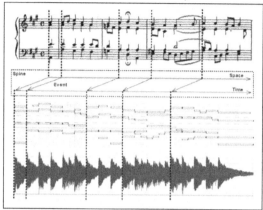

branch of the source element. The conceptual hierarchy is represented in Figure 15.We are not interested here in describing all MX layers, for a complete treatment of the subject, see for example Longari (2005).

We will limit our description to the *structural* layer.

```
<!ELEMENT mx (general, structural?,
             logic, notational?,
             performance?, audio?)
>
```

The *structural level* of information was developed in order to contain the explicit description of musical objects and their causal relationships, both from musicological and compositional points of view. That is to say, musical objects can be described as transformations of previously described musical objects.

Those objects are usually the results of segmentation processes made by different musicologists together with their own different musical points of view, or also by an automatic score segmenter like *Scoresegmenter* (Haus & Sametti, 1991; Haus & Pollastri, 2000).

At the moment there is not a definitive standard for this layer and efforts are especially directed towards the definition of a common acceptable standard.

In this framework it is evident that the introduction in this layer of MIR-oriented metadata, for example attributes of objects as **Theme** for music indexes, are extremely useful.

Below we list the part of DTD related to the structural layer which implements the concept of melodic theme.

Invariant Representation

In the code you may have noticed the introduction of melodic invariant quantities, such as **order**, **size,** and **complexity**, which are attributes of the object **Theme**: the same could be done for similar invariants related to the graphs derived from audio.

The inclusion-monotone graph invariants play an important role in the retrieval process and are necessary in order to avoid unproductive comparisons.

```
<!-- Structural Layer -->
<!ELEMENT structural (analysis*, PN*)>
<!-- Melodic themes -->
<!ELEMENT analysis (theme*, segment*,
                transformation*,
                relationship*)
>

<!ATTLIST theme
        id ID #REQUIRED
        ordinal CDATA #IMPLIED
        desc CDATA #IMPLIED
>
<!--
Desc attribute provides a textual descrip-
tion of the theme.
Ordinal attribute describes the possible
numeric characterization of the theme.
It should be encoded in roman numbers: I,
II, III, IV, V, etc (e.g. I and II themes
in a Sonata.)
-->

<!ELEMENT theme (occurrence+)>
<!ELEMENT occurrence (thm_desc?,
        thm_spine_ref+,
        transposition | inversion
        | retrogradation)*)
>
<!ATTLIST occurrence
        id ID #REQUIRED
>
```

Continued on following page

```
<!ELEMENT thm_spine_ref EMPTY>
<!--
This element is needed for generalization
of theme representation,
since there could be themes split in dif-
ferent sequences of notes belonging
to the same part or even to different
parts.
-->
<!ATTLIST thm_spine_ref
          spine_start_ref IDREF #REQUIRED
          spine_end_ref IDREF #REQUIRED
          part_ref IDREF #REQUIRED
          voice_ref IDREF #REQUIRED
>
<!ELEMENT thm_desc (#PCDATA)>
<!ELEMENT transposition EMPTY>
<!--
Interval is an integer number, indicates
the interval of transposition
and its interpretation is related to the type
attribute. When type is real interval
indicates the distance in semitones, oth-
erwise it indicates distance in tonal
scale.
-->
<!ATTLIST transposition
          type (real | tonal) #REQUIRED
          interval CDATA #REQUIRED
>
<!ELEMENT inversion EMPTY>
<!--
Staffstep attribute must have the same in-
terpretation as the staff_step
attribute of noteheads.
-->
<!ATTLIST inversion
          type (real | tonal) #REQUIRED
          staff_step CDATA #REQUIRED
>
<!ELEMENT retrogradation EMPTY>
<--
Invariants are quantities that refer to a
theme and do not vary
even if the theme is transformed by canoni-
cal transformations

-->

<!ELEMENT theme (invariants?)>
<!ELEMENT invariants (order, size, complex-
ity)>
<!ELEMENT order (#PCDATA)>
<!ELEMENT size (#PCDATA)>
<!ELEMENT complexity (#PCDATA)>
<!-- Petri Nets -->
<!ELEMENT PN EMPTY>
<!ATTLIST PN
          file_name CDATA #REQUIRED
>
<!-- Segments -->
<!ATTLIST relationship
          id ID #REQUIRED
```

```
          segmentAref IDREF #REQUIRED
          segmentBref IDREF #REQUIRED
          transformationref IDREF #RE-
QUIRED
>
<!ELEMENT relationship EMPTY>
<!ATTLIST segment
    id ID #REQUIRED
>

<!ELEMENT segment (segment_event+)>
<!ELEMENT transformation EMPTY>
<!ATTLIST transformation
          id ID #REQUIRED
          description CDATA #REQUIRED
          gis CDATA #IMPLIED
>
<!ATTLIST segment_event
          id_ref IDREF #REQUIRED
>
```

Those quantities, which depend upon the structural characteristics, are extremely useful to deal with musical objects together with all their possible transformations.

Example of a Melodic Sequence

In Figure 18 there is an example of an MX file and it is possible to identify the **general**, **structural**, and **logic** layers.

In the structural layer it is possible to identify the subelement **invariants** and its subelements **order**, **size**, and **complexity**.

THE ARCHITECTURE OF A MIR SYSTEM

In this section we introduce the architecture of a MIR system which exploits the MX language in order to handle different formats of music data.

The most innovative features of this MIR

Figure 17. Example: Notational layer

architecture is that it provides tools for efficient storage of structural musical data and for performing content-based queries on such data.

The overall architecture of the Musical Data Management module is illustrated in Figure 19.

```xml
<?xml version="1.0" encoding="UTF-8"?>
<mx>
  <general>
    <description>
      <movement_title>Inventio #4
      </movement_title>
    </description>
  </general>
  <structural>
    <themes>
      <theme id="theme0">
        <thm_spineref endref="v1_12"
            partref="part0" stafref="v1_0"
            voiceref="voice0" />
        <thm_spineref endref="v2_12"
            partref="part1" stafref="v2_0"
            voiceref="voice0" />
        <invariants>
          <order="7">
          <size="12">
          <complexity="54">
        </invariants>
      </theme>
    </themes>
  </structural>
  <logic>
    <spine>
    <event id="timesig_0" timing="0" hpos="0"/>
    <event id="keysig_0" timing="0" hpos="0"/>
    <event id="clef_0" timing="0" hpos="0"/>
    <event id="clef_1" timing="0" hpos="0"/>
    <event id="p1v1_0" timing="0" hpos="0"/>
    <event id="p1v1_1" timing="256" hpos="256"/>
    <event id="p1v1_2" timing="256" hpos="256"/>
    <event id="p1v1_3" timing="256" hpos="256"/>
    <event id="p1v1_4" timing="256" hpos="256"/>
    <event id="p1v1_5" timing="256" hpos="256"/>
    <event id="p1v1_6" timing="256" hpos="256"/>
    <event id="p1v1_7" timing="256" hpos="256"/>
    <event id="p1v1_8" timing="256" hpos="256"/>
    <event id="p1v1_9" timing="256" hpos="256"/>
    <event id="p1v1_10" timing="256" hpos="256"/>
    <event id="p1v1_11" timing="256" hpos="256"/>
    <event id="p1v1_12" timing="256" hpos="256"/>
    <event id="p2v1_0" timing="0" hpos="0"/>
    <event id="p2v1_1" timing="256" hpos="256"/>
    <event id="p1v1_13" timing="256" hpos="256"/>
    <event id="p2v1_2" timing="0" hpos="0"/>
    <event id="p2v1_3" timing="256" hpos="256"/>
    <event id="p1v1_14" timing="256" hpos="256"/>
    <event id="p2v1_4" timing="0" hpos="0"/>
    <event id="p2v1_5" timing="256" hpos="256"/>
    <event id="p1v1_15" timing="256" hpos="256"/>
    <event id="p2v1_6" timing="0" hpos="0"/>
    <event id="p2v1_7" timing="256" hpos="256"/>
    <event id="p1v1_16" timing="256" hpos="256"/>
    <event id="p2v1_8" timing="0" hpos="0"/>
    <event id="p2v1_9" timing="256" hpos="256"/>
    <event id="p1v1_17" timing="256" hpos="256"/>
    <event id="p2v1_10" timing="0" hpos="0"/>
    <event id="p2v1_11" timing="256" hpos="256"/>
    <event id="p1v1_18" timing="256" hpos="256"/>
    <event id="p2v1_12" timing="0" hpos="0"/>
    <event id="p1v1_19" timing="256" hpos="256"/>
    <event id="p1v1_20" timing="256" hpos="256"/>
    <event id="p2v1_13" timing="0" hpos="0"/>
    <event id="p1v1_21" timing="256" hpos="256"/>
```

```xml
    <event id="p1v1_22" timing="256" hpos="256"/>
    <event id="p2v1_14" timing="0" hpos="0"/>
    <event id="p1v1_23" timing="256" hpos="256"/>
    </spine>
  ...
</mx>
```

Figure 18. Embedding of MIR metadata in an XML environment

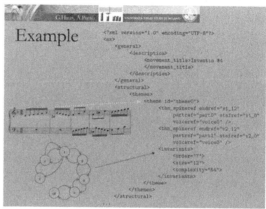

The module consists of two main environments: the Musical Storage Environment and the Musical Query Environment. The musical storage environment has the purpose of representing musical information in the database, to make query by content efficient. The musical query environment provides methods to perform query by content on music scores, starting from a score or an audio fragment given as input.

The matching between the input and the scores stored into DB is performed in several steps, graphically illustrated in Figure 19. The input can be either an audio file or a score fragment, played by the user on a keyboard or sung or whistled into a microphone connected to the computer (Haus & Pollastri, 2000).

- **Musical Storage Environment:** From the audio files, note-like attributes are extracted by converting the input into a sequence of note-numbers, that is, the concatenation of pitch and duration of each input note. Such a step is performed by the Symbolic Music Code Extractor module (Figure 19). The

Figure 19. General architecture

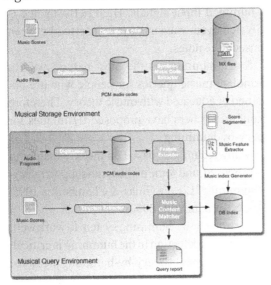

The processing phase is characterized also by other feature extraction techniques and parameters typical of audio processing. All those techniques will be analyzed in the next sections.

MUSICAL FEATURE EXTRACTION

A musical feature extraction system is a part contained in a MIR system that works requiring brute force and sophisticated signal-processing technology, which provides objective information about music content (Pachet, 2003).

This section will describe the common tasks performed by this system.

Pitch Tracking

conversion uses different pitch-tracking algorithms. If the input is entered from a keyboard or it is a score fragment, conversion is not necessary and the sequence can be directly built.

- **Musical Query Environment:** The Feature Extractor converts acoustic input first into an audio feature sequence and then into its related symbolic representation. Then the similarity function is computed.

The system we described allows to organize, manage, and utilize information of a heterogeneous set of music source material.

This work is an improvement of the information system described in the context of the "Teatro Alla Scala" project. The improvements regard the use of the graph model of musical data at different levels, the XML format for the representation of musical work and the new user interfaces for the navigation of musical source material.

Such a system takes advantage of organizing, managing, and utilizing information of a heterogeneous set of music source material through the XML multilayered structure.

The conventional fashion of organization of music collection using singer's names, album's name, or any other text-based manner is becoming inadequate for effective and efficient usage of the music collection for average users. People sometimes prefer to access the music database by its musical content rather than textual keywords. Content-based music retrieval has thus become an active research area in recent years.

Pitch extraction or estimation, more often called pitch tracking, is a simple form of automatic music transcription which converts musical sound into a symbolic representation (Martin, 1996; Scheirer, 1997).

The basic idea of this approach is quite simple. Each note of music (including the query) is represented by its pitch. So a musical piece or segment is represented as a sequence or string of pitches. The retrieval decision is based on the similarity between the query and candidate strings.

Pitch is normally defined as the fundamental frequency of a sound. To find the pitch for each note, the input music must first be segmented into individual notes. Segmentation of continuous music, especially humming and singing, is very difficult. Therefore, it is normally assumed that music is monophonic (produced using a single instrument) and stored as scores in the database. The pitch of each note is known. The common query input form is humming. To improve pitch tracking performance on the query input, a pause is normally required between consecutive notes.

There are two pitch representations. In the first method, each pitch except the first one is represented as pitch direction (or change) relative to the previous note. The pitch direction is either U(up), D(down) or S(similar). Thus, each musical piece is represented as a string of three symbols or characters.

The second pitch representation method represents each note as a value based on a chosen reference note. The value is assigned from a set of standard pitch values that is closest to the estimated pitch. If we represent each allowed value as a character, each musical piece or segment is represented as a string of characters. But in this case, the number of allowed symbols is much greater than the three that are used in the first pitch representation.

After each musical piece is represented as a string of characters, the final stage is to find a match or similarity between the strings. Considering that humming is not exact and the user may be interested in find similar musical pieces instead of just the same one, approximate matching is used instead of exact matching. The approximate matching problem is that of string matching with k mismatches. The variable k can be determined by the user of the system. The problem consists of finding all instances of a query string $Q = q1q2q3 \ldots qm$ in a reference string $R = r1r2r3 \ldots rn$ such that there are at most k mismatches (characters that are not the same). There are several algorithms that have developed to address the problem of approximate string matching (Wold et al., 1996).

Both the systems of Muscle Fish LLC (Wold et al., 1996) and the University Waikato produced good retrieval performance. But the perform-

ance depends on the accuracy of pitch tracking of hummed input signals. High performance is only achieved when a pause is inserted between consecutive notes.

Since humming is the most natural way to formulate music queries for people who are not trained or educated with music theory. Therefore many researchers have proposed techniques for query-by-humming.

Many techniques based on melody matching are proposed, and some of them can support query-by-humming (Logan, Ghias, & Chamberlin, 1995; Zhu & Kankanhalli, 2002).

For a query-by-humming system to work well, reliable pitch detection in the humming is critical. There are 2 types of query-by-humming methods: (1) the method based on music notes segmentation and matching; (2) and the method based on continuous pitch contour matching.

The first type of methods (Pollastri, 2002) requires the user to separate each music note with a short silence or hum with a particular syllable (such as "Da"). By such restrictions, it is assumed that each individual note can he accurately segmented by using signal energy. The pitch for the segmented note is then estimated. The restrictions, however, make the methods less practical for a real-world music retrieval system, since a user cannot always be aware of the note boundaries particularly when there are tied notes in the melody. Figure 20 illustrates the flow of such pitch detection method.

The second type of query-by-humming methods does not impose the above mentioned restrictions. The pitch value for each audio (a short time window) is estimated, and then melody is represented using a pitch contour, or a time series of pitch values with no music note identities.

Music retrieval is done by similarity matching of the pitch contours (Jang, 2001; Zhu, 2002). These approaches have shown a better performance than the first type of method. Although note segmentation error does not exist in this

Figure 20. Illustrates the flow of such pitch

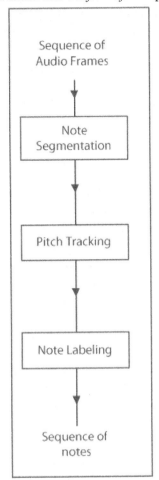

Figure 21. Illustrates the flow of such pitch

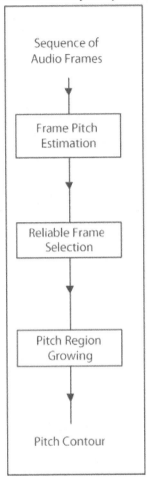

method, the reliable pitch detection for each frame is difficult due to various dynamics in the singer's voice, like pitch transitions and vocal registers. It can be a hard decision that whether an audio frame has a pitch and how reliable the detected pitch is. We have so far not seen a pitch detection method that is designed for this problem.

Zhu and Kankanhalli (2003) present a pitch tracking method for pitch contour extraction from humming voice, and propose a harmonic analysis technique to efficiently group partials of a harmony in the power spectrum. A harmonic energy can be computed to estimate the reliability of a pitch value for a frame. The pitch tracking method operates by initially finding the frames

with reliable pitch and subsequently finalizing the pitch detection of other frames.

Music and human voice are rich in harmonics. For a signal with a pitch there are quite a number of partials that are multiples of the fundamental frequency. The pitch is measured by the fundamental frequency; however, the fundamental frequency may not be outstanding in the power spectrum. The partials can then be explored for robust pitch detection. The proposed techniques analyze the harmonic structure for each audio frame (about 500 milliseconds). The analysis techniques can help determine whether there is pitch and what is the pitch in the signal. The analysis techniques

Figure 22. Illustrates the flow of such pitch

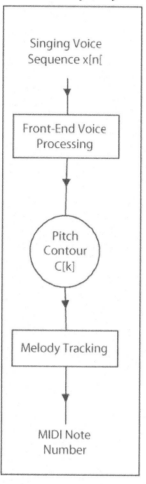

converts a pitch contour of singing voice to a sequence of music notes. The pitch of singing voice is usually much more unstable than that of musical instruments.

Furthermore, by adding on the transcription process, a heuristic music grammar constraints based on music theory, the error rate can be reduced to the lowest.

Beat/Tempo Tracking

In this section we will describe beat and tempo tracking contest; to define these contests we want to cite Simon Dixon (2001):

The task of beat tracking or tempo following is perhaps best described by analogy to the human activities of foot-tapping or hand-clapping in time with music, tasks of which average human listeners are capable. Despite its apparent intuitiveness and simplicity compared to the rest of music perception, beat tracking has remained a difficult task to define, and still more difficult to implement in an algorithm or computer program.

These algorithms should be able to estimate the tempo and the times of musical beats in expressively performed music. The input data may be either digital audio or a symbolic representation of music such as MIDI (Zoia, 2004).

This kind of program finds application in tasks like beat-driven real-time computer graphics, computer accompaniment of a human performer, lighting control, and many others. Tempo and beat tracking are directly implemented in MIR systems, in fact every song has a distinctive beat and metronome BPM.

It should be noted that these tasks are not restricted to music with drums; in fact the human ear can identify beats and tempo even if the song does not have a strong rhythmical accentuation. Obviously these tasks are more difficult in music without drums. The algorithms that implement tempo and beat tracking actually have less accuracy in music without drums.

include power spectrum analysis, peak grouping, and harmonic energy estimation.

Wang, Lyu, and Chiang (2003) describe a singing transcription system, which could he divided into two modules. One is for the front-end voicing processing, including voice acquisition, end-point detection, and pitch tracking, which deal with the raw singing signal and convert it to a pitch contour. The other is for the melody tracking, which maps the relatively variation pitch level of human singing into accurate music notes, represented as MIDI note number. The overall system block diagram can be shown as Figure 22.

The melody tracker is based on Adaptive Round Semitones (ARS) algorithm, which

In this contest it is difficult to point out the accuracy rate of the various algorithms because some widespread dataset and common methodological evaluation routine are not yet accepted. This situation is partly due to the choice of dataset, which often depends on the goals of the system (Dixon, 2001).

Various models have been proposed in order to extract the beat from performance data. The primary distinction we want to point out is between real-time and batch algorithms. For example automatic accompaniment systems have to use real-time algorithms. Transcription and analysis software tends to process data off-line, because rhythmically ambiguous sections can be frequently determined analyzing all the beat information found in the song. Thus the choice between real-time and off-line systems it is directly related to algorithm aim.

Actually the beat tracking system works on a two-stage model. The first stage is an onset detector, the second one is an interpretative system, which gets the onset detector output and tries to understand the tempo of the song and the correct beat position.

For music with drums to develop an onset detector system the simplest way is to high pass the signal and then clustering the filtered signal and introduce a threshold to the cluster energies. Obviously this trivial algorithm does not work very well, but it permits understanding that a drums beat has a spectral frequency with rich high components.

With the interpretative system, it is possible to find many different solutions like the agents model (Dixon, 2001; Goto, 2001), or probabilistic systems (Sethares, Sethares, & Morris, 2005) and so on.

We will present two different solutions to the interpretative problem that use the agents model.

In the next sections, four different tempo-beat tracking algorithms (one solely dedicated to tempo tracking) will be described. The algorithms

(Dixon 2001; Goto, 2001) work in PCM format, the algorithms presented in (D'Aguanno, Haus, & Vercellesi, 2006;Wang, & Vilernmo, 2001) are dedicated to MP3 standard.

The Goto Algorithm

The first algorithm was developed by Masataka and Goto (2001). This algorithm is based on the previous Goto and Marauroka (1998; 1999) works, one for music with drums and the other for music without drums. In Figure 23 is presented the algorithm scheme.

This algorithm describes a real-time beat-tracking system that can deal with the audio signals of popular-music compact discs in real time regardless of whether or not those signals contain drum sounds. The system can recognize the hierarchical beat structure comprising the quarter-note level (almost regularly spaced beat times), the half-note level, and the measure level (Goto, 2001)

The algorithm consists of two components: the first one extracts the musical elements from audio signals; the second component tries to understand the beat structure.

The first step detects three kinds of musical elements as the beat tracking cues:

- Onset times
- Chord changes
- Drum patterns

These elements are extracted from the frequency spectrum calculated with the FFT (1024 samples) of the input (16 bit / 22.05 kHz) using the Hanning window. The frequency spectrum is subdivided into seven critical bands. The onset times can be detected by a frequency analysis process that takes into account the rapidity of an increase in power and the power present in nearby time frequency bands. The results of this algorithm are stored in an onset-time vector. By using autocorrelation and crosscorrelation of the

Figure 23. Overview of the Beat tracking system proposed in (Goto, 2001)

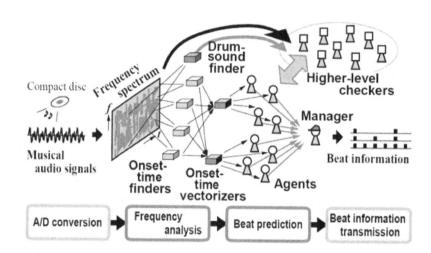

onset-time vectors, the model determines the inter-beat interval and predicts the next beat time. The output of this stage is the provisional beat times vector. The provisional beat times obtained is just a single hypothesis of the quarter-note level.

To calculate the chord-changes, the frequency spectrum is sliced into the point indicated by the provisional beat times component. In this point the dominant frequencies of the spectrum are estimated by using a histogram of frequency components. Chord-change possibilities are then obtained by comparing dominant frequencies between adjacent point indicated by the provisional beat times element.

The drum patterns are restricted to bass drum and snare. A drum-sound finder detects the onset time of the bass drum; the onset time of the snare is found using a noise detector.

The second step handled ambiguous situations when the beat-tracking cues are interpreted; a multiple-agent model in which multiple agents examine various hypotheses of the beat structure in parallel was developed. Each agent uses it's own strategy and makes various hypotheses. The agent manager gathers all hypotheses and then determines the final output on the basis of the most

reliable one. It should be noted in Figure 23 that the drums line is not mandatory, but it helps the algorithm furnishing more information.

In Figure 24 we present the algorithm results on music without drums and in Figure 25 we present the results on music with drums.

Goto (2001) proposes a quantitative measure of the rhythmic difficulty, called the *power-difference measure* (see also Goto (1999) for further information) that considers differences between the power on beats and the power on other positions. This measure is defined as the mean of all the normalized power difference ${diff}_{pow}(n)$ in the song:

Figure 24. Histogram for 40 songs without drum-sounds (Wang, 2001)

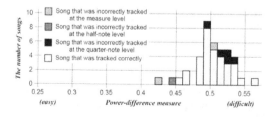

Figure 25. Histogram for 45 songs with drum-sounds (Wang, 2001)

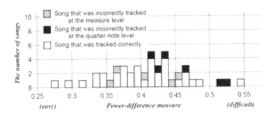

$$diff_{pow}(n) = 0.5 \frac{pow_{other}(n) - pow_{beat}(n)}{max(pow_{other}(n), pow_{beat}(n))} + 0.5$$

where $pow_{beat}(n)$ represents the local maximum power on the n-th beat and $pow_{other}(n)$ represents the local maximum power on positions between the n-th beat and $(n + 1)$-th beat. The power-difference measure takes a value between 0 (easiest) and 1 (most difficult). For a regular pulse sequence with a constant interval, for example, this measure takes a value of 0 (Goto, 2001).

The Dixon Algorithm

Dixon (2001) describes an audio beat tracking system using multiple identical agents, each of which represents a hypothesis of the current tempo and synchronization (phase) of the beat. The system works well for pop music, where tempo variations are minimal, but does not perform well with larger tempo changes. Dixon and Cambouropoulos (2000) extend this work to provide for significant tempo variations as found in expressive performances of classical music. They use the duration, amplitude and pitch information available in MIDI data to estimate the relative rhythmic salience (importance) of notes, and prefer that beats coincide with the onsets of strong notes. In this chapter, the salience calculation is modified to ignore note durations because they are not correctly recorded in the data. Processing is performed in two stages: tempo induction is performed by clustering of the time intervals between near note onsets, to generate the initial tempo hypotheses, which are fed into the second stage, and beat tracking, which searches for sequences of events which support the given tempo hypothesis. Agents perform the search. Any agent represents a hypothesized tempo and beat phase, and tries to match their predictions to the incoming data. The closeness of the match is used to evaluate the quality of the agents' beat tracking, and the discrepancies are used to update the agents' hypotheses. Multiple reasonable paths of action result in new agents being created, and agents are destroyed when they duplicate each other's work or are continuously unable to match their predictions to the data. The agent with the highest final score is selected, and its sequence of beat times becomes the solution (Dixon, 2001)

Beat Tracking in Compressed Domain

In order to better understand the rest of the section, a brief overview of the basic concepts about MP3 audio standard is provided. We focus on the Window-Switching pattern and its onset detector behaviour.

Further information about MPEG standards can be found in ISO/IEC 11172-3, ISO/IEC 13818-3, (Noll, 1997; Pan 1995).

MP3 uses four different MDCT window types: long, long-to-short, short, short-to-long indexed with 0,1,2,3 respectively. The long window, allows greater frequency resolution for audio signals with stationary characteristics, while the short one provides better time resolution for transients (Pan, 1995). In short blocks there are 3 sets of window values for a given frequency, in a window there are 32 frequency sub bands, further subdivided into 6 finer sub bands by MDCT. Three short windows are then grouped in one granule. The values are ordered by frequency, then by window. The switch between long and short blocks is not instantaneous. The two-window type long-to-short and short-to-long serves to transition between long and short window types. Because

Figure 26. The comparison between song waveform (gray) and its corresponding MP3 window-switching pattern (black line). Horizontal axis is the MP3 granule index. The four window types (long, long-to-short, short and short-to-long) are indexed with 0, 1, 2 and 3 respectively. The metronome template is represented by black line with -1 peaks (D'Aguanno et al., 2006).

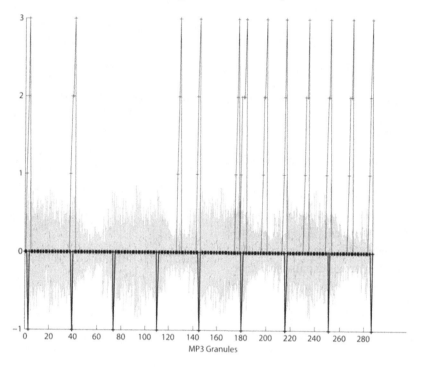

MDCT processing of a subband signal provides better frequency resolution, it consequently has poorer time resolution. The quantization of MDCT values will cause errors that are spread over the long time window so it is more likely that this quantization will produce audible distortions. Such distortions usually manifest themselves as pre-echo because the temporal masking of noise occurring before a given signal is weaker than the masking of noise afterward (Pan, 1995; Zhaorong 2001). This situation appears frequently in music, with strong drum lines, when the drummer plays snare or bass drum and then the Window-Switching Pattern may be used as simple onset detector with a high threshold.

Wang and Vilermo (2001) propose the Window-Switching Pattern (WSP) as information to refine the output of an MDCT\footnote{Modified

Discrete Cosine Transform} coefficient analysis in a beat tracking contest in order to perform better error concealment for music transmission in a noisy channel. The algorithm extracts the subband MDCT coefficients and than it calculates any subband energy. A search window is defined. The basic principle of onset selection is setting a proper threshold for the extracted subband energy values. The local maxima within a search window, which fulfils certain conditions, are selected to be beat candidates. This process is performed in each band separately. Than the WSP identified by the encoder is used to refine the MDCT analysis. The algorithm extracts the subband MDCT coefficients and then it calculates any subband energy. A Statistical model selects the correct beat from the beat candidate set.

D'Aguanno et al. (2006) presents a template matching technique (based on WSP only) to reach a general-purpose tempo tracker on music with drums. Because the WSP is structured coherently with the drum line, it is possible to compare this pattern with a simple template made up by a vector filled with 0 and with a 1 value where is a metronome beat. Any elements of this array represent an MP3 granule. This array has to be matched with the WSP found by the MP3 encoder. An estimation function is required. This function has to yield the distance between the metronome template examined and the real MP3 window-switching pattern. In figure 26 the metronome template is represented by the darkest line with -1 peak. Any peak is a metronome beat. In this figure is clear the WSP structure is coherent with song time even if the song has a very complex drums line.

A first implementation reached a correct BPM recognition in the 50% songs and in another 30% it is possible to estimate the correct BPM by the program results. The algorithm fails in the 20% of the songs. These values come from an experimentation finalized to demonstrate the WSP capabilities. Obviously the WSP alone is not sufficient to act like a beat tracker, but it is adequate to solve a tempo tracking contest.

Score Extraction

Score extraction can be defined as the act of listening to a piece of music and to write down the score for the musical events that constitute the piece. This implies the extraction of specific features out of a musical acoustic signal, resulting in a symbolic representation that comprises notes, pitches, timings, dynamics, timbre, and so on.

The score extraction task is not simple and intuitive like beat tracking. People without musical education find this task very difficult and they are not be able to perform it. The automatic transcription of music is a well-understood prob-

lem just for monophonic music. To transcribe monophonic music many solution algorithms have been proposed, including time-domain techniques based on zero-crossing and autocorrelation, as well as frequency frequency-domain based on the discrete Fourier transform and the cepstrum (Brown, 1992; Brown & Puckette 1993; Brown & Zhang, 1991). These algorithms proved to be reliable and commercially applicable. In polyphonic music transcription the situation is not so positive. These results are not so encouraging because of the increased complexity of the signals in question. It should be noted that score extraction is a composed task. In fact, we can subdivide this problem in a set of different tasks: pitch tracking to get information about the notes, beat tracking to understand the correct rhythmical figures, source separation to separate a single instrument part from the other, timbre extraction to understand which instruments have to be insert in the score, and so on. Many algorithms have been proposed to solve the problem constrained to monotimbrical music (i.e., a piano score with many voices simultaneously). These algorithms are very similar to the algorithm presented in section *Pitch Tracking* using the same low-level feature extractor but with a second stage dedicated to interpret the low-level results. The low-level features are often identified with the term "midlevel representation". A good mid-level representation for audio should be able to separate individual sources, be invertible in a perceptual sense, reduce the number of components, and reveal the most important attributes of the sound. Current methods for automatic music transcription are often based on modeling the music spectrum as a sum of harmonic sources and estimating the fundamental frequencies of these sources. This information constitutes an ad hoc midlevel representation. In order to successfully create a system for automatic music transcription, the information contained in the analyzed audio signal must be combined with knowledge of the structure of music (Klapuri, 2004).

Genre Extraction

Musical genres are categorical descriptions that are used to characterize music in music stores, radio stations, and now on the Internet. Although the division of music into genres is somewhat subjective and arbitrary, there are perceptual criteria related to the texture, instrumentation, and rhythmic structure of music that can be used to characterize a particular genre. Humans are remarkably good at genre classification as investigated in Pachet and Cazaly (2000) where it is shown that humans can accurately predict a musical genre based on 250 milliseconds of audio. This finding suggests that humans can judge genres using only the musical surface without constructing any higher level theoretic descriptions as has been argued in Davis and Mermelstein (1980). Up to now genre classification for digitally available music has been performed manually. Therefore techniques for automatic genre classification would be a valuable addition to the development of audio information retrieval systems for music.

Cook (2002) addresses the problem of automatically classifying audio signals into a hierarchy of musical genres. More specifically, three sets of features for representing timbral texture, rhythmic content, and pitch content are proposed. Although there has been significant work in the development of features for speech recognition and music-speech discrimination, there has been relatively little work in the development of features specifically designed for music signals. Although the timbral texture feature set is based on features used for speech and general sound classification, the other two feature sets (rhythmic and pitch content) are new and specifically designed to represent aspects of musical content (rhythm and harmony). The performance and relative importance of the proposed feature sets is evaluated by training statistical pattern recognition classifiers using audio collections collected from compact disks, radio, and the Web. Audio signals can be classified into a hierarchy of music genres, augmented with speech categories. The speech categories are useful for radio and television broadcasts.

Both whole-file classification and real-time frame classification schemes are proposed. Cook (2002) identifies and reviews two different approaches to Automatic Musical Genre Classification. The first approach is prescriptive, as it tries to classify songs in an arbitrary taxonomy, given a priori. The second approach adopts a reversed point-of-view, in which the classification emerges from the songs.

- **Prescriptive approach:** it makes the same assumption that a genre taxonomy is given and should be superimposed on the database of songs. They all proceed in two steps:
  - **Frame-based feature extraction:** the music signal is cut into frames, and a feature vector of low-level descriptors of timbre, rhythm, and so forth is computed for each frame.
  - **Machine learning/classification:** a classification algorithm is then applied on the set of feature vectors to label each frame with its most probable class: its "genre." The class models used in this phase are trained beforehand, in a supervised way.

The features used in the first step of automatic, prescriptive genre classification systems can be classified in three sets: timbre related, rhythm related, and pitch related.

There have been numerous attempts at extracting genre information automatically from the audio signal, using signal processing techniques and machine learning schemes.

- **Similarity relations approach:** the second approach to automatic genre classification is exactly opposite to the prescriptive approach just reviewed. Instead of assuming that a genre taxonomy is given a priori, it tries to emerge a classification from the database, by clustering songs according to a given measure of similarity. While the prescriptive approach adopts the framework of supervised learning, this second point-of-view is unsupervised. Another important difference is that in the first approach, genre classifications are considered as natural and objective, whereas in this approach it is similarity relations which are considered as objective.

AUDIO-SCORE AUTOMATIC SYNCHRONIZATION

Music language is made up of many different and complementary aspects. Music is the composition itself, as well as the sound a listener hears, and is the score that a performer reads as well as the execution provided by a computer system.

The encoding formats are commonly accepted and employed and often characterized by a partial perspective of the whole matter: they describe data or metadata for score, audio tracks, computer performances of music pieces, but they seldom encode all these aspects together. Nowadays, we have at our disposal many encoding formats aimed at a precise characterization of only one (or few) music aspect(s). For example, MP3, AAC, and PCM formats provide ways to encode audio recordings; MIDI represents—among other things—a well known standard for computer—driven performance; TIFF and JPEG files can result from a scanning process of scores; NIFF, Enigma, Finale formats are aimed at score typing and publishing.

The first problem to face is finding a comprehensive way to encode all these different aspects in a common framework, without repudiating the accepted formats. An important advantage of such effort is keeping together all the information related to a single music piece, in order to appreciate the richness of heterogeneous representations of music (aural, visual, logical, structural descriptions). But this key advantage has an interesting consequence: the possibility to create a strongly interconnected and synchronized environment to enjoy music. The purpose of our MXDemo is illustrating the full potentialities of an integrated approach to music description.

This goal can be achieved thanks to three cooperating elements:

- A comprehensive XML-based format to encode music in all its aspects.
- A software environment aimed to the integrated representation. The software application will provide a graphic interface to read, watch, and listen to music, keeping the different levels synchronized.
- An automatic system to synchronize music score and the related audio signal.

About point number one, some examples of XML-based formats used to encode music are presented in Haus and Longari (2002) and Roland (2002). They are not discussed in this section.

About the second one, Kurth, Muller, Ribbrock, Roder, Damm, and Fremerey (2004) propose a generic service for realtime access to context-based music information such as lyrics or score data. In our Web-based client-server scenario, a client application plays back a particular (waveform) audio recording. During playback, the client connects to a server which in turn identifies the particular piece of audio as well as the current playback position. Subsequently, the server delivers local, that is, position specific, context-based information on the audio piece to the client. The client then synchronously displays the received information during acoustic playback. Kurth et al. (2004) demonstrates how such a service can be established using recent MIR (Music Information Retrieval) techniques such as audio identification and synchronization.

Baraté (2005) proposes the MXDemo, a stand-alone software which illustrates the full potentialities of an integrated approach to music description. In order to solve the third point, all present approaches to score-to audio synchronization proceed in two stages: in the first stage, suitable parameters are extracted from the score and audio data streams making them comparable; in the second stage, an optimal alignment is computed by means of dynamic programming (DP) based on a suitable local distance measure.

Turetsky et al. [§7], first to convert the score data (given in MIDI format) into an audio data stream using a synthesizer. Then, the two audio data streams are analyzed by means of a short-time Fourier transform (STFT) which in turn yields a sequence of suitable feature vectors.

Based on an adequate local distance measure permitting a pairwise comparison of these feature vectors, the best alignment is derived by means of DTW. The approach of Soulez, Rodet, and Schwarz (2003) is similar to Turetsky et al. [§7] with one fundamental difference: In Turetsky et al. [§7], the score data is first converted into the much more complex audio format—in the actual synchronization step the explicit knowledge of note parameters is not used. Contrary to Soulez et al. (2003) who explicitly uses note parameters such as onset times and pitches to generate a sequence of attack, sustain and silence models which are used in the synchronization process. This results in a more robust algorithm with respect to local time deviations and small spectral variations.

Since the STFT is used for the analysis of the audio data stream, both approaches have the following drawbacks:

Firstly, the STFT computes spectral coefficients which are linearly spread over the spectrum resulting in a bad low-frequency resolution. Therefore, one has to rely on the harmonics in the case of low notes. This is problematic in polyphonic music where harmonics and fundamental frequencies of different notes often coincide. Secondly, in order to obtain a sufficient time resolution one has to work with a relatively large number of feature vectors on the audio side. (For example, even with

a rough time resolution of 46 ms as suggested in Turetsky et al. [§7] more than 20 feature vectors per second are required.) This leads to huge memory requirements as well as long running times in the DTW computation.

In the approach of Arifi (2004), note parameters such as onset times and pitches are extracted from the audio data stream (piano music). The alignment process is then performed in the score-like domain by means of a suitably designed cost measure on the note level. Due to the expressiveness of such note parameters only a small number of features is sufficient to solve the synchronization task, allowing for a more efficient alignment. One major drawback of this approach is that the extraction of score-like note parameters from the audio data—a kind of music transcription—constitutes a difficult and time-consuming problem, possibly leading to many wrongly extracted audio features. This makes the subsequent alignment step a delicate task.

Muller, Kurth, and Roder (2004) present an algorithm, which solves the synchronization problem accurately and efficiently for complex, polyphonic piano music. In a first step, they extract from the audio data stream a set of highly expressive features encoding note onset candidates separately for all pitches. This makes computations efficient since only a small number of such features are sufficient to solve the synchronization task. Based on a suitable matching model, the best match between the score and the feature parameters is computed by dynamic programming (DP). To further cut down the computational cost in the synchronization process, they introduce the concept of anchor matches, matches which can be easily established. Then the DP-based technique is locally applied between adjacent anchor matches.

REFERENCES

Bollobás Béla (1998). *Modern graph theory*. New York: Springer-Verlag.

Brown, J. C. (1992). Musical fundamental frequency tracking using a pattern recognition method. *Journal of the Acoustical Society of America, 92*(3), 1394-1402.

Brown J. C., & Puckette, M. S. (1993). A high resolution fundamental frequency determination based on phase changes of the fourier transform. *Journal of the Acoustical Society of America, 94,* 662-667.

Brown, J. C., & Zhang, B. (1991). Musical frequency tracking using the methods of conventional and narrowed autocorrelation. *Journal of the Acoustical Society of America, 89*(5), 2346-2354.

Buckley, F., & Harary, F. (1990). *Distance in graphs.* Redwood City: Addison-Wesley.

Clausen, M., Kurth, F., Muller, M., & Arifi, V. (2004). *Automatic synchronization of musical data: A mathematical approach.* MIT Press.

D'Aguanno, A., Haus, G., & Vercellesi, G. (2006). Mp3 window-switching pattern preliminary analysis for general purposes beat tracking. In *Proceedings of the 120th AES Convention*, Paris, France.

Davis, S., & Mermelstein, P. (1980). Experiments in syllable-based recognition of continuous speech. IEEE Trans. Acoust., Speech, Signal Processing (vol. 28, pp. 357-366).

Dixon, S. (2001). An empirical comparison of tempo trackers. In *Proceedings of the 8th Brazilian Symposium on Computer Music.*

Dixon, S. (2001). Automatic extraction of tempo and beat from expressive performances. *Journal of New Music Research, 30*(1), 39-58.

Dixon, S., & Cambouropoulos, E. (2000). Beat tracking with musical knowledge. In *Proceedings of the 14th European Conference on Artificial Intelligence*, pages 626-630.

Godsil, C., & Royle, G. (2001). Algebraic graph theory. *Vol. 207. Graduate texts in mathematics.* Springer Verlag.

Goto, M., & Muraoka, Y. (1998). Music understanding at the beat level real-time beat tracking for audio signals. D. F. Rosenthal & H. G. Okuno (Eds.), *Computational auditoryscene analysis* (pp. 157-176).

Goto, M., & Muraoka, Y. (1999). Real-time beat tracking for drumless audio signals: Chord change detection for musical decisions. *Speech Communication, 27*(34), 311-335.

Goto, M. (2001). An audio-based real-time beat tracking system for music with or withoutdrumsounds. *Journal of New Music Research, 30*(2), 159 - 171.

Haus, G., & Longari, M. (2002). Towards a symbolic/tim-based music language based on xml. In *Proceedings of the First International IEEE Conference on Musical Applications Using XML (MAX2002).*

Haus, G., & Longari, M. (2005). A multi-layered, timebased music description approach based on xml. *Computer Music Journal, 29*(1), 70-85.

Haus, G., & Pinto, A. (2005). *A graph theoretic approach to melodic similarity* (vol. 3310).

Haus, G., & Pollastri, E. (2000). *A multimodal framework for music inputs.* Poster session presented at ACM Multimedia, pages 382-384.

Haus, G., & Sametti, A. (1991). Scoresynth: A system for the synthesis of music scores based on petri nets and a music algebra. *IEEE Computer, 24*(7), 56-60.

Haus, G, Longari, M., & Emanuele, P. (2004). A score-driven approach to music information retrieval. *JASIST, 55*(12), 1045-1052.

Haus, G., Ludovico, L. A., Vercelesi, G., & Barate' A. (2005). Mxdemo: A case study about audio, video, and score synchronization. In *Proceedings of IEEE Conference on Automatic Production of Cross Media Content for Multi-Channel Distribution (AXMEDIS)* (pp. 45-52).

Hewlett, W. B., & Selfridge-Field, E. (2005). *Music query*. Cambridge: MIT Press.

ISO/IEC International Standard IS 11172-3. Information technology - coding of moving pictures and associated audio for digital storage media at up to about 1.5 mbits/s - part 3: Audio.

ISO/IEC International Standard IS 13818-3. Information technology - generic coding of moving pictures and associated audio, part 3: Audio.

Klapuri, A. P. (2004). Automatic music transcription as we know it today. *Journal of New Music Research, 33*(3), 269-282.

Kurth, F., Muller, M., Ribbrock, A., Roder, T., Damm, D., & Fremerey, C. (2004). *A prototypical service for real-time access to local context-based music information*. Barcelona, Spain: ISMIR.

Lee, H., Jang, J. R., & Kao, M. (2001). Content-based music retrieval using linear scaling and branch-and-bound tree search. In *Proceedings of IEEE International Conference on Multimedia and Expo*.

Lerdahl, F., & Jackendoff, Ray. (1996). *A generative theory of tonal music*. Cambridge: MIT Press.

Logan, J., Ghias, A., & Chamberlin, D. (1995). Query by humming. In *Proceedings of ACM Multimedia, 95*, 231-236.

Longari, M. (2004). *Formal and software tools for a commonly acceptable musical application using the XML language*. Unpublished doctoral thesis, Università degli Studi di Milano, Milano, IT 20135. Also available as Università degli Studi di Milano, Department of Computer Science Report.

Martin, K. D. (1996). *Automatic transcription of simple polyphonic music: Robust front end processing* (Tech. Rep. No. 399). M.I.T. Media Laboratory Perceptual Computing Section.

Muller, M., Kurth, F., & Roder, T. (2004). Towards an efficient algorithm for automatic score-to-audio synchronization. In *Proceedings of the 5th International Conference on Music Information Retrieval*, Barcelona, Spain.

Noll, D. (1997). Mpeg digital audio coding. *IEEE Signal Processing Magazine, 14*(5), 59-81.

Pachet, F., & Cazaly, D. (2000). A classification of musical genre. In *Proceedings of the RIAO Content-Based Multimedia Information Access Conference*.

Pachet, F. (2003). Content management for electronic music distribution. *Commun. ACM, 46*(4), 71-75.

Pan, D. (1995). A tutorial on mpeg/audio compression. *IEEE Multimedia, 2*(2), 60 - 74.

Pinto, A. (2003). Modelli formali per misure di similarità musicale. Master's thesis, Universit'a degli Studi di Milano, Milano I 20135. Also available as Università degli Studi di Milano, Department of Mathematics Report.

Polansky, L. (1996). Morphological metrics. *Journal of New Music Research, 25*, 289-368.

Pollastri, E. (2002). A pitch tracking system dedicated to process smging voice for music retrieval. In *Proceedings of IEEE International Conference on Multimedia and Expo*.

Roland, P. (2002). The music encoding initiative (mei). In *Proceedings of the First International IEEE Conference on Musical Applications Using XML (MAX2002)*.

Scaringella, N., & Zoia, G. (2004). A real-time beat tracker for unrestricted audio signals. In *Proceedings of the SMC'04 Conference*, Paris, France.

Scheirer, E. D. (1997). Using musical knowledge to extract expressive performance information from audio recordings. In *Proceedings Readings in Computational Auditory Scene Analysis.*

Sethares, J. C., Sethares, W. A., & Morris, R. D. (2005). Beat tracking of musical performances using low-level audio features. *IEEE Transactions On Speech and Audio Processing, 13*(2), 275-285.

Soulez, F., Rodet, X., & Schwarz, D. (2003). Improving polyphonic and poly-instrumental music to score alignment. In *Proceedings of the 4th International Conference on Music Information Retrieval* (pp. 143-148).

Tian, Q., Zhu, Y., & Kankanhalli, M. (2002). Similarity matching of continuous melody contours for humming querying of melody databases. In *Proceeedings of the International Workshop on Multimedia Signal Processing.*

Tzanetakis, G., & Cook, P. (2002). *Musical genre classification of audio signals.*

Wang, C., Lyu, R., & Chiang, Y. (2003). A robust singing melody tracker using adaptive round semi-tones (ars). In *Proceedings of the 3rd International Symposium on Image and Signal Processing and Analysis,* (pp. 549-554).

Wang, Y., & Vilermo, M. (2001). A compressed domain beat detector using mp3 audio bitst,reams. In *Proceedings of the 9th ACM International Conference on Multimedia* (pp. 194-202). Ottawa, Canada.

Weibei, D., Zhaorong, H., & Zaiwang, D. (2001). New window-switching criterion of audio compression. In *Proceedings of the Multimedia Signal Processing, 2001 IEEE Fourth Workshop,* (pp. 319-323), Cannes, France.

Wold, E. et al. (1996). Content-based classification, search, and retrieval of audio. *IEEE Multimedia, 3*(3), 27-36.

Zhu, Y., & Kankanhalli, M. S. (2003). Robust and efficient pitch tracking for query-by-humming. Information, Communications and Signal Processing, 2003 and the Fourth Pacific Rim Conference on Multimedia. In *Proceedings of the 2003 Joint Conference of the Fourth International Conference* (pp. 1586-1590).

Section III
P2P and Distributed System

Chapter VII
Collaborative Use of Features in a Distributed System for the Organization of Music Collections

Ingo Mierswa
University of Dortmund, Germany

Katharina Morik
University of Dortmund, Germany

Michael Wurst
University of Dortmund, Germany

ABSTRACT

Today, large audio collections are stored in computers. Their organization can be supported by machine learning, but this demands a more abstract representation than is the time series of audio values. We have developed a unifying framework which decomposes the complex extraction methods into their building blocks. This allows us to move beyond the manual composition of feature extraction methods. Several of the well-known features, as well as some new ones, have been composed automatically by a genetic learning algorithm. While this has delivered good classifications it needs long training times. Hence, we additionally follow a metalearning approach. We have developed a method of feature transfer which exploits the similarity of learning tasks to retrieve similar feature extractions. This method achieves almost optimal accuracies while it is very efficient. Nemoz, an intelligent media management system, incorporates adaptive feature extraction and feature transfer which allows for personalized services in peer-to-peer settings.

INTRODUCTION

Collecting and playing music has become a primary use of personal computers and large digital music libraries offer services to the public. Private collections often consist of about 10,000 audio files. Hence, the *organization* of collections has become an issue. The large central music stores organize and index their collections according to artist, album, song as expressed by metadata. Also, users apply this organization principle. However, there are far more structuring styles to be observed. A user study showed that several categories are used to structure a private collection (Jones, Cuuningham, & Jones, 2004). Another one observes that hierarchical structures (taxonomies) are used. Remarkably, the study states that all the users had a folder for music which does not fit the structure (Vignoli, 2004). In a student project, we received 39 different hierarchical organizations for the same music collection (Homburg, Mierswa, Möller, Morik, & Wurst, 2005). We also experienced that there were leftover nodes in the taxonomies where the students no longer wanted to annotate the music, or where they could not make up their mind where to put a song. Beyond the well-studied classification into genres, there seems to be a need of automatically classifying music into individual, hierarchical structures.

Observations of users also indicate a retrieval task beyond searching for a particular song. Users search for yet unknown music which might be interesting (Aucouturier & Pachet, 2002). New music which fits a user's taste is most often recommended by friends, as was clearly stated by an empirical analysis of (music) information seeking behavior (Lee & Downie, 2004). Recommending music is a retrieval task in its own right with a link to social networks (friend of a friend) (Celma, Ramirez, & Herrera, 2005), also marked as sociocultural aspect (Baumann, Pohle, & Shankar, 2004). For the structuring of music, the co-occurrence in personal collections was found the most useful ground truth (Berenzweig, Logan, Ellis, & Whitman, 2003). This, again, stresses the *collaborative* nature of building up private music collections. Another empirical study shows that—in addition to searching for a particular song— users want to browse through collections of other users (Taheri-Panah & MacFarlane, 2004). The Nemoz system allows users to browse through the collection of another user in a peer-to-peer network (Aksoy, Burgard, Flasch, Kaspari, Lüttgens, Martens, & Möller, 2005). In addition to simply looking at the collection, the extra service of what we called "goggling" allows users to look at the other collection through their "own glasses". This enables users to discover new, interesting music according to their own taste. It moves beyond finding yet another song of a favorite artist. Each user has its own taxonomy which stores the personal collection. We exploit the structure of these taxonomies in order to guide a tour through the media collections of other users. This ensures that users navigate through other media collections in a similar way like they navigate through their own collection. More technically spoken, the learner classifiers used to automatically sort songs into the own taxonomy are applied to another user's collection.

The service of classifying songs automatically into the user's taxonomy is rather straight-forward from a user's point of view. An intelligent music management system inputs the user's taxonomy and a set of music files— the not yet tagged ones from their own collection or from that of another user. The system outputs the set of music pieces together with tags, which correspond to the user's taxonomy. From a technical point of view, this is not at all straight-forward. The system needs to learn the implicit classification of the user. Considering each taxonomy node (i.e., tag) a class and the songs which are stored at that node (i.e., labeled by the tag). To its members, this looks like the standard machine learning task of classification. Each audio file is represented by a set of random variables, such as X, that describe features of this audio file. Y is another random variable that denotes to which class the audio file belongs. These obey a fixed, but unknown probability distribution $Pr(X, Y)$. The objective of *classification* is to find a function $h(X)$ which predicts the value of Y. The major challenge in audio classification, and the reason why the user's requirements are hard to fulfill, is to find those features of *X* which allow the program to perform the prediction with high accuracy.

A large variety of features for audio data were proposed in the literature (e.g., Pampalk, Flexer, & Widmer, 2005; Tzanetakis, 2002; Tzanetakis & Cook, 1999). However, it has been shown in several investigations that there does not exist one set of features which is well suited for all tasks. For instance, clustering rock music requires completely different features than does clustering music according to the mood (Pohle, Pamplak, & Widmer, 2005). Even in genre classification, for two different data sets different feature sets perform better (Lidy & Rauber, 2005). As will be shown later (Section 4.5), classifying user preferences requires a different feature set for each user. Personal taxonomies are far from being standardized. We cannot even hope to achieve an appropriate common feature set for the classification into diverse user taxonomies— even if we would tailor our feature extractions in a tremendous effort. The principled problem is that the particular data set and taxonomy cannot be foreseen so that there is no standard data set for which a feature set could be developed. Hence, we see one opportunity, namely to use machine learning for the construction of the feature set itself.

Following this idea, we propose a framework consisting of two main ideas: first, we systemize all basic methods of feature extraction and introduce a new concept of constrained combinations, namely *method trees*. We will then discuss how these method trees can be automatically found by means of a genetic programming approach. Second, we observe that this approach, although it delivers very accurate feature sets and classifiers, is very time consuming and we propose a solution for this problem by transferring successfully created feature sets to other, similar learning tasks.

After a more detailed overview of related research, we present a unifying framework which decomposes the complex feature extractions into their building blocks (Section 3). This allows us to automatically learn a feature set for a certain classification-learning task (Section 4). Since learning feature sets for learning classifiers is computationally demanding, we exploit its result for new, similar classifier learning tasks. Instead of training the feature extraction anew, we transfer feature sets to similar classification tasks (Section 5). The new measure of similarity of learning tasks is interesting also for those who want to manually tailor feature extraction to a new classification task, quickly. Finally, in Section 6, we come back to the user's requirements and illustrate the use of learning feature extraction and transferring features by the Nemoz system, a peer-to-peer music management system.

RELATED RESEARCH

The automatic organization of music collections into a hierarchical structure often uses self-organizing maps (SOMs) (Kohonen, 1988). The islands of music, for instance, organizes music into regions of a map taking into account a fixed set of features (Pampalk, 2001, Pampalk, Dixon, & Widmer, 2004). Due to their pleasant visualization, SOMs are used to build intelligent user interfaces to large collections (Rauber, Pampalk, & Merkl, 2002). The burden of structuring a collection is handed over to the system when applying SOMs. However, this also means that personal aspects are not taken into account. A first step towards personalization is the approach of Baumann and colleagues (Baumann, Pohle, & Shankar, 2004). They use feedback of users in order to adjust their clustering. In addition to audio features they use lyrics and cultural metadata. Where we share the goal of hierarchical organization, we rely on audio features only. Moreover, we want to include the taxonomies which the users have built. Instead of replacing the user-made structures, we aim at enhancing them automatically.

Feature extraction for audio classification is the dominant issue investigated in the proceedings of conferences and workshops about music information retrieval. Since 1998 (Liu, Wang, & Chen, 1998; Tzanetakis, 2002; Zhang & Kuo, 1998), an ever increasing set of feature extractions has been developed. There are still new features proposed even for the genre classification task (Pampalk et al., 2005). We expect that there will never be the complete and appropriate feature set for all tasks. Hence, we do not participate in the effort of constructing new features manually, but have machine learning methods constructing features for us. Funny enough, our first publication on automatic extraction of audio features (Mierswa & Morik, 2005) was not perceived as it was meant to. Readers cited this publication as the presentation of a new feature type, namely features in the phase space. This state space reconstruction is included in our general framework of building blocks for feature construction in order to complete the general basis transformations. In fact, it delivers good results sometimes. However, our aim is far more challenging, namely to automatically adapt feature construction to a classification task at hand. In the following, we will describe this automatic process, where phase space features are just another building block which might be combined with other building blocks.

Computational support in constructing features usually means a library of mathematical functions, for instance using MATLAB (Pampalk et al., 2004). System support is also included in the MARSYAS system, but it is fixed to 30 feature extractions in version 1.0 and 80 feature extractions in version 2.0 (Bray & Tzanetakis, 2005; Tzanetakis & Cook, 1999,). Also libraries of some known feature extractions are made publicly available, for example, in the ACE and the jAudio system (McEnnis, McKay, Fujinaga, & Depalle, 2005; McKay, Fiebrink, McEnnis, Li, & Fujinaga, 2005). The YALE environment with its audio and value series plug-in moves beyond this library approach[1] (Fischer, Klinkenberg,

Figure 1. The machine learning environment YALE includes a plugin containing all described building blocks and methods for feature extraction together with operators for machine learning and model evaluation

Mierswa, & Ritthoff, 2002). It does not publish a set of complex feature extractions, but offers a set of building blocks for feature construction (cf. Section 3). A large variety of machine learning algorithms including all WEKA algorithms is provided to users. It allows users to run experiments which automatically construct a feature set for a certain learning task and performance measure (Section 4). The YALE user chooses which classification learner the user wants to couple with the automatic feature extraction in the experiment. Since the output is in standard representation, it cannot only be used by the YALE environment, but also by other learning environments. Hence, the support in running a learning experiment does not prescribe a particular classification learner. In contrast, the user is in complete control of designing the experiment (see Figure 1).

Our claim that feature extraction needs to be adapted to a particular classification task and dataset is supported by the extensive comparison of seven feature sets in Mörchen, Ultsch, Nöcker, and Stamm (2005). They eagerly enumerate

66,000 audio features from the space of features which could be constructed using YALE. Then, they evaluate the contribution of each feature to the classification task at hand. This tremendous effort is rewarded by the best performance of this tailored feature set when compared to fixed feature sets. It is interesting that the general-purpose feature set of Tzanetakis ranks in the middle of the feature sets, where a feature set adapted to a *different* classification task performs the worst. General-purpose features cannot achieve the best performance in all tasks. Tailoring to one classification task also means to fail in other, different ones. Most likely, their hand-tailored feature set would fail in another classification task. Without noticing, the authors provide another justification for the need of automatic adaptive feature construction.

To the best of our knowledge, in addition to YALE there exists only one approach, the EDS, to automatic feature construction (Zils & Pachet, 2004). Developed at the same time, the two systems are similar in the tree structure of feature extractions, its XML representation format, and the choice of genetic programming for the construction. However, the fitness function of EDS and YALE differ. EDS employs a heuristic score which evaluates the composition of operators (building blocks) independent of the classification task for which the features are to be extracted. In contrast, we use the performance of classification learning as the fitness function for evolving feature construction. Therefore, the YALE feature construction adapts rigorously to the classification task at hand. Also the method of growing the tree of feature extractions differs. Their procedure is similar to that of a grammar producing well-formed sentences. EDS instantiates a set of general patterns. We shall describe the YALE procedure in detail below (Section 4).

The choice of the method for classifier learning seems to have less impact on the result than has the chosen feature set. Primarily we use the support vector machine (SVM) as did, for example, Maddage, Xu, and Wang (2003), Mandel and Ellis (2005), and Meng and Shawe-Taylor (2005).

Recently, some authors embed music information retrieval into a peer-to-peer (p2p) setting (Wang, Li, & Shi, 2002). Despite the run-time advantages, we see the support of user collaboration as the crucial advantage and have developed the Nemoz system as a p2p system. Tzanetakis and colleagues have pushed forward this view (Tzanetakis, Gao, & Steenkiste, 2003):

"One of the greatest potential benefits of p2p networks is the ability to harness the collaborative efforts of users to provide semantic, subjective and community-based tags to describe musical content."

A UNIFYING FRAMEWORK FOR FEATURE EXTRACTION

Audio data are time series, where the y-axis is the current amplitude corresponding to a loudspeaker's membrane and the x-axis corresponds to the time. They are univariate, finite, and equidistant. We may generalize the type of series which we want to investigate to *value series*. Each element x_i of the series consists of two components. The first is the *index component*, which indicates a position on a straight line (e.g., time). The second component is a m-dimensional vector of values which is an element of the *value space*.

Definition 1 *A* VALUE SERIES *is a mapping* $x : \mathbb{N} \rightarrow \mathbb{R} \times \mathbb{C}^m$ *where we write* x_n *instead of* $x(n)$ *and* $(x)_i \in \{1,...,n\}$ *for a series of length n.*

This general definition covers time series as well as their transformations. All the methods described in the following refer to value series. They are of course not only applicable to audio data, but to value series in general. The usage of a complex number value space instead of a real number value space allows a convenient way to use basis transformations like the Fourier transformation. Finally, the introduction of the index component allows both equidistant and nonequidistant value series.

The value series cannot be directly used as representation for classification learners since the number of values is usually too large and the interaction of values is not adequately represented. Therefore, only a small set of features is derived from the raw series data, which are then used by the classification algorithm. In this section[2], we propose a principled view of the building blocks from which audio features are constructed from series data. Later on, this systematization will allow us to flexibly construct sequences in an automatic way.

Basis Transformations

Basis transformations map the data from the given vector space into another space. Audio data—like all univariate time series—are originally elements of the vector space $\mathbb{R}^2$. The basis B of a vector space V is a set of vectors which can represent all vectors in V by their linear combination. The only required operation on vector spaces as the domain of transformations is the scalar product. Since the most common basis transformation performed on audio data is the transformation into the infinite space of harmonic oscillations we assume *Hilbert spaces*.

Definition 2 *Let H be a vector space with an inner product* $\langle f, g \rangle$. *H is called* HILBERT SPACE *if the norm defined by* $|f| = \sqrt{\langle f, f \rangle}$ *turns H into a complete metric space, i.e. any Cauchy sequence of elements of the space converges to an element in the space.*

The assumption of Hilbert spaces is no constraint, because all finite-dimensional spaces with a scalar product (such as Euclidean space with ordinary scalar product) are Hilbert spaces. However, we use Hilbert spaces with an infinite number of dimensions to introduce the concept of Fourier transformations. Therefore, we need an infinite-dimensional Hilbert space of functions.

Definition 3 *Let P be a Hilbert space. If the elements* $f \in P$ *are functions, P is called a* FUNCTION SPACE.

Example 1 *The set of all functions* $f : \mathbb{R} \to \mathbb{R}$ *with a finite integral*

$$\int_{-\infty}^{\infty} f^2(x)dx$$

together with the inner product

$$\langle f, g \rangle = \int_{-\infty}^{\infty} f(x)g(x)dx$$

form a well known function space: L^2.

Figure 2. Overlay of two curves, $v_1 = 2Hz$, $a_1 = 3$ and $v_2 = 8Hz$, $a_2 = 1$, shown left in time space, right in frequency space after a Fourier transformation.

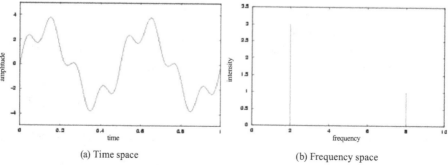

(a) Time space   (b) Frequency space

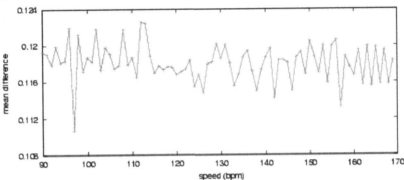

Figure 3. Autocorrelation differences for a phase shift depending on speeds ranging from 90 to 170 beats per minute

The goal of *Fourier analysis* is to write the series $(x_i)_{i \in \{1,...,n\}}$ as a (possibly infinite) sum of multiples of the given base functions, which are e^{ivx} for all frequencies v. A Fast Fourier Transformation (Cooley & Tukey, 1965) maps the given time space into this frequency space and is valid for audio data (Figure 2). The frequency space is a special case of a function space. Therefore, the transformation uses the infinite number of complex valued dimensions of a Hilbert space. Complex numbers are necessary because Fourier transformations actually deliver two values: the intensity of occurring frequencies and the phase shifts.

The frequency space expresses a sort of correlation between values in terms of frequencies. For some features it would be more appropriate to express the correlation in terms of time dependencies. Therefore, the transformation into another space is used.

Definition 4 *The calculation of correlations of values between two points in time, i and i + k, produce the* CORRELATION SPACE, *where for each lag k their correlation coefficient in (-1,+1) is indicated.*

Transforming audio data into the correlation space eases the recognition of the speed of the music, measured in beats per minute. Assuming T is the number of beats per measure and SR the sampling rate. If we shift the original time series by $shift = T \cdot SR \cdot 60 / Z$ for several values of Z we can determine the correlation between the original and the shifted time series. Maximal correlation corresponds to minimal difference between the shifted and the original series. Figure 3 shows the differences of original values with the shifted ones. Clearly, the difference at 97 beats per minute is minimal.

Nonlinear dynamic systems can be described with the aid of nonlinear differential equations. The number of variables, which must be known to completely describe the behavior of such a system, corresponds to the number of dimensions of this system. These variables are called *state variables*.

Definition 5 *The basis of the* STATE SPACE *of a dynamic system is given by the* STATE VARIABLES *of the system, that is, the variables which must be known to describe the system. The elements of a state space represent the values of the state variables at the examined (time) points.*

The *state space* emphasizes characteristics which can hardly be seen in the original space. Since the state variables are often unknown, a topologically equivalent space is constructed (Takens, 1980). This is known as *reconstruction of state space.*

Figure 4. Phase space representation of a popular song (left) and a classical piece (right)

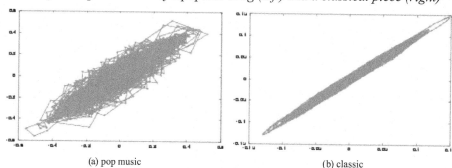

(a) pop music   (b) classic

Figure 5. Intervals found in the index dimension are summarized.

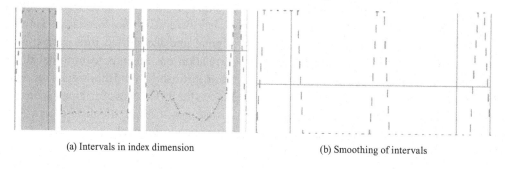

(a) Intervals in index dimension   (b) Smoothing of intervals

Definition 6 *Vectors within* PHASE SPACE *are constructed, where the components are parts of the original series:*

$$p_i = (x_i, x_{i+d}, x_{i+2d}, ..., x_{i+(m-1)d})$$

where d is the delay, and m the dimension of the phase space. The set

$$P_{d,m} = \{p_i \mid i = 1, ..., n - (m-1)d\}$$

is the phase space representation of the original series $(xi)_{i \in \{1,...,n\}}$.

Within the phase space, several features can be extracted, for example, the angles between vectors. Small variances of angles indicate smooth changes of the state variables, large variances harsh changes. This is a dominant feature when separating classic from the more percussive pop music as shown in Figure 4.

Basis transformations most often are reversible, because only the basis, not the position of the elements is changed. In contrast, if intervals in the index dimension are used, the transformation is not reversible. If, for instance, we summarize the original series by some time intervals and assign a value to each interval, the transformed series has still the same number of elements but fewer different values (see Figure 5 for illustration). We will discuss some possible ways to detect intervals in different dimensions of a value series in Section 3.3.

Filters

Filters transform elements of a series to another location within the same space. Moving average and exponential smoothing, for instance, are filters. Many known transformations are subsumed by weighting functions. We consider the window functions Bartlett, Hanning, Hamming, Blackman-Harris, linear and exponential functions as particular instances of a function $f_w(i)$ which weights the position within the window.

Definition 7 *Given a value series* $(x_i)_i \in \{1,...,n\}$, *a filter* $y_i = f_w(i) \cdot x_i$ *is a* WEIGHT FILTER. *The weighting function* f_w *only depends on the position i.*

Other filters are the frequency passes, filtering the extremes, the Bark-filter, and the ERB filter, which are all often used when analyzing music data.

Mark-Up of Intervals

In analogy to mark-up languages for documents, which annotate segments within a text, also segments within a value series can be annotated.

Definition 8 *A* MARK-UP $M : S \rightarrow C$ *assigns an arbitrary characteristic C to a segment S.*

We define special instances of mark-up by assigning characteristic value types to intervals in one of the dimensions of the considered space.

Definition 9 *An* INTERVAL $I : S \rightarrow C$ *is a mark-up within one dimension. The segment* $S = (d,s,e)$ *is given by the dimension d, the starting point s, and the end point e. The characteristic* $E = (t, \rho)$ *indicates a type t and a density* ρ.

Often clustering (e.g., k-means) is used in order to detect suitable intervals (Hastie, Tibshirani, & Friedman, 2001). A clustering scheme is only usable in dimensions with a nonequidistant value distribution. Additionally, clustering in one or several dimensions is a batch process to be applied to the complete series. An incremental process is the signal to symbol process (Morik & Wessel, 1999):

Signal to symbol processing:

- Given the series $(x_i)_i \in {}_{\{1,...,n\}}$ with *n* values, a decision function f_e and an interval dimension,

Figure 6. The process of finding intervals in a series (a), first in the value dimension (b), then projected on the index dimension (c), delivering (d).

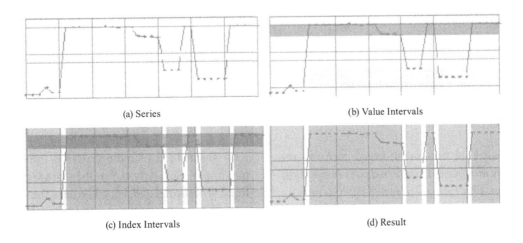

(a) Series	(b) Value Intervals
(c) Index Intervals	(d) Result

- Initialize the interval counter with $t = 1$, start a new interval I_t and add the first point.
- For the remaining points of the series, do:
  1. If $f_e(I_{t,xi}) = 1$, then add x_i to the current interval I_t.
  2. Else close I_t, increase t by 1, and add x_i to the new I_t.

Typical examples of the decision function f_e refer to the gradient, delivering characteristics such as, for example, *increase, decrease*. Signal to symbol processing is applied to the index dimension (time). If intervals have already been found in the value dimension, these can be used to induce intervals in the index dimension. For instance, whenever an interval change in the value dimension has been found, the current interval in the index dimension is closed and a new one is started. Figure 6 illustrates this combination.

Generalized Windowing

Many known operators on times series involve windowing. Separating the notion of windows over the index dimension from the functions applied to the values within the window segment allows it to construct many operators of the kind.

Definition 10 *Given the series* $(x_i)_{i \in \{1,...,n\}}$, *a transformation is called* WINDOWING, *if it shifts a window of width w over* $(x_i)_{i \in \{1,...,n\}}$, *using a step size s and evaluates in each window the function F:*

$$y_j = F(x_i)_{i \in \{j \cdot s + 1, ..., j \cdot s + w\}}$$

All y_j *together form again a series:*

$$(y_j)_{j \in \{0,...,\lfloor (n-w)/s \rfloor\}}$$

Definition 11 *A windowing which performs an arbitrary number of transformations in addition to the function F is called* GENERAL WINDOWING.

The function F summarizes values within a window and thus prevents general windowing from enlarging the data set too much. Since the size of audio data is already rather large, it is necessary to consider carefully the number of data points which is handled more than once.

Definition 12 *The* OVERLAP *of a general windowing with step size s and width w is defined as g = w / s.*

Only for windowings with overlap $g = 1$ the function can be omitted. Such a windowing performs transformations for each window and is called *piecewise filtering*.

Combining general windowing with the mark-up of intervals allows consideration at each interval being a window. This results in an adaptive window width w and no overlap, that is, $g = 1$. Of course, this speeds up processing considerably.

Functions

Transformations convert a series into another series. In contrast, functions calculate single values from a series. The group of functions includes all kinds of statistics like different averages, variance and standard deviation. They refer to the value dimension. We may also consider the index dimension, for instance, the point with the largest value or highest amplitude. Often used functions are those indicating peaks.

Definition 13 (*k*-**Peaks function**) *The k-peak function delivers for a series* $(x_i)_{i \in \{1,...,n\}}$ *the position (index dimension), the height, and the width of the k largest peaks.*

It is an instance of finding extremes (minimum, maximum). Similarly, the gradient of a regression line can be formulated. For audio data, the spectral

Figure 7. Constructing the mel-frequency cepstral coefficients method from elementary extraction operators. Solid arrows show the data flow; dashed lines define the tree structure.

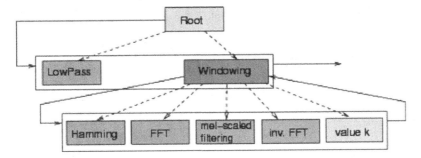

flatness measure or the spectral crest factor can be expressed as an arithmetic combination of simple functions (Jayant & Noll, 1984).

From Low-Level to High-Level Features

In this chapter, we discussed most of the current methods to work on series data and grouped them into transformations (basic transformations and filters) and functionals. In the next chapter, we will see how this systematization will help to constraint the search space for automatic feature extraction methods. Before we describe this automatic process we would like to point out that these basic feature extraction methods can be combined to form more complex features. As an example we describe how the *mel-frequency cepstral coefficients* can be constructed as a general windowing, where the frequency spectrum of the window is calculated, its logarithm is determined and a psychoacoustic filtering is performed, and the inverse Fourier transformation is applied to the result. Figure 7 shows how the methods for feature extraction are put together to compute the cepstral coefficients. From these coefficients additional features can be extracted. It is easy to see how variants of this series can be generated, for example, replacing the frequency spectrum and its logarithm by the gradient of a regression

line. In the next chapter, we will describe the concept of method trees like the one depicted in Figure 7 and we will also see how these method trees can automatically constructed for a given learning task.

Similar to the tree for mel-frequency cepstral coefficients more complex trees for high-level features could be constructed. For example, other trees exist calculating the used chroma vector in a time window of a song. The set of high-level features is only limited by the set of basic extraction methods. If a basic feature is absolutely necessary for the high-level feature method tree, but it is not part of the method repository than the corresponding high-level feature cannot be constructed. This can usually be fixed easily by adding the necessary basic extraction method to the used method repository.

AUTOMATIC CONSTRUCTION OF FEATURE EXTRACTION METHODS

The elementary methods described earlier can be manually combined in order to construct more complex features for classification tasks. Figure 7 already showed how elementary methods could be used for the reconstruction of known complex feature extraction methods. There are many more complex feature extraction methods which can

Figure 8. A method tree for feature extraction built of elementary methods. Solid arrows show the data flow, dashed lines define the tree structure

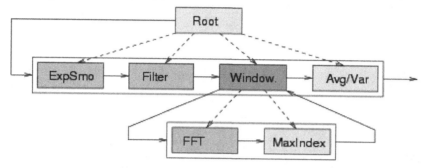

be built using the framework described above (Section 3). For instance, the general windowing may apply a Fourier transformation so that the peaks of the transformed series can be related with windows in time:

$$y_j = \max_{index}(FT(\{x_i\}_{i \in \{j \cdot s + 1, ..., j \cdot s + w\}}))$$

The result is a value series, where the value of y_j denotes the highest frequency for each window. From this series, the average and variance is built, yielding a good feature for the separation of techno and pop music—the variance is greater in pop music.

It is rather cumbersome to find such combinations that perform well for a classification task. We are looking for chains of method applications. Moreover, there might be some windowing within which such chains are applied. The search space is too large to be inspected manually. Hence, *genetic programming* is applied in order to look for the best combination of methods (Holland, 1986; Koza, 1992). The result is a complex method tree. Its use for the classifier learning will be shown in experiments (Sections 4.4 and 4.5).

In order to structure the huge search space, we may separate functions, chains of method applications, and general windowing, where a chain of method applications is applied to each window.

Definition 14 *A* CHAIN *consists of an arbitrary number of transformations and a function at the end.*

A function is a chain with no transformations. It has the length 1. A longer chain consists of some transformations followed by a function. In

Figure 9. Overall process of automatic feature construction for classification

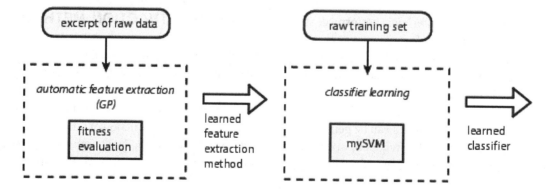

Figure 10. Automatic feature extraction using genetic programming

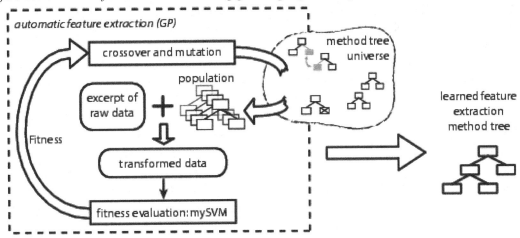

any case, a chain delivers one value. Incorporating windowings leads to the concept of method trees:

Definition 15 *A* METHOD TREE *is a general windowing whose children build a chain. If the chain entails a windowing, this becomes the root of a new, embedded method tree.*

The methods, which are performed on each window, can be seen as children of the windowing operator. Together they output a value series. The tree structure emerges from the nesting of windowing operators.

An example of a method tree is shown in Figure 8, where the root identifies the element within the search space. Its four children are exponential smoothing, a filtering, another method tree consisting of the chain just described (Fourier transformation with peaks applied to windows), and the average of the peaks. This last child returns the desired features. Before the genetic programming approach is technically described, Figure 9 presents the process of automatically extracting features for a given classification task and data set.

The search space within which the best method tree is to be found is called the universe of method trees. Evolutionary algorithms in general search in such a universe by maintaining populations of elements in this universe. Hence, a population is a set of (different) method trees. The navigation

Figure 11. XML method tree representation for YALE.

```
<operator name="Root" class="ValueSeriesPreprocessing">
  <operator name="Chain 1" class="OperatorChain">
    <operator name="ExpSm" class="ExponentialSmoothing" />
    <operator name="Filter" class="FilterTransformation" />
    <operator name="Windowing" class="Windowing">
      <parameter key="overlap"  value="2"/>
      <operator name="Chain 2" class="OperatorChain">
        <operator name="FFT" class="FastFourierTransform" />
        <operator name="MaxIndex" class="MaxIndexPoint" />
      </operator>
    </operator>
    <operator name="Avg" class="AverageFunction" />
  </operator>
</operator>
```

within the universe of method trees is a cycle of selecting a population, applying the method trees to the raw data, evaluating the fitness of the population, and enhancing the fittest method trees further to build a new population (Section 4.2). This cycle corresponds to the standard process of genetic algorithms. What differs from the standard is that method trees instead of binary vectors form the search space, that the search space is structured, and that the fitness evaluation is not merely a function but the result of running another learning algorithm. Figure 10 details the left box of the overall picture.

Representation

Genetic programming constructs finite automata. Here, method trees are to be constructed. They are represented by XML expressions. Figure 11 shows the representation of the method tree from Figure 8. The YALE system executes such trees and takes care of the syntactic well-formedness.

The restriction that chains are concluded by a function implies a level-wise structure of all possible method trees. The lowest level 1 entails only functions. These are chains of length 1. The next level, 2, covers chains with a concluding function. Levels 3 and above entail windowing. Method trees are constructed according to their levels. The level-wise growing means small changes to a current method tree. On the one hand, this reduces the probability of missing the optimal method tree. On the other hand, it may slow down the search, if the fitness of the lower levels does not distinguish between good and bad method trees.

Mutation, Crossover, and Selection

The operations of genetic programming are mutation and crossover. By random, mutations insert a new method into the current tree, delete a method from the tree, or replace a method by one of the same class, that is by a function or transformation. For all operations it is ensured that the resulting tree still obeys the constraints discussed above. Another possible mutation is to allow parameter changes like the size of the used windows. This further increases the size of the search space which must not necessarily mean that the problem gets harder. In fact, in our experiments allowing also parameter optimizations further increases the achieved accuracies while the additional effort is approximately 20% of run time. Crossover replaces a subtree from one method tree by a subtree from another method tree, respecting the well-formedness conditions. This means that the roots of the subtrees must be of the same type of methods.

For selection purposes, the fitness of all method trees might be expressed by a *roulette wheel*, that is, fitness proportional parts of a wheel's 360 degrees. The larger the portion, the more likely it becomes that the particular individual is selected for the next generation or crossover. Other possible selection schemes include *tournament selection*, where t method trees are randomly chosen from the population and the winner of this set, i.e. the method tree with the largest fitness, is added to the next generation. The parameter t allows the definition of selection pressure.

Fitness Evaluation

Since method trees serve classification in the end, the quality of classification is the ultimate criterion of fitness. Each audio file is represented by a set of random variables X that describe features of this audio file. This feature set X is the one obtained by the method tree constructed by the genetic search operations described above. For each method tree (individual) another feature set X will be constructed and evaluated. Y is another random variable that denotes to which class the audio file belongs. These obey a fixed but unknown probability distribution $Pr(X,Y)$. The objective of classification is to find a function

$h(X)$ which predicts the value of Y. Individuals which provide better classification results when used as features for the classification task at hand should have a greater probability to survive into the next generation. To evaluate the fitness of each method tree in a population the following steps are performed:

1. Each individual method tree is applied to an excerpt of the raw data.
2. This method application returns a transformed dataset, which is used by classifier learning.
3. A k-fold cross validation is executed to estimate the performances of the learning scheme in combination with the feature sets provided by the method trees.
4. The mean accuracy, recall, and/or precision of the result become the fitness value of the applied feature construction method trees.
5. The fitness values of the method trees are used to build the next population with one of the selection schemes described above.

We use a Support Vector Machine (SVM) as the inner learning scheme. The SVM classification is done by calculating an optimal hyperplane separating the classes. Following the notion of statistical learning theory, the optimal hyperplane is the one with the largest safety margin on both sides (Schölkopf & Smola, 2002). Hence, SVMs belong to a group of learners called "large margin methods". Minimizing the number of training errors and maximizing the margin between the examples and the hyperplane lead to a constrained optimization problem, which is solved by introducing Lagrange multipliers. The resulting optimization problem can be efficiently solved, for example by quadratic programming approaches, and allows for another interesting property: the examples are only used in dot products which might be replaced by other (nonlinear) similarity functions. The introduction of these nonlinear kernel functions and the efficiency are the reasons for the great success of this learning paradigm. We will later discuss some other properties of SVM learning in chapter 5 where we exploit these properties in order to speed up the process of feature set discovery.

Classifying Genres

Since results are published for the genre classification task, we have applied our approach to this task, too. Note, however, that no published benchmark data sets exist. Hence, the comparison can only show that feature construction and selection leads to similar performance as achieved by other approaches. For the classification of genres, three data sets have been built.

- **Classic/pop:** 100 pieces for each class were available in Ogg Vorbis format.

Table 1. Classification of genres with a linear SVM using the task specific feature sets

	Classic/pop	Techno/pop	Hiphop/pop
Accuracy	100%	93.12%	82.50%
Precision	100%	94.80%	85.27%
Recall	100%	93.22%	79.41%
Error	0%	6.88%	17.50%

Table 2. Classification performance using the same non-tailored standard feature set for all classification tasks (linear SVM)

	Classic/pop	Techno/pop	Hiphop/pop
Accuracy	96.50%	64.38%	72.08%
Precision	94.12%	60.38%	70.41%
Recall	95.31%	64.00%	67.65%
Error	3.50%	35.63%	27.92%

Table 3. Classification errors with respect to different learning schemes

	Classic/pop	Techno/pop
SVM (linear)	0.00%	6.88%
SVM (rbf)	1.50%	14.38%
C4.5	0.00%	7.50%
k-NN	3.00%	9.38%
Naive Bayes	2.50%	10.63%

Table 4. Classification according to user preferences

	User$_1$	User$_2$	User$_3$	User$_4$
Accuracy	95.19%	92.14%	90.56%	84.55%
Precision	92.70%	98.33%	90.83%	85.87%
Recall	99.00%	84.67%	93.00%	83.74%
Error	4.81%	7.86%	9.44%	15.45%

- **Techno/pop:** 80 songs for each class from a large variety of artists in Ogg Vorbis.
- **Hiphop/pop:** 120 songs for each class from few records were available in MP3 format with a coding of 128 kbits/s.

The classification tasks are of increasing difficulty. Using mySVM with a linear kernel, the performance was determined by a 10-fold cross validation and is shown in Table 1. Concerning classic vs. pop, 93% accuracy, and concerning hiphop vs. pop, 66% accuracy have been published (Tzanetakis, 2002; Tzanetakis et al., 2001).

41 features have been constructed for all genre classification tasks (the full list is available in (Mierswa, 2004). For the distinction between classic and pop, 21 features have been selected for mySVM by the evolutionary approach. Most runs selected features referring to the phase space (angle and variance). The use of features can also be inspected by restricting a top-down induction of decision trees to a few levels. For a one level stump, 93% accuracy could be achieved by just using the RMS volume, i.e. the root mean square average of the series. For the separation of techno and pop, 18 features were selected for mySVM, the most frequently selected ones being the filtering of those positions in the index dimension where the curve crosses the zero line. The decision tree starts with a phase space feature, the average of angles. A one level stump uses the starting value of the second frequency band, giving a benchmark of 76% accuracy. For the classification into hiphop and pop, 22 features were selected with the mere

volume being the most frequently selected feature. The decision tree classifying hiphop against pop is rather complex. It starts with the length of the songs. Experiments with naive Bayes and k-NN did not change the picture: an accuracy of about 75% can easily be achieved, increasing the performance further demands better features.

To demonstrate the effect of tailored feature sets for each classification task we performed experiments with the same feature set for all data sets. We used only features which were used in at least 50% of all subsets produced by feature selection for all data sets to simulate a reasonable standard feature set. Table 2 shows the classification performance for a linear SVM estimated with a 10-fold cross validation. The performance is significantly lower than the performance which can be achieved using the tailored feature sets (see Table 1).

Table 3 shows the achieved classification errors with respect to different learning schemes. Since the extraction of features and the transformation in another feature space is performed by the applied method tree, the usage of a linear kernel function is actually no restriction. Therefore, we use a linear SVM for all our experiments and as inner learner to estimate the fitness of the method trees. The conclusions which can be drawn from Table 2 and 3 indicate that a tailored set of task specific features and not the quality of the learning scheme is the crucial aspect for the successful classification of audio data. More details on this can be found in Mierswa and Morik (2005).

User Preferences

Recommendations of songs to possible customers are currently based on the individual correlation of record sales. This collaborative filtering approach ignores the content of the music. A high correlation is only achieved within genres, because the preferences traversing a type of music are less frequent. The combination of favorite songs into a set is a very individual and rare classification. It is not a generalization of many instances. Therefore, the classification of user preferences beyond genres is a challenging task, where for each user the feature set has to be learned. Of course, sometimes a user is interested only in pieces of a particular genre. This does not decrease the difficulty of the classification task. In contrast, if positive and negative examples stem from the same genre, it is hard to construct distinguishing features. Genre characteristics might dominate the user-specific features. As has been seen in the difficulty of the data set for hiphop vs. pop, sampling from few records also increases the difficulty of learning. Hence, four learning tasks of increasing difficulty have been investigated.

Four users brought 50 to 80 pieces of their favorite music ranging through diverse genres. They also selected the same number of negative examples. User 1 selected positive examples from rock music with a dominating electric guitar. User 2 selected positive as well as negative examples from jazz music. User 3 selected music from a large set of different genres containing classic, Latin, soul, rock, and jazz. User 4 selected pieces from different genres but only from few records. Using a 10-fold cross validation, mySVM was applied to the constructed and selected features, one feature set per learning task (user). Table 4 shows the results.

The excellent learning result for a set of positive instances which are all from a certain style of music corresponds to our expectation (User$_1$). The expectation that learning performance would decrease if positive and negative examples are taken from the same genre is not supported (User$_2$). Surprisingly good is the learning result for a broad variety of genres among the favorites (User$_3$). This fact indicates that for this user the constructed feature set supports the building of preference clusters in feature space instead of dominating genre clusters. In contrast to this result the (negative) effect of sampling from few records can be seen clearly (User$_4$). Applying the learned decision function to a database of records allowed the users to assess the recommendations. They were found very reasonable. Users agree that no music which was disliked was recommended to the user, but unknown plays and those, which could have been selected as the top 50.

It has already been shown in several investigations that there does not exist one set of features which is well suited for all tasks (Lidy & Rauber, 2005; Pohle et al., 2005). The same applies in our case where automatic feature extraction finds optimal feature sets by means of genetic programming. The difference between feature sets found for different users seems to be even greater compared to those found for genre classification. The features most often used for User$_1$ are those modeling timbre distance, that is both the peaks in the spectrum of the given audio files and measurements like the quotient of minimum or maximum and average (like spectral crest factor). This is reasonable since the differences between the positive and negative classes can be explained by different sound characteristics. For User$_2$, very simple features were extracted like the length of the songs and the root mean square average and variance which measures the loudness and its variance. In addition, some features in time space were extracted, namely zero crossing rate and autocorrelation. For User$_3$ a broad range of very different features were extracted, including spectral features similar to those extracted for the classification task posed by the first user. In addition, the differences and variances between the time space extrema together with features in phase space were also extracted for this user. It seems that the variety of genres is reflected in the variety of extracted features. The classification task of User$_4$ again requires a completely different feature set. For this user, interval features in different spaces were extracted. Another interesting feature newly discovered for this user was the slope of a linear regression function in a filtered frequency space. As a result, we can state that no feature exists which was extracted for all tasks and only a few which were extracted for more than one task. Hence, different user preference classifications require totally different feature sets which, in a weaker fashion, was also detected for genre classifications.

FEATURE TRANSFER

As already stated, no generic feature set exists for all possible audio classification tasks. While learning the feature extraction for a particular classification task delivers good results, training the feature extraction is time-consuming and demands a sufficient set of examples. The feature extraction process itself takes some time and for fitness evaluation a full cross-validation on a learning scheme is performed. For large classification problems, the whole optimization process might take up to several days. Therefore, we discuss an important improvement for the automatic feature extraction method discussed above. The basic idea of this improvement is to check if former work or work of others might be exploited to reduce the total runtime or to skip the feature extraction process at all.

Given only one learning task, we cannot do much about this. In a networked media organizer system, however, individual nodes are connected and may share information and data. Most p2p systems are focused on primarily sharing media content. In the following we propose an efficient approach allowing nodes to share features, as well. Although many different user taxonomies exist, it is at the same time reasonable to assume

that some of the taxonomies resemble each other to some extent. This is based on the observation of sociocultural aspects of music indicating communities or friend of a friend networks which share their view of music. We exploit this fact by transferring successful features among such similar classification tasks. Thus, instead of searching for suitable transformations using a genetic algorithm, we first query other nodes for features. If relevant features are indeed available, the given classification task can be learned with high accuracy and only minimal effort.

This scenario poses some additional constraints on the methods used to compare learning tasks and to share features. First, the retrieval of similar learning tasks and relevant features has to be very efficient, as the system is designed for interactive work. This also means that methods should enable a best effort strategy, such that the user can stop the retrieval process at any point and get the current best result. Second, the system should scale well with an increasing number of users and thus learning tasks. Also, it has to deal with a large variety of heterogeneous learning tasks, as we cannot make any strict assumptions on the classification problems users create. Finally, as the system is distributed, communication cost should be as low as possible. As a consequence, methods that are based on exchanging complete data sets or many feature vectors are not applicable.

We have developed a new similarity measure of learning tasks from audio data which is based on already learned feature weights. This measure is efficient and produces only minimal communication cost. In this way we obtain specialized feature sets that achieve high performance in near real-time.

Let T be the set of all learning tasks, a single task is denoted by t_i. In our scenario each learning task corresponds to a taxonomy node. Using the approach discussed in Section 4, we can extract a feature set X_i for task t_i. The components of X_i are called *features* X_{ik}. The objective of every *learning task* t_i is to find a function $h_i(X_i)$ which predicts the value of Y_i. We assume that each set of features X_i is partitioned in a set of *base features* X_B which are common for all learning tasks $t_i \in T$ and a set of *constructed features* $X_i \setminus X_B$.

We now introduce a very simple model of feature relevance and interaction. The feature X_{ik} is assumed to be irrelevant for a learning task t_i if it does not improve the classification accuracy:

Definition 16 *A feature X_{ik} is called* IRRELEVANT *for a learning task t_i iff X_{ik} is not correlated to the target feature Y_i, that is if $Pr(Y_i|X_{ik}) = Pr(Y_i)$.*

The set of all irrelevant features for a learning task t_i is denoted by IF_i.

Two features X_{ik} and X_{il} are alternative for a learning task t_i, denoted by $X_{ik} \sim X_{il}$ if they can be replaced by each other without affecting the classification accuracy. For linear learning schemes this leads to the linear correlation of two features:

Definition 17 *Two features X_{ik} and X_{il} are called* ALTERNATIVE *for a learning task t_i (written as $X_{ik} \sim X_{il}$) iff $X_{il} = a + b \cdot X_{ik}$ with $b > 0$.*

This is a very limited definition of alternative features. However, we will show that most weighting algorithms are already ruled out by conditions based on this simple definition.

We assume that a learning task t_i is completely represented by a feature weight vector w_i. The vector w_i is calculated from the base features X_B only. This representation of learning tasks is motivated by the idea that a given learning scheme approximate similar constructed features by a set of base features in a similar way, for example if the constructed feature "$\sin(X_{ik} \cdot X_{il})$" is highly relevant, the features X_{ik} and X_{il} are relevant as well.

Our approach works as follows: for a given learning task t_i we first calculate the relevance

of all base features X_B. We then send a query to all other nodes in the network by range limited broadcast. Each node compares the weight vector to the weight vectors representing the locally stored tasks and corresponding feature sets. This comparison is based on a function $d(t_i, t_j)$. Finally, we create a set of constructed features as union of the constructed features associated with these tasks.

This set is then evaluated on the learning task t_i. If the performance gain is sufficiently high (above a given threshold) we store task t_i as additional case. Otherwise, the constructed features are only used as initialization for a feature construction that is performed locally (Section 4). If this leads to a sufficiently high increase in performance, the task t_i is also stored to the local case base along with the locally generated features.

LEARNING TASK SIMILARITY FOR AUDIO CLASSIFICATION

While feature weighting and feature construction are well-studied tasks, the core of our algorithm is the calculation of d using only the relevance values of the base features X_B. In a first step, we define a set of conditions which must be met by feature weighting schemes. In a second step, a set of conditions for learning task distance is defined which makes use of the weighting conditions.

Weighting Conditions 1 *Let w be a* WEIGHTING FUNCTION $w : X_B \rightarrow \mathbb{R}$. *Then the following must hold:*

(W1) $w(X_{ik}) = 0$ if $X_{ik} \in X_B$ is irrelevant
(W2) $X_i \subseteq X_B$ is a set of alternative features.
Then

$$\forall S \subset X_i, S \neq \emptyset: \sum_{X_k \in S} w(X_k) = \sum_{X_k \in X_i} w(X_k) = \hat{w}$$

(W3) $w(X_{ik}) = w(X_{il})$ *if* $X_{ik} \sim X_{il}$

(W4) Let AF be a set of features where

$$\forall X_{ik} \in AF : (X_{ik} \in IF_i \lor \exists X_{il} \in X_B : X_{ik} \sim X_{il}).$$

Then

$$\forall X_{il} \in X_B : \neg\exists X_{ik} \in AF : X_{il} \sim X_{ik} \land w'(X_{il}) = w(X_{il})$$

where w' is a weighting function for $X'_B = X_B \cup AF.$

These conditions state that irrelevant features have weight 0 and that the sum of weights of alternative features must be constant independently of the actual number of alternative features used. Together with the last conditions it will be guaranteed that a set of alternative features is not more important than a single feature. In the following we assume that for a modified space of base features X'_B the function w' denotes the weighting function for X'_B according to the definition in (W4).

Additionally, we can define a set of conditions which must be met by distance measures for learning tasks which are based on feature weights only:

Distance Conditions 1 *A* DISTANCE MEASURE *d for learning tasks is a mapping $d : T \times T \to \mathbb{R}^+$ which should fulfill at least the following conditions:*

(D1) $d(t_{1,t2}) = 0 \Leftrightarrow t_1 = t_2$
(D2) $d(t_{1,t2}) = d(t_{2,t1})$
(D3) $d(t_{1,t3}) \leq d(t_{1,t2}) + d(t_{2,t3})$
(D4) $d(t_{1,t2}) = d(t_{1',t2'})$ *if* $X_{B'} = X_B \cup IF$ *and* $IF \subseteq IF_1 \cap IF_2$
(D5) $d(t_{1,t2}) = d(t_{1',t2'})$ *if* $X_{B'} = X_B \cup AF$ *and* $\forall X_k \in AF : \exists X_l \in X_B : X_k \sim X_l$

(D1)–(D3) represent the conditions for a metric. These conditions are required for efficient

case retrieval and indexing, using, for example, M-Trees (Ciaccia, Patella, & Zezula, 1997). (D4) states that irrelevant features should not have an influence on the distance. Finally, (D5) states that adding alternative features should not have an influence on distance.

Negative Results

In this section we will show that many feature weighting approaches do not fulfill the conditions (W1)–(W4). Furthermore, one of most popular distance measures, the Euclidian distance, cannot be used as a learning task distance measure.

Lemma 1 *Any feature selection method does not fulfill the conditions (W1)–(W4).*

Proof: For a feature selection method, weights are always binary, that is, $w(X_{ik}) \in \{0,1\}$. We assume a learning task t_i with no alternative features and $X'_B = C_B \cup \{X_{ik}\}$ with $\exists X_{il} \in X_B : X_{il} \sim X_{ik}$, then either $w'(X_{il}) = w'(X_{ik}) = w(X_{il}) = 1$, leading to a contradiction with (W2), or $w'(X_{il}) \neq w'(X_{ik})$ leading to a contradiction with (W3).

Lemma 2 *Any feature weighting method for which $w(X_{ik})$ is calculated independently of $X_B \setminus X_{ik}$ does not fulfill the conditions (W1)–(W4).*

Proof: We assume a learning task t_i with no alternative features and $X'_B = X_{B \cup} \{X_{ik}\}$ with $\exists X_{il} \in X_B : X_{il} \sim X_{ik}$. If w is independent of $X_{B \setminus Xik}$ adding X_{ik} would not change the weight $w'(X_{il})$ in the new feature space X'_B. From (W3) follows that $w'(X_{ik}) = w'(X_{il}) = w(X_{il})$ which is a violation of (W2).

Lemma 2 essentially covers all feature weighting methods that treat features independently. Important examples for such weighting schemes are information gain (Quinlan, 1986) or Relief (Kira & Rendell, 1992).

The next theorem states that the Euclidean distance cannot be used as a distance measure based on feature weights.

Theorem 3 *Euclidean distance does not fulfill the conditions (D1)–(D5).*

Proof: We give a counterexample. We assume that a weighting function w is given which fulfills the conditions (W1)–(W4). Further assume that learning tasks $t_{i,tj}$ are given with no alternative features. We add an alternative feature X_{ik} to X_B and get $X'_B = X_B \cup \{X_{ik}\}$ with $\exists X_{il} \in X_B : X_{il} \sim X_{ik}$. We infer from conditions (W2) and (W3) that

$$w'(X_{ik}) = w'(X_{il}) = \frac{w(X_{il})}{2} \text{ and } w'(X_{ik}) = w'(X_{il}) = \frac{w(X_{il})}{2}$$

and from condition (W4) that

$$\forall p \neq k : w'(X_{ip}) = w(X_{ip}) \text{ and } \forall p \neq k : w'(X_{jp}) = w(X_{jp})$$

In this case the following holds for the Euclidean distance

$$d(t'_i, t'_j) = \sqrt{S + 2(w'(X_k) - w'(X_k))^2} = \sqrt{S + 2\left(\frac{w(X_k)}{2} - \frac{w(X_k)}{2}\right)^2}$$
$$= \sqrt{S + \frac{1}{2}(w(X_k) - w(X_k))^2} \neq \sqrt{S + (w(X_k) - w(X_k))^2}$$
$$= d(t_i, t_j)$$

With

$$S = \sum_{p=1, p \neq k}^{|X_B|}(w'(X_p) - w'(X_p))^2 = \sum_{p=1, p \neq k}^{|X_B|}(w(X_p) - w(X_p))^2$$

Hence, alternative features here do make a difference, violating (D5).

Positive Results

We have shown that many common feature weighting algorithms and distance measures cannot be used for learning task distance in our scenario. In this section, we will prove that the feature weights delivered by a linear Support Vector Machine (SVM) obeys the proposed weighting conditions. Afterwards, we also discuss a distance measure fulfilling the distance conditions.

Support Vector Machines are based on the work of Vapnik in statistical learning theory (Vapnik, 1995). They aim to minimize the regularized risk $R_{reg}(f)$ of a learned function f which is the weighted sum of the empirical risk $R_{emp}(f)$ and a complexity term $\|w\|^2$:

$$R_{reg}[f] = R_{emp}[f] + \lambda \|w\|^2$$

The result is a linear decision function $y = \text{sgn}(w \cdot x + b)$ with a minimal length of w. The vector w is the normal vector of an optimal hyperplane with a maximal margin to both classes. One of the strengths of SVMs is the use of kernel functions to extend the feature space and allow linear decision boundaries after efficient nonlinear transformations of the input (Schölkopf and Smola, 2002). Since our goal is the construction of (nonlinear) features during preprocessing we can just use the most simple kernel function which is the dot product. In this case the components of the vector w can be interpreted as weights for all features.

Theorem 4 *The feature weight calculation of SVMs with linear kernel function meets the conditions (W1)–(W4).*

Proof: Since these conditions can be proved for a single learning task t_i we write X_k and w_k as a shortcut for X_{ik} and $w(X_{ik})$.

(W1) Sketch We assume that the SVM finds an optimal hyperplane. The algorithm tries to minimize both the length of w and the empirical error. This naturally corresponds to a maximum margin hyperplane where the weights of irrelevant features are 0 if enough data points are given.

(W2) SVMs find the optimal hyperplane by minimizing the weight vector w. Using the optimal classification hyperplane with weight vector w can be written as $y = \text{sgn}(w_1 x_1 + \ldots + w_i x_i + \ldots + w_m x_m + b)$. We will show that this vector cannot be changed by adding the same feature more than

one time. We assume that all alternative features can be transformed into identical features by normalizing the data. Adding k - 1 alternative features will result in:

$$y = \text{sgn}\left(... + \underbrace{(w_i^1 + ... + w_i^k)}_{\substack{\text{alternative} \\ \text{features}}} x_i + ... + b \right)$$

However, the optimal hyperplane will remain the same and does not depend on the number of alternative attributes. This means that the other values w_j will not be changed. This leads to

$$w_i = \sum_{l=1}^{k} w_i^l$$

which proves condition (W2).

(W3) The SVM optimization minimizes the length of the weight vector w. This can be written as

$$w_1^2 + ... + w_i^2 + ... + w_m^2 \overset{!}{=} \min.$$

We replace w_i using condition (W2):

$$w_1^2 + ... + \left(\hat{w} - \sum_{j \neq i} w_j \right)^2 + ... + w_m^2 \overset{!}{=} \min.$$

In order to find the minimum we have to partially differentiate the last equation for all weights w_k:

$$\frac{\partial}{\partial w_k}\left(... + \left(\hat{w} - \sum_{j \neq i} w_j \right)^2 + w_k^2 + ... \right) = 0$$

$$\Leftrightarrow 2w_k - 2\left(\hat{w} - \sum_{j \neq i} w_j \right) = 0 \Leftrightarrow w_k + \sum_{j \neq i} w_j = \hat{w}$$

The sum on the left side contains another w_k. This leads to a system of linear equations of the form $... + 0 \cdot w_i + ... + 2 \cdot w_k + ... = \hat{w}$. Solving this system of equations leads to $w_p = w_q$ (condition (W3)).

(W4) Sketch: We again assume that a SVM finds an optimal hyperplane given enough data points. Since condition (W1) holds adding an irrelevant feature would not change the hyperplane and thus the weighting vector w for the base features will remain. The proofs of conditions (W2) and (W3) state that the optimal hyperplane is not affected by alternative features as well.

In order to calculate the distance of learning tasks based only on a set of base feature weights we still need a distance measure that meets the conditions (D1)–(D5).

Theorem 5 *Manhattan distance does fulfill the conditions (D1)–(D5).*

Proof: The conditions (D1)–(D3) are fulfilled due to basic properties of the Manhattan distance. Therefore, we only give proofs for conditions (D4) and (D5).

(D4) We follow from the definition of the Manhattan distance that

$$d(t'_i, t'_j) = \sum_{X_{ip}, X_{jp} \in X_B} \left| w'_i(X_{ip}) - W'_j(X_{jp}) \right| + \underbrace{\sum_{X_{iq}, X_{jq} \in IF} \left| w'_i(X_{iq}) - w'_j(X_{jq}) \right|}_{0}$$

$$= d(t_i, t_j)$$

from (W4).

(D5) Sketch We show the case for adding k features with $\forall X_{ik} : X_{ik} \sim X_{il}$ for a fixed $X_{il} \in X_B$:

$$d(t'_i, t'_j) = \sum_{p=1, p \neq k}^{|X_B|} \left| w'_i(X_{ip}) - W'_j(X_{jp}) \right| + (k+1) \cdot \left| w'_i(X_{ik}) - w'_j(X_{jk}) \right|$$

$$= \sum_{p=1, p \neq k}^{|X_B|} \left| w_i(X_{ip}) - w_j(X_{jp}) \right| \left| w_i(X_{ik}) - w_j(X_{jk}) \right|$$

$$= d(t_i, t_j)$$

from (W4) and (W2).

Therefore, we conclude that SVM feature weights in combination with Manhattan distance fulfill the necessary constraints for a learning task distance measure based on feature weights.

Experiments

In this section, we evaluate the ability of our approach to speed up the extraction of essential features, while the accuracy is preserved. As mentioned before, finding the optimal feature set is a very demanding task which must be performed for each unknown learning task anew. For our experiments, we can tackle this problem in a simpler way. Since we know all training taxonomies in advance, we can extract a large feature set for several prototypical training taxonomies. We then perform a feature selection to determine the best feature set for each learning task. Using only a small subset of base features X_B we regard the additionally selected features as the set of specially extracted features $X \setminus X_B$ for each learning task. Additional experiments for synthetic data can be found in Mierswa and Wurst (2005).

We used the benchmark dataset containing 39 user made taxonomies (Homburg, Mierswa, Möller, Morik, & Wurst, 2005). The taxonomies were split into a training set of 28 taxonomies and a test set of 11 taxonomies. For both, a set of flat binary classification tasks was generated by splitting the items at each inner node according to subconcepts. As stated before we selected the set of optimal features for each of the learning tasks using a wrapper approach (forward selection) in combination with a nearest neighbor learner evaluated by 10-fold cross validation. We used classification accuracy as the optimization

Table 5 Average accuracy and effort for learning using base features, optimized features and feature transfer (ft)

	Accuracy	Time	Optimization cycles
base features	0.79	-	-
optimal features	0.92	42s	3970
ft (k = 1)	0.85	3s	257
ft (k = 3)	0.88	5s	389
ft (k = 9)	0.89	8s	678

Figure 12. The base feature weights of the audio test cases after a dimensionality reduction on two dimensions

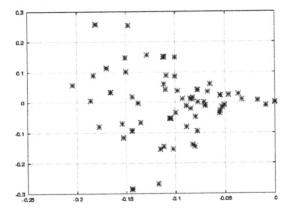

Figure 13. Architecture of Nemoz: the core is the data model; the service layer accesses the data model implementing various functions; the application layer around provides developers with generic operations; the GUI interacts with the user, the ScriptEngine with the developer

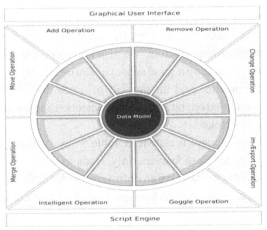

Figure 14. Different taxonomies created with Nemoz. The upper one structures the audio files according to mood, the other according to the singer's voice.

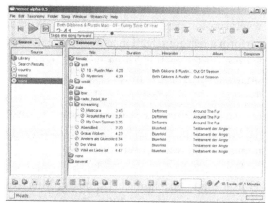

(a) Mood taxonomy   (b) Voice taxonomy

criterion. The underlying feature set contained 20 "allround" features (Mörchen, Ultsch, Thies, Löhken, Nöcker, & Stamm, 2004) and 123 specialized features created by the approach described in Mierswa and Morik (2005). We selected 10 base features which performed well on a wide range of learning tasks in order to allow for an efficient comparison. We then generated base feature weights for each learning task in the training set and test set using a SVM (Rüping, 2000). The average accuracy was measured for all learning tasks in the test set. We used the base feature set only, the selected set of optimal features for each learning task, and features recommended by case-based feature construction with a varying number of predictors. We also measured the effort of finding a good subset of features in terms of run-time and the number of times the inner evaluation operator for feature selection approach was invoked.

The result is shown in Table 5. As expected, using the base features only, leads to the lowest accuracy. Choosing an optimal set of features for each task separately leads to the highest accuracy. Using the features of the k most similar taxonomies

with respect to the similarity measure described in this section performs in between. However, this feature transfer efficiently achieves accuracy close to the optimal one. This empirically supports our hypothesis, that our approach can combine the best of both worlds: very fast learning while a high accuracy is preserved. In real-world applications the described approach performs even better. Applying an automatic feature extraction method instead of merely applying a feature selection is very demanding and might take up to several days while the run-time of the transfer approach basically remains the same.

In addition to the aforemetioned evaluation, we visualized the notion of related tasks. Figure 12 shows the base feature vectors of all learning tasks after a singular value decomposition to transform the data into two dimensions. On the one hand, we can see the heterogeneity of learning tasks. On the other hand, several learning tasks form groups of tasks with similar base weights. This approves our hypothesis: while in general different learning tasks require different features, some of the learning tasks resemble each other at least to some extent.

NEMOZ

Together with a group of students we have developed Nemoz as a framework for studying collaborative music organization[3]. It has a graphical user interface with several visualizations, an application layer with generic operations which offer various ways to exploit the services which, in turn, access the data model, and a developer's interface for fast modification of system behavior. The architecture of the system is shown in Figure 13.

Nemoz is implemented such that it can be tailored to:

- Different learning tasks
- Different media
- Different network architectures

Introducing new learning tasks is easy because of the connection (LabService) to the YALE system (Fischer et al., 2002), in which diverse classification, clustering, and preprocessing operators can be composed to form an experiment. Storing other than music data is easy because the DescriptorService calls feature extraction methods, which result in complete or stripped sets of attributes for given raw data. The NetworkService currently implements communication among LAN nodes via TCP and UDP. In addition to tailoring the system behavior using the implemented functions, the abstract classes and interfaces can be implemented in order to enlarge the scope of the system. Moreover, the PluginService together with the ScriptEngine allows introduction of new codes and connects Nemoz to other systems.

Nemoz is made for experimenting with intelligent functionality of media organization systems. Of course, the basic functionality is implemented: download and import of songs, playing music, retrieving music from a collection based on given metadata, and creating play lists. The data model covers not only the standard metadata (performer, composer, album, year, duration of the song, genre, and comment) and a reference to the location of the song, but also features which are extracted from the raw data. The feature extraction is the application of the results of the automatic feature construction (Section 4). Since the learning experiment delivers different results for different learning tasks, the set of features may vary. Developers can, however, use a fixed set of features, if running a learning experiment is too time consuming.

For intelligent functions, the data structure of taxonomies is implemented. A collection can be organized using several taxonomies in parallel. For an example, see Figure 14. At each taxonomy node, a classification function can be stored, which decides whether a new song belongs to this node, or not. This classifier is the learned model, where the learning task has been performed by one of the methods supplied by Yale. Based on this data structure Nemoz already implements several intelligent functions:

- The taxonomies can be defined extensionally by the user, or
- Automatically be learned using hierarchical clustering.
- Taxonomy nodes can be intensionally defined by a (learned) model.
- New music can be classified into the taxonomy.
- Users can view the audio collections of other users in terms of an own classification scheme by temporarily classifying the content of this collection into an own taxonomy (goggling).
- Search queries can be composed using AND and OR, quantor-free logic formulas without negation allowing queries such as "users who are less than 18 years old and who own a taxonomy with the word grunge in a node's title".
- Users can search for similar taxonomies in the network.

- Users can search for music similar to a selected song.
- A taxonomy can be enhanced through the taxonomies of other users automatically (distributed collaborative clustering (Wurst & Morik, 2006)).

Which methods are used in a particular function can easily be configured through the learning component provided by the YALE system. Currently, we apply hierarchical single-link clustering for the automatic construction of taxonomies using a fixed set of audio features. For classifier learning we used instance-based learning, decision-tree learning, and the support vector machine together with forward feature selection.

Nemoz is implemented as a p2p network and allows nodes to share arbitrary information. A major focus of Nemoz is on sharing features that are used to learn classification functions. A node uses the procedure described in Section 5 to query other nodes for features given a particular classification task. When a node receives responses to its query, it applies the feature construction procedures in the response set to extract the corresponding features from the local audio data and then repeats the learning process. All successful features are stored for future use and to respond to the queries of other nodes.

Nemoz supports still another form of feature sharing, based on extensional queries. A node queries other nodes with a set of IDs representing audio files. Other nodes then respond with feature values directly instead of feature construction procedures. This approach is more expensive in terms of communication costs, can however be applied even to nominal features like label information or ID3 tags (Wurst & Morik, 2006).

Beside feature sharing, we exploit the p2p structure for other kinds of queries as well, such as search and distributed clustering. Nemoz is designed to be extendible, that is, additional functionality and communication patterns can be added easily.

CONCLUSION

In this chapter we analyzed the problem of supervised feature extraction and transfer for organizing personal music collections. Audio classification enables users to maintain arbitrary personal organization schemes easily. New audio files are assigned automatically to the user specified classes, such that the effort for the user is minimal. While this approach is very attractive, one problem needs to be solved in order to apply automatic classification techniques to audio files. Audio classification needs an adequate feature representation of the given data set. Which features are well suited strongly depends on the classification task at hand.

We described a unifying framework which decomposes the complex extraction methods into their building blocks. This systematization allows us to move beyond the manual composition of feature extraction methods for a given classification task. This way, the design of an appropriate feature set has become a learning task in its own right. Our genetic learning approach discovered several of the well-known features as well as some new ones. The automatic feature extraction approach delivers excellent results in terms of accuracy for a wide range of different learning tasks and is able to replace the phase of manual feature tuning in future applications.

A drawback of this and similar methods is, however, that they are computationally very demanding. In addition, it is required that the user classifies a considerably large amount of audio files. We therefore embedded the new learning task of feature extraction in a (distributed) meta-learning setting. We exploit the fact that there is not only one, but several audio classification tasks faced by many different users or by the same user in different points of time. The idea is to exploit the former, time-consuming runs of feature extraction learning and transfer the resulting feature sets to similar new classification tasks. We hence allow users to share features among similar learning tasks. The similarity measure of learning tasks is based on relevance weights on a common set of base features only. This avoids the need to calculate or transfer large amounts of data so that an efficient feature transfer is guaranteed with minimal communication overhead. Thus, we cannot only find accurate features by searching them locally but also very fast by querying other nodes or reusing the results of former runs.

We have exemplified this scenario on Nemoz, which is a distributed media organization framework that focuses on the application of data mining in p2p networks. It supports users in structuring their private media collections by exploiting information from other peers in the described way. It contains traditional functions as file sharing as well as intelligent functionality, for example classifying and clustering music files or advanced visualization. The Nemoz framework allows for the incorporatation of a large variety of different data mining algorithms and cooperation protocols.

The amount of media available is ever increasing. Organizing personal music collection by machine learning is a key to manage this information overload. We think that collaborative computation will play a central role in this process.

REFERENCES

Aksoy, M., Burgard, D., Flasch, O., Kaspari, A., Lüttgens, M., Martens, M., Möller, B., Öztürk, U., & Thome, P. (2005). Kollaboratives Strukturieren von Multimediadaten für Peer-to-Peer Netze. Technical report, Fachbereich Informatik, Universität Dortmund. Endbericht der Projektgruppe 461.

Aucouturier, J.-J., & Pachet, F. (2002). Music similarity measures: What's the use? In *Proceedings of the International Symposium on Music Information Retrieval*.

Baumann, S., Pohle, T., & Shankar, V. (2004). Towards a socio-cultural compatibility of MIR systems. In *Proceedings of the International Conference on Music Information Retrieval*.

Berenzweig, A., Logan, B., Ellis, D. P. W., & Whitman, B. (2003). A large-scale evaluation of acoustic and subjective music similarity measures. In *Proceedings of the International Conference on Music Information Retrieval*.

Bray, S. & Tzanetakis, G. (2005). Distributed audio feature extraction for music. In *Proceedings of the International Conference on Music Information Retrieval*.

Celma, O., Ramirez, M., & Herrera, P. (2005). Foafing the music: A music recommendation system based on RSS feeds and user preferences. In *Proceedings of the International Conference on Music Information Retrieval*.

Ciaccia, P., Patella, M., & Zezula, P. (1997). M-tree: An efficient access method for similarity search in metric spaces. In *Proceedings of International Conference on Very Large Data Bases* (pp. 426-435). Morgan Kaufmann.

Cooley, J. W., & Tukey, J. W. (1965). An algorithm for the machine computation of the complex Fourier series. *Mathematics of Computation, 19*, 297-301.

Fischer, S., Klinkenberg, R., Mierswa, I., & Ritthoff, O. (2002). *Yale: Yet another learning environment— Tutorial* (Tech. Rep. CI-136/02). Collaborative Research Center 531, University of Dortmund.

Hastie, T., Tibshirani, R., & Friedman, J. (2001). *The elements of statistical learning: Data mining, inference, and prediction*. New York: Springer.

Holland, J. H. (1986). Escaping brittleness: The possibilities of general-purpose learning algorithms applied to parallel rule-based systems. In R. S. Michalski, J. G. Carbonell, & T. M. Mitchell (Eds.), *Machine learning: An artificial intelligence approach* (Vol. 2, pp. 593-624). Palo Alto, CA: Morgan Kaufmann.

Homburg, H., Mierswa, I., Möller, B., Morik, K., & Wurst, M. (2005). A benchmark dataset for audio classification and clustering. In *Proceedings of the International Conference on Music Information Retrieval*.

Jayant, N. S., & Noll, P. (1984). *Digital coding of waveforms: Principles and applications to speech and video.* Englewood Cliffs, NJ: Prentice Hall.

Jones, S., Cunningham, S. J., & Jones, M. (2004). Organizing digital music for use: An examination of personal music collections. In *Proceedings of the International Conference on Music Information Retrieval*.

Kira, K., & Rendell, I. A. (1992). The feature selection problem: Traditional methods and a new algoirthm. In *Proceedings of the National Conference on Artificial Intelligence* (pp. 129-134). MIT Press.

Kohonen, T. (1988). *Self-organization and associative memory.* Berlin: Springer-Verlag.

Koza, J. R. (1992). *Genetic programming: On the programming of computers by means of natural selection.* Cambridge: MIT Press.

Lee, J. H., & Downie, J. S. (2004). Survey of music information needs, uses, and seeking behaviours: Preliminary findings. In *Proceedings of the International Conference on Music Information Retrieval*.

Lidy, T., & Rauber, A. (2005). Evaluation of feature extractors and psycho-acoustic transformations for music genre classification. In *Proceedings of the International Conference on Music Information Retrieval* (pp. 34-41).

Liu, Z., Wang, Y., & Chen, T. (1998). Audio feature extraction and analysis for scene segmentation and classification. *Journal of VLSI Signal Processing System, 20*(1-2).

Maddage, N. C., Xu, C., & Wang, Y. (2003). A SVM-based classification approach to musical audio. In *Proceedings of the International Conference on Music Information Retrieval*.

Mandel, M. I., & Ellis, D. P. W. (2005). Song-level features and support vector machines for music classification. In *Proceedings of the International Conference on Music Information Retrieval*.

McEnnis, D., McKay, C., Fujinaga, I., & Depalle, P. (2005). JAUDIO: A feature extraction library. In *Proceedings of the International Conference on Music Information Retrieval*.

McKay, C., Fiebrink, R., McEnnis, D., Li, B., & Fujinaga, I. (2005). Ace: A framework for optimizing music classification. In *Proceedings of the International Conference on Music Information Retrieval*.

Meng, A., & Shawe-Taylor, J. (2005). An investigation of feature models for music genre classification using the support vector classifier. In *Proceedings of the International Conference on Music Information Retrieval* (pp. 604-609).

Mierswa, I. (2004). Automatisierte Merkmalsextraktion aus Audiodaten. Fachbereich Informatik, Universität Dortmund, 2004.

Mierswa, I., & Morik, K. (2005). Automatic feature extraction for classifying audio data. *Machine Learning Journal, 58,* 127-149.

Mierswa, I., & Wurst, M. (2005). Efficient feature construction by meta learning: Guiding the search in meta hypothesis space. In *Proceedings of the International Conference on Machine Learning Workshop on Meta Learning*.

Mörchen, F., Ultsch, A., Thies, M., Löhken, I., Nöcker, M., Stamm, C., Efthymiou, N., & Kümmerer, M. (2004). *MusicMiner: Visualizing perceptual distances of music as topograpical maps* (Tech. Rep.). Dept. of Mathematics and Computer Science, University of Marburg, Germany.

Mörchen, F., Ultsch, A., Nöcker, M., & Stamm, C. (2005). Databionic visualization of music collections according to perceptual distance. In *Proceedings of the International Conference on Music Information Retrieval.*

Morik, K., & Wessel, S. (1999). Incremental signal to symbol processing. In K. Morik, M. Kaiser, & V. Klingspor (Eds.), *Making robots smarter: Combining sensing and action through robot learning* (pp. 185-198). Boston: Kluwer Academic.

Pampalk, E. (2001). *Islands of music: Analysis, organization, and visualization of music archives.* Unpublished master's thesis, Department of Software Technology and Interactive Systems, Vienna University of Technology.

Pampalk, E., Dixon, S., & Widmer, G. (2004). Exploring music collections by browsing different views. *Computer Music Journal, 28*(2), 49-62.

Pampalk, E., Flexer, A., & Widmer, G. (2005). Improvements of audio-based music similarity and genre classification. In *Proceedings of the International Conference on Music Information Retrieval.*

Pohle, T., Pampalk, E., & Widmer, G. (2005). Evaluation of frequently used audio features for classification of music into perceptual categories. In *Proceedings of the Fourth International Workshop on Content-Based Multimedia Indexing (CBMI'05).*

Quinlan, R. J. (1986). Induction of decision trees. *Machine Learning, 1*(1), 81-106.

Rauber, A., Pampalk, E., & Merkl, D. (2002). Using psycho-acoustic models and self-organizing maps to create a hierarchical structuring of music by sound similarity. In *Proceedings of the International Symposium on Music Information Retrieval.*

Rüping, S. (2000). *mySVM Manual.* Universität Dortmund, Lehrstuhl Informatik VIII. http://

www-ai.cs.uni-dortmund.de/SOFTWARE/MYSVM/.

Schölkopf, B. & Smola, A. J. (2002). *Learning with kernels— Support vector machines, regularization, optimization, and beyond.* MIT Press.

Taheri-Panah, S. & MacFarlane, A. (2004). Music information retrieval systems: Why do individuals use them and what are their needs? In *Proceedings of the International Conference on Music Information Retrieval.*

Takens, F. (1980). Detecting strange attractors in turbulence. In D. A. Rand & L. S. Young (Eds.), *Dynamical systems and turbulence* (Vol. 898), *Lecture Notes in Mathematics* (pp. 366-381). Berlin: Springer.

Tzanetakis, G. (2002). *Manipulation, analysis and retrieval systems for audio signals.* Unpublished doctoral thesis, Computer Science Department, Princeton University.

Tzanetakis, G., & Cook, P. (1999). A framework for audio analysis based on classification and temporal segmentation. In *EUROMICRO 1999 (25th EUROMICRO '99 Conference, Informatics: Theory and Practice for the New Millenium).*

Tzanetakis, G., Essl, G., & Cook, P. (2001). Automatic musical genre classification of audio signals. In *Proceedings of the International Symposium on Music Information Retrieval* (pp. 205-210).

Tzanetakis, G., Gao, J., & Steenkiste, P. (2003). A scalable peer-to-peer system for music content and information retrieval. In *Proceedings of the International Conference on Music Information Retrieval.*

Vapnik, V. N. (1995). *The nature of statistical learning theory.* New York: Springer.

Vignoli, F. (2004). Digital music interaction concepts: A user study. In *Proceedings of the Intern. Conference on Music Information Retrieval.*

Wang, C., Li, J., & Shi, S. (2002). A kind of content-based music information retrieval method in a peer-to-peer environment. In *Proceedings of the International Symposium on Music Information Retrieval*.

Wurst, M., Mierswa, I., & Morik, K. (2005). *Structuring music collections by exploting peers' processing* (Tech. Rep. 43/2005), Collaborative Research Center 475, University of Dortmund.

Wurst, M., & Morik, K. (2006). Distributed feature extraction in a p2p setting: A case study (Special Issue). *Future Generation Computer Systems, 23*(1).

Zhang, T., & Kuo, C. (1998). Content-based classification and retrieval of audio. In *SPIE's 43rd Annual Meeting - Conference on Advanced Signal Processing Algorithms, Architectures, and Implementations VIII*.

Zils, A., & Pachet, F. (2004). Automatic extraction of music descriptors from acoustic signals using EDS. In *Proceedings of the 116th Convention of the AES*.

ENDNOTES

[1] YALE is available under GNU GPL license at http: //yale.sf.net

[2] This section and the next one include material from (Mierswa & Morik, 2005).

[3] Nemoz is implemented in Java. The Nemoz system can be downloaded under http://nemoz.sf.net.

Chapter VIII
A P2P Based Secure Digital Music Distribution Channel:
The Next Generation

Marc Fetscherin
Rollins College, USA

ABSTRACT

This chapter presents a conceptual framework enabling content providers to successfully sell digital music. We show that content providers must overcome three main hurdles to successfully sell digital music. The first is to establish an efficient and economically viable distribution channel. Second, they need to develop a secure and interoperable framework for protecting copyrighted digital music from piracy by integrating digital rights management systems into the distribution channel. The third hurdle is to set-up a robust payment mechanism that meets the content providers' needs for revenue capturing and the consumers' needs for hassle-free and legal content acquisition and usage. This chapter finally presents a conceptual framework for the next generation of digital music distribution which could address and overcome the three hurdles. We conclude that a DRM supported P2P network gives content providers as well as consumers the secure, legal and most cost-efficient and user friendly digital distribution channel they have been searching for.

INTRODUCTION

Over the last few years, technology advances such as IP-Networks, CD-R(w) and the development of compression formats such as MP3 have enabled individuals to easily copy and distribute digital music on a mass scale. These technologies have significantly impacted the businesses of content providers, especially the music industry. The result has been the desegregation of the value chain, an increasing digitisation of content, and a faster, simpler, and cheaper distribution channel. These technologies, and resulting trends, are a double-edge sword to content providers. On the one hand, they provide enormous opportunities, such as access to new markets, direct distribution to consumers, and opportunities for new products and business models like pay-per-listen and superdistribution. On the other hand, they provide enormous threats of increasing piracy and the unlawful storage, usage, manipulation, and sharing of billions of pieces of intellectual property (IP) content. This has become worse with the emergence of decentralized peer-to-peer (P2P) networks. In that respect, content providers must carefully choose how to deliver their digital content to their consumers by simultaneously enabling copyright protection on one hand and the sales on the other hand throughout the life cycle of their product.

The aim of this chapter is to show that there are three main hurdles content providers must overcome to conduct business with digital music. The first is establishing an efficient and economically viable distribution channel. So far, most legal music downloads are based on centralized systems such as client-server based models. However, most users today use decentralized systems to access and download music files such as peer-to-peer networks. Despite the fact that sharing of copyrighted content on those networks is illegal, they have found wide spread usage. This chapter compares the two distribution systems along various dimensions such as cost of ownership, scalability, performance, security, quality of services/control, and concludes that decentralized systems have many advantages over centralized ones, where the main weakness is security and control.

The second hurdle to overcome is to develop a secure and interoperable framework for protecting copyrighted digital music from piracy. The emergence of Digital Rights Management Systems (DRM) enables content providers to control the access and usage of their digital content. This chapter outlines the key components of a DRM, the core entities involved, discusses the pros and cons of DRM, and concludes that DRM has the potential to overcome some of the weaknesses of decentralized distribution systems by offering additional and augmenting functionalities for security and control.

The third hurdle is to establish a robust payment mechanism that meets the content providers'

needs for revenue capturing and the consumers' needs for hassle-free and legal content acquisition and use.

Finally, this chapter presents a DRM supported peer-to-peer network which could address and overcome the three hurdles mentioned previously. It presents a framework, which is different to the existing ones by outlining and describing in detail the key components needed such as the log server, the index server, the licensing server with key management, and rights management functions. Furthermore, we discuss the various technological, business, and legal mechanisms to overcome like fault tolerance, free riding behavior, denial up service attack, access control, and usage tracking. We conclude that integrating DRM into a P2P network gives content providers the secure, legal and most cost-efficient and user-friendly digital distribution channel they have been searching for.

THE FIRST HURDLE: DIGITAL DISTRIBUTION

Choice Between Client-Server and Peer-to-Peer

Computer systems can be classified into two groups: centralized or stand-alone systems, and distributed or network systems. This chapter defines a digital content distribution system as a distributed computer system enabling the delivery or exchange of digital content from one computer to another. Figure 1, adapted from Milojicic et al. (2002), provides a good classification of computer systems with respect to digital content distribution systems.

Distributed systems consist of different components located at networked computers, which communicate, collaborate, and coordinate actions such as sharing resources or content. There are many examples of distributed systems (Nelson, 2002) at various scales such as LAN, Intranet,

Figure 1. Classification of computer systems

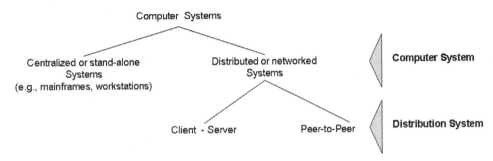

WAN, or the Internet. They can be based on the client-server model or peer-to-peer model which will both be discussed further in the following sections.

Client–Server Model

The client-server model describes the relationship between two computer programs in which one program, the client, makes a service request to another program, the server, which fulfils the request. Although the client-server model idea can be used by programs within a single computer, it is a more important idea in network computing. In a network, the client-server model provides a convenient way to interconnect programs, computers, or devices that are distributed across different locations. This model has become one of the central ideas of network computing and most digital music distribution systems (Minar & Hedlung, 2001).

Peer-to-Peer Model

The idea of P2P in a network environment is not new. In 1996 for example, a young Israeli firm called Mirabilit launched its popular ICQ ("I seek you") instant messenger services using a P2P architecture to send messages between personal computers connected to the Internet (Shirky, 2001). Despite its existence for several years, there is no unique definition for the term

"peer-to-peer" and there are only few attempts to classify peer-to-peer technologies (Kant, Iyer, & Tewari, 2002). In a P2P model, each node or peer has both server and client capabilities. Thus, each peer can store, send, and receive service requests, data or music files to each other's peers (Schoder & Fischbach, 2002). In addition, each peer makes a portion of its own resources (e.g., part of hard disk, bandwidth, CPU) available to other peers (Lesavich, 2002). P2P networks build the infrastructure for the following three applications: resource sharing, virtual communities, and for this chapter the most relevant one which is file sharing (Schoder, Fischbach, 2002). There are, on one hand, the centralized P2P, and on the other hand, the decentralized P2P systems. Also there are lots of P2P systems in between, we will present shortly those two opposing ones.

Centralized Peer-to-Peer
Centralized or mediated P2P networks utilize the client-server network structure. The server facilitates the interaction between peers by maintaining directories of the shared files stored on the respective personal computers of the registered users of the network. A centralized directory server maintains an index with the metadata, all control and search messages are sent to the central server. The first type of peer-to-peer music sharing networks where based on this structure, where the most prominent example was Napster (Minar & Hedlung, 2001).

Pure Peer-to-Peer

In a pure P2P network, peers communicate directly without a centralized authority or server. Thus, all peers have the same capabilities in respect to client-server functions. The index and the metadata of the shared files are stored locally among all peers. The most prominent examples were Gnutella and Kazaa, or more recently LimeWire or Morpheus.

Napster was by far the most familiar P2P network (centralized). However, there are multiple P2P applications, lesser known to the press, but sometimes even more popular and accessed by a larger number of users such as AOL Instant Messenger™ or more recently so called LAN-parties.

Comparison Between Client-Server and Peer-to-Peer Model

There is no unique set of characteristics through which a client-server model and a P2P model can be compared. Though extensive literature review (Burghardt, & Schumann, 2002; Eggs et al., 2002; Gehrke, Homayounfar, Wang, & Areibi, 2002; Milojicic et al., 2002) and expert discussion, we came up with the following five key dimensions with which they can be compared:

- Cost of ownership
- Scalability
- Performance
- Security (in the view of peer and content provider)
- Quality of service / control

There are other important aspects like trust, interoperability, metadata, reputation, and firewalls (Lethin, 2001; Milojicic et al., 2001; Waldman, Cranor, & Rubin, 2001) which are also taken into account to some extend in this analysis as well as business, legal, and technical challenges which Schoder and Fischbach (2002) discussed in their paper, as well as technical and nontechnical challenges (Milojicic et al., 2002).

Table 1 compares the client-server and P2P model along the 5 dimensions already mentioned. In the P2P column, if not mentioned otherwise, the arguments are applicable to both types of P2P systems, pure and centralized P2P. The rating of HIGH to LOW is taken from a content provider's perspective. The rating reflects the sum of the arguments in the table which are based on literature review and expert discussions.

P2P will not replace the client-server model. But as Table 1 shows, P2P networks provide many advantages over the client-server model in respect to cost of ownership and scalability (Parameswaran, Susarla, & Whinston, 2001; Schollmeier, 2001). Centralized P2P networks could provide the same quality of service and control as currently used by client-server model. However, in terms of performance and security, P2P networks, and especially pure P2P networks, lack behind the client-server model. Today, P2P networks are used on a voluntary basis and do not follow any economical principles (Eggs et al., 2002). If P2P networks should support business transactions such as purchasing a music file, they should integrate not only functionalities like the distribution of the digital content, but information exchange (Gehrke, Burghardt, & Schumann 2002), billing systems, and Digital Rights Management (Fetscherin, 2002). If content providers want to use P2P networks for distributing their intellectual property content, they have to overcome these weaknesses.

Therefore we can argue that P2P networks have a significant cost and scalability advantage over the client server model, where the latter has a security and performance advantage. Centralized or mediated P2P networks (Schollmeier, 2001) combine the benefits of both, client-server model and pure P2P networks. Figure 2 summarizes these findings.

Figure 2 is especially true if the centralized P2P networks integrate DRM which enables to overcome the challenges of pure P2P networks in terms of security and control.

Table 1. Comparison between client-server vs. peer-to-peer

Dimension	Client–Server Model	Peer-to-Peer Model
Costs of Ownership (e.g., infrastructure, distribution, maintenance costs)	**LOW: Requires Capital Outlays to Build and Maintain** • Requires servers with high purchase, hosting, and maintenance costs. • Centralized model, with no sharing of resources, resulting in higher overhead.	**HIGH: More Economical** • No overhead costs as the peers constitute the network (O'Reilly, 2001). • For centralized P2P, very low infrastructure and maintenance costs (Rosenblatt, Trippe, & Mooney, 2002).
Scalability	**MIDDLE: Hardware and Infrastructure Dependent** • Low, as scalability is limited by centralized operations such as coordination. • High dependency on centralized point (Milojicic et al., 2002).	**HIGH: Inherently Organic, Scales with Users** • Scales by avoiding dependency on centralized point (Milojicic et al., 2002). • P2P are more suitable for the large number of computers on the Internet or mobile devices (Minar & Hedlung, 2001).
Performance (e.g., fault tolerance, free riding problem)	**HIGH: Dependent on Centralized Infrastructure** • Poor, as single point of failure resulting in crashed and busy servers. • Low risk of fault tolerance. • Low risk of free riding (Schoder & Fischbach, 2002). • Content is always accessible, does not depend on number of users connected to the server. • Only one point for maintenance of digital data.	**MIDDLE: Dependent on Bandwidth of Peers and Number of Peers** • High: reduction of redundancy through replicating information at multiple nodes (Kini & Shetty, 2001). • High: P2P can help to break the IT bottleneck. More effective use of Internet resources by edge service. • On peer level, poor for pure P2P: as sending/receiving and keeping communication requires lot of traffic. • Offering download to other peers' means sharing bandwidth and perhaps slowing down own connection speed (Kwok, Lang & Kar, 2002).
Security For Peer (e.g., denial access attacks)	**HIGH: Less Vulnerable due to direct link to content provider** • Does not "open" up a certain part of their computer to others, unknown peers. • Central authority increases control, thus reducing risk of virus attack.	**MIDDLE: Vulnerable by Forcing Peers to Have Server Functionalities** • Peer must "open" several parts and/or ports, which render peers vulnerable to hackers and virus attacks (Kwok, Lang, & Kar, 2002).
Security For Content Provider (e.g., access control, usage tracking, piracy)	**Centralized and Controlled** • Can easily be determined who request the digital content, which digital content, how many copies of the digital content was utilized, how many time, and so forth (Lesavich, 2002). • Content providers can exercise control through the server and manage rights digitally (Fetscherin, 2002).	**LOW: Distributed and Vulnerable** • For pure P2P, the control over where and how the content is shared is lost but not in a centralized P2P network (Lesavich, 2002). • For pure P2P, peer devices are owned by individuals instead of ISP's; it is not easy to locale or initiate litigation against individuals (Lesavich, 2002). • Poor search possibilities as on P2P networks it begins when the user logs into the networks.
Quality of Service / Control (e.g., authenticity, integrity of data)	**HIGH: Assured and Controlled** • High, as it is simple to control the uniqueness of a digital content. As the server is on a centralized control. • Quality check done by centralized server.	**HIGH: Organic Service** • Dynamic availability of content and information as the amount of data depends on the number of peers • Free riding issue, but positive externalities. • For pure P2P, poor quality of service.

Figure 2. Matrix distributed systems

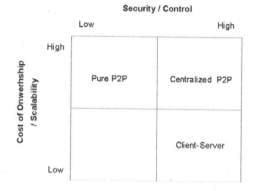

SECOND AND THIRD HURDLE: SECURITY AND MONITIZATION

What can content providers do to both, protect on one hand their digital music and on the other hand make money with it? DRM has the potential to accomplish both goals. First, by protecting digital content through access and usage control by using a set of technologies such as encryption and by ensuring its authenticity and integrity through watermarking or digital signature. Second, to enable the monetarization of digital music by providing billing systems processes and systems enabling to manage rights in the digital environment (Bechtold, 2002). In their weakest form, they prevent or make it difficult to copy digital content, in their strongest form DRM enables the individual billing of the digital content on a per usage unit.

Definition

The Association of American Publishers (2002) defines DRM as "the technologies, tools and processes that protect intellectual property during digital content commerce," Gordon (2001) defines it as "a system of information technology (IT) components and services that strive to distribute and control digital products" and Einhorn (2001) argues "digital rights management entails the operation of a control system that can moni-

tor, regulate, and price each subsequent use of a computer file that contains media content, such as video, audio, photos, or print." Although there is not a unique definition of DRM, it provides opportunities as well as limitations for the different stakeholders involved (Fetscherin, 2002; Rosenblatt, Trippe & Mooney, 2002).

Components of Digital Rights Management (DRM)

The role of any DRM is to protect and manage intellectual property content as it travels through the value chain from the content provider to consumers, and even from consumer to consumer (C2C). While an in-depth analysis of DRM components and the underlying technologies goes beyond the scope of this chapter, a short overview of these is needed to highlight the advantages and disadvantages of those systems. Table 2 outlines and summarizes the key components of any DRM.

It is important to recognize that there is no unique DRM technology or standard. A DRM will change to include different components according to the type of content (e.g., audio, video, text), the desired level of security and technology vendor used. Despite standardization efforts like the Open Mobile Alliance (OMA) for mobile digital content distribution, this variability and lack of a common standards in general has ensured that there are many different DRM in place.

Core Entities of DRM

There are three core entities involved in any DRM: The user, the content, and the rights as Figure 3 illustrates. The USER can be any type of user, such as a publisher, a record company, a film studio, a corporate enterprise, or an individual. This entity creates the content, and the same or another uses the content. The CONTENT is any type of digital content, such as games, software, films, or in this case a music file. The RIGHTS

Table 2. Key components of DRM

Component	Short description
Access and Usage Control	• Controls who has access to the content and how it is used. • Technologies used are encryption (e.g., symmetric, asymmetric), passwords, and copy protection systems.
Protection of Authenticity and Integrity	• Protects the authenticity and integrity of the digital content. Integrity: securing that the object has not be changed or altered. Authenticity: securing that the object is an object which claims to be. • Different types of objects exist such as digital content, rights owner, and user. • Technologies used are watermarks and digital signature.
Identification by Metadata	• Allows the identification of a digital content by metadata. • Different types of objects exist such as digital content, rights owner, and user. • Different identification mechanisms are used. Metadata can be a part of the digital content or be added to the digital content.
Specific Hardware and Software for End-Devices	• Includes all hardware and software used by the end-device where the digital content is being played, viewed, or printed. • For hardware this could be a personal computer, laptop, or a PDA. For software this might be the Windows Media Player or Real Player.
Copy Detection Systems	• Search engines which search the network for illegal copies of digital content, integrity of digital content, or user registration. • Technologies used are search engines looking for watermarks or digital fingerprints.
Billing Systems	• Billing systems should be able to handle different pricing models such as pay per use, monthly subscription. • Different types of billing systems. From Monthly billing, credit card systems (Secure Electronic Transaction Systems), electronic payment systems, or micro-payment systems.
Integrated E-Commerce Systems	• DRM systems must as well include systems, which support contract negotiation, accounting information and all other sort of information. • Different standards exist such as Electronic Data Interchange (EDI) or extensible Markup Language (XML) -based systems.

are the permissions, constraints, and obligations that are granted to or placed on the user and which they apply to the content.

As Figure 3 shows, the content is created by an entity called the user. Either the user also uses this content, or the content is used by another user. The creator of the content, which can also use the content, owns certain rights that can be exercised over the content.

At the core of any DRM is the rights model. It describes the type of rights as well as their attributes/constraints associated with these rights. There are three sets of rights. First, render rights including the right to print, view, and play. Second, transport rights including the rights to copy, move or loan the digital content from one place or device to another. Finally derivative work rights including the right to extract, edit, augments, or embed the digital content. It deals with all kind of manipulations of digital content.

Another important part of the rights model are the rights attributes. They change relative to each of the three main rights. For example, an attribute of a render right might be the type of devices on which the content can be played (e.g., a computer

Figure 3. Core entities in DRM

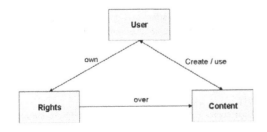

screen but not movie screen) or how many times a song may be played on a computer.

The combination of the type of rights and attributes of these rights enable new ways to control access to and the usage of digital content. This in turn enables new business models, such as superdistribution. For example, in June 2002 IBM worked with Spero Communications and other companies to launch a free promotional CD of the rock band, Oasis. Nearly two million newspaper readers in the United Kingdom received the CD. It contained music and video tracks from the band's forthcoming album and was distributed a week before the album's release. The CD allowed consumers to prelisten to three of the album's new tracks on their personal computer, and a DRM restricted play access to the one-week period before the album's launch.

Advantages and Disadvantages of DRM

After defining what a DRM is and outlining the key components and technologies used, the following table summarizes the main advantages and disadvantages of the usage of DRM for digital music.

Table 3 shows that DRM has the potential to overcome some of the weaknesses of centralized P2P networks by offering additional security and control. The next section presents the marriage of P2P networks and DRM which should enable content providers to overcome the three main hurdles for the successful distribution of digital music.

DIGITAL MUSIC DISTRIBUTION: THE NEXT GENERATION

Introduction

Peer-to-peer is not only fundamental to the architecture of today's Internet, but it is showing the directions in the future evolution of networking (O'Reilly, 2001). Therefore, content providers should learn to exploit those networks instead of spending large amount of resources on lobbying for legislation that would ban them (Gayer, 2002). If content providers want to produce music that cannot be copied, they have to make music that cannot be heard (Alexander, 2002). In addition, file sharing systems might well continue

Table 3. Advantages and disadvantages of DRMS

Advantages of DRM	Disadvantages of DRM
• DRM enables to protect the intellectual property of content creators or artists. • DRM protects and controls the access to and usage of digital content (e.g., tracking of content through the life cycle) (Bechtold, 2002). • DRM ensures the authenticity and integrity of digital music (e.g., prevent manipulation) (Bechtold, 2002). • Consumers have to pay only for the effective usage of the content (e.g., pay-per-view, pay-per-listen) (Pack, 2001). • DRM enables easy cross selling. • DRM automates the "rights management" faced by content providers in the digital environment. • DRM enables new business opportunities and business models such as superdistribution (Cox, 2002). • Current DRM improved significantly in the areas of usability, flexibility, and security compared with first generation DRM.	• DRM needs also to protect the rights of consumers and privacy (Cope & Freeman, 2001). • Restricting innovation, research. • Restricting access to digital content. As no access to digital content is possible except by copying and complete control of copying would mean control of access (Fetscherin, 2002). • Inoperability issues (e.g., across media, functions, levels of metadata, technology platforms) (Cope & Freeman, 2001). • DRM is conceptually simple but extremely difficult to implement (Mulholland, 2001). • Copyright in the physical world has never sought to capture, register, and take commercial benefits from every use of every part of every creation work ever produced (Cope & Freeman, 2001). • Pirated copies could sometimes, as in the software industry, serve as a positive marketing tool (Hui, 2002).

to operate, despite proposed bills such as the Peer-to-Peer Piracy Prevention Act (PPPA) or stronger law enforcement (Gehrke, Burghardt & Schumann, 2002). This could even drive users to "underground" systems, especially, when only one unprotected copy is made available is sufficient to be globally distributed (Buhse, 2002). Therefore, the most effective way for the music industry to fight against piracy and successfully sell digital music is to join and provide sites and networks that become the best source for high quality music downloads (O'Reilly, 2001).

Whatever the answer to the content providers' quandary, it must address the following two questions: First, why should users subscribe to a DRM supported P2P network to search, purchase and exchange music files? Second, why should content providers offer their intellectual property on such file sharing systems?

For the users, it does not only provide a platform where they can easily and legally search, purchase, and exchange high quality digital music, but they are already used to use such neworks. The proposed framework should provide the legal platform for an attractive and secure digital music distribution channel.

For content providers, it must provide the legal, secure, and cost-effective digital distribution channel that will accurately track sales and usage data to compensate copyright holders. However, protecting any digital content in a P2P environment is difficult without employing some type of DRM (Lesavich, 2002) and centralized control (Gehrke, Burghardt, & Schumann, 2002). Thus, integrating DRM into a P2P network provides the required legal, secure solution content providers have been searching for. But, a pure technological solution (like DRM) cannot overcome all the challenges faced with digital music and P2P networks, such as free-riding. Therefore, business and legal mechanisms have also to be taken into account. Only the appropriate mix of these three mechanisms will enable content providers to sell successfully digital music.

P2P Based Secure Digital Music Framework

A first attempt to such a network has been presented by Lesavich (2002) and Kini and Shetty (2001), but they have not included DRM as well as other functionalities have been missing. In a centralized P2P system which is supported by DRM, digital content is encrypted, a digital watermark is also embedded and finally cataloged the first time on a **content server** before it is made available on the network. This server can also be seen as a peer to the network acting as a super node which means, this peer is always connected to the network and provides many music files. More specifically this peer "injects" into the network new released songs and assures that songs which are not very popular in terms of storing and sharing among other peers are still provided in order to assure a high quality of service. As mentioned previously, the content and the rights can be managed separately where metadata can be part of the digital content and the type of rights and attributes of those rights granted to the user.

The **index server** includes a directory of all digital content available on the network, access points, available bandwidth, download/upload speed of peers, and so on. This information made transparent to all peers, increases the overall performance of the network. Moreover, some quality control on the digital content being traded could also be included in the index server. The index server increases the authenticity and integrity of the digital content exchanged over the P2P network. This would increase the overall P2P performance (e.g., search time, traffic on the network) quality of service, and trust of the P2P network.

Another server is the **log server** which authenticates the peers when they connect themselves into the P2P network. This enables the control of access to the network, and to some extent, to the content. The user registration information enables the identification of the user, marked "ID" in Figure 4, which increases the security and trust in the network. It also enables the redistribution of the compensation of the user through the reward system in place or to track the user in case of fraud suspicion. This is similar to other systems already in place such as Wedelmusic (www.wedelmusic.org) and the Potatoe Systems (www.potatoesystem.com).

Once the song is in the network, it stays protected against unauthorized use and access. In addition, if the content "leaves" the P2P network, it cannot be opened, because it requires a decryption key. When a peer requests a song, the peer gets a response from the content provider alias super node or another peer in the network indicating who has stored this piece of music on the user's hard disk. The encrypted license, which includes the rights and the key for decrypting the song, as well as the encrypted content package, including the content and the metadata, are sent to the peer. If the consumer is using this service for the first time, the DRM controller creates a user identity (ID). This may entail getting the user to fill out a registration form (e.g., including a number, name, address, gender, age, credit card details) and clicking to accept an end-user license or software agreement. This may be happen already when the user first downloaded and installed the P2P software. The user's identity is passed to the license server for storage in the identity database.

The **licensing servers** including the **rights management** and the **key managements server** have the following functions. The license generator authenticates the peer's identity against it's identity database and uses the content identifier to look up the rights information about the content, manage and issues licenses for legally purchased music files. In addition, they track the files (e.g., who downloaded which files, who is providing which files to other peers). This information is important for incentive systems of peers, rights management, and business models. The license

server increases the security and quality of service of the centralized P2P network.

Finally, on the peer's side the DRM controller decrypts both files and forward it to the render application and the file can be downloaded, played, stored, copied, modified according to the rights granted to the user. This exchange can happen between the super node and peers or directly between peers.

The DRM in place also includes tampering detection technologies (e.g., watermarking, digital fingerprinting) to protect the authenticity and integrity of the content. Thus, the user is guaranteed to receive the same high quality content that the content provider would have released in the case of the client-server model used.

The following figure shows a simplified centralized P2P architecture consisting of three main players: the network consisting of thousands or millions of users; the super nodes representing super users or content providers; the individual peer user.

The peer or client in Figure 4 refers to components that reside on the peer or user's side, such as the DRM controller and the rendering application. Examples of the rendering application are Windows Media Player from Microsoft or RealPlayer from RealNetworks, or they might be integrated in the peer-to-peer software. The DRM controller is the real "nerve center" of a DRM. It pulls the content package with the content and metadata, the license with the associated keys and rights together. It can be an independent piece of software, an integral part of a rendering application, or a hardware device. A DRM controller will carry out a number of functions as mentioned earlier such as exercising certain rights over content that the user requests, clarifying and authenticating content, and performing all encryption and decryption functions.

The super nodes do not need to store all digital content, they act more as a "broker" or enabler for the exchange of digital content. The key reasons

Figure 4. Digital music distribution framework

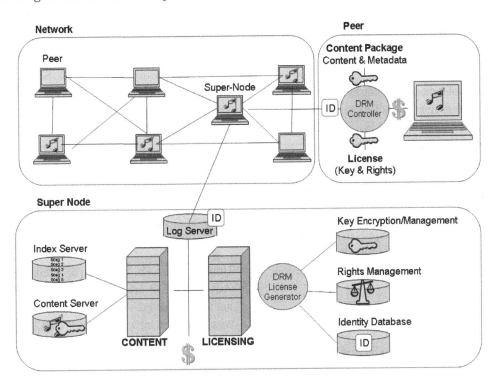

for those super nodes with their "centralized server functions" are increasing security and performance, both weaknesses of pure P2P networks. By integrating DRM into a P2P system, this enables to reduce performance issues such as fault tolerance as they integrate intelligent routing and caching or automatically mirrors popular data. It should also reduce the free-riding problem by integrating reward systems, asking users for their identification (log server) or possible review of peer recommendations. Parameswaran, Susarla, and Whinston (2001) have shown that an internal currency system can effectively privatize a public good by compensating contributors with credits toward network content and services. Finally, the integration of a DRM into a P2P enables also to solve many other security issues such as denial of service attacks, access control or usage tracking and overall piracy.

CONCLUSION

Despite huge latent demand from the consumer side, content providers have not been able to significantly extract value out of the distribution of digital music. Today, most content providers are using the client-server model to offer digital music. However, this chapter has outlined how P2P networks provide some advantages over the client-server model in terms of cost of ownership and scalability. Performance and security are the major weaknesses. But, by integrating into a P2P systems DRM, it enables to overcome these weaknesses. Therefore, this framwork gives content providers the secure, legal and cost-effective digital distribution channel they have been searching for.

REFERENCES

Alexander, P. (2002). Peer-to-peer file sharing: The case of the music recording industry. *Review of Industrial Organization*, 151-161.

Association of American Publishers (2002). AAP: Digital rights management for Ebooks: Publisher requirements. Retrieved May 27, 2007, from http://www.publishers.org/home/drm.pdf

Bechtold, S. (2002). Vom Urheber- zum Informationsrecht, Implikationen des Digital Rights Management. München, Verlag C.H. Beck oHG.

Buhse, W. (2002). Digital rights management for music filesharing communities. Retrieved May 27, 2007, from http://iab.fhbb.ch/eb/publications. nsf/id/94

Cope, B., & Freeman, R. (2001). *Digital rights management and content development technology drivers across the book production supply chain, from creator to consumer.* Australia: Common Ground Publishing Pty Ltd.

Cox, B. (2002). Finding an oasis for DRM. Retrieved May 27, 2007, from http://www.internet-news.com/ec-news/article.php/1369601

Eggs, H., et al. (2002). Vertrauensgenerierende Institutionen für P2P-Netzwerke. In C. Weinhardt & C. Holtmann (Eds.), *E-Commerce: Netze, Märkte, Technologien* (pp. 43-54). Physica-Berlag, Heidelberg.

Einhorn, M. (2001). *Digital rights management and access protection: An economic analysis.* Retrieved May 27, 2007, from http://www.law.columbia. edu/conferences/2001/1_program_en.htm

Fetscherin, M. (2002). Present state and emerging scenario of Digital Rights Management Systems. *The International Journal on Media Management, 4*, 3.

Gayer, A. (2002). Internet, peer-to-peer, and intellectual property in markets for digital products. Retrieved May 27, 2007, from http://econ.haifa. ac.il/~ozshy/freeware19.pdf

Gehrke, N., Burghardt, M., & Schumann, M. (2002). Ein Peer-to-Peer basiertes Modell zur Dezentralisierung elektronischer Marktplätze. In C. Weinhardt & C. Holtmann (Eds.), *E-Commerce: Netze, Märkte, Technologien. Physica-Verlag* (pp. 101-116). Heidelberg.

Gordon, L. (2002). *The Internet marketplace and digital rights management.* Retrieved May 27, 2007, from http://www.itl.nist.gov/div895/docs/ GLyonDRM Whitepaper.pdf

Homayounfar, H., Wang, F., & Areibi, S. (2002). Advanced P2P architecture using autonomous agents. Retrieved May 27, 2007, from http://wolf-man.eos.uoguelph.ca/~sareibi/PUBLICATIONS_ dr/docs/CAINE02-paper-agent-initial.pdf

Horne, B., Pinkasa, B., & Sander, T. (2002). *Escrow services and incentives in peer-to-peer networks.* Retrieved May 27, 2007, from http:// www.star-lab.com/bpinkas/PAPERS/p2p.ps

Hui, K. (2002). *Piracy and the legitimate demand for recorded music.* Retrieved May 27, 2007, from http://www.comp.nus.edu.sg/~ipng/research/Piracy_3.pdf

Kant, K., Iyer, R., & Tewari, V. (2002). *A framework for classifying peer-to-peer technologies.* Retrieved May 27, 2007, from http://kkant.ccweb-host.com/papers/taxonomy.pdf

Kini, A., & Shetty, S. (2002). *Peer-to-peer networking - Is this the future of network computing?* Retrieved May 27, 2007, from http://www.ias.ac.in/ resonance/Dec2001/pdf/Dec2001p69-79.pdf

Kwok, S., & Lui, S. (2000). *A license management model to support B2C and C2C music sharing.*

Retrieved May 27, 2007, from http://www10. org/cdrom/posters/1008.pdf

Kwok, S., & Lui, S. (2002). A license management model for peer-to-peer music sharing. *World Scientific Publishing Company, 1*(3), 541-558.

Kwok, S., Lang, & Kar, Y. (2002). Peer-to-peer technology business and service models: Risks and opportunities. *Electronic Markets, 12*(3), 175-183.

Lesavich, S. (2002). *Protecting digital content in a peer-to-peer world.* Retrieved May 27, 2007, from http://www.hightech-iplaw.com/wibardrm.pdf

Lethin, R. (2001). Reputation. In A. Oram (Ed.), *Harnessing the power of disruptive technologies* (pp. 341-353). Sebastopol: O'Reilly.

Milojicic, D., et al. (2002). Peer-to-peer computing, HP laboratories. Retrieved May 27, 2007, from http://www.hpl.hp.com/techreports/2002/HPL-2002-57.pdf

Minar, N., & Hedlung, M. (2001). Network of peers: Peer-to-peer models through the history of the internet. In A. Oram (Ed.), *Harnessing the power of disruptive technologies* (pp. 3-20). Sebastopol: O'Reilly.

Mulholland, J. (2001). Digital rights (mis)management, W3C DRM workshop. Retrieved May 27, 2007, from http://www. w3.org/2000/12/drm-ws/pp/fsu-mulholland.html

Nelson, M. (2002). *Distributed systems topologies: Part 2.* Retrieved May 27, 2007, from http://www. openp2p.com/pub/a/p2p/2002/01/08/p2p_topologies_pt2.html

O'Reilly, T. (2001). Remaking the peer-to-peer meme. In A. Oram (Ed.), *Harnessing the power of disruptive technologies* (pp. 38-59). Sebastopol: O'Reilly.

Pack, T. (2001). Digital rights management: Can technology provide long-term solutions? *E-Content, 5*(6), 22-27.

Parameswaran, M., Susarla, A., & Whinston, A. (2002). *P2P networking: An information-sharing alternative.* Retrieved May 27, 2007, from http://cism.bus.utexas.edu/works/articles/PARA. Cxs2final.pdf

Rosenblatt, B., Trippe, B., & Mooney, S. (2002). *Digital rights management: Business and technology.* New York: M&T Books.

Schoder, D., & Fischbach, K. (2002). Peer-to-peer - Anwendungsbereiche und herausforderungen. Retrieved May 27, 2007, from http://www. whu-koblenz.de/ebusiness/p2p-buch/buch/P2P-Buch_04_Schoder-Fischbach_P2P-Anwendungsbereiche-Herausforderungen.pdf

Schollmeier, R. (2002). *Peer-to-peer networking. Applications for and impacts on future IP-based networks.* Retrieved May 27, 2007, from http://www.lkn.ei.tum.de/lkn/mitarbeiter/hrs/ Komponenten/paper/Peer1f.pdf

Shirky, C. (2001). Listening to napster. In A. Oram (Ed.), *Harnessing the power of disruptive technologies* (pp. 21-37). Sebastopol: O'Reilly.

Waldman, M., Cranor, L., & Rubin, A. (2002). Trust. In A. Oram (Ed.), *Harnessing the power of disruptive technologies* (pp. 242-270). Sebastopol: O'Reilly.

Chapter IX
Music Information Retrieval in P2P Networks[1]

Ioannis Karydis
Aristotle University of Thessaloniki, Greece

Yannis Manolopoulos
Aristotle University of Thessaloniki, Greece

ABSTRACT

In this chapter we present the most significant trends in recent research in the field of content-based music information retrieval in peer-to-peer networks. Despite the diminished attention the area has received in general terms, the relatively close area of metadata MIR in P2P is by far new. As metadata prove to be inefficient for the purposes of MIR as well as the peculiarities of music in comparison to text and image data, developing dedicated solutions for CBMIR in P2P networks becomes a necessity while the challenges faced therein, unique. Depending on the type of P2P network, a number of prominent research works are presented and compared in this chapter.

INTRODUCTION

The World Wide Web (WWW) is being used for commercial, entertainment, and educational purposes and has become the primary means for information dissemination. One popular type of data that is being disseminated over WWW is digitised music. Recently, the new opportunities that emerge from this activity have been recognized and led to the development of systems like iTune (www.apple.com/itunes), iMusic (www.imusic. com), and Napster (www.napster.com). Although abundantly used, even nowadays, traditional metadata (title, composer, performer, genre, date, etc.) of a music object give rather minimal information regarding the actual content of the music object itself. On the other hand, research efforts in the field of music information retrieval (MIR) have developed efficient methods for searching music data collections by **content**. For instance, queries based on humming (using a microphone) or on a small piece of musical file, are far more natural an approach to MIR. This type of queries lies within the content-based MIR (CBMIR). In CBMIR, an actual music piece is required in order to compare its content with the content of the music pieces already available in a database.

As with regard to the infrastructure for exchanging music data, peer-to-peer networks over the WWW have gain significant popularity. A peer-to-peer (P2P) network is a distributed system in which peers employ resources that are distributed in the network of peers in order to perform a function in a decentralized manner. Nodes in P2P networks normally hold equivalent roles, thus, also called peers. Within the advantageous qualities of the P2P networks lie the increased size of the overall database offered by a P2P network, its fault tolerance support to peer failure by other peers and the workload distribution over a network of available CPUs, since CBMIR is computationally highly intensive, the absence of the requirement of special administration or financial arrangements and their self-organzation capability and adaptability. Additionally, P2P networks offer the ability to harness the collaborative efforts of users to provide various semantic tags aiming at musical content description. Nonetheless, the very advantages of the P2P network are the same parameters that make P2P information retrieval much more complex than in the traditional server-client model. That is, the lack of a central repository for the documents to be retrieved, the large number of documents available and the dynamic character of the network, introduce an increased degree of difficulty in the retrieval process. Accordingly, as collections become larger, CBMIR in P2P networks presents new and challenging requirements the highlights of which are:

- Richer set of search semantics that can support efficient CBMIR
- Appropriate P2P models that ensure scalability
- Distribution of the workload over a network of available CPUs, as CBMIR is computationally intensive.

Though, despite the previously mentioned advantages of P2P networks, the trend of musical data dissemination over P2P networks became obscure by the illegal exchange of copyrighted material. One of the key advantages of P2P networks, as previously discussed, is the lack of necessity for an administration, which acted as a loophole. Accordingly, numerous approaches (Chu, Su, Prabhu, Gadh, Kurup, Sridhar et al., 2006; Kalker, Epema, Hartel, Lagendijk, & Steen, 2004; Praveen, Sridhar, Sridhar, & Gadh, 2005) for the protection and reproduction of intellectual property have been proposed, while the field is still developing (Dhamija & Wallenberg, 2003; Dubosson-Torbay, Pigneur, & Usunier, 2004; Sastry, 2005; Schyndel, 2005), both in terms of technology as well as ethics. CBMIR applications in P2P networks can, and must, adopt any such developments.

The field of music information retrieval has received increased attention during the last decade. Numerous surveys examine the state of the art developments in the area (Byrd & Crawford, 2002; Karydis, Nanopoulos, & Manolopoulos, 2006; Orio, 2006; Typke, Wiering, & Veltkamp, 2005) while a litany of works spawns rapidly in all directions of MIR.

Although outside the scope of this chapter, work in multimedia (other than music) information retrieval in P2P networks (Lew, Sebe, Djeraba, & Jain, 2006) shows a wealth of research issues that still remain open. Moreover, multimedia IR in P2P faces similar problems (such as indexing high-dimensionality data) appearing to MIR in P2P, though the difference of the nature of the data, such as interfaces, data representation as well as data volume issues, requires, in many cases, a completely differentiated approach. Additionally, multimedia IR research is naturally complemented by streaming in P2P networks research as many of the retrieved multimedia documents are videos. Therein lie more open research issues (Liu, Kundur, Merabti, & Yu, 2006).

In what follows this chapter, we summarize existing work on music content-based information retrieval in peer-to-peer networks. First, necessary background information on P2P networks such as classification and searching methods are provided in Section "Networks". Next, in Section "CBMIR in Wired P2P Networks" we examine the task of CBMIR in wired P2P networks, which has attracted significant attention in research related to CBMIR. A number of methods as well as systems that have been proposed are presented therein, classified according to their degree of centralization and structure. In the section to follow, we study methods for CBMIR in wireless ad-hoc networks and present the challenges this new field introduces. In the final section, we conclude this chapter and present the perspective of P2P CBMIR.

P2P NETWORKS

This section of the chapter offers a concise presentation of the common classification of P2P systems based on their attributes, as well as some of the prominent searching methods for both wired and wireless such systems.

P2P Classification

P2P networks can be classified based on the control over data location and network topology in *unstructured, loosely structured* and *highly structured* (Li & Wu, 2004). Unstructured P2P networks follow no rule in where data is stored while the network topology is arbitrary (Gnutella). Loosely structured P2P networks have both data location and network architecture nonprecisely determined (Freenet). Finally, in highly structured networks data storage and network topology are explicitly defined (Chord). What is more, P2P networks can also be classified according to the number of central directories of document loca-

tions in *centralized, hybrid,* and *decentralized.* Centralized networks maintain a central directory in a single location (Napster), hybrid networks maintain more than one directories in super-peers (Kazaa) while for the decentralized (Chord) no central directory is kept. P2P networks can also be classified into hierarchical and nonhierarchical based on whether their overlay structure is a hierarchy or not. It is common for decentralized systems to have no hierarchy, while hybrid and most centralized systems ordinarily incorporate some degree of hierarchy. Hierarchical systems provide increased scalability, ease in exploiting peer heterogeneity and high routing efficiency. On the other hand systems with no hierarchy offer load-balance and increased resilience.

Searching Methods in Unstructured P2P Networks

In unstructured P2P systems, no rule exists that strictly defines where data is stored and which nodes are neighbors of each other. Many alternative schemes (Li & Wu, 2004 offer a survey of searching techniques in P2P networks) have been proposed to address the problems of the original flooding search. These works include iterative deepening, k-walker random walk, modified random Breadth First Search (BFS), two-level k-walker random walk, directed BFS, intelligent search, local indices based search, routing indices based search, attenuated bloom filter based search, adaptive probabilistic search and dominating set based search. Following are some prominent searching methods for decentralized unstructured P2P networks.

Early works such as the original Gnutella used flooding algorithms, which is the BFS of the overlay network graph with depth limit D. In the BFS, a query peer Q propagates the query q to all its neighbor peers. Each peer P receiving the q initially searches its local repository for any documents matching q and then passes on q to all its neighbors. In case, a P has a match in its local repository then a *QueryMatch* message is created containing information about the match. The *QueryMatch* messages are then transmitted back, using reversely the path q travelled, to Q. Finally, since more than one *QueryMatch* message may have been received by Q, it can select the peer with best connectivity attributes for direct transfer of the match. It is obvious that the BFS sacrifices performance and network traffic for simplicity and high-hit rates. In order to reduce network traffic, the TTL parameter is used, which is the number of peers a query should be forwarded to. In a modified version of this algorithm, the Random BFS (RBFS) (Kalogeraki, Gunopulos, & Zeinalipour-Yazti, 2002), the query peer Q propagates the query q not to all but a fraction of its neighbor peers.

In an attempt to rectify the inability of the RBFS to select a path of the network leading to large network segments, the *>RES* algorithm was developed (Yang & Garcial-Molina, 2002). In this approach, the query peer Q propagates the query q to a subset of its neighbor peers based on an aggregated statistic. That is, Q propagates the q to k neighboring peers, all of which returned the most results during the last m queries, with k and m being configurable parameters. *>RES* is a significant amelioration in comparison to the RBFS algorithm, however its attitude is rather quantitative than qualitative, since it does not select the neighbors to propagate the query q based on the similarity of the content of q with the previous queries.

To overcome this quantitative behavior of the *>RES* approach, the *ISM* approach emerged (Kalogeraki et al., 2002). In *ISM*, for each query, a peer propagates the query q to the peers that are more likely to reply the query based on the following two parameters; a profile mechanism and a relevance rank. The profile is built and maintained by each peer for each of its neighboring peers. The information included in this profile consists of the t most recent queries with matches and their matches as well as the number

of matches the neighboring peer reported. The relevance rank (*RR*) function is computed by comparison of the query q to all the queries for which there is a match in each profile. Thus, for a querying peer P_Q the *RR* function is calculated by the following formula:

$$RR_Q(P_i, Q) = Qsim(q_j, q)^a \times S(P_i, q_j)$$

where Qsim is the similarity function used between queries and $S(P_i, q_j)$ is the number of the results returned by P_i for query q_j. The *ISM* allows for higher ranking of the neighboring peers that return more results by adjustment of the α parameter. Obviously, the strong point of the *ISM* approach reveals in environments that show increased degree of document locality.

Searching Methods In Structured P2P Networks

In strictly structured P2P systems, the neighbor relationship between peers and data locations is explicitly defined. Thus, the particular network architecture of such systems determines the searching process. Of the alternative strictly structured systems available, some implement the Distributed Hash Table (DHT), others have flat overlay structures while some have hierarchical overlay structures.

A DHT is a hash table whose table entries are distributed among different peers located in arbitrary locations. In such systems each node is assigned with a region in a virtual address space, while each shared document is associated with a value of this address space. Thus, locating a document requires only a key lookup of the node responsible for the key. Numerous different flat data structures can be used to implement the DHT, including ring, mesh, hypercube, and other special graphs such as de Bruijn graph.

Hierarchical DHT P2P systems organize peers into different groups or clusters, where each group forms its own overlay. The entire hierarchical overlay is formed by the entirety of all groups. Typically, the overlay hierarchies are two-tier or three-tier. Their key difference refers on the number of groups each tier has, the structure of the overlay each group forms and whether super-peers do exist. The existence of such super-peers offers increased computing resources, stability, and effectiveness in routing.

In an attempt to solve the deficiencies of DHT, the nonDHT P2Ps avoid hashing. Hashing ignores data locality and cannot support range queries, two serious disadvantages. SkipNet, SkipGraph and TerraDir are three of the most representative such systems (Li & Wu, 2004). SkipNet stores data close to users, SkipGraph offers support to range queries, while TerraDir is targeted for hierarchical name searches. Searching in these systems is achieved based on the specified neighboring relationships between nodes.

In loosely structured P2Ps, the overlay structure is not strictly specified. It is either formed based on hints or formed probabilistically. Some systems develop their structure based on hints or preferences, while in others the overlay is constructed probabilistically. Searching in loosely structured P2P systems depends on the overlay structure and how the data is stored. Approaches do exist, where searching is application dependent, based on hints or done by reducing the numerical distance from the querying source to the node that stores the desired data.

Information Discovery/Provision In Wireless Mobile Ad-hoc Networks

A Mobile Ad-hoc NETwork (MANET) is a collection of wireless Mobile Hosts (MH) forming a temporary network without the aid of any centralized administration or standard support services regularly available on the wide area network to which the hosts may normally be connected. When a source node desires to send a message to some destination node and does not already have a valid route to that node, it initiates a path discovery process to locate the destination. It broadcasts a route request to its neighbors, which then forward the request to their neighbors and so on, until the destination or an intermediate node with a route to the destination is located. Nodes are identified by their IP address and maintain a broadcast ID, which is incremented after every route request they initiate. The broadcast ID together with the node's IP address, uniquely identify a route request. In the same manner, the transmitted data requests can be identified.

Routing algorithms for MANETs are radically different from the traditional routing (e.g., Open Shortest Path First) and information search protocols (e.g., Distributed Hash Table) used in hardwired networks, due to the absence of "fixed" infrastructure (servers, access points, routers, and cables) in a MANET as well as the mobility of the nodes. For wireless ad-hoc networks, there have been proposed various routing/discovery protocols, which roughly fall into the following categories (Agrawal & Zeng, 2003): (a) table-driven routing protocols, (b) source-initiated on-demand routing protocols, and (c) hybrid routing protocols. Apart from the former, which require consistent, up-to-date routing information from each node to every other node in the network and thus are practically unfeasible for large-scale and dynamic MANETs, the remaining two families of information (node) discovery protocols rely on some form of *broadcasting*; broadcasting is best suited in cases where information packets are transmitted to multiple hosts in the network. *Flooding* is the simplest broadcasting approach, where every node in the network forwards the packet exactly once; flooding ensures full coverage of the MANET provided that there are no network partitions. Flooding, though, generates too many redundant transmissions, causing the *broadcast storm problem* (Ni, Tseng, Chen, & Sheu, 1999).

Numerous algorithms have been proposed to address this problem (Lou & Wu, 2004). They can be classified as follows: (a) *probabilistic approaches* (counter-based, distance-based, location-based) and (b) *deterministic approaches* (global, quasi-global, quasi-local, local). The former methods do not guarantee full coverage of the network, whereas the latter does provide coverage guarantee, and thus are preferable.

The *deterministic approaches* provide full coverage of the network for a broadcast operation, by selecting only a subset of nodes to forward the broadcast packet (*forward nodes*), and the remaining nodes are adjacent to the nodes that forward the packet. The selection of nodes is done by exploiting the "state" information, that is, network topology and broadcast state (e.g., next selected node to forward the packet, recently visited nodes and their neighbor sets). All the categories of the deterministic algorithms, apart from the *local algorithms*, require (full or partial) global state information, thus being impractical. The local or *neighbor-designating* algorithms maintain some local state information, that is, 1-hop neighborhood information by periodic exchange of "HELLO" messages, which is feasible and not costly. In the neighbor-designating methods, the forwarding status of each node is determined by its neighbors. As a matter of fact, the source node selects a subset of its 1-hop neighbors as forward nodes to cover its 2-hop neighbors. This forward node list is piggybacked in the broadcast packet. Each forward node in turn designates its own forward node list.

Remotely related to the topic of this chapter is the issue of multicasting streaming media (audio/video) to MANETs (Dutta, Chennikara, Chen, Altintas, & Schulzrinne, 2003) or unicasting audio to 3G UMTS devices (Roccetti, Salomoni, Ghini, & Ferretti, 2005). These works though assume the existence of a central server (supplier), which provisions the mobile clients with multimedia data.

CBMIR IN WIRED P2P NETWORKS

The field of combined CBMIR and P2P networks is definitely very young as the inaugural research paper dates back to 2002 (Wang, Li, & Shi, 2002).

In this first attempt, the authors of Wang et al. (2002) present four P2P models for CBMIR (Sections "Generalised", "PsPs Model", & "Hybrid"). The four models include all centralized, decentralized, and hybrid categories. Another research based on a hybrid configuration is presented in Tzanetakis, Gao, and Steenkiste (2004) (Section "Decentralized Structured"). Therein the authors propose a scalable and load balanced P2P system with an underlying DHT-based system. C. Yang (2003) proposed the utilization of the feature selection and extraction process that is described in Yang (2002) for CBMIR in a decentralized unstructured P2P system (Section "MACSIS-P2P"). Finally, Karydis, Nanopoulos, and Manolopoulos (2005) (Section "Sampling Framework") focus on similarity searching for similar acoustic data over unstructured decentralized P2P networks, proposing a framework, which takes advantage of unstructured P2P networks and minimises the required traffic for all operations with the use of a sampling scheme.

The following sections contain an overall description of the systems that have been proposed for the purposes of CBMIR in P2P networks, classified by their degree of centralization and structure.

Centralized

Wang et al. (2002) introduced CBMIR in peer-to-peer environments by developing four systems based on different P2P models. Two of these models, PsCM & PsC+M, have a centralized architecture.

PsC Model

In the peers-coordinator model (PsCM) peers contain a music set as well as sharing a common feature extraction method. A coordinator maintains a data structure to store all music features in the P2P system and a feature matching method to compute the distance between two music features. Queries are content requests proposed by a user. In this model, any query PC in the system connects with the coordinator, while peers connect with each other via the coordinator, though they directly transfer music data from one to another. During the query process the feature of the music request is extracted from the music request by an extraction method and sent to the coordinator. The coordinator receives the feature, compares it with all music features uploaded during peers registration and sends the result to the request PC. Results contain the locations of the peers which store the music similar to the requested.

PsC+ Model

A slightly differentiated implementation of a centralized system, PsC+M, assigns the feature matching process on each peer. In the peers-coordinator+ model (PsC+M) each peer has additionally to the PsC model a commonly shared feature matching method. The coordinator consists of a data structure which stores the network identifiers of all peers. The main steps of a query process are the following: Each peer shares some music stored on the local hard disk and registers its location at the coordinator. A query by any peer sends the coordinator the extracted feature of the music request. The coordinator forwards the feature of the query to all registered peers, each peer compares it with the features of the local shared music and sends the local result to the coordinator. The coordinator in turn passes on the results to the querier.

In both the previously mentioned models, the role of the coordinator can significantly ease the process of retrieval due to its supervising character in terms of route to peers discovery and knowledge of the available content on other peers (PsCM). Though, centralized P2P networks are subject to the same drawbacks for which the traditional server-client model was originally not used (network failures due to central peer failure, impaired scalability, joining/leaving of peers not easily handled and possible undesirable dominion of coordinator controllers). In other words the coordinator is easily overloaded and becomes the bottleneck of the whole system, leading to poor stability. As for these two models (PsCM & PsC+M) Wang et al. (2002) conclude that the load for a given query produced by PsCM is less than that of PsC+M. Though comparing time requirements for the completion of the same query PsC+M is faster than PsCM.

Decentralized Structured

In the system proposed by Tzanetakis et al. (2004) each node in the network stores music files for sharing as well as information about the location of other music files in the network. Shared files in the system are described by a Music File Description (MFD) which is essentially a set of AV pairs (artist = "Jennifer Warnes", album = "Dirty Dancing", song = "The Time Of My Life", ..., specCentroid = 0.65, mfcc2 = 0.85, ...). A Music Feature Extraction Engine (MFEE) calculates the features from the audio files, while others are manually appointed. Two operations are supported by the system, the registration of a music file based on its associated MFD and the search where the user query is converted into an appropriate MFD that is then used to locate nodes containing files matching the search criteria. The MFD of either registration or search query is passed to the content discovery system (CDS), which runs on top of a

DHT-based P2P system (see Section "Searching Methods in Structured P2P Networks").

The MFEE component takes as input an audio file and produces a feature vector of AV pairs that characterises the particular musical content of the file as proposed by Tzanetakis and Cook (2002). Features based on the Short Time Fourier Transform as well as Mel-Frequency Cepstral Coefficients are used to represent sound texture, and features based on Beat and Pitch Histograms are used to represent rhythm and pitch content.

Scalable Content Discovery

Unlike centralized systems in which files are registered at a single place, or broadcast-based (decentralized unstructured) systems where a query may potentially be sent to all peers in the system, CDS uses a scalable approach based on Rendez-vous Points (RPs) for registration and query resolution. Essentially, the P2P network is structured to efficiently represent the space of AV pairs for the tasks of searching and retrieving music.

MFD Registration

To register an MFD, the CDS applies a uniform hash function such as SHA-1 to each AV pair in the MFD to obtain n node IDs. The MFD is then sent to each of these n peers, while this set of peers is known as the Rendez-vous Point (RP) set for this MFD. Upon receiving an MFD, the peer inserts it into its database. Hence, each peer is responsible for the AV pairs that are mapped onto it. Obviously, the load on each node depends on the distribution of specific AV pairs, addressed by a load-balancing scheme.

MFD Searching

Searching has been divided into two categories: exact search and similarity search. In an exact search, the user is looking for MFDs that match

simultaneously all the AV pairs of the query, while extra AV pairs that may be in the MFDs but not in the query are ignored. For a query Q with m AV pairs, the MFDs that match Q are registered at RP peers N_1 through N_m, while the CDS chooses the peer that has the smallest MFD database, to fully resolve the query. Once a query is received, the peer conducts a pair-wise comparison between the query and all the entries in its database to find the matching MFDs.

In a similarity search, the user is trying to find music files that have a similar feature vector to what is specified in the query. Thus, a pair of feature-value selected from the extracted feature vector of the query is sent to a peer designated by the hash function. The receiving peer computes the "distance" between the query vector and each MFD in its database, using a distance function (Manhattan). The distances are then ranked, and the k top MFDs that have the smallest distance are returned to the user. For the discovery of MFDs that slightly differ from the query, in a selected pair of feature-value, but are similar or identical regarding other features, the query is also sent either by the peer that received the query or querier to peers corresponding to values near the originally selected pair of feature-value.

Load Balancing

The use of RPs, ensures the absence of network-wide message flooding at both registration and query. Though, some AV pairs may be much more common or popular in MFDs than others, causing a few peers to be overloaded by registrations or queries, while the majority of peers in the system stay underutilised. The system's throughput is improved by deployment of a distributed dynamic load-balancing mechanism where multiple peers are used as RP points to share the heavy load incurred by popular AV pairs.

The work of Tzanetakis et al. (2004) addresses a number of important issues concerning both MIR as well as P2P networking factors. On one hand, the use of both metadata and content-based features confronts a number of real life scenarios where a user may query based on a sample-file or humming as well as by the singer's name or song title. On the other hand, the disadvantages of the use of metadata, such as the fact that there are not always available, the inconsistencies introduced by their manual appointment, the fact that their sole use in MIR requires knowledge for the query not provided by listening and the fact that their description lacks customization since it relies on predefined descriptors are compromised by the co-existence of the feature extraction process. On the networking side of their proposal, the use of an decentralized system avoids scalability issues as well as potential coordinator problems. Additionally, given the assumption that the proposed system is structured, the use of an underlying DHT-like scheme alleviates problems concerning networking searching in order to identify the host that may have a match to a query. Though, such an advantage comes at the cost of requiring the peers to host foreign data. Finally, the use of the load-balancing scheme ensures that no peer is over exploited due to the use of the underlying DHT-based system, at the cost of redundant data replication and increased processing requirements for the distributed dynamic load-balancing mechanism to work efficiently.

Decentralized Unstructured

PsPs Model

Wang et al. (2002) presented a distributed CBMIR P2P model, where the system is formed by a numerous of peers without a coordinator, while the width of the system is m and the depth is n. Peers consist of a music set, a same feature extraction method, a common feature matching method and a data structure that stores the network identifiers of neighboring peers. The main steps of a query process in this system, PsPsM, are the following: Each peer shares some music and gets the

network identifiers of its neighbors by broadcast or other algorithms. Upon a query by any peer, the feature of the query is extracted and sent to m peers, randomly selected from the neighboring set. After receiving the feature of a query, each peer sends it to m random neighbor peers, as long as a maximum allowed hop number is less than n, examines the local content and returns the results to the querying peer.

This approach is identical to the random breadth first search (RBFS) as also presented by Kalogeraki et al. (2002), aside from the domain of MIR, where the querying peer Q propagates the query q not to all but at a fraction of its neighbor peers.

In comparison to the centralized P2P CBMIR systems, the stability of their distributed version, such as the PsPsM, is far better since no coordinator exists that can easily overload and become the bottleneck of the whole system. However the number of messages that are sent by PCs of distributed P2P CBMIR systems increases when the scale of the system expands. Accordingly, the load produced for a given query by PsPsM is smaller than that of either PsCM or PsC+M, but by no means smaller than that of the hybrid approach PsPsCM, as it will be seen in section "Hybrid".

MACSIS-P2P

C. Yang (2003) proposed a peer-to-peer model for music retrieval, where nodes are interconnected as an undirected graph and each node stores a collection of music files. Following the MACSIS system, analysis of raw audio and conversion to characteristic sequences are done locally at each node, for both the database and queries. While building the database, characteristic sequences for each music file are stored in multiple LSH hashing instances (each with its own set of randomised parameters). The same music file may appear in many different nodes and indexed under different sets of hashing instances. At any time, every node maintains a variable "CPU Availability" which indicates how much CPU power it can offer to run peers' search tasks. When the node is busy with other tasks or when the owner wants to start using the node, CPU-Availability is set to zero.

Feature Extraction

The music indexing framework (MACSIS) (C. Yang, 2002) consists of three phases: (1) Raw audio goes through a series of transformations, including Fourier Transformation, leading to a stream of characteristic sequences, which are high-dimensional vectors representing a short segment of music data. (2) Characteristic sequences for the audio database are then indexed in a high-dimensional indexing scheme known as Locality-Sensitive Hashing, or LSH (Indyk & Motwani, 1998). (3) During retrieval, Phase 2 finds a list of matches on characteristic sequences, representing short segments of music, which require joining together to determine which song is the best "global" match.

Searching Phase

A music query issued by one node (querier) in the network, is processed by a set of other nodes, which may include the querier itself. Due to the symmetric nature of P2P networks, any node can become a querier and a node may be simultaneously a querier and response node for different queries. A query is sent as a stream of characteristic sequences, obtained by analysing user-input audio at the querier. Each query has two required parameters: expiration-time and search depth, indicating the time at which the query expires, and the maximum number of links through which the query can be passed in the P2P network graph. The query is sent from the querier to its neighbors, which may in turn pass it on to other neighbors of their own (while decrementing search-depth by 1) as long as search depth is greater than zero. The processing of all

query vectors is not obligatory, since one way to speed up retrieval is to process only a fraction of such query vectors.

A common method between peers for hashing binary files to a signature value is assumed, so that identical files must have identical signatures and the chance of different files having identical signatures to be very low.

The work considers both a replicated database and a general P2P scenario, while special attention is given on the control of the workload produced at queried peers during query time. Each query is divided into two phases, the first of which includes only a subpart of the actual query vectors, in order to distinguish high probability response peers. Accordingly, a peer ranking occurs and the full query vectors are sent to all peers. Given that a peer has free CPU resources, it decides whether to process a query or not based on the ranking that the specific query received, among other factors.

The work proposed by C. Yang (2003), is based on music indexing framework (MACSIS), which reports high accuracy levels in most of the five levels of musical similarity: (1) identical digital copies; (2) same analog source, different digital copies, possibly with noise; (3) same instrumental performance, different vocal components; (4) same score different performances, possibly at different tempo; (5) same underlying melody, different otherwise, with possible transposition) used therein. As the MACSIS framework is highly computationally intensive, its proposed utilization in a P2P environment is safeguarded by a the "CPU-availability" variable, allowing peers to select their engagement to the retrieval process. Moreover, the use of different sampling levels of the query vectors as well as a two staged search phase, in the later of which higher probability response candidates may perform more demanding tasks, allows a further level of security in terms peer CPU-availability as well as network utilization.

Sampling Framework

The work of Karydis, Nanopoulos, and Manolopoulos (2005) examines the problem of searching for similar acoustic data over unstructured decentralized P2P networks using Dynamic Time Warping (DTW) as a distance measure.

DTW can express similarity between two time series even if they are out of phase in the time axis, or they do not have the same length. The DTW distance $D_{DTW}(S,T)$ between time series S and T is essentially a way to map S to T and vice-versa. The most important disadvantage of the DTW method is that it does not satisfy the triangular inequality, which is a desirable property for constructing efficient indexing schemes and pruning the search space. Moreover, the calculation of $D_{DTW}(S,T)$ is significantly more CPU intensive than the calculation of $D_{Euclidean}(S,T)$. Therefore, a performance improvement is the definition of a lower bound, that would take advantage of indexing schemes and avoid the computation of DTW when there is a guarantee that the two time series are not similar. One such lower bound, as proposed in Keogh and Ratanamahatana (2005), is termed *LB_Keogh* and defined as follows:

$$LB\_Keogh\ (S,T) = \begin{cases} \sqrt{\sum_{i=1}^{n}(T[i]-[i])^2} & T[i] \geq U[i] \\ \sqrt{\sum_{i=1}^{n}(T[i]-[i])^2} & T[i] < L[i] \\ 0 & otherwise \end{cases} \quad (1)$$

where U and L is the upper and lower bound respectively for the time series S. Essentially, for each i, the upper bound guarantees that $U[i] \geq S[i]$ and the lower bound guarantees that $L[i] \leq S[i]$. In Keogh and Ratanamahatana (2005) it has been proven that $LB\_Keogh \leq D_{DTW}(S,T)$, and therefore the distance measure *LB_Keogh(S,T)* can be effectively used for pruning, resulting in considerably less number of D_{DTW} computations.

Due to the selected similarity model, the information that is propagated between nodes

comprises the U and L sequences of the query sequence. A node receiving these sequences computes the LB value between its documents and envelope. When a LB value is smaller than the user-specified similarity threshold, then the query sequence is propagated to this node and the actual DTW distance is computed between the query and corresponding document.

As acoustic data tend to be very large, the number of elements in a phrase of even few seconds can be several hundred thousands. The length of the U and L sequences is equal to the length of the query sequence, meaning that a straightforward approach, which directly propagates U and L sequences between nodes, will result into an extremely large traffic over the P2P network. Moreover, the computation of LB in each node can become rather costly, violating the need of a P2P network to burden the participating nodes as little as possible.

A two-fold optimization scheme is used for the reduction of the traffic over the P2P network when querying music documents by content. The scheme works as follows:

- It reduces the length of the envelope's sequences by sampling them. However, plain sampling can be ineffective, since it leads to underestimation of LB, thus a sampling method to reduce the length of the sequences without significantly affecting the computation of LB or introducing false-negatives is provided.
- The scheme uses (whenever possible) a compact representation of the sampled sequences of the envelope. The representation comprises a form of compression for the sequences, but does not burden the nodes with the cost of decompression.

Sampling and Representation Methods

Let the considered phrase length be equal to N. The length of each query Q, and therefore of its upper (U) and lower (L) sequences, will also be equal to

N. The goal is to sample *U* and *L*, so as to obtain two sequences *U'* and *L'*, each of length $M < N$. Initially, it is assumed that uniform sampling is performed. In this case, each time the $(i \times N/M)$-th element of *U* and *L* is selected, where $1 \le i \le M$. When the LB Keogh between the query sequence *Q* and a data sequence is computed, each phrase *C* of length *N* in *Q* is considered. Thus, each phrase has to be sampled in the same way as *U* and *L*. This leads to a sampled phrase *C'*. Therefore, the lower-bound measure *B'*, is given as:

$$LB' = \sqrt{\sum_{i=1}^{M} \begin{cases} (C_i'-U_i')^2 & f \quad C_i'>U_i' \\ (C_i'-L_i')^2 & f \quad C_i'<L_i' \\ 0 & otherwise \end{cases}} \quad (2)$$

In the aforementioned equation, the third case (i.e., when $L_i' \le C_i \le U_i'$) does not contribute in the computation of *B'*. The problem of uniform sampling is that, as it selects elements without following any particular criterion, it tends to select many elements from *U* and *L* that result to this third case. Therefore, *B'* may become a significantly bad underestimation of *B* that would have been computed if sampling was not used. The underestimation of the lower-bound value will result to an increase in false-alarms, which will in turn incur high traffic.

To overcome this problem, an alternative sampling method is therein proposed. *U* and *L* are sampled separately. Initially, the elements of U are stored in ascending order. In *U'* the first *M* elements of this ordering are selected. Respectively, *L* is sorted in descending order and the first *M* elements in *L'* are selected. The intuition is that the selection of the smallest *M* values of *U*, helps in increasing the number of occurrences of the first case (i.e., when $C_i > U_i'$), since the smallest the value of U_i' is, the more expected is to have a C_i' larger than it. Accordingly, it is easy to prove (Karydis, Nanopoulos, & Manolopoulos, 2005)

that the sampling of *U* and *L* does not produce any false negatives.

The separate sampling of *U* and *L* presents the requirement of having to store the positions from which elements are being selected in *U'* and *L'*. If the positions are stored explicitly, then this doubles the amount of information kept (2M numbers for storing *U'* and *L'* and additionally 2*M* numbers for storing the positions of selected elements). Since this information is propagated during querying, traffic is increased. For this reason an alternative representation is proposed. To represent *U'*, a bitmap of length *N* (the phrase length) is used. Each bit corresponds to an element in *U*. If an element is selected in the sample *U'*, then its bit is set to 1, otherwise it is set to 0. Therefore, the combination of the bitmap and the *M* values that are selected in *U'* are used to represent *U'*. The same applies for *L'*. This representation proves to be efficient: the space required for *U'* is $M + \lceil N/8 \rceil$ bytes[2].

The plain representation requires 5*M* bytes (since it requires only one integer, i.e., 4 bytes, to store the position of each selected element). Thus, the proposed method is advantageous when $N<32M$, i.e., for sample larger than about 3% (experimentation showed that samples with size 10% are the best choice).

In the following, existing algorithms for searching in P2P networks that can be used in a modified version within the framework are presented.

The BFSS Algorithm

The simplest similarity searching algorithm is on the basis of breadth-first-search over the nodes of the P2P network. The adapted algorithm, which uses the proposed sampling and representation methods, is denoted as BFSS (breadth-first-search with sampling). Each time, the current node *n* is considered. A TTL (time-to-leave or Maxhop) value denotes how many valid hops are remaining for *n*, whereas T_s is the user-defined similarity threshold. It is assumed that sequences U' and L' carry also the associated bitmaps.

Evidently, the movement of the actual query sequence from the querier to the currently visited node, increases the traffic (not being sampled, the query sequence has rather large length). For this reason, it is important not to have a large number of false-alarms.

The algorithm that does not use sampling (denoted as BFS) may produce less false-alarms. However, between each pair of peers it has to propagate U and L sequences, with length equal to the one of the query sequence. Therefore, it is clear that there is a trade-off between the number of additional false-alarms produced due to sampling and the gains in traffic from propagating sampled (i.e., smaller) envelopes.

The >RESS Algorithm

The >RES algorithm tries to reduce the number of paths that are pursued during searching. Instead of selecting, at random, a subset of the peers of the currently visited node, it maintains a profile for each such peer and bases its decision on this profile. In particular, each node maintains for each of its peers the number of positive answers that it has replied. Then, it selects the k peers that provided the most answers during the previous m queries. Both k and m are user specified.

It is clear that >RES algorithm can be easily adapted in the framework. The query sequence is sampled and represented according to the method previously mentioned. This does not affect the profile that is maintained by >RES. The resulting method is denoted as >RESS (>RES with sampling).

Since only a subset of peers is actually visited, >RESS tries to reduce traffic without missing a large number of answers. However, compared to BFSS, >RESS is proved experimentally to produce fewer answers.

The ISMS Algorithm

The ISM algorithm shares the same objective with >RES, i.e., it tries to reduce the number of examined paths. However, the profile maintained for each peer is different. ISM does not base its decision only on the number of answers to previous queries, but also examines the similarity between the previously answered queries and the current one. Therefore, for each peer, a node maintains the t most recent queries that were answered by the peer. When a new query q arrives in the node, then it computes the similarity Qsim between q and all queries that are maintained in the profile of each node. A relative-ranking measure is given to each peer P_i, using the following formula:

$$RR_Q(P_i, q) = Qsim\,(q_j, q)^a \times S(P_i, q_j)$$

where $S(P_i, q_j)$ is the number of the results returned by P_i for query q_j. Thus, ISM ranks higher the neighboring peers that return more results by adjustment of the α parameter. The comparison is made more clear when α is set equal to 1, therefore focusing only on the criterion of similarity. We also have to notice that ISM may become biased towards the nodes that have answered somewhat similar queries in the past and may not give the chance to new nodes to be explored. For this reason, the following heuristic is used in Kalogeraki et al. (2002): besides the peers selected with the aforementioned criterion, ISM also selects at random an additional very small subset of peers (e.g., one node). In total, k peers are selected, where k is user-defined. The length of each profile (the number of queries stored in it) is also user-defined.

In order to adapt ISM to the sampling framework, one has to consider how to maintain the previously answered queries. In this framework, query sequences are represented by their samples. Therefore, the similarity between the current query's sample and the samples of previously answered queries is measured. For this reason the samples of the answered queries are maintained in the profiles of the peers. To save time during the computation of the ranking, instead of measuring the actual similarity (through the DTW measure), the *LB_Keogh* value is computed. The resulting algorithm is denoted as ISMS (ISM with sampling).

ISMS is expected to have slightly larger traffic than >RES, since it propagates the sample of an answered query to all nodes involved in the search (in order to update their profiles). However, by testing the content of the queries, it tries to reduce the number of missed answers.

The work proposed by Karydis et al. (2005) focuses mainly on developing a framework for similarity searching algorithms using a sampling method, while musical pieces are treated as sequences and their similarity based on DTW. Accordingly, three algorithms (BFS, >RES and ISM) used for searching similar text documents in P2P networks are examined and adapted for CBMIR. The use of DTW proves too expensive and thus a lower bound is used therein. Though, the cheap lower bound calculation advantage is alleviated whenever a real match is available, by requiring the full DTW measurement. Nevertheless, DTW's characteristic being able to withstand distortion of the comparing series in the time axis has had great appeal in the MIR research community.

Hybrid

The fourth model proposed by Wang et al. (2002), PsPsC, is a hybrid approach that combines characteristics from the centralized models PsC & PsC+ (Section "Centralized") and the decentralized unstructured PsPs (Section "PsPs Model"), as previously described.

PsPsC Model

In the PsPsC model there is one coordinator peers registers at, which collects and manages their statistical data. The architecture of the system is similar to the PsPs model (see Section "PsPs Model") with the addition of a peer character-

ization feature and a common method to obtain such features. The coordinator consists of a data structure to store the network identifiers of all peers, a data structure to store the PC features of all peers and an accelerating structure which can utilize the peer features to locate proper peers for faster CBMIR. The query process steps are the following: Each peer shares musical content and registers at the coordinator information including its network identifier and PC feature. Upon a query the peer feature of the querier, that is, the peer feature of the music set which includes only the music request, can be extracted from the music request by the PC feature extraction method and sent to the coordinator. Based on the PC feature of the music request and the accelerating algorithm, the coordinator selects a high probability subset of the peers which may have similar music to the query and the querier directly addresses this subset. In this case, these peers act as some short of super-peers.

In this approach, the balance of stability and cost can be obtained by selecting the proper number of high probability peers. Moreover, Wang et al. (2002) report that PsPsCM has the best load and time attitude in comparison to the family of presented models, thus supporting the further development of the accelerating algorithm solely on this model.

CBMIR IN WIRELESS P2P NETWORKS

As already discussed in the introduction of this chapter, the sovereign of the traditional music distribution has undergone a significant alteration under the auspices of new technologies like MP3 and the penetration of the World Wide Web. Brand new opportunities for music delivery are additionally introduced by the widespread penetration of the wireless networks (wireless LANs, GPRS, UMTS as described by DeVriendt, Lerouge, & Xu, 2002) such as the pioneering applications

(Roccetti et al., 2005) supporting the distribution of MP3-based songs to 3G UMTS devices. These applications rely on the existence of a central server, which receives requests from and delivers audio files to the mobile clients. Sadly enough, CBMIR research in this type of infrastructures has not yet received attention and is currently considering only metadata MIR. Though, aside from these single-hop infrastructure wireless networks, music delivery can also unfold over the emerging wireless ad-hoc networks. The wireless ad-hoc networks are peer-to-peer, multi-hop, mobile wireless networks, where information packets are transmitted in a store-and-forward fashion from source to destination, via intermediate nodes. The salient characteristics of these networks, that is, dynamic topology, bandwidth-constrained communication links and energy-constraint operation, introduce significant design challenges.

This section of the chapter focuses on CBMIR in wireless ad-hoc networks. Consider a number of mobile hosts that participate in a wireless ad-hoc network, where each host may store several audio musical pieces. Assume a user that wants to search in the wireless network, to find audio pieces that are similar to a given one. For instance, the user can provide an audio snippet (e.g., a song excerpt) and query the network to find the peers that store similar pieces. As will be described in the following, the definition of similarity can be based on several features that have been developed for Content-Based Music Information Retrieval. It is important to notice that the querying host is assumed to have no prior knowledge of both the qualifying music pieces and the hosts' locations that contain them. This is the key differentiation from existing researches that are interested in just identifying the hosts, in a wireless ad-hoc network, that contain a known datum. Moreover, the issues discussed in this section are complementary to the problem of delivering streaming media, such as audio and video, as considered by Baochun and Wang (2003) in wireless ad-hoc networks, since the latter does not involve any searching for similar

audio pieces, and just focuses on transferring data from one host to another.

Requirements Set by the Wireless Medium

This section focuses on methods for searching audio music by content in wireless ad-hoc networks, where the querier receives music excerpts matching to a posed query. The actual searching procedure can benefit from the latest approaches for CBMIR in wired P2P networks (see Section "CBMIR in Wired Networks"). Nevertheless, the combination of the characteristics of the wireless medium and the audio-music data pose challenging requirements:

1. CBMIR methods for wired P2P networks do not consider the continuous alteration of the network topology, which is inherent in wireless ad-hoc networks, since Mobile Hosts (MHs, the terms MH and peer are similar in this context and thus interchangeable) are moving and become in and out of range of the others continuously. One impact of this mobility is that selective propagation of the query among MHs, e.g., by using data indexing like DHT as proposed by Tzanetakis et al. (2004) or caching past queries (Kalogeraki et al. (2002) for text documents and Karydis, Nanopoulos, Papadopoulos, and Manolopoulos (2005b) for music), is not feasible. Additionally, the recall of the searching procedure is affected by the possibility of unsuccessful routing of the query, as well as the answers, over the changing network topology.

2. The need to reduce traffic, which results from the size of audio-music data (approx. 8 MBytes for a 3 minute query). This is can be achieved by replacing the original query with a representation that utilizes appropriate transcoding schemes. Although traffic concerns CBMIR in wired P2P networks

too, the requirement of traffic reduction is much more compelling in wireless ad-hoc networks, where the communication bandwidth ability is usually limited to approximately 1 MBps. It is worth noticing, that the reduction of traffic also reduces the involvement of other MHs, due to constraints in their processing power and autonomy.

3   In CBMIR over wired P2P networks, should a matching music excerpt be found, it can immediately be returned to the querying node, since the querier is directly accessible (through its IP address). In contrast, in wireless ad-hoc networks the answers to a query have to be propagated back to the querier via the network (the querier is not directly accessible), burdening further traffic.

The aforementioned issues can be addressed, to a certain extent, by algorithms proposed for the problem of routing in wireless ad-hoc networks, though, these approaches consider neither the peculiarities of searching for CBMIR purposes nor the size of the transferred data, since music data are considerably larger than routing packets.

Research related to the application of CBMIR in wireless ad-hoc P2P networks is so young, that to our best knowledge the work by Karydis, Nanopoulos, Papadopoulos, Katsaros, and Manolopoulos (in press) is the only one to examine the issue of CBMIR in ad-hoc wireless networks.

Accordingly, to address the requirements posed by the wireless medium, Karydis et al. (in press) proposed the following techniques:

1.   To fulfil the first requirement, breadth-first searching is performed over the wireless ad-hoc network using knowledge about neighboring MHs (obtained by probing neighborhood at specific time points). This approach can cope with mobility, maintain increased final recall and constraint the drawbacks of flooding, for example, excessive traffic due to multiple broadcasts (as

already explained in Section "Information Discovery/Provision In Wireless Mobile Ad-hoc Networks").

2.   The second requirement is addressed by a technique that uses a concise, feature-based representation of the query with reducing length. The reducing-length representation (a.k.a transcoding) drastically degrades traffic, while reducing the computation performed at each MH as well.

3.   The additional traffic produced by the third requirement is addressed by a twofold technique: (1) Policies to constraint the number of MHs involved for the propagation of the answers, by exploiting any MHs that were involved during the propagation of the query. (2) By allowing such MHs to prune the propagation of answers, based on a property of the previously described representation.

Outline of the Searching Procedure

The problem of finding similar music sequences in a MANET requires a searching procedure, which will detect MHs in the MANET that have similar sequences, find those sequences in the MHs and return them back to the querier. The already described requirements of the wireless framework formulate the examined searching procedure in the following way:

1.   There is no prior knowledge of the data MHs store; that is, the querier has no knowledge of the location of the required data.

2.   MHs that have qualifying sequences have to be reached in a way that addresses their mobility and minimises traffic. Due to their relative positions and the preferred tolerance to traffic (see Figure 1) all such nodes may not be possible to reach.

3.   At each reached MH, the qualifying sequences have to be detected by detaining

the MHs, in terms of CPU cost, as little as possible.

4. Each qualifying sequence has to reach the querier in a way that reduces traffic. Notice that the answers may have to be routed back to the querier following paths different from those through which the MHs with qualifying sequences were reached, since intermediate MHs may have changed their position and therefore be out of range. Due to this, every detected answer may not be possible to reach the querier.

The searching procedure is initiated at the querying MH, aiming at detecting sequences in other MHs, which contain excerpts whose similarity from the query sequence Q is within user-defined boundaries, a threshold ε. The definition of the distance measure is detailed in Section "Features and Indexing". Just for now, one can intuitively think of the distance as a measure of how dissimilar two music sequences are. The length of detected excerpts is equal to the length of the query sequence Q.

To address traffic minimization, Q has to be transformed to a representation form, denoted as R, through which qualifying sequences are detected.

Due to this transformation, it is possible that false-positive results may appear. A false positive result is a result that appears to be a true result when comparing with the transformed represen-

tation, though, under the non-transformed query is not a real result. Moreover, R must present no false-negatives (real results that were missed due to the transformation). However, its particular implementation determines whether false-positives may be produced or if they will be completely avoided. Based on all the aforementioned issues, an abstract scheme to describe the entire searching procedure consists of the steps depicted in Figure 1(a). These steps are summarised in four events according to Figure 1(b).

To avoid duplicate effort, the procedure tags R with an ID (see Section "Information Discovery/ Provision In Wireless Mobile Ad-hoc Networks"). This way, MHs that have already received it will perform no further action. Additionally, the propagation of R to the neighboring MHs is controlled by a parameter called h, which acts as a counter that is decreased at each receiving MH (denotes the available number of hops). Its initial value, at the querier, is equal to *MaxHop*. This value corresponds to the preferred tolerance to traffic and network reach/coverage. The propagation of answer sets (resulting from step 5) is handled similarly.

As already mentioned, the searching process consists of a forward and a backward phase. During the former, R is propagated and during the latter answers are routed back to the querier. The two phases are interleaved, since during the propagation of R by some MHs, other MHs are returning answers to the querier. The backward

Figure 1. Searching process and basic events

1.	User poses a query Q
2.	Q is transformed to a representation form R
3.	R is broadcast to all peers in range
4.	Qualifying sequences (true- and false-positives) detected at each peer comprise an answer set
5.	Each answer set is broadcast back to the querier
6.	Resolution of false-positives (possible places are: at answer providing peers, the querier or intermediate peers)
7.	Return of actual matches to user/application

Event name	Involved steps
query initialization	1,2,3
reception of R	4,5
reception of an answer set	5,6
answer set reaching the querier	7

(a) seaching process

(b) events

phase's volume mainly depends on the existence of answers and the number of false-positives, while the forward phase depends on the size of R, the user defined coverage willingness as well as the network reachability. In general, the volume of information transferred during the backward phase is larger than that of the forward phase.

Having outlined the searching procedure, the following sections detail its parts, starting with the features selected for the formation of R. Next, a method for the acceleration of similarity searching within each MH, using indexing, is presented. Based on these, follow two searching algorithms, which rely on different choices with respect to the formation of R, while, finally, methods to improve the backward phase are described.

Features and Indexing

The most typically encountered features for the acoustic representation are produced by time analysis (Papaodysseus, Roussopoulos, Fragoulis, Panagopoulos, & Alexiou, 2001; Paraskevas & Mourjopoulos, 1996), spectral analysis (Kostek & Wieczorkowska, 1997; Papaodysseus et al., 2001; Paraskevas & Mourjopoulos, 1996;), and wavelet analysis (Wieczorkowska, 2001).

Karydis et al. (2006) do not concentrate on devising new features, while their interest remains in the searching procedure and their methodology is able to embrace any high performance feature extraction procedure. Accordingly, a feature extraction process based on the wavelet transform is utilised. Wavelet transforms provide a simple but yet efficient representation of audio by taking into consideration both nonuniform frequency resolution and impulsive characteristics, as shown by (Li, Li, Zhu, & Ogihara, 2002; Li, Ogihara, & Li, 2003; Roads, Pope, Piccialli, & Poli, 1997).

More particularly, they consider the Haar wavelet transformation for its simple incremental computation, its capability concerning the capture of time dependant properties of data and overall multiresolution representation of signals (Chan,

Fu, & Yu, 2003) as well as for the incorporation of the previously mentioned properties. However, the approach can easily be extended to other types of wavelet transforms.

Moving on to the indexing procedure within peers to facilitate the searching, they propose the following approach. In a peer, each original audio sequence is transformed to a number of multidimensional points. A sliding window of length n is used over the sequence and apply Discrete Wavelet Transform (DWT) to the contents of each window, producing n coefficients per window. An example is depicted in Figure 2a. Therefore, each audio sequence produces a set of n-dimensional points in the feature space. Since n depends on the query length and, thus, takes relatively large values (e.g., 64 K), in order to efficiently index them in the feature space, only the first d dimensions from each point (experiments with d = 64 are presented therein) are selected. This procedure dramatically reduces both the size of the index and the number of dimensions without affecting much the quality of the index. The reason for the latter is the merit of DWT to concentrate the energy of the sequence in the first few coefficients. However, false-positives remain a possibility and thus require resolution.

Most importantly, it has been proven by Chan and Fu (1999) that no false dismissals are introduced when using only the d first coefficients (due to Parseval's theorem). Notice that this property is proven in (Chan & Fu, 1999) for the Euclidean distance. Although this distance measure is simple, it is known to have several advantages, as it has been illustrated by Keogh and Kasetty (2002). Nevertheless, the methodology proposed by Karydis et al. (2006) does not decisively depend on the particular features and distance measure.

To speed-up the retrieval, for each sequence the collection of the resulting d-dimensional points is organised in Minimum Bounding Rectangles (MBRs), which are, then, stored in an R*-tree (Beckmann, Kriegel, & Seeger, 1990). Answering

Figure 2. Feature extraction process

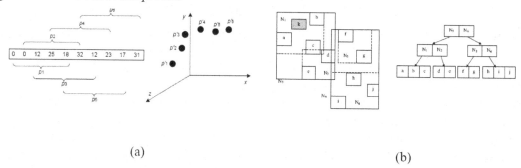

(a)　　　　　　　　　　　　　　　　　　　　　　　　　(b)

Figure 3. The ML algorithm

> **Query initialization.** The querier assigns to *R* the entire query sequence (plus the few query coefficients) and propagates (broadcasts) it to all its neighbors.
>
> **Reception of R.** Upon the reception of *R*, each MH *P* probes its indexes, resolves the false-positives, and produces a list of results (only true-positives). The answer-set is propagated back to the querier, by broadcasting it to *all* the neighbors of *P* (backward phase). Accordingly, should there be available *h*, *R* is conveyed to all P's neighboring MHs (forward phase).
>
> **Reception of an answer-set.** Each MH *P*, that is not the querier, receiving an answer-set, continues the propagation (backward phase) to *all* its neighboring MHs as long as there is available *h*.
>
> **An answer-set reaches the querier.** When an answer-set reaches the querier, then the results are immediately presented to the user.

to a query, the root is initially retrieved and its entries that intersect the query are only further examined recursively until reaching a leaf. All nonintersecting nodes are not included in the search. An example is given in Figure 2b. Therefore, when searching for similar subsequence, candidates from the R*-tree are first retrieved. The candidates are ranked so as to process the most promising ones first and then, those candidates are examined against the provided query representation. When the latter is reduced (as in the case of transcoding that will be explained), false-positives are still possible. Nevertheless, their number is significantly reduced. More details about indexing can be found in Karydis, Nanopoulos, Papadopoulos, and Manolopoulos (2005a).

Searching Algorithms

This section presents the two algorithms that implement the searching procedure, as described in Karydis et al. (2006). The first is based on simple choices concerning the representation *R* of the query sequence and its propagation during the forward and backward phases, while the second is based on more advanced choices with respect to the latter issues.

Algorithm Based on Maximal Query Representation

A simplistic approach for the representation *R* is to set it identical to the query sequence. The advantage is that no false-positives occur, since when a possible match has been found by index probing, it can be immediately tested against the query itself (i.e., R). Thus, no false-positives will be included in the answer-sets, which could negatively impact the backward-phase traffic, as they would be propagated to the querier just to discover that they are not actual matches. It should be noticed that, to be able to perform index probing (i.e., to avoid sequential searching at each MH), a small number of DWT coefficients are included in R as well. However, their size is negligible compared to the size of the query sequence.

The resulting algorithm is denoted as ML (full *M*aximum representation with *L*ocal resolution at MHs). ML is summarised in Figure 3 according to the actions performed for each occurring event (see Figure 1(b)).

Algorithm Based on Reduced Query Representation and Transcoding

Section "Algorithm based on Maximal Query Representation" made apparent that a trade-off exists between the forward and backward traffic. ML focuses only on the improvement of backward traffic and incurs high forward traffic. In this section a different algorithm is presented, which has a two-fold objective. The first is to produce a representation R that achieves a balance between the two phases and minimizes the overall traffic. The second is to develop selective routing policies for the propagation of the answer-sets, leading to significant reduction of the backward traffic.

The first objective is confronted by setting R between the two extremes cases: (1) the minimum possible representation with only the d DWT coefficients that are required for the local index-searching (minimising forward traffic), and (2) the maximum possible representation with all n elements in the query sequence itself (eliminating the burden of false-positives in terms of computation and backward traffic). Therefore, between the two extremes, R can consist of the l greater DWT coefficients, where $d \leq l \leq n$. Notice that this type of representation generalises the

two extreme cases: by setting $l = d$, R becomes identical to the first (1) case; in contrast, by setting $l = n$, R becomes identical to the second (2) case, since the n DWT coefficients are equivalent to the n elements of the query sequence (due to the Parseval's theorem)[3]. As described in Section "Features and Indexing", a number l of the greater DWT coefficients can effectively capture the energy of the music sequence and reduce the number of false-positives. The result is that, compared to the second (2) case, the forward traffic is smaller, because $l \leq n$. Compared to the first (1) case, the backward traffic is smaller too, due to the number of false-positives being significantly reduced, since $d \leq l$.

The tuning of l, however, is difficult, as it depends on several factors, like the topology of the MANET, which are changeable. Accordingly, the following approach can be used: Initially, l takes an adequately large value and this value is monotonically reduced during the propagation of R in the forward phase. This constitutes a *transcoding* scheme, as it involves sequences with varying number of DWT coefficients that correspond to varying approximations of the initial query sequence. The transcoding scheme:

- Keeps forward traffic low, since the size of R is reducing during its propagation in the forward phase.
- Reduces backward traffic by letting the MHs involved in the forward phase to cache the transcoded representation and, during the backward phase, to use it for early resolving false-positives, before these reach the querier. The problem of caching depends on several network parameters and is independent to the theme of this section of the chapter, while effective solutions can be found in Fang, Haas, Liang, and Lin (2004). Experimentation in Karydis et al. (2006), shows that by simply caching the representations for a small, fixed amount of time, adequate performance is attained.

- Reduces the processing (CPU) time at each MH, as the cost of resolving false-positives at each MH depends on the size of *R*.

The reduction is performed by getting *l* values according to an inverse sigmoid function (Figure 4b). Due to the shape of this function, the immediate neighborhood of the querier, which can provide results faster, receives a larger *R*, whereas the burden posed on MHs that are far is appreciably smaller. Additionally, this way the exponential growth of traffic that results by plain broadcasting of a full-size representation is controlled. An example is depicted in Figure 4a. P_1 is the querier and P_4 is the node that starts propagating the answer-set. The MHs in the path from P_1 to P_4 are depicted gray shaded, and they are annotated with the size of *R* that reaches them (P_1 starts with 10K DWT coefficients). Figure 4b illustrates that these sizes are reducing, following an inverse sigmoid function. During the backward phase, starting from P_4, MHs P_3 and P_5 can be reached (depicted with dashed arrows). The cached representation in P_3 can help resolving possible false-positives in the answer-set. This is due to the fact that in P_4 the false-positives were examined against a smaller *R* than the one in P_3. In contrast, P_5 was not in the path, thus cannot resolve any false-positives.

Henceforth, the size of the initial query representation is given as a factor (denoted as *I*) of the complete query size, whereas the slope of the inverse sigmoid function is controlled by a pa-

Figure 5. The RT algorithm

Query initialization. The querier sets *R* equal to a sample with an initial size (parameter) plus the query coefficients, and propagates (broadcasts) it to all its neighbors.
Reception of R. Upon the reception of *R*, each MH *P* probes its indexes, resolves as many false-positives as possible based on the received query sample of *R*, and produces a list of results. The answer-set is propagated back to the querier, by following the described policy for the backward phase. Accordingly, should there be available *h*, *R*'s size is reduced, and the reduced *R* is conveyed to all P's neighboring MHs (forward phase).
Reception of an answer-set. When a MH receives a reply, it checks if it can resolve any false-positives. This is true, should it have received (if any) a representation that was larger than the one that the sequences in the answer set were examined previously (i.e., at the sending MH). After any possible pruning, as long as there is available *h*, the answer-set is routed backwards following a policy.
An answer-set reaches the querier. When an answer-set reaches the querier, initially any remaining false positives requiring resolution are examined, and then the results are presented to the user.

rameter denoted as α (higher values of α produce a steeper slope).

Regarding the second objective, in contrast to the simplistic approach of ML, which propagates the answer-sets to all neighbors, during the forward phase, as it is typical in any dynamic source routing protocol (Johnson & Maltz, 1996), each MH that receives *R*, additionally receives the ID of all MHs in the path that were used from the querier to it. These IDs can be maintained along with *R* with minimal cost (only some bytes). When a MH starts propagating answer-sets, it selects among its current neighbors those that will propagate the answer-set (not all of them). To make this selection, it applies a policy that focuses on the neighbors that were included in the path from the querier to it. Since several such policies can be developed, Section "Routing Policies for the Backward Phase" elaborates further on them. All the policies, despite their differences, emphasise on selecting neighboring MHs that were included in the path, due to the cached representations they maintain, which can resolve some false-positives in situ.

The algorithm that combines all the aforementioned characteristics is denoted as RT (querying

Figure 4. Searching procedure example

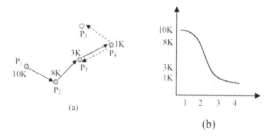

(a)

(b)

by *R*educed representation with *T*ranscoding) and is illustrated in Figure 5.

Routing Policies for the Backward Phase

Accordingly, Karydis et al. (2006) describe three policies for routing the answer-sets in the backward phase. The first two policies (global and local counter) are based on existing methods (Castaneda, Das, & Marina, 2002). As mentioned, all policies try to select nodes that were included in the path during the forward phase. Nevertheless, the backward phase cannot be based only on such nodes. Due to the mobility of MHs, it may be impossible to reach the querier unless other MHs (not included in the path) are additionally involved. The objective of all policies is to control the number of involved MHs so as to reduce backward traffic. These policies constitute a hybrid approach between probabilistic broadcasting, where the broadcasting decision is completely local to each mobile host and the deterministic broadcasting which relies on the discovery of some form of connected dominating set (Lou & Wu, 2004).

Global and Local Counter Policies

To clarify the description of the first two policies, consider the example of Figure 6a, which depicts the path from MH P_1 to MH P_6, which was followed in the forward phase. Figure 6b depicts the routing of the answer-set from P_6 back to P_1. Comparing the two phases, several MHs have

Figure 6. Propagation in a MANET: (a) forward phase, (b) backward phase.

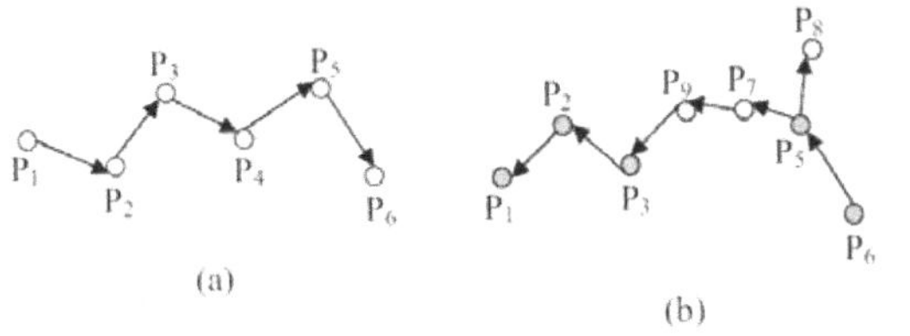

changed their location, others have switched off, and some new ones have become reachable. The MHs that are greyed are the ones that were included in the forward path too, whereas the rest are new ones that were involved only in the backward phase.

With the *global-counter* (GC) policy, when selecting the MHs to route back the answer-set, GC tries to follow the MHs included in the forward path. However, to overcome problems from the alteration of the MANET (like the disappearance of P_4 in this example), it allows an amount of discrepancy by resorting to broadcasting. To control the discrepancy, and thus the backward traffic, it uses the value of e. Notice that with a very large e, GC resorts to broadcasting for a very large number of times, thus becoming equivalent to the simplistic policy used by the ML searching algorithm. In contrast, with a very small e, the querier may not become reachable, especially when the MANET changes very fast.

A variation of GC works as follows. After a discrepancy, when a MH from the path has been reached again, h is reset to its initial value. In the previous example, when P_3 is reached again, available hop is reset to 6 (initial value). Thus, h acts as a decreasing local counter, because it is reset independently at several MHs. For this reason this policy is denoted as *local-counter* (LC). Its objective is to increase the probability of reaching the querier, by rewarding the identification of the forward path. Nevertheless, this can increase the backward traffic.

Critical Mass Policy

With the *critical-mass* (CM) policy, if at least a number, denoted as *critical-mass factor* (*CMF*), of the current neighbors was in the forward path, they are selected as the only ones to propagate the answer-set. If their number is less than *CMF*, then some of the current neighbors (not in the path) are additionally randomly selected in order to have at least *CMF* MHs to propagate the answer-set.

Figure 7. MHs' relative locations in forward and backward phase example.

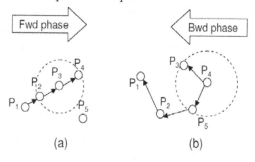

In contrast, if their number is larger than *CMF*, then they are all selected. For example, consider the case in Figure 7. Figure 7a depicts the forward phase, whereas Figure 7b presents the backward case. As shown, during the backward phase some MHs have now relocated. Let *CMF* be 2. When P_4 starts propagating the answer-set, it first selects P_3, because it belongs to the forward path. Since this is the only such MH and *CMF* is 2, it also selects P_5 at random, among the other reachable MHs.

The nodes that were selected at random in order to fulfil *CMF*, are still provided with the path of the MH that initiated the propagation of the answer-set (for the previous example, P_5 that is selected by P_4, will also know the path from P_1 to P_4). This way, due to mobility, it is possible for such nodes during the backward phase to find neighbors that appear in the forwarded path (in the same example, P_5 finds P_2 that was in the path). Therefore, the impact of such randomly selected

MHs on the proposed policy may be kept at a moderate level.

Experimental Results

Four of the most prominent experimental results presented in Karydis et al. (2006) are discussed in this section. The first experiment, examines the traffic against MaxHop. The results are illustrated in Figure 8a. As expected, ML produces the highest forward traffic in all cases, whereas the forward traffic of CM, LC and GC are about the same. Regarding the backward traffic, ML attains a decreased number of returning results. However, due to the absence of an efficient backward routing policy, this advantage is invalidated. The rest approaches, considerably improve backward traffic, with CM performing better for MaxHop greater than seven. From this result it becomes obvious that, although the backward phase is in general more demanding for all algorithms, due to the reduction of backward traffic attained by CM, LC and GC, the requirement for optimization of the forward phase, is fair.

This result can be further clarified by the results on time of the first and last results, which are depicted in Figure 8b. As expected, increase in available MaxHop produces longer times, since more MHs are examined. In all cases, the increase in time is far steeper for ML, while CM presents an advantage over LC and GC.

Next, the impact of query range ε is examined.

Figure 8. Traffic, number and time of results vs. MaxHop

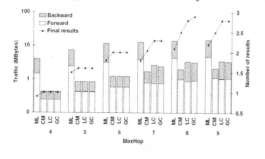

(a)   (b)

Figure 9. Traffic vs. query range (ε)

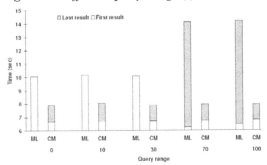

Figure 10. Traffic & number of results vs. CMF

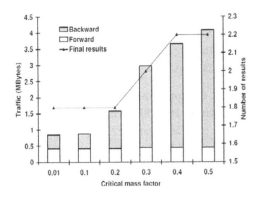

Figure 9 shows the results for traffic with respect to ε. CM, LC, and GC perform similarly, thus only the results for the former are included. As ε increases, more results are found and, consequently, backward traffic increases too (forward traffic is unaffected). However, the increase is much more obvious for ML, whereas CM, due the effectiveness of the policy for the backward phase, has a very smooth increase.

The last experiment, examines the sensitivity of CM against *CMF*. The traffic and number of results of CM, for varying *CMF* values, are depicted in Figure 10. When *CMF* is high, the effectiveness of the policy for the backward phase is limited, since most MHs are selected at random by this policy, resulting to high backward traffic.

SUMMARY AND PERSPECTIVES

We have presented the most significant trends in recent research in the field of content based music information retrieval in peer-to-peer networks. Despite the diminished attention the area has received in general terms, its relatively close area of metadata MIR in P2P is by far new. On the contrary, it could be argued that it was actually one of the key threads that lead to the widespread acceptance of P2P systems.

Though, as metadata prove to be inefficient for the purposes of MIR as well as the peculiarities of music in comparison to text and image data, the development of dedicated solutions for CBMIR in P2P networks becomes obvious. As described, CBMIR in P2P networks presents unique challenges.

P2P networks can be classified according to numerous of their characteristics. A number of prominent research works have been presented in this chapter falling within all categories. Despite an obvious tendency towards decentralized unstructured models, solutions for other categories of P2P models do exist. Additionally, we have presented an initial attempt of CBMIR to invade the area of wireless P2P networks, as well as the challenges presented in that case.

The prospects of MIR in P2P networks, both in terms of research and applications, seem to be encouraging. As it is relatively new a research field, it contains several open research issues. Following ethics, a very important area of possible further development is the implementation of data rights management. As the previously mentioned widespread penetration of P2P systems based on the illegal exchange of copyrighted material, methods are required to enforce rights on data. Another field is music e-commerce. Attempts like iTune or iMusic changed the paradigm that music is merchandised. Moreover, applications in P2P environments (such as Napster and Kazaa) can only set the path for commercial CBMIR in P2P networks. Additionally, with the development of high CPU capability mobile computing devices, one can envisage an ubiquitous exchange of ring-tones (cell phones) and music (PDAs, portable and tablet computers or even dedicated devices) while on the go.

REFERENCES

Agrawal, D.-P., & Zeng, Q.-A. (2003). *Introduction to wireless and mobile systems*. Thomson, Brooks/Cole, Minnesota, USA.

Baochun, L., & Wang, K.-H. (2003). NonStop: Continuous multimedia streaming in wireless ad-hoc networks with node mobility. *IEEE Journal on Selected Areas in Communications, 21*(10), 1627-1641.

Beckmann, N., Kriegel, H., & Seeger, B. (1990). The R*-tree: An efficient and robust method for points and rectangles. In *Proceedings ACM International Conference on Knowledge Discovery and Data Mining (SIGKDD)* (pp. 322-331).

Byrd, D., & Crawford, T. (2002). Problems of music information retrieval in the real world. *Information Processing and Management, 38*(2), 249-272.

Castaneda, R., Das, S. R., & Marina, M. K. (2002). Query localization techniques for on-demand routing protocols in ad-hoc networks. *Wireless Networks, 8*(2/3), 137-151.

Chan, K., & Fu, A.-C. (1999). Efficient time series matching by wavelets. In *Proceedings International Conference on Data Engineering (ICDE)* (pp. 126-133).

Chan, K.-P., Fu, A.-C., & Yu, C. (2003). Haar wavelets for efficient similarity search of time-series: With and without time warping. *IEEE Transactions on Knowledge and Data Engineering, 15*(3).

Chu, C.-C., Su, X., Prabhu, B., Gadh, R., Kurup, S., Sridhar, G., et al. (2006). Mobile drm for multimedia content commerce in p2p networks. In *Proceedings*

IEEE Workshop on Digital Rights Management Impact on Consumer Communications.

DeVriendt, J. C., Lerouge, P. L., & Xu, X. (2002). Mobile network evolution: A revolution on the move. *IEEE Communications Magazine*, p. 104-111.

Dhamija, R., & Wallenberg, F. (2003). A framework for evaluating digital rights management proposals. In *Proceedings International Mobile IPR Workshop: Rights Management of Information Products on the Mobile Internet.*

Dubosson-Torbay, M., Pigneur, Y., & Usunier, J.-C. (2004). Business models for music distribution after the p2p revolution. In *Proceedings Wedelmusic* (pp. 172-179).

Dutta, A., Chennikara, J., Chen, W., Altintas, O., & Schulzrinne, H. (2003). Multicasting streaming media to mobile users. *IEEE Communications Magazine*, p. 81-89.

Fang, Y., Haas, Z., Liang, B., & Lin, Y.-B. (2004). TTL prediction schemes and the effects of inter-update time distribution on wireless data access. *Wireless Networks, 10*(5), 607-619.

Indyk, P., & Motwani, R. (1998). Approximate nearest neighbors: Towards removing the curse of dimensionality. In *Proceedings of the Thirtieth Annual ACM Symposium on theory of Computing.* NY: ACM Press.

Johnson, D., & Maltz, D. (1996). Dynamic source routing in ad-hoc wireless networks. *Mobile computing* (Vol. 353). MA: Kluwer Academic Publishers.

Kalker, T., Epema, D., Hartel, P., Lagendijk, R., & Steen, M. van. (2004). Music2share -copyright-compliant music sharing in p2p systems. In *Proceedings of the IEEE* (pp. 961-970).

Kalogeraki, V., Gunopulos, D., & Zeinalipour-Yazti, D. (2002). A local search mechanism for peer-to-peer networks. In *Proceedings Confer-*

ence on Information and Knowledge Management (CIKM) (pp. 300-307).

Karydis, I., Nanopoulos, A., & Manolopoulos, Y. (2005). Evaluation of similarity searching methods for music data in peer-to-peer networks. *International Journal of Business Intelligence and Data Mining, 1*(2), 210-228.

Karydis, I., Nanopoulos, A., & Manolopoulos, Y. (2006). Mining in music databases. *Processing and managing complex data for decision support* (pp. 340-374). Hershey, PA: Idea Group Publishing.

Karydis, I., Nanopoulos, A., Papadopoulos, A., Katsaros, D., & Manolopoulos, Y. (in press). Audio music retrieval in wireless ad-hoc networks. *IEEE Transactions on Audio, Speech and Language Processing*.

Karydis, I., Nanopoulos, A., Papadopoulos, A., & Manolopoulos, Y. (2005a). Audio indexing for efficient music information retrieval. In *Proceedings Multimedia Modelling Conference (MMM)* (pp. 22-29).

Karydis, I., Nanopoulos, A., Papadopoulos, A. N., & Manolopoulos, Y. (2005b). Music retrieval in p2p networks under the warping distance. In *Proceedings International Conference on Enterprise Information Systems (ICEIS)* (p. 100-107).

Keogh, E., & Kasetty, S. (2002). On the need for time series data mining benchmarks: A survey and empirical demonstration. In *Proceedings ACM International Conference on Knowledge Discovery and Data Mining (SIGKDD)* (pp. 102-111).

Keogh, E., & Ratanamahatana, A. (2005). Exact indexing of dynamic time warping. *Knowledge and Information Systems, 7*(3), 358-386.

Kostek, B., & Wieczorkowska, A. (1997). Parametric representation of musical sound. *Archive of Acoustics* (pp. 3-26).

Lew, M. S., Sebe, N., Djeraba, C., & Jain, R. (2006). Content-based multimedia information retrieval: State of the art and challenges. *ACM Transactions on Multimedia Computing, Communications and Applications, 2*(1), 1-19.

Li, T., Li, Q., Zhu, S., & Ogihara, M. (2002). A survey on wavelet applications in data mining. *Special Interest Group on Knowledge Discovery and Data Mining (SIGKDD) Explorations, 4*(2), 49-68.

Li, T., Ogihara, M., & Li, Q. (2003). A comparative study on content-based music genre classification. In *Proceedings ACM Conference on Research and Development in Information Retrieval (SIGIR)* (pp. 282-289).

Li, X., & Wu, J. (2004). Searching techniques in peer-to-peer networks. In *Handbook of Theoretical and Algorithmic Aspects of Ad hoc, Sensor, and Peer-to-peer Networks*. FL: CRC Press.

Liu, Z., Kundur, D., Merabti, M., & Yu, H. (2006). On peer-to-peer multimedia content access and distribution. In *Proceedings of the IEEE International Conference on Multimedia and Expo (ICME)*.

Lou, W., & Wu, J. (2004). Broadcasting in ad-hoc networks using neighbor designating. In *Handbook of Mobile Computing*. FL: CRC Press.

Ni, S.-Y., Tseng, Y.-C., Chen, Y.-S., & Sheu, J. (1999). The broadcast storm problem in a mobile ad-hoc networks. In *Proceedings ACM/IEEE International Conference on Mobile Computing and Networking (MOBICOM)* (pp. 151-162).

Orio, N. (2006). Music retrieval: A tutorial and review. *Foundations and Trends in Information Retrieval, 1*(1), 1-90.

Papaodysseus, C., Roussopoulos, G., Fragoulis, D., Panagopoulos, T., & Alexiou, C. (2001). A new approach to the automatic recognition of musical recordings. *Journal of Acoustical Engineering Society, 49*(1/2), 23-35.

Paraskevas, M., & Mourjopoulos, J. (1996). A Statistical Study of the Variability and Features of Audio Signals: Some Preliminary Results. In *Audio Engineering Society 100th Convention.* Copenhagen, Sweden.

Praveen, K., Sridhar, G., Sridhar, V., & Gadh, R. (2005). Dmw - A middleware for digital rights management in peer-to-peer networks. In *Proceedings International Workshop on Secure and Ubiquitous Networks.*

Roads, C., Pope, S., Piccialli, A., & Poli, G. D. (Eds.). (1997). *Musical signal processing.* Royal Swets & Zeitlinger, Lisse, The Netherlands.

Roccetti, M., Salomoni, P., Ghini, V., & Ferretti, S. (2005). Bringing the wireless Internet to UMTS devices: A case study with music distribution. *Multimedia Tools and Applications, 25*(2), 217-251.

Sastry, N. (2005). *Stealing (from) the music industry* (Tech. Rep.). Computer Science Dept., University of Berkeley.

Schyndel, R. G. van. (2005). A preliminary design for a privacy-friendly free p2p media file distribution system. *International Workshop on Intelligent Information Hiding and Multimedia Signal Processing (IIHMSP) part of Knowledge-Based Intelligent Information and Engineering Systems (KES), 3,* 1018-1024.

Typke, R., Wiering, F., Veltkamp, R. C. (2005). A survey of music information retrieval systems. *In Proceedings International Conference on Music Information Retrieval (ISMIR)* (pp. 153-160).

Tzanetakis, G., & Cook, P. (2002). Musical genre classification of audio signals. *IEEE Transactions on Speech and Audio Processing, 10*(5), 293-302.

Tzanetakis, G., Gao, J., & Steenkiste, P. (2004). A scalable peer-to-peer system for music information retrieval. *Computer Music Journal, 28*(2), 24-33.

Wang, C., Li, J., & Shi, S. (2002). A kind of content-based music information retrieval method in a peer-to-peer environment. In *Proceedings International Symposium on Music Information Retrieval (ISMIR)* (pp. 178-186).

Wieczorkowska, A. (2001). Musical sound classification based on wavelet analysis. *Fundamenta Informaticae, 47*(1/2), 175-188.

Yang, B., & Garcial-Molina, H. (2002). Improving search in peer-to-peer networks. In *Proceedings Conference of Distributed Computer Systems* (pp. 5-15).

Yang, C. (2002). Efficient acoustic index for music retrieval with various degrees of similarity. In *Proceedings ACM Multimedia Conference* (pp. 584-591).

Yang, C. (2003). Peer-to-peer architecture for content-based music retrieval on acoustic data. In *Proceedings international World Wide Web Conference (WWW)* (pp. 376-383).

ENDNOTES

[1] This research is supported by the ΗΡΑΚΛΕΙΤΟΣ and ΠΥΘΑΓΟΡΑΣ II national programs funded by the ΕΠΕΑΕΚ.

[2] Each element in an acoustic sequence is in the range 0-255, thus it requires one byte.

[3] In the case of ML, R could consist of all the n DWT coefficients. However, the n sequence elements in the time domain are selected just to avoid the computation of the inverse DWT, since the time domain presents a smaller storage requirement as the data values are in range 0-255.

Chapter X
DART:
A Framework for Distributed Audio Analysis and Music Information Retrieval

Eddie Al-Shakarchi
Cardiff University, UK

Ian Taylor
Cardiff University, UK

Stephen David Beck
Louisiana State University, USA

ABSTRACT

This chapter introduces the DART (Distributed Audio Retrieval using Triana) project as a framework for facilitating the distributed processing and analysis of audio and Music Information Retrieval. The chapter begins by discussing the background and history of Grid and P2P technologies, the Triana framework, the current tools already developed for audio-rate signal processing, and also gives a description of how Triana is employing a decentralized P2P framework to support MIR applications. A music recommendation system is proposed to demonstrate the DART framework, and the chapter also documents the DART team's progress towards the creation of a working system. The authors hope that introducing the DART system to the MIR community will not only inform them of a research tool that will benefit the entire field of MIR, but also establish DART as an important tool for the rest of the audio and research communities.

INTRODUCTION

Over the past five years, there have been significant advancements made in the field of distributed systems technologies with applications being deployed on an Internet scale. On the one hand, Grid computing has evolved from core toolkits, such as Globus (http://www.globus.org/) providing the underlying mechanisms for executing and managing jobs and data, to using service oriented architectures (SOAs) in the form of Open Grid Services Architecture (OGSA) (Foster, Kesselman, Nick, Tuecke, 2002) that capitalises on Web Services standards set out by W3C (2000, 2003) for exposing the low level functionality on a network. The recent advancement to WS-RF (http://www.globus.org/wsrf/) provides decoupled mechanisms for representing *stateful* resource capabilities *through stateless* Web services interfaces, which allows a system to manage lifetime without using a tightly coupled approach like previous distributed object systems, such as Corba (http://www.corba.org/) or Jini (http://www.jini.org/). Grid computing is built on standardized technologies and extended through other standardization efforts often initiated through the various research and working groups hosted within the Open Grid Forum (OGF) conference (http://www.ogf.org/).

Peer-to-peer (P2P) technologies on the other hand, have grown through grass roots Internet culture, initiated by specific applications such as file sharing systems like Napster (http://www.napster.com/) or Gnutella (http://gnutella.wego.com/) and CPU sharing systems like SETI (Search for Extra Terrestrial Intelligence (http://setiathome.ssl.berkeley.edu/)). At its essence, P2P is about connecting people so that users can share information or participate in projects by being offered a various range of incentives to do so. P2P therefore is much more focused on solving scalability and robustness issues when faced with huge numbers of connected participants, which are extremely unreliable in that they can disconnect frequently and are hosted behind application-unfriendly mechanisms, such as Network Address Translation (NAT) systems and firewalls. With such a high number of highly transient participants, writing applications for such a networking environment requires various design issues to be tackled in order to cope with such a dynamic environment, for example, scalability, reliability, interoperability, and so on.

The growth of these two largely independent areas has been exponential with enormous momentum and diversity. However, there is also an obvious convergence as production Grids move forward into deployment over significantly more participants. The scalability techniques offered through P2P algorithms not only balance the load through encouraging the use of *servents*, where each peer is both a client and a server, but also address robustness through the use of more decentralized network overlays that can adapt to random failures across the network.

In this chapter we describe the DART (Distributed Audio Retrieval using Triana) project that is being researched jointly between Cardiff University and the Laboratory for Creative arts and Technologies (LCAT) in Louisiana State University that capitalises on these developments to provide a decentralized overlay for the processing of audio information for application in Music Information Retrieval (MIR). The design of the system is based on a BOINC-like (http://boinc.berkeley.edu/) paradigm; similar to the way SETI@home works. Under these scenarios, users provide CPU cycles to projects to help in the analysis of data for searching for both scientific and non-scientific events. Within DART we use the same type of philosophy to enable users to provide metadata to the network that is created through the analysis of the audio files located on their individual hard drives. The local processing on the network participants is achieved though the use of a popular Grid and P2P enabled workflow environment, called Triana, which allows the specification of data flows, to provide pipelines for processing the data in specific ways. Triana enables extremely rapid prototyping and code reusability of analysis algorithms exposed by a graphical interface, where units (representing audio analysis tools) can be dragged, dropped and connected together in order to create the algorithms. Such algorithms can be deployed that is, uploaded to the peers in the network, through the use of decentralized P2P structures that can enable caching and file replication for speed and efficiency. Although, in an early stage of development, DART provides insight into the aggregation of P2P, Grid and MIR technologies to provide next generation capabilities for navigating new audio information spaces for extracting statistical and content-based analysis of the audio across the Internet.

This chapter touches on several objectives for Intelligent Music Information Systems: Tools and Methodologies. Firstly, it provides a new P2P framework for MIR applications. Secondly, it exposes a new paradigm for the way we create massively distributed MIR applications by enabling users to contribute their own audio to the network, which is an alternative approach to the standard pull model employed currently. Lastly, it represents a shift away from centralized control and management of information by employing the use of a decentralized MIR metadata database, which is stored across the network participants as a whole. We believe that this approach is scalable and escapes from the bottlenecks associated with management and configurability, not to mention cost, of the alternative centralized approaches. We believe the ideas presented here would be of great interest to the readers of this book.

This chapter is organized as follows. In the background section, we discuss the background and history of Grid and P2P technologies, and also look at related research and work in the field of MIR. The next section focuses on the Triana framework, the current tools already in place for audio-rate signal processing, and gives a description of how Triana is employing a decentralized P2P framework to support MIR applications, as well as our progress towards that goal. The third section looks in detail at the DART system, explaining the work package assignment and results retrieval protocols, detailing the various peers in the DART system and illustrating their connectivity. The last main section then looks towards the future and discusses how DART hopes to lead the way when building next-generation MIR applications. Finally, we finish with a conclusion and a summary of the DART framework.

BACKGROUND

Recently, P2P networks have been broadly classified as using "unstructured" or "structured" approaches to locate resources. Gnutella (http://gnutella.wego.com/) and Kazaa (http://www.kazaa.com/) are examples of unstructured P2P networks, with hosts and resources being made available through dynamic network overlays, and without any global overlay planning. Distributed Hash Table (DHT) based systems such as FreeNet (Miller, Hong, Sandberg, & Brandon, 2002) and Chord (http://www.pdos.lcs.mit.edu/chord/) use a so-called "structured network" overlay of peers. This structuring consists of a logical identifier space (using hash keys) to which peers and resources are mapped. Peers maintain a neighborhood state about each other enabling application level routing of messages through the network based on the identifier space.

Within DART, we are more interested in the creation of unstructured technologies that can adapt to the types of connectivity associated with Internet scale applications. To this end, we have adopted the use of a middleware framework, called P2PS (Wang 2005), which is capable of creating super-peer networks across a range of heterogeneous devices. P2PS is a lightweight peer-to-peer infrastructure based on XML discovery and communication and provides a simple interface on which to develop peer-to-peer style applications, hiding the complexity of other architectures such as JXTA (Brookshier, Govoni, Krishnan, & Soto, 2002) and Jini (http://www.jini.org/). Due to its adoption of XML, P2PS is independent of any implementation language, and through the use of virtual pipes, it can support different transport protocol (such as TCP/IP, Multicast, UDP). Further, the reference implementation is in Java and can therefore run on most operating systems.

BOINC is a software platform for distributed computing using volunteered computer resources, developed at U.C. Berkeley Spaces Sciences Laboratory. The main goal of BOINC is to advance the public resource-computing paradigm: to encourage the creation of many projects, and to encourage a large fraction of the world's computer owners to participate. BOINC has been used in a number of projects, ranging from searching for extraterrestrial intelligence to searching for gravitational waves. The DART project described here builds on BOINC by extending it by two ways: firstly, it provides a decentralized overlay for accessing information across the system; and secondly, it reverses the role of the participants. In BOINC the participants provide CPU cycles for the analysis of external data (downloaded from a central point), whereas, in DART, the participants provide MIR metadata information to the network by analysing their own data that is, audio that is stored on their hard drives.

Related MIR Studies

Audio analysis algorithms and frameworks for Music Information Retrieval (MIR) are expanding rapidly, providing new ways to garnish information from audio sources well beyond what can be ascertained from ID3 tags. Modest successes have been made in audio-based musical genre classification audio-analysis algorithms such as musical genre classification (Tzanetakis & Cook 2002; Aucouturier & Pachet 2003), beat detection and analysis (Foote & Cooper 2002), similarity retrieval (Aucouturier & Pachet 2002; Logan & Salomon 2001; Yang, 2002), and audio finger-printing (Haitsma & Kalker, 2002). This work uses Short-Time Fourier Transforms to track the means and variances of the Spectral Centroid, standard deviations of the spectrum around its centroid, spectral envelopes, and signal power to represent sound textures, beat and pitch content (Tummarello, Morbidoni, Puliti, & Piazza, 2005). These values are then transformed into attribute-value pairs for pattern matching and semantic retrieval. There is still much to be done in this field. Refinements to existing strategies, as well as new strategies are still needed.

The analysis component of MIR requires extensive computational resources. Distributed environments and P2P networks are already being used for this purpose (Tzanetakis, Gao, & Steenkiste, 2005). The idea of using MIR over P2P was proposed in Wang, Li, and Shi (2002), however this system suffered from problems with scalability. More recently, the JXTA programming framework was used by Baumann (2003) to aid in the content-based retrieval over a P2P network. The proposed DART system differs from the distributed MIR system proposed in Tzanetakis, Gao, and Steenkiste (2005) however, in that only metadata is returned to the main Triana server for analysis, as opposed to actual audio data files, and has a different overall goal; DART is not intended to act as a file sharing system, but instead a distributed P2P MIR system with the main application scenario focussing on the recommendation of music based on the audio files the users hard drive.

Pandora (http://www.pandora.com/) is a novel music recommendation system from the makers of the Music Genome Project (http://www.pandora.com/mgp.shtml). Pandora allows users to enter the names of artists or songs they like, and Pandora will consult return a play list of artists and songs that the user may like. Again, DART hopes to build on these concepts by using the user's actual audio files to base the recommendations on, and analysing a much broader range of music, potentially across millions of users.

In summary, DART's P2P architecture aims to build upon all of these developments to provide an advanced, fully scalable platform for developing, testing and deploying new search and analysis algorithms on an Internet scale. Furthermore, as explained later in the chapter, the DART system can be adapted to fulfil a variety of applications other than music recommendation by modifying the Triana workflow that is distributed to the worker nodes. The Triana framework and Triana workflows are discussed in the next section.

THE TRIANA WORKFLOW ENVIRONMENT

Triana (http://www.trianacode.org) is a graphical Problem Solving Environment (PSE) for composing data-driven applications. Workflows (or data-flows) are constructed by dragging programming components, called tools, from the toolbox onto a workspace, and then drawing cables between these components to create a block diagram. Components can be aggregated visually to group functionality and compose new algorithm from existing components. For example, to add a digital Schroeder reverb to a piece of audio (see Figure 1), the file could be loaded (using the LoadSound unit), then passed to a SchroderVerb group unit before being passed to the Play unit to hear the result. The SchroderVerb unit is itself a group, which consists of a number of summed comb delays and all-pass filters, representing the inner workings of such an algorithm.

Within Triana, large suites of Java tools exist in a range of domains including signal, image and text processing. The signal processing tools are the most advanced, as Triana was initially developed for signal analysis within the GEO600 Gravitational Wave Project (GEO 600 Project 2004), who use the system to visualize and analyze one-dimensional signals (rather like an audio channel but sampled at a lower rate). Therefore a number of core mathematical, statistical and high-quality digital-signal processing algorithms already exist (around 300 signal processing and visualization units, and in total there are around 500 units in Triana that cover a broad range of applications).

Audio Processing in Triana

Triana integrates both Grid and P2P technologies and has been used in a number of domains, from bioinformatics, investigating biodiversity

Figure 1. A simple audio processing work-flow, showing how a Schroeder reverb is applied to a signal by using a group, which contains the underlying algorithmic details

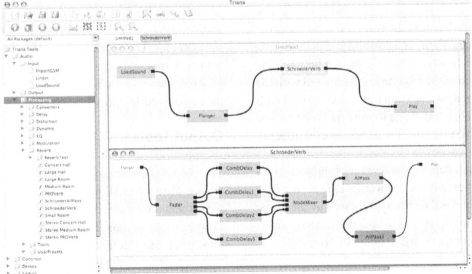

patterns, to gravitational wave observation, using computational Grids to process one-dimensional signals using standard digital signal-processing techniques. The goal of the DART project is to leverage this technology such that the same kind of DSP processing can be achieved with audio rate signals for the purposes of signal analysis, feature extraction, synthesis, and music information retrieval.

Given its modularity, its support for high quality audio, and its ability to distribute processes across a Grid of computers, Triana has the potential to be an extremely useful piece of software that allows users to implement custom audio processing algorithms from their constituent elements, no matter their computational complexity.

Triana Data Types

Triana units are programmed in a logical and robust manor and only ever need to be written and compiled once. When the unit is written, the programmer specifies the data type that the unit can receive and output. When connecting two units together, the input and output types of both units are checked in order to confirm the compatibility of the units. This means programmers can create units that can be guaranteed to work sensibly with other units because the run-time type checking guarantees their compatibility. Furthermore, since the data types that are passed between the units contain the parameters associated with the particular data, each unit knows how to deal with the data object whatever it contains. It is therefore impossible to crash a Triana network due to array size mismatches.

Triana's data type classes are fundamental to Triana's flexibility and power. Data Types are containers for the data being processed by the units. The two main types in Triana that are relevant to the processing of digital audio in Triana are:

- MultipleChannel
- MultipleAudio

MultipleChannel is a base class for representing multiple channelled data. Each channel can have its own particular format, specified within an object that implements the *ChannelFormat* interface. Furthermore, each channel can contain complex data so that, for example, multiple channels of complex spectra could be stored.

MutipleAudio stores many channels of sampled data. Each channel can have its own particular audio format of the data for example, the encoding, such as MU_LAW, PCM and number of bits used to record the data. This is essential for performing sound transformations and writing audio data. In essence, *MultipleAudio* provides the support for high quality audio to be utilized in Triana.

The Triana audio toolkit consists of several categorized hierarchical folders, each with an assortment of units based on the *MultipleAudio* Triana data type. This type utilizes the *JavaSound API* classes in order to allow the use of high fidelity audio. The Audio toolkit tree is split into three main folders: Input, Output, and Processing.

Input Tools

The audio input section houses one of the most important tools for Audio in Triana—the Load-Sound unit. This unit allows the user to select an audio file (WAV, Aiff, Au) and outputs the data to the next unit. The user can select if the audio file is to be output in its entirety, or if the data should be streamed on to the next unit by chunking the data into fixed-length segments.

Output Tools

The output tools section contains a varied collection of tools to allow the user to hear—and see—the audio data loaded, allowing for thorough analysis of the sounds. The *Play* unit is one of the most often used in this toolbox, and allows the user to play the audio (both streamed, or as one large file). Triana gives the user a useful selection of other output tools, such as the *WaveViewer* unit

Figure 2. A screenshot of the WaveViewer unit from the Audio/Output folder, displaying a waveform

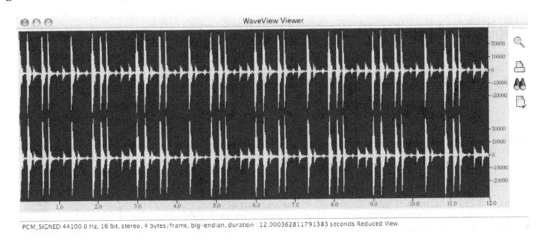

PCM_SIGNED 44100.0 Hz, 16 bit, stereo, 4 bytes/frame, big-endian, duration : 12.000362811791383 seconds Reduced View

(see Figure 2), which shows the current waveform with a time-amplitude relationship. This allows for a much more thorough visual scrutiny of the audio. Also included in the *Output* section is a group of audio writing tools (such as *WriteWav*, *WriteAiff*), allowing the user to (re)save the audio after any amount of processing in Triana is complete.

Audio Processing Tools

The audio processing tools form the core of its audio manipulation capabilities. Inside the audio processing toolkit is another level of categorized folders, covering a wide range of applications:

- **Converters:** for converting between audio formats and for separating stereo streams into two independent channels and vice versa.
- **Delay:** single delays, all pass filters and comb delays.
- **Distortion:** distortion algorithms and fuzz boxes.
- **Dynamic:** compressors, limiters and expanders.
- **EQ:** low pass, high pass and parametric EQ (in progress).

- **Modulation:** chorus, flanger, phaser and variable delays.
- **Reverb:** Schroeder verbs, and various presents from small rooms to large concert halls.
- **Signal Analysis:** FFT analysis for use in spectral processing, analysis/resynthesis, and signal analysis for music information retrieval
- **Tools:** faders, resampling modules, wave inverters, rectifiers and reversal algorithms.
- **UserPresets:** combinational effects (i.e., group units) encompassing several of the above algorithms with particular settings for example, distorted flangers, exuberant reverbs, and so forth.

The categories should be recognizable to regular users of audio processing or production software. Each folder contains units which are in themselves effects but also allow the user to create their custom algorithms from the smaller building blocks supplied. It is possible to break down complex algorithms into a group of functions (units) that when linked together in a particular fashion, are able to perform the task as a whole. This was demonstrated earlier, with the example of Triana's ability to group the comb and allpass

Figure 3. Audio is split and converted to a SampleSet data type, in order to subtract all music that is panned down the middle of the stereo field. This conversion is then reversed and played back.

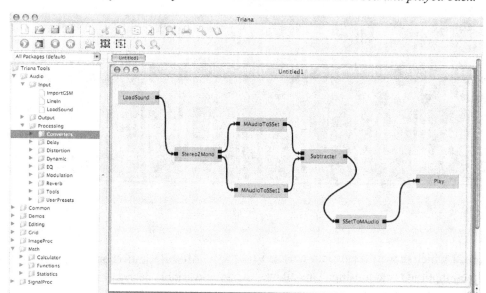

filters in order to create a *Schreoder Reverberator* algorithm, which is then grouped, saved and reused as if it were a single unit. This unit aggregation gives the user more freedom to take advantage of Triana's modularity.

One feature of interest resides in the *Converters* folder; two units are available that allow the user to convert from *MultipleAudio* to *a SampleSet* Triana data type—and back again (*MAudioToSSet* and *SSetToMAudio* respectively). This opens up a whole range of possibilities to the user, enabling them to utilize many of the numerous math and signal-processing units to process the audio, and then convert data back to a *MultipleAudio* data type for playback. One example of how this technique could be used is shown in Figure 3.

In Figure 3, a *Stereo2Mono* unit (also in the converters folder) is used to split the stereo channels of an audio file or stream into two distinct mono channels. Each side is then converted to a *SampleSet* and fed into a *Subtractor* unit from the *Math* folder. This subtracts the left from the

right stereo channel, which results in the removal of sound that is contained in both that is, those panned in the middle of the stereo field. This is a simple way of removing vocals from many songs and leaving the (majority) of the backing track (as vocals in particular are normally panned down the centre). This is just a simple example of how a few of the converter units could help users create their own algorithms. It must be remembered that the user is encouraged to try create different algorithms themselves, and experiment with different unit connection chains—and not only using the presets given in Triana.

As mentioned previously, Triana also contains hundreds of statistical, mathematical, and signal processing units, which can be used in conjunction to all of the *MultipleAudio* compatible units, opening up an vast range of units to facilitate and aid MIR and the creation of useful MIR algorithms. Triana includes *Fast Fourier Transform* units, a range of filters, graphs, and histogram viewers, spectrum analyzers and more, meaning that algorithms can be broken down into their constituent elements, and programmers can take advantage of prewritten software modules within Triana to aid in the development of new algorithms. This allows the user to bypass the conventional approach to programming, creating various methods and coding a core program to connect the set of related method procedures together.

Distributing Triana Taskgraphs

Triana is capable of working within P2P environments through the use of P2PS and JXTA and it can work within Grid environments through the use of the Globus toolkit accessed via the GAT interface. Further, it has the capability of fusing these environments through the use of WSPeer (Harrison & Taylor, 2005), which can host Web Services and OGSA implementations, such as WS-RF, within P2P environments like P2PS.

The Triana Underlying Toolkits

Triana builds on distributing systems technologies by integrating the Grid Application Toolkit (GAT) (Allen et al., 2003) and its peer-to-peer subset, called the GAP (Taylor et al. 2003), which is illustrated in Figure 4. These interfaces provide application-level capabilities for a number of different types of middleware. So, for example, within a Grid computing scenario, Triana could use the GAT's Globus GRAM (Grid Resource Allocation Manager) binding to execute applications on distributed resources or similarly it could use the GAP's JXTA or P2PS (Wang, 2005) discovery and pipe mechanisms to discover and communicate with peers in a P2P environment.

The GAT interface provides a generalized collection of calls to shield Grid applications from the implementation details of the underlying Grid middleware, and was developed in the European GridLab Project. The GAT utilizes adaptors that provide specific bindings from the GAT interface to underlying mechanisms that implement this functionality. The GAT may be referred to as upperware, which distinguishes it from middleware (which provides the actual implementation of the underlying functionality). Until recently, application developers typically interact with the middleware directly. However it is becoming increasingly apparent that this transition from one type of middleware to another is not a trivial one. Using interfaces like the GAT, migrating from one middleware environment is easier and typically achieved by setting an environment variable. The GAT is currently being standardized through the SAGA working group efforts within the OGF consortium.

The Grid Application Prototype Interface (GAP interface) is a generic application interface that provides P2P-based discovery and communication mechanisms. It is also middleware independent and defines common high-level capabilities with bindings provided for different service-oriented middleware, such as P2P middleware for example, JXTA and P2P, and also middleware for interacting with Web and Grid services, as illustrated in Figure 4. The GAP interface hides many of the complexities of dealing with the various environments and provides a uniform view of how to deploy, discover, and communicate with distributed services. Specific details for each environment are typically set using a configuration file (or GUI in Triana). Such details can include attributes such as: specifying which transport protocols to use; providing rules for specifying Rendezvous peers; or naming which UDDI servers to use. The GAP massively simplifies the implementation for an application as it provides a clean dividing line between simple distributed interactions, such as discovery and communication, and low-level details that are middleware dependent. This allows the application developer to develop switchable interfaces that interact with the underlying middleware in a coherent fashion but then also allow the flexibility of being to add tools for manipulating the behavior environments that they run within.

For example, to a user in an MIR system, he/she may have no interest in the fact that a "publish to network" command involves flooding the super peers to connect with a suitable rendezvous for publication using UDP with NACK enabled reliability, but still he/she may understand well that a publish will make their information available to others on the network. The GAP is this high level view, whereas the configuration of the network designers will specify the low-level details of how this happens.

Currently there are three GAP bindings implemented:

- **P2PS:** a lightweight Peer-to-Peer middleware.
- **Web Services:** allows applications to discover and interact with Web and WS-RF Services—using WSPeer, which can use standard Web-based tools, such as a UDDI registry and the Web Service Invocation Framework (WSIF), or indeed run on top of P2PS to host Web services within a P2P environment.
- **JXTA:** the original GAP Interface binding was to JXTA, which has been not bee updated, and superceded by P2PS.

In DART, we are interested in forming unstructured P2P networks and therefore need to employ technologies that can adapt and scale within such an environment. We therefore, use the GAP interface and employ the use of the P2PS middleware binding to achieve this goal. P2PS is described in the next section.

P2P Simplified

For distribution across dynamic networks, we use the P2PS binding. Peer-to-Peer Simplified (P2PS)

Figure 4. The GAP interface provides a middleware independent interface for developing P2P applications, whilst the GAT provides access to Grid tools and middleware.

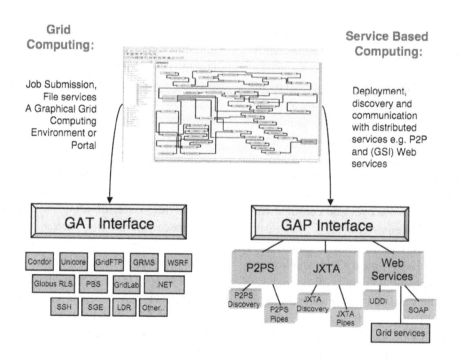

came into being as a response to the complexity and overhead associated with JXTA. As its name suggests, it is a simple yet generic API for developing peer-to-peer systems. P2PS encompasses intelligent discovery mechanisms, pipe based communication and makes it possible to easily create desirable network topologies for searching, such as decentralized ad-hoc networks with super peers or rendezvous nodes. P2PS is designed to cope with rapidly changing environments, where peers may come and go at frequent intervals.

At the core of P2PS is the notion of a pipe: a virtual communication channel that is only bound to specific endpoints at connection time. When a peer publishes a pipe advertisement it only identifies the pipe by its name, ID, and the ID of its host peer. A remote peer wishing to connect to a pipe must query an endpoint resolver for the host peer in order to determine an actual endpoint address that it can contact. In P2PS a peer can have multiple endpoint resolvers (e.g., TCP, UDP etc), with each resolving endpoints in different transport protocols or returning relay endpoints that bridge between protocols (e.g., to traverse a firewall). Also, the P2PS infrastructure employs XML in its discovery and communication protocols, which allows it to be independent of any implementation language and computing hardware. Assuming that suitable P2PS implementations exist, it should be possible to form a P2PS network that includes everything from super-computer peers to PDA peers.

Distributing Triana Units or Groups

Triana units (or groups of units) can be distributed to a number of Triana launcher services, according to a distribution policy. A Triana launcher service is a GAP-based service that, when sent a workflow subsection (serialized in XML) via its control pipe, uses the GAP Interface to launch that subsection as a new Triana service. This capability has led to a number of interesting demonstrations. For example, by dynamically sending the *Play*

audio unit to distributed Triana service, you can playback the audio on another person's computer. You can also use this mechanism to perform distributed calculations across a number of services by dynamically sending the analysis you wish to perform across the various distributed services and then passing them data to process.

However, in the DART framework the distribution policy for Triana is more loosely coupled. Although Triana acts as a manager and processor in the system, the distributed functionality is provided by the DART framework, which implements a decentralized discovery and communication system based on P2PS. This allows Triana workflows to be uploaded to peers for execution and enables users to query the network to locate results and to perform custom searches. The DART system therefore manages the specifics of the network and Triana acts as a client (i.e., the DART manager or user) that both accesses DART via the GAP and also acts as an end processor to execute data-flows that have been previously uploaded for the analysis of the audio. Therefore, Triana does not tie the network together, rather it accesses a loosely coupled framework that allows wide-range distributed Triana entities to communicate via the Internet. The next section of this chapter discusses the DART framework in more detail and details the mechanisms to facilitate so-called *work package assignment* and the retrieval of the results.

DART: A FRAMEWORK FOR DISTRIBUTED INFORMATION RETRIEVAL

Work Package Assignment and Results Retrieval

A process-intensive DART application can require the distributed analysis of a large number of audio files, in order to provide some useful, nontrivial feedback to the user. One sample application for the use of the DART system would be a music recommendation system, whereby the audio (typically in mp3 format) on a user's machine is analyzed and suitable recommendations are made to the user based on the results of the analysis carried out. The analysis of the files could be index-based, including statistical correlations of song names to extract commonalities in order to make a recommendation— or the analysis could be content based, actually searching for track tempos, timbre, pitch, mood, frequency range, and so forth. Algorithms for statistical and audio-based analysis consist of workflows that are created by the so-called *DART Manager*. Such workflows are bundled into a *package* (containing the Java code and their required resources) that is propagated onto the network in order to upload the new analysis to the users' machines. As the algorithms are updated and refined by the DART Manager, the updated Triana task graph and any new tools are bundled into a new package, and distributed onto the network.

The scenario described here discusses the decentralized DART network, in which nodes are organized in a super-peer topology using the P2PS middleware. In P2PS producers (e.g., providers of packages containing algorithms or results) create *adverts* to advertise that they have something that is of interest to other participants in the network. Consumers (i.e., the peers that wish to use available packages, result sets and so on) issue a *query* in order to search for relevant adverts. P2PS *rendezvous* nodes are then responsible for matching queries, with adverts within their local cache, in order to search for matches and respond accordingly. Consumers receive adverts when their query matches, and can be used to retrieve the relevant information they require that is, download the new package to perform the analysis. The *DART Manager* node produces and advertises the bundle representing the new DART package (called *DART Package Adverts*) containing algorithms that the worker nodes need to run (new Triana units and task

graphs). With the DART system, the data files that undergo analysis (the music files and mp3s) are on the users local system, and therefore all data processing is local so network bandwidth is not consumed transferring large data files over the DART infrastructure. Although local, the processing is massively parallel, as participants analyze their own audio files in parallel.

Simple peers, or *workers*, are available for package execution, and therefore issue a *package query* to download a package in order to start their analysis. Super-peer interconnections are exploited to make package queries travel the network rapidly; super peers play the role of rendezvous *nodes*, since they can store package adverts (and potentially the packages themselves if the super peers are also functioning as *Package Repositories*, as discussed shortly) and compare these files with queries issued to discover them; thereby acting as a meeting place for both package providers and consumers. Since packages could require a reasonable amount of storage memory, it is assumed that only some of the peers in the network will cache such files. These peers are referred to as *Package Repositories* (*PR*) nodes and can be located on super peers or worker peers. Each user or node in the system would decide if they want to be a super peer and/or package repositories, as well as a worker.

Figure 5 shows a sample topology with 5 super-peers (2 of which are also package repositories), and the sequence of messages exchanged among workers, super-peers and package repositories to perform the package submission protocol. These messages are related to the execution of a packager by a single worker, labelled as W0. Note that in this example, normal peers are not considered as package repositories.

The protocol requires that job execution be preceded by two matching phases that exploit the features of the super-peer network: the *package-advertisement* phase and the *results-query* phase. In the *package-advertisement* phase, the *DART manager* generates a number of *package adverts*,

Figure 5. Super-peer package submission protocol: Sample network topology and sequence of exchanged messages to execute one package cycle

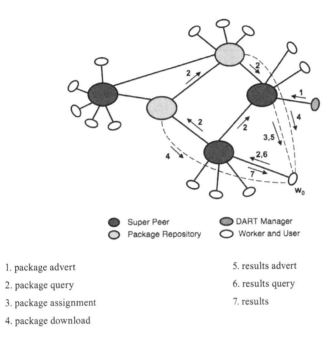

1. package advert
2. package query
3. package assignment
4. package download

5. results advert
6. results query
7. results

which are XML files describing the properties of the algorithms to be executed (task graph parameters containing the units/tools, platform requirements if any, information about required input audio data files, etc.), and sends them to the local rendezvous super peer, which stores the adverts. Each worker, when ready to offer a fraction of its CPU time, either sends a new *package query* that travels the network through the super-peer interconnections or continues working on its current workflow. A package query is expressed by an XML document that requests if there are any updates to the package it is currently using to perform the analysis. The query can also contain hardware and software features of the worker node, if this is necessary—for example, available RAM, disk space or JDK version. As soon as the package query finds a matching package advert, that is, an advert describing a package that can be actually executed by the requesting worker, a package assignment is made to the worker.

Package assignment is sent by the rendezvous that stores the advert directly to the worker. The actual packages are also stored locally on the package repositories (whose adverts are cached by the super peers), which query for new packages to download and store, and then re-advertise the packages in order to propagate them onto the network in a more decentralized fashion, rather than relying on one node to do this, which is the case for systems like SETI or BOINC. It may be the case that a super peer is also a package repository, if the peer chooses to donate these resources, and has them to spare.

Since more than one package repository can match the query, the package repository does not directly send the package to the worker. Rather, it returns a small *package advertisement* to the worker, possibly via other super peers. The worker itself initiates the download operation after receiving the first package advertisement that has matched its query and simply discards

Figure 6. High-level overview of the DART system, showing the various peers and their connectivity

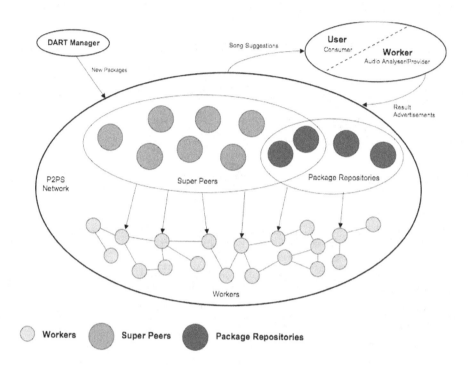

the subsequent adverts. Moreover, when a super peer in this scenario also plays the role of package repository, it caches the downloaded file so that in the future another package query can be matched directly by this package repository. Replication of the package on multiple package repositories allows for a significant saving of time in the querying phase and enables the concurrent retrieving of packages from different repositories.

Once the worker has received the most up to date package that it can find on the network, the Triana taskgraphs are run and the algorithms begin to analyze the audio files on the workers system during the system's idle time. Once a package *cycle* is complete and the worker has results to present, the worker then creates an XML advert containing the results and metadata that generated by the algorithm specified in the package (a *results advertisement*). As the actual results generated would extremely small in size in this DART system, the functionality of the Super

Peer has been extended in order to also cache and make available.

The worker, who can be thought of a results *provider* on the DART system, can also act as a *user*, as it can query for results (in this case a suitable music/song suggestion as generated on the super-peer). There is not a central results collector, but rather DART utilizes a fully decentralized model and allows the results to propagate through the network hop by hop, to be stored on the super peers. The super peers can process the metadata and issue an XML *results advertisement* on receipt of a *results query* from the user. Once the query is received, the results may be sent to the user.

In the package assignment phase the protocol works in a way similar to the BOINC software, except that package (or "job") queries are not sent directly to the DART manager, as in BOINC, but travel the super-peer network hop by hop. Conversely, the data download phase differs from

BOINC in that it exploits the presence of multiple data centres in order to replicate input data files across the Grid network.

Peer Overview

This section gives a brief overview of what role each node on the network plays, and the jobs associated with that role:

DART Manager

- Creates new task graphs and Triana units
- Advertises new DART Packages

User

- Queries Results
- Downloads/Receives Results

Worker Nodes

- Queries New Packages
- Downloads Package
- Works/processes Taskgraph
- Advertises Results

Package Repositories

- Query and Download New Packages (Stored locally)
- Advertise Packages

Super Peers

- Caches Advertisements
- Does simple analysis of results received from workers

Workflow Design

The workflow created by the DART manager and propagated onto the other peers on the network,

will always be evolving. Initially, it is easier to concentrate on statistical methods for recommending music to the users of the DART system (searching for correlations between artists found on the users machines), however this will soon evolve, and become more involved as the Triana workflow is refined and more MIR algorithms are incorporated into the package sent to the worker nodes. The algorithms used for the recommendation of music files to the DART users will be made available to the MIR community for refinement, suggestions, and also to allow for the advancement of this field of research as MIR-algorithm specialists provide input ideas and offer improvements to refine and maximise the benefit of the use of the DART system.

DART Flexibility

The chapter so far has focussed on the creation of a distributed P2P MIR system to facilitate the recommendation of music to users intelligently, and the framework created in order to achieve this. However the DART infrastructure can be used for a variety of applications, musical, and otherwise. One application scenario is a DART system installed on a local/closed network; scanning sound effect audio files on separate systems in networked commercial studio facilities, to search for sound effect files (or for example, drum sounds) that match a specific criteria. For example, if a DART user requires a 'snare' drum sample, usual search mechanisms cannot search for suitable sounds unless the audio files filename contains the word "snare" or other suitable identifier—the search mechanism would do no more than string matching.

In contrast to this, given the appropriate algorithm created in Triana by the DART manager, then propagated onto the network, the DART system would allow the user to search all the audio content in the distributed sound library, and suggest files with suitable characteristics which match the specific search criteria set by the user.

This would also be able to return further results to the user, which would not be returned via conventional methods— any samples that match the users search criteria, will be returned. This means that when ignoring criteria such as pitch and tempo and investigating the timbre of the sound file, new sounds that could be adapted to work for the user, could be suggested. For example, a sped up sample of a car collision may easily work well in place of a snare sample!

Another example consists of a scenario that requires speech recognition algorithms to detect a certain caller from a large amount of recorded telephone audio data. Given a sophisticated enough algorithm (created in Triana as a workflow), the DART framework could be used to scan terabytes of recorded audio data to help trace calls from a specific caller.

The flexibility of the DART system stems from the ability to easily refine and change the Triana workflow that dictates what the worker nodes will be processing in their screensaver/idle/nice time.

FUTURE TRENDS

DART is a new research project that is attempting to provide a platform for addressing future-looking MIR applications. DART attempts to gain access to the participants of the Internet as a whole rather than providing an access point or a main database for storing global information. We believe such a decentralized approach is key to the future possibilities of MIR applications. DART assumes zero configurability and administrations and aims to scale and reuse the resources already available on the Internet. It does this by involving the participation of end users in all aspects of the system. The DART system has no single point of control but rather it organically lives across the network. The DART database, for example, evolves across a decentralized layer of super peers, which are simply Internet users that

can spare some disk space for the greater good of the system. Such approaches have been shown to work elsewhere where incentives are given in order to participate, for example, ability to download files, point scoring for recognition, and so forth. In DART, the motivation will be provided by the usefulness of the applications that will make use of this framework by allowing users to search a global audio information space to, for example, find other similar music they may like. Although, the database is decentralized and therefore consists of transient participants (who may disconnect for example), the caching scheme employed ensures replication across the various nodes in order to retain the information. This mechanism is useful because the distributed database is persisted based on the users' demand and therefore will help prune and optimise the process.

The change in use of the Internet over the past five years clearly points to approaches such as this for building next-generation MIR applications. DART maybe a first step in this direction but we hope it will lead to further frameworks or take-up of this type of technology.

CONCLUSION

In this chapter, we provided an overview of a new framework called DART, which attempts to extend the state-of-the-art in the application of P2P networks for MIR. At its essence, DART enables users to provide input to a massively distributed database through the analysis of their audio files for application in MIR. DART provides decentralized P2P mechanisms to allow the scalability of such a database for dynamic construction and manageability. DART is a research project that aims to provide this framework as open source to the community for simplifying the development of Internet scale MIR applications. The framework is based on Java and our interests lie in the ability to create a global music information space that allows us to investigate novel ways of searching between music genres and tastes. Further, we provide high-level tools for creating data processing pipelines, which can be deployed onto the network. Users or developers can easily extend this framework for their specific needs.

REFERENCES

Allen, G., et al. (2003). The Grid Application Toolkit: Towards Generic and Easy Application Programming Interfaces for the Grid. *Submitted to IEEE*

Aucouturier, J. and Pachet, F. 2003. Representing musical genre: A state of the art. *Journal of New Music Research, 32*(1), 83–93.

Baumann, S. (2003). Music Similarity Analysis in a P2P environment. In *Proceedings of the 4th European Workshop on Image Analysis for Multimedia Interactive Services*, pages 314–319, London, UK

BOINC. See http://boinc.berkeley.edu/

Brookshier, D., Govoni, D., Krishnan, N., and Soto, J C,. 2002. JXTA: Java P2P Programming. SAMS.

Chord. See http://www.pdos.lcs.mit.edu/chord/

Clarke, I., Miller, S., Hong, T., Sandberg, O., and Wiley, B. Jan/Feb 2002. Protecting Free Expression Online with Freenet. In *IEEE Internet Computing, 6*(1), 40-49.

Corba. See http://www.corba.org/

Dabek, F., Brunskill, E., Kaashoek, M., Karger, D., Morris, R., Stoica, I., and Balakrishnan, H. 2001. Building Peer-to-Peer Systems with Chord, a Distributed Lookup Service. In *Eighth Workshop on Hot Topics in Operating Systems*, page 81.

Foote, J., Cooper, M., and Nam, U. 2002. Audio retrieval by rhythmic similarity. In *Proceedings of the International Conference on Music Information Retrieval*. Paris: IRCAM.

Foster, I., and Iamnitchi, A. 2003. On Death, Taxes, and the Convergence of Peer- to-Peer and Grid Computing. In *Proceedings of the 2nd International Workshop on Peer-to-Peer Systems (IPTPS '03)*.

Foster, I., Kesselman, C., Nick, S., and Tuecke, S. 2002. The Physiology of the Grid: An Open Grid Services Architecture for Distributed Systems Integration. *Open Grid Service Infrastructure WG, Global Grid Forum*, June 22, 2002. See website http://www.gridforum.org/ogsi-wg/

GEO 600, July 2005. http://www.geo600.uni-hannover.de/.

Global Grid Forum (GGF). See http://www.ggf.org/

Globus Project. See http://www.globus.org/

Gnutella. See http://gnutella.wego.com/

Harrison, A., and Taylor, I. J. 2005. WSPeer - An Interface to Web Service Hosting and Invocation. In *Joint Workshop on High-Performance Grid Computing and High-Level Parallel Programming Models*.

Haitsma, J., and Kalker, T. 2002. A highly robust audio fingerprinting system. In *Proceedings of the 3rd International Conference on Music Information Retrieval*. Paris: IRCAM.

Jini. See http://www.jini.org/

KaZaA. See http://www.kazaa.com/

Logan, B. and Salomon, A. (2001). A Music Similarity Function based on Signal Analysis. In *International Conference on Multimedia and Expo* (ICME). IEEE

Napster. See http://www.napster.com/

OGSI working group. See https://forge.gridforum.org/projects/ogsi-wg

Pandora. See http://www.pandora.com/

Pastry. See http://research.microsoft.com/<antr/pastry/

SETI@Home. See http://setiathome.ssl.berkeley.edu/

Taylor, I. J., et al. (2003). Triana as a Graphical Web Services Composition Toolkit. Web Services. In *Proceedings of the IEEE International Conference.*

The GridLab Project. See http://www.gridlab.org

The Triana Project. See http://www.trianacode.org/

Tummarello, G., Morbidoni, C., Puliti, P., and Piazza, P. 2005. Semantic audio hyperlinking: a multimedia-semantic web scenario. In *Proceedings of the 1st International Conference on Automated Production of Cross Media Content for Multi-channel Distribution.*

Tzanetakis, G., Gao, J., and Steenkiste, P. (Summer 2004). A scalable peer-to-peer system for music information retrieval. *Computer Music Journal, 28*(2), 24-33.

Tzanetakis, G., Ermolinskyi, A., and Cook, P. (2002). Beyond the query-by-example paradigm: New query interfaces for music information retrieval. In *Proceedings of the 2002 International Computer Music Conference.*

Tzanetakis, G., and Cook, P. (2002). Music Genre Classification of Audio Signals. In *IEEE Transactions on Speech and Audio Processing, 10*(5), 293-302, 2002.

Wang, C., Li, J., and Shi, S. (2002). A kind of content-based music information retrieval method in a peer-to-peer environment. In *Proceedings 2nd ISMIR.*

Wang, I. P2PS (Peer-to-Peer Simplified). In *Proceedings of 13th Annual Mardi Gras Conference - Frontiers of Grid Applications and Technologies*, pages 54-59. Louisiana State University, February 2005.

Web Services Description Language, version 2.0 draft. See http://www.w3.org/TR/2003/WD-wsdl20-20031110/

WS-Resource Framework home page. See http://www.globus.org/wsrf/

W3C Document, Extensible Markup Language 1.0. (1988), second edition (2000), http://www.w3.org/TR/REC-xml/, Third Edition, W3C Recommendation 04 February 2004, see http://www.w3.org/TR/2004/REC-xml-20040204/

Yang, C. (2002). The MACSIS Acoustic Indexing Framework for Music Retrieval: An Experimental Study. In *Proceedings of the International Conference on Music Information Retrieval.* Paris, France.

Section IV
Music Analysis

Chapter XI
Motivic Pattern Extraction in Symbolic Domain

Olivier Lartillot
University of Jyväskylä, Finland

ABSTRACT

This chapter offers an overview of computational research in motivic pattern extraction. The central questions underlying the topic, concerning the formalization of the motivic structures, the matching strategies and the filtering of the results, have been addressed in various ways. A detailed analysis of these problems leads to the proposal of a new methodology, which will be developed throughout the study. One main conclusion of this review is that the problems cannot be tackled using purely mathematic or geometric heuristics or classical engineering tools, but require also a detailed understanding of the multiple constraints derived by the underlying cognitive context.

INTRODUCTION

Motives are series of notes (or chords) that are highlighted in different manners, related to their temporal location (such at the beginning of a piece), the use of particular punctuations or articulations (such as silence, pitch, or timbral contrast, etc.), or their multiple repetitions throughout the piece (Lerdahl & Jackendoff, 1983; Temperley, 1988). As such, they form one of the most characteristic descriptions of music. The themes of a piece correspond to the most prominent and original motives.

A more detailed analysis shows the existence of deeper motivic structures proliferating throughout the work. Some of these cells are specific material created in the context of the piece, while others are common stylistic features, also known as "signatures", corresponding to particular musical styles (Cope, 1996).

The automated extraction of motives in music databases is an important topic related to the domain of music knowledge discovery. First, it would enable an automated description of the melodic and rhythmic characteristics of musical pieces and of musical styles and genres in general. Second, the automated description allows more advanced comparisons between pieces, based on a comparison between salient structures, instead of a matching of local structural configurations that often present less perceptual or musical relevance. We may conjecture also that the motivic pattern extraction task might be beneficial to music information retrieval: the automated description of musical databases allows a reduction of the size of the search, a focus on the most salient structures and therefore a probable increase of the relevance of the results.

The motivic structure is often highly complex. Detailed analysis of the deeper motivic structures contained in music has been undertaken during the 20th century (Reti, 1951). Systematic approaches have been suggested, with the view to augmenting the analytic capabilities, both in quantitative and qualitative terms (Lerdahl & Jackendoff, 1983; Nattiez, 1990; Ruwet, 1987). Computational modeling offers the possibility to automate the process, enabling the fast annotation of large scores, and the extraction of complex and detailed structures without much effort.

The pattern discovery system described in this chapter is applied uniquely to symbolic representation (such as score or MIDI format). A direct analysis on the signal level would arouse tremendous difficulties. In fact, even when restricted to the symbolic level, the pattern extraction task still remains a difficult challenge. The pattern discovery task seems therefore too complex for a direct examination from the audio signal, but requires rather a prior transcription from the audio to the symbolic representations, in order to carry out the analysis on a conceptual level.

This chapter presents an overview of computational research in motivic pattern extraction, discusses the main underlying questions, and suggests a partial answer to the problem. We will show that the central questions underlying the topic, concerning the nature of the motivic structures, the matching strategies and the filter-

ing of the results, have been tackled in alternative ways by the different approaches. The detailed analysis of these problems leads to the proposal of a new methodology developed throughout the study. Combinatorial redundancy constitutes, in our view, one major difficulty aroused by the task. A solution is proposed, through an adaptive filtering based on closed patterns and cyclic patterns. Important questions that need to be considered in future works concern, among others, the validation of the alternative approaches, the taking into account of complex musical configurations such as polyphony and the integration of multiple segmentation factors into one synthetic model.

MOTIVE FORMALIZATION

Definition of Motives

The basic principle of *motivic pattern extraction* consists of identifying several short extracts or subsequences—from one or several pieces—as instances, or *occurrences*, of a same model called *pattern*. A *motivic pattern* is a succession of notes that forms a melodic sequence, or motive, repeated several times in the piece or the corpus. Each pattern presents two main properties: the "intentional" property is related to the musical description common to all its occurrences; the "extensional" property corresponds to its *class*, that is, the set of occurrences itself (Rolland, 1999). This dichotomy between intentional and extensional properties plays a core role since it implies a Gallois correspondence (Ganter & Wille, 1999) that offers interesting mathematic properties, as we will later.

A complete description of the motivic pattern extraction task requires further specifications: in particular the explicit formalization of the concept of motive and the description of the matching process. The formalization of motives is of high importance because it determines the way pattern occurrences are extracted from pieces.

Two opposite paradigms have been proposed in previous works, based respectively on set and string paradigms.

Set-Based Formalization

In Meredith, Lemström, and Wiggins (2002; 2003), score are formalized as *sets* of notes, and motives as *subsets* of the scores. The broad generality of this approach enables the taking into account of a large range of musical structures and configurations—such as polyphony—that are outside the scope of the more constrained string-based paradigm, as we will see in the next subsection. The extraction strategy is founded on geometrical principles: notes are represented by points in a multi-dimensional representation of the score, and melodic patterns are defined as

subsets of points that are translated in that space. One particular difficulty in this approach is that it cannot be easily applied—and it has not been applied yet—to the detection of patterns that present temporal fluctuations.

Among the configurations allowed by this broad characterization of motives appears a large range of structures that do not convey much perceptive and musical relevance.[1] One reason for this poor selectivity is that no constraint is initially defined, regarding the relationship between successive notes composing each pattern. Hence patterns may be composed of notes taken from very distinct temporal contexts—for instance one note from the beginning of a piece and another note from the end, which is generally counterintuitive. The solution proposed by the authors consists in defining the "compactness" of a pattern to be

Figure 1. In the set paradigm, motives are considered as subsets of the notes of the score. Here, the notes of Twinkle Twinkle Little Star reduced theme (i.e., without pitch repetitions) are circled in the first theme exposition and the beginning of the first variation in Mozart's theme and variations (K. 300e). The compactness of each motive is assessed with respect to the corresponding "time segments" (between crochets), "bounding-boxes" (gray rectangles) or "convex hulls" (black triangles).

the ratio of the number of notes in the pattern to the total number of notes in the piece that occur within the region spanned by the pattern. The "region spanned by a pattern" is defined in a number of different ways: either as the smallest "time segment" that contains the pattern, or as the "bounding-box" or the "convex hull" spanned by the pattern in the bi-dimensional representation (time/pitch) of the score. See Figure 1 for an illustration of these geometrical objects. The underlying assumption is that typically at least one occurrence of the pattern should have a high compactness value, even if the other occurrences are highly embellished.

For instance, in Mozart's Theme and Variations on *Twinkle, Twinkle, Little Star* (K. 300e), the basic theme common to all the variations does not contain the pitch repetition and is therefore reduced to only one note per bar (circled in the figure). During the exposition of the theme (first occurrence), its compactness with respect to the corresponding "time segment" (between crochets) is very low: 8 notes out of 31, or 26%. The results are better for "bounding box" (gray rectangle, 8 notes out of 16, or 50%) and for "convex hull" (black triangle, 8 notes out of 14, or 57%) but not particularly high. Hence the main theme is likely to be rejected by the heuristics, unless the minimum compactness threshold is fixed to a low value, below 57%. But a low threshold value may dramatically increase the proportion of false positives, without necessarily insuring a significant reduction of false negatives.

String-Based Formalization

The alternate approach is focused on monodic sequences, which are formalized as *strings* of notes. This follows the idea that music sequences are perceived as a succession of events closely connected one after the other. This hypothesis can be associated with the phenomenological idea of primary retention (Husserl, 1905) and the linguistic concept of syntagmatic relation

(Saussure, 1916). Yet, in general, music takes the form of a complex polyphonic flux that cannot easily be reduced to a single string of events. For instance, the Mozart example, as shown in Figure 2, features two strings, one for each voice[2]. The adaptation of this approach to polyphony will require extensive subsequent works.

Following the string paradigm, each voice is considered separately, and motives are formalized as *substrings* of the monodic string that contain *all* the notes of the string between two given limits. In its very simple version, this approach can only formalize exact repetition of patterns, transpositions, or similar simple transformations. Ornamented motives on the contrary,—like in the Mozart example, where *secondary notes* are added in the temporal neighbourhood of the *primary notes* (i.e., the notes forming the reduced theme itself) –, are beyond the compass of this simple framework. Primary notes may be retrieved through an automated filtering of secondary notes, for instance, by focusing on metrically strong positions (Conklin & Anagnostopoulou, 2001; Eerola, Järvinen, Louhivuori, & Toiviainen, 2001). This heuristic does not, however, work correctly for appoggiaturas, where secondary notes, instead of primary notes, are placed on downbeats. For instance, the pattern repetition of the theme could not be detected in this way in the first variation of the *Twinkle* theme (Figure 2, staves 2 and 3).

Another solution (Mongeau & Sankoff, 1990; Rolland, 1999) consists of tolerating gaps, using alignment strategies based on dynamic programming. The idea is that a substring may be compared to another substring through a successive sequence of transformations, such as insertion of notes from the second substring, suppression of notes in the initial first substring, modification of one note, and so forth. With each transformation is associated a cost, whose summation defines a global dissimilarity distance between the two motives, from which identification decision can be inferred. As explained in the next section, this decision is based on a dissimilarity threshold,

Figure 2. Mozart's theme and first variation on Twinkle Twinkle Little Star feature two monodic streams, one for each voice, represented by the lines in the figure. In the string paradigm, motives are considered as substrings of the monodic streams, and are represented here with thick lines. The notes forming the occurrences of the reduced theme are circled.

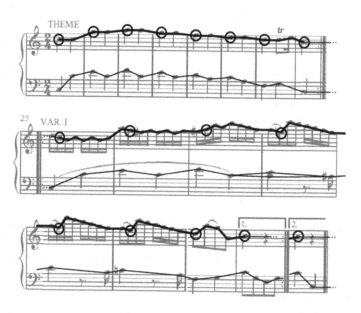

Figure 3. Syntagmatic graph (both solid and dotted lines) suggesting the network of connections perceived between temporally close notes. Occurrences of the reduced theme (whose notes are circled) are modelled here as strings without gap, forming continuous chains in the syntagmatic graph.

which implies that a substring will be aligned to another substring (or a pattern) only if the total dissimilarity does not exceed a certain threshold. For instance, in Figure 2, the alignment of the beginning of the theme exposition (stave 1) with the reduced theme (circled notes) requires the deletion of one note per retained note. But the alignment of the beginning of the first variation (staves 2 and 3) with the same reduced theme requires the deletion of *seven* notes per retained note. If the dissimilarity threshold is lower than such high value, the second occurrence will not be detected.

Syntagmatic-Graph Approach

In order to solve this problem, we hypothesize that the extraction of the reduced theme from the highly ornamented phrase may be explained by the listeners' ability to perceive not only one single monodic line, as previously shown in Figure 2, but also a more complex network of interconnections between notes that are not immediately successive, as shown in Figure 3. In other word, from the "*syntagmatic chain*" (Saussure, 1916) that form the monodic string may be constructed a *syntagmatic graph* of relations of succession. The direct application of the pattern extraction algorithm to this syntagmatic graph would hence enable the detection of ornamented repetitions.

MATCHING STRATEGIES

The discovery of a repeated pattern results from the *matching* between different candidate subsets or substrings of the score. If the matching succeeds, the candidates form occurrences of a new pattern. The recognition of new occurrences of the pattern results from a matching between new candidates and the pattern description. This section discusses the different matching strategies considered in the literature.

Distance-Based Matching

In some approaches of automated motivic analysis, the instances are compared along one or several given musical dimensions, and a numerical similarity (or dissimilarity) distance is computed. The matching is inferred when the similarity distance is lower than a prespecified threshold (or if the dissimilarity distance is higher that a pre-specified threshold). For instance, concerning the melodic dimension, candidates are compared along the *chromatic pitch interval* dimension, which consists of the intervals in semitones between the successive notes of the candidates. The taking into consideration of intervals, instead of exact pitch values, enables the detection of transposed repetitions as well. Chromatic pitch-interval sequences are δ-*approximately repeated* when each corresponding pair of chromatic interval values are not more distant than δ semitones (Cambouropoulos, Crochemore, Iliopoulos, Mouchard, & Pinzon, 2002; Cope, 1996). Chromatic interval sequences are γ-*approximately repeated* if the summation of differences between all successive couples of chromatic interval values is not higher than γ semitones (Cambouropoulos et al., 2002). Concerning δ-approximation, a threshold of $\delta=1$ semitone is commonly used in order to identify a melody played in both major and minor keys (Cope, 1996; Cambouropoulos et al., 2002). However, this threshold also tolerates other transformations that are not directly related to the major/minor configuration (for instance, the dilatation of a major third into a perfect fourth). Users may be offered the option to fix the dissimilarity threshold by themselves (Cope, 1996; Rolland, 1999). However, no study has shown how it could be possible in this way to find a good threshold value for each analysis. Numerical distance may also be used in order to detect rhythmic patterns. Here also, different patterns can be identified if the successive values forming their description are sufficiently similar, with respect to a given similarity threshold.

Figure 4. Motivic analysis of the beginning of Beethoven's Fifth Symphony (piano reduction), using the numerical distance paradigm. Under the score are indicated the chromatic pitch interval values in semitones between successive notes. Chains represents pattern occurrences, where nodes represent successive notes and transition parameters describe the chromatic pitch interval values. The first line of chains below each stave shows patterns featuring exact descriptions. Following lines are related to patterns with approximate descriptions.

For instance, in Figure 4, the analysis of the beginning of Beethoven's *Fifth Symphony*, along the chromatic dimension, may show different pattern classes depending on the tuning of the similarity threshold. For a threshold of zero semitone, corresponding to a search for exact repetition, we obtain several possible melodic patterns depending on the values of the last pitch interval of the motive: either major third (0,0,-4), minor third (0,0,-3), or minor second (0,0,-1). The other possible interval values such as (0,0,-5), since not repeated several times in the example, do not form patterns. For a threshold of one semitone, minor and major third can be combined into one pattern (0,0,-3±1). For a threshold of two semitones, minor second intervals can be included in the pattern notated (0,0,-3±2). For a threshold of four semitones, the last motive, containing a fifth-interval can be included in pattern (0,0,-3±4).

Pattern (0,0±1,0±2) is problematical since its class and description are not very intuitive. Another obscure example is pattern (0,-1±1,-1±2): due to its description, its class includes the motive at bar 14 (0,-2,-2), the minor second motive (0,0,-1), the minor due to its description, the motive includes the minor third motive (0,0,-3), but excludes the major third motive (0,0,-4).

According to the numerical distance paradigm, a pattern class can accept occurrences that are not completely identical one with each other. The description of the pattern is therefore not explicitly given and requires further processing. For example, in Figure 4, the pattern (0,0,-3±1) could be described as (0,0,-4±1) as well for the particular excerpts, but the choice of the description may lead to a significant divergence of results when analyzing the whole piece. One method of pattern description has been proposed by Rolland (1999): the *Star-Center* methodology, influenced by works in molecular biology, consists in first constructing a graph whose vertices represent the different substrings of the score, and whose valued edges represent the corresponding similarity distances between each couple of substrings. For each vertex is computed the sum of the similarity values associated with the connected edges. The vertices with maximum sum are considered as "pattern paradigms": they form the description of the corresponding patterns, and the occurrences of the patterns are the set of vertices around these centers. The cognitive and musical relevance of this algorithm has however not been studied.

Multiple-Viewpoint Approach

Instead of using numerical distances, melodic comparison can be carried out through an *exact matching* along a multiple set of musical dimensions (Conklin & Anagnostopoulou, 2001). For instance, instead of computing numerical distance between chromatic-pitch-interval descriptions, motives are compared along chromatic-pitch-interval and diatonic pitch-interval descriptions in parallel. Diatonic pitches represent positions of the notes on a given tonal scale, and diatonic pitch intervals indicate the successive scale transitions on this tonal scale. If two motives have exactly the same chromatic-pitch-interval descriptions, then they are considered as chromatically matched. For instance, in Figure 5, pattern *a* contains occurrences that present exactly the same chromatic description. If on the contrary, there is a major-minor difference between the two motives, then the two motives are not chromatically matched, but they are still diatonically matched. In Figure 5, the "major-third" (*a*) and "minor-third" (*a'*) patterns can be unified into a "third" pattern *b* that represents the identification along the diatonic representation. Pattern *b* is considered as *less specific* than patterns *a* (or *a'*), which is notated "*a > b*" in Figure 5, since the description

of pattern *b* is included in the description of pattern *a* (or *a'*).

The diatonic description can be directly obtained from the score when the tonality of a piece strictly follows the indication given by the key signature. But in more general cases, local modulations need to be taken into account through a proper harmonic analysis. In particular, when analyzing MIDI files where no tonality is specified explicitly, diatonic pitch representations need to be reconstructed using pitch-spelling algorithms (Cambouropoulos, 2003; Chew & Chen, 2005).

If the compared motives cannot be exactly matched along the diatonic-pitch-interval dimension, then they are compared along the *gross contour* dimension, which simply indicates the sense of variation—ascending ("+"), descending ("-"), constant ("0")—of the pitch intervals. For instance, in Figure 5, all the occurrences of patterns *a*, *a'* and *a''*, and two more motives (bar 10 and 59) are occurrences of the contour pattern *c*. This strategy may sound at first sight rather simplistic, since the actual interval distortion is not taken here into account in the matching process. Nevertheless, this strategy is grounded by cognitive studies (cf., for instance, Deutsch, 1972; DeWitt & Crowder, 1986; Dowling, 1978; Dowling & Fujitani, 1971; Dowling & Harwood, 1986; Edworthy, 1985). Studies have shown the perceptual importance of gross contour dimensions (Dowling & Harwood, 1986; White, 1960): distorted repetitions of the same motive can be recognized even if the interval values have been significantly changed, as long as the gross contour remains constant.

Similarly, motives can be compared through a matching of the rhythmic parameters. Two dimensions are considered in particular: the rhythmic values indicating the temporal distance between successive notes, and the position of each note with respect to the metrical pulsation. These parameters are directly available in score, and can be expressed with respect to the implicit metrical unit. For instance, in Figure 5, with

Figure 5. Motivic analysis of the beginning of Beethoven's Fifth Symphony in the multiple viewpoint approach. Different musical dimensions are considered: chromatic (chro) and diatonic (diat) pitch intervals, gross contours (cont), rhythmic values (rhyt) and position with respect to the metrical pulsation (puls). The patterns that are discovered form a hierarchy: i.e., in decreasing order of specificity, the "major-third" (a), "minor-third" (a') and "minor-second" (a") chromatic patterns, the "third" diatonic pattern (b), the "decreasing" contour pattern (c), all including a same rhythmic sequence, described by pattern d.

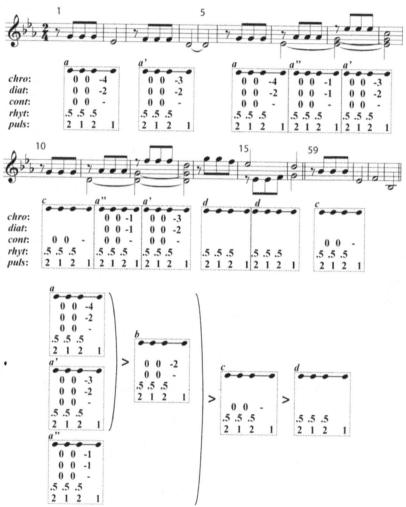

time signature of 2/4, the beat reiterates every fourth note (4) and the rhythmic values of eighth notes are indicated therefore by the value .5. On a higher metrical level, downbeats are indicated on the "pulsation" dimension by the value 1 and offbeats by the value 2.

In MIDI files, on the contrary, the metrical structure is not specified explicitly, and needs to be reconstructed using beat-tracking (Dannenberg & Mont-Reynaud, 1987; Large & Kolen, 1994; Toiviainen, 1998), quantization (Cemgil & Kappen, 2003; Desain & Honing, 1991), or meter induction algorithms (Eck & Casagrande, 2005; Toiviainen & Eerola, 2006).

Cambouropoulos (2006) suggested other representations for pitch intervals, such as a step-leap profile comprising five distinct symbols (ascending step or leap, descending step or leap, unison) coupled with rhythmic information. As a further refinement of the algorithm, instances are allowed to be members of more than one category. For that purpose, a variant of the pattern extraction algorithm has been developed using "don't care" symbols for elements that may belong to two categories (Cambouropoulos, Crochemore, Iliopoulos, Mohamed, & Sagot, 2005).

Adaptive Matching in a Multi-Parametric Space

We propose a generalization of the multiple viewpoint approach that allows *variability* in the set of musical dimensions used during the construction of each musical pattern. This enables to take into consideration a more general type of pattern, called *heterogeneous pattern*, which despite its structural complexity seems to catch an important aspect of musical structure. An example of heterogeneous pattern is the first theme of Mozart's *Sonata in A*, K. 331 (Fig. 6), which contains two

phrases that repeat the same pattern. This pattern, enclosed in a solid box in the figure, is decomposed into two parts: a *melodico-rhythmic* antecedent, and a *rhythmic* consequent[3].

Another example is the finale theme of Beethoven's *Ninth Symphony* (Figure 7), which begins with an antecedent/consequent repetition of a phrase, with identities both in pitch and time domains, except a slight modification at the ending of each phrase.

Due to the very limited degree of specificity of the gross contour parameter, patterns made of ascendant and descendant intervals are not easily recognised if the occurrences are too distant in time (Dowling & Harwood, 1986). It has been suggested, therefore, that repetition of gross contour sequences can be identified only when sufficiently close in time such that, when the second occurrence is heard, the first one remains in short-term memory. Indeed, gross contour sequences can more easily be searched in short-term memory due to the limited size of the memory store, and availability of its content. On the other hand, a search in long-term memory

Figure 6. Heterogeneous motivic description of the first theme of Mozart's Sonata in A, K. 331, bars 1-8 (slightly simplified): each line repeats a same pattern, whose first half is melodico-rhythmic, and its second half purely rhythmic.

Figure 7. Heterogeneous motivic description of Ode to Joy, from Beethoven's Ninth Symphony. The 13-note motive is exactly repeated, except the modification of a unison (diat = 0) into a decreasing second interval (diat = -1) between the 10th and 11th notes of each occurrence.

seems cognitively implausible because of the large size of its content, the resulting combinatory explosion of possible results, and the insufficient specificity of the query (cf. Dowling & Harwood, 1986). However, this restriction leads to paradoxes (Dowling & Fujitani, 1971; Dowling & Harwood, 1986): if gross contour has no impact on long-term memory, how could the different occurrences of the familiar four-note theme throughout the first movement of Beethoven's *Fifth Symphony* (Figure 5) actually be detected? One suggested explanation is that the numerous repetitions of the motive enable a memorization of the contour pattern in long-term memory. Yet, could not this motive be detected, due to its intrinsic construction, even when repeated only a couple of times throughout the piece (such as in Figure 8)?

The heterogeneous pattern representation may offer an answer to this question, through a decoupling of the choice of musical dimensions and the construction of patterns. A full understanding of the perceptive properties of motivic patterns requires a chronological view of the construction of these structures, in terms of an incremental concatenation of successive intervals. The dependency of such constructions upon long- and short-term memory may be understood in this incremental approach. More precisely, the initiation of a new occurrence of a pattern requires, as previously, a matching in long-term memory along interval dimensions. However, in this framework, it may be suggested that the further extensions of a discovered new occurrence do not require such a demanding computational effort. Indeed, once the first in-

Figure 8. The famous four-note pattern at the beginning of the first movement of Beethoven's Fifth Symphony is considered here as a concatenation of two unison intervals and a decreasing contour, in a uniform quaver rhythm. Any new instance of this pattern, such as the instance far later at bar 59 is detected following a two-step process: The specific description of the first two intervals triggers the matching, whereas the extension of the matching can follow a less specific contour description.

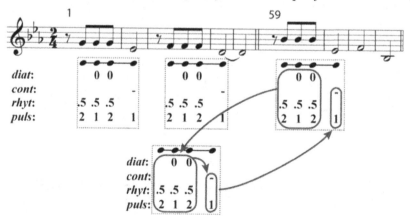

tervals have been initiated, the discovery of the progressive extensions simply requires a matching of the successive intervals with the corresponding successive intervals in the pattern.

The four-note pattern of Beethoven's *Fifth Symphony* (Figure 8) may be considered in this respect as a concatenation of two specific unison intervals (or three repetitions of the same note), followed by a less specific descending contour. Each new occurrence of the pattern can be easily perceived due to the high specificity of its three first notes, which allows an interval-based matching in long-term memory.

CONTROLLING THE COMBINATORIAL REDUNDANCY

Let us consider now a third central difficulty encountered by automated motivic algorithms, related to the control of the complexity of the results.

Review of the Filtering Strategies

In Conklin and Anagnostopoulou (2001), pattern discovery is performed by building a suffix tree along several parametric dimensions. Due to the large size of the set of discovered patterns, a subset of the extracted patterns are selected in a subsequent step, namely those occurring in a specified minimum number of pieces k, and showing sufficient statistical significance. The criterion of statistical significance of a given pattern is based on p-value, that is, the probability that a random viewpoint sequences would contain an equal or higher number of occurrences of that pattern. In this view the p-value should be lower than a predefined cut-off value. A further filtering step globally selected the longest significant patterns within the set of discovered patterns, by reporting the leaves of the suffix tree structure.

Cambouropoulos (2006) searched for exact pattern repetition, using Crochemore's (1981)

approach, in different parametric descriptions of musical sequences. A prominence value is attached to each of the discovered patterns in order to prefer most frequently occurring patterns and in the same time longer patterns and to avoid overlapping. More precisely, a *selection function* associates a numerical strength value with each pattern following the formula:

$$f(L,F,DOL)=L^a \cdot F^b/10^{c \cdot DOL}$$

where L is the pattern length, F the frequency of occurrence of each pattern, DOL the degree of overlapping, and a, *b, c* are constants that give different weights to the three factors. For every pattern discovered by the above pattern induction algorithm a value is calculated by the selection function. The patterns that score the highest are considered as the most significant ones. The author acknowledges the need for further processing that will lead to a 'good' description of the surface (in terms of exhaustiveness, economy, simplicity, etc.). It is likely that some instances of the selected pitch patterns should be dropped out or that a combination of patterns that rate slightly lower than the top rating patterns may give a better description of the musical surface. In order to overcome this problem, a simple methodology has been devised, following which no pattern is disregarded but each pattern (both its beginning and ending point) contributes to each possible boundary of the melodic sequence by a value that is proportional to its Selection Function value. That is, for each point in the melodic surface all the patterns are found that have one of their edges falling at that point and all their Selection Function values are summed. This way a pattern boundary strength profile is created (normalized from 0-1). It is hypothesized that points in the surface for which local maxima appear are more likely to be perceived as boundaries because of musical similarity. The modeling has been subsequently revised by restricting the definition of the strength of the pattern boundary profile to the starting points of patterns only, usually conveying more importance than endings.

Rolland (1999) defined a numerical similarity distance between sub-sequences based on edit distance. In order to extract patterns, similarity distances were computed between all possible pairs of sub-sequences of a certain range of lengths, and only similarity exceeding a user-defined arbitrary threshold was selected. From the resulting similarity graph, patterns are extracted using the Star-Center categorization algorithm (detailed in last section). The set of discovered patterns is reduced even further using pre-defined constraints such as minimal or maximal length, maximal length difference between pattern occurrences, and minimal number of pieces where the pattern can be found. The last constraint, called "quorum", corresponds to the k factor in Conklin & Anagnostopoulou (2001).

Discussion

As we can see, all approaches[4] in motivic pattern extraction propose diverse ways to solve the major problem of combinatorial explosion of redundant structures: the core pattern extraction process results in a very large set of candidates, of poor interest to musicology or music information retrieval. All approaches therefore include post-processing algorithms that filter the results in order to select the most relevant structures. The main limitation of this strategy comes from the lack of selectivity of the global criteria. Hence, by selecting longest patterns, one may discard frequent short motives (such as the 4-note pattern from Beethoven's *Fifth Symphony*), or nonfrequent long patterns, that may nevertheless be considered as highly relevant by listeners.

Closed Pattern Mining

The problem of reducing the combinatorial complexity of pattern structure is largely studied in current research in computer science, and several

distinct strategies have been proposed. The *frequent pattern mining* approach is restricted to patterns that have a number of occurrences (or *support*) exceeding a given minimum threshold (Lin et al., 2002). The main drawback of this strategy comes from the arbitrariness and poor adaptation of the definition of the threshold value. Another approach is based on the search for *maximal patterns*, that is, patterns that are not included in any other pattern (Zaki, 2005; Agrawal & Srikant, 1995). This heuristic enables a more selective filtering of redundancy. For instance, in figure 9, the suffix *aij* can be immediately discarded following this strategy, since it is included in the longer pattern *abcde*: its properties can be directly induced from the long pattern itself. However, this approach still leads to an excessive filtering of important structures. For instance, in Figure 10, the same 3-note pattern *aij* presents a specific configuration that cannot be directly deduced from the longer pattern *abcde*, for the simple reason that its *support* (or number of occurrences) is higher than the support of *abcde*. This corresponds to

Figure 9. Occurrences of patterns are extracted from the score. These occurrences are displayed below the score, and the patterns are grouped in a tree above the score. Pattern aij, a suffix of abcde with identical support (i.e., two occurrences), is therefore non-closed, and should not be explicitly represented.

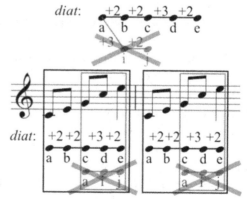

Figure 10. Pattern aij, now featuring more occurrences than abcde or abcdefgh (namely, four occurrences instead of two), is now explicitly represented.

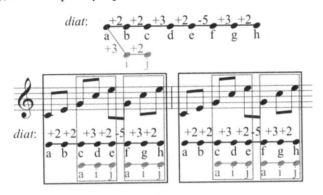

Figure 11. The rhythmic pattern afghi is less specific than the melodico-rhythmic pattern abcde.

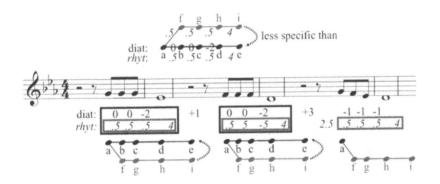

the concept of *closed patterns*, which are patterns whose support is higher than the support of the pattern in which they are included (Zaki, 2005). A filtering of non-closed patterns is therefore more selective than a filtering of non-maximal patterns. In fact, it ensures a more compact representation of the pattern configuration *without any loss of information.*

The model presented in this article looks for closed patterns in musical sequences. For this purpose, the notion of inclusion relation between patterns founding the definition of closed patterns is generalized to the multidimensional paramet-

ric space of music. A mathematical description of this operation can be formalized using the Gallois correspondence between pattern classes and pattern description (Ganter & Wille, 1999; Lartillot, 2005). For instance, pattern *abcde* in Figure 11 features melodic and rhythmical descriptions, whereas pattern *afghi* only features the rhythmic part. Hence pattern *abcde* can be considered as more specific than pattern *afghi*, since its description contains more information. When only the first two occurrences are analyzed, both patterns having same support, only the more specific pattern *abcde* should be explicitly

Figure 12. Multiple successive repetitions of pattern abcd logically lead to extensions into patterns e, f, etc. which form a complex intertwining of structures

represented. But the less specific pattern *afghi* will be represented once the last occurrence is discovered, as it is not an occurrence of the more specific pattern *abcde*.

Cyclic Patterns

Combinatory explosions can be caused by another common phenomenon provoked by successive repetitions of a same pattern (for instance, in Figure 12, the simple pattern *abcd*, a succession of one fourth note and two eighth notes forming two ascending and one descending contours). As each occurrence is followed by the beginning of a new occurrence, each pattern can be extended (leading to pattern *e*) by a new interval whose description (an ascending crochet interval) is identical to the description of the first interval of the same pattern (i.e., between states *a* and *b*). This extension can be prolonged recursively (into *f, g, h, i*, etc.), leading to a combinatorial explosion of patterns that are not perceived due to their complex intertwining (Cambouropoulos, 1998).

The graph-based representation (Figure 12) shows that the last state of each occurrence of pattern *d* is synchronised with the first state of the following occurrence. Listeners tend to fuse these two states, and to perceive a loop from the last state (*d*) to the first state (*a*) (Figure 13). The initial acyclic pattern *d* leads, therefore, to a cyclic pattern that oscillates between three *phases b', c'* and *d'*. Indeed, when listening to the remainder of the musical sequence, we actually perceive this progressive cycling. Hence this cycle-based modeling seems to explain a common listening strategy, and resolves the problem of combinatorial redundancy.

This cyclic pattern (with three phases *b', c'* and *d'* at the top of Figure 13) is considered as a continuation of the original acyclic pattern *abcd*. Indeed, the first repetition of the rhythmic period is not perceived as a period as such but rather as a simple pattern: its successive notes are simply linked to the progressive states *a, b, c* and *d* of the acyclic pattern. On the contrary, the following notes extend the occurrence, which cannot be associated with the acyclic pattern anymore, and are therefore linked to the successive states of the cyclic pattern (*b', c'* and *d'*). The whole periodic sequence is therefore represented as a single chain of states representing the traversal of the acyclic pattern followed by multiple rotations in the cyclic pattern.

This additional concept immediately solves the redundancy problem. Indeed, each type of redundant structure considered previously is

Figure 13. Listening to successive repetitions of pattern abcd leads to the induction of its cyclicity, and thus to an oscillation between states b', c' and d'.

Figure 14. Heterogeneous cyclic pattern, including two complete layers of rhythmic and contour descriptions, plus two local descriptions: the diatonic pitch-class value C associated to the first note of each period (diat-pc = 0), and the constant pitch interval value of ascending major third between the second and the third note of each period (diat = +2).

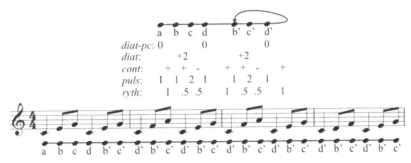

Figure 15. The periodic sequence is initiated with a different phase, since it begins on an upbeat instead of the downbeat. Nevertheless, the sequence can be still related to the same cyclic pattern (b'c'd').

a non-closed suffix of a prefix of the long and unique chain of states, and will therefore not be represented anymore. But this compact representation will be possible only if the initial period (corresponding to the acyclic pattern chain) is considered and extended before the other possible periods. This implies that scores need to be analyzed in a chronological fashion.

Heterogeneous descriptions, presented in previous section, can be applied to cyclic patterns too. For instance, in Figure 14, the cyclic pattern is a little more specific than the cyclic pattern presented in Figure 13, since the first note of each period is always C (diat-pc = 0), and the interval between the second and third notes is always an ascending major third (diat = +2). This can therefore be added to the representation of the pattern, as shown in the Figure.

A mechanism has been added that unifies all the possible rotations of the periodic pattern (*b'c'd'*, *c'd'b'*, *d'b'c'*) into one single cyclic pattern. For instance, in Figure 15, the periodic sequence beginning in a different phase than previously (on an upbeat instead of a downbeat) is still identified with the same cyclic pattern.

By construction of the cyclic pattern, no segmentation is explicitly represented between successive repetitions. Indeed, the listener may be inclined to segment at any phase of the cyclic chain (or to not segment at all). However it would be interesting to estimate the positions in the cycle where listeners would tend to segment. Several factors need to be taken into consideration, such as primacy, local segmentation or global context. For instance, a primacy-based segmentation will favor the period that appears first in the sequence, depending on the phase at which the cyclic sequence begins. Global context corresponds to the general segmentation of the piece, based on the major motives and the metrical structure. This might be considered in future work.

RESULTS

Review of Other Approaches

Conklin and Anagnostopoulou's study (2001) analyzes 185 Bach chorales, comprising a total of about 40000 notes. About 20 viewpoints were encoded; most of them pertain to melodic and rhythmic aspects of the chorales. Several viewpoints are test viewpoints used for combination ("linking") with other viewpoints, or in order to restrict certain viewpoints to precise temporal or metrical locations within the piece ("threading"). Additional viewpoints model harmonic or vertical structures. The adjusted p-value cut-off for patterns was set to 0.01 and the parameter k (the minimum number of pieces a pattern must occur in) was set to 10. For the soprano line, 33 longest significant melodic interval patterns were found. For the alto line, 29 were found. One single significant melodic contour pattern has been detected. A total of 57 longest significant pitch class interval patterns were found in the bass lines. Chromatic stepwise movements, a well-known common pattern in the bass line of the chorales, have been detected too. The combination of melodic intervals and duration leads to the discovery of 23 longest significant patterns. Hence this method offers a synthetic description of most common patterns in a given corpus of music.

Cambouropoulos's model (2006) is aimed at studying some particular problems in melody segmentation. It suggests segmentation boundaries on a given selection of short melodic examples (*Frère Jacques*, finale theme from Beethoven's *Ninth Symphony*, opening melody of Mozart's *A-Major Sonata*, K. 331, etc.) but is not supposed to work on more complex repertoire, neither to highlight the motivic patterns that have an impact on the inference of these global segmentations.

Rolland's approach (1999) was primarily dedicated to the analysis of Charlie Parker's improvised playing, and to the characterization of recurrent melodic patterns ("formulae") in a corpus of 250 solos transcribed by the musicologist T. Owens (1974). A restricted corpus made of 10 Parker solos in the "C major—Blues" category of Owens' corpus (3 takes on "Cool Blues", 3 on "Relaxin' at Camarillo" and 4 on "Perhaps") is used for the computational experiment. The cumulative length is about 2000 notes and rests, each solo (except one) comprising between 25 and 40 bars and between 130 and 250 notes. The similarity graph obtained from the analysis contains about 12000 vertices and 40000 edges; the largest star has a size of 35 edges (plus its own center). The longest pattern has a prototype of length 27 notes. 58 patterns have been found whose occurrences are spread out in all 10 of the corpus' sequences.

These patterns have a length less than or equal to 4 notes and possess at most 21 occurrences. Owens established a hierarchically classified lexicon of 193 patterns from his corpus (Owens, 1974). A large number of Owens' patterns were satisfactorily extracted by the system, in particular patterns designated by 11A, 4Ea and 5B in Owens' nomenclature. Moreover, a number of new patterns, not signalled by Owens, have been effectively "discovered" by the system, and are considered by Rolland as "musically meaningful" (p. 348). Significantly different sets of musical descriptions lead to the extraction of significantly different patterns. In particular, the use of too-restrictive sets leads to the extraction of patterns without any musical pertinence.

Meredith et al. approach (2002) has been illustrated with one single practical example: the analysis of the beginning of Bach's two-part *Invention in C major* (BWV 772), where only one pattern is presented in the paper, composed of the seven eighth notes forming the entry of the main theme.

Results Obtained Using our Proposed Approach

Our own approach can be applied for the moment to the analysis of simple melodies. The model has been tested using different musical sequences taken from several musical genres (classical music, pop, jazz, etc.), and featuring various level of complexity. The experiment has been run using version 0.8 of our algorithm, called *kanthus*. This section presents the analysis of two pieces: a medieval *Geisslerlied* and a Bach *Invention*. A large set of

Figure 16. Analysis of the Geisslerlied "Maria muoter reinû maît" (Ruwet, 1987). Each motivic repetition is represented by a line below the corresponding stave, each labelled with a letter.

musical parameters has been taken into account (Lartillot & Toiviainen, 2007) and all patterns longer than 3 notes are displayed. These analyses have been validated through a comparison with musicological analyses found in the literature. Figure 16 and 17 shows examples of analysis. Detailed explanation of these analyses and their comparison with musicological analyses are developed in Lartillot and Toiviainen (2007).

Figure 16 shows the analysis of a XIV-century German *Geisslerlied*, "Maria muoter reinû maît". According to Nicolas Ruwet's analysis (1987), the piece is composed of a repetition of an eight-bar phrase *A* followed by a repetition of a four-bar phrase *B*. The algorithm extracts pattern *A* but fails to segment pattern *B* correctly, because the presence of a suffix of *B* at the end of pattern *A* leads to an incorrect segmentation (represented by *B'*). This segmentation needs to be controlled using additional heuristics, as suggested in Lartillot and Toiviainan (2007). Pattern *b*, its melodic variation *b'*, and pattern *d* can also be found in Ruwet's analysis. A certain number of patterns proposed by Ruwet are not explicitly represented in the computational analysis, because they do not convey additional information concerning the pattern structure of the piece. Following the terminology introduced in previous section, these patterns are non-closed subsequences of others pattern. In Ruwet's analysis, the selection of these patterns is based on segmentation processes, which are not taken into account in our modeling. On the other hand, the algorithm proposes short patterns, such as e and f, that have no correspondence with Ruwet's analysis. The assessment of their perceptual or musical relevance will require further study.

Figure 17 shows the results of the computational analysis of the first 14 bars of J.S. Bach's *Invention in D minor* BWV 775, which can be compared with Jeffrey Kresky's analysis (1977). The opening motive *A,* with all its occurrences throughout the piece, has been exactly retrieved

by the machine. The ascending and descending lines within the motive (gray arrows) have been detected, too. On the other hand, the inversion of the motive shape *a1* in the second half of motive *A*, has not been detected since inversions are not taken into account in the model yet. The accompanying figure *B* has been detected, and is decomposed into a succession of two successive and similar shapes *c*. However, the similarity of these shapes with motive *a1*, suggested by Kresky, has not been discovered. The first sequence unit *A'* is detected and identified as a variation of the opening motive *A*, but not exactly for the same reasons offered by Kresky. The second sequence unit *a3* has been detected and identified as a variation of the original motive shape *a*. The successive repetition of the three-note scale *b* in bars 11 and 13 is also identified with the first three notes of the original scale form at the beginning of the motive shape *a*. The repeated bass line during the first sequence is detected (*C*), but cannot be identified with the motive shape *a*. Finally, the descending scale F-E-D-C (first note of bars 7, 9, 11, and 13) has not been detected due to the incapacity of the algorithm to consider motivic configurations between distant notes.

The computational analysis also includes additional motivic structures that do not seem to offer much musical interest or perceptive relevance. Pattern *D*, featuring a succession of a descending second interval followed by a series of ascending second intervals, sounds poorly salient due to its weak position in the metrical structure, and the limited size of its description. The second occurrence of pattern *D* is also considered by the model as the beginning of a variant *a4* of motive *a2*, which is, once again, not very salient due to the weak position of this motive in the metrical structure. Pattern *E* shows similar limitations: it corresponds to a series of pitches (E5, F5, D5, E5, F5) starting offbeat. In order to filter patterns *D* and *E*, a higher-level metrical representation may be integrated in future works that would show the

Figure 17. Automated motivic analysis of J.S. Bach's Invention in D minor BWV 775, first 14 bars. The representation of the motives follows the convention adopted in the previous figure. The motives for each voice are shown below the respective staves. The class of each motive is indicated on the left side of the lines.

position of each pattern in the bar structure, and would, in particular cases, force pattern occurrences to conserve the same metrical information. The model also includes evident structural configurations, such as the oscillations between ascending and descending contour, and other patterns that are mostly redundant descriptions incorrectly filtered. This results partly from un-solved errors in the modeling process, but also shows the necessity of taking into account other heuristics. Finally, in order to obtain the compact representation displayed in Figure 17, some manual ordering of the computational results was required. For more results, see Lartillot (2005b) and Lartillot and Toiviainen (2007).

FUTURE TRENDS

Objective Validation and Comparison Between Approaches

The analyses produced by the different computational models are evaluated for the moment in a mostly qualitative manner: the results are searched for the most important motives of the piece, and the additional unexpected structures proposed by the algorithm are rated intuitively. In future works, the computational results need to be compared each other and with analyses available in the music literature. A more precise and refined validation of the results will require the establishment of a "ground truth": a corpus of pieces of diverse style will be collected, on which manual motivic analyses will be carried out by a board of musicologists. The comparison of the manual analyses and the computational results will enable a more precise determination of the precision and recall factors offered by the different models.

Generalization of the String Approach to Polyphony

String-based approaches are currently limited to the detection of repeated monodic patterns. Music in general is polyphonic, where simultaneous notes form chords and parallel voices. Research carried out in this topic (Dovey, 2001; Meredith et al., 2002), generally focuses on the discovery of exact repetitions along different separate dimensions, following the set-based paradigm. On the other hand, the string-based approach may be generalized to polyphony, if the polyphony is first decomposed into monodic stream and if the pattern detection is applied to each stream (Cambouropoulos, 2006). More generally, as explained previously, these different streams may be intertwined, forming complex "syntagmatic graphs" along which the pattern discovery algo-

rithm could be applied. The additional factors of combinatorial explosion resulting from this generalized framework will require further adaptive filtering mechanisms. Patterns of chords might also be studied in future works.

Articulating Global Patterns and Local Discontinuities

As explained in the introduction, this study is focused on the extraction of repeated patterns. Another important heuristic for motivic analysis is based on local discontinuities of the sequential structure of music along its different dimensions, which imply the inference of segmentations (Lerdahl & Jackendoff, 1983). The strength of each segmentation depends on the size of the corresponding discontinuities. A local maximum of pitch and/or temporal interval amplitude, or the accentuation of one particular note, are common examples of such local discontinuities. These segmentations result in a rich structural configuration. The multiple principles ruling these segmentations, such as Lerdahl and Jackendoff's Grouping Preference Rules (Lerdahl & Jackendoff, 1983), can be ordered relative to their perceptive salience (Deliège, 1987).

Local discontinuities impose some important constraints on the pattern extraction process. Hence pattern extraction needs to be studied in interaction with local segmentation. Lerdahl and Jackendoff (1983) have proposed a coupling of the two principles, and Temperley (1988) has suggested a computational formalization. But in these approaches, as acknowledged by their authors, pattern extraction (called here "parallelism") is theoretically considered without actual systematic modeling. Cambouropoulos (2006) proposed a way of modeling the interaction between the two principles. In a first step, both local segmentation and pattern extraction are performed in parallel, but only the boundaries of the segments and motives are taken into consideration. These boundaries are summed together, leading to a segmentation curve, and global segmentations are performed at local maxima of the curve. The resulting segments are then classified based on similarity measurement, following the paradigmatic analysis approach (Cambouropoulos & Widmer, 2000).

Ahlbäck (in press) has elaborated a set of Gestalt theory-based principles for melodic grouping. The core of this model is the classification of the different grouping principles according to the role they play in the cognition of grouping structure in melody. The model postulates that groups can be formed by implication based on properties of grouping determined by primary grouping principles, reflecting the general coherence principle. Secondary grouping principles refer to grouping by good continuation, which involves both selection of grouping and implicative grouping by means of periodicity and symmetry. A third class, tertiary grouping principles, is defined as involving perceptual and cognitive selection of grouping, reflecting principles of cognitive economy, significance and intelligibility.

Motives of Motives

Throughout the chapter, motives have been defined as series of notes that feature particular invariants related to the relative configurations between the successive elements of these series. Several approaches propose to accept as building blocks of these series not only elementary notes, but also motives themselves. This recursive definition would enable in particular a multi-leveled hierarchical construction of motivic structures. Previous works in music cognition have studied the structural particularities of successive repetitions of patterns (Deutsch & Feroe, 1981). The recent development of Conklin and Anagnostopoulou's project (2006) is dedicated to the formalization of interval relationships between successive motives.

CONCLUSION

This chapter presented the state of the art in motivic pattern extraction, and has shown that, however simple the task may appear according to its basic purpose, its computational realization remains a very difficult challenge. The review of the different approaches and underlying difficulties suggests the idea that the question cannot be answered using solely mathematic or geometric heuristics and classical engineering tools inspired from artificial intelligence, but requires also a detailed understanding of the multiple constraints derived by the cognitive situation of the process. This philosophy implies a vision of the question of pattern extraction that is tightly interdependent with other issues such as pitch spelling, rhythm quantification or stream segregation. This is, in our vision, the price to pay in order to reach a complete and sound automation of this challenging task.

ACKNOWLEDGMENT

This work has been supported by the European Commission (NEST project "Tuning the Brain for Music," code 028570). Some ideas presented in this paper emerged after fruitful conversations with my colleague Petri Toiviainen. Their formalization have also benefitted from valuable feedback offered by reviewers of this chapter and reviewers of our previous publicatios as well.

REFERENCES

Agrawal, R., & Srikant, R. (1995). Mining sequential patterns. In *Proceedings of the International Conference on Data Engineering* (pp. 3-14).

Ahlbäck, S. (2007). Melodic similarity as determinant of melody structure. *Musicae Scientiae*, Discussion Forum 4A, 235-280.

Cambouropoulos, E. (1998). *Towards a general computational theory of musical structure.* Unpublished doctoral dissertation, University of Edinburgh, UK.

Cambouropoulos, E. (2003). Pitch spelling: A computational model. *Music Perception, 20*(4), 411-429.

Cambouropoulos, E. (2006). Musical parallelism and melodic segmentation: A computational approach. *Music Perception, 23*(3), 249-268.

Cambouropoulos E., Crochemore, M., Iliopoulos, C., Mohamed, M., & Sagot, M.-F. (2005). A pattern extraction algorithm for abstract melodic representations that allow partial overlapping intervallic categories. In *Proceedings of the International Conference on Music Information Retrieval* (pp. 167-174).

Cambouropoulos, E., Crochemore, M., Iliopoulos, C., Mouchard, L., & Pinzon, Y. (2002). Algorithms for computing approximate repetitions in musical sequences. *Journal of Computer Mathematics, 79*(11), 1135-1148.

Cambouropoulos, E., & Widmer, G. (2000). Automated motivic analysis via melodic clustering. *Journal of New Music Research, 29*(4), 347-370.

Cemgil, A. T., & Kappen, B. (2003). Monte Carlo methods for tempo tracking and rhythm quantization. *Journal of Artificial Intelligence Research, 18,* 45-81.

Chew, E., & Chen, Y. C. (2005). Real-time pitch spelling using the spiral array. *Computer Music Journal, 29*(2), 61-76.

Conklin, D., & Anagnostopoulou, C. (2001). Representation and discovery of multiple viewpoint patterns. In *Proceedings of the International Computer Music Conference* (pp. 479-485).

Conklin, D., & Anagnostopoulou, C. (2006). Segmental pattern discovery in music. *INFORMS Journal on Computing, 18*(3), 285-293.

Cope, D. (1996). *Experiments in musical intelligence.* Middleton, WI: A-R Editions.

Crochemore, M. (1981). An optimal algorithm for computing the repetitions in a word. *Information Processing Letters, 12*(3), 244-250.

Dannenberg, R., & Mont-Reynaud, B. (1987). Following an improvisation in real-time. In *Proceedings of the International Computer Music Conference* (pp. 241-248).

Deliège, I. (1987). Grouping conditions in listening to music: An approach to Lerdahl and Jackendoff's grouping preference rules. *Music Perception, 4*(4), 325-350.

Desain, P., & Honing, H. (1991). Quantization of musical time: A connectionist approach. In P. M. Todd & D. G. Loy (Eds.), *Music and connectionism* (pp. 150-167). Cambridge, MA: MIT Press.

Deutsch, D. (1972). Octave generalization and tune recognition. *Perception & Psychophysics, 11,* 411-412.

Deutsch, D., & Feroe, J. (1981). The internal representation of pitch sequences in tonal music. *Psychological Review, 88*(6), 503-522.

DeWitt, L. A., & Crowder, R. G. (1986). Recognition of novel melodies after brief delays. *Music Perception, 3,* 259-274.

Dovey, M. J. (2001). A technique for "regular expression" style searching in polyphonic music. In *Proceedings of the International Conference on Music Information Retrieval* (pp. 179-185).

Dowling, W. J. (1978). Scale and contour: Two components of a theory of memory for melodies. *Psychological Review, 85*(4), 341-354.

Dowling, W. J., & Fujitani, D. S. (1971). Contour, interval, and pitch recognition in memory for melodies. *Journal of the Acoustical Society of America, 49,* 524-531.

Dowling, W. J., & Harwood, D. L. (1986). *Music cognition.* London: Academic Press.

Eck, D. & Casagrande, N. (2005). Finding meter in music using an autocorrelation phase matrix and Shannon Entropy. In *Proceedings of the International Conference on Music Information Retrieval* (pp. 504-509).

Edworthy, J. (1985). Melodic contour and musical structure. In P. Howell, I. Cross, & R. West (Eds.), *Musical structure and cognition* (pp. 169-188). London: Academic Press.

Eerola, T., Järvinen, T., Louhivuori, J., & Toiviainen, P. (2001). Statistical features and perceived similarity of folk melodies. *Music Perception, 18*, 275-296.

Ganter, B., & Wille, R. (1999). *Formal concept analysis: Mathematical foundations.* Springer-Verlag.

Husserl, E. (1905). On the phenomenology of the consciousness of internal time. (trans. J. B. Brough, 1991). In E. Husserl (Ed.), *Collected works, 4.* The Hague, Netherlands: Kluwer Academic Publishers.

Large, E. W., & Kolen, J. F. (1994). Resonance and the perception of musical meter. *Connection Science, 6*(2/3), 177-208.

Lartillot, O. (2005). Efficient extraction of closed motivic patterns in multi-dimensional symbolic representations of music. In *Proceedings of the International Conference on Music Information Retrieval* (pp. 191-198).

Lartillot, O., & Toiviainen, P. (2007). Motivic matching strategies for automated pattern extraction. *Musicae Scientiae*, Discussion Forum 4A, 281-314.

Lerdahl, F., & Jackendoff, R. (1983). *A generative theory of tonal music.* Cambridge, MA: MIT Press.

Lin, J., Keogh, J., Lonardi, S., & Patel, P. (2002). Finding motifs in time series. In *Proceedings of the Workshop on Temporal Data Mining* (pp. 53-68).

Meredith, D., Lemström, K., & Wiggins, G. (2002). Algorithms for discovering repeated patterns in multidimensional representations of polyphonic music. *Journal of New Music Research, 31*(4), 321-345.

Meredith, D., Lemström K., & Wiggins G. (2003). Algorithms for discovering repeated patterns in multidimensional representations of polyphonic music. In *Proceedings of the Cambridge Music Processing Colloquium* (pp. 46-56).

Mongeau, M., & Sankoff, D. (1990). Comparison of musical sequences. *Computers and the Humanities, 24*, 161-175.

Nattiez, J.-J. (1990). *Music and discourse: Towards a semiology of music.* Princeton, NJ: Princeton University Press.

Owens, T. (1974). Charlie Parker: Techniques of Improvisation. Doctoral dissertation, UCLA.

Reti, R. (1951). *The thematic process in music.* NewYork: Macmillan.

Rolland, P.-Y. (1999). Discovering patterns in musical sequences. *Journal of New Music Research, 28*(4), 334-350.

Ruwet, N. (1987). Methods of analysis in musicology. *Music Analysis, 6*(1-2), 4-39.

Saussure, F. de (1916). *Course in general linguistics* (trans. Roy Harris, 1983). London: Duckworth.

Temperley, D. (1988). *The cognition of basic musical structures.* Cambridge, MA: MIT Press.

Toiviainen, P. (1998). An interactive MIDI accompanist. *Computer Music Journal, 22*(4), 63-75.

Toiviainen, P., & Eerola, T. (2006). Autocorrelation in meter induction: The role of accent structure. *Journal of Acoustical Society of America, 119*(2), 1164-1170.

White, B. (1960). Recognition of distorted melodies. *American Journal of Psychology, 73,* 100–107.

Zaki, M. (2005). Efficient algorithms for mining closed itemsets and their lattice structure. *IEEE Transactions on Knowledge and Data Engineering, 17,* 462-478.

ENDNOTES

[1] As stated by the authors themselves, "only a very small proportion of the patterns generated by SIA would be considered musically interesting by an analyst or expert listener. For example, SIA discovers over 70000 [patterns] in Rachmaninoff's Prelude, Op.3 No.2 and probably fewer than 100 of these would be considered interesting by a music analyst" (Meredith et al. 2003, p. 52).

[2] We can note also that the presence of a chord, in the bass voice of the last bar of the second stave, induces the creation of a local graph.

[3] The antecedent itself contains an exact repetition with transposition of a short cell (indicated with dotted lines). In the actual piece, the ending of the first phrase contains a little melodic ornamentation indicated here by short notes.

[4] The particular difficulties aroused by the geometrical approach proposed by Meredith, Lemström and Wiggins (2002) have been studied in the first section of the chapter.

Chapter XII
Pen–Based Interaction for Intuitive Music Composition and Editing

Sébastien Macé
Campus Universitaire de Beaulieu, France

Eric Anquetil
Campus Universitaire de Beaulieu, France

Bruno Bossis
Campus Universitaire de Villejan, France

ABSTRACT

This chapter deals with pen interaction and its use for musical notation composition and editing. The authors first present existing pen-based musical notation editors and argue that they are dedicated to classical musical notations and are often constraining for the user. They then focus on their generic method that is in particular based on a formalism that models how to interpret the strokes drawn in online structured documents. To analyze an element, it models a coupling of a global vision (its position relatively to the other elements of the document) with a local vision (its shape and that of its components). The authors also present the hand-drawn stroke analyzer associated to this formalism. Finally, they demonstrate how the presented method can be used to design pen-based systems not only for classical musical score notations, but also for plainchant scores, drum tablatures and stringed-instrument tablatures.

INTRODUCTION

This chapter deals with a new computer system approach, based on pen interaction, for music composition and editing: thanks to a pen, the user creates and modifies digital documents by drawing on a touch screen. The use of a pen is very intuitive, because it reproduces the "paper-pen" metaphor, media everybody knows: it makes it possible to use computer systems the same way as a sheet of paper. Figure 1 presents a tablet PC, which is a computer system with such an interaction: the user writes musical scores in a traditional way by drawing the symbols on the screen. This system is an example of system developed thanks to the methodology presented in this chapter: the user draws musical

Figure 1. A tablet PC with a pen-based interface

symbols the same way as on paper. The drawings are recognized and retranscribed neatly directly as the user composes the document. The user can then check the recognition process and interact with the system to easily modify the document, for instance move some of its elements, erase them, and so forth.

Pen-based interaction offers various advantages for the composition and the editing of digital documents. Indeed, the user can benefit from the possibilities of both paper and computer systems. On the one hand, the user can write symbols as he usually does on paper. As stated by many authors, like for instance Anstice, Bell, Cockburn, and Setchell (1996), Macé and Anquetil (2006a) or George (2003), it is more user-friendly and faster than classical mouse-based composition and editing systems which consist in clicking on a menu to select a symbol and dragging it to the appropriate place. Moreover, as presented in Figure 1, a tablet PC is almost as mobile as a sheet of paper, which simplifies its use in various situations. On the other hand, computer systems offer a direct retranscription which is easier to read than hand-drawn symbols. The user can also easily modify the documents, erase or move some of their components, copy, cut and paste some of them, and so forth, and then avoid the loss of quality and neatness of the paper document.

Finally, the user benefits from the traditional computer functionalities; for example, a digital musical score can be played, perfectly formatted, archived, distributed, and so forth.

Actually, there are very few pen-based interfaces for digital document composition and editing, and in particular for musical notations. This is due to the fact that developing such systems is complex. Indeed, the recognition of symbols drawn on the touch screen is a difficult problem of pattern recognition due to the diversity of handwriting styles. This recognition process is even more complex in the context of highly structured document analysis, since these documents are constituted of many elements of various natures. Moreover, a same drawing can have different meanings according to the context in which it has been realized, which must therefore be taken into account.

This chapter deals with the exploitation of pen interaction to compose and edit structured documents, and, more specifically, documents with musical notations. Before going further, let us introduce the vocabulary used in this chapter. We use the word *composition* for the action of writing music symbols, and the word *editing* for the action of modifying one or more of these symbols or more generally the document. We designate as *structured documents*, documents which present a predefined structural arrangement, and for which it is possible to express *composition conventions*, that is the way they are classically drawn. Concerned documents come from various domains, such as diagrams, plans, electronic figures, and so forth. Traditional musical scores, plainchant scores, drum tablatures or stringed-instrument tablatures are examples of structured documents with musical notations that we are going to focus on in this chapter. *Online interpretation* deals with the interpretation of the hand-drawn user strokes, which are the sequences of points captured by the touch screen between a pen-down and a pen-up. Online interpretation can be either *lazy* (i.e., occurring only when explicitly

Figure 2. Illustration of the lazy interpretation process

Figure 3. Illustration of the eager interpretation process

requested by the user) or *eager* (*on the fly*, that is occurring directly while the user is drawing). As presented on Figure 2, lazy interpretation offers the advantage of not intruding into the user's creative phase during the composition because he can write everything he has in mind before asking the system to interpret the document (Nakagawa, Machii, Kato, & Souya, 1993). Nevertheless, once the recognition process applied at once on all of his strokes, he has to examine the entire document to look for possible incorrect interpretations. Besides, it turns out that lazy systems are so far not robust enough and make too many mistakes, which reduces their usability. We believe that lazy recognition is a promising approach to offer unconstrained understanding of ink, but the difficulties to design automatic parsing coupled with a robust hand-drawn shape recognition system show that it remains an open problem.

Eager interpretation is then another way to consider online structured document analysis. As presented on Figure 3, every time the user draws a stroke, the system interprets it immediately (Blostein, Lank, Rose, & Zanibbi, 2002; Macé, Anquetil, & Coüasnon, 2005a); it then has to deal with documents directly during their composition and to make a decision as quickly as possible so that the user does not have to wait to continue his drawing. Eager interpretation allows exploiting the interaction with the user, who is aware of the system answers, and can then validate or refute them progressively. We believe that eager interpretation is the most pertinent compromise for online structured document interpretation because systems based on this kind of interaction are often more robust and more efficient than lazy ones, which makes them more usable. The work we present aims at exploiting a generic approach in

order to eagerly interpret various forms of hand-drawn musical notations and various composition conventions.

Whereas the existing approaches only enable users to draw classical musical score notations, our approach aims at making it possible to easily adapt the system to different ones. In this chapter, we focus on the composition and the editing of various musical notations, such as classical musical scores, plainchant scores, drum tablatures and stringed-instrument tablatures, but the method is generic and has already been exploited for two others structured document domains, which are diagrams and unified modelling language (UML) class diagrams.

In the following section, we present a state of the art in pen-based interface development in the domain of musical notation composition and editing. We first state that, so far, systems are dedicated to classical musical scores. We emphasize, on the one hand, their differences with traditional composition conventions, and, on the other hand, their limitations in term of musical notations. In section "A Generic Approach for Hand-Drawn Structured Document Composition and Editing", we introduce our generic approach and present each of its components. In section "Pen-Based Systems for Music Composition and Editing with the Presented Approach", we present how this generic approach can be used to compose and edit four different natures of musical structured documents: classical musical scores, plainchant scores, drum tablatures and stringed-instrument tablatures. Finally, we conclude this chapter by highlighting future trends in the exploitation of pen-based interaction for musical notation composition and editing and by presenting our future works.

STATE OF THE ART IN PEN-BASED MUSICAL SCORE COMPOSITION AND EDITING

Before going further, it is interesting to notice that, so far, there are little pen-based software for musical notation composition and editing. In particular, as far as we know, only systems for classical musical score notations exist.

In this section, we first present the main difficulties that make pen-based musical score editors complex software to develop. We would like to note that these problems also exist in other pen-based structured document composition and editing software. Then, we present the existing approaches and highlight the way they deal with each of these problems.

Difficulties in Developing Pen-Based Musical Score Editors

The two main difficulties in the development of pen-based musical score editors are the interpretation of the user strokes in the context of structured documents and the management of symbols drawn with more than one stroke.

Interpreting the Strokes of Structured Documents

Musical scores contain a lot of symbols of various natures, such as clefs (G-clefs, C-clefs, F-clefs, etc.), notes (whole-notes, half-notes, quarter-notes, etc.), accidentals (flat, sharp, natural, etc.), figures (time signature, etc.), characters (dynamics, lyrics, etc.). Powerful hand-drawn shape recognizers can be developed to interpret these symbols (Plamondon & Srihari, 2000), but we have to take into account the fact that the more symbols a recognizer has to discriminate, the less robust and efficient it is. Thus, it is not possible to use a unique recognizer for all symbols a musical score can contain. It is then necessary to exploit *dedicated recognizers*, that is recognizers able to

interpret subsets of these symbols, for instance one recognizer to discriminate between clefs, one to discriminate between accidentals, and so forth. As a consequence, the first difficulty consists in interpreting the user hand-drawn strokes, which is furthermore complicated by the fact that every scripter has its own way to realize a musical score and draw the musical symbols. Finally, the fact that some of these symbols have the same shape (for instance a whole note, a half note, the figure "0", the character "o") complicates even more the problem. It is then essential to take into account the context in which a stroke has been drawn in order to interpret it: depending on the context, which can be for instance structural and/or temporal, the same drawing is interpreted differently (for instance, a circle on a staff is more likely a head note, whereas a circle below a staff is more likely part of lyrics, i.e., the character "o").

Dealing with Multi-Stroke Symbols

Some of the classical musical symbols cannot be, or are not traditionally, drawn with only one stroke: they are called *multistroke* symbols (in opposition to *unistroke* symbols). For instance, the sharp symbol is constituted of two horizontal segments and two vertical segments; as a consequence, such a symbol is classically drawn with four strokes. This presents a second difficulty for the eager interpretation process. Indeed, the system is faced with the dynamic segmentation problem: it has to eagerly decide if a stroke is sufficient to form a symbol, and interpret it as such, or if it should wait for the following strokes. Once again, the solution can be based on the exploitation of structural and/or temporal contexts.

Some authors avoid part of or all these problems, for instance by assuming that each musical symbol has already been isolated before trying to interpret it. Thus, George (2003) proposed to exploit artificial neural networks in order to recognize already segmented symbols. But the use of this method in an online musical notation editor is not straightforward because the segmentation of the symbols is a complex problem, ever more with an eager interpretation process.

Existing Pen-Based Musical Score Editors

In order to deal with both of the problems presented in previous section, the main solution consists in changing the *gestures*, that is the way musical symbols are drawn, and to constrain the user to a new way of writing musical scores. Therefore, the authors often define new alphabets, which are designed to reduce the similarity between the different symbols in order to make their discrimination easier. These new alphabets are generally unistrokes, in order to facilitate the interpretation process: as a symbol is always drawn with only one stroke, the hand-drawn shape recognizers can be called each time the user draws a stroke. If an interpretation for this stroke is found, then it is replaced by the corresponding musical symbol. On the contrary, if no possible interpretation is found, then the system has been unable to recognize the stroke: it is *rejected*. It disappears from the screen, and the user has to draw it again. Naturally, the definition of new alphabets for musical symbol composition tends to find the best compromise between ease of recognition for systems and ease of learning for users. Nevertheless, this solution has a major drawback: the user has to get used to this new alphabet, and does not write musical notations the same way as on paper. We believe that this creates a gap between the musician and the computer which often implies, for instance, a rupture in the creation process in comparison with the use of paper.

One of the first pen-based systems was proposed in 1996 by Anstice et al. and then enriched in 1998 by Ng, Bell, and Cockburn; it was based on this idea. The authors exploited the three primary criteria proposed by Goldberg and Richardson (1993) for their pen-based text input system, which are: *ease of learning, high*

distinction between the input symbols and *fast writing speed*. Actually, one of the goals of the proposed system, called "*Presto*", was to make it possible to write music in a faster way than on paper thanks to the use of pen interaction and the definition of new faster gestures to replace the classical way to draw musical symbols. As a consequence, the gestures are also thought to be as small as possible. Of course, in order to facilitate their learning, the new gestures are as intuitive for musicians as possible, but are still different from the classical ones. For instance, the gesture to draw a filled-note head is a dot. In order to add an accidental to a note head, the user has to draw a small vertical segment starting on this head, uprising for a sharp, descending for a flat. In the same manner, a durational dot is added to a note head by drawing a small horizontal segment starting on this head. The second column of Table 1 presents some of the gestures of this system. Finally, in terms of input process speed, the performances of Presto are positive, because experimentations highlight that the software enables musicians to copy music in the average time of 72% of that required to copy on paper.

Forsberg, Dieterich, and Zeleznik presented in 1998 a pen-based musical score editor, called the "*Music Notepad*"; a more recent version of this composition system is available on the internet (Forsberg, Holden, Miller, & Zeleznik, 2005); the gestures we explicit in this paragraph and in the third column of Table 1 corresponds to this last version. Once again, the authors exploit a new alphabet to write classical musical notations, which is in fact quite close to the one proposed by Anstice et al. (1996) and Ng et al. (1998). For instance, quarter-notes can be drawn almost the same way as on paper, but accidentals can not: a gesture starting on a note head and uprising on the right is interpreted as a sharp, descending on the right as a flat. A durational dot is added by tapping on the note head.

We proposed a pen-based system dedicated to the editing of musical scores (Macé, Anquetil,

Garrivier & Bossis, 2005). In order to facilitate the recognition process, we used a unistroke alphabet, but we just changed the symbols that cannot be draw with only one gesture. The goal was to keep gestures as close as possible to the classical ones in order to make a more user-friendly and more usable system and to limit as much as possible the rupture in the creation process. For instance, a durational dot is drawn as a small dot on the right of a note head; an accidental is drawn close to a note head on its left: a flat is drawn with one stroke the same way as on paper, but the gestures for the sharp and the natural are changed, for a horizontal segment and a vertical segment respectively. We also proposed different gestures for a same symbol when it seemed appropriate. Thus, a filled-note head can be done in several ways, for instance by drawing a dot, a slash, a scribble, and so forth. The originality of our approach was to exploit the structural context of a stroke to interpret it. For example, a stroke drawn close to a note head on its left has a high probability of being an accidental; then, instead of trying to recognize any possible symbol, we try to recognize an accidental. Actually, we kept some of the concepts of this system to design the generic approach we present in the continuation of this chapter. The fourth column of Table 1 presents some of the gestures of this system.

In 2004, Miyao and Maruyama, and then Mitobe, Miyao, and Maruyama, presented an online musical score recognition system, which is able to deal with multistroke symbols. As far as we know, with the exception of the work we present in this chapter, there is no other system with such a capability. The gestures they propose are almost the same as the classical one, with one exception (a filled-note head is drawn with a circle with a slash in order to reduce the input time). The analysis process consists then in two steps. In the first one, each user stroke is interpreted as a primitive form, that is as one of the unitary symbols that can exist in musical scores: they are all the unistroke symbols (whole-notes, half-notes, clefs, flat, etc.) and all the components of the multistroke ones (horizontal and vertical segments, which can be part of a sharp, etc.). In the second step, the system tries to combine the primitive forms to produce multistroke elements. Although the system they present does not propose enough available symbols to be usable, we believe that their approach is interesting. Actually, some of the concepts we present in the following section are close to some of these authors. The fifth column of Table 1 presents some of the gestures of this system.

In the next section, we introduce the generic approach we designed to develop pen-based structured document composition and editing software. We have in particular exploited this approach to develop a system for classical musical score notations, which aims at letting the user

Figure 4. Screenshots of the pen-based musical score editor developed with the presented methodology: On the left, the user draws a beam between two quarter-notes, and on the right it is replaced by its neatly re-transcribed symbol thanks to an eager interpretation process

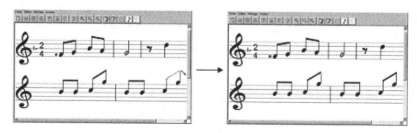

Table 1. Alphabet of existing pen-based musical score editors; when the direction of a gesture is constrained, a pen indicates its last point

Symbols to draw	*Presto* Anstice et al. (1995) Ng et al. (1998)	*Music Notepad* Forsberg et al. (1998)	Macé, et al. (2005)	Miyao, Mitobe et al. (2004a, 2004b)	*Presented approach:* Macé, Anquetil and Bossis
	Apparently not available	Apparently not available			
	Apparently not available	Apparently not available			
			Not available	Not available	
				Not available	
			Not available		

compose musical symbols the same way as on a sheet of paper. The gestures are then as classical as possible, as presented in the sixth column of Table 1. Figure 4 presents two screenshots of the editor: on the left, the user draws a beam between two quarter-notes, and on the right, this drawing is interpreted and retranscribed neatly.

Screenshots of the pen-based musical score editor developed with the presented methodology: on the left, the user draws a beam between two quarter-notes, and on the right it is replaced by its neatly retranscribed symbol thanks to an eager interpretation process.

A GENERIC APPROACH FOR HAND-DRAWN STRUCTURED DOCUMENT COMPOSITION AND EDITING

In this section, we present a new generic approach that aims at interpreting hand-drawn structured documents from various domains and with different constraints, such as musical scores, but also diagrams, plans, electronic figures, and so forth. The architecture of the system is illustrated in Figure 5. It is based on a framework constituted of three main components:

- *A formalism for eager interpretation of hand-drawn structured documents* (1), which models how to eagerly interpret the elements of hand-drawn structured documents from a given domain. It permits to write interpretation rules that represent composition conventions (for instance chronological information: it models which element can or must be drawn before another one) and physical information, such as the spatial structure of the document. Finally, they model the driving of the use of hand-drawn shape recognizers depending on the document structural context of a stroke, that is depending on its location in relation

to the other elements of the document; this is its main originality. This formalism can be applied to different notation domains and composition conventions, in order to model how to eagerly interpret a very large panel of hand-drawn structured documents. The interpretation rules written for one domain according to this formalism are externalized from the system: they are easily modifiable. They just need to be transformed by the generic compiler of the system. This formalism is presented more in detail in the first subsection.

- *A hand-drawn stroke analyzer* (2), which exploits the knowledge modeled by the formalism to eagerly interpret hand-drawn structured documents. It is able to call the pertinent hand-drawn shape recognizers (for example clef recognizer, accidental recognizer, etc.) depending on the structural context of the stroke, and then update the document contexts that will help recognizing the following strokes. This analyzer is generic: it does not need to be adapted to each specific domain. This analyzer is presented more in detail in the second subsection.

- A set of graphical functions and pen-based editing functions (3), which can be exploited by any pen-based system; such functions deal with the user interface and the display of the document. They exploit graphical information, such as images of the neatly retranscribed symbols, which are externalized because they are dependent on the domain. These functions also deal with pen-based interaction and editing: the user can for instance select graphical elements, move them to another part of the document, erase them, and so forth. It is also possible to undo the last element, zoom in or out, save or load a document. All these actions can be done just using the pen. These functions are presented more in detail in the last subsection.

Figure 5. Architecture of the generic system

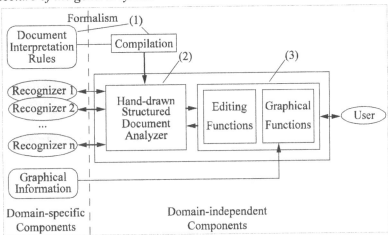

The graphical and pen-based editing functions and the hand-drawn stroke analyzer are *domain-independent components*; they do not need to be rewritten for each pen-based system. The development of such systems with our approach only requires realizing the *domain-specific components*: writing the interpretation rules (embedded under a compiled form), designing the necessary hand-drawn shape recognizers (which can be reused from one system to another) and specifying the graphical information. The components of our system are well separated and can be modified and adapted independently of the others.

We present these components more in detail in the next subsections.

A Formalism for Eager Interpretation of Structured Documents

The main component of our approach is a formalism which aims at defining how to eagerly interpret the elements of structured documents from various domains. The goal is to propose a formalism which is as generic as possible in order to be able to deal with a large panel of documents. We previously (Macé et al., 2005a) defined the four basic concepts that are, in our opinion, associated to the modelling of eager interpretation of online structured documents:

- **The modeling of the composition conventions:** As the interpretation process is eager, the system has to deal with incomplete documents; a way to do so is to model how a document is typically drawn, for instance, which element after which other.

- **The representation of the document spatial structure:** It is necessary to exploit the relative positioning of the document elements in order to model, on the one hand, in which document structural contexts an element can be identified, and, on the other hand, which of these contexts are generated due to the creation of an element.

- **The driving of the recognition process by the document context analysis:** We have stated that it is not possible to have a unique recognizer for all the symbols that a document can contain. By exploiting the document context of an element, the system must reduce the likely symbols and choose which dedicated recognizers to use.

- **The pen-based human-computer interaction:** As the result of the interpretation process is directly displayed on the screen, the user is aware of it. Consequently we can take into account the human-computer interaction and exploit it on an as user-friendly way as possible.

Figure 6. Drawings of a filled-note head (on the left) and a sharp (on the right)

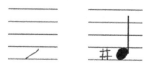

The formalism we propose takes all these concepts into account. We present its syntax and explain it on two classical musical score notation examples, which are the filled-note head and the sharp.

The description of the interpretation of a structured document with our formalism is composed of interpretation rules which define the generating of the element which name they bear. Several rules can have the same name, which makes it possible to model different ways to compose the same element. A rule takes a set of elements as parameters, enounced in its heading, and returns a new one that can replace them; the parameters are the *components*, or *sub-elements*, of the new element. A parameter can be either a stroke or an already interpreted element, which makes possible a hierarchical shape description. For instance, as presented in Figure 6, a filled-note head is typically drawn with one stroke, whereas a sharp is typically drawn with two horizontal segments and two vertical segments. The corresponding rule headings can then be:

FilledNoteHead (Stroke s) ...

Sharp (HorizontalSeg hs1 , HorizontalSeg hs2, VecticalSeg vs1 , VecticalSeg vs2) ...

The structure of a rule is composed of four blocks: a *document context verification (DCV)* block, a *shape context verification (SCV)* block,

a *shape recognition (SR)* block and a *document context creation (DCC)* block, in the following order:

SymbolName (Parameter 1 , ... , Parameter n)
Document Context Verification block (DCV).
Shape Context Verification block (SCV).
Shape Recognition block (SR).
Document Context Creation block (DCC).

DCV and DCC blocks enable a global vision of the document in order to define in which document structural contexts an element must be located. A DCV block specifies the document structural contexts in which the symbol created by the rule has to be identified, whereas a DCC block indicates the contexts that are generated due to the creation of this element. The SCV and SR blocks enable, given a document context, a local vision of the element to recognize; it distributes the recognition process among local constraints, formalized in the SCV block, and recognizers, formalized in the SR block; it drives the interpretation process by calling dedicated recognizers depending on the context of elements.

The proposed formalism is based on the definition of structural contexts which model, on the one hand, specific locations in the document, and, on the other hand, which elements can or must exist at these positioning. The syntax of a structural context is as follows:

R[position,part]A.

This means that the involved structural context is located at the relative positioning *position* (e.g., in, on the left, above, etc.) of a reference *R*. In order to satisfy this context, an element *A* must have its part *part* (e.g., one point, all the points, the first point, the highest point, etc.) in this positioning.

Document Context Verification Block (DCV)

The document context verification block specifies a list of document structural contexts in which the symbol has to be identified; they thus have to be verified by the parameters of the rule. Its syntax is as follows:

$$DCV: R_1[position_1, part_1]A_1, ..., R_n[position_n, part_n]A_n.$$

As introduced previously, this means that at the relative position $position_i$ of a reference R_i, the part $part_i$ of an analyzed element A_i exists. In this block, R_i and A_i do not have to be part of the parameters.

For example, a sharp can be drawn on the left of any note head that does not already have an accidental; this means that the four segments forming this symbol must be drawn on the left of a note head. A DCV block for such an interpretation rule can be written as (as seen previously, the parameters of the sharp interpretation rule are two horizontal segments *hs1* and *hs2* and two vertical segments *vs1* and *vs2*):

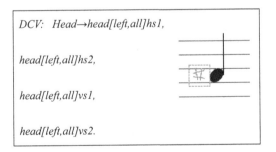

An alias is defined to specify that a *Head* can be a *WholeNote*, a *HalfNote* or a *QuarterNote*. We would like to note that in this block, we use a saving operator "→" to save an element and reuse it afterwards. Here, it aims at modelling that the four segments forming the sharp symbol must be on the left of the same head, denoted by *head*.

Shape Context Verification Block (SCV)

Once we know that the symbol that the rule generates can exist in the document structural context in which the element is located, we locally focus on its shape in order to check if it corresponds to this symbol. The shape context verification block is a first step: it models local structural constraints about the parameters of a rule in order to interpret an element constituted of several sub-elements: it makes it possible to identify which part of the new element corresponds to each parameter. The syntax is the same as in the DCV block, but this time R_i and A_i must be parameters. By default, there is no constraint on the drawing order of the elements; if necessary, a chronological operator can be used.

For example, a sharp is constituted of four segments which can be drawn in any order. A SCV block (in which the alias *[intersects]* is used for the structural context *[in,one]*) can be written as:

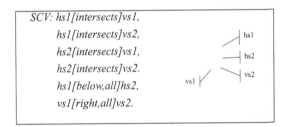

These local structural constraints are not necessarily enough to ensure that the four segments constitute a sharp. So, we may want to exploit a classical hand-drawn shape recognizer; this can be done thanks to the SR block.

Shape Recognition Block (SR)

The shape recognition block is the second step of the local interpretation of the analysed element shape: it corresponds to the call to a hand-drawn shape recognizer. It makes it possible to invoke

Table 2. Interpretation rules for quarter-notes and sharps

Interpretation rules	Structural contexts before recognition – Hand-drawn strokes	Structural contexts after recognition – Re-transcribed symbols
FilledNoteHead (Stroke s) DCV: Staff→staff[on,all]s. SCV: . SR: HeadNotes, { FilledNoteHead }. DCC: this[left,all]Accidental^i, this[right,all]Dot^i, (this[rightUprising,all] UprisingStem^i | this[leftDescending,all] DescendingStem^i).		
Sharp (HorizontalSegment hs1 , HorizontalSegment hs2, VecticalSegment vs1 , VecticalSegment vs2) DCV: Head→head[left,all]hs1, head[left,all]hs2, head[left,all]vs1, head[left,all]vs2. SCV: hs1[intersects]vs1, hs1[intersects]vs2, hs2[intersects]vs1, hs2[intersects]vs2, hs1[below,all]hs2, vs1[right,all]vs2. SR: Accidentals, {Sharp}. DCC: .		

only the relevant recognizers, depending on the context of an element. It is essential to increase the interpretation process robustness, since the less symbols a recognizer must interpret, the more efficient and the more reliable it is. The SR block syntax is:

SR: SymbolFamily , {AcceptedAnswers}.

This expression means that the recognizer of *SymbolFamily* is called, with the rule parameters as input. If its answer is included in *{AcceptedAnswers}* the recognition process is a success. If no *{AcceptedAnswers}* is specified, then any answer of the recognizer is acceptable. The order of the elements presented to the recognizer is the order of the parameters in the declaration of the rule; so it is always the same. As a result, its work is relieved, because it has to interpret the elements always in the same order.

For example, to interpret a sharp, we exploit a recognizer able to recognize accidentals, and we want its answer to be a sharp. This way, the coupling of the global and the local visions model that it is more pertinent to call an accidental recognizer than a stem recognizer or a dot recognizer on elements located on the left of a note head. A SR block modelling this can be written as:

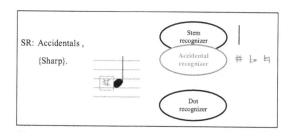

Document Context Creation Block (DCC)

The document context creation block specifies a list of document structural contexts which are created due to the recognition of an element. They explain which rules will have to be activated on an element drawn there. Its syntax is:

$$DCC: R_1[position_1, part_1]A_1^{m\_1}, \ldots, R_n[position_n, part_n]A_n^{m\_n}$$

This means that at the relative position *position$_i$* of an element R_i, the part *part$_i$* of an element A_i can exist. The current element, in process of creation, is referenced as *"this"*. The number *m_i* indicates how many A_i can exist in this context and is * if there is no limit.

For example, the creation of a sharp on the left of a note head does not imply the possibility to draw a specific symbol. On the contrary, the creation of a note head allows drawing one accidental on its left, one durational dot on its right and one stem, either uprising or descending; then, document structural contexts modelling where these symbols can now exist are created and will help in interpreting them. A DCC block for such a rule can be written as:

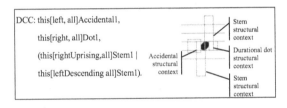

We would like to emphasize that the accidental document structural context created in this DCC block corresponds to the one exploited by the DCV block of the sharp interpretation rule defined previously and to note that disjunction between contexts is possible. Finally, an alias is defined to specify that an *Accidental* can be a *Flat*, a *Sharp* or a *Natural*.

The complete *QuarterNote* and *Sharp* interpretation rules are given in Table 2.

As presented in previous section, our goal is to design a pen-based musical score composition software as close as possible to classical notations, in order to be as user-friendly and as usable as

possible so as to limit the rupture in the creative process. Thus, in the presented rules and figures, the gestures are the same as the classical ones. We would like to highlight the possibility, with this system, to model different ways to draw the same symbol. This implies that it is possible, if necessary, to use new alphabets such as the ones presented in previous section and in Table 1.

A Stroke Analyzer

The second component of the system is a hand-drawn stroke analyzer that eagerly interprets the drawings of the user thanks to the knowledge modelled by the formalism. In this section, we first explain how we deal with multistroke symbols. Then, we present the analysis process more in detail, and finally highlight the exploitation of the human-computer interaction.

An Incremental Interpretation Process to Deal with Multi-Stroke Symbols

The system we propose interprets the user strokes dynamically and incrementally. This means that the analysis is applied every time the user draws a stroke, like in unistroke symbol systems. If no interpretation is found for a hand-drawn stroke, it is rejected. On the contrary, if it can be interpreted, that is, if such a stroke can exist in such a context, it is replaced by its neatly retranscribed corresponding symbol and the system tries to associate it with other elements of the document in order to constitute multistroke symbols. Thus, the dynamic segmentation process is deduced from the formalism. For instance, the *Sharp* interpretation rule presented in Table 2 models that where a sharp can exist, two horizontal and two vertical segments can also exist; but once they do, they can be replaced by a sharp if their shape is coherent. This analysis process is close to the one proposed by Miyao et al. (2004) and Mitobe et al. (2004).

Presentation of the Analysis Process

The formal analysis process algorithm is given Figure 7, and it is illustrated by Figure 8. When a new stroke, or more generally a new element, is analyzed, the goal is to find the sequence of interpretation rules to apply. As introduced in previous section, an existing document is constituted, on the one hand, of the already interpreted elements it contains and, on the other hand, of its structural contexts. This knowledge defines a global vision of the document which must be exploited to interpret new elements. The analyzer identifies the document structural contexts in which the analyzed element is located and activates the corresponding associated rules.

Each activated rule is tested. The analyzer searches for possible parameters for the current rule that is, the elements of the document that can be associated to the analyzed element to constitute a more complex one. For each applicable rule, the analyzer verifies the coherence of its parameters

Figure 7. Algorithm of the analysis process

```
AnalysisProcess
Input    Element    e /*element of the document to analyse*/
Data     List       possibleRules = {}
Data     Rule       chosenRule = null
begin
    for each document structural context c that e satisfies do
        /* Rule activation */
        for each possible interpretation rule pr associated to c do
            for each list of parameters lp (containing e) for the rule pr do
                /* DCV block */
                if all structural contexts of the DCV block are satisfied then
                    /* SCV block */
                    if all local constraints of the SCV block are satisfied then
                        /* SR block */
                        if the recognizer is able to interpret the parameters then
                            add pr to possibleRules
                        end if
                    end if
                end if
            end for
        end for
    end for

    /* Rule Selection */
    chosenRule = findBestSatisfiedRule(possibleRules)

    if chosenRule is not null then
        replace the parameters of chosenRule by the element this rule creates
        /* DCC block */
        create the structural contexts specified by the DCC block of chosenRule
        apply AnalysisProcess to the new element
    else if chosenRule is null and e is a stroke then
        reject the stroke
    end if
end
```

Figure 8. Illustration of the analysis process

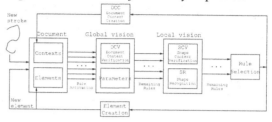

Figure 9. Illustration of the sharp symbol analysis process

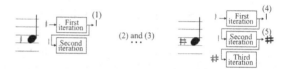

with the structural context in which the new element should be located; this is modelled by the DCV block. Only the rules that satisfy both of these criteria remain.

The verification of the coherence of the new element with the document structural context thanks to a global vision means that the corresponding element can exist at this positioning; the next step consists in trying to identify the shape of the parameters of the rule. For that purpose, a local vision of these parameters is exploited to analyze their structural arrangement; this is modeled by the SCV block. A shape recognition system can be used on the parameters of the rule in order to identify their shape thanks to the SR block. The recognition systems that are exploited by our system have a particular characteristic: they have reject options, which means they do not give an answer unless their confidence in it is high enough (Mouchère & Anquetil, 2006). The advantage is to filter possible interpretations, and to prevent from displaying an answer which has a high probability of being wrong. The rules that satisfy the SCV and SR blocks remain: they are applicable.

As more than one rule can be applicable, a *Rule Selection* component is exploited to make a decision. This component evaluates the degree to which the parameters of each rule belong to the document structural contexts and selects the rule with the higher degree. If the difference between the degrees of the best solutions is negligible, the analyzer decides that it is unable to make a decision and rejects the element. We do not present this rule selection component more in detail, because we believe that it is outside the scope of this chapter.

Once interpreted, the new element is created; it replaces the parameters of the applied rule in the document. New structural contexts are created to help interpreting the following elements; this is modelled by the DCC block. Once a rule is applied, the current iteration of the analysis process is finished. Then, a new iteration begins, in order to check if this new element interacts with other elements of the document to constitute a more complex symbol: we try to eventually apply a rule on the new element, and so on until stability; as a consequence, a stroke can imply a sequence of transformations. If no rule can be applied on a stroke (i.e., if the first iteration does not succeed), it is rejected and disappears from the editing window.

In order to explicit this interpretation process, Figure 9 presents its mechanism on one particular example, which is the interpretation of a sharp. In this example, the user first draws a vertical segment on the left of a filled-note head (1). This hand-drawn stroke is recognized by the system, and replaced by its neatly retranscribed symbol. This segment does not, for now, interact with other existing elements of the document to from a more complex one: the analysis process is over. The

mechanism is the same when the user adds two horizontal segments on the left of this note head (2 and 3). Finally, the user draws a stroke which is supposed to be the second vertical segment that ends the sharp symbol. In the first iteration of the interpretation process, the stroke is interpreted as a vertical segment (4). This new element is then analyzed in the second iteration: it interacts with the three other segments to constitute a sharp (5). As this new symbol does not interact with other existing elements of the document to constitute a more complex symbol, the analysis process is over. We would like to remind the fact that the order in which these four segments are drawn is not constrained.

User Validation

As the recognition process is eager, the result of the analysis is displayed directly as the user is drawing. We can then exploit the human-computer interaction and integrate the user in the interpretation process to validate or reject the results. Thus, if after the display of the answer, the user goes on with the drawing of the document, he implicitly accepts and validates it; on the contrary, if he does not agree, he can delete the new element with a deletion gesture and so explicitly reject it. The main consequence of this process is that it is not necessary for the analyzer to question a decision made beforehand because it has been validated by the user. We believe that it is pertinent because it could be perturbing for the user to see the interpretation of an element changing after drawing another one. It is a major

Figure 10. Three different visualization modes: novice mode (left), expert mode (middle), and contextual mode (right)

advantage of the eager interpretation process over the lazy one: indeed, the user limits the ambiguities, which makes the system more robust and more efficient, increasing its user-friendliness and its usability. The system is also faster because it only has to find the sequence of rules to apply on the last hand-drawn stroke.

A Set of Graphical Functions and Pen-Based Editing Functions

The last component of the system is a set of graphical and pen-based editing functions: it deals with the human-computer interaction. In this section, we present these functions that are independent of the domain of the documents that are drawn, more in detail. Their principle is to enable the user to draw *graphical gestures*, which are not interpreted by the system as drawings of symbols, but as editing actions. Although we have developed our own graphical and pen-based editing functions, this component is not the main contribution of our method, because other authors have proposed similar functions (Lank, 2003).

Graphical Functions

Graphical functions correspond to the way the system displays its messages to the user. Their main functionality is the display of the results of the analysis process, i.e., the neatly retranscribed symbols, directly as the user is drawing his document. They exploit graphical information, such as images of these symbols, which are externalized of the system because they are dependent of the domain of the documents.

Graphical functions also propose solutions to guide the user in the drawing process. Indeed, to help him to have reference marks, rectangles giving an indication of the document structural contexts that are generated in DCC blocks can be displayed. We would like to note that whereas these displayed rectangles are strict, structural contexts are not: the user does not have to draw

Figure 11. Selection and moving mechanisms: Example on a quarter-note

the elements exactly in the rectangles. To lighten the editing area, a context is visible provided that it is not already filled with an element. Thus, as presented on Figure 10, it is possible to switch between a *novice mode*, in which empty contexts are visible, and an *expert mode*, in which they are not. It is also possible to show only the contexts that are near the pen position, once again to lighten the editing area: it corresponds to a *contextual mode*. The experience shows that this last mode seems to be the most user-friendly because it allows to only focus on potentially interesting structural contexts according to the pen position. The authors would like to note that the filled-note head structural contexts presented on Figure 10 correspond to those declared in the *FilledNote* interpretation rule defined in Table 2.

Graphical functions also make it possible to display the neatly retranscribed symbols and/or handwritten strokes, as presented for instance in Figure 12 and Figure 13. Moreover, a document can be constituted of as many pages as possible; it is then, for instance, possible to switch form one page to another. Some classical functions, such as zooming in or out, displaying an outline of some of the pages of the composed document or printing, are also already available.

Editing Functions

Editing functions correspond to the way the user expresses his requests to the system thanks to pen interaction. Concerned functions can be divided into two main categories, on the one hand the *document functions* that involve the management of the document, and on the other hand the *element functions* that involve the modification of the document elements.

Document functions are, for instance, adding or removing one page to the composed document, undoing the last action, saving or loading a document, and so forth. All these actions can be done using the pen, which offers an alternative to classical menu and button-based interaction.

Element functions are, for instance, selecting graphical symbols, moving them to another part of the document, deleting them, copying, cutting or pasting them, etc. For that purpose, every element of the document has a selection dot, which is a small red anchor point (which it is possible to make disappear, as presented in some figures of this chapter). In order to select an element, the user just has to circle its selection dot. This way, it is not necessary to draw a stroke as big as the element. Several elements can be selected or other elements can be added to the selection in the same manner. When an element is selected, the document elements associated to it are also selected; they actually correspond to the elements which have been drawn in the different contexts it has created. Once selected, elements can be moved to another part of the document by pointing to one of them and moving the pen to the appropriate place. It is also possible to move an element directly by pointing at its selection dot and moving the pen (by drag and drop). Moreover, selected elements can be copied or cut, and then pasted to another part of the document. To delete an element, the user can, for instance, move it outside the editing window. These mechanisms are illustrated by Figure 11: on the left, the user draws a stroke around the selection dot of a filled-note head; in the middle, the head and its associated elements (i.e., its stem and its flat) are selected, and the user moves them with the pen; on the right, he raises the pen to drop the elements. We would like to notice that the action of moving elements in the document requires the exploitation of the knowledge in the formalism, in order to check if the arrival position of the element is consistent with the rules associated to the document. Thus, the analysis process presented previously is also exploited for the moving of elements of the document.

Figure 12. Screenshots of two pen-based composition and editing systems designed thanks to the presented methodology

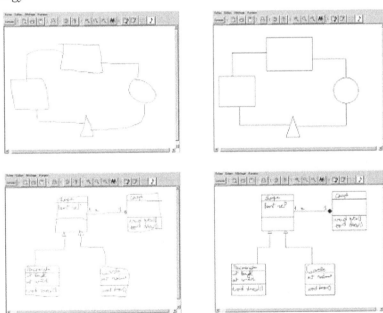

Table 3. Examples of rules used in the pen-based musical score editor and the corresponding strokes and interpreted symbols

Interpretation rules	Structural contexts before recognition – Hand-drawn strokes	Structural contexts after recognition – Re-transcribed symbols
UpStem *(Stroke s)* DCV: *HalfNote→head[rightUp,all]s.* SCV: . SR: *GeometricalShapes , {VerticalSeg}.* DCC: .		
UpStem *(Stroke s)* DCV: *FilledNoteHead→head[rightUp,all]s.* SCV: . SR: *GeometricalShapes , {VerticalSeg}.* DCC: *(this[top,extremity]Beam¹ |* *this[top,extremity]Flag¹).*		
DescStem *(Stroke s)* DCV: *FilledNoteHead→head[leftDesc,all]s.* SCV: . SR: *GeometricalShapes , {VerticalSeg}.* DCC: *(this[bottom,extremity]Beam¹ |* *this[bottom,extremity]Flag¹).*		
Beam *(Stroke s)* DCV: *UpStem→stemL[top,left]s,* *UpStem→stemR[top,right]s,* *stemR.head.staff = stemL.head.staff,* *stemL ≠ stemR.* SCV: . SR: *GeometricalShapes , {Segment}.* DCC: .		
Beam *(Stroke s)* DCV: *DescStem→stemL[bottom,left]s,* *DescStem→stemR[bottom,right]s,* *stemR.head.staff = stemL.head.staff,* *stemL ≠ stemR.* SCV: . SR: *GeometricalShapes , {Segment}.* DCC: .		

Figure 13. Screenshots of the pen-based classical musical score composition and editing system: on the left the hand-drawn strokes and on the right the corresponding retranscribed document

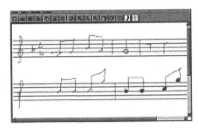 

PEN-BASED SYSTEMS FOR MUSIC COMPOSITION AND EDITING WITH THE PRESENTED APPROACH

Thanks to the methodology we present in this chapter, we have already developed various pen-based prototypes for the composition and the editing of structured documents from different domains:

- Pen-based editors adapted to classical musical score notations, plainchant score notations, drum tablature notations and finally stringed-instrument tablature notations. We are going to present these systems more in detail in this section.

- A pen-based graph editor, that allows to draw geometrical shapes and to connect them thanks to arcs; it also enables the user to write text in the geometrical shapes; the top of Figure 12 presents two screenshots of this editing prototype, on the left the user hand-drawn strokes, and on the right the corresponding interpreted document.

- A pen-based UML class diagram editor, that makes it possible to draw classes, represented as rectangles, and to connect them to model associations; inheritance and aggregation are among already available symbols; the bottom of Figure 12 presents two screenshots of this editing prototype.

Table 4. Interpretation rules for basic plainchant notations

Interpretation rules		Hand-drawn strokes	Re-transcribed symbols
Punctum *(Stroke s)*			
DCV:	*Staff[in,all]s.*		
SCV:	*.*		
SR:	*GeometricalShapes , {Square}.*		
DCC:	*.*		
VerticalSeg *(Stroke s)*			
DCV:	*Staff[in,all]s.*		
SCV:	*.*		
SR:	*GeometricalShapes , {VerticalSeg}.*		
DCC:	*.*		
Virga *(Punctum punctum , VerticalSeg vSeg)*			
DCV:	*Staff→staff[in,all]punctum,*		
	staff[in,all]vSeg.		
SCV:	*vSeg[topLeft]punctum.*		
SR:	*.*		
DCC:	*.*		

Table 5. Integration rules of more complex plainchant symbols; examples of keys and several neumes

Interpretation rules	Hand-drawn strokes	Re-transcribed symbols
FKey *(Punctum punctum1 , Punctum punctum2 , Punctum punctum3)* *DCV:* *Staff→staff[left,all]punctum1,* *staff[left,all]punctum2,* *staff[left,all]punctum3.* *SCV:* *punctum2[aboveRight]punctum1,* *punctum2[belowRight]punctum3.* *SR:* . *DCC:* .		
CKey *(VerticalSegment vSeg , Punctum punctum1 , Punctum punctum2)* *DCV:* *Staff→staff[left,all]punctum1,* *staff[left,all]vSeg,* *staff[left,all]punctum2.* *SCV:* *vSeg[topRight,all]punctum1,* *vSeg[bottomRight,all]punctum2.* *SR:* . *DCC:* .		
Pes *(Virga virga , Punctum punctum)* *DCV:* *Staff→staff[in,all]virga,* *staff[in,all]punctum.* *SCV:* *virga[bottomLeft,all]punctum.* *SR:* . *DCC:* .		
Clivis *(VerticalSeg vSeg , Virga virga , Punctum punctum)* *DCV:* *Staff→staff[in,all]vSeg,* *stuff[in,all]virga,* *staff[in,all]punctum.* *SCV:* *virga[left,all]vSeg,* *virga[bottomRight,all]punctum.* *SR:* . *DCC:* .		
Scandicus *(Pes pes , Virga virga)* *DCV:* *Staff→staff[in,all]pes,* *staff[in,all]virga.* *SCV:* *pes[topRight,all]virga.* *SR:* . *DCC:* .		

We would like to note that although it is not visible in Figure 12, the interpretation process of the systems that are developed thanks to the presented methodology is eager.

As indicated previously, the development of a composition and editing system based on pen interaction thanks to the presented methodology only requires:

- The writing of the interpretation rules thanks to the presented formalism.
- The design of the necessary hand-drawn shape recognizers (Plamondon & Srihari, 2000; Anquetil & Bouchereau, 2002).

- The specification of the graphical information, such as the images of the retranscribed elements.

In the next subsections, we focus on how this methodology can be exploited to develop pen-based composition and editing systems for various musical notations, whatever the desired associated composition conventions.

Classical Musical Score Notations

We first developed a pen-based musical score editor adapted to classical notations. In order to

Table 6. Interpretation rules for drum tablature notations

Interpretation rules	Hand-drawn strokes	Re-transcribed symbols
DrumTablatureLine (Stroke s) DCV: Document[in,all]s. SCV: . SR: GeometricalShapes , {HorizontalSeg} . DCC: this[left,all]Instrument² , this[in,all]DrumStroke* , (this[above,all]DrumTabLine* | this[in,highestP]LineBar*) , (this[below,all]DrumTabLine* | this[in,lowestP] LineBar*) .		
Instrument (Stroke s) DCV: DrumTabLine[left,all]s. SCV: . SR: Characters , {C , H , S , D , B}. DCC: .		
DrumStroke (Stroke s) DCV: DrumTabLine[in,all]s. SCV: . SR: Character , {x , o , d} . DCC: .		
LineBar (Stroke s) DCV: DrumTabLine→firstL[top,highestP]s , DrumTabLine→lastL[bottom,lowestP]s , firstL ≠ lastL . SCV: . SR: GeometricalShapes , {VerticalSeg} . DCC: .		

Table 7. Interpretation rules for stringed-instrument tablatures

Interpretation rules		Structural contexts before recognition – Hand-drawn strokes	Structural contexts after recognition – Re-transcribed symbols
Fret *(Stroke s)*			
DCV:	*TablatureLine[in,all]s.*		
SCV:	*.*		
SR:	*Numeral .*		
DCC:	*this[above,extremity]Connexion[1] ,*		
	this[below,top]Stem[1] .		
Connexion *(Stroke s)*			
DCV:	*Fret→ firstFret[above,left]s ,*		
	Fret →lastFret[above,right]s ,		
	firstFret ≠ lastFret .		
SCV:	*.*		
SR:	*GeometricalShapes , {CircularArc} .*		
DCC:	*this[above,all]PlayingMode[1] .*		
Stem (Stroke s)			
DCV:	*Fret[below,top]s ,*		
	Staff[below,bottom]s ,		
SCV:	*.*		
SR:	*GeometricalShapes , {VerticalSeg} .*		
DCC:	*this[below,extremity]Beam[1]*		
Beam *(Stroke s)*			
DCV:	*Stem→firstStem[below,left]s ,*		
	Stem→lastStem[below,right]s ,		
	firstStem ≠ lastStem .		
SCV:	*.*		
SR:	*GeometricalShapes , {HorizontalSeg} .*		
DCC:	*.*		

develop a system as usable and as intuitive as possible, professional musicians have guided us, in particular in the process of interpretation rule writing. Figure 13 presents two screenshots of the same musical score document: on the left only the user hand-drawn strokes are visible, and on the right the elements of the document are in their neatly retranscribed aspect (in order to lighten the screenshots, selection dots and document structural contexts are not shown).

Among the available symbols, the user can draw clefs (F-Clefs and G-Clefs), notes (from whole-notes to sixty-fourth notes) with uprising or descending stems, accidentals (flats, naturals, sharps, double-flats, double sharps) and durational

dots. Beams are also available. Silences (from rests to sixty-fourth rests), bar lines (simple and double bar lines) can be drawn on the staves, and dynamics (crescendo, decrescendo, pppp, ppp, pp, p, mp, mf, f, ff, fff, ffff) can be drawn under them. Table 3 presents some of these available symbols and some of their corresponding interpretation rules used in the developed system: it highlights in particular how the rules model that a flag or a beam can only be added to a quarter-note, and not to a half-note. The reader can also notice how the beam rule models that such a symbol must have its left and right points on the extremity (top or bottom) of two different quarter-notes of a same staff.

Figure 14. Antiphonary of the Middle of the XII Century, with an Example of Plainchant Score

About 80 rules have been written in order to develop this system. The duration of the analysis process, that is, the duration between the moment when the user raises the pen and the moment when the corresponding neatly retranscribed symbol is displayed, is mostly less than 400 milliseconds, and always less than one second. We, as well as musicians, believe that it is short enough to be considered as quasi-instantaneous and to not disturb the user.

We would like to notice that our software does not constrain the user to write semantically correct notations. For instance, the user can draw any number of notes in any measure. Naturally, such functionality could be added.

Musical score notations used traditionally for classical and popular music is not the only one:

Figure 15. Screenshots of the Plainchant Composition and Editing System

other systems exist. Even though they are more specialized, they are often necessary for composers, interprets, pedagogues, etc. We present three of these notations (for plainchant scores, drum tablatures and stringed-instrument tablatures), and highlight the genericity of the presented approach by showing how it is exploited to generate the corresponding composition and editing pen-based systems.

Plainchant Score Notations

The "Plainchant", or "Gregorian singing", is a type of occidental music, essentially based on a cappella singing. Generally, it is not written with the classical musical notations. Staves are constituted of only four lines and have one key. Notes are replaced by squares or diamonds isolated or gathered in *neumes*, which are short melodic figures executed in one breathing. Figure 14 pres-

Figure 17. Screenshot of the stringed-instrument tablature composition and editing prototype: example of a simple document

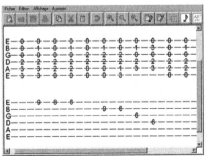

Figure 16. Screenshot of the drum tablature composition and editing system

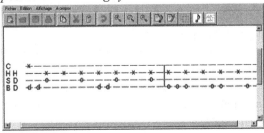

Figure 18. Screenshot of the stringed-instrument tablature composition and editing prototype: example of a more complex document

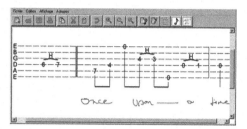

ents an antiphonary of the middle of the twelfth century with such notations.

One of the main characteristic of the plainchant score notations is the diversity of the existing systems. Contrary to classical musical score notations, very standardized since the classical epoch, plainchant melodies have been written with very different notations. For instance, rhythms can be represented according to a modal system (i.e., based on the representation of short rhythmic cells), like for the "Ecole de Notre-Dame de Paris" in the XII century. On the opposite, the mensuralist notation, since last century, adopts a connection between the duration of a sound and the shape of the isolated note. This is the cause of lots of difficulties for usual musical composition software, which are therefore often adapted to very simplified plainchant notations. Only a formalism like the one we propose makes it possible to deal with such difficulties, by offering the possibility to easily modify composition conventions in order to adapt to different notations.

Among different variants for plainchant notations, some have started to be standardized since the XIVth century. In the continuation of this section, we focus on one example of these notations. It includes two kinds of simple notes: the *punctum*, which is a filled-square, and the *virga*, which is a filled-square with a stem. Table 4 presents three interpretation rules, which model the eager recognition of punctums, vertical segments (which can become, afterwards, stems) and virgas.

Then, punctums, and virgas can be joined to constitute various neumes. Most current neumes are constituted of one to three notes. Table 5 introduces some of these symbols as well as the two existing clefs (the C-Clef and the F-Clef), and some interpretation rules which have been used to design the corresponding pen-based composition and editing system. The authors would like to highlight the fact that there are no constraints in the order of the drawings in the sub-elements of all the presented symbols. As a consequence, the resulting system is very user-friendly, because the user can draw the symbols in any order, as he does on a sheet of paper.

The developed system enables the user to draw as many staves as possible; it is possible to write the lyrics under these staves. Figure 15 presents two screenshots of this system, on the left the user strokes and on the right the corresponding interpreted document. As it can be seen on this figure, we have not yet coupled this prototype with a handwritten text recognizer: thanks to the context in which they are drawn, such strokes are identified as being text, but are not interpreted; as a consequence, we keep the strokes under their handwritten form.

About 20 rules model the eager interpretation process for this system. Its performances are even slightly better than the one for traditional musical score notations because the number of available symbols (and as a consequence of interpretation rules) is reduced.

Drum Tablature Notations

Notations for percussion instruments are less normalized than notations for other instruments. We focus here on drum tablatures. Contrary to traditional musical scores, which can represent music for any singer or instrument, tablatures are musical notations adapted to specific instruments. The graphical metaphor is no longer based on the pitch in the acoustic sense of the term, but on the physical constitution of the instrument: it is not about "what to play" any more, but about "how to play".

A drum tablature is constituted of horizontal lines; each line is associated to one of the instruments of the drum set. On the left of each line, the name of the corresponding instrument is identified by one or two letters, for instance "C" for the cymbal, "HH" for the hi-hat, "SD" for the snare drum, "BD" for the bass drum, etc. Then, on each line, symbols depict how the corresponding instrument must be played: for the cymbal and the hi-hat, an "x" indicates that the player has to beat, like an "o" for the snare drum and the bass drum. A double stroke is denoted by "dd". Bar lines can make it possible to delimitate the content of one tablature measure.

The developed system enables the user to draw as many tablatures as necessary, and each of these tablatures can be constituted of as many lines, that is, instruments, as necessary. All the symbols presented above are available and can be drawn in any order. Table 6 presents some of these symbols and the corresponding interpretation rules; in order to lighten the figures, the document structural contexts are not represented. A screenshot of the developed system is given on Figure 16.

Less than 10 rules have been necessary to develop this prototype. Its performances are of the same order than the other ones. We would like to emphasize that, although this composition and editing system is so far quite simple and only adapted to drum, it can easily be completed with other symbols and adapted to other types of percussion instruments.

Stringed-Instrument Tablature Notations

We now present another example of modern tablatures, adapted to fretted stringed-instruments, like for instance the guitar. As defined previously, a tablature does not represent "what to play", but

"how to play"; a stringed-instrument tablature tells the player where to place his fingers.

A tablature is constituted of horizontal lines representing the strings of the instrument. On the left of each line, the pitch of the corresponding opened string can be specified. Figures located on a line correspond to the fret of the instrument that the player must press down to produce the awaited sound, and "0" denotes an opened string. More complex notations can be introduced. Rhythm can be written under each figure thanks to symbols coming from the classical representation: a quarter-note is limited to its stem, two flags are indicated by a beam, etc. Other symbols make it possible to express particular playing modes, for instance "H" to represent a harmonic, "T" for a thumb, that is, a slap with the thumb, "P" for a pop, that is, a slap with another finger, and so forth.

We would like to note that, when limited to the most common symbols, stringed-instrument tablature notations are very close to drum tablature ones. As a consequence, it is easy to derive one from another, and to obtain a system with quite the same performances. Figure 17 presents a screenshot of a simple composition and editing system for stringed-instrument tablatures and whose interpretation rules are very close to the ones presented Table 6.

This basic prototype can be enriched with more symbols, for instance to model rhythm and particular playing modes. Table 7 presents some of the interpretation rules modelling the interpretation of such a document, and a screenshot of the corresponding system is on Figure 18.

CONCLUSION AND FUTURE TRENDS

In this chapter, we have faced the lack of software taking advantage of pen-interaction in order to compose and edit online structured documents with musical notations. We have presented a new generic approach to design such pen-based systems. It aims at interpreting the strokes eagerly, that is, directly as the user composes his documents. The main component of this approach is a formalism modelling how each symbol of the document can be interpreted: its originality is the coupling of a global vision of the analysed document in order to model in which structural context an element can be identified, with a local vision of this element in order to interpret its shape and that of its components. This formalism can be adapted to a large panel of structured documents. In order to emphasize its genericity, we have presented how it can be applied to interpret documents with various notations, such as traditional musical scores, plainchant scores, drum tablatures and finally stringed-instrument tablatures.

Future trends will aim at exploiting such pen-based systems at a larger scale, in order to offer an access to this technology to a larger public. People from various domains can potentially be interested in pen interaction. First, thanks to its aspect of play, pen-based software for pedagogue purposes will facilitate the initiation and learning of music and its notations. Pedagogy concerns the learning of music theory, the intuitive and instantaneous composition (e.g., harmonisation exercises), ear formation exercises (e.g., musical dictations), and so forth. Examples of potentially interested targets are music schools, conservatoires, and universities. Secondly, pen-based music software is of great interest for composers and arrangers, whether they are amateurs or professionals. Such systems can be very useful in the process of composition itself (archiving of the drafts and of new ideas) as well as for the deposit of scores to author-composer society.

As far as the prototypes we have developed are concerned, many improvements can be achieved in order to make them more usable systems. Of course, we will have to add new symbols in the classical music notation system, for instance articulations (staccato, bow strokes, etc.), expressions, all the clefs, ties, and so forth. A composition on at least the two staves of the piano is often used: it will thus be conceivable. Thanks to the formalism associated to our method, such improvements will be straightforward. It will be essential to be able to hear the music and so for instance to propose an output in the MIDI format. The play of the music can be done, on the one hand, incrementally, that is, each time a new hand-drawn note is recognized, or, on the other hand, once the document is finished, that is, with the rhythm. A main step would be to couple pen-based systems with more traditional, keyboard and mouse-based musical editing software. Then, the user could exploit the advantages of both: on the one hand, he could draw musical notations from very different domains in a very intuitive and user-friendly way, as he usually does on paper, and, on the other hand, he could benefit of all the functionalities of classical software, such as the verification of the coherency of the notations, the formatting of the documents (e.g., the alignment of its elements), and so forth. Of course, pen-based systems could propose to save the documents in very widespread formats, such as MusicXML, in order to use them afterwards in any software able to deal with a file in such a format.

Finally, we will also have to define well-formalized test protocols in order to evaluate the usability and the user-friendliness of such pen-based prototypes.

ACKNOWLEDGMENT

The authors would like to thank Guy Lorette, Professor at the University of Rennes 1, from the IMADOC (IMAges and DOCuments) team of the IRISA (Institut de Recherche en Informatique et Systèmes Aléatoires) for his contribution to this work and his precious advices.

This project partially benefits from the financial support of the Brittany Region.

REFERENCES

Anquetil, E., & Bouchereau, H. (2002). Integration of an online handwriting recognition system in a smart phone device. In *Proceedings of the Sixteenth International Conference on Pattern Recognition (ICPR'02)* (pp. 192-195).

Anstice, J., Bell, T., Cockburn, A., & Setchell, M. (1996). The design of a pen-based musical input system. In *Proceedings of the Sixth Australian Conference on Computer-Human Interaction (OzChi 96)* (pp. 260-267).

Blostein, D., Lank, E., Rose, A., & Zanibbi, R. (2002). User interfaces for on-line diagram recognition. In D. Blostein & Y. B. Kwon (Eds.), *Graphics recognition: Algorithms and applications, Lecture notes in computer science* (Vol. 2390, pp. 92-103). Springer.

Forsberg, A. S., Dieterich, M., & Zeleznik, R. C. (1998). The music notepad. In *Proceedings of the ACM Symposium on User Interface Software and Technology* (pp. 203-210).

Forsberg, A., Holden, L., Miller, T., & Zeleznik, R. (October 2002; 2005). The music notepad for tablet PC, Retrieved May 29, 2007, from http://graphics.cs.brown.edu/research/music/tpc.html

George, S. (2003). Online pen-based recognition of music notation with artificial neural networks. *Computer Music Journal, 27*(2), 70-79.

Goldberg, D., & Richardson, C. (1993). Touch-typing with a stylus. In *Proceedings of InterCHI'93 Conference on Human Factors in Computing Systems* (pp. 80-87).

Lank, E. H. (2003). A retargetable framework for interactive diagram recognition. In *Proceedings of the International Conference on Document Analysis and Recognition (ICDAR'03)* (pp. 185-189).

Macé, S., & Anquetil, E. (2006). A generic approach for pen-based user interface development. In C. Pribeanu, G. Santucci, J. Vanderdonckt, & G. Calvary (Eds.), *Computer-aided design of user interfaces V*. In *Proceedings of the Sixth International Conference on Computer-Aided Design of User Interfaces (CADUI'06)* (pp. 57-70). Springer-Verlag.

Macé, S., & Anquetil, E. (2006). A generic approach for eager interpretation of online handwritten structured documents. In *Proceedings of the Eighteenth International Conference on Pattern Recognition (ICPR'06)* (pp. 1106-1109).

Macé, S., Anquetil, E., & Coüasnon, B. (2005). A generic method to design pen-based systems for structured document composition: Development of a musical score editor. In *Proceedings of the first Workshop on Improving and Assessing Pen-Based Input Techniques* (pp. 15-22).

Macé, S., Anquetil, E., Garrivier, E., & Bossis, B. (2005). A pen-based musical score editor. In *Proceedings of the International Computer Music Conference (ICMC'05)* (pp. 415-418).

Mitobe, Y., Miyao, H., & Maruyama, M. (2004). A fast HMM algorithm based on stroke lengths for online recognition of handwritten music scores. In *Proceedings of the Ninth International Workshop on Frontiers in Handwriting Recognition (IWFHR'04)* (pp. 521-526).

Miyao, H., & Maruyama, M. (2004). An online handwritten music score recognition system. In *Proceedings of the Seventeenth International Conference on Pattern Recognition (ICPR'04)* (pp. 461-464).

Mouchère, H., & Anquetil, E. (2006). A unify strategy to deal with different natures of reject. In *Proceedings of the Eighteenth International Conference on Pattern Recognition (ICPR'06)* (pp. 792-795).

Nakagawa, M., Machii, K., Kato, N., & Souya, T. (1993). Lazy recognition as a principle of pen interfaces. In *Proceedings of the ACM Conference Companion on Human Factors in Computing Systems (InterCHI'93)* (pp. 89-90).

Ng, E., Bell, T., & Cockburn, A. (1998). Improvements to a pen-based musical input system. In *Proceedings of the Australian Conference on Computer-Human Interaction (OzCHI'98)* (pp. 239-252).

Plamondon, R., & Srihari, S. (2000). On-line and off-line handwriting recognition: A comprehensive survey. *IEEE Transactions on Pattern Analysis and Machine Intelligence, 1*(22), 63-84.

Silberger, K. (1996). Putting composers in control. *IBM Research, 34*(4), 14-15.

Chapter XIII
MusicStory:
An Autonomous, Personalized Music Video Creator

David A. Shamma
Yahoo! Research Berkeley, USA

John Woodruff
Ohio State University, USA

Bryan Pardo
Northwestern University, USA

ABSTRACT

This chapter covers some of the challenges in storytelling with music. We describe the MusicStory system which creates music videos from personal media (audio and image) collections. Using a song's lyrics, MusicStory finds and presents word/image associations. It takes the emotional experience of listening to music, amplifies it and heightens its visceral appeal by externalizing concrete and visual imagery intrinsic in the music. The retrieved images vary in their association—some semantically on point and some distant. The flow of imagery moves with the pace of the song: providing quick transitions through fast songs, and leisurely transitions through slower songs. In addition, MusicStory uses vocal segmentation to direct the video and alter how images are displayed. We discuss the creative and technical challenges in this work as well as how it was deployed in several fashions.

INTRODUCTION

Our personal media collections, from the music on an iPod to the images in a photo album, reflect who we are as individuals. Public media collections, from commercial image repositories, to the songs in a band's MySpace account, reflect who we are as a culture. Today, these media collections are increasingly stored online. Visual images can be found on such photo sharing Web sites as Flickr. Music sites, such as iTunes, eMusic, and Rhapsody make large collections of music audio available on the internet. Lyrics are available at sites such as Leos Lyrics. This provides unprecedented opportunity to explore the relationships between imagery, audio, and text documents through the use of autonomous information systems.

In the work described in this chapter, we illustrate the construction of MusicStory. MusicStory is an autonomous music video creator that takes an audio file (such as an mp3 or wma file) as input and outputs a music video file (MPG, or mpv). The music video is created by finding links between the audio file and associated image and text documents. The approach we take is hybrid and autonomous. Many approaches in music information systems, or information systems for that matter, use task constraints to limit the scope of the problem at hand to provide a more tractable solution. In building MusicStory, an autonomous music video creator, we identify the task as what defines the domain. Its constraint is the starting point, a single audio file. Using this file as a search key, MusicStory finds, and collects all the necessary files to create a music video. This approach is hybrid as it uses both audio and the metadata text to build a complete photo narrative. It is also autonomous because the user simply selects the audio document for which to build a video and clicks "go." MusicStory then creates the music video, without any need for text querying by the user. Figure 1 shows an example of a created photo narrative from MusicStory.

In this chapter, we first discuss several similar music video creation systems, then turning to our music video creator, we identify several components needed to make a music video, autonomous or otherwise. Next, we discuss how to search and find the necessary supporting media for the video track as well as discuss features of the source audio and how it can be used in music video creation and how it can be found autonomously. Finally, we discuss how to make the final composition.

BACKGROUND

Network Arts

In 2004, Shamma, Owlsey, Hammond, Bradshaw, and Budzik began working with autonomous photo narrative generation using various video sources using images found from online communities. They codified installation pieces that form linkages between video and image sources available on the Internet as "Network Arts." These installations place the computer as a reflector of popular culture. Moving away from the traditional role of a computational tool, Network Arts fuses art and the Internet to expose cultural connections people draw implicitly but rarely consider directly. Creating new media experiences using World Wide Web as a reflection of cultural reality to highlight and explore the relations between ideas that compose the fabric of our daily lives. The first Network Arts installation, *Imagination Environment* (see Figure 2) reflects these links back to us; from the virtual world into the real. Using any video stream as its starting point, it discovers images linked to the words being said, and shows us the flow of connections between ideas and images that we ourselves crafted. Exploiting the connectivity of

Figure 1. Salient Flickr Images found from the lyrics of a Radiohead song Street Spirit (Fade Out). *"Rows of houses, all bearing down on me". Flickr Photos from left to right by: Locutis, brappy!, Jan the mason, and yoppy. Used under Creative Commons licensing: see endnotes 1–4 for more photo details.*

Figure 2. The Imagination Environment at Second City Chicago

the Web and the core technologies of information retrieval, it opens a window to our world that is a machine's "imagination" of who and what we are. Search engines, Web logs (blogs), Web portals, and individual Web sites are reflections of our cultural reality. They represent a set of created systems that expose and heighten the connections we use, but rarely see, both in our minds and in the online world. The images and media online are linked and indexed by how we refer to them in a variety of contexts: blogs, news feeds, and Web pages. By exposing both their results and processes, these systems reflect and reuse the mundane, the available, and the purely popular as art. In doing so, the system itself is an artistic agent, gathering, sifting, and presenting our own reality back to us as it moves through the Web, seeking information.

The *Imagination Environment* uses advanced information retrieval techniques on media streams that are invisible to us. When we "watch" TV, the TV receiver is reading (actually decoding) the closed captioning (CC) stream and using it to identify what is being said. Then, by exploiting indexing mechanisms within search engines, it

finds distinct images and displays them as juxtaposition, to externalize either the canonical or the popular culture.

The TV, here the 2003 State of the Union address, plays on the center tile as related media is presented in the surrounding tiles. The installation uses the words and phrases in the dialog to build the context of the scenes portrayed through the surrounding screens of images.

President George W. Bush mentions that Saddam Hussein is in violation of several United Nations agreements during the 2003 State of the Union address. He says the word 'agreement,' and the image of a proposed Palestine-Israel partition from the second Oslo Interim Agreement of 1995 is displayed on the neighboring screen. See Figure 3. The audience is reminded of other senses of the word agreement in the world, juxtaposed with the source's (President Bush's) words.

The Imagination Environment externalizes the zeitgeist of the online community. It is an autonomous emotional amplifier that is built to externalize media broadcasts in real time as illustrated in Figure 3. It watches movies as either a DVD or TV feed. While it watches, it searches

Figure 3. An example of visually expanding the space of free association found by the Imagination Environment. Here the term 'agreement,' from G. W. Bush's 2003 State of the Union Address, is juxtaposed with a picture of the Oslo II Interim Agreement of 1995, one of the Google Image results for that term.

Agreement

``He (Saddam Hussein) systematically violated that agreement"

online sources to find images and media clips related to the content of the media. It presents a selection of the results, images as found objects, during its performance. The Imagination Environment understands the structure of a scene of video; it builds a representation of the scene's context, uses that context to find new media and run a performance. The Imagination Environment has been reviewed in the *New York Times* (Mirapaul, 2004) and shown as a public display at Second City Chicago from April 2004 to July 2005, ACM SIGGRAPH ETECH 2004, and *Wired Magazine*'s NextFest 2005 (Anderson, 2005) and NextFest 2006. MusicStory builds on the foundation of the Imagination Environment by incorporating tagged image search with automated examination of audio cues and lyrics search to create a unified artistic experience. Instead of externalizing the online zeitgeist, MusicStory seeks to invoke personal memories by using private media content (mp3s and photos). This is described in greater detail in a later section.

Related Work

There has been much work in automatic music video creation. Our work bears the most likeness to P-Karaoke from Microsoft Research Asia (Hua, Lu, & Zhang, 2004). P-Karaoke selects personal home videos and images from a user's local documents to uses as the backdrop video projection during a karaoke performance. Since a user's local documents are often unstructured, it filters out the undesirable images. Undesirable images are typically those which are damaged by being burred or through bad exposure. Images which are duplicated on the user's local disk are also avoided.

P-Karaoke relies on the Microsoft DirectX framework for the video creation and both systems examine the beat of the audio track. P-Karaoke (blurred, bad exposure, duplicates, etc.) selects capriciously from the final candidate list. P-Karaoke uses the beat of the audio track, relying on exact beat transitions to structure the video creation.

This requires a syllable by syllable time-stamped lyric file to be associated with the audio file. Since such files must be created manually through a time-consuming process, this limits the wider applicability of P-Karaoke.

In addition to P-Karaoke, Microsoft Research Asia developed Photo2Video (Hua, Lu, et al. 2003). Starting with the user selecting a set of photographs or a photo-graphic series, Photo-2Video identifies a set of key-frame sequences. With the key frames, several motion trajectories are generated in a Ken Burn's documentary style. Here the camera pans across several salient elements in the photo as determined through face recognition or attention maps. The motion sequences are then aligned with a user specified song, using event onsets detected in the frequency domain of the song as starting candidate points for the sequences.

Existing commercial music video creators, such as Muvee's AutoProducer and Microsoft's PhotoStory 3 require significant user interaction to create the video. Typically, the user must specify the song's speed and hand select the desired local photos. These systems provide assisted music video creation; they construct photo narratives with an audio soundtrack.

MusicStory produces videos autonomously, building a video from person photo collections when possible and public collections when needed. MusicStory discovers images (locally or online) linked to the words in the lyrics. The end result is a video which brings new and unexpected imagery to the viewer, based on images, textually indexed, and related to the song itself. Since MusicStory's images are semantically tied (via Web-indexing and community tagging) to the song and its lyrics, it brings a new experience, a musical narrative with discovered imagery that requires no work on the users part. The following section describes MusicStory in depth.

MusicStory

Like a human listener, MusicStory processes the lyrics in the music and these lyrics bring forth associations with images. The imagery chosen by MusicStory is defined by the set of links between words drawn from the lyrics and image-word associations contained in a social network, either private or public. As the images are found, it presents them to the audience, creating an on-the fly music video, heightening, clarifying, and exposing the connections between words, ideas, and images that we are often unaware of, until shown. Figure 1 shows a slide-by-slide expansion of the imagery from the lyrics of a Radiohead song.

The image associations that MusicStory presents amplify the emotional experience and heighten its visceral appeal by externalizing the concrete imagery intrinsic in the lyrics. Some images depict the expected relation found in the song, while others present a juxtaposition between the song's meaning and the meaning found within the social network. Our approach focuses on the creation of a photo narrative, to compliment the music and not the strict alignment of images to lyrics, as we have shown in the Imagination Environment. Artistically speaking, the strict alignment of images-word pairs to lyrics or spoken dialog provides an amplification of meaning through free association (Shamma, 2005). For MusicStory, we rely on this amplification of meaning in the context of the song itself, and not the individual words being communicated.

MusicStory uses public media to retrieve images with popular relevance, relying on Web frequency as a measure of familiarity and salience (Shamma, Owsley, Bradshaw, & Hammond, 2004), returning images that reflect current pop-culture meanings. More personal images can be found by focusing the retrieval to smaller social networks, such as personal photo-sharing sites.

For example, the word "home" from the song *Sweet Home Alabama*, retrieves different associations from different repositories. Google's ranking returns a canonical photo of a home from a realtor's Web site. Flickr, in contrast, returns photos people took in their home, in this case of their child. The combination of image repositories (popular, canonical, and personal) provide a balance of associations which the agent uses to aid in the art's creation and assists in the audience's understanding of the work (Kandinsky, 1994; Shamma, 2005).

While it is possible to use simple search to create a sequence of images overlaying music, that does not make for a successful piece. Successful integration of sound and image relies on an intimate knowledge of the media itself, considering available image resources (repositories, number of images per term), musical parameters (tempo, dynamics, density, lyrics) and the output format (screen size, playback bit rate). To do this, MusicStory assumes the role of a director, concerning itself with the overall flow and pacing of the resulting multimedia performance. In order to build a music video, MusicStory must identify three features of the song. First, it must find the lyrics to guide the narrative. It must identify the overall pace of the song. Finally, it must identify points of significant structural change in the music. Currently MusicStory searches for the points where a lead instrument or vocalist starts and stops in a performance.

MusicStory's director is an Artistic Information Agent. This agent is a variant of the Information Management Assistant (Budzik, 2003) used in Information Retrieval. The agent's architecture shows several adapters that let it access online information sources. The core functionality is separated into four basic components. The Artistic Analyzers for the MusicStory consist of a listener and a presenter. The listener feeds in the audio information from a source and the metadata (some metadata, such as lyrics, is not carried within the source file). The presenter controls how the final movie is created. Table 1 outlines MusicStory's general workflow.

Fetch Metadata

To make music videos, MusicStory borrows from the Imagination Environment's information flow (Shamma, Owlsey, Hammond, & Bradshaw, 2004). Starting with an audio file (MP3, wav, wma, etc.), the metadata must be extracted. MusicStory uses populated metadata to identify song, album, and artist name. If the audio file is not populated with metadata, MusicStory queries the user for the missing information. Alternatively, a music audio fingerprinting service, such as Shazam (Wang, 2003) may be used by the to identify the song.

Finding Lyrics

Speech-to-text on singing is a well-known unsolved problem (Mellody, Bartsch, & Wakefield, 2003), due to the nonstandard nature of the speech and the large amount of background noise (read: the musical accompaniment) present in the recording. In fact, many humans have great difficulty in performing this task (see http://www.kissthisguy.com/ for examples of misheard lyrics). For this reason, we concentrated on finding song lyrics in online lyric repositories. There are many strategies for finding song lyrics from audio metadata like artist, title, and album information. Using a general-purpose search engine to find lyrics introduces difficulties. As an alternative, MusicStory uses Leos Lyrics, an online lyrics library whose specialized search engines allow a direct lookup from the metadata.

Table 1. MusicStory's steps in music video creation

1.	Fetch Metadata
2.	Lyrics Search
3.	Image Search
4.	Pace/Beat Match
5.	Find Vocal Segments
6.	Determine Slide Transition and Duration Times
7.	Make Slideshow

Direct search does not always work. For example, the song *Smells Like Teen Spirit* by Nirvana appeared first on the 1991 album *Nevermind*, then on numerous compilations. If MusicStory looks up *Smells Like Teen Spirit* lyrics from Nirvana's self-titled 2002 compilation, our lyrics database will return no results. Similarly, Tori Amos's cover of this song may not also return any results. When a search failure is encountered, the agent performs a roll back strategy, dropping the album from the query. If no results are returned again, the artist is dropped from the search key and only the song is used. This ensures the most exact lyric match can be found. If the song is not in the database, we prompt for lyrics. As search extraction improves, it is possible to "screen scrape" the lyrics from a general-purpose search using engines like Yahoo! Search. A similar rollback strategy would be equally applicable in this situation.

Finding Images

MusicStory searches for images from a user's social network space. While many users keep photos on their personal computers, often they are unorganized, uncommented, and untagged. We use Flickr to find images within the personal network of an individual. First, the lyrics are stripped of common stop words (common words, "if", "he", "the", and so forth, in the English and Spanish languages). It then searches for each salient term in the lyrics, using Flickr's public API. MusicStory looks for the photos which match each term by searching tags and comments. If the personalized (user-specific) search returns no images, MusicStory then begins searching through the user's Flickr contacts, first searching contacts marked Family then contacts marked Friends and finally, upon failure, a general Flickr search is performed. Like the lyric search, MusicStory uses this rollback strategy to ensure an image is found for each candidate term, while providing the most personalized relevant image.

Finding Pace

When building a Network Arts installation, one must remember the audience. It is important the audience be engaged and connected with the installation and its performance. Keeping this connection will allow the piece to create more emotional and captivating moments with the viewer, following Kandinsky's model of expressionism (Kandinsky, 1994). Foremost, the agent must determine the pacing of the installation and hence performance. There are two pacing metrics, the tempo of the source (input) media and the desired tempo of the overall (output) performance.

The tempo of a slow ballad does not match that of a live speech or a fast hip-hop song. MusicStory bases its rate for presenting images on the pace of the media. To accommodate several media sources, we created a model of presentation for the agent. The model's presentation pace is set to complement the pace of the source media. As a result, an effective flow state for the overall installation is achieved. To keep the flow state engaging, thresholds are set to keep the images from changing too quickly or too slowly, which prevents the audience from being overwhelmed or becoming bored.

A simple implementation of Mihaly Csikszentmihalyi's flow model (Csikszentmihalyi, 1990) suffices for our purposes. While, Csikszentmihalyi describes human activities as a compromise between two components, challenges and skills, we focus on the flow channel itself and the neighboring anxiety and boredom outside the channel. MusicStory needed a descriptor of the pace of the song to implement our modified Csikszentmihalyi pacing model. In a previous Network Arts installation, which used broadcast media, Shamma et al. (2004) estimated pace by using the rate of the closed captioning feed. Given the input rate and knowledge of how fast information can be displayed (output rate), Csikszentmihalyi's flow model can be put to use by the agent to optimize the display and interaction.

In our current work, pacing is affected by song tempo and the agent's artistic intent. The directing agent adjusts how long a image is displayed and the speed of transition between images, influenced by placement of peaks in the volume of the audio. The final slide show pacing does not map strictly to beat-by-beat image transitions, but visually moves at a speed complimentary to a multiple of the beat. To make this adjustment, the agent first needs to know the general pace of the song. For many kinds of popular music, good synchronization points for the video correspond to peaks in the root-mean-squared amplitude of the audio signal (RMS). To use RMS for this application, we must look at the structure of the digitally encoded song.

Finding the beat in music is often problematic (Pardo, 2004), especially in cases of odd-meter and shifting metric levels. It is, however, simple to find the average pace at which percussive events occur in a passage of music. For the purposes of video pacing, this turns out to be an important and useful measure

$$RMS = \sqrt{\frac{\sum_{i=1}^{n} x_i^2}{n}}, where \begin{cases} x = \text{sample's amplitude} \\ n = \text{window size} \end{cases}$$

$$(1)$$

To find the event pace, we compute the RMS amplitude of the audio at time t by applying basic RMS to a 100 millisecond window, centered on time t, where n is the number of samples in the window and x is the amplitude of a single sample. For simplicity, a compressed audio file is converted to linearly encoded PCM audio before RMS amplitude is calculated.

Figure 4 shows the RMS amplitude for the first 10 seconds of Michael Jackson's *Billie Jean*. An average of the peak distances (1025ms) yields the overall pace for the song (about 59 pulses per minute). By walking through the entire song, one can easily detect sections whose pacing gives the

music a half-time feel. This works quite well in the Pop/Rock genre. More complex music styles require more sophisticated techniques (Pikrakis, Antonopoulos, & Theodoridis, 2004).

Finding Structure

The next step requires MusicStory to identify the presence of vocals (hence lyrics) during a song. The ability to detect vocal segments allows the directing agent to tighten its focus on the photo narrative aspects of the music video. Considering the ease with which human listeners can detect whether or not a singing voice is present in a musical recording, it may be surprising that automatic detection of singing voice is an active area of research within the music information retrieval community. Identifying whether a vocal part is present in a given segment of an audio signal is challenging because of both the timbral diversity the human voice is capable of and that many commercial recordings include dozens of instrument parts and are laden with effects processing, which often obstructs any salient characteristics of the voice. Without prior structural knowledge of the vocal or instrument signals, or knowledge of how many or what types of signals are in the recording, we cannot directly attribute components or sound events (notes or percussion hits) in the song to

Figure 4. The RMS values for the intro to Billie Jean. An average of the peak distances (1025ms) yields an overall pace for the song.

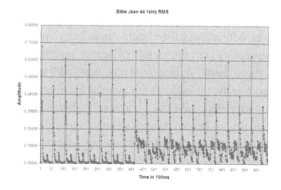

individual instrument or vocal parts. As a result, researchers must search for signal features that are common to all voices, whether they are male or female and whether the singer is Etta James or John Ashcroft. These features and the classification method used must also be salient in the face of significant obstruction from instruments in the recording. Both of these constraints motivate looking for characteristic differences between purely instrumental audio segments and instrument plus voice segments rather than directly searching for the vocal waveform or spectrum.

Berenzweig and Ellis (2001) locate singing voice segments by incorporating the acoustic classifier of a speech recognizer to identify speech-like sounds in the music signal. The speech classifier is trained to identify English phonemes, so when the input signal is English speech, clear-cut classification to a particular phoneme is achieved for the majority of time segments (or syllables). Berenzweig and Ellis make novel use of this classifier and show that when music signals with and without singing voice are processed, the classification of those segments that contain a vocal part is somewhat similar to the classification of speech and is characteristically different than the classification of the purely instrumental segments. Berenzweig and Ellis propose a number of statistical measures to identify transitions in the nature of the speech classifier's output—which are then treated as transitions between vocal and nonvocal segments.

Kim and Whitman (2002) use a band-pass filter (200-2000 Hz) to eliminate energy from signals that fall outside of the probable vocal range. They argue that any remaining instruments within this range will likely be broadband in nature (percussion instruments), and thus propose using *harmonicity*—the proportion of harmonic vs. inharmonic energy—as an additional feature to distinguish between vocal and percussive sounds. However, the assertion that only voice and percussive instruments have significant energy in the 200-2000 Hz frequency band is unrealistic

because nearly all harmonic instruments could also have energy concentrated in this range, thus the success of this approach seems largely dependent on the vocal part having significantly more energy in this range than other harmonic instruments.

Maddage, Wan, Xu, and Wang (2004) propose incorporating top-down musical knowledge in identifying vocal segments. They use rhythm tracking in order to segment the audio signal according to quarter-note length frames. Each frame is then processed using the *twice-iterated composite Fourier transform* (TICFT). They claim that voice signals tend to have a narrower bandwidth than most instrument signals, and that this characteristic is exaggerated in the lower order coefficients of the TICFT. A simple linear threshold on the cumulative energy in the low TICFT coefficients is used to determine whether a singing voice was active in a particular frame. Three heuristic rules based on simple musical knowledge and beat information are used to refine the determination of vocal segments. While the heuristics do improve classification for music that adheres to the imposed constraints (the meter of the song is 4/4, vocal segments must be at least two measures long, etc.), testing on a larger database of recordings is necessary to determine whether the approach is robust when given any musical input. Also, while certainly some instruments commonly found in popular music do have a wider bandwidth than vocal signals—percussion, guitar or piano—this claim is not well substantiated in the general case, and it is unclear that this characteristic would be robust in recordings with many instruments present.

Nwe and Wang (2004) observe that audio segments that contain both voice and instruments tend to have more high-frequency energy than purely instrumental segments. They report a systematic difference in *log-frequency power coefficients* (LFPCs) between instrumental and instrument plus vocal segments. They show that the instrument plus voice segments have more power than instrumental segments in frequency sub-bands above 1 kHz, with the largest difference in the highest frequencies, where vocal segments have over 10 dB greater signal power than nonvocal segments. This feature along with a measure of rhythmic tempo and overall signal loudness are used in conjunction with a hidden Markov model for the identification of vocal segments.

This systematic spectral difference between audio segments with and without singing voice is a promising detection feature because it does not impose specific constraints on the structure of the vocal part (e.g., pitch range, formant structure, bandwidth) and appears to be robust in the face of obstruction from different types of instrument signals. However, such a simple feature hardly seems adequate to truly identify whether a human voice is present in the audio, and most likely reflects a difference between audio segments that do and do not contain their lead musical part (whether that part is a voice or a saxophone). Most likely, the systematic increase in high-frequency energy in the segments that contain a vocal part is due to either conscious or subconscious decisions by the recording and mixing engineers to make the leading musical part (the voice in this case) the *brightest* and most audible component of the recording. For MusicStory, the goal is to find significant structural events in the music to help guide video creation. We use the systematic spectral difference cue to find the places where a lead harmonic instrument (typically the singer, in a song with lyrics) is introduced, letting us structure the video in a way that responds to the introduction and removal of musically important elements in the audio. While the current system uses the systematic spectral difference between vocal and nonvocal segments in pop songs, future versions of VocalSearch may use more in-depth methods to find musically salient points to change the video presentation style.

To explore the validity of this systematic difference between vocal and nonvocal audio segments, we conducted an informal study on 155, 3-6 second

audio segments from 25 rock and popular music recordings. We calculated log-frequency power coefficients for each segment and compared the average LFPCs over all segments that contained a vocal part (75 segments) to the average LFPCs over all instrumental segments (80 segments). Table 2 lists the songs that these short segments were extracted from.

LFPCs function as a low dimensional representation of the magnitude of each segment's frequency spectrum and capture the general spectral shape of the audio signal. To calculate LFPCs, the short-time Fourier transform (STFT) of each segment is taken using Equation (2). Here, W represents a 93 ms Hanning window, τ is the center of a time index and ω is the frequency of analysis.

$$X(\tau, \omega) = \frac{1}{\sqrt{2p}} \int_{-\infty}^{\infty} W(t-\tau)\, x(t)e^{-iwt}\, dt \quad (2)$$

The Fourier transform captures detailed information about how the signal energy is distributed as a function of frequency and time. In order to create a more general characterization of the frequency content over the entire audio segment, we take the mean over all time steps and divide the signal into 13 frequency sub-bands using Equation (3). Frequency sub-bands are spaced between 130 Hz and 16 kHz according to the equivalent rectangular bandwidth (ERB) scale (Moore & Glasberg, 1983). In Equation (3), k represents the index of the frequency sub-band, N is the number of time steps in $X(\tau, \omega)$, f_k represents the center frequency of the sub-band in Hz, and b_k is the sub-band bandwidth in Hz.

$$S(k) = \frac{1}{N} \sum_{w=f_k-\frac{b_k}{2}}^{f_k+\frac{b_k}{2}} \sum_{\forall t} |X(t,w)| \quad (3)$$

We then calculate log-frequency power coefficients using (4), where M denotes the number of

Table 2. A list of songs of varying genres used to determine the presence of vocal segments

Artist	Song	Genre
Fiona Apple	Get Gone	Pop/Rock
Ben Folds Five	Narcolepsy	Pop/Rock
The Dave Matthews Band	Lie In Our Graves	Pop/Rock
Ronnie James Dio	Holy Diver	Classic Rock, Heavy Metal
Astrud Gilberto and Stan Getz	The Girl from Ipanema	Jazz, World Music
Al Green	Not Tonight	R & B
Hall & Oates	Private Eyes	Pop/Rock
Hall & Oates	You Make My Dreams	Pop/Rock
Jimi Hendrix	All Along the Watchtower	Classic Rock
Michael Jackson	Rock With You	Pop, R & B
Jane's Addiction	Been Caught Stealing	Alternative Rock
Led Zeppelin	The Song Remains the Same	Classic Rock
Bob Marley	Three Little Birds	Reggae
Juana Molina	Martin Fierro	World Music, Electronic, Pop
Nirvana	Drain You	Alternative Rock
Nirvana	Heart Shaped Box	Alternative Rock
Jim O'Rourke	Memory Lame	Pop/Rock
Pearl Jam	Alive	Alternative Rock
Pearl Jam	Last Exit	Alternative Rock
Pink Floyd	Time	Classic Rock
Radiohead	The Tourist	Alternative Rock
Lionel Ritchie	All Night Long	Pop, R & B
Stereolab	Diagonals	Pop/Rock, Electronic
U2	Where the Streets Have No Name	Pop/Rock
Wilco	Hummingbird	Alternative Rock

analysis frequencies, ω, associated with frequency sub-band, k.

$$LFPC(k) = 10\log_{10}\left(\frac{S(k)}{M}\right) \qquad (4)$$

In Figure 5, we show the mean LFPCs for both vocal and instrumental segments and the difference between the two. The figure supports Nwe and Wang's claim that vocal segments tend to have more high-frequency energy than purely instrumental segments, however the difference found here is considerably more subtle than the one New and Wang presented (2004). We notice the greatest LFPC difference in the 11th, 12th, and 13th sub-bands (roughly 5-16 kHz) where we see an average difference of about 4 dB.

Since volumes tend to swell and drop over the duration of the song, this must be determined locally, across 25-30 second segments (about five or six slices in Figure 5). Simple k-means clustering can be used to identify the onset of vocal or nonvocal segments within a localized slice. We find this technique to be effective for MusicStory's purpose, which is to say the technique works well on standard rock/pop recordings one might find on an iPod or personal video device. Our end result is a song segmented into vocal and nonvocal partitions (see Figure 6).

Figure 5. (left) The mean log-frequency power coefficients for 80 instrumental and 75 vocal audio segments. (right) The mean difference in log-frequency power coefficients between vocal and instrumental audio segments (LFPC$_{vocal}$ - LFPC$_{inst}$).

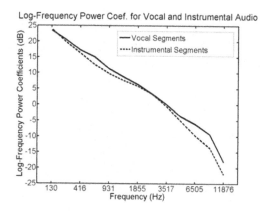 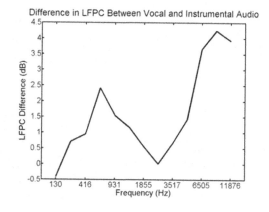

Using Transitions

MusicStory creates a photo slide show of the lyrics set to the source music. The images tell a different narrative during the vocal segments. The lyrics tell a story. To preserve the story, during these segments, images are shown in the order of the lyrics. During the nonvocal segments, a more general thematic slideshow is shown, using lyric terms with high frequency, ordered by frequency, see Figure 7. An introduction segment is added with images from the search for the band's name and the song's title.

To make the actual transitions, MusicStory uses the hint from our RMS pace estimate. From previous work, we find that images need to be visible for at least 900 ms for the viewer to be able to see and gather the image association (Shamma et al, 2004). The agent adjusts each photo's duration and the dissolve transition speed between photos using the RMS pace hint. The initial version of MusicStory uses the hint to select one of three categories: slow, medium, and fast. Table 3 shows the average display time per frame and number of transition frames for each category. Each category has a preset slide duration and transition speed. The duration and transition times for each

Figure 6. A wave form with annotated vocal and nonvocal segments

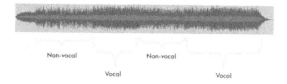

category follow common video direction practice (Groening & Cohen, 2002). The output video file contains the audio in the same or similar format as the source audio. The video can be encoded with any variable bit-rate suitable for JPEG based videos, we chose to use Microsoft's ImageVideo Codec v9, which is designed for this style of application.

Targeting Demographics

By looking at onset in the amplitude and frequency domains, we can determine the overall pace of a song and some vocal segmentation information. Our results are positive albeit fragile with respect towards our demographic. We targeted MusicStory towards a 25-35 year old, iPodded techno-savvy group, which implies a certain genre

Figure 7. A song tagged with vocal and non-vocal segments is composed into lyrical sections and thematic (salient terms) sections

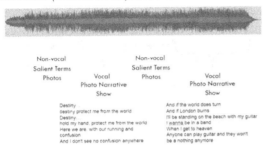

Table 3. The frame duration time and transition frame count for each given hint from the RMS pace estimate. Each photo is displayed for 60 frames plus the transition times for that rate.

Hint	Transition Duration	Number of Frames
Slow (≤ 55 bmp)	33.3 ms	90 frames
Medium (56—85 bmp)	25.0 ms	80 frames
Fast (>85 bmp)	16.6 ms	70 frames

of pop/rock songs which have been professionally engineered and recorded. Even within our genre, we had to handle certain exceptions. Bands like Radiohead and My Bloody Valentine often have slow moving songs with guitars covered in modulation effects, like flange and reverb. Looking for amplitude onset in these songs, using our method, returns abnormally high beats per minute (BPM) estimates greater than 175 BPM. We catch these exceptions by assuming high estimates are indeed slow songs. In the event that a *really* fast song is misclassified, a slow paced slideshow offers a stronger performance via juxtaposition than fast images to an even faster song. This works because MusicStory does not particularly rely on any one metric, rather it uses the information it can gather to help assist in the music video. Songs outside the genre, such as Chinese opera, will likely result in a poor video.

INSTALLATIONS

Our motivations for MusicStory centered on autonomous music video creation for new media devices. The hand held music/MP3 player has grown both in its ability and ubiquity. Stand alone players, now play DVD-like quality video. Integrated players, like cellphones, have large color displays also capable of video playback. The use case for these video enabled devices

provides something to hold and look at, and not something to hide in a jacket pocked during playback. MusicStory transforms the pure audio into a compelling multimedia experience. The personal version is available at http://www.infolab. northwestern.edu/musicstory.

Moving from the small to the silver screen, we deployed MusicStory in a large-scale, concert venue. We developed a five song set list, which was presented as one of three acts at Wired Magazine's NextMusic show on June 22, 2005. Jeff Tweedy of the band Wilco, the NextMusic's curator, used MusicStory to create lyric based photo narratives and presented the music videos between two live acts.

FUTURE WORK

Currently, MusicStory connects our personal audio with visuals from public and personal media sources accessible through search engines (Yahoo!, Google , etc.). MusicStory incorporates photo sharing Web sites, like Flickr.com, where tagged images are shared amongst a social network. There, personal music can be joined with personal images or the images from only the music of those listed as friends.

Each MusicStory music video is unique to one's personal experiences and photos—creating one's own personalized music video soundtrack.

We are working on incorporating more sophisticated techniques for finding hints. Instead of using an overall multiple of the beat of the song, we wish to find where the song changes time or introduces an interlude or a break and have the agent direct the visual performance accordingly. Additionally, we will introduce work on song structure identification to find such things as verse/chorus boundaries (Cooper & Foote, 2003) in the song to provide further direction. MusicStory could perform a call back to a prior image during a later chorus in the song.

Currently, we look for features present in 20 and 30 something pop/rock. MusicStory could be expanded to more demographics by first using genre classification. Genre knowledge can be used to identify which features and metrics to look for within the song. We also plan to incorporate our existing work on affect detection to steer the direction of the music video. High affect lyrics can be matched to similar high affect images, which can be found from reading the affect in the image's captions, tags, and comments as well as image analysis.

MusicStory is what is known as a "mashup," an application which combines media and content from several sources to make a new application. Flickr itself has an entire gallery of mashups submitted by third parties. Since MusicStory (and the Imagination Environment), mashup for storytelling through appropriated images has appeared in several installations. For instance, September 23, 2006 brought *StoryMashup* to the streets of New York City. Two hundred and fifty participants of this game, covered midtown Manhattan with Nokia camera phones. Each phone was sent a stream of keywords. Participants were scored with how quickly they could take a representative photo of words like "taxi," "fire," and "harmony." The game continued for 90 minutes. When the game was over, the photos served as illustrated images to stories presented on the Reuters billboard in Times Square (Tuulos & Scheible, 2006).

New directions in automated content creation incorporate new media content from our social spaces. As automatic music video creation moves forward, it will include new techniques in video remixing and location based content creation. These directions must be approached paying careful attention to the domain semantics, relying on techniques described via filmmakers, and hybrid approaches which utilize content found autonomously.

ACKNOWLEDGMENT

The authors thank Victor Friedberg and Melanie Cornwell from NextFest & Wired Magazine, Jeff Tweedy from the band Wilco, and Flickr. In addition, continuing thanks to the guiding comments of Kristian Hammond, Larry Birnbaum, and other members of the Intelligent Information Laboratory at Northwestern University.

REFERENCES

Anderson, C. (Ed.). (2005, June). NextFest.2005. *Wired Magazine, 13*(6), p. 24.

Berenzweig, A., & Ellis, D. (2001). Locating singing voice segments within music signals. In *Proceedings of the IEEE Workshop on Applications of Signal Processing to Audio and Acoustics,* New York.

Budzik, J. (2003, June). *Information access in context: Experiences with the Watson System.* Unpublished doctoral dissertation. Evanston, IL: Northwestern University.

Cooper, M., & Foote, J. (2003). Summarizing popular music via structural similarity analysis. In *Proceedings of the IEEE Workshop on Ap-*

plications of Signal Processing to Audio and Acoustics.

Csikszentmihalyi, M. (1990). *Flow: The psychology of optimal experience.* New York: Harper & Row.

Groening, M., & Cohen, D. X. (2002). The Simpsons. *DVD, Creator, director and producers notes from the season commentary.*

Hua, X.-S., Lu, L. et al. (2003). *Photo2Video.* ACM Multimedia (ACM MM 2003). Berkeley, CA.

Hua, X. S., Lu, L., & Zhang, H. J. (2004). P-karaoke: Personalized karaoke system. In *Proceedings of the 12th annual ACM international conference on Multimedia* (pp. 172-173). New York: ACM Press.

Kandinsky, W. (1994). Point and line to plane: A contribution to the analysis of pictoral elements. In W. Kandinsky, K. C. Lindsay, & P. Vergo (Eds.), *Complete writings on art* (pp. 528-699). Da Capo Press.

Kim, Y., & Whitman, B. (2002). Singer identification in popular music recordings using voice coding features. In *Proceedings of the International Symposium on Music Information Retrieval.*

Maddage, N., Wan, K. W., Xu, C., & Wang, Y. (2004). Singing voice detection using twice-iterated composite fourier transform. In *Proceedings of the IEEE International Conference on Multimedia and Expo.*

Mellody, M., Bartsch, M. A., & Wakefield, G. H. (2003). Analysis of vowels in sung queries for a music information retrieval system. *Journal of Intelligent Information Systems, 21*(1), 35-52.

Mirapaul, M. (2004, June 17). Art unfolds in a search for keywords. *The New York Times, CLIII(52883),* E5. New York.

Moore, B. C., & Glasberg, B. (1983). Suggested formulae for calculating auditory-filter band-widths and excitation patterns. *The Journal of the Acoustical Society of America, 74*(3), 750-753.

Nwe, T. L., & Wang, Y. (2004). Automatic detection of vocal segments in popular songs. In *Proceedings of the International Conference on Music Information Retrieval.* Barcelona, Spain.

Pardo, B. (2004). Tempo tracking with a single oscillator. In *Proceedings of the International Conference on Music Information Retrieval.* Barcelona, Spain.

Pikrakis, A., Antonopoulos, I., & Theodoridis, S. (2004). Music meter & tempo tracking from audio. In *Proceedings of the International Conference on Music Information Retrieval.* Barcelona, Spain.

Shamma, D. A. (2005, December). *Network arts: Defining emotional interaction in media arts and information retrieval.* Evanston, IL: Northwestern University.

Shamma, D. A., Owlsey, S., Hammond, K. J., Bradshaw, S., & Budzik, J. (2004). Network arts: Exposing cultural reality. In *Alternate track papers & posters of the 13th International Conference on World Wide Web* (pp. 41-47). New York: ACM Press.

Shamma, D. A., Owsley, S., Bradshaw, S., & Hammond, K. J. (2004). Using web frequency within multi-media exhibitions. In *Proceedings of the 12th International Conference on Multi-Media.* New York: ACM Press.

Tuulos, V., & Scheible, J. (2006) StoryMashup. Retrieved May 29, 2007, from http://www.story-mashup.org/

Wang, A. (2003). An industrial strength audio search algorithm. In *Proceedings of the 4th International Conference on Music Information Retrieval (ISMIR 2003),* Baltimore.

ENDNOTES

[1]   Locutis: *Rowing* http://www.flickr.com/photos/locutis/128808976/

[2]   brappy!: houses along Bellevue PI.E http://www.flickr.com/photos/aep/448564993/

[3]   Jan the mason: *hi-tech* http://www.flickr.com/photos/janthemanson/151503088/

[4]   yoppy: *R00012955* http://www.flickr.com/photos/spilt-milk/178059694/

Chapter XIV
Music Representation of Score, Sound, MIDI, Structure and Metadata All Integrated in a Single Multilayer Environment Based on XML

Adriano Baratè
Università degli Studi di Milano, Italy

Goffredo Haus
Università degli Studi di Milano, Italy

Luca A. Ludovico
Università degli Studi di Milano, Italy

ABSTRACT

In this chapter, we will analyze the heterogeneous contents involved in a comprehensive description of music, organizing them according to a multilayer structure. Each layer we can identify corresponds to a different degree of abstraction in music information. In particular, our approach arranges music contents in six layers: General, Music Logic, Structural, Notational, Performance, and Audio. In order to reflect such organization, we will introduce a new XML-based format, called MX, which is currently undergoing the IEEE standardization process (IEEE SA PAR1599). In an MX file, music symbols, printed scores, audio tracks, computer-driven performances, catalogue metadata, and graphic contents related to a single music piece can be linked and mutually synchronized within the same encoding. The aforementioned multilayer structure allows us to gather and organize heterogeneous contents, leaving them encoded in well-known and commonly used formats aimed at music description.

INTRODUCTION

Nowadays, music is considered an important matter in information and communication technology. Production, reproduction and representation of music by computer are different facets of the same problem: all these terms should be taken into account for a comprehensive description of music. In fact, if we want to provide an accurate and detailed description of a music piece, we cannot consider only its score. On the contrary, our approach requires a deep knowledge about the processes that bring to the final result, including compositional ideas, music structures and relationships, notated signs, sound generation, recording and reproduction.

Today it is possible to produce music and sound also by computer. In this context, the term *production* can mean generation, composition, but also transformation and manipulation of existent audio material. Computer based production is not only allowed, but even made easier and richer as regards expressive possibilities. We can cite the examples of computer aided composition, notation and editing software, digital instruments and effects, and so on.

Not only music production, but also *music reproduction* has gained benefit from digital knowledge and techniques. As regards digital music availability for its consumers, information technology has recently reached good results: let us cite portable and wearable audio devices or the phenomenon of online music sharing. In other words, music availability is now achieved both in space and in time, and music can be enjoyed both by remote and by future recipients.

About music reproduction on digital devices, a significant example is constituted by digital media supports and by file formats that make music available on computers. If we were able to include audio information coming from one or more media files as well as score symbolic representation, the overall description of the music piece would be more complete, opening a number of new scenarios that will be discussed later.

A directly related aspect is represented by music digitalization, in its most comprehensive meaning: not only performances, but also scores, graphic material, and related physical objects. We know that digital information is not intrinsically eternal (see Rothenberg, 1995 for a throughout discussion about the longevity of digital information), however—thanks to digitalization campaigns—documents can be preserved from the wearing out due to time and physical phenomena. After digitalization process, storage and networking technologies allow the preservation, the transmission, and the worldwide diffusion of music.

As regards information and communication technology, the state of the art of music production and reproduction by computer-based systems is noticeably advanced. But what about *music description*?

Before jumping into an in-depth discussion of the matter, let us claim the relevance of computer-based music description. In our opinion, the audience of potential recipients is very wide: music producers (publishers, editors, composers, major, and indie record labels, and multimedia entertainment industries), music consumers (both educated listeners and kccns), and finally researchers (analysts, musicologists, etc.) Each of the aforementioned actors faces the problem of music description from a different point of view, and expects an answer to the actor's requirements and demands.

Needless to say, the locution *music description* can embrace a number of different meanings, and understanding its exact sense is the first key problem. When we describe a music work, we usually list the metadata about its title, its author(s), its performers, its instrumental ensemble, and so on; but we could also want to catch the symbols that compose the piece, or give a description of physical objects related to music itself and to music performance; finally, also audio/video recordings should be considered music descriptions. We will face the matter of a comprehensive description of music in the next section; at the moment, for our purposes it is sufficient to realize that music communication is very rich, thus also the number of its possible descriptions will be high.

Any meaning we assign to the term "description", the problem of describing music in a computer-based system is not a technological one. In general, we can choose the most appropriate between already existing file formats aimed at music description, according to the interpretation we consider. The evidence comes from the large number of available file formats addressed to music enjoyment. For example, AAC, MP3, and PCM formats are commonly used to encode audio recordings; MIDI represents a well known standard for computer-driven performance; GIF, JPEG and TIFF files can contain the results of a scanning process of scores; DARMS, NIFF, and MusicXML formats are aimed at score typing and publishing, and so forth.

So, the problem of music description on computer systems is not technological, rather there exists a theoretical problem. The latter can be summarized through the following key questions: Which facets of music information should be described? Are heterogeneous communication levels involved? Is an encoding format currently available to catch the different aspects of music information? In the next section we will try to answer these questions.

A COMPREHENSIVE DESCRIPTION OF MUSIC

In our opinion, it is necessary to conceive music description in a comprehensive way. Before investigating this concept, let us recall that music communication is made up of many different and complementary aspects: music can be (and actually is) the idea that the composer translates to symbols as well as their performance, the printed

score that musicians read as well as a number of other related contents. Let us cite the example of opera houses (Haus, 1998) or music publishers (Haus, & Ludovico, 2005), where a great amount of heterogeneous music documents are available: scores, audio/video recordings, fliers, playbills, posters, photos, stage maps, sketches, and so forth. Our definition of comprehensive description of music embraces all the aspects we have cited.

As we have affirmed before, specific encoding formats to represent peculiar music features are already commonly accepted and used. But such formats are characterized by an intrinsic limitation: they can describe music data or metadata for score, audio tracks, computer performances of music pieces, but they are not intended to encode all these aspects together. On the contrary, we are interested in a "comprehensive" representation and enjoyment of music, addressed to musicologists as well as to performers, to music students as well as to untrained people simply interested in music. The key characteristics that a comprehensive format should support can be summarized as follows:

- Richness in the multimedia descriptions related to the same music piece (graphical, audio, and video contents).
- Possibility to link and perform a number of media objects of the same type (for instance, many performances of the same piece or many score scans coming from different editions).

In addition, we want this comprehensive format to support complete synchronization among time-based contents, meaning that audio and video contents are kept synchronized with score advancing, even when the user switches from a particular performance to another, or from a particular score edition to another.

Interaction should be supported as well. Of course, this aspect cannot be realized by a format, rather by applications working on the format. The matter will be developed in Section 5, devoted to MX applications. At the moment, in order to provide a broad picture, we underline the possibility for the users to click any point of the score and jump there also in the audio content currently performed, as well as the possibility to navigate the audio track moving a slider control and highlight the related portion of the score.

Achieving the aforementioned goals implies: (1) designing and adopting a suitable format to represent music, (2) encoding music pieces and all the related material in such format, and (3) implementing software applications to achieve synchronization and user interaction.

The first step is represented by the design of a comprehensive representation format for music. A formal and complete analysis of music richness and complexity is provided by Haus and Longari (2005), where six different levels of music description are identified—namely General, Structural, Logical, Notational, Audio, and Performance layers. This multilayer structure, suitable for our concept of comprehensive description of music, is reflected by the encoding format we will describe in Section 4.

XML-BASED REPRESENTATION OF MUSIC DATA AND METADATA

In the previous section, we have provided our definition of "comprehensive description" applied to music. In this sense, the inadequacy of current file formats should be evident. As a satisfactory standard is still unavailable, we propose some guidelines to face the matter, introducing a new approach for computer-based music description.

A possible solution to the problem could reside in the adoption of an XML-based format. There are many advantages in choosing XML[1] to describe information in general, and music information in particular. Many texts and scientific papers have already described the advantages of XML-based formats applied to information representation.

Here we are more interested in the reason why XML and music make a good couple.

First, XML is a formal meta-language suitable for declarative representations. It is capable to describe entities (in our case music objects) as they are, without unnecessary information overload. This kind of representation is modular and hierarchical; nevertheless it allows explicit interaction among modules. Internal relationships are formal and explicit. All these aspects have an important counterpart in music language, which is formal and hierarchical too.

XML modularity can solve the problem of a well-organized comprehensive description: each part constitutes a separate plug of the overall description, still maintaining its own identity. However, interdependencies are allowed and made explicit by an XML-based format.

Languages derived from XML are extensible, as they support extensions and external entities. This aspect is fundamental to take into account further developments of music language or still unforeseen uses of the description format.

Finally, XML is open to user contributions, easy to be read, decoded, edited, and understood. In principle, anyone can give suggestions and implement specific parts of the format. Even if easier than binary formats, XML in general is not intended to be managed directly: rather, it should be read and written by computer-based systems. For instance, music XML cannot be printed in its text form in order to be played at first sight by a human performer; on the contrary, we need specific software to decode the format and represent it as a sequence of music symbols. Fortunately, applications to edit XML files can be easily found on the marketplace and usually basic editors are free. Besides, specific software able to work on a peculiar XML-based format can be implemented without paying royalties or licences, as most formats are free.

In conclusion, an XML-based language allows inherent readability, extensibility, and durability. A specific coverage of the matter is presented by

Steyn (2002). These are the main reasons why the format we propose relies on XML in order to represent and organize music information in a comprehensive way.

AN OVERVIEW ON MX OVERVIEW AND BASIC CONCEPTS

MX is the code name for a new file format officially called IEEE SA PAR1599[2] (XML Musical Application Working Group, 2001). This project is aimed at a comprehensive symbolic music representation, and opens up new possibilities to make both the message and the internal structure of music available to musicologists, performers and non-practitioners. Its ultimate goal is providing a highly integrated representation of music, where score, audio, video, and related graphical contents can be enjoyed together.

MX inherits all the peculiarities of an XML-based format: for example, it is open, free, easily readable by humans and computers and editable by common software applications. Moreover, some of the typical features of an XML format well suit to music: XML is strongly structured, as well as most music scores; an XML format can be extended, supporting new notations and new music symbols; XML provides a means of interchange for music over the Net.

All the characteristics we have mentioned before represent themselves valid reasons to adopt an XML-based encoding for music. But our own XML format, namely MX, presents further advantages. First, the music description provided by an MX file is flexible and potentially very rich, as regards both the number and the type of media involved. In fact, thanks to our approach a single file could contain one or more descriptions of the same music piece in each layer. For example, if we had to provide a description of an operatic aria, the MX file could house: the catalogue metadata about the piece, its author(s) and genre; the corresponding portion of the libretto; the scans of the

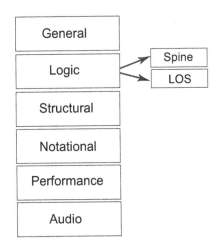

Figure 1. The six-layer MX structure

autographical version and of a number of printed versions; many audio files containing different performances; related iconographic contents such as sketches, on-stage photographs, and playbills. Thanks to the rich information provided by MX, software applications based on such format allow an integrated fruition of music in all its aspects.

Another key feature from both a theoretical and an applicative point of view is the full synchronization among layers, involving both time and space dimensions. This characteristic lets the user switch from a representation to another in real-time. For instance, he/she can compare the vocal performance of Enrico Caruso to the one of Luciano Pavarotti, or the signs notated on the autographical score to their translation on the printed version. At the same time, the user can view the structure of the piece he/she is listening to and open a number of iconographic related files.

As mentioned before, a thorough description of music must encompass different layers to represent information (see Figure 1):

- **General:** Catalog information about the piece

- **Logic:** The symbols that compose the score as intended by its author(s)
- **Structural:** Music objects and their relationship
- **Notational:** Graphical representations of the score
- **Performance:** Computer-based descriptions and executions of music
- **Audio:** Digital or digitized recordings of the piece

Figure 2 shows the relationship between the group constituted by General, Structural, and Logic layers and the one encompassing Notational (e.g., GIF, JPEG, TIFF for a score), Audio (e.g., AAC, MP3, WAV), and Performance (e.g., Csound, MIDI, MPEG) layers. It should be evident that our approach consists in keeping intrinsic music descriptions inside the MX file (the upper block in Figure 2), whereas media objects are external (the lower block in Figure 2). Let us cite some clarifying examples. The symbols that belong to the score, such as chords and notes, are directly described in XML format, in the so-called Logic

Figure 2. Relationships among MX layers and external media objects

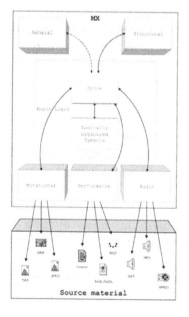

layer; on the contrary, MP3 files and other audio descriptions are not translated into XML format, rather they are linked and mapped inside the corresponding MX layer, namely Audio layer.

Needless to say, not all layers must or can be present for a given music piece. Of course, the higher their number, the richer the piece's description is. Besides, each layer could contain one or more object instances: for example, Audio layer could link 3 audio tracks and Structural layer could provide two different analyses for the same piece. The concept of multilayer description (i.e., potentially many different types of descriptions, all correlated and synchronized) together with the concept of multiinstance support (i.e., potentially many different media objects for each layer) provide a very rich and flexible means of encoding music in all its aspects. Section 5 will illustrate possible applications of these characteristics.

MX layers will be soon analyzed in greater detail and made clearer by some example, but first we have to introduce the main concept MX is based on: the idea of spine.

Spine

According to our comprehensive approach to music description, the MX standard provides different layers to represent information. Of course, these levels cannot be independent: in order to achieve richness in information description, each music event can have one or more descriptions in different layers. Thus, we should be able to create a common data structure in order to link the different representations of each music event within the MX file. For instance, let us refer to a hypothetical event named e12, corresponding to a B quaver somehow described in Logical layer: we should be able to refer to its representation also in audio, video, score parts of the MX file.

Accordingly, we have introduced the concept of spine, which is an overall structure that relates time and space information. Spine contains no

Box 1. MX spine

```
<spine>
    <event id="timesig _ 0" timing="0" hpos="0" />
    <event id="keysig _ 0" timing="0" hpos="0" />
    <event id="clef _ 0" timing="0" hpos="0" />
    <event id="clef _ 1" timing="0" hpos="0" />
    <event id="p1 _ 0" timing="0" hpos="0" />
    <event id="p2 _ 0" timing="0" hpos="0" />
    <event id="p1 _ 1" timing="256" hpos="256" />
    <event id="p1 _ 2" timing="256" hpos="256" />
    <event id="p1 _ 3" timing="256" hpos="256" />
    <event id="p1 _ 4" timing="256" hpos="256" />
    ...

</spine>
```

more than an ordered list of event identifiers, whereas the events are later described in Logic layer as regards their musical meaning. Events correspond to the music entities of the piece we want to describe. This definition is intentionally vague, as our approach is aimed at allowing a high degree of flexibility. In general, events are all the notes, rests, time signatures, key signatures, clefs, and symbols of the score; but the aforementioned definition allows also to map only the C notes in the trumpet part or the dotted crotchets of string instruments. The choice of what should be referenced by the spine list of events is very subjective, and depends on the characteristics of the piece and on the purpose of the description. For instance, in jazz improvisation only the harmonic grid can be mapped; in this case, spine contains identifiers for chords instead of including identifiers for single notes.

In Box 1, the first 10 events of an MX spine are shown.

A first problem is: how can we put in a one-dimensional ordered list a two-dimensional sequence of events? Notes, rests and other symbols in a score are disposed according to a vertical juxtaposition (related to harmony) and to a horizontal development (corresponding to temporal evolution of music). Our solution is referring each event in spine to the previous one, following a path that scans music in vertical from upper staves to lower

staves; when all the simultaneous events have been considered, we move to the next event on the right, and so on. In a certain sense, the list of events achieved by this process "meanders" through the score, from top to bottom and from left to right. Timing and hpos attributes (shown in the example) are calculated in function of previous events: timing = "0" means simultaneous occurrence in time, and hpos = "0" means vertical alignment. Values are expressed in virtual timing units and in virtual positioning units, in order to achieve a high degree of abstraction. In this layer, music is equally spaced in time and space by applying a concept similar to beat spacing. The actual occurrences of music events inside digital objects such as scores and clips will be mapped inside Notational, Performance and Audio layers.

Now we have described what spine contains. But how does spine provide synchronization to the whole multilayer structure? Each music event, later described in any MX layer, is listed inside the spine and associated to a unique identifier. This identifier represents the key that other layers use in order to refer to such particular event. In this way, all the layers reference (and are referenced by) a common structure that relates them from a spatial and temporal point of view. Figure 3 illustrates the principle spine is based on: by a number of links between spine and other layers, it is possible to create a global net of relationships. For the sake of

Figure 3. Mappings of the notational layer and synchronization of the spine event named `e12`

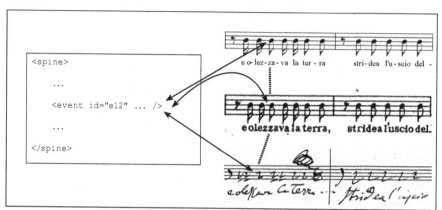

greater clearness, Figure 3 shows the relationships among three graphical representations of the same score[3]: in this case, synchronization takes place among instances of the same layer.

The arrows represent the mapping from and towards Notational layer. Even if this is a simplified example, please note that Figure 3 does not represent a trivial star schema: if we consider the vertical dotted lines, they are the graphical counterparts of a structure intrinsically and automatically produced by spine mappings. Thus, the resulting layout is a star-ring scheme, where the star is given by the relationships among the identifiers listed in spine and their occurrence in other layers, whereas the ring represents synchronization among instances. This process can be generalized to heterogeneous representations aimed at music description, as Figure 4 illustrates.

MX Layers

After presenting the idea of multilayered structure to represent music and the concept of time-space construct to achieve synchronization, let us briefly define the meaning and the contents of each MX layer.

The first MX layer, namely General layer, is not directly related to score and audio contents. It describes some fundamental catalog information about the encoded music work. The situation is reflected by Figure 2, where General block appears disconnected from other levels, even if it clearly belongs to the overall description as well. A particular importance is given to its subelement Description, devoted to author, genre and title information. Such music metadata are not music events, so they are not directly related to music symbols, scores or audio performances; never-

Box 2. General layer: Catalog metadata

```
<general>
  <description>
    <main _title>E lucevan le stelle</main _title>
    <author type="composer">Giacomo Puccini</author>
    <author type="librettist">Luigi Illica</author>
    <author type="librettist">Giuseppe Giacosa</author>
    <work _title>Tosca</work _title>
  </description>
</general>
```

Figure 4. Synchronization among notational, performance and audio layers provided by spine

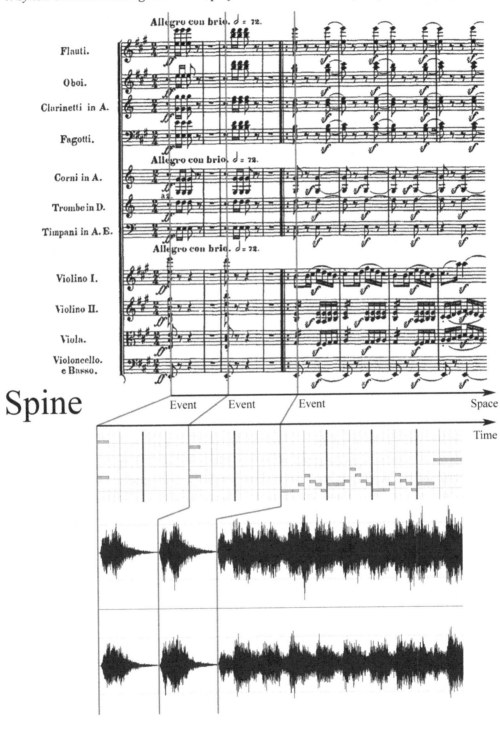

Box 3. General layer: Other data

```
<general>
    <description>
    ...
    </description>
    <related_files>
        <related_file file_name="playbill01.jpg"
                      file_format="image_jpeg"
                      encoding_format="image_jpeg"
                      description="Playbill" />
    <related_file>...</related_file>
    ...
    </related_files>
</general>
```

theless, these labels are particularly interesting for music classification and retrieval. The XML block displayed in Box 2 provides an example of catalog metadata.

In addition, General layer can contain links towards files that do not describe directly the piece and its music events, but are strongly related and can provide further information. For instance, related files can contain iconographic material and text contents. Needless to say, such objects cannot be synchronized with music execution, and they do not present any reference to spine structure; nevertheless they belong to our concept of comprehensive description of music.

As regards the aforementioned Puccini's aria, our MX description could provide link towards sketches, on stage photos, libretto, and score covers. Box 3 illustrates this case.

Logic layer contains what the author(s) intended to put in the piece. If we look at a score as a sequence of music symbols, we should refer to its "abstract" layout. For instance, characteristics of a score such as the number of measures per system, page margins, fonts, paper type, and format are described in Notational layer, as they derive from a graphical implementation of the score. In Logic layer we find the same information, but unformatted and disposed on a sort of virtual score. The difference is illustrated by Figure 5, where we can compare an abstract description of a chord to its corresponding printed version: the former is the logical description of the chord, where—among a number of possible descriptions—we have chosen an XML-based one; on the contrary, the latter is the kind of description referred by Notational layer, as we will explain later. Please note that the XML

Figure 5. A logic representation of a chord vs. a graphical one

```
<chord event_ref="p7v1_69">
    <notehead>
        <pitch step="E" octave="5"/>
        <duration num="1" den="1"/>
    </notehead>
    <notehead>
        <pitch step="G" octave="5"/>
        <duration num="1" den="1"/>
    </notehead>
    <notehead>
        <pitch step="C" octave="6"/>
        <duration num="1" den="1"/>
    </notehead>
</chord>
```

Figure 6. The measure encoded in MX format

```
<measure number="1">
  <voice voice_item_ref="Clarinetto_I_voice_1">
    <chord event_ref="p5v1_0">
      <duration num="1" den="4" />
      <augmentation_dots number="1" />
      <notehead>
        <pitch step="B" octave="5" />
      </notehead>
    </chord>
    <chord event_ref="p5v1_1">
      <duration num="1" den="8" />
      <notehead>
        <pitch step="B" octave="5" />
      </notehead>
    </chord>
    <chord event_ref="p5v1_2">
      <duration num="1" den="8" />
      <notehead>
        <pitch step="C" octave="6" actual_accidental="sharp" />
      </notehead>
    </chord>
    <chord event_ref="p5v1_3">
      <duration num="1" den="8" />
      <notehead>
        <pitch step="D" octave="6" />
      </notehead>
    </chord>
  </voice>
</measure>
```

logic description is encoded inside MX Logic layer, whereas the digital image of a printed score remains external and it is only linked and mapped within Notational layer (see Figure 2).

Logic layer is composed of two sub-elements: (1) spine, which lists the significant events referable by other layers and (2) logically organized symbols (LOS), that describes the score from a symbolic point of view.

Spine has been illustrated and explained in the previous sub-section. As regards LOS sub-layer, it is based on the hierarchical structure typical of XML formats. Generally speaking, music can be considered strongly structured in a hierarchical fashion: a complete score is made of pages, each page of systems, each system of staves, each staff of measures, and so on. Unfortunately, this tree structure suffers from problems when applied both to staves and to instrumental parts. In

fact, the standard situation is having a biunique relationship between staves and parts: a violinist reads the violin staff, as well as a trumpeter performs the notes written on the trumpet staff. But pianists, harpists, and organists have their part usually split into two or even three staves[4]. These examples could suggest that staves are at a lower level of instrumental parts in the hierarchy; in other words, a score seems to be made of parts, and each part takes one or more staves. But all the scores represent a counterexample where many instrumental parts are written on the same staff: for instance, flute and piccolo parts, or three different melodic lines for as many horns. The solution is providing two different structures and a device of crossmapping: an instrumental hierarchy for parts and voices and a layout hierarchy for systems and staves. A part/voice will be assigned to a standard

Box 4. Horizontal symbol representation

```
<lyrics part _ ref="Cavaradossi" voice _ ref="Voice1">
    …
  <syllable start _ event _ ref="p1v1 _ 1" end _ event _ ref="p1v1 _ 1" hyphen="yes">
     e o
  </syllable>
  <syllable start _ event _ ref="p1v1 _ 2" end _ event _ ref="p1v1 _ 2" hyphen="yes">
     lez
  </syllable>
  <syllable start _ event _ ref="p1v1 _ 3" end _ event _ ref="p1v1 _ 3" hyphen="yes">
     za
  </syllable>
  <syllable start _ event _ ref="p1v1 _ 4" end _ event _ ref="p1v1 _ 4">
     va
  </syllable>
    …
</lyrics>
```

Box 5. Structural layer: Music analyses

```
<structural>
   <chord _ grid description="Harmony">
      <chord _ name root _ id="e1">I _ 3 _ 5</chord _ name>
      <chord _ name root _ id="e2">IV _ 3 _ 6</chord _ name>
      <chord _ name root _ id="e3">V _ 3 _ 5</chord _ name>
      <chord _ name root _ id="e4">V _ 7</chord _ name>
      <chord _ name root _ id="e5">VI _ 3 _ 5</chord _ name>
         …
   </chord _ grid>
      …
</structural>
```

staff, with the possibility to change this setting with single-notehead granularity.

Figure 6 shows a graphical representation of a measure encoded in MX format.

At the end of LOS subelement, after describing symbols such as clefs, notes and rests, there are the sections to represent horizontal symbols (slurs, hairpins, embellishments) and lyrics (Box 4).

Structural layer contains explicit descriptions of music objects together with their causal relationships, from both a compositional and a musicological point of view. In this context, we can define "music object" as every type of structured information in any musical language. Given this definition, Structural layer identifies a number of music objects and describes how they interact in the overall structure and how they can be described as a transformation of previous music objects.

Thanks to the meaning we assigned at Structural layer, this is the right place to host music analyses. A simple application of music analysis is the identification of chords, whose concatenation gives the harmonic path. In this case, music objects are constituted by simultaneous sets of notes, namely chords (Box 5).

Other applications are the identification of the themes of a sonata form, of the subject of fugues, of particularly important melodic or rhythmic patterns.

Structural layer, thanks to MX multiinstance approach, can contain one or more analyses. In addition, many forms of analysis and segmentation are supported.

Notational layer links all the possible visual instances of a music piece, by organizing single digital objects in collections called graphic or notational instance groups. In this way, for a

Box 6. Notational layer: Spine event mapping

```
<notational>
  <graphic _ instance _ group description="Manuscript">
    <graphic _ instance file _ name="images\page _ 1.tif"
        file _ format="image _ tiff" encoding _ format="image _ tiff"
        position _ in _ group="1" measurement _ unit="pixels">
      <graphic _ event event _ ref="p1v1 _ 1"
          upper _ left _ x="977" upper _ left _ y="451"
          lower _ right _ x="999"lower _ right _ y="483" />
      <graphic _ event event _ ref="p1v1 _ 2"
          upper _ left _ x="999" upper _ left _ y="458"
          lower _ right _ x="1011" lower _ right _ y="483" />
      <graphic _ event event _ ref="p1v1 _ 3"
          upper _ left _ x="1026" upper _ left _ y="462"
          lower _ right _ x="1042" lower _ right _ y="493" />
      ...
    </graphic _ instance>
    <graphic _ instance file _ name="images\page _ 2.tif"
        file _ format="image _ tiff" encoding _ format="image _ tiff"
        position _ in _ group="2" measurement _ unit="pixels">
      <graphic _ event event _ ref="p1v1 _ 100"
          upper _ left _ x="710" upper _ left _ y="123"
          lower _ right _ x="732" lower _ right _ y="170" />
      <graphic _ event event _ ref="p1v1 _ 101"
          upper _ left _ x="738" upper _ left _ y="90"
          lower _ right _ x="775" lower _ right _ y="149" />
      <graphic _ event event _ ref="p1v1 _ 102"
          upper _ left _ x="813" upper _ left _ y="105"
          lower _ right _ x="836" lower _ right _ y="154" />
      ...
    </graphic _ instance>
  </graphic _ instance _ group>
  ...
</notational>
```

given piece, MX can link and map not only *n* files belonging to a particular version, but also the files coming from *m* different versions. The *m* x *n* graphic instances are grouped and numbered, to keep trace of their original position in the collection.

Representations mainly belong to two classes: notational and graphical. A notational instance is often in a binary format, such as NIFF[5]; nevertheless, there exist also text-based and XML-based formats. In this case, the occurrence of music events is identified by the offset between the event-related binary encoding and the beginning of file. On the contrary, a graphical instance contains images representing the score, usually in a binary format like JPEG or TIFF. The occurrence

of events is expressed in term of space measurement units (e.g., pixels, inches, centimetres) and is directly related to virtual space coordinates in the Spine structure. The way to map spine events in digital images is creating a sort of bounding box for each event, using corner coordinates in pixels or other absolute measurement units. Box 6 illustrates this technique.

Performance layer lies between Notational and Audio layers. File formats supported by this level encode parameters of notes to be played and parameters of sounds to be created by computer performances. This layer supports symbolic formats such as Csound, MIDI and SASL/SAOL files.

Finally, Audio layer describes the properties of the audio material related to the piece. Once

Box 7. Audio layer: Mapping music events based on timing values

```
<audio>
  <track file_name="audio\tosca1984.wav"
      file_format="audio_wav" encoding_format="audio_wav">
    <track_indexing start_time_type="seconds">
      <track_event start_time="0.00" event_ref="p1v1_0"/>
      <track_event start_time="0.00" event_ref="p1v1_1"/>
      <track_event start_time="0.00" event_ref="p1v1_2"/>
      <track_event start_time="1.05" event_ref="p1v1_3"/>
      <track_event start_time="2.07" event_ref="p1v1_4"/>
      ...
    </track_indexing>
  </track>
  ...
</audio>
```

again, many audio/video clips in a number of formats are supported. Here the device used to map music events is based on timing values, as shown in Box 7.

The complete DTD of MX[6] is downloadable at http://mx.dico.unimi.it, together with complete music examples encoded in MX format.

MX APPLICATIONS

As stated before, MX format allows a rich and comprehensive description of music contents. MX technology represents a base for the development of applications that allow a full musical experience. Richness is just a possibility: a piece could be described only in terms of its music symbols, without multimedia objects attached, and the MX file would be validated in any case. However, if the file has as many related material as possible, a more comprehensive description of music is achieved.

Before enjoying music contents, the MX file has to be created. Like any other XML-based encoding, files in this format can be written and edited even by a simple text editor. It is virtually possible to encode all the score symbols and all the synchronization information by hand and in plain text format. Nevertheless, this approach would be very cumbersome and time-consuming. First, for a musician the task of writing notes

and rests according to XML formal rules (that are substantially different from score notation) is unacceptable. Besides, after obtaining a well-formed, valid, complete, and semantically correct encoding of the piece, the author of the MX file should face other complex tasks: for example, the author should manually find the symbols to map, synchronize heterogeneous media objects, and enter those values in the MX file.

Since the central part, and in a certain sense the skeleton, of an MX file is represented by Logic layer, this is the first part to be produced. A practical way to perform this task is implementing conversion tools that take in input widely used formats of music representation and translate them to a basic MX file. At the moment, we have developed an application that converts ETF[7] and MIDI files into MX format. The simple interface of this tool is shown in Figure 7.

This tool prepares a basic MX file as regards only Logic layer, creating a spine structure and LOS sub-layer.

After describing symbolic information from a logic perspective, we have to face the problems related to heterogeneous media linking and synchronization. As a solution, we have implemented two of utilities to support the creation and management of rich MX files, namely MX Graphic Mapper and MX Audio Mapper. Their general purpose is simplifying the assemblage process

Figure 7. The application to convert ETF and MIDI files into MX files

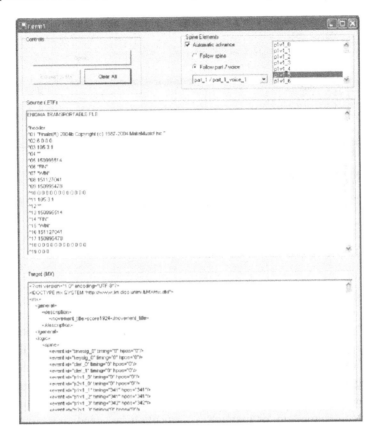

Figure 8. The MX graphic mapper

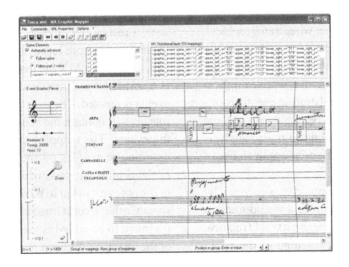

Figure 9. The MX audio mapper

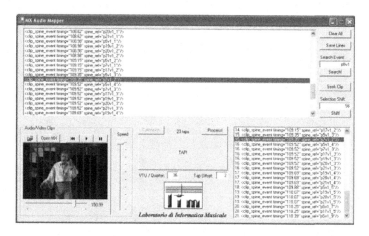

of heterogeneous contents within a single music description.

Since a key concept of the MX format is the mutual synchronization of all associated media, the process of adding a certain kind of material cannot be viewed merely as linking a file, but it needs an automatic, semiautomatic, or manual synchronization procedure. Unfortunately, the process required to map and synchronize heterogeneous media at the moment cannot be performed automatically with a high precision degree. As regards notational contents, this would require a reliable OMR[8] system in order to recognize musical symbols in scores, even when autographical. Besides, such symbols should be automatically put in relationship with the spine structure. As regards audio information, an effective application to extract automatically music events from a complex audio track should be employed, but some well-known limits in automated music analysis techniques prevent the extensive applicability of this approach.

On the other hand, mapping music events by a completely hand-made process would imply a terrible waste of time and energy: it would require, for instance, an accurate listening of the audio tracks in a sound editing environment, or the precise computation of the "bounding box" around each music event in a digital imaging software. Calculating milliseconds and pixels by hand is neither effective nor efficient. A better solution is designing and implementing some aiding applications to speed up the mapping process.

MX Graphic Mapper is the application devoted to link the logic events of an MX file to their corresponding graphic counterparts within one or more score images (see Figure 8); in this way, the final MX file will contain a new block of information defining where a particular event—a note, a rest, a clef, and so forth—is graphically located in the score representation. Through this tool, an existing MX file that needs to be mapped is opened and scanned, and a list of all note/rest events is created. The user can open one or more images that contain the score in order to map all the events. The mapping procedure is done by dragging rectangles on the score image loaded in the central window, while the representation of the note/rest event to be mapped is graphically shown in the "Event Graphic Parser" and the XML fragment to be added is visible in the upper part of the interface. When a rectangle is created, the

Figure 10. The ScoreSynth application

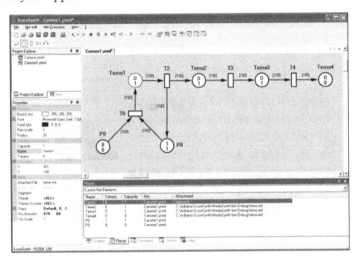

application generates the XML line by reading the current event in the "Spine Elements" list box, and by computing the coordinates of the rectangle. After adding a new line, the current element indicator is moved forward and the mapping process continues. When this procedure comes to an end, each logic event in the LOS part of the original MX file has at least one element associated in Notational layer, indicating where it is represented in the score image.

On the other side, MX Audio Mapper is the application used to map the logic events in audio/video clips (see Figure 9). This software is similar to the previous one, but—instead of mapping the graphic representations of scores—it maps audio/video performances. The mapping process is achieved by "tapping" the rhythm on a button. To map a clip, some parameters must be defined in advance: the timing unit per quarter used in Logic layer and the rhythm figure to be processed (crotchet, quaver, etc.). The user opens the MX file (already containing a Logic layer) and the audio/video clip and starts hitting the "TAP!" button (with the mouse or the space bar): the result is the hand-made synchronization of the selected

rhythmic figures. When this process is completed, the MX spine is processed and all the timings of the events are computed (in seconds), interpolating events between two consecutive taps. Finally, the computed points of synchronization can be fine-tuned by hearing the selected position in the clip and adjusting the wrong timings.

As stated in Section 4, the MX format has a layer devoted to structural information. The software tool, which we have developed to compile this layer, is ScoreSynth (see Figure 10). This application works with Petri Nets (Petri, 1976), a formalism used at LIM since 1980 as the basic tool for music description and processing. In Music Petri Nets we manage music objects (MOs), that is anything that could have a musical meaning and that we consider an entity, either simple or complex, either abstract or detailed. Such entities, identified by unique names, can present some relationship with other music objects. We can treat music objects at various abstraction levels within a hierarchical context of description, applying to them transformation algorithms in order to create new modified objects (Haus, 1997). Through ScoreSynth, a user can describe the structure of a

Figure 11. The MX jazz demo

music piece coded in MX format simply drawing the corresponding Music Petri Nets. The model created by ScoreSynth is saved in MX too, and it is linked to Structural layer of the file itself.

An important advantage of the MX standard is represented by its usability in a multimodal environment. Thanks to the multilayer approach in music description, we have developed a number of applications devoted to MX enjoyment, that is, to process an MX file in order to offer an integrated environment where the user can appreciate the advantages of the MX format. In the following, two applications will be presented: one dedicated to jazz compositions and another one based on an aria from Puccini's *Tosca*.

MX Jazz Demo (Baratè, Haus, Ludovico, & Vercellesi, 2005), shown in Figure 11, features two jazz pieces: *King Porter Stomp*, with two versions of scores and three mapped audio/video clips, and *Crazy Rhythm*, constituted by some improvisations on a fixed harmonic grid. The aim of the application is providing a tool to "navigate" an MX file and its associated media files, maintaining synchronization among all layers. From this point of view, in MX Jazz Demo we

can load an MX file and open its heterogeneous linked material. When a linked clip is played, other media are shown synchronously: there is a small rectangle which highlights the note being played in the score part of the window, while the active part of the MX file is shown, and the Chord grid advances. The main part of the window is dedicated to represent the current score. On the top the currently playing MX element is shown, according to the selected layer.

MX Jazz Demo faces some interesting representational problems, such as structural descriptions for those pieces that cannot be represented by traditional notation. For instance, harmonic grid is supported for jazz improvisation. Besides, virtually any type of graphical representation of music can be mapped in an MX file, even if not explicitly supported by the original format (as in *Crazy Rhythm*); this confers great flexibility and power to MX descriptive possibilities. An interesting consequence of our approach is the possibility to select a particular point of music (a timing in a media file, a location in a score image, a tag in the MX window), and have all the other media automatically synchronized in real time, thus allowing an integrated and evolved enjoyment of music contents.

Before describing the second application aimed at user interaction with music contents, some words on real-time synchronization among MX layers must be spent. In MX, some layers contain only the concept of *relative time*, some others have also the idea of *absolute time*, and layers such as General do not have a time concept at all. The *relative time* concept resembles the execution of a music score: even if the score presents its own internal temporal relationships, in absolute terms music can be performed slowly or quickly. Similarly, the spine of an MX file contains an internal temporization, not in absolute terms (such as seconds) but in relative terms: each event is related to the previous one through a relative time and space distance. The main layer presenting this form of time specification is Logic layer. LOS, Notational, and Structural layers inherit this behavior, as their time parameters are specified only in function of the spine. On the other hand, the concept of *absolute time* is present in Performance and Audio layers. Here, in addition to spine links, the events must have an absolute timing associated (expressed either in seconds, ticks, or frames, depending on the file format). The absolute timing lets the application determine the precise time occurrence of a given event within the clip. In this way, when an audio/video file is played, the relative time specifications of the spine are translated to absolute timings. This mechanism allows association of different performances (with different absolute time values) to the same logical representation (where events are characterized by relative time relationships).

In summary, a symbolic score contains only relative timing indications (rhythmical values, vertical overlaps), but our mapping lets us associate different performances of a piece to a single spine along with their different agogics. As a consequence, the real-time execution of an MX file is possible only in two cases: (1) by specifying a relative/absolute time ratio, or (2) by running

one and only one associated performance/clip. In fact, multiple simultaneous performances/clips would actualize in different ways the concept of relative time, and this would represent a problematic issue.

In MX Jazz Demo, our approach follows the latter method. As a consequence, when *play* command is activated in a performance/clip window, previously running files are stopped. This is the only case of non-concurrent execution: all the linked objects from all the other layers can be shown at the same time and kept synchronized. On the contrary, a file containing a temporized performance (e.g., a MIDI file) cannot be played during the execution of another audio or video file (e.g., an MP3 file).

The second MX demo aimed at music enjoyment was installed at the exhibition "Tema con Variazioni. Musica e innovazione tecnologica" (Theme with variations. Music and technological innovation), a voyage into the Italian musical heritage through the rooms held at Rome's Music Park Auditorium in December 2005. All the images shown are courtesy of Italian publishing house Ricordi[9], which owns the manuscripts of the most important Italian composers of the last two centuries.

One of the purposes of the exhibition was making music tangible and visible bringing together the five senses, not just hearing. In this context we have designed a simple user interface, conceived for untrained people, in order to listen to and visualize a track alongside variously interpreted scores. This application, entitled MX Navigator, represents the natural evolution of MX Jazz Demo. The main differences between MX Jazz Demo and MX Navigator are the following two:

- The latter is a generalized version of the former, as MX Jazz Demo was designed only to demonstrate MX format characteristics and worked on the limited number of pieces consequently chosen, whereas MX Navigator is virtually able to open any MX file. In

Figure 12. The MX Navigator

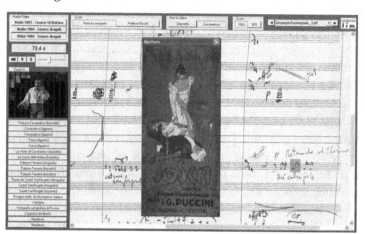

fact, this new version is able to adapt itself in real time to the different kind and number of media contained in the MX file[10].

- MX Navigator is necessarily characterized by an improved usability and by a simpler user interface. In fact, MX Jazz Demo had to be presented to a scientific audience by its authors, whereas MX Navigator is at untrained users' disposal in public exhibitions.

MX Navigator allows an integrated enjoyment of different media contents related to the same music piece. For the exhibition held in Rome, we translated into MX the aria "E lucevan le stelle..." from Puccini's *Tosca* – III Act. The choice of the piece was imposed by the *leitmotiv* of the exhibition "Tema con Variazioni", nevertheless MX Navigator could open and play any MX file.

Apart from a number of multimedia objects such as greeting cards, playbills, historical photos and sketches, the software mainly shows two versions of the score (an autographical and a printed one), a video and two audio performances of the aforementioned aria.

The central part of the interface contains the score in one of its versions, since this is the main media in terms of interaction and visual extent.

The upper left part of the window hosts the controls related to audio/video interaction. In this application, three different clips are shown: an audio clip of a 1953 version performed by the Italian tenor Di Stefano and both an audio and a video clip of the 1984 version performed by Aragall at Verona's Arena. When a particular version is selected, the music and/or video clip is played, and in the score window a red rectangle highlights the current event (thanks to the synchronization achieved by MX Audio Mapper and MX Graphic Mapper).

Since there are many instrumental parts in the score, and they all have been coded into the MX file, it should be possible to choose any part to follow. But this application is intended to be used even by nonmusicians, so the choice is simplified and only two parts can be selected. Thus, in the top of the interface there are two buttons that control which part can be followed by the red rectangle in the score: either the Clarinet or the Tenor (Cavaradossi). Please note that this limitation has been discarded in more recent versions of the application.

In the upper area of the interface, the controls are devoted to manage score visualization. This MX file includes two score instances: the autographical version by Puccini and the Ricordi printed version. The upper left buttons switch (even when running an audio/video clip) between this two scores. The upper right buttons control the zoom level (50% or 100%) and the current page to be displayed. Of course, this takes place only in the Pause state; otherwise the current page is automatically selected by the audio/video clip execution.

The bottom left part of the interface is simply used to open some iconographic objects related to the piece.

MX Navigator provides a visual interface that supports different ways to enjoy music. First, it is possible to select a score version, an audio track, and a leading instrument and simply follow the instrument part evolution. This is a basic level of music enjoyment, and yet music can be listened and watched in a synchronized fashion. But a second way to enjoy music through MX Navigator is even more interesting: it consists in switching from an aural/visual representation to another. In other words, it is possible to compare in real time different versions of the score (the hand-made and the printed one) and different performances. When the user decides to switch from a representation to another, MX Navigator continues just from the point previously reached. Finally, the application suggests a third way to enjoy music, by the possibility to alter the original sequence of music events. For instance, it is possible to jump – forward or back – from a point to another point of the score, both in its visual and aural representations, maintaining the overall synchronization.

RELATED AND FUTURE WORKS

The idea of representing music for computer applications goes back several decades, as shown by Plaine-And-Easie Code (Brook, 1970) and DARMS (Erickson, 1975).

As regards recent attempts to face the problem of a comprehensive description of music, we can cite the Standard Music Description Language (SMDL) (Newcomb, 1991) and the Music Encoding Initiative (MEI, by Perry Roland) (Roland, 2002). The former provides a markup language for any kind of music, of any time, of any geographical region, of any style; the latter is primarily concerned with the markup of all the written forms of musical expression, and in particular those referable to common music notation. Though well defined, SMDL probably failed to attract much attention because of lack of applications. On the other hand, MEI strives to be a sort of framework for music description languages, and MX was deeply influenced in its main peculiarities by Roland's suggestions.

Presently, there are some de-facto standards based on XML. MusicXML is a proprietary standard by Recordare[11], used in dozens of existing applications on the market, including the aforementioned MakeMusic Finale. This standard has been in existence for over four years, and new Version 1.1 has been recently released. Even if MusicXML provides an XML-based description of music, its approach is different from MX's one as the former is aimed at a complete description of the logic and the notational aspects of music, disregarding other features such as structural and audio contents. However, it is interesting to note that most current attempts are based on the markup concept, which confirms that XML-based languages can provide an effective representation of music.

Currently, the most prominent international initiatives to encode music in all its facets are referable to IEEE Standard Association Working Group on Music Application of XML and to ISO/IEC JTC1/SC29/WG11 Audio Subgroup.

Since 1992, the IEEE Computer Society has supported the establishment of a Technical Committee on Computer-Generated Music. The purpose was investigating the vast interdisciplinary area of computer science, electrical engineering and music: a field that ranges from artistic music —composed or played with computers—to audio signal processing (Baggi, 1995). Nowadays the efforts of the working group are mainly aimed at creating the MX standard. The MX project, officially named "Definition of a Commonly Acceptable Musical Application Using the XML Language", was accepted by IEEE and labelled PAR1599. MX is currently undergoing the IEEE balloting process, which is the final step to become officially an international standard.

We can find a similar target in the Call for Proposals on Symbolic Music Representation, submitted by ISO/IEC JTC1/SC29/WG11 Audio Subgroup and already approved. This workgroup solicits technology responses that propose solutions for the specification of a Symbolic Music Representation. The resulting format should be capable of coding symbolic representations of music in a manner that allows its integration in MPEG-4 (International Organisation for Standardisation, 2004). Even if "MPEG-oriented", such declaration of intents is aimed at the same purpose of IEEE: an approach to overcome the limits of partial descriptions of music by establishing relationships with other data and metadata.

Some differences between the two approaches should be evident. ISO/IEC considers music as one media in a multimedia context, and establishes links towards other multimedia levels. On the other hand, IEEE is working on a standard uniquely aimed at music description, and in such encoding music in treated in a multilayer environment. Also in IEEE format audio, video, and text are supported, but the role played by the music piece is central. IEEE proposal is based on links towards other file formats: audio, video, and text will be treated as a part of music information; whereas ISO/IEC approach is aimed at the integration of a symbolic music layer in the already existing MPEG standards.

The two perspectives are different concerning implementation, but quite similar about theoretical motivations. The fact that both IEEE and ISO/IEC are working on a comprehensive music description makes us sense the importance of this matter in computer music field.

As regards future developments of our research, some aspects of our work should be further investigated, even if the overall approach can be considered stable and consolidated.

First, supported music notation should be completed and integrated with symbols coming from cultures different from Common Western Notation. A detailed test phase is required to validate the completeness and the effectiveness of the adopted data structures. Tests should embrace music from all historical periods, styles, and geographical regions. Needless to say, jazz music grammar is different from early neumes, tablatures, or 20th century experimental notations. In our ambitious attempt to describe all the aspects of music in a comprehensive way, each type of music should be supported.

Second, a number of contributions coming from other XML-based formats should be integrated: we can cite formalisms to represent music in Braille language, or descriptions of intrinsic music structures through Petri Nets Markup Language (PNML).

Finally, a particular attention will be devoted to the problem of genre classification. In particular, General layer will be soon enriched to achieve a flexible and Semantic Web compatible representation of the metadata associated with MX resources.

Another research field will be the investigation of music structures, their relationships and the ways to describe them. The results of this study will enrich MX Structural layer, taking into account the opinions of experts in information technology as well as in musicology.

ACKNOWLEDGMENT

The MX standard, on which this work is based, has been sponsored by the IEEE CS Standards Activity Board and financially supported by the global fund Intelligent Manufacturing Systems (www.ims.org). The authors want to acknowledge researchers and graduate students at LIM, and the members of the IEEE Standards Association Working Group on Music Application of XML (PAR1599) for their cooperation and efforts. Special acknowledgments are due to: Denis Baggi for his invaluable work as working group chair of the IEEE Standard Association WG on MX (PAR1599); Mariapia Ferraris and Cristiano Ostinelli (Ricordi) for their fundamental contributions as regards the original material (autographic and printed scores, sketches, pictures, photos) used in MX Navigator.

REFERENCES

Baggi, D. (1995, November). Presentation of the Technical Committee on Computer-Generated Music. Computer.

Baratè, A., Haus, G., Ludovico, L. A., & Vercellesi, G. (2005). MXDemo: A case study about audio, video, and score synchronization. In *Proceedings of Axmedis 2005*.

Brook, B. S. (1970). The Plaine and Easie code. *Musicology and the computer* (pp 53-56). New York: City University of New York Press.

Erickson, R. F. (1975). The Darms project: A status report. *Computers and the Humanities, 9*(6), 291-298.

Haus, G. (1997). Describing and processing multimedia objects by Petri Nets. In *Proceedings of the 1997 IEEE International Conference on Systems, Man, and Cybernetics*. IEEE Computer Society Press, 3906-3911.

Haus, G. (1998). Rescuing La Scala's music archives. *Computer, 31*(3), 88-89.

Haus, G., & Longari, M. (2005). A multilayered time-based music description approach based on XML. *Computer Music Journal, 29*(1), 70-85. MIT Press.

Haus, G., & Ludovico, L. A. (2005). The digital opera house: An architecture for multimedia databases. *Journal of Cultural Heritage, 7*(2), 92-97.

International Organisation for Standardisation (2004). ISO/IEC JTC1/SC29/WG11, Call for Proposals on Symbolic Music Representation. Redmond, USA.

Newcomb, S. R. (1991). Standard music description language complies with hypermedia standard. *IEEE Computer*, 76-79.

Petri, C. A. (1976). General net theory. In *Proceedings of the Joint IBM & Newcastle upon Tyne Seminar on Computer Systems Design*.

Roland, P. (2002). The music encoding initiative (MEI). In *Proceedings of IEEE 1st International Conference on Musical Application Using XML (MAX 2002)*. Milano, Italy.

Rothenberg, J. (1995). Ensuring the longevity of digital documents. *Scientific American, 272*(1), 42-47.

Steyn, J. (2002). Framework for a music markup language. In *Proceedings of IEEE 1st International Conference on Musical Applications Using XML (MAX2002)*. Milano, Italy.

XML Musical Application Working Group (2001). Recommended practice for the definition of a commonly acceptable musical application using the XML language. IEEE SA 1599, PAR approval date 09/27/2001.

ENDNOTES

[1] XML stands for eXtensible Markup Language. XML is a W3C-recommended general-purpose markup language for creating special-purpose markup languages.

[2] Institute of Electrical and Electronics Engineers Standards Association, Project Approval Request 1599.

[3] Here and in the following examples, we refer to the aria "E lucean le stelle..." from Giacomo Puccini's *Tosca*. The iconographic material shown in this paper and in the software applications we will describe is property of Archivio Storico Ricordi (Milan, Italy) and is copyrighted.

[4] In piano pieces by Claude Debussy, piano part is sometimes arranged in three staves (e.g., in the piece entitled *D'un cahier d'esquisses*).

[5] NIFF stands for Notation Interchange File Format. It is a file format primarily designed for music typing and publishing. Another key element is transferring music notation among different score writers.

[6] Current MX release, namely version Release Candidate 1 (RC1), was updated in March 2007.

[7] ETF stands for Enigma Transportable File, a format produced by the well-known notation software MakeMusic Finale. An ETF file mainly contains score information.

[8] OMR stands for Optical Music Recognition.

[9] http://www.ricordi.it.

[10] As a matter of fact, MX Navigator at the moment has been employed in three other exhibitions, with different music contents: "Antonio Vivaldi e il suo tempo" (National Library of Turin, February – June 2006), "Ottobre: Piovono Libri" (Bari, October 2006), and "Celeste Aida" (Teatro alla Scala, Milan, December 2006 – January 2007).

[11] http://www.recordare.com/xml.html.

Compilation of References

Ackerman, W. (1982). *Dataflow languages, IEEE Computer, 15*(2), 15-25.

Adams, W. W., & Loustaunau, P. (1994). *An introduction to Gröbner Bases*. Providende, RI: Graduate Studies in Mathematics, American Mathematical Society.

Agosti, M., Bombi, F., Melucci, M. & Mian, G. A. (2000). Towards a digital library for the Venetian music of the eighteenth century. In J. Anderson, M. Deegan, S. Ross & S. Harold (Eds.), *DRH 98: Selected papers from digital resources for the humanities* (pp. 1-16). Office for Humanities Communication.

Agrawal, D.-P., & Zeng, Q.-A. (2003). *Introduction to wireless and mobile systems*. Thomson, Brooks/Cole, Minnesota, USA.

Agrawal, R., & Srikant, R. (1995). Mining sequential patterns. In *Proceedings of the International Conference on Data Engineering* (pp. 3-14).

Ahlbäck, S. (2007). Melodic similarity as determinant of melody structure. *Musicae Scientiae*, Discussion Forum 4A, 235-280.

Aksoy, M., Burgard, D., Flasch, O., Kaspari, A., Lüttgens, M., Martens, M., Möller, B., Öztürk, U., & Thome, P. (2005). Kollaboratives Strukturieren von Multimediadaten für Peer-to-Peer Netze. Technical report, Fachbereich Informatik, Universität Dortmund. Endbericht der Projektgruppe 461.

Alexander, P. (2002). Peer-to-peer file sharing: The case of the music recording industry. *Review of Industrial Organization*, 151-161.

Allen, G., et al. (2003). The Grid Application Toolkit: Towards Generic and Easy Application Programming Interfaces for the Grid. *Submitted to IEEE*

Alonso, J. A., Briales, E., & Riscos, A. (1990). Preuve Automatique dans le Calcul Propositionnel et des Logiques Trivalentes. In *Proceedings of the Congress on Computational Geometry and Topology and Computation* (pp.15-24). Seville, Spain: Universidad de Sevilla.

Amatriain, X. (2005). *An object-oriented metamodel for digital signal processing with a focus on audio and music*. Unpublished doctoral dissertation, Univesity of Pompeu Fabra, Spain.

Anderson, C. (Ed.). (2005, June). NextFest.2005. *Wired Magazine, 13*(6), p. 24.

Anquetil, E., & Bouchereau, H. (2002). Integration of an online handwriting recognition system in a smart phone device. In *Proceedings of the Sixteenth International Conference on Pattern Recognition (ICPR'02)* (pp. 192-195).

Anstice, J., Bell, T., Cockburn, A., & Setchell, M. (1996). The design of a pen-based musical input system. In *Proceedings of the Sixth Australian Conference on Computer-Human Interaction (OzChi 96)* (pp. 260-267).

Apel, W. (1972). *Harvard dictionary of music* (2nd ed.). Cambridge, MA: Belknap Press of Harvard University Press.

Association of American Publishers (2002). AAP: Digital rights management for Ebooks: Publisher requirements. Retrieved May 27, 2007, from http://www.publishers.org/home/drm.pdf

Attneave, F. & Olson, R. K. (1971). Pitch as a medium: A new approach to psychophysical scaling. *American Journal of Psychology, 84*, 147-166.

Aucouturier, J. and Pachet , F. (2003). Representing musical genre: A state of the art. *Journal of New Music Research, 32*(1), 83–93.

Aucouturier, J.-J., & Pachet, F. (2002). Music similarity measures: What's the use? In *Proceedings of the International Symposium on Music Information Retrieval.*

Baeza-Yates, R. & Ribeiro-Neto, B. (1999). *Modern information retrieval.* New York: ACM Press.

Baggi, D. (1995, November). Presentation of the Technical Committee on Computer-Generated Music. Computer.

Bainbridge, D., Nevill-Manning, C. G., Witten, I. H., Smith, L. A. & McNab, R. J. (1999). Towards a digital library of popular music. In *Proceedings of the Fourth ACM International Conference on Digital Libraries (DL'99)* (pp. 161-169). Berkeley, California.

Balaban, M., Ebcioglu, K., & Laske, O. (1992). Understanding music with AI. *Perspectives on music cognition.* Boston: The MIT Press.

Baochun, L., & Wang, K.-H. (2003). NonStop: Continuous multimedia streaming in wireless ad-hoc networks with node mobility. *IEEE Journal on Selected Areas in Communications, 21*(10), 1627-1641.

Baratè, A., Haus, G., Ludovico, L. A., & Vercellesi, G. (2005). MXDemo: A case study about audio, video, and score synchronization. In *Proceedings of Axmedis 2005.*

Bartlett, J. C. & Dowling, W. J. (1980). Recognition of transposed melodies: A key-distance effect in developmental perspective. *Journal of Experimental Psychology: Human Perception and Performance, 6*(3), 501-515.

Basaldella, D. & Orio, N. (2006). An application of weighted transducers to music information retrieval. *In Proceedings of Electronic Imaging* (pp. 607306/1-607306/10).

Baumann, S. (2003). Music Similarity Analysis in a P2P environment. In *Proceedings of the 4th European Workshop on Image Analysis for Multimedia Interactive Services,* pages 314–319, London, UK

Baumann, S., Pohle, T., & Shankar, V. (2004). Towards a socio-cultural compatibility of MIR systems. In *Proceedings of the International Conference on Music Information Retrieval.*

Bechtold, S. (2002). Vom Urheber- zum Informationsrecht, Implikationen des Digital Rights Management. München, Verlag C.H. Beck oHG.

Beckmann, N., Kriegel, H., & Seeger, B. (1990). The R*-tree: An efficient and robust method for points and rectangles. In *Proceedings ACM International Conference on Knowledge Discovery and Data Mining (SIGKDD)* (pp. 322-331).

Berenzweig, A., & Ellis, D. (2001). Locating singing voice segments within music signals. In *Proceedings of the IEEE Workshop on Applications of Signal Processing to Audio and Acoustics,* New York.

Berenzweig, A., Logan, B., Ellis, D. P. W. & Whitman, B. (2004). A large-scale evaluation of acoustic and subjective music-similarity measures. *Computer Music Journal, 28*(2), 63-76.

Bernstein, A. D., & Cooper E. D. (1976, July/August). The piecewise-linear technique of electronic music synthesis. *J. Audio Eng. Soc., 24*(6).

Birmingham, W. P., Dannenberg, R. B., Wakefield, G. H., Bartsch, M., Bykowski, D., Mazzoni, D., Meek, C., Mellody, M. & Rand, W. (2001). MUSART: Music retrieval via aural queries. *In Proceedings of the International Conference on Music Information Retrieval* (pp. 73-82).

Blackburn, S. & DeRoure, D. (1998). A tool for content-based navigation of music. *In Proceedings of the ACM Multimedia Conference* (pp. 361-368).

Blostein, D., Lank, E., Rose, A., & Zanibbi, R. (2002). User interfaces for on-line diagram recognition. In D. Blostein & Y. B. Kwon (Eds.), *Graphics recognition:*

Algorithms and applications, Lecture notes in computer science (Vol. 2390, pp. 92-103). Springer.

BOINC. See http://boinc.berkeley.edu/

Bollobás Béla (1998). *Modern graph theory.* New York: Springer-Verlag.

Borko, H. & Bernier, C. L. (1978). *Indexing concepts and methods.* New York: Academic Press.

Bray, S. & Tzanetakis, G. (2005). Distributed audio feature extraction for music. In *Proceedings of the International Conference on Music Information Retrieval.*

Bray, S. & Tzanetakis, G. (2005). Implicit patching for dataflow-based audio analysis and syntehsis. In *Proceedings of the International Computer Music Conference (ICMC).*

Bresin, R. (2002). Articulation rules for automatic music performance. In *Proceedings of the 2001 International Computer Music Conference*, San Francisco, California.

Brook, B. S. (1970). The Plaine and Easie code. *Musicology and the computer* (pp 53-56). New York: City University of New York Press.

Brookshier, D., Govoni, D., Krishnan, N., and Soto, J C,. 2002. JXTA: Java P2P Programming. SAMS.

Brown J. C., & Puckette, M. S. (1993). A high resolution fundamental frequency determination based on phase changes of the fourier transform. *Journal of the Acoustical Society of America, 94*, 662-667.

Brown, J. C. (1992). Musical fundamental frequency tracking using a pattern recognition method. *Journal of the Acoustical Society of America, 92*(3), 1394-1402.

Brown, J. C., & Zhang, B. (1991). Musical frequency tracking using the methods of conventional and narrowed autocorrelation. *Journal of the Acoustical Society of America, 89*(5), 2346-2354.

Buchberger, B. (1965). *An algorithm for finding a basis for the residue class ring of a zero-dimensional polynomial ideal.* Unpublished doctoral disseration. Insbruck, Austria: Math. Institute - University of Innsbruck.

Buchberger, B. (1988). Applications of Gröbner Bases in non-linear computational geometry. In J. R. Rice (Ed.), *Mathematical aspects of scientific software.* IMA Vol. 14 (pp. 60-88). New York: Springer-Verlag.

Buckley, F., & Harary, F. (1990). *Distance in graphs.* Redwood City: Addison-Wesley.

Budzik, J. (2003, June). *Information access in context: Experiences with the Watson System.* Unpublished doctoral dissertation. Evanston, IL: Northwestern University.

Buhse, W. (2002). Digital rights management for music filesharing communities. Retrieved May 27, 2007, from http://iab.fhbb.ch/eb/publications.nsf/id/94

Burroughs, N., Parkin, A. & Tzanetakis, G. (2006). Flexible scheduling for dataFlow audio processing. In *Proceedings of the International Computer Music Conference (ICMC)*, New Orleans, USA.

Byrd, D. (2006). Candidate music IR test collections: A list. Retrieved May 21, 2007, from *http://php.indiana.edu/~donbyrd/MusicTestCollections.HTML*

Byrd, D., & Crawford, T. (2002). Problems of music information retrieval in the real world. *Information Processing and Management, 38*(2), 249-272.

Cambouropoulos E., Crochemore, M., Iliopoulos, C., Mohamed, M., & Sagot, M.-F. (2005). A pattern extraction algorithm for abstract melodic representations that allow partial overlapping intervallic categories. In *Proceedings of the International Conference on Music Information Retrieval* (pp. 167-174).

Cambouropoulos, E. (1997). Musical rhythm: A formal model for determining local boundaries. In E. Leman (Ed.), *Music, gestalt and computing* (pp. 277-293). Berlin: Springer-Verlag.

Cambouropoulos, E. (1998). *Towards a general computational theory of musical structure.* Unpublished doctoral dissertation, University of Edinburgh, UK.

Cambouropoulos, E. (2003). Pitch spelling: A computational model. *Music Perception, 20*(4), 411-429.

Cambouropoulos, E. (2006). Musical parallelism and melodic segmentation: A computational approach. *Music Perception, 23*(3), 249-268.

Cambouropoulos, E., & Widmer, G. (2000). Automated motivic analysis via melodic clustering. *Journal of New Music Research, 29*(4), 347-370.

Cambouropoulos, E., Crochemore, M., Iliopoulos, C., Mouchard, L., & Pinzon, Y. (2002). Algorithms for computing approximate repetitions in musical sequences. *Journal of Computer Mathematics, 79*(11), 1135-1148.

Canazza, S., De Poli, G., Roda, A., & Vidolin, A. (1997). Analysis and synthesis of expressive intention in a clarinet performance. In *Proceedings of the 1997 International Computer Music Conference* (pp. 113-120). San Francisco, California.

Cano, P. (1998). Fundamental frequency estimation in the SMS analysis. In *Proceedings of the Digital AudioEffects Workshop (DAFx)*, Barcelona, Spain.

Cano, P., Batlle, E., Kalker, T. & Haitsma, J. (2005). A review of audio fingerprinting. *Journal of VLSI Signal Processing, 41*, 271-284.

Cano, P., Gomez, E., Gouyon, F., Herrera, P., Koppenberger, M. et al. (2006). ISMIR 2004 audio description contest. Retrieved May 21, 2007, from *http://www.iua.upf.edu/mtg/publications/MTG-TR-2006-02.pdf*

Cantate (2006). Computer access to notation and text in music libraries. Retrieved May 17, 2007, from *http://projects.fnb.nl/cantate/*

Capani, A., & Niesi, G. (1996). *CoCoA user's manual v. 3.0b.* Genova, Italy: Dept. of Mathematics, University of Genova.

Castaneda, R., Das, S. R., & Marina, M. K. (2002). Query localization techniques for on-demand routing protocols in ad-hoc networks. *Wireless Networks, 8*(2/3), 137-151.

Celma, O., Ramirez, M., & Herrera, P. (2005). Foafing the music: A music recommendation system based on RSS feeds and user preferences. In *Proceedings of the International Conference on Music Information Retrieval*.

Cemgil, A. T., & Kappen, B. (2003). Monte Carlo methods for tempo tracking and rhythm quantization. *Journal of Artificial Intelligence Research, 18*, 45-81.

Chan, K., & Fu, A.-C. (1999). Efficient time series matching by wavelets. In *Proceedings International Conference on Data Engineering (ICDE)* (pp. 126-133).

Chan, K.-P., Fu, A.-C., & Yu, C. (2003). Haar wavelets for efficient similarity search of time-series: With and without time warping. *IEEE Transactions on Knowledge and Data Engineering, 15*(3).

Chauvin, Y. et al. (1995). *Backpropagation: Theory, architectures and applications.* Lawrence Erlbaum Assoc.

Chazarain, J., Riscos, A., Alonso, J. A., & Briales, E. (1991). Multivalued logic and Gröbner Bases with applications to modal logic. *Journal of Symbolic Computation, 11*, 181-194.

Chew, E., & Chen, Y. C. (2005). Real-time pitch spelling using the spiral array. *Computer Music Journal, 29*(2), 61-76.

Chord. See http://www.pdos.lcs.mit.edu/chord/

Chu, C.-C., Su, X., Prabhu, B., Gadh, R., Kurup, S., Sridhar, G., et al. (2006). Mobile drm for multimedia content commerce in p2p networks. In *Proceedings IEEE Workshop on Digital Rights Management Impact on Consumer Communications*.

Ciaccia, P., Patella, M., & Zezula, P. (1997). M-tree: An efficient access method for similarity search in metric spaces. In *Proceedings of International Conference on Very Large Data Bases* (pp. 426-435). Morgan Kaufmann.

Clarke, I., Miller, S., Hong, T., Sandberg, O., and Wiley, B. Jan/Feb 2002. Protecting Free Expression Online with Freenet. In *IEEE Internet Computing, 6*(1), 40-49.

Clausen, M., Kurth, F., Muller, M., & Arifi, V. (2004). *Automatic synchronization of musical data: A mathematical approach.* MIT Press.

Clegg, M., Edmonds, J., & Impagliazzo, R. (1996). Using the Groebner basis algorithm to find proofs of unsatisfiability. In *Proceedings of the twenty-eighth annual ACM Symposium on Theory of Computing*. Philadelphia.

Colmenauer A. (1990). An introduction to PROLOG-III. *Communications of the ACM, 33*(7).

Conklin, D., & Anagnostopoulou, C. (2001). Representation and discovery of multiple viewpoint patterns. In *Proceedings of the International Computer Music Conference* (pp. 479-485).

Conklin, D., & Anagnostopoulou, C. (2006). Segmental pattern discovery in music. *INFORMS Journal on Computing, 18*(3), 285-293.

Cook, P. & Scavone, G. (1999). The synthesis toolkit (STK) version 2.1. In *Proceedings of the International Computer Music Conference (ICMC)*, Beijing, China.

Cooley, J. W., & Tukey, J. W. (1965). An algorithm for the machine computation of the complex Fourier series. *Mathematics of Computation, 19*, 297-301.

Cooper, M., & Foote, J. (2003). Summarizing popular music via structural similarity analysis. In *Proceedings of the IEEE Workshop on Applications of Signal Processing to Audio and Acoustics*.

Cope, B., & Freeman, R. (2001). *Digital rights management and content development technology drivers across the book production supply chain, from creator to consumer*. Australia: Common Ground Publishing Pty Ltd.

Cope, D. (1996). *Experiments in musical intelligence*. Middleton, WI: A-R Editions.

Corba. See http://www.corba.org/

Cox, B. (2002). Finding an oasis for DRM. Retrieved May 27, 2007, from http://www.internetnews.com/ec-news/article.php/1369601

Cox, D., Little, J., & O'Shea, D. (1992). *Ideals, varieties, and algorithms*. New York: Springer-Verlag.

Cristianini N., & Shawe-Taylor J. (2000). *An introduction to support vector machines*. Cambridge University Press

Crochemore, M. (1981). An optimal algorithm for computing the repetitions in a word. *Information Processing Letters, 12*(3), 244-250.

Csikszentmihalyi, M. (1990). *Flow: The psychology of optimal experience*. New York: Harper & Row.

Cuddy, L. L. & Cohen, A. J. (1976). Recognition of transposed melodic sequences. *Quarterly Journal of Experimental Psychology, 28*, 255-270.

D'Aguanno, A., Haus, G., & Vercellesi, G. (2006). Mp3 window-switching pattern preliminary analysis for general purposes beat tracking. In *Proceedings of the 120th AES Convention*, Paris, France.

Dabek, F., Brunskill, E., Kaashoek, M., Karger, D., Morris, R., Stoica, I., and Balakrishnan, H. 2001. Building Peer-to-Peer Systems with Chord, a Distributed Lookup Service. In *Eighth Workshop on Hot Topics in Operating Systems*, page 81.

Dannenberg, R. B., & Derenyi, I. (1998). Combining instrument and performance models for high-quality music synthesis. *Journal of New Music Research, 27*(3), 211-238.

Dannenberg, R. D., Pellerin, H., & Derenyi (1998). A study of trumpet envelopes. In *Proceedings of the International Computer Music Conference (ICMC)*, San Francisco, California.

Dannenberg, R., & Mont-Reynaud, B. (1987). Following an improvisation in real-time. In *Proceedings of the International Computer Music Conference* (pp. 241-248).

Dannengerg, R. & Brandt, E. (1996). A flexible real-time software synthesis system. In *Proceedings of the International Computer Music Conference (ICMC)* (pp. 270-273).

Davis, S., & Mermelstein, P. (1980). Experiments in syllable-based recognition of continuous speech. IEEE Trans. Acoust., Speech, Signal Processing (vol. 28, pp. 357-366).

de Cheveigné, A. & Baskind, A. (2003). F0 extimation. *In Proceedings of Eurospeech* (pp. 833-836).

Deliège, I. (1987). Grouping conditions in listening to music: An approach to Lerdahl and Jackendoff's grouping preference rules. *Music Perception, 4*(4), 325-350.

Desain, P., & Honing, H. (1991). Quantization of musical time: A connectionist approach. In P. M. Todd & D. G. Loy (Eds.), *Music and connectionism* (pp. 150-167). Cambridge, MA: MIT Press.

Deutsch, D. (1972). Octave generalization and tune recognition. *Perception & Psychophysics, 11*, 411-412.

Deutsch, D. (Ed.) (1982). *The psychology of music*. Academic Press.

Deutsch, D., & Feroe, J. (1981). The internal representation of pitch sequences in tonal music. *Psychological Review, 88*(6), 503-522.

DeVriendt, J. C., Lerouge, P. L., & Xu, X. (2002). Mobile network evolution: A revolution on the move. *IEEE Communications Magazine*, p. 104-111.

DeWitt, L. A., & Crowder, R. G. (1986). Recognition of novel melodies after brief delays. *Music Perception, 3*, 259-274.

Dhamija, R., & Wallenberg, F. (2003). A framework for evaluating digital rights management proposals. In *Proceedings International Mobile IPR Workshop: Rights Management of Information Products on the Mobile Internet*.

Dixon, S. (2001). An empirical comparison of tempo trackers. In *Proceedings of the 8th Brazilian Symposium on Computer Music*.

Dixon, S. (2001). Automatic extraction of tempo and beat from expressive performances. *Journal of New Music Research, 30*(1), 39-58.

Dixon, S., & Cambouropoulos, E. (2000). Beat tracking with musical knowledge. In *Proceedings of the 14th European Conference on Artificial Intelligence*, pages 626-630.

Doraisamy, S. & Rüger, S. (2004). A polyphonic music retrieval system using N-grams. *In Proceedings of the*

International Conference on Music Information Retrieval (pp. 204-209).

Dovey, M. J. (1995). *Analysis of Rachmaninoff's piano performances using inductive logic programming*. European Conference on Machine Learning, Springer-Verlag.

Dovey, M. J. (2001). A technique for "regular expression" style searching in polyphonic music. In *Proceedings of the International Conference on Music Information Retrieval* (pp. 179-185).

Dowling, W. J. & Fujitani, D. S. (1971). Contour, interval, and pitch recognition in memory for melodies. *Journal of the Acoustical Society of America, 49*, 524-531.

Dowling, W. J. (1978). Scale and contour: Two components of a theory of memory for melodies. *Psychological Review, 85*(4), 341-354.

Dowling, W. J. (1986). Context effects on melody recognition: Scale-step versus interval representations. *Music Perception, 3*(3), 281-296.

Dowling, W. J., & Harwood, D. L. (1986). *Music cognition*. London: Academic Press.

Dowling, W. J., Kwak, S. & Andrews, M. W. (1995). The time course recognition of novel melodies. *Perception and Psychophysics, 57*(2), 136-149.

Downie, J. S. & Nelson, M. (2000). Evaluation of a simple and effective music information retrieval method. In *Proceedings of the 23rd ACM Conference on Research and Development in Information Retrieval (SIGIR '00)* (pp. 73-80) Athens, Greece.

Downie, J. S. (2003). Music information retrieval. *Annual Review of Information Science and Technology, 37*, 295-340.

Downie, J. S., Futrelle, J. & Tcheng, D. (2004). The international music information retrieval systems evaluation laboratory: Governance, access and security. *In Proceedings of the International Conference on Music Information Retrieval* (pp. 9-14).

Downie, S. & Nelson, M. (2000). Evaluation of a simple and effective music information retrieval method. *In Proceedings of the ACM International Conference on Research and Development in Information Retrieval* (pp. 73-80).

Downie, S. J. & Futrelle, J. (2005). Terascale music mining. In *Proceedings of the ACM/IEEE Super Computing Conference*, 2005.

Drake, C. (1993). Reproduction of musical rhythms by children, adult musicians, and adult nonmusicians. *Perception and Psychophysics, 53*(1), 25-33.

Drake, C., Dowling, W. J. & Palmer, C. (1991). Accent structures in the reproduction of simple tunes by children and adult pianists. *Music Perception, 8*(3), 315-334.

Dubosson-Torbay, M., Pigneur, Y., & Usunier, J.-C. (2004). Business models for music distribution after the p2p revolution. In *Proceedings Wedelmusic* (pp. 172-179).

Dunn, J. & Mayer, C. (1999). VARIATIONS: A Digital Music Library System at Indiana University. *In Proceedings of ACM Conference on Digital Libraries* (pp. 12-19).

Dutta, A., Chennikara, J., Chen, W., Altintas, O., & Schulzrinne, H. (2003). Multicasting streaming media to mobile users. *IEEE Communications Magazine*, p. 81-89.

Eck, D. & Casagrande, N. (2005). Finding meter in music using an autocorrelation phase matrix and Shannon Entropy. In *Proceedings of the International Conference on Music Information Retrieval* (pp. 504-509).

Edworthy, J. (1985). Interval and contour in melody processing. *Music Perception, 2*(3), 375-388.

Edworthy, J. (1985). Melodic contour and musical structure. In P. Howell, I. Cross, & R. West (Eds.), *Musical structure and cognition* (pp. 169-188). London: Academic Press.

Eerola, T. & Toiviainen, P. (2004). MIR in Matlab: The Midi Toolbox. *In Proceedings of the International Conference on Music Information Retrieval* (pp. 22-27).

Eerola, T., Järvinen, T., Louhivuori, J., & Toiviainen, P. (2001). Statistical features and perceived similarity of folk melodies. *Music Perception, 18*, 275-296.

Eggs, H., et al. (2002). Vertrauensgenerierende Institutionen für P2P-Netzwerke. In C. Weinhardt & C. Holtmann (Eds.), *E-Commerce: Netze, Märkte, Technologien* (pp. 43-54). Physica-Berlag, Heidelberg.

Einhorn, M. (2001). *Digital rights management and access protection: An economic analysis*. Retrieved May 27, 2007, from http://www.law.columbia.edu/conferences/2001/1_program_en.htm

Erickson, R. F. (1975). The Darms project: A status report. *Computers and the Humanities, 9*(6), 291-298.

Fang, Y., Haas, Z., Liang, B., & Lin, Y.-B. (2004). TTL prediction schemes and the effects of inter-update time distribution on wireless data access. *Wireless Networks, 10*(5), 607-619.

Fernández de Sevilla, M. A. (2001). Desarrollo musical por medio de técnicas informáticas. Doce Notas, 28, 25-26.

Fernández de Sevilla, M. A. (2002). Informática musical al servicio de la formación de profesionales. *Música y Educación, 49*, 69-81.

Fernández de Sevilla, M. A. (2005). *Sistema Computacional para reconocimiento de Actitudes y Estilos en Música Culta*. Unpublished doctoral dissertation, Universidad de Alcalá, España.

Fernández de Sevilla, M. A., & Fernández del Castillo, J. R. (2002). Estudio Comparativo de editores musicales utilizando técnicas fuzzy. *Base Informática, 38*, 58-64.

Fernández de Sevilla, M. A., & Gutiérrez de Mesa, J. A. (2002). El software musical y su aplicación a la enseñanza de la música. *PCWorld, 7*, 194-202.

Fernández de Sevilla, M. A., & Hilera, J. R. (2001). Conservación y restauración del patrimonio musical. *Cuadernos de Documentación multimedia, 8*, 25-26.

Fernández de Sevilla, M. A., Jiménez, L., & Fernández del Castillo, J. R. (2003). Tool selection under uncertainty by fuzzy aggregation operators. In *Proceedings of AGOP2003* (pp 67-72). Alcalá de Henares, España: Universidad de Alcalá.

Ferrari, E. & Haus, G. (1999). The musical archive information system at Teatro alla Scala. *In Proceedings of the IEEE International Conference on Multimedia Computing and Systems* (Vol. 2, pp. 817-821).

Fetscherin, M. (2002). Present state and emerging scenario of Digital Rights Management Systems. *The International Journal on Media Management, 4*, 3.

Fischer, S., Klinkenberg, R., Mierswa, I., & Ritthoff, O. (2002). *Yale: Yet another learning environment—Tutorial* (Tech. Rep. CI-136/02). Collaborative Research Center 531, University of Dortmund.

Foote, J., Cooper, M., and Nam, U. 2002. Audio retrieval by rhythmic similarity. In *Proceedings of the International Conference on Music Information Retrieval*. Paris: IRCAM.

Forsberg, A. S., Dieterich, M., & Zeleznik, R. C. (1998). The music notepad. In *Proceedings of the ACM Symposium on User Interface Software and Technology* (pp. 203-210).

Forsberg, A., Holden, L., Miller, T., & Zeleznik, R. (October 2002; 2005). The music notepad for tablet PC, Retrieved May 29, 2007, from http://graphics.cs.brown.edu/research/music/tpc.html

Foster, I., & Iamnitchi, A. 2003. On Death, Taxes, and the Convergence of Peer- to-Peer and Grid Computing. In *Proceedings of the 2nd International Workshop on Peer-to-Peer Systems (IPTPS '03)*.

Foster, I., Kesselman, C., Nick, S., & Tuecke, S. 2002. The Physiology of the Grid: An Open Grid Services Architecture for Distributed Systems Integration. *Open Grid Service Infrastructure WG, Global Grid Forum*, June 22, 2002. See website http://www.gridforum.org/ogsi-wg/

Fox, E. A., & Shaw, J. A. (1994). Combination of multiple searches. *In The Second Text REtrieval Conference*, TREC-2 (pp. 243-249).

Friberg, A., Bresin, R., Fryden, L. (2000). Music from motion: Sound level envelopes of tones expressing human locomotion. *Journal of New Music Research, 29*(3), 199-210.

Friberg, A., Bresin, R., Fryden, L., & Sunberg, J. (1998). Musical punctuation on the microlevel: Automatic identification and performance of small melodic units. *Journal of New Music Research, 27*(3), 217-292.

Friedman, M. L. (1985). A methodology for the discussion of contour: Its application to Schoenberg's music. *Journal of Music Theory, 29*(2), 223-248.

Futrelle, J. & Downie, S. J. (2002). Interdisciplinary communities and research issues in music information retrieval. In *Proceedings of the International Conference on Music Information Retrieval (ISMIR)*, Paris.

Gabrielsson, A. (1999). The performance of music. In D. Deutsch (Ed.), *The psychology of music* (2nd ed.) Academic Press.

Gamma, E., Helm, R., Johnson, R. & Vlissides, J. (1995). *Design patterns: Elements of reusable object-oriented software*. Addison Wesley.

Ganter, B., & Wille, R. (1999). *Formal concept analysis: Mathematical foundations*. Springer-Verlag.

Gayer, A. (2002). Internet, peer-to-peer, and intellectual property in markets for digital products. Retrieved May 27, 2007, from http://econ.haifa.ac.il/~ozshy/freeware19.pdf

Gehrke, N., Burghardt, M., & Schumann, M. (2002). Ein Peer-to-Peer basiertes Modell zur Dezentralisierung elektronischer Marktplätze. In C. Weinhardt & C. Holtmann (Eds.), *E-Commerce: Netze, Märkte, Technologien. Physica-Verlag* (pp. 101-116). Heidelberg.

GEO 600, July 2005. http://www.geo600.uni-hannover.de/.

George, S. (2003). Online pen-based recognition of music notation with artificial neural networks. *Computer Music Journal, 27*(2), 70-79.

Ghias, A., Logan, J., Chamberlin, D. & Smith, B. C. (1995). Query by humming: Musical information retrieval in an audio database. *In Proceedings of the ACM Conference on Digital Libraries* (pp. 231-236).

Global Grid Forum (GGF). See http://www.ggf.org/

Globus Project. See http://www.globus.org/

Gnutella. See http://gnutella.wego.com/

Godsil, C., & Royle, G. (2001). Algebraic graph theory. *Vol. 207. Graduate texts in mathematics.* Springer Verlag.

Goldberg, D., & Richardson, C. (1993). Touch-typing with a stylus. In *Proceedings of InterCHI'93 Conference on Human Factors in Computing Systems* (pp. 80-87).

Gómez, E. & Herrera, P. (2004). Estimating the tonality of polyphonic audio files: Cognitive versus machine learning modelling strategies. *In Proceedings of the International Conference on Music Information Retrieval* (pp. 92-95).

Gomez, E., Gouyon, F., Herrera, P. & Amatriain, X. (2003). Using and enhancing the current MPEG-7 standard for a music content processing tool. In *Proceedings of the Audio Engineering Society, 114th Convention,* Mar. 22-25, Amsterdam, NL. Retrieved May 21, 2007, from http://www.iua.upf.es/mtg/publications/AES114-GomezEtAl.pdf

Gordon, L. (2002). *The Internet marketplace and digital rights management.* Retrieved May 27, 2007, from http://www.itl.nist.gov/div895/docs/GLyonDRM Whitepaper.pdf

Goto & Goto (2005). Musicream: New music playback interface for streaming, sticking, sorting and recalling musical pieces. In *Proceedings of the International Conference on Music Information Retrieval (ISMIR),* London.

Goto, M. (2001). An audio-based real-time beat tracking system for music with or without drum-sounds. *Journal of New Music Research, 30*(2), 159 - 171.

Goto, M., & Muraoka, Y. (1998). Music understanding at the beat level real-time beat tracking for audio signals. D. F. Rosenthal & H. G. Okuno (Eds.), *Computational auditoryscene analysis* (pp. 157-176).

Goto, M., & Muraoka, Y. (1999). Real-time beat tracking for drumless audio signals: Chord change detection for musical decisions. *Speech Communication, 27*(34), 311-335.

Greenhaus, D. et al. (n.d.) Digital tradition folksong database. Retrieved May 21, 2007, from *http://www.mudcat.org*

Groening, M., & Cohen, D. X. (2002). The Simpsons. *DVD, Creator, director and producers notes from the season commentary.*

Groutald, D. J., & Palisca, C. V. (2004). *Historia de la música occidental I, II.* Madrid: Alianza Editorial.

Haitsma, J., and Kalker, T. 2002. A highly robust audio fingerprinting system. In *Proceedings of the 3rd International Conference on Music Information Retrieval.* Paris: IRCAM.

Halpern, A. R. (1988). Perceived and imagined tempos of familiar songs. *Music Perception, 6*(2), 193-202.

Halpern, A. R. (1989). Memory for the absolute pitch of familiar songs. *Memory and Cognition, 17*(5), 572-581.

Harmonica (2006). Accompanying action on music information in libraries. Retrieved May 17, 2007, from *http://projects.fnb.nl/harmonica/*

Harrison, A., and Taylor, I. J. 2005. WSPeer - An Interface to Web Service Hosting and Invocation. In *Joint Workshop on High-Performance Grid Computing and High-Level Parallel Programming Models.*

Harte, C., Sandler, M., Abdallah, S. & Gómez, E. (2005). Symbolic representation of musical chords: A proposed syntax for text annotations. *In Proceedings of the International Conference on Music Information Retrieval* (pp. 66-71).

Harvell, J. & Clark, C. (1995). Analysis of the quantitative data of system performance. Deliverable 7c, LIB-JUKE-

BOX/4-1049: Music across borders. Retrieved May 17, 2007, from *http://www.statsbiblioteket.dk/Jukebox/edit-report-1.html*

Hastie, T., Tibshirani, R., & Friedman, J. (2001). *The elements of statistical learning: Data mining, inference, and prediction.* New York: Springer.

Haus, G, Longari, M., & Emanuele, P. (2004). A score-driven approach to music information retrieval. *JASIST, 55*(12), 1045-1052.

Haus, G. & Pollastri, E. (2001). An audio front end for query-by-humming systems. In *Proceedings of the Second International Symposium on Music Information Retrieval (ISMIR 2001)* (pp. 65-72) Bloomington, Indiana.

Haus, G. (1997). Describing and processing multimedia objects by Petri Nets. In *Proceedings of the 1997 IEEE International Conference on Systems, Man, and Cybernetics.* IEEE Computer Society Press, 3906-3911.

Haus, G. (1998). Rescuing La Scala's music archives. *Computer, 31*(3), 88-89.

Haus, G., & Longari, M. (2002). Towards a symbolic/tim-based music language based on xml. In *Proceedings of the First International IEEE Conference on Musical Applications Using XML (MAX2002).*

Haus, G., & Longari, M. (2005). A multilayered time-based music description approach based on XML. *Computer Music Journal, 29*(1), 70-85. MIT Press.

Haus, G., & Ludovico, L. A. (2005). The digital opera house: An architecture for multimedia databases. *Journal of Cultural Heritage, 7*(2), 92-97.

Haus, G., & Pinto, A. (2005). *A graph theoretic approach to melodic similarity* (vol. 3310).

Haus, G., & Pollastri, E. (2000). *A multimodal framework for music inputs.* Poster session presented at ACM Multimedia, pages 382-384.

Haus, G., & Sametti, A. (1991). Scoresynth: A system for the synthesis of music scores based on petri nets and a music algebra. *IEEE Computer, 24*(7), 56-60.

Haus, G., Ludovico, L. A., Vercelesi, G., & Barate' A. (2005). Mxdemo: A case study about audio, video, and score synchronization. In *Proceedings of IEEE Conference on Automatic Production of Cross Media Content for Multi-Channel Distribution (AXMEDIS)* (pp. 45-52.

Herrera, P., & Bonada, J. (1998). Vibrato extraction and parameterization in the SMS framework. In *Proceedings of COST G6 Conference on Digital Audio Effects (DAFx).* Barcelona, Spain.

Hewlett, W. B., & Selfridge-Field, E. (2005). *Music query.* Cambridge: MIT Press.

Hoashi, K., Matsumoto, K. & Inoue, N. (2003). Personalization of user profiles for content-based music retrieval based on relevance feedback. *In Proceedings of the ACM International Conference on Multimedia* (pp. 110-119).

Holland, J. H. (1986). Escaping brittleness: The possibilities of general-purpose learning algorithms applied to parallel rule-based systems. In R. S. Michalski, J. G. Carbonell, & T. M. Mitchell (Eds.), *Machine learning: An artificial intelligence approach* (Vol. 2, pp. 593-624). Palo Alto, CA: Morgan Kaufmann.

Homayounfar, H., Wang, F., & Areibi, S. (2002). Advanced P2P architecture using autonomous agents. Retrieved May 27, 2007, from http://wolfman.eos.uoguelph.ca/~sareibi/PUBLICATIONS_dr/docs/CAINE02-paper-agent-initial.pdf

Homburg, H., Mierswa, I., Möller, B., Morik, K., & Wurst, M. (2005). A benchmark dataset for audio classification and clustering. In *Proceedings of the International Conference on Music Information Retrieval.*

Horne, B., Pinkasa, B., & Sander, T. (2002). *Escrow services and incentives in peer-to-peer networks.* Retrieved May 27, 2007, from http://www.star-lab.com/bpinkas/PAPERS/p2p.ps

Hsiang, J. (1985). Refutational theorem proving using term-rewriting systems. *Artificial Intelligence, 25,* 255-300.

Hsu, J.-L., Liu, C. C. & Chen, A. L. P. (1998). Efficient repeating pattern finding in music databases. *In Proceeding of the International Conference on Information and Knowledge Management* (pp. 281-288).

Hu, N., & Dannenberg, R. B. (2002). A comparison of melodic database retrieval techniques using sung queries. *In Proceedings of the ACM/IEEE Joint Conference on Digital Libraries* (pp. 301-307).

Hua, X. S., Lu, L., & Zhang, H. J. (2004). P-karaoke: Personalized karaoke system. In *Proceedings of the 12th annual ACM international conference on Multimedia* (pp. 172-173). New York: ACM Press.

Hua, X.-S., Lu, L. et al. (2003). *Photo2Video.*ACM Multimedia (ACM MM 2003). Berkeley, CA.

Hui, K. (2002). *Piracy and the legitimate demand for recorded music.* Retrieved May 27, 2007, from http://www.comp.nus.edu.sg/~ipng/research/Piracy_3.pdf

Humdrum. The Humdram toolkit: Software for music research. Retrieved May 17, 2007, from *http://www.music-cog.ohio-state.edu/Humdrum/*

Huron D. (1995). *The Humdrum toolkit: Reference manual.*, Menlo Park, CA: Center for Computer Assisted Research in the Humanities.

Husserl, E. (1905). On the phenomenology of the consciousness of internal time. (trans. J. B. Brough, 1991). In E. Husserl (Ed.), *Collected works, 4.* The Hague, Netherlands: Kluwer Academic Publishers.

IMIRSEL (2006). The international music information retrieval system evaluation laboratory project. Retrieved May 17, 2007, from *http://www.music-ir.org/evaluation/*

Indyk, P., & Motwani, R. (1998). Approximate nearest neighbors: Towards removing the curse of dimensionality. In *Proceedings of the Thirtieth Annual ACM Symposium on theory of Computing.* NY: ACM Press.

International Conferences on Music Information Retrieval, http://www.ismir.net

International Organisation for Standardisation (2004). ISO/IEC JTC1/SC29/WG11, Call for Proposals on Symbolic Music Representation. Redmond, USA.

ISMIR (2004). ISMIR 2004 audio description contest. Retrieved May 21, 2007, from *http://ismir2004.ismir.net/ISMIR_Contest.html*

ISO/IEC International Standard IS 11172-3. Information technology - coding of moving pictures and associated audio for digital storage media at up to about 1.5 mbits/s - part 3: Audio.

ISO/IEC International Standard IS 13818-3. Information technology - generic coding of moving pictures and associatedaudio, part 3: Audio.

Jang, J.-S. R., Chen, J.-C. & Kao, M.-Y. (2001a). MIRACLE: A music information retrieval system with clustered computing engines. In *Proceedings of the Second International Symposium on Music Information Retrieval (ISMIR 2001)* (pp. 11-12) Bloomington, Indiana.

Jang, J.-S. R., Lee, H.-R. & Kao, M.-Y (n.d.). SuperMBox computer software. Retrieved May 21, 2007, from http://neural.cs.nthu.edu.tw/jang/demo

Jang, J.-S. R., Lee, H.-R. & Kao, M.-Y. (2001b). Content-based music retrieval using linear scaling and branch-and-bound tree search. In *IEEE International Conference on Multimedia and Expo*, Tokyo, Japan.

Jayant, N. S., & Noll, P. (1984). *Digital coding of waveforms: Principles and applications to speech and video.* Englewood Cliffs, NJ: Prentice Hall.

Jenssen, K. (1999). Envelope model of isolated musical sounds. In *Proceedings of COST G-6 Workshop on Digital Audio Effects (DAFx)*, Trondheim.

Jini. See http://www.jini.org/

Johnson, D., & Maltz, D. (1996). Dynamic source routing in ad-hoc wireless networks. *Mobile computing* (Vol. 353). MA: Kluwer Academic Publishers.

Johnson, M. L. (1992). An expert system for the articulation of Bach fugue melodies. In D. L. Baggi (Ed.),

Readings in computer-generated music (pp. 41-51). IEEE Computer Society.

Johnston, W. Hanna, J.P., & Millar, R. (2004). Advances in dataflow programming languages. *ACM Computing Surveys, 36*(1), 1-34.

Jones, S., Cunningham, S. J., & Jones, M. (2004). Organizing digital music for use: An examination of personal music collections. In *Proceedings of the International Conference on Music Information Retrieval.*

Juslin, P. N. (2001). Communicating emotion in music performance: A review and theoretical framework. In P. N. Juslin, & J. A. Sloboda (Eds.), *Music and Emotion: Theory and Research.* Oxford University Press.

Kageyama, T., & Takashima, Y. (1994). A melody retrieval method with hummed melody (language: Japanese). *Transactions of the Institute of Electronics, Information and Communication Engineers D-II, J77D-II*(8), 1543-1551.

Kageyama, T., Mochizuki, K. & Takashima, Y. (1993). Melody retrieval with humming. In *Proceedings of the 1993 International Computer Music Conference (ICMC'93)* (pp. 349-351) Tokyo, Japan.

Kalker, T., Epema, D., Hartel, P., Lagendijk, R., & Steen, M. van. (2004). Music2share -copyright-compliant music sharing in p2p systems. In *Proceedings of the IEEE* (pp. 961-970).

Kalogeraki, V., Gunopulos, D., & Zeinalipour-Yazti, D. (2002). A local search mechanism for peer-to-peer networks. In *Proceedings Conference on Information and Knowledge Management (CIKM)* (pp. 300-307).

Kandinsky, W. (1994). Point and line to plane: A contribution to the analysis of pictoral elements. In W. Kandinsky, K. C. Lindsay, & P. Vergo (Eds.), *Complete writings on art* (pp. 528-699). Da Capo Press.

Kant, K., Iyer, R., & Tewari, V. (2002). *A framework for classifying peer-to-peer technologies.* Retrieved May 27, 2007, from http://kkant.ccwebhost.com/papers/taxonomy.pdf

Kapur, D., & Narendran, P. (1984). *An equational approach to theorem proving in first-order predicate calculus* (Rep. No. 84CRD296). Schenectady, NY: General Electric Corporate Research and Development.

Karydis, I., Nanopoulos, A., & Manolopoulos, Y. (2005). Evaluation of similarity searching methods for music data in peer-to-peer networks. *International Journal of Business Intelligence and Data Mining, 1*(2), 210-228.

Karydis, I., Nanopoulos, A., & Manolopoulos, Y. (2006). Mining in music databases. *Processing and managing complex data for decision support* (pp. 340-374). Hershey, PA: Idea Group Publishing.

Karydis, I., Nanopoulos, A., Papadopoulos, A. N., & Manolopoulos, Y. (2005b). Music retrieval in p2p networks under the warping distance. In *Proceedings International Conference on Enterprise Information Systems (ICEIS)* (p. 100-107).

Karydis, I., Nanopoulos, A., Papadopoulos, A., & Manolopoulos, Y. (2005a). Audio indexing for efficient music information retrieval. In *Proceedings Multimedia Modelling Conference (MMM)* (pp. 22-29).

Karydis, I., Nanopoulos, A., Papadopoulos, A., Katsaros, D., & Manolopoulos, Y. (in press). Audio music retrieval in wireless ad-hoc networks. *IEEE Transactions on Audio, Speech and Language Processing.*

KaZaA. See http://www.kazaa.com/

Kendall, R. A. & Carterette, E. C. (1990). The Communication of Musical Expression. *Musical Perception 8.*

Keogh, E., & Kasetty, S. (2002). On the need for time series data mining benchmarks: A survey and empirical demonstration. In *Proceedings ACM International Conference on Knowledge Discovery and Data Mining (SIGKDD)* (pp. 102-111).

Keogh, E., & Ratanamahatana, A. (2005). Exact indexing of dynamic time warping. *Knowledge and Information Systems, 7*(3), 358-386.

Kim, Y., & Whitman, B. (2002). Singer identification in popular music recordings using voice coding features. In

Proceedings of the International Symposium on Music Information Retrieval.

Kini, A., & Shetty, S. (2002). *Peer-to-peer networking - Is this the future of network computing?* Retrieved May 27, 2007, from http://www.ias.ac.in/resonance/Dec2001/pdf/Dec2001p69-79.pdf

Kira, K., & Rendell, I. A. (1992). The feature selection problem: Traditional methods and a new algoirthm. In *Proceedings of the National Conference on Artificial Intelligence* (pp. 129-134). MIT Press.

Klapuri, A. (1999). Sound onset detection by applying psychoacoustic knowledge. In *Proceedings of the IEEE International Conference on Acoustics, Speech and Signal Processing, ICASSP.*

Klapuri, A. (n.d.) Automatic transcription of music: Literature review. Retrieved May 21, 2007, from *http://www.cs.tut.fi/~klap/iiro/literature.html*

Klapuri, A. P. (2004). Automatic music transcription as we know it today. *Journal of New Music Research, 33*(3), 269-282.

Kline, R. L. & Glinert, E. P. (2003). Approximate matching algorithms for music information retrieval using vocal input. In *Proceedings of the 11th ACM Conference on Multimedia (MM'03)* (pp. 130-139) Berkeley, California.

Kline, R. L. (2002). Algorithms for error tolerant information retrieval from music databases using vocal input. Unpublished doctoral dissertation. Rensselaer Polytechnic Institute, Troy, NY.

Kohonen, T. (1988). *Self-organization and associative memory.* Berlin: Springer-Verlag.

Kostek, B., & Wieczorkowska, A. (1997). Parametric representation of musical sound. *Archive of Acoustics* (pp. 3-26).

Kosugi, N., Nishihara, Y., Sakata, T., Yamamuro, M. & Kushima, K. (2000). A practical query-by-humming system for a large music database. In *Proceedings of the 8th ACM Conference on Multimedia (MM'00)* (pp. 333-342) Marina del Rey, California.

Kosugi, N., Sakurai, Y. & Morimoto, M. (2004). SoundCompass: A practical query-by-humming system; Normalization of scalable and shiftable time-series data and effective subsequence generation. In *Proceedings of the 2004 ACM SIGMOD international Conference on Management of Data* (pp. 881-886) Paris, France.

Koza, J. R. (1992). *Genetic programming: On the programming of computers by means of natural selection.* Cambridge: MIT Press.

Kreuzer, M., & Robbiano, L. (2000). *Computational commutative algebra.* Berlin - Heidelgeberg, Germany: Springer-Verlag.

Krumhansl, C. L. (1989). Why is musical timbre so hard to understand? In S. Nielsen and O. Olsson (Eds.), *Structure and perception electroacoustic sound and music* (pp. 45-53). Amsterdam, NL: Elsevier.

Kuhn, W. B. (1990). A real-time pitch recognition algorithm for music applications. *Computer Music Journal, 14*(3), 60-71.

Kurth, F., Muller, M., Ribbrock, A., Roder, T., Damm, D., & Fremerey, C. (2004). *A prototypical service for real-time access to local context-based music information.* Barcelona, Spain: ISMIR.

Kwok, S., & Lui, S. (2000). *A license management model to support B2C and C2C music sharing.* Retrieved May 27, 2007, from http://www10.org/cdrom/posters/1008.pdf

Kwok, S., & Lui, S. (2002). A license management model for peer-to-peer music sharing. *World Scientific Publishing Company, 1*(3), 541-558.

Kwok, S., Lang, & Kar, Y. (2002). Peer-to-peer technology business and service models: Risks and opportunities. *Electronic Markets, 12*(3), 175-183.

Laita, L. M., Roanes Lozano, E., & Alonso, J. A. (Guest Eds.). (2004). Symbolic computation in logic and artificial intelligence [Special Issue]. *RACSAM, Revista de la Real Academia de Ciencias de España, Serie "A" Matemáticas, 98*(1-2).

Laita, L. M., Roanes-Lozano, E., de Ledesma, L., & Alonso, J. A. (1999). A computer algebra approach to verification and deduction in many-valued knowledge systems. *Soft Computing, 3*(1), 7-19.

Laita, L. M., Roanes-Lozano, E., Maojo, V., de Ledesma, L., & Laita, L. (2000). An expert system for managing medical appropriateness criteria based on computer algebra techniques. *Computers and Mathematics with Applications, 51*(5), 473-481.

Lank, E. H. (2003). A retargetable framework for interactive diagram recognition. In *Proceedings of the International Conference on Document Analysis and Recognition (ICDAR'03)* (pp. 185-189).

Large, E. W., & Kolen, J. F. (1994). Resonance and the perception of musical meter. *Connection Science, 6*(2/3), 177-208.

Lartillot, O. (2005). Efficient extraction of closed motivic patterns in multi-dimensional symbolic representations of music. In *Proceedings of the International Conference on Music Information Retrieval* (pp. 191-198).

Lartillot, O., & Toiviainen, P. (2007). Motivic matching strategies for automated pattern extraction. *Musicae Scientiae*, Discussion Forum 4A, 281-314.

Lavrenko, V. & Pickens, J. (2003). Polyphonic music modeling with random fields. *In Proceedings of the ACM International Conference on Multimedia* (pp. 120-129).

Lee, II., Jang, J. R., & Kao, M. (2001). Content-based music retrieval using linear scaling and branch-and-bound tree search. In *Proceedings of IEEE International Conference on Multimedia and Expo.*

Lee, J. H. & Downie, J. S. (2004). Survey of music information needs, uses, and seeking behaviours: Preliminary findings. *In Proceedings of the International Conference on Music Information Retrieval* (pp. 441-446).

Lee, J. H. (1997). Analysis of multiple evidence combination. *In Proceedings of the ACM International Conference on Research and Development in Information Retrieval* (pp. 267-275).

Lee, J. H., & Downie, J. S. (2004). Survey of music information needs, uses, and seeking behaviours: Preliminary findings. In *Proceedings of the International Conference on Music Information Retrieval*.

Lerdahl, F., & Jackendoff, R. (1983). *A generative theory of tonal music.* Cambridge, MA: MIT Press.

Lerdhal, F. & Jackendoff, R. (1983). *A generative theory of tonal music.* Cambridge: The MIT Press.

Lesaffre, M., Leman, M., Tanghe, K., De Baets, B., De Meyer, H. & Martens, J.-P. (2003). User-dependent taxonomy of musical features as a conceptual framework for musical audio-mining technology. *In Proceedings of the Stockholm Music Acoustics Conference* (pp. 635-638).

Lesavich, S. (2002). *Protecting digital content in a peer-to-peer world.* Retrieved May 27, 2007, from http://www.hightech-iplaw.com/wibardrm.pdf

Lethin, R. (2001). Reputation. In A. Oram (Ed.), *Harnessing the power of disruptive technologies* (pp. 341-353). Sebastopol: O'Reilly.

Levitin, D. J., & Cook, P. R. (1996). Memory for musical tempo: Additional evidence that auditory memory is absolute. *Perception and Psychophysics, 58*(6), 927-935.

Levitin, D. J. (1994). Absolute memory for musical pitch: Evidence from the production of learned melodies. *Perception and Psychophysics, 56*(4), 414-423.

Lew, M. S., Sebe, N., Djeraba, C., & Jain, R. (2006). Content-based multimedia information retrieval: State of the art and challenges. *ACM Transactions on Multimedia Computing, Communications and Applications, 2*(1), 1-19.

Li, G. (1985). Robust regression. In D. C. Hoaglin, F. Mosteller & J. W. Tukey (Eds.), *Exploring data tables, trends, and shapes* (pp. 281-343). New York: John Wiley and Sons.

Li, T. & Tzanetakis, G. (2003). Factors in automatic musical genre classification of audio signals. In *Proceedings of the IEEE Workshop on Applications of Signal Processing to Audio and Acoustics (WASPAA)* New Paltz, New York.

Li, T., Li, Q., Zhu, S., & Ogihara, M. (2002). A survey on wavelet applications in data mining. *Special Interest Group on Knowledge Discovery and Data Mining (SIGKDD) Explorations, 4*(2), 49-68.

Li, T., Ogihara, M., & Li, Q. (2003). A comparative study on content-based music genre classification. In *Proceedings ACM Conference on Research and Development in Information Retrieval (SIGIR)* (pp. 282-289).

Li, X., & Wu, J. (2004). Searching techniques in peer-to-peer networks. In *Handbook of Theoretical and Algorithmic Aspects of Ad hoc, Sensor, and Peer-to-peer Networks.* FL: CRC Press.

Lidy, T., & Rauber, A. (2005). Evaluation of feature extractors and psycho-acoustic transformations for music genre classification. In *Proceedings of the International Conference on Music Information Retrieval* (pp. 34-41).

Lin, J., Keogh, J., Lonardi, S., & Patel, P. (2002). Finding motifs in time series. In *Proceedings of the Workshop on Temporal Data Mining* (pp. 53-68).

Lindsay, A. T. (1996). *Using contour as a mid-level representation of melody.* Unpublished master's thesis, Massachusetts Institute of Technology.

Lippens, S. et al. (2004). A comparison of human and automatic musical genre classification. In *Proceedings of the IEEE International Conference on Audio, Speech and Signal Processing,* Montreal, Canada.

Liu, Z., Kundur, D., Merabti, M., & Yu, H. (2006). On peer-to-peer multimedia content access and distribution. In *Proceedings of the IEEE International Conference on Multimedia and Expo (ICME).*

Liu, Z., Wang, Y., & Chen, T. (1998). Audio feature extraction and analysis for scene segmentation and classification. *Journal of VLSI Signal Processing System, 20*(1-2).

Logan, B. and Salomon, A. (2001). A Music Similarity Function based on Signal Analysis. In *International Conference on Multimedia and Expo* (ICME). IEEE

Logan, J., Ghias, A., & Chamberlin, D. (1995). Query by humming. In *Proceedings of ACM Multimedia, 95,* 231-236.

Longari, M. (2004). *Formal and software tools for a commonly acceptable musical application using the XML language.* Unpublished doctoral thesis, Università degli Studi di Milano, Milano, IT 20135. Also available as Università degli Studi di Milano, Department of Computer Science Report.

Lopez de Mantaras, R., & Arcos, J. L. (2002). AI and music, from composition to expressive performance. *AI Magazine, 23*, 3.

Lou, W., & Wu, J. (2004). Broadcasting in ad-hoc networks using neighbor designating. In *Handbook of Mobile Computing.* FL: CRC Press.

Macé, S., & Anquetil, E. (2006). A generic approach for pen-based user interface development. In C. Pribeanu, G. Santucci, J. Vanderdonckt, & G. Calvary (Eds.), *Computer-aided design of user interfaces V.* In *Proceedings of the Sixth International Conference on Computer-Aided Design of User Interfaces (CADUI'06)* (pp. 57-70). Springer-Verlag.

Macé, S., Anquetil, E., & Coüasnon, B. (2005). A generic method to design pen-based systems for structured document composition: Development of a musical score editor. In *Proceedings of the first Workshop on Improving and Assessing Pen-Based Input Techniques* (pp. 15-22).

Macé, S., Anquetil, E., Garrivier, E., & Bossis, B. (2005). A pen-based musical score editor. In *Proceedings of the International Computer Music Conference (ICMC'05)* (pp. 415-418).

Maddage, N. C., Xu, C., & Wang, Y. (2003). A SVM-based classification approach to musical audio. In *Proceedings of the International Conference on Music Information Retrieval.*

Maddage, N., Wan, K. W., Xu, C., & Wang, Y. (2004). Singing voice detection using twice-iterated composite fourier transform. In *Proceedings of the IEEE International Conference on Multimedia and Expo.*

Maher, R. C., & Beauchamp, J. W. (1994). Fundamental frequency estimation of musical signals using a two-way mismatch procedure. *Journal of the Acoustic Society of America, 95,* 2254-2263.

Mandel, M. I., & Ellis, D. P. W. (2005). Song-level features and support vector machines for music classification. In *Proceedings of the International Conference on Music Information Retrieval.*

Manjunath, B. S., Salembier, P. & Sikora, T. (2002). *Introduction to MPEG-7.* New York: John Wiley and Sons.

Manulescu, D. A. (1997). A dataflow pattern language. In *Proceedings of Pattern Languages of Programming,* Monticello, Illinois.

Marco, T. A. (2002). *Historia de la música occidental del siglo XX.* Madrid, España: Alpuerto.

Martin, K. D. (1996). *Automatic transcription of simple polyphonic music: Robust front end processing* (Tech. Rep. No. 399). M.I.T. Media Laboratory Perceptual Computing Section.

Martinez, J. M. (Ed.) (2004). MPEG-7 overview (version 10). ISO/IEC JTC1/SC29/WG11, Palma de Mallorca. Retrieved May 21, 2007, from *http://www.chiariglione. org/MPEG/standards/mpeg-7/mpeg-7.htm*

Marvin, E. W. & Laprade, P. A. (1987). Relating musical contours: Extensions of a theory for contours. *Journal of Music Theory, 31*(2), 225-267.

McEnnis, D., McKay, C., Fujinaga, I., & Depalle, P. (2005). JAUDIO: A feature extraction library. In *Proceedings of the International Conference on Music Information Retrieval.*

McKay, C., Fiebrink, R., McEnnis, D., Li, B., & Fujinaga, I. (2005). Ace: A framework for optimizing music classification. In *Proceedings of the International Conference on Music Information Retrieval.*

McLane, A. (1996). Music as information. In M. E. Williams (Ed.), *Arist* (Vol. 31, pp. 225-262). American Society for Information Science.

McNab, R. J., Smith, L. A., Bainbridge, D. & Witten, I. H. (1997). The New Zealand digital library MELody inDEX. *D-Lib Magazine.* Retrieved May 21, 2007, from *http://www.dlib.org/dlib/may97/meldex/05witten.html*

McNab, R. J., Smith, L. A., Witten, I. H., Henderson, C. L. & Cunningham, S. J. (1996). Towards the digital music library: Tune retrieval from acoustic input. In *Proceedings of the First ACM Conference on Digital Libraries (DL'96)* (pp. 11-18) Bethesda, Maryland.

McNab, R. J., Smith, L. l. A., & Witten I. H. (1996). Signal processing for melody transcription. (SIG Working Paper vol. 95-22).

Meek, C. & Birmingham, W. (2003). Automatic thematic extractor. *Journal of Intelligent Information Systems, 21*(1), 9-33.

Mellody, M., Bartsch, M. A., & Wakefield, G. H. (2003). Analysis of vowels in sung queries for a music information retrieval system. *Journal of Intelligent Information Systems, 21*(1), 35-52.

Melucci, M. & Orio, N. (1999). Musical information retrieval using melodic surface. *In Proceedings of the ACM Conference on Digital Libraries* (pp. 152-160).

Melucci, M. & Orio, N. (2004). Combining melody processing and information retrieval techniques: Methodology, evaluation, and system implementation. *Journal of the American Society for Information Science and Technology, 55*(12), 1058-1066.

Meng, A., & Shawe-Taylor, J. (2005). An investigation of feature models for music genre classification using the support vector classifier. In *Proceedings of the International Conference on Music Information Retrieval* (pp. 604-609).

Meredith, D., Lemström K., & Wiggins G. (2003). Algorithms for discovering repeated patterns in multidimensional representations of polyphonic music. In *Proceedings of the Cambridge Music Processing Colloquium* (pp. 46-56).

Meredith, D., Lemström, K., & Wiggins, G. (2002). Algorithms for discovering repeated patterns in multidimensional representations of polyphonic music. *Journal of New Music Research, 31*(4), 321-345.

Middleton, R. (2002). *Studying popular music*. Philadelphia: Open University Press.

MIDI (1993). *MIDI 1.0 detailed specification, version 4.3*. Los Angeles, CA: International MIDI Association.

Mierswa, I. (2004). Automatisierte Merkmalsextraktion aus Audiodaten. Fachbereich Informatik, Universität Dortmund, 2004.

Mierswa, I., & Morik, K. (2005). Automatic feature extraction for classifying audio data. *Machine Learning Journal, 58*, 127-149.

Mierswa, I., & Wurst, M. (2005). Efficient feature construction by meta learning: Guiding the search in meta hypothesis space. In *Proceedings of the International Conference on Machine Learning Workshop on Meta Learning*.

Milojicic, D., et al. (2002). Peer-to-peer computing, HP laboratories. Retrieved May 27, 2007, from http://www.hpl.hp.com/techreports/2002/HPL-2002-57.pdf

Minar, N., & Hedlung, M. (2001). Network of peers: Peer-to-peer models through the history of the internet. In A. Oram (Ed.), *Harnessing the power of disruptive technologies* (pp. 3-20). Sebastopol: O'Reilly.

Mirapaul, M. (2004, June 17). Art unfolds in a search for keywords. *The New York Times, CLIII(52883)*, E5. New York.

Misra, A., Wang, G. & Cook, P. (2005). SndTools: Real-time audio DSP and 3D visualization. In *Proceedings of the International Computer Music Conference (ICMC)*, Barcelona, Spain.

Mitchell, T. M. (1997). Machine learning. McGraw-Hill.

Mitobe, Y., Miyao, H., & Maruyama, M. (2004). A fast HMM algorithm based on stroke lengths for online recognition of handwritten music scores. In *Proceedings of the Ninth International Workshop on Frontiers in Handwriting Recognition (IWFHR'04)* (pp. 521-526).

Miyao, H., & Maruyama, M. (2004). An online handwritten music score recognition system. In *Proceedings of the Seventeenth International Conference on Pattern Recognition (ICPR'04)* (pp. 461-464).

Moen, W. E. (1998). Accessing distributed cultural heritage information. *Communications of the ACM, 41*(4), 45-48.

Mongeau, M. & Sankoff, D. (1990). Comparison of musical sequences. *Computers and the Humanities, 24*, 161-175.

Moore, B. C., & Glasberg, B. (1983). Suggested formulae for calculating auditory-filter bandwidths and excitation patterns. *The Journal of the Acoustical Society of America, 74*(3), 750-753.

Mörchen, F., Ultsch, A., Nöcker, M., & Stamm, C. (2005). Databionic visualization of music collections according to perceptual distance. In *Proceedings of the International Conference on Music Information Retrieval*.

Mörchen, F., Ultsch, A., Thies, M., Löhken, I., Nöcker, M., Stamm, C., Efthymiou, N., & Kümmerer, M. (2004). *MusicMiner: Visualizing perceptual distances of music as topographical maps* (Tech. Rep.). Dept. of Mathematics and Computer Science, University of Marburg, Germany.

Morik, K., & Wessel, S. (1999). Incremental signal to symbol processing. In K. Morik, M. Kaiser, & V. Klingspor (Eds.), *Making robots smarter: Combining sensing and action through robot learning* (pp. 185-198). Boston: Kluwer Academic.

Mouchère, H., & Anquetil, E. (2006). A unify strategy to deal with different natures of reject. In *Proceedings of the Eighteenth International Conference on Pattern Recognition (ICPR'06)* (pp. 792-795).

Mulholland, J. (2001). Digital rights (mis)management, W3C DRM workshop. Retrieved May 27, 2007, from http://www.w3.org/2000/12/drm-ws/pp/fsu-mulholland.html

Muller, M., Kurth, F., & Roder, T. (2004). Towards an efficient algorithm for automatic score-to-audio synchronization. In *Proceedings of the 5th International*

Conference on Music Information Retrieval, Barcelona, Spain.

Musica. The international database of choral repertoire. Retrieved May 17, 2007, from *http: //www.musicanet. org/*

Nakagawa, M., Machii, K., Kato, N., & Souya, T. (1993). Lazy recognition as a principle of pen interfaces. In *Proceedings of the ACM Conference Companion on Human Factors in Computing Systems (InterCHI'93)* (pp. 89-90).

Napster. See http://www.napster.com/

Narmour, E. (1990). *The analysis and cognition of basic melodic structures.* Chicago, MI: University of Chicago Press.

Narmour, E. (1991). *The analysis and cognition of melodic complexity: The implication realization model.* University of Chicago Press.

Nattiez, J.-J. (1990). *Music and discourse: Towards a semiology of music.* Princeton, NJ: Princeton University Press.

Nelson, M. (2002). *Distributed systems topologies: Part 2.* Retrieved May 27, 2007, from http://www.openp2p. com/ pub/a/p2p/2002/01/08/p2p_topologies_pt2.html

Neve, G. & Orio, N. (2004). Indexing and retrieval of music documents through pattern analysis and data fusion techniques. *In Proceedings of the International Conference on Music Information Retrieval* (pp. 216-223).

Newcomb, S. R. (1991). Standard music description language complies with hypermedia standard. *IEEE Computer,* 76-79.

Ng, E., Bell, T., & Cockburn, A. (1998). Improvements to a pen-based musical input system. In *Proceedings of the Australian Conference on Computer-Human Interaction (OzCHI'98)* (pp. 239-252).

Ni, S.-Y., Tseng, Y.-C., Chen, Y.-S., & Sheu, J. (1999). The broadcast storm problem in a mobile ad-hoc networks. In *Proceedings ACM/IEEE International Conference on Mobile Computing and Networking (MOBICOM)* (pp. 151-162).

Noll, D. (1997). Mpeg digital audio coding. *IEEE Signal Processing Magazine, 14*(5), 59-81.

Nwe, T. L., & Wang, Y. (2004). Automatic detection of vocal segments in popular songs. In *Proceedings of the International Conference on Music Information Retrieval.* Barcelona, Spain.

O'Reilly, T. (2001). Remaking the peer-to-peer meme. In A. Oram (Ed.), *Harnessing the power of disruptive technologies* (pp. 38-59). Sebastopol: O'Reilly.

OGSI working group. See https://forge.gridforum.org/ projects/ogsi-wg

Orio, N. (2006). Music retrieval: A tutorial and review. *Foundations and Trends in Information Retrieval, 1*(1), 1-90.

Owens, T. (1974). Charlie Parker: Techniques of Improvisation. Doctoral dissertation, UCLA.

Pachet, F. (2003). Content management for electronic music distribution. *Commun. ACM, 46*(4), 71-75.

Pachet, F., & Cazaly, D. (2000). A classification of musical genre. In *Proceedings of the RIAO Content-Based Multimedia Information Access Conference.*

Pack, T. (2001). Digital rights management: Can technology provide long-term solutions? *E-Content, 5*(6), 22-27.

Pampalk, E. (2001). *Islands of music: Analysis, organization, and visualization of music archives.* Unpublished master's thesis, Department of Software Technology and Interactive Systems, Vienna University of Technology.

Pampalk, E., Dixon, S., & Widmer, G. (2004). Exploring music collections by browsing different views. *Computer Music Journal, 28*(2), 49-62.

Pampalk, E., Flexer, A., & Widmer, G. (2005). Improvements of audio-based music similarity and genre classification. In *Proceedings of the International Conference on Music Information Retrieval.*

Pan, D. (1995). A tutorial on mpeg/audio compression. *IEEE Multimedia, 2*(2), 60 - 74.

Pandora. See http://www.pandora.com/

Papaodysseus, C., Roussopoulos, G., Fragoulis, D., Panagopoulos, T., & Alexiou, C. (2001). A new approach to the automatic recognition of musical recordings. *Jounal of Acoustical Engineering Society, 49*(1/2), 23-35.

Parameswaran, M., Susarla, A., & Whinston, A. (2002). *P2P networking: An information-sharing alternative.* Retrieved May 27, 2007, from http://cism.bus.utexas. edu/works/articles/ PARA.Cxs2final.pdf

Paraskevas, M., & Mourjopoulos, J. (1996). A Statistical Study of the Variability and Features of Audio Signals: Some Preliminary Results. In *Audio Engineering Society 100th Convention.* Copenhagen, Sweden.

Pardo, B. (2004). Tempo tracking with a single oscillator. In *Proceedings of the International Conference on Music Information Retrieval.* Barcelona, Spain.

Pastry. See http://research.microsoft.com/<antr/pastry/

Pauws, S. (2002). CubyHum: A fully operational query by humming system. In *Proceedings of the 3rd International Symposium on Music Information Retrieval (ISMIR'02)* (pp. 187-196). Paris, France.

Pérez Carretero, C., Laita L. M., Roanes-Lozano, E., & Laita, L. (2002). A logic and computer algebra-based expert system for diagnosis of anorexia. *Mathematics and Computers in Simulation, 58,* 183-202.

Perkinson, D. (n.d.). *CoCoA 4.0 Online Help.* Genova, Italy: Dept. of Mathematics - University of Genova.

Petri, C. A. (1976). General net theory. In *Proceedings of the Joint IBM & Newcastle upon Tyne Seminar on Computer Systems Design.*

Pfalzgraf, J. (2004). On logical fiberings and automated deduction in many-valued logics using Gröbner Bases. *RACSAM Revista de la Real Academia de Ciencias, Serie A "matemáticas", 98*(1-2), 213-228.

Pienimäki, A. (2002). Indexing music database using automatic extraction of frequent phrases. *In Proceedings of the International Conference on Music Information Retrieval* (pp. 25-30).

Pikrakis, A., Antonopoulos, I., & Theodoridis, S. (2004). Music meter & tempo tracking from audio. In *Proceedings of the International Conference on Music Information Retrieval.* Barcelona, Spain.

Pinto, A. (2003). Modelli formali per misure di similarità musicale. Master's thesis, Universit`a degli Studi di Milano, Milano I 20135. Also available as Università degli Studi di Milano, Department of Mathematics Report.

Plamondon, R., & Srihari, S. (2000). On-line and off-line handwriting recognition: A comprehensive survey. *IEEE Transactions on Pattern Analysis and Machine Intelligence, 1*(22), 63-84.

Pohle, T., Pampalk, E., & Widmer, G. (2005). Evaluation of frequently used audio features for classification of music into perceptual categories. In *Proceedings of the Fourth International Workshop on Content-Based Multimedia Indexing (CBMI'05).*

Polansky, L., & Bassein, R. (1992). Possible and impossible melody: Some formal aspects of contour. *Journal of Music Theory, 36*(2), 259-284.

Polansky, L. (1996). Morphological metrics. *Journal of New Music Research, 25,* 289-368.

Pollastri, E. (2002). A pitch tracking system dedicated to process smging voice for music retrieval. In *Proceedings of IEEE International Conference on Multimedia and Expo.*

Praveen, K., Sridhar, G., Sridhar, V., & Gadh, R. (2005). Dmw - A middleware for digital rights management in peer-to-peer networks. In *Proceedings International Workshop on Secure and Ubiquitous Networks.*

Puckette, M. (2002). Max at seventeen. *Computer Music Journal, 26*(4).

Quinlan, J. R. (1993). *C4.5: Programs for machine learning.* San Francisco: Morgan Kaufmann.

Quinlan, R. J. (1986). Induction of decision trees. *Machine Learning, 1*(1), 81-106.

Ramirez, R., & Hazan, A. (2005). In *Proceedings of the 18th Florida Artificial Intelligence Research Society Conference (FLAIRS 2005)*, Clearwater Beach, Florida.

Ramirez, R., Hazan, A., Maestre, E., & Serra, X. (2006). A data mining approach to expressive music performance modeling. In *Multimedia data mining and knowledge discovery*. Springer.

Rauber, A., Pampalk, E., & Merkl, D. (2002). Using psycho-acoustic models and self-organizing maps to create a hierarchical structuring of music by sound similarity. In *Proceedings of the International Symposium on Music Information Retrieval*.

Repp, B. H. (1992). Diversity and commonality in music performance: An analysis of timing microstructure in Schumann's "Traumerei". *Journal of the Acoustical Society of America, 104*.

Reti, R. (1951). *The thematic process in music*. New York: Macmillan.

Roads, C., Pope, S., Piccialli, A., & Poli, G. D. (Eds.). (1997). *Musical signal processing*. Royal Swets & Zeitlinger, Lisse, The Netherlands.

Roanes-Lozano, E., Laita, L. M., & Roanes-Macías, E. (1998). A polynomial model for multivalued logics with a touch of algebraic geometry and computer algebra. *Mathematics and Computers in Simulation, 45*(1), 83-99.

Roanes-Lozano, E., Roanes-Macías, E., & L.M. Laita. (2000). Railway interlocking systems and Gröbner Bases. *Mathematics and Computers in Simulation, 51*(5), 473-481.

Roanes-Macías, E., & Roanes-Lozano, E. (2001). Automatic determination of geometric loci. 3D-extension of Simson-Steiner theorem. In J. A. Campbell & E. Roanes Lozano (Eds.), *Artificial Intelligence and Symbolic Computation; International Conference AISC 2000*. Revised Papers. LNCS 1930 (pp.157-173). Berlin-Heidelberg, Germany: Springer-Verlag.

Roccetti, M., Salomoni, P., Ghini, V., & Ferretti, S. (2005). Bringing the wireless Internet to UMTS devices: A case study with music distribution. *Multimedia Tools and Applications, 25*(2), 217-251.

Roland, P. (2002). The music encoding initiative (MEI). In *Proceedings of IEEE 1st International Conference on Musical Application Using XML (MAX 2002)*. Milano, Italy.

Rolland, P.-Y. (1999). Discovering patterns in musical sequences. *Journal of New Music Research, 28*(4), 334-350.

Rosenblatt, B., Trippe, B., & Mooney, S. (2002). *Digital rights management: Business and technology*. New York: M&T Books.

Rothenberg, J. (1995). Ensuring the longevity of digital documents. *Scientific American, 272*(1), 42-47.

Rothstein, J. (1991). *MIDI: A comprehensive introduction*. Madison, WI: A-R Editions.

Rothstein, J. (1995). *MIDI: A comprehensive introduction* (2nd ed.). A-R Editions.

Rüping, S. (2000). *mySVM Manual*. Universität Dortmund, Lehrstuhl Informatik VIII. http://www-ai.cs.uni-dortmund.de/SOFTWARE/MYSVM/.

Ruwet, N. (1987). Methods of analysis in musicology. *Music Analysis, 6*(1-2), 4-39.

Sastry, N. (2005). *Stealing (from) the music industry* (Tech. Rep.). Computer Science Dept., University of Berkeley.

Saunders C., Hardoon, D., Shawe-Taylor, J., & Widmer, G. (2004). Using string kernels to identify famous performers from their playing style. In *Proceedings of the 15th European Conference on Machine Learning (ECML'2004)*, Pisa, Italy.

Saussure, F. de (1916). *Course in general linguistics* (trans. Roy Harris, 1983). London: Duckworth.

Scaringella, N., & Zoia, G. (2004). A real-time beat tracker for unrestricted audio signals. In *Proceedings of the SMC'04 Conference*, Paris, France.

Scheirer, E. D. (1997). Using musical knowledge to extract expressive performance information from audio recordings. In *Proceedings Readings in Computational Auditory Scene Analysis.*

Scheirer, E. & Slaney, M. (1997). Construction and evaluation of a robust multi-feature music/speech discriminator. In *Proceedings of the IEEE Int. Conf. on Audio, Speech and Signal Processing (ICASSP).*

Schoder, D., & Fischbach, K. (2002). Peer-to-peer - Anwendungsbereiche und herausforderungen. Retrieved May 27, 2007, from http://www.whu-koblenz.de/ebusiness/p2p-buch/buch/P2P-Buch_04_Schoder-Fischbach_P2P-Anwendungsbereiche-Herausforderungen.pdf

Schölkopf, B. & Smola, A. J. (2002). *Learning with kernels—Support vector machines, regularization, optimization, and beyond.* MIT Press.

Schollmeier, R. (2002). *Peer-to-peer networking. Applications for and impacts on future IP-based networks.* Retrieved May 27, 2007, from http://www.lkn.ei.tum.de/lkn/mitarbeiter/hrs/ Komponenten/paper/Peer1f.pdf

Schwarz, D., & Wright, M. (2000). Extensions and applications of the SDIF sound description interchange format. In *Proceedings of the International Computer Music Conf (ICMC).*

Schyndel, R. G. van. (2005). A preliminary design for a privacy-friendly free p2p media file distribution system. *International Workshop on Intelligent Information Hiding and Multimedia Signal Processing (IIHMSP) part of Knowledge-Based Intelligent Information and Engineering Systems (KES), 3*, 1018-1024.

Seashore, C. E. (Ed.) (1936). *Objective analysis of music performance.* University of Iowa Press.

Selfridge-Field, E. (Ed.) (1997). *Beyond MIDI: The handbook of musical codes.*, Cambridge: MIT Press.

Serra, X., & Smith, S. (1990). Spectral modeling synthesis: A sound analysis/synthesis system based on a deterministic plus stochastic decomposition. *Computer Music Journal, 14*(4).

Sethares, J. C., Sethares, W. A., & Morris, R. D. (2005). Beat tracking of musical performances using low-level audio features. *IEEE Transactions On Speech and Audio Processing, 13*(2), 275-285.

SETI@Home. See http://setiathome.ssl.berkeley.edu/

Shamma, D. A. (2005, December). *Network arts: Defining emotional interaction in media arts and information retrieval.* Evanston, IL: Northwestern University.

Shamma, D. A., Owlsey, S., Hammond, K. J., Bradshaw, S., & Budzik, J. (2004). Network arts: Exposing cultural reality. In *Alternate track papers & posters of the 13th International Conference on World Wide Web* (pp. 41-47). New York: ACM Press.

Shamma, D. A., Owsley, S., Bradshaw, S., & Hammond, K. J. (2004). Using web frequency within multi-media exhibitions. In *Proceedings of the 12th International Conference on Multi-Media.* New York: ACM Press.

Shifrin, J., Pardo, B., Meek, C. & Birmingham, W. (2002). HMM-based musical query retrieval. *In Proceedings of the ACM/IEEE Joint Conference on Digital Libraries* (pp. 295–300).

Shirky, C. (2001). Listening to napster. In A. Oram (Ed.), *Harnessing the power of disruptive technologies* (pp. 21-37). Sebastopol: O'Reilly.

Silberger, K. (1996). Putting composers in control. *IBM Research, 34*(4), 14-15.

Smith, J. D., Nelson, D. G. K., Grohskopf, L. A. & Appleton, T. (1994). What child is this? What interval was that? Familiar tunes and music perception in novice listeners. *Cognition, 52*, 23-54.

Smith, T. F. & Waterman, M. S. (1981). Identification of common molecular subsequences. *Journal of Molecular Biology, 147*, 195-197.

SMSTools. Retrieved May 26, 2007, from http://www.iua.upf.es/sms

Soulez, F., Rodet, X., & Schwarz, D. (2003). Improving polyphonic and poly-instrumental music to score alignment. In *Proceedings of the 4th International Conference on Music Information Retrieval* (pp. 143-148).

Sparck Jones, K., & Willett, P. (1997). *Readings in information retrieval.*, San Francisco: Morgan Kaufmann.

Stamatatos, E., & Widmer, G. (2005). Automatic identification of music performers with learning ensembles. *Artificial Intelligence, 165*(1), 37-56.

Stenzel, R. & Kamps, T. (2005). Improving content-based similarity measures by training a collaborative model. *In Proceedings of the International Conference on Music Information Retrieval* (pp. 264-271).

Steyn, J. (2002). Framework for a music markup language. In *Proceedings of IEEE 1st International Conference on Musical Applications Using XML (MAX2002)*. Milano, Italy.

Taheri-Panah, S. & MacFarlane, A. (2004). Music information retrieval systems: Why do individuals use them and what are their needs? In *Proceedings of the International Conference on Music Information Retrieval*.

Takens, F. (1980). Detecting strange attractors in turbulence. In D. A. Rand & L. S. Young (Eds.), *Dynamical systems and turbulence* (Vol. 898), *Lecture Notes in Mathematics* (pp. 366-381). Berlin: Springer.

Taylor, I. J., et al. (2003). Triana as a Graphical Web Services Composition Toolkit. Web Services. In *Proceedings of the IEEE International Conference*.

Temperley, D. (1988). *The cognition of basic musical structures*. Cambridge, MA: MIT Press.

Tenney, J. & Polansky, L. (1980). Temporal gestalt perception in music. *Journal of Music Theory, 24*(2), 205-241.

The GridLab Project. See http://www.gridlab.org

The Triana Project. See http://www.trianacode.org/

Tian, Q., Zhu, Y., & Kankanhalli, M. (2002). Similarity matching of continuous melody contours for humming querying of melody databases. In *Proceeedings of the International Workshop on Multimedia Signal Processing*.

Tobudic A., & Widmer, G. (2003). Relational IBL in music with a new structural similarity measure. In *Proceedings of the International Conference on Inductive Logic Programming*.

Todd, N. (1992). The dynamics of dynamics: A model of musical expression. *Journal of the Acoustical Society of America, 91*.

Toiviainen, P. (1998). An interactive MIDI accompanist. *Computer Music Journal, 22*(4), 63-75.

Toiviainen, P., & Eerola, T. (2006). Autocorrelation in meter induction: The role of accent structure. *Journal of Acoustical Society of America, 119*(2), 1164-1170.

TREC. Text REtrieval conference home page. Retrieved May 17, 2007, from *http://trec.nist.gov/*

Trehub, S. E. (1987). Infants' perception of musical patterns. *Perception and Psychophysics, 41*(6), 635-641.

Tummarello, G., Morbidoni, C., Puliti, P., and Piazza, P. 2005. Semantic audio hyperlinking: a multimedia-semantic web scenario. In *Proceedings of the 1ˢᵗ International Conference on Automated Production of Cross Media Content for Multi-channel Distribution*.

Tuulos, V., & Scheible, J. (2006) StoryMashup. Retrieved May 29, 2007, from http://www.storymashup.org/

Typke, R., den Hoed, M., de Nooijer, J., Wiering, F. & Veltkamp, R.C. (2005). A ground truth for half a million musical incipits. *Journal of Digital Information Management, 3*(1), 34-39.

Typke, R., Wiering, F., Veltkamp, R. C. (2005). A survey of music information retrieval systems. *In Proceedings International Conference on Music Information Retrieval (ISMIR)* (pp. 153-160).

Tzanetakis, G. & Cook, P. (2000). MARSYAS: A framework for audio analysis. *Organized Sound, Cambridge University Press*, 4(3).

Tzanetakis, G. & Cook, P. (2002). Musical genre classification of audio signals. *IEEE Trans. on Speech and Audio Processing, 10*(5).

Tzanetakis, G. (2002). *Manipulation, analysis and retrieval systems for audio signals.* Unpublished doctoral thesis, Computer Science Department, Princeton University.

Tzanetakis, G., & Cook, P. (1999). A framework for audio analysis based on classification and temporal segmentation. In *EUROMICRO 1999 (25th EUROMICRO '99 Conference, Informatics: Theory and Practice for the New Millenium).*

Tzanetakis, G., & Cook, P. (2002). Musical genre classification of audio signals. *IEEE Transactions on Speech and Audio Processing, 10*(5), 293-302.

Tzanetakis, G., Ermolinskyi, A., & Cook, P. (2002). Beyond the query-by-example paradigm: New query interfaces for music information retrieval. In *Proceedings of the 2002 International Computer Music Conference.*

Tzanetakis, G., Essl, G., & Cook, P. (2001). Automatic musical genre classification of audio signals. In *Proceedings of the International Symposium on Music Information Retrieval* (pp. 205-210).

Tzanetakis, G., Gao, J., & Steenkiste, P. (2003). A scalable peer-to-peer system for music content and information retrieval. In *Proceedings of the International Conference on Music Information Retrieval.*

Tzanetakis, G., Gao, J., & Steenkiste, P. (2004). A scalable peer-to-peer system for music information retrieval. *Computer Music Journal, 28*(2), 24-33.

Uitdenbogerd, A., & Zobel, J. (1998). Manipulation of music for melody matching. In *Proceedings of the 6th ACM Conference on Multimedia (MM'98)* (pp. 235-240). Bristol, UK.

Uitdenbogerd, A., & Zobel, J. (1999). Melodic matching techniques for large music databases. In *Proceedings of the 7th ACM Conference on Multimedia (MM'99)* (pp. 57-66) Orlando, Florida.

Ukkonen, E. (1992). Approximate string-matching with q-grams and maximal matches. *Theoretical Computer Science, 92,* 191-211.

Unal, E., Narayanan, S. S. & Chew, E. (2004). A statistical approach to retrieval under user-dependent uncertainty in query-by-humming systems. In *Proceedings of the 6th ACM SIGMM International Workshop on Multimedia Information Retrieval (MIR'04)* (pp. 113–118) New York, New York.

Unal, E., Narayanan, S. S., Shih, H. H., Chew, E. & Kuo, C. C. (2003). Creating data resources for designing user-centric frontends for query by humming systems. In *Proceedings of the 5th ACM SIGMM International Workshop on Multimedia Information Retrieval (MIR'03)* (pp. 116-121) Berkeley, California.

University of Waikato (n.d.). New Zealand digital library. Retrieved May 21, 2007, from http://www.nzdl.org

Van Baelen, E., & De Raedt, L. (1996). Analysis and prediction of piano performances using inductive logic programming. *International Conference in Inductive Logic Programming, 55-71.*

van Rijsbergen, C. J., (1979). *Information retrieval* (2nd ed.). London: Butterworths.

Vapnik, V. N. (1995). *The nature of statistical learning theory.* New York: Springer.

Vignoli, F. (2004). Digital music interaction concepts: A user study. In *Proceedings of the Intern. Conference on Music Information Retrieval.*

W3C Document, Extensible Markup Language 1.0. (1988), second edition (2000), http://www.w3.org/TR/REC-xml/, Third Edition, W3C Recommendation 04 February 2004, see http://www.w3.org/TR/2004/REC-xml-20040204/

Wadge, W. and Ashcroft, E. (1985). Lucid, the dataflow programming language. *APIC Studies in Data Processing.* New York: Academic Press.

Waldman, M., Cranor, L., & Rubin, A. (2002). Trust. In A. Oram (Ed.), *Harnessing the power of disruptive technologies* (pp. 242-270). Sebastopol: O'Reilly.

Wang, A. (2003). An industrial strength audio search algorithm. In *Proceedings of the 4th International*

Conference on Music Information Retrieval (ISMIR 2003), Baltimore.

Wang, C., Li, J., & Shi, S. (2002). A kind of content-based music information retrieval method in a peer-to-peer environment. In *Proceedings International Symposium on Music Information Retrieval (ISMIR)* (pp. 178-186).

Wang, C., Lyu, R., & Chiang, Y. (2003). A robust singing melody tracker using adaptive round semitones (ars). In *Proceedings of the 3rd International Symposium on Image and Signal Processing and Analysis*, (pp. 549-554).

Wang, G., & Cook, P. (2003). Chuck: A concurrent, on-the-fly audio programming language. In *Proceedings of the International Computer Music Conference. (ICMC)*, Singapore.

Wang, I. P2PS (Peer-to-Peer Simplified). In *Proceedings of 13th Annual Mardi Gras Conference - Frontiers of Grid Applications and Technologies*, pages 54-59. Louisiana State University, February 2005.

Wang, Y., & Vilermo, M. (2001). A compressed domain beat detector using mp3 audio bitst,reams. In *Proceedings of the 9th ACM International Conference on Multimedia* (pp. 194-202). Ottawa, Canada.

Web Services Description Language, version 2.0 draft. See http://www.w3.org/TR/2003/WD-wsdl20-20031110/

Weibei, D., Zhaorong, H., & Zaiwang, D. (2001). New window-switching criterion of audio compression. In *Proceedings of the Multimedia Signal Processing, 2001 IEEE Fourth Workshop*, (pp. 319-323), Cannes, France.

White, B. (1960). Recognition of distorted melodies. *American Journal of Psychology, 73*, 100–107.

Widmer, G. (2001). Discovering strong principles of expressive music performance with the PLCG rule learning strategy. In *Proceedings of the 12th European Conference on Machine Learning (ECML'01)*, Freiburg, Germany.

Widmer, G. (2002). Machine discoveries: A few simple, robust local expression principles. *Journal of New Music Research, 31*(1), 37-50.

Wieczorkowska, A. (2001). Musical sound classification based on wavelet analysis. *Fundamenta Informaticae, 47*(1/2), 175-188.

Witten, I. H. (1999). Data mining, practical machine learning tools and techniques with JAVA implementation. Morgan Kaufmann Publishers.

Wold, E. et al. (1996). Content-based classification, search, and retrieval of audio. *IEEE Multimedia, 3*(3), 27-36.

Wright, M. & Freed, A. (1997). Open sound control: A new protocol for communicating with sound synthesizers. In *Proceedings of the International Computer Music Conference (ICMC)*, Thessaloniki, Greece.

WS-Resource Framework home page. See http://www.globus.org/wsrf/

Wurst, M., & Morik, K. (2006). Distributed feature extraction in a p2p setting: A case study (Special Issue). *Future Generation Computer Systems, 23*(1).

Wurst, M., Mierswa, I., & Morik, K. (2005). *Structuring music collections by exploting peers' processing* (Tech. Rep. 43/2005), Collaborative Research Center 475, University of Dortmund.

XML Musical Application Working Group (2001). Recommended practice for the definition of a commonly acceptable musical application using the XML language. IEEE SA 1599, PAR approval date 09/27/2001.

Yang, B., & Garcial-Molina, H. (2002). Improving search in peer-to-peer networks. In *Proceedings Conference of Distributed Computer Systems* (pp. 5-15).

Yang, C. (2002). Efficient acoustic index for music retrieval with various degrees of similarity. In *Proceedings ACM Multimedia Conference* (pp. 584-591).

Yang, C. (2002). The MACSIS Acoustic Indexing Framework for Music Retrieval: An Experimental Study. In

Proceedings of the International Conference on Music Information Retrieval. Paris, France.

Yang, C. (2003). Peer-to-peer architecture for content-based music retrieval on acoustic data. In *Proceedings international World Wide Web Conference (WWW)* (pp. 376-383).

Zaki, M. (2005). Efficient algorithms for mining closed itemsets and their lattice structure. *IEEE Transactions on Knowledge and Data Engineering, 17*, 462-478.

Zampronha, E. S. (2000). *Notação, Representação e Composição: Um Novo Paradigma da Escritura Musical*. Lisboa, Portugal: Annablume/FAPESP.

Zhang, T., & Kuo, C. (1998). Content-based classification and retrieval of audio. In *SPIE's 43rd Annual Meeting - Conference on Advanced Signal Processing Algorithms, Architectures, and Implementations VIII*.

Zhu, Y. & Shasha, D. (2003). Warping indexes with envelope transforms for query by humming. In *Proceedings of the 2003 ACM SIGMOD international conference on Management of data (SIGMOD'03)* (pp. 181-192).

Zhu, Y., & Kankanhalli, M. S. (2003). Robust and efficient pitch tracking for query-by-humming. Information, Communications and Signal Processing, 2003 and the Fourth Pacific Rim Conference on Multimedia. In *Proceedings of the 2003 Joint Conference of the Fourth International Conference* (pp. 1586-1590).

Zicarelli, D. (2002). How I learned to love a program that does nothing. *Computer Music Journal, 26*(4), 44-51.

Zils, A., & Pachet, F. (2004). Automatic extraction of music descriptors from acoustic signals using EDS. In *Proceedings of the 116th Convention of the AES*.

About the Contributors

Jialie Shen is an assistant professor in the School of Information Systems at Singapore Management University. His research interests can be summarized as developing effective and efficient data analysis and retrieval techniques for novel data intensive applications. Particularly, he is currently interested in various techniques of multimedia data mining, multimedia information retrieval and database systems. His research results have been published in *ACM SIGIR, ACM SIGMOD,* and *IEEE Transactions on Multimedia*. He has served as a reviewer for a number of major journals and conferences such as *SIGKDD, SIGMOD, ICDE, ICDM, IEEE TMM, IEEE TKDE,* and *ACM TOIS*. He is also a member of ACM SIGMOD and SIGIR.

John Shepherd received his PhD in 1990 from the University of Melbourne. He is a seniorlecturer at the School of Computer Science and Engineerng, University of New South Wales, Sydney, Australia. His main research interests are query processing for both relational and nonrelational (e.g., multimedia) databases, information organization/retrieval and applications of information technology to teaching and learning. Dr. Shepherd has served on the program committees of conferences such as VLDB, WISE and DASFAAA.

Bin Cui is a professor in the Department of Computer Science, Peking University. He obtained his BSc from Xi'an Jiaotong University in 1996, and PhD from the National University of Singapore in 2004, respectively. From 2004 to 2006, he worked as a research fellow in Singapore-MIT Alliance. His current research interests cover various aspects of database management systems, including high performance query processing, indexing techniques, multi/high-dimensional databases, multimedia databases, location based services, time series databases, bioinformatics, etc., and he has published over 30 international journal and conference papers in these areas. Dr. Cui has served as a member of the technical program committee for international conferences including SIGMOD, VLDB, SIGIR, ICDE, etc.

Ling Liu is an associate professor in the College of Computing at Georgia Institute of Technology. There she directs the research programs in Distributed Data Intensive Systems Lab (DiSL), examining performance, security, privacy, and data management issues in building large scale distributed computing systems. Dr. Liu and the DiSL research group have been working on various aspects of distributed data intensive systems, ranging from decentralized overlay networks, mobile computing and location based services, sensor network and event stream processing, to service oriented computing and architectures. She has published over 200 international journal and conference articles in the areas of Internet computing systems, distributed systems, and information security. Her research group has produced a number of open source software systems, among which the most popular ones include WebCQ, XWRAPElite, PeerCrawl. She has chaired a number of conferences as a PC chair, vice PC chair, or a general chair, and the most recent ones include IEEE International Conference on Data Engineering (2006, 2007), IEEE International Conference on Distributed Computing (2006). Dr. Liu is currently on the editorial board of several international journals, including *IEEE Transactions on Knowledge and Data Engineering* and *International Journal of Very Large Database systems (VLDBJ)*. Dr. Liu is the recipient of the best paper award of ICDCS 2003 and the best paper award of WWW 2004.

* * *

Eddie Al-Shakarachi is a final year PhD student at Cardiff University, researching the distributed processing and analysis of music, and with a focus on MIR techniques. He created the audio processing toolkit for Triana (http://www.trianacode.org), enabling Triana to be used to process and analyze high quality audio files. Al-Shakarachi recently spent several months at Louisiana State University working closely in conjunction with Dr. Stephen Beck and Dr. Ian Taylor at the Laboratory for Creative Arts & Technologies on the Distributed Audio Retrieval using Triana (DART) project, and recently introduced the plans for the DART framework at the 2006 International Computer Music Conference (ICMC) in New Orleans. He is also a freelance mix-engineer and producer.

Eric Anquetil received his PhD in computer science from the Université de Rennes 1 (1997). Currently he is an associate professor in the Department of Computer Science at the Institut National des Sciences Appliquées (INSA) in Rennes, France. He is in the IMADOC research team at the IRISA laboratory (Institut de Recherche en Informatique et Systèmes Aléatoires). His research interests include pattern recognition, fuzzy logic, handwriting recognition and pen-based interaction.

Adriano Baratè obtained the university degree in computer science at the State University of Milan with the thesis *A Petri Nets-Based System for the Generation of XML Music Documents*. He is currently the beneficiary of a research grant for contributing to the IEEE Standards Association PAR1599 project with particular attention to structural aspects. His research activities include music description through XML, music petri nets, and music programming.

Stephen David Beck is the area head for the human & social world (HSW) focus area and director of the Laboratory for Creative Arts & Technologies at the Center for Computation & Technology, Louisiana State University. He is also professor of composition and computer music at the LSU School of Music. He received his PhD in music composition and theory from the University of California, Los Angeles (1988), and was a Fulbright researcher at the Institut de Recherche et Coordination Acoustique/Musique (IRCAM) in Paris. His current research includes sound diffusion systems, computer music composition, and HPC applications in the arts & humanities.

Bruno Bossis was born in France. He, after scientific studies, began as a teacher of digital transmissions in telecommunications. He received his PhD in musicology (Paris-Sorbonne University) and he is currently a lecturer in analysis, electroacoustic and musicology at Rennes University. He is also part-time lecturer and permanent researcher at Paris – Sorbonne University (OMF/MINT lab). Bossis collaborated or collaborates with UNESCO, CCMIX, GRM and Ircam. He is the author of many papers on electroacoustic music. His book, *La Voix et la Machine, la Vocalité Artificielle dans la Musique Contemporaine* (The Voice and the Machine, Artificial Vocality in Contemporary Music), was published in 2005.

Antonello D'Aguanno obtained the university degree in computer science at the State University of Milan with a thesis about audio and score synchronization in compressed domain. He is currently a member of Laboratorio di Informatica Musicale (LIM) of the State University of Milan. His research activities are focused in music information retrieval and music analysis in compressed domain.

Marc Fetscherin is an assistant professor in the International Business Department at Rollins College. He teaches various courses related to international business and information systems. He was a fellow at Harvard University, a researcher at the University of California at Berkeley. He received his PhD from the University of Bern, Switzerland. He also has an MBA from the London School of Economics (LSE), UK; and a master in management (MIM) from the University of Lausanne, Switzerland. He was also consultant at McKinsey & Company in the areas of e-commerce and telecom. He is in various review boards and has more than 40 publications ranging from a book, book chapters, journal articles, case studies and presentations.

León González-Sotos is a computer science full professor and is the chairman of the Computer Science School at the Universidad de Alcalá. He holds a MS in mathematics from the Universidad de Valencia, and a PhD in computer science from the Universidad de Alcalá. He has been the advisor of four PhD theses in computer science.

Goffredo Haus is known for his research in computer science for music and multimedia. He has established at the Computer Science and Communication Department of the State University of Milan (1985) and, since then, directed the Laboratorio di Informatica Musicale (LIM). He is currently the dean of that department. He is currnetly full professor in the computer science area at the State University of Milan and teaches computer science applications in music, foundations of computer science, multimedia digital archives. He has also directed computer music and multimedia projects of industrial interest, and carried out didactic and other cultural activities, both inside and outside academy. The most relevant are the projects concerning the rescuing of the Musical Archive at Teatro alla Scala in Milan and the Bolshoi Theatre in Moscow. Haus published about 100 scientific papers, and also dozens of other kinds of publications, including a number of books and CD-ROMs concerning computer applications in music. He started the IEEE Technical Committee on Computer Generated Music (1992); he is the vice-chair of the TC. In 2001 he started the IEEE Standards Association Working Group on Music Application of XML; he is the official reporter of the WG.

Ioannis Karydis was born in Athens, Greece in 1979. He received a BEng (2000) in engineering science & technology from Brunel University, UK, an MSc (2001) in advanced methods in computer science from Queen Mary University, UK and a PhD (2006) in mining and retrieval methods for acoustic and symbolic music data from the Aristotle University of Thessaloniki, Greece. Currently he is researching as a post doctorate in music databases. His research interests include music databases, music information retrieval (indexing & searching), music mining and music object representation.

Richard L. Kline, PhD, is an assistant professor in the Computer Science Department at Pace University, New York. He earned his PhD in computer science at Rensselaer Polytechnic Institute, Troy, NY (2002). His research interests include user interface design and testing, universal access and assistive technology, and information visualization and retrieval.

Luis M. Laita is a senior professor of logic in computer science and artificial intelligence at the Universidad Politécnica de Madrid. He holds a MS in physics and a PhD in mathematics from the Universidad Complutense de Madrid, and a PhD in history and philosophy of science (with a major in logic) from the American University of Notre Dame. He has been elected correspondent academician of the Royal Academy of Sciences of Spain. He formed a research group in artificial intelligence in the early 1990's to which these researchers belong. He has been the advisor of 13 PhD theses and 55 master's theses (in mathematics and computer science).

Olivier Lartillot is a post doctoral researcher at the Music Cognition Team of the University of Jyväskylä. His research covers the fields of computational musicology and music information retrieval. He currently takes part in the project "Tuning the Brain for Music" funded by the 6th framework program of the European Union and coordinated by the Brain and Music Team at the Cognitive Brain Research Unit of the University of Helsinki. This project is devoted to resolve the neural determinants of music emotion and appreciation, and to reveal the relationship between musical structure and emotion. Olivier Lartillot is author of several publications.

Luca A. Ludovico is a researcher at Laboratorio di Informatica Musicale (LIM) of the State University of Milan. His education includes engineering, computer science and music composition. At present, he is aggregate professor of programming languages for Music 2 and Music Informatics Laboratory at the Computer Science and Communication Department of the aforementioned university. His main research activity consists in the exploration of computer-based encoding for symbolic aspects of music. As the Italian coordinator of the project PAR1599, he is one of the authors of the MX standard draft submitted to IEEE Standards Association.

Sébastien Macé is a French PhD student in computer science from the INSA (Institut National des Sciences Appliquées) in Rennes, France; he holds a master's degree in computer science. He is in the IMADOC (IMAges et DOCuments) research team at the IRISA (Institut de Recherche en Informatique et Systèmes Aléatoires). His works concern pattern recognition and pen interaction. He is more precisely interested in the design of generic methods for the recognition of online hand-drawn structured documents.

Yannis Manolopoulos received his B.Eng. (1981) in electrical engineering and his PhD (1986) in computer engineering from the Aristotle University of Thessaloniki. He is professor at the Department of Informatics of the latter university. He has been with the University of Toronto, the University of Maryland at College Park and the University of Cyprus. He has co-authored over 160 refereed publications and four monographs published by Kluwer and Springer. Recently, he served as general chair of the 10th ADBIS Conference and the 8th ICEIS Conf. (2006). His research interests include databases, data mining, Web and geographical information systems.

Ingo Mierswa studied computer science at the University of Dortmund from 1998 to 2004. He worked as a student assistant in the collaborative research center 531 where he started to develop the machine learning environment YALE. Since April 2004 he is a research assistant and PhD student at the Artificial Intelligence Unit of the University of Dortmund. He is mainly working on multi-objective optimization for numerical learning and feature engineering. Today, he is a member of the project A4 of the collaborative research center 475.

Katharina Morik received her PhD at the University of Hamburg (1981) and worked in the well-known natural language project HAM-ANS at Hamburg (1982 to 1984). Then, she moved to the technical university Berlin and became the project leader of the first German machine learning project. From 1989 to 1991 she led a research group for machine learning at the German National Research Center for Computer Science at Bonn. In 1991, she became full professor at the University of Dortmund. She is interested in all kinds of applications of machine learning. This also covers cognitive modeling of theory acquisition and revision.

Nicola Orio, PhD, is assistant professor of computer engineering at the Department of Information Engineering at the University of Padova, Italy. He is the author of journal and conference papers in the area of music processing and multimedia retrieval. His research interests are on music retrieval, audio recognition and alignment, and multimedia digital libraries. He works on approaches and techniques for a compact and effective representation of the content of music documents, aimed at efficient retrieval, while the work on audio recognition and alignment aims at by providing new tools for music access and browsing. He participates to the DELOS Network of Excellences in Digital Libraries.

Bryan Pardo is an assistant professor in the Northwestern University Department of Electrical Engineering and Computer Science with a courtesy appointment in Northwestern University's School of Music. He received both a master's degree in music and a PhD in computer science from the University of Michigan. In addition to his academic career, he has worked as a software developer for the Speech & Hearing Science Department of Ohio State and the statistical software company SPSS. When he's not programming, writing or teaching, he performs on saxophone and clarinet throughout the Midwest.

Alberto Pinto received his Laurea (MS) degree in pure mathematics from the University of Milan and the diploma (MA) degree in organ and composition from the "G. Verdi" Conservatory of Milan. Since his degree thesis, he has been associated with the Laboratorio di Informatica Musicale (LIM), where he has been working on music information retrieval. Pinto is currently a PhD candidate in computer science at the University of Milan. He is also visiting researcher at Stanford University, CA (USA) and Utrecht University (NL). His current research activity focuses on both the theoretical aspects and applications of similarity measures. His other research interests include mathematical models for music, audio and musical acoustics.

Rafael Ramirez is an assistant professor at the Technology Department of the Pompeu Fabra University in Barcelona. He received a BS in mathematics from the National University of Mexico, an MSc in artificial intelligence from The University of Bristol, UK, and a PhD in computer science also from the University of Bristol. Prior to joining the Pompeu Fabra University he was a lecturer at the Department of Computer Science in the National University of Singapore, Singapore, and researcher at the National Research Institute in Computer Science (INRIA), France. His research interests include artificial intelligence, music information retrieval, declarative languages and music perception and cognition.

Eugenio Roanes-Lozano is an associate professor of algebra at the Universidad Complutense de Madrid. He holds a PhD in mathematics (algebra) from the Universidad de Sevilla, and a second PhD in computer science from the Univ. Politécnica de Madrid. He has developed theoretical approaches and implementations of applications of computer algebra in different fields: logic, expert systems, railway traffic control, airport traffic control, automatic theorem proving in geometry, education. He was in charge of a project for developing a passengers' movement simulation software for the Spanish airport authority (AENA). He is the author or one of the co-authors of more than 30 papers in journals referenced in SCI-JCR.

María Angeles Fernández de Sevilla is an assistant professor of computer science at the Polytechnic School at the Universidad de Alcalá. She holds an MS in mathematics (computer science section, Universidad Complutense de Madrid) and a PhD in computer science from the Universidad de Alcalá. She holds a piano degree from the Royal Music Conservatory of Madrid and has taught piano at the Professional Conservatory of Rodolfo Halffter. Her research has focused for nine years in the applications of computers in music. Nowadays, she teaches computer science at the Universidad de Alcala and also coordinates at this university the "Opera Oberta" project of the Gran Teatre del Liceu de Barcelona.

David A. Shamma is a researcher at Yahoo! Research Berkeley. He received a BS and MS from the Institute for Human and Machine Cognition at The University of West Florida and a PhD. in computer science from the Intelligent Information Laboratory at Northwestern University. Prior to receiving his PhD, he was a visiting research scientist for the Center for Mars Exploration at NASA Ames Research Center. His research on media experience and design focuses on building new creative process models and tools. He also creates and builds media art installations which have been exhibited and reviewed internationally.

Ian Taylor has been a lecturer at Cardiff University's School of Computer Science since 2002. He concurrently holds an adjunct assistant professorship at the Center for Computation & Technology at Louisiana State University and regularly offers consultations in the USA. He has a PhD in physics and music and is the co-ordinator of Triana activities at Cardiff (http://www.trianacode.org). Through this he has been active in many major projects including GridLab, CoreGrid and GridOneD. His research interests include distributed techniques and workflow for grid and P2P computing, which take in applications ranging from astrophysics and healthcare to distributed audio. Taylor has written a professional book for Springer on P2P, Web services and grids, edited another with 3 coeditors, called *Workflows for eScience*, and has published over 50 scientific papers. He has also coedited a special edition for *Journal of Grid Computing on Scientific Workflow*.

George Tzanetakis is currently an assistant professor in computer science at the University of Victoria in Canada. He received his PhD in computer science from Princeton University (May 2002) and was a post doctoral fellow at Carnegie Mellon University. His research deals with all stages of audio content analysis such as feature extraction, segmentation, classification.He is also an active musician and has studied saxophone performance, music theory and composition. More information can be found at http://www.cs.uvic.ca/~gtzan.

Giancarlo Vercellesi is researcher and a member of Laboratorio di Informatica Musicale (LIM), Dipartimento di Informatica e Comunicazione (DICo), Università degli Studi di Milano. He received the degree and the PhD in computer science (2003 and 2006, respectively). His education includes computer science, engineering, music performance and digital audio signal processing. At present, he is external teacher of DRM technologies and audio compression at the Dipartimento di Informatica e Comunicazione (DICo), Università degli Studi di Milano. His researches are mainly focused on analysis and manipulation of signal audio in compressed domain. Furthermore, he is studying methods to evaluate perceived audio quality by subjective and objective approaches and new technologies on DRM field.

John Woodruff is a doctoral student in the Ohio State University Department of Computer Science and Engineering. He received a BFA in media arts and a BSc in mathematics from the University of Michigan, and an MMus in music technology from Northwestern University. At Michigan, Woodruff was a laboratory instructor for the School of Music and the sound recording facilities at the Duderstadt Center. At Northwestern, he was a research assistant in the Department of Electrical Engineering and Computer Science and a teaching assistant in the School of Music. He is also an active recording engineer and electroacoustic composer.

Michael Wurst studied computer science with a minor in philosophy at the University of Stuttgart. He specialized in artificial intelligence and distributed systems. He had an academic stay in Prague, Czech Republic (2000 to 2001) and worked on the student research project, *Application of Machine Learning Methods in a Multi-Agent System*, at the Electrotechnical Department of the Czech Technical University. Since 2001 he is a PhD student at the Artificial Intelligence Unit where he mainly works on distributed knowledge management, clustering, and distributed data mining.

Index